Corruption and Justice in Colonial Mexico, 1650–1755

Corruption is one of the most prominent issues in Latin American news cycles, with charges deciding the recent elections in Mexico, Brazil, and Guatemala. Despite the urgency of the matter, few recent historical studies on the topic exist, especially on Mexico. For this reason, Christoph Rosenmüller explores the enigma of historical corruption. By drawing upon thorough archival research and a multi-lingual collection of printed primary sources and secondary literature, Rosenmüller demonstrates how corruption in the past differed markedly from today. Corruption in Mexico's colonial period connoted the obstruction of justice; judges, for example, tortured prisoners to extract cash or accepted bribes to alter judicial verdicts. In addition, the concept evolved over time to include several forms of self-advantage in the bureaucracy. Rosenmüller embeds this important shift from judicial to administrative corruption within the changing Atlantic world, while also providing insightful perspectives from the lower social echelons of colonial Mexico.

Christoph Rosenmüller is a professor at Middle Tennessee State University. His publications include the edited volumes *Corruption in the Iberian Empires: Greed, Custom, and Colonial Networks* (2017), *"Dávidas, Dones, Dinero": Aportes a la nueva historia de la corrupción* (2016, with Stephan Ruderer), and the book *Patrons, Partisans, and Palace Intrigues: The Court Society of Colonial Mexico, 1702–1710* (2008).

CAMBRIDGE LATIN AMERICAN STUDIES

General Editors
KRIS LANE, Tulane University
MATTHEW RESTALL, Pennsylvania State University

Editor Emeritus
HERBERT S. KLEIN
Gouverneur Morris Emeritus Professor of History, Columbia University and Hoover Research Fellow, Stanford University

Other Books in the Series

113. *Corruption and Justice in Colonial Mexico, 1650–1755*, Christoph Rosenmüller
112. *Blacks of the Land: Indian Slavery, Settler Society, and the Portuguese Colonial Enterprise in South America*, Weinstein/Woodard/Montiero
111. *The Street Is Ours: Community, the Car, and the Nature of Public Space in Rio de Janeiro*, Shawn William Miller
110. *Laywomen and the Making of Colonial Catholicism in New Spain, 1630–1790*, Jessica L. Delgado
109. *Urban Slavery in Colonial Mexico: Puebla de los Ángeles, 1531–1706*, Pablo Miguel Sierra Silva
108. *The Mexican Revolution's Wake: The Making of a Political System, 1920–1929*, Sarah Osten
107. *Latin America's Radical Left: Rebellion and Cold War in the Global 1960s*, Aldo Marchesi
106. *Liberalism as Utopia: The Rise and Fall of Legal Rule in Post-Colonial Mexico, 1820–1900*, Timo H. Schaefer
105. *Before Mestizaje: The Frontiers of Race and Caste in Colonial Mexico*, Ben Vinson III
104. *The Lords of Tetzcoco: The Transformation of Indigenous Rule in Postconquest Central Mexico*, Bradley Benton
103. *Theater of a Thousand Wonders: A History of Miraculous Images and Shrines in New Spain*, William B. Taylor
102. *Indian and Slave Royalists in the Age of Revolution*, Marcela Echeverri
101. *Indigenous Elites and Creole Identity in Colonial Mexico, 1500–1800*, Peter Villella
100. *Asian Slaves in Colonial Mexico: From Chinos to Indians*, Tatiana Seijas

(*Continued after the Index*)

Corruption and Justice in Colonial Mexico, 1650–1755

CHRISTOPH ROSENMÜLLER
Middle Tennessee State University

CAMBRIDGE
UNIVERSITY PRESS

University Printing House, Cambridge CB2 8BS, United Kingdom

One Liberty Plaza, 20th Floor, New York, NY 10006, USA

477 Williamstown Road, Port Melbourne, VIC 3207, Australia

314–321, 3rd Floor, Plot 3, Splendor Forum, Jasola District Centre,
New Delhi – 110025, India

79 Anson Road, #06-04/06, Singapore 079906

Cambridge University Press is part of the University of Cambridge.

It furthers the University's mission by disseminating knowledge in the pursuit of
education, learning, and research at the highest international levels of excellence.

www.cambridge.org
Information on this title: www.cambridge.org/9781108477116
DOI: 10.1017/9781108756761

© Christoph Rosenmüller 2019

This publication is in copyright. Subject to statutory exception
and to the provisions of relevant collective licensing agreements,
no reproduction of any part may take place without the written
permission of Cambridge University Press.

First published 2019

A catalogue record for this publication is available from the British Library.

Library of Congress Cataloging-in-Publication Data
NAMES: Rosenmüller, Christoph, 1969– author.
TITLE: Corruption and justice in colonial Mexico, 1650–1755 / Christoph
Rosenmüller.
DESCRIPTION: Cambridge, United Kingdom ; New York, NY : Cambridge University
Press, .2019. | Series: Cambridge Latin American studies | Includes bibliographical
references and index.
IDENTIFIERS: LCCN 2018061284 | ISBN 9781108477116 (alk. paper)
SUBJECTS: LCSH: Mexico – Politics and government – 1540–1810. | Mexico – History –
Spanish colony, 1540–1810. | Political corruption – Mexico – History.
CLASSIFICATION: LCC F1231 .R765 2019 | DDC 972/.02–dc23
LC record available at https://lccn.loc.gov/2018061284

ISBN 978-1-108-47711-6 Hardback

Cambridge University Press has no responsibility for the persistence or accuracy of
URLs for external or third-party internet websites referred to in this publication
and does not guarantee that any content on such websites is, or will remain,
accurate or appropriate.

Contents

List of Maps, Tables and Figures		page vi
Acknowledgments		vii
A Note on Terms		xi
List of Abbreviations		xiv
	Introduction	1
1	Empire of Justice	11
2	From Judicial to Administrative Corruption	53
3	"This Custom or Better Said Corruption": Legal Strategies and the Native Trade with the *Alcaldes Mayores*	92
4	"Vile and Abominable Pacts": The Sale of Judicial Appointments and the Great Decline of Viceregal Patronage	123
5	Criminal Process and the "Judge Who Is Corrupted by Money"	153
6	Guilt and Punishments for Fraud, Theft, and the "Grave Offense of Bribery or Corruption"	196
7	The Politics of Justice: Francisco Garzarón's *Visita* (1716–1727)	222
	Conclusion: Approaching Historical Corruption	255
Appendix		273
Glossary		283
Bibliography		289
Index		334

Maps, Tables, and Figures

MAPS

1 The Viceroyalty of New Spain in 1700	page 5
2 The Global *Ius Commune*	22
3 The Iberian Peninsula in 1700	43
4 The Jurisdiction or *Alcaldía Mayor* of Huejotzingo	157

TABLES

1 Absolute Cochineal Export Prices in the Harbor of Veracruz	109
2 Mean Inflation-Adjusted Cochineal Prices in Amsterdam	109
3 The Beginnings of the *Beneficio* of *Alcaldías Mayores*	140
4 Viceregal Appointments to *Alcaldías Mayores* of New Spain	149
5 Suspended and Absolved Ministers	243
6 Verdicts against Ministers in Garzarón's *Visita*	274
7 The Eleven Dismissed *Audiencia* Officials	281

FIGURES

1 *The Decree of the Unjust Judge*	59
2 Unknown artist, *Mexican Biombo of the first half of the eighteenth century, representing the entry of a Spanish king* (detail)	68
3 Unknown artist, *Refugium Peccatorum/ Virgen del Refugio de los Pecadores* (detail)	76
4 Unknown artist, *The King Reforms Justice, 1764*	88
5 José Antonio de Alzate, *Indian Who Gathers Cochineal with a Deer Tail*, Mexico City, 1777	99

Acknowledgments

MEPHISTOPHELES. But choose some faculty, I pray!
STUDENT. I feel a strong dislike to try the legal college.
MEPHISTOPHELES. I cannot blame you much, I must acknowledge.
    I know how this profession stands today.
    Statutes and laws through all the ages
    Like a transmitted malady you trace;
    In every generation still it rages
    And softly creeps from place to place.
    Reason is nonsense, right an impudent suggestion;
    Alas for thee, that thou a grandson art!
    Of inborn law in which each man has part,
    Of that, unfortunately, there's no question.

    JOHANN WOLFGANG VON GOETHE, *Faust: A Tragedy*, chap. 7,
    the study chamber, transl. Charles T. Brooks, 7th ed.
    Boston: Ticknor and Fields, 1868, http://www.gutenberg.org/
    cache/epub/14460/pg14460.html.

I am grateful to the series editors Kris Lane and Matthew Restall and to acquisitions editor Deborah Gershenowitz for their thoughtful suggestions and for including the book in the Latin American Series of Cambridge University Press.

    Several grants supported research and writing. A Fulbright García Robles Grant took me to Mexico in the academic year 2014–15. The Center for Historical Studies at *El Colegio de México* accepted me as a visiting scholar and offered fabulous working conditions during this fellowship and on later occasions. I particularly wish to thank Erika

Pani and Ariel Rodríguez Kuri, the Center's directors. In addition, Bernd Hausberger, Andrés Lira, Carlos Marichal, Adrian Pearce, Gabriel Torres Puga, and Guillermo Zermeño discussed with me ideas of justice on many occasions. Sandra Kuntz kindly invited me to present my work in her *Permanent Seminar on Economic History*.

Subsequently, a German Academic Exchange Service (Deutscher Akademischer Austauschdienst) Grant in the fall 2015 allowed me to continue my research at the University of Münster, where I profited much from discussions with Silke Hensel and Stephan Ruderer. In the winter 2015, I returned to Mexico to research and lecture, supported by a Fulbright Specialist Grant. During the academic year 2016–17, the Max Planck Institute for Legal History in Frankfurt, Germany, gave me the chance to advance the manuscript and use its wonderful facilities. I am especially grateful to its director, Thomas Duve, for this opportunity. The conversations at the Institute with Alejandro Agüero, Angela Ballone, Pamela Cacciavillani, Álvaro Caso Bello, Fernanda Bretones Lane, Peter Colin, Macarena Cordero, Otto Danwerth, Dora Dávila, Max Deardorff, Wim Decock, José Luis Egío, Karl Härter, José María Humanes, Constanza López Lamerain, María del Pilar Mejía Quiroga, Heinz Mohnhaupt, Osvaldo Rodolfo Moutin, José Luis Paz Nomey, Jakob Fortunat Stagl, Michael Stolleis, and Javier Villa Flores considerably shaped my thinking about corruption.

I finished the manuscript and added sources while on a fellowship sponsored by the Gerda Henkel Foundation, to which I am much indebted. The Foundation also provided support for the index and substantial editing work. In addition, the Middle Tennessee State University has awarded me three Faculty Creative Arts and Research grants to travel to international archives. I am also thankful to the library of the University of Florida for supporting travel in 2006 to read the microfilmed Archive of the Counts of Revillagigedo.

Mark Burkholder, Susan Deeds, Marc Eagle, Tamar Herzog, Renzo Honores, Renate Pieper, Susan Schroeder, and Brad Wright read chapters of the manuscript and gave very insightful suggestions. The 2018 Southwestern Seminar and especially Mark Lentz, Ryan Kashanipour, José Carlos de la Puente Luna, Kevin Gosner, Eva Mehl, Bianca Premo, Joaquín Rivaya-Martínez, Dana Velasco Murillo, and Juliet Wiersema commented insightfully on chapter three. The working group on *Empire in the Long Eighteenth Century*, composed of Iván Escamilla, Francisco Eissa-Barroso, Gibrán Bautista Lugo, Guadalupe Pinzón, Frances Ramos, Antonio Rubial García, and Matilde Souto also discussed three chapters of this book. In addition, Felipe Castro, Brígida von Mentz, María Teresa Álvarez Icaza and the seminar on the *Sociedad Indiana* (Colonial Society), and Guillermina del Valle Pavón, Antonio Ibarra, and their seminar on *Corporations and Corruption* perspicaciously critiqued one chapter. Horst Pietschmann has offered much shrewd advice over the years, while Linda Arnold was always willing to discuss new ideas and showed me around the vast Mexican repositories. Sherry Johnson very kindly invited me to stay at her fine home near Gainesville, Florida, and remarked shrewdly on my topic. I owe knowledge of the painting *Refugium Peccatorum* to Nelly Sigaut. Asunción Lavrín suggested treatises, while Eric Van Young and David Rex Galindo both commented meaningfully on the proposal. Two anonymous reviewers for Cambridge University Press gave very detailed and thoughtful suggestions. In addition, Iván D. Alcántar gave footnotes, glossary, and bibliography a solid read. My gratitude goes to all these scholars, and any errors that remain in this book are mine.

Furthermore, the working group headed by Francisco Andújar Castillo and Pilar Ponce-Leyva in Spain have successfully rekindled the discussion on corruption in the *Ancien Regime*. They graciously invited me to participate at their conference in Madrid in 2017. Hannes Ziegler and María Ángeles Martín Romera also brought me to a German Historical Institute Conference in London in the fall of 2017, and Miguel Costa, Carlos Gálvez, José de la Puente Bruncke, and Margarita Suárez gave me the chance to give two talks in Lima. In addition, Agustín Grajales (*Benemérita Universidad de Puebla*), Cristina Torales Pacheco (*Iberoamericana*, Santa Fe), Stefan Rincke (Berlin), Jens Ivo Engels (Darmstadt), Renate Pieper (Graz), the Early Modern Seminar (Münster), and Klaus Buchenau (Regensburg) invited me to lecture at their home institutions.

I also profited from many conversations and friendship with Arne Bialuschewski, Jürgen Buchenau, Alejandro Cañeque, William Connell, James Cordova, José Enrique Covarrubias (since we met in Hamburg over twenty years ago), Rafael Diego-Fernández, Marshall C. Eakin, James Garza, Carlos Garriga, Catherine Tracy Goode, Ana Hontanilla, Jane Landers, Pilar Latasa, Mark Lentz, Jeremy Mumford, Guillermo Náñez Falcón, Luis Navarro García, Allan J. Kuethe, Caterina Pizzigoni, Fabricio Prado, Cynthia Radding, and Dorothy Tanck de Estrada.

I am thankful to the staff of the *Archivo General de la Nación* in Mexico City, the *Archivo Histórico de la Ciudad de México*, and the *Biblioteca Nacional*. The *Archivo General de Indias* was instrumental, while the staff at *the Archivo Histórico Nacional* and the *Biblioteca Nacional* in Madrid were very helpful. I also thank Paula Covington and the Vanderbilt Humanities Library, the staff at the MTSU library, the library of the Max Planck Institute for Legal History for helping me on many instances. In addition, James Beeby, Kevin Leonhard, Susan Myers-Shirk, and Amy Sayward, the chairs of the history department at MTSU, have continually supported my work.

Finally, thanks to my parents and my sisters for their lucid ideas. Certainly not least, Marcela Saldaña Solís has always accompanied me, inspired me, and helped me develop new ideas. *Con agradecimiento y mucho cariño.* An earlier version of chapter four appeared in the *Hispanic American Historical Review* 96:1 and is republished by permission of the copyright holder, Duke University Press.

GERDA HENKEL STIFTUNG

A Note on Terms

Colonial Mexico was known as *Nueva España* (New Spain), and its inhabitants were the colonial Mexicans or the *novohispanas* and *novohispanos*, including Indians, blacks, and mestizos. Those originating from the Spanish peninsula are called peninsular Spaniards in this book, while I call all residents of the empire Spaniards, in lack of a better word. Americans refers to the inhabitants of the Spanish Americas in tune with eighteenth-century usage when "America" rivaled "the Indies." Even today, Latin Americans often refer to themselves as *Americanos/as* (Americans). *Novohispanos* also had a range of labels for racial groups. I have not translated all of them, as their English equivalents are sometimes offensive, and for this reason *mulata/o* (a person of mixed African descent), *mestiza/o* (of mixed indigenous descent), and other terms appear in the text in italics.[1]

In addition, historians have usually translated the offices of *alcaldes mayores* and *corregidores* as district officials or provincial administrators, because they levied taxes and tributes and commanded the local militia. Yet the *alcaldes mayores* derived their name from the Arabic *al-qadi* for judge, and they ruled on justice, which was their most distinctive feature for the colonial society. The best translation for these ministers is district judge in my view. Meanwhile, the first-instance magistrates of the Native and Spanish-speaking towns were the *alcaldes* and *alcaldes ordinarios*. The *audiencia* (appeals or high court) of Mexico City consisted of *oidores*

---

[1] On this usage of terms, see Jaime Rodríguez O., "*We Are Now the True Spaniards.*" *Sovereignty, Revolution, Independence, and the Emergence of the Federal Republic of Mexico, 1808–1824* (Stanford, CA: Stanford University Press, 2012), xvi–xvii.

(civil judges) and *alcaldes de crimen* (criminal judges). A *fiscal del crimen* (criminal prosecutor) and a *fiscal de lo civil* (civil prosecutor) joined them. In the sources, these prosecutors and judges were sometimes called *ministros superiores* (superior ministers) and sometimes even *jueces* (judges), although they had different roles. I occasionally refer with judges to both judges and prosecutors of the *audiencia* to make the prose flow easier, as long as the context is clear.

Spaniards rarely labeled the district, municipal, or high court judges as *oficiales* (officials) and usually reserved this term for those without judicial powers, including notaries, scribes, or jailers. These officials also appeared as *oficiales subalternos* (subaltern officials) or *ministros inferiores* (lower ministers). Town council members, for example, assessed tax burdens and coordinated public works, and they "had some administration of justice," as one notary put it.[2] Yet they differed from judges in the colonial understanding. When speaking of both judges and officials at the same time, the word *ministros* (ministers) often appears in the sources, and I follow this usage. I have also employed the terms "legal experts" or "legal practitioners" when referring to procurators and other officials who learned their legal skills mostly on the job, as well as academically trained civil and canon jurists. Moreover, I have translated the legal terms as much as possible but have kept the word *prueba*, which connotes the reasoning of a judge for a verdict.[3]

---

[2] Pedro Robledo to Francisco Garzarón, Mexico City, 2 June 1719, Archivo General de Indias, Seville (hereinafter cited as AGI), Escribanía 280 C, Q[uader]no 12, fols. 453v–454.

[3] On *ministros subalternos*, see Rodrigo de Zepeda to king, n. d., attached to the *consulta* of the Council of the Indies, 5 Dec. 1721, AGI, México 670 A. Early modern sources were not always consistent on distinguishing officials from judges. Viceroy Count of Revillagigedo to Marquis of la Ensenada, Mexico City, 23 Jan. 1752, AGI, México 1506, separated robed ministers from *alcaldes mayores* and financial officials. The issue hinges in part on whether the kings had the exclusive right to appoint ministers of justice. Jerónimo Castillo de Bobadilla, *Política para corregidores y señores de vasallos, en tiempo de paz, y de guerra* [...] (Barcelona: Jerónimo Margarit, 1616), book 5, chap. 1, para. 227, distinguished between the "judge or the official," while in book 2, chap. 11, para. 17, esp. note e, he translated the term *agentes* in Justinian's *Novels* 8.1. in *Corpus Iuris Civilis*, eds. Paul Krueger and Theodor Mommsen (Berlin: Apud Weidmannos, 1954), accessed under Y. Lassard, and A. Koptev, eds., *The Roman Law Library*, http://webu2.upmf-grenoble.fr/DroitRomain, as *oficiales de justicia* (judicial officials). Judges are at least sometimes labeled *officiales* in Latin. Antonio Fernández de Otero, *Tractatus de Oficialibus Reipublicae, necnon oppidorum utriusque Castellae, tum de eorundem electione, usu, exercitio. Opus non solum tironibus, sed etiam magistris pernecessarium, duplici indice, capitum scilicet, & rerum locupletatum. Editio Tertia, auctior et accuratior* (Colonia [Geneva]: Fratres de Fonties, 1732), part 1, chap. 1, for example, maintained that

A Note on Terms

Despite all scholarly claims to the contrary, the term *state* increasingly appeared in seventeenth-century sources in various shades of meaning. In 1687, for example, Juan Alfonso de Lancina spoke of *materias de Estado* (state matters) and of *secretos de los Estados* (state secrets) to indicate a more unified understanding of government over territory.[4] In addition, English speakers today rarely use the word *functionary* and prefer civil servant or officer. In early eighteenth-century Spanish, the word *función* (function) referred to "the exercise of an employment, faculty, or office."[5] Within a broader Atlantic perspective, a jurist from the Holy Roman Empire writing in Latin demanded in 1695 an oath from "those who are accepted to public function," indicating that the term was older.[6] French encyclopedists recorded the term *fonctionnaire* (functionary) for the first time in 1770 in tune with the professionalizing of administrations. The Spanish pendant *funcionario* is attested in dictionaries in 1835. Yet lexicons usually delayed recording political innovations, and there is a good chance that the Spanish term emerged earlier.[7] Finally, the early modern word *prince* referred to supreme rulers of a state who recognized no superior, and they could have been kings, queens, dukes, or have other titles, while today the notion is largely restricted to the heirs of the reigning families.

"officials are derived ... from office, and they use this name to describe magistrates or those who look after public service."

[4] Juan Alfonso de Lancina, *Commentarios politicos a los Annales de Cayo Vero Cornelio Tácito* [...] (Madrid: Oficina de Melchor Álvarez, 1687), 37, 354; for Jean-Frédéric Schaub, "El pasado republicano del espacio público," in *Los espacios públicos en Iberoamérica: Ambigüedades y problemas, siglos XVIII–XIX*, eds. François-Xavier Guerra, Annick Lempérière, et al. (Mexico City: Fondo de Cultura Económica, 1998), 29–35, the term state referred principally to foreign policy until the nineteenth century.

[5] *Diccionario de la lengua castellana, en que se explica el verdadero sentido de las voces, su naturaleza y calidad, con las phrases o modos de hablar, los proverbios o refranes, y otras cosas convenientes al uso de la lengua*, ed. Real Academia Española (Madrid: Imprenta de Francisco del Hierro, 1732). http://buscon.rae.es/ntlle/SrvltGUILoginNtlle, 811.

[6] Benjamin Heinrich Schwartz and Heinrich Linck, *De iuramento ambitus et repetundarum, ex l. fin. C. ad L. Jul. repetund. Sub Praesidio Dn. Henrici Linckens* (PhD diss., University of Altdorf: Henricus Meyerus, 1695), 16.

[7] Word coined by Anne Robert Jacques Turgot; see the entry *fonctionnaire* in *Dictionaire de la Academie Francaise*, http://atilf.atilf.fr/dendien/scripts/tlfiv4/showps.exe?p=combi.htm;java=no, accessed July 29, 2018; Ramón Joaquín Domínguez, *Diccionario Nacional o Gran Diccionario Clásico de la Lengua Española (1846–47)*, 5th ed. (Madrid–Paris: Establecimiento de Mellado, 1853), vol. 2, p. 830.

Abbreviations

AEA	*Anuario de Estudios Americanos*, Seville, Spain
ACR	*Archive of the Counts of Revillagigedo*, Special Collections of the University of Florida Library, Gainesville, USA
AGI	*Archivo General de las Indias*, Seville, Spain
AGN	*Archivo General de la Nación*, Mexico City
AHCM	*Archivo Histórico de la Ciudad de México*, Mexico City
EEHA	*Escuela de Estudios Hispano-Americanos*, Seville, Spain
exp.	*expediente* (file)
HAHR	*Hispanic American Historical Review*
JbLA	*Jahrbuch für Geschichte Lateinamerikas*, Cologne, Germany
Law of the Indies	*Recopilación de leyes de los reynos de las Indias* [...]. 1741. Facsimile. Madrid: Consejo de la Hispanidad, 1953. http://www.leyes.congreso.gob.pe/leyes_indias.aspx.
leg.	*legajo* (folder)
Law of Castile	*Recopilación de las leyes destos reynos hecha por mandado de la Magestad Catholica del Rey don Philipe Segundo [...]. Alcalá de Henares: Juan Iñiguez de Liquerica, 1581.*
Q.no	*Quaderno* or *cuaderno* (folder)

Siete Partidas   (Seven Parts) Sanponts y Barba, Ignacio, Ramon Marti de Eixalá, and José Ferrer y Subirana, eds. *Las Siete Partidas del sabio rey Don Alfonso el IX, con las variantes de mas interés, y con la glosa del Lic. Gregorio Lopez, vertida al castellano y estensamente adicionada con nuevas notas y comentarios y unas tablas sinópticas comparativas, sobre la legislacion española, antigua y moderna, hasta su actual estado.* Barcelona: Bergnes, vol. 1 (1843)–vol. 4 (1844).

Introduction

Millions have marched in the past years to protest corruption scandals in Latin America. Popular discontent and politicians have forced out the presidents of Brazil and Guatemala. The Mexican president also plunged deeply in the polls when sordid scandals became public. Amidst the backlash, new allegations of malfeasance hit the headlines of newspapers almost every day. At least in Mexico, many citizens have resigned themselves to thinking that corruption has pervaded their country since the Spanish conquest (1519–1521). These Mexicans are right in believing that there has always been some form of corruption in their country, just as in most other regions of the world. Yet the idea of corruption in the past differed markedly from today and has largely been forgotten.[1]

Corruption in Mexico's colonial period meant violating the proper finding of justice. Judges who accepted bribes to alter judicial verdicts committed this crime, for example, and early modern people roundly condemned the injustice.[2] At the same time, the concept of corruption changed slowly and grew beyond the judiciary in the period 1650–1755. The concept evolved to include several forms of self-advantage in the bureaucracy. Scholars of Latin America have overlooked this conceptual expansion from judicial to administrative corruption, as they have tended to ignore the subject in the past years. This book sets out to explore the

---

[1] The Mexican jurist Alejandro Mayagoitia, "Notas sobre las Reglas ciertas y precisamente necessarias para juezes y ministros [...] de Fray Jerónimo Moreno, O. P.," *Anuario Mexicano de Historia del Derecho* 8 (1996): 334, for instance, underlines "the general corruption in which our forebears lived," indicating that this abuse has always existed in some shade in Mexico.

[2] See, for example, Print *por Don Miguel Truxillo*, AGI, México 670 A, fol. 4; see also Gabriel Berart y Gassol, *Speculum visitationis secularis omnium magistratum* [...] (Barcinone [Barcelona]: Ex Typographia Sebastiani Mathenat, 1627), chap. 17, para. 5.

enigma of historical corruption by studying fresh sources in Spanish and other, less consulted, languages.

Rumors about wayward judges and officials in Mexico City reached Madrid in the early eighteenth century. The crown ordered the inquisitor Francisco Garzarón to conduct a *visita general* (comprehensive investigation) from 1716 to 1727 to get to the root of the allegations. Garzarón called on residents to report what they had experienced. Three indigenous noblemen from Santiago Tecali (Puebla) stepped forward in early 1724. They complained about the "great extortions that they suffered for a year and a half since the *alcalde mayor* (district judge) took office ... arresting us and confiscating property and sending us to the public jail in Puebla without ever raising any formal charges." In their view, the *alcalde mayor* also connived with a notary to sell mules and oxen in the district at 300 percent profit. As a result, the *alcalde mayor* "today owns 30,000 pesos from his *baraterías* (corruption) in administering justice," the Natives lamented. What is worse, the notary had raped a "*mulata* [a person of mixed African descent] from Tepeaca ... whom he had maliciously hired as a cook under false pretenses, and he forced her so that it was necessary to give her the last rites at midnight."[3]

According to the noblemen, the *alcalde mayor* had traded with and extorted his subjects, and he had also tolerated that others physically harmed his subjects. Colonial Mexicans considered these offenses as corrupt. In addition, many literati rejected candidates for office because of their alleged racial and social insufficiencies. One jurist averred in 1673 that commoners of unworthy ethnic or social descent were "corrupted by ambition and avarice and shamed by their blood."[4] These people lacked the proper bloodline and therefore the qualities to resist the manifold temptations of judicial office. They most certainly issued wrongful verdicts. Moreover, the term corruption frequently referred to those inappropriate customs that displaced the just laws. This aspect even included the clergy. For this reason, a friar in Quito

---

[3] Pedro, Bartolomé, and Antonio Tellez of Santiago Tecali (Tecali de Herrera, Puebla) to Garzarón, Mexico City, 9 Feb. 1724, Archivo General de la Nación, Mexico City (hereinafter cited as AGN), Historia 102, *expediente* (exp.) 20, fols. 491–492. The other petitioners included an inmate awaiting his execution, a nun of the Saint Jerome convent seeking to sell her black slave, and a jailed merchant; see Sebastian Garzón to Garzarón, Mexico City, 11 Jan. 1724, AGN, Historia 102, exp. 20, fols. 494–503; Francisco Ruiz de Fonseca to Garzarón, Mexico City, 11 Jan. 1724, AGN, Historia 102, exp. 20, fol. 504–504v, 508–509; Catarina del Sacramento to Garzarón; decree of Garzarón, Mexico City, 4 Nov. 1721, AGN, Historia 102, exp. 20, fol. 505–505v.

[4] Domingo Antunez Portugal, *Tractatus de donationibus jurium et bonorum regiae coronae* (Lisbon: Ioannis a Costa, 1673), second part, book 1, chap. 14, para. 7.

(Ecuador) excoriated his colleagues who demanded excessive contributions from Natives in 1684. He ended his sermon with the words: "God help me! What gives birth to all this soulless corruption?"[5] The friar used the term corruption to attack the malicious and pervasive practice that replaced the just rules governing Natives and priests. Finally, the idea of corrupt customs and judges sometimes overlapped. The trade of the *alcalde mayor* with the Native subjects in Santiago Tecali, for instance, was corrupt in both senses. The judges skewed justice by favoring their interests, and commerce with the Natives was so ingrained in New Spain (colonial Mexico) that it displaced all legal prohibitions against it.

Yet in the period 1650–1755, the laws defining corruption and other crimes were not as precise and clear-cut as today. The crown was not the only authority producing rules, and printed texts and unwritten norms of different origins coexisted with one other.[6] Legal pluralism reigned and practitioners discussed in the courts and in treatises which laws best applied to specific offenses. In addition, justice was usually casuistic; in other words, it was decided on a case-by-case basis. This was true for corruption cases too. Many suspects maintained, for example, that they had only ever exchanged legitimate gifts with family and litigants and denied that they had committed corruption. Their defense could well be successful, depending on the cases, especially as politics often shaped verdicts. Powerful friends helped suspects and shielded them from prosecution. Impunity was widespread and judges frequently faced few consequences for their actions.

Nonetheless, most *novohispanos* (those living in New Spain) and peninsular Spaniards saw corruption as an actionable crime under certain circumstances. As a result, Francisco Garzarón suspended thirteen judges from the *audiencia* (high court) of Mexico City. He proved, according to the standards of the time, that the ministers had accepted gifts with the malicious intent to rule in favor of the givers. They had also tortured prisoners to obtain their cash and delayed rulings because litigants refused to pay. The Council of the Indies (the highest court for American affairs)

---

[5] Cited in Pilar Ponce-Leiva, "Percepciones sobre la corrupción en la monarquía hispánica, siglos XVI y XVII," in *Mérito, venalidad y corrupción en España y América*, eds. Francisco Andújar Castillo and Pilar Ponce-Leiva (Valencia: Albatros, 2016), 195. Judith Francis Zeitlin, *Cultural Politics in Colonial Tehuantepec: Community and State among the Isthmus Zapotec, 1500–1750* (Stanford, CA: Stanford University Press, 2005), 131–132, shows, for example, that the vicar of Zanatepec (near Tehuantepec) required local children to raise his five hundred chickens and ended his practice as late as 1635.

[6] José Carlos de la Puente Luna and Renzo Honores, "Guardianes de la real justicia: alcaldes de indios, costumbre y justicia local en Huarochirí colonial," *Histórica* 40, no. 2 (2016): 31–32.

in Madrid agreed in 1721, and permanently removed the thirteen judges from the bench for corruption.

In addition, Garzarón suspended 156 subaltern officials, including jailers and notaries, for committing fraud or theft, overcharging their clients, and keeping careless records. Yet these offenses were usually not seen as corruption. One notary explained, in 1719, that his "office was ... bare of any administration of justice." He and other officials merely executed orders and rarely contributed to flawed verdicts, and for this reason he could not have acted corruptly.[7] The Council of the Indies largely agreed with this point. Yet the Council removed him and ten other officials for offenses such as forging papers, stealing property, and other illegalities. The Council also sentenced several officials to pay meaningful fines or extended painful suspensions without salary. At the same time, those who had merely levied excessive fees or improperly filed records received relatively lenient punishments and returned to their positions.

Not all violations of justice therefore equaled corruption. Murder or robbery were serious crimes and punishable, yet these one-time breaches of justice did not bend judicial rulings. The following example also shows a slave's sense of injury about his bondage in a religious institution, but this was not corruption in the colonial sense and did not concern Garzarón. Juan Esteban Madrigal deplored, in 1724, that the friars of the Saint Augustine monastery in Mexico City held him as a cook. Madrigal sent Garzarón "his mother's letter of liberty, which she received in 1700 ... and I was born in 1702, and Your Lordship will decide whether I am a slave when I was born two years after my mother was released." Madrigal implored Garzarón to confirm his status as a free man. Yet Garzarón suggested seeking justice elsewhere, because he did not venture into misconduct within the Church and mostly prosecuted judges and officials at the *audiencia*.[8] This book follows Garzarón's path in this regard. Although ecclesiastical malfeasance is an enticing subject, as Madrigal's story shows, such an approach would require significant additional research on canon law and colonial religion. Nor is it my aim to sleuth out the true culprits of the past and sentence them posthumously. This would be a difficult task anyway, because the sources are often incomplete and the standards for crimes and investigations have shifted substantially. Instead, studying the

---

[7] Pedro Robledo to Garzarón, Mexico City, 15 Apr. 1719, AGI, Escribanía 280 C, *Quaderno* (*Q.no*) 12, fols. 453v–454; defense of Pedro Robledo, AGI, México 670 B, *Relación*, fol. 352v.
[8] Juan Esteban Madrigal to Garzarón, Mexico City, 9 Feb. 1724, AGN, Historia 102, exp. 20, fol. 493; *auto* of Garzarón, n. d., AGN, Historia 102, exp. 20, fol. 493v.

MAP 1 The Viceroyalty of New Spain in 1700
Map adapted by Gabriela Chávez from Christoph Rosenmüller, *Patrons, Partisans, and Palace Intrigues: The Court Society of Colonial Mexico, 1702–1710* (Calgary: Calgary University Press, 2008), 26.

combined discourses about wayward ministers from various angles opens a wide panorama on past ideas of fairness.

The purpose of scrutinizing the strategies of the suspects is cultural, seeking to illuminate how *novohispano* and peninsular Spaniards thought, felt, and communicated about justice. To this end, I have combined the analysis of the day-to-day practices on the ground, the law and its learned interpretations, and politics. In this vein, Eric Van Young perceptively pointed out some twenty years ago that assessing politics also reveals cultural notions. Yet rather than to "elbow aside" the "metanarratives" of power, as he suggested then, we can join them today with the view from below to understand what early modern people "believed about the world around them."[9] Examining the defenses of culprits and accusations of victims, the political scheming, and the

[9] Eric Van Young, "The New Cultural History Comes to Old Mexico," *HAHR* 79, no. 2 (1999): 247, see also 213–218, 246–47; see also Frances Ramos, *Identity, Ritual, and Power in Colonial Puebla* (Tucson: University of Arizona Press, 2012), xxviii–xxx; and Peter Burke, *What Is Cultural History* (Cambridge: Polity Press, 2008), 29–30, 37–39, 52–64.

claims to authority show how *novohispanos* imagined themselves. They also clarify notions of equity, as the speech about corruption did "take place within a network of socially constructed meanings."[10]

Historians have discussed historical corruption with great controversy. Stuart Schwartz, Colin MacLachlan, and Horst Pietschmann forged a consensus starting in the 1970s, that corruption was a matter of excess, because community standards frequently refrained from censuring bribery or contraband trade. Breaching the laws for self-interest, therefore, provided a flexible balance between local and crown interests.[11] Tamar Herzog and others have pushed this view even further. She argues in her excellent study, that it is "impossible to speak about corruption in the early modern period," because judges in Quito (Ecuador) before 1750 oscillated between their own interests and social harmony instead of observing the royal laws.[12]

---

[10] Hans Vorlander, "What is constitutional culture," in *Constitutional Cultures. On the Concept and Representation of Constitutions in the Atlantic World*, eds. Silke Hensel, Ulrike Bock, Katrin Dircksen, and Hans-Ulrich Thamer (Newcastle, UK: Cambridge Scholars Publishing, 2012), 25.

[11] Stuart B. Schwartz, *Sovereignty and Society in Colonial Brazil. The High Court of Bahia and its Judges, 1609–1751* (Berkeley: University of California Press, 1973), 181–182, 281, 325, 360–368; Colin M. MacLachlan, *Spain's Empire in the New World: The Role of Ideas in Institutional and Social Change* (Berkeley: University of California Press, 1988), 37; Horst Pietschmann, "Corrupción en las Indias Españolas: Revisión de un debate en la historiografía sobre Hispanoamérica colonial," *Memorias de la Academia Mexicana de la Historia* 40 (1997): 40, 46–54; Pietschmann, "'Corrupción' en el virreinato novohispano: Un tercer intento de valoración," *E-Spania: Revue interdisciplinaire d'études hispaniques médiévales et modernes* 16 (2013); Kenneth J. Andrien, "Corruption, Self-Interest, and the Political Culture of Eighteenth-Century Quito," in *Virtue, Corruption, and Self-Interest: Political Values in the Eighteenth Century*, ed. Richard K. Matthews (Bethlehem, PA: Lehigh University Press, 1994), 270–271; Anthony McFarlane, "Political Corruption and Reform in Bourbon Spanish America," in *Political Corruption in Europe and Latin America*, eds. Walter Little and Eduardo Posada Carbó (London: Palgrave, Macmillan, 1996), 46–47, 57. See the Conclusion for a full discussion of the scholarship.

[12] Tamar Herzog, *Upholding Justice. Society, State, and the Penal System in Quito (1650–1750)* (Ann Arbor: University of Michigan Press, 2004), 157, see also 154–160. Herzog, "Ritos de control, prácticas de negociación: pesquisas, visitas y residencias y las relaciones entre Quito y Madrid (1650–1750)," in *Nuevas Aportaciones a la historia jurídica de Iberoamérica* (Madrid: Fundación Histórica Tavera, Hernando de Larramendi, Mapfre, 2000), 22, adds that "notions of corruption and peddling favors were omnipresent in the political and social discourse of the time, yet they rarely occurred ... in the space surrounding Quito and perhaps in America as a whole." Similarly, Solange Alberro, "Control de la iglesia y transgresiones eclesiásticas durante el periodo colonial," in *Vicios públicos, virtudes privadas: La corrupción en México*, ed. Claudio Lomnitz (Mexico City: CIESAS, 2000), 35; Pierre Ragon, "Abusivo o corrupto? El conde de Baños, virrey de la Nueva España (1660–1664): De la voz pública al testimonio en derecho," in Andújar Castillo and Ponce-Leiva, *Mérito, venalidad*

While these scholars have provided many insights, their views cannot fully explain corruption as colonial Mexicans understood the idea. It is true that both the legal norms and many practices were malleable and multi-faceted, and they also hinged in many ways on political interests. Nonetheless, the term corruption existed as a meaningful doctrine, and even commoners understood and opposed the offense in some fashion. The Indians of Santiago Tecali accused their own *alcalde mayor* of *baratería* for this reason. They, and most commoners, had relatively easy access to the courts. They hired procurators and attorneys to sue their *alcaldes mayores* for breaching justice, which met the early modern definition of corruption. The judges who heard the cases against the *alcaldes mayores* often awarded redress to the Natives, demonstrating that the doctrine had significance.[13] This is one reason why historians are walking away from the view that corruption did not exist in the early modern period. Scholars instead emphasize the power of the discourse against political opponents, especially in the judicial arena.[14]

---

y corrupción, 277–278; Alejandro Cañeque, *The King's Living Image: The Culture and Politics of Viceregal Power in Colonial Mexico* (New York: Routledge, 2004), 177. According to Anne Dubet, "La moralidad de los mentirosos: por un estudio comprensivo de la corrupción," in Andújar Castillo and Ponce-Leiva, *Mérito, venalidad y corrupción*, 213–214, fraud was largely a moral and not a criminal matter.

[13] Woodrow Borah, *Justice by Insurance: The General Indian Court of Colonial Mexico and the Legal Aides of the Half-Real* (Berkeley: University of California Press, 1983), 91–97; Richard L. Kagan, *Lawsuits and Litigants in Castile, 1500–1700* (Chapel Hill: University of North Carolina Press, 1981); Charles Cutter, "The Legal System as a Touchstone of Identity in Colonial New Mexico," in *The Collective and the Public in Latin America: Cultural Identities and Political Order*, eds. Luis Roniger and Tamar Herzog (Brighton, UK: Sussex Academic Press, 2000), 59–63; Brian Owensby, *Empire of Law and Indian Justice in Colonial Mexico* (Stanford, CA: Stanford University Press, 2008); Yanna Yannakakis, *The Art of Being In-Between: Native Intermediaries, Indian Identity, and Local Rule in Colonial Oaxaca* (Durham, NC: Duke University Press, 2008); Michelle A. McKinley, *Fractional Freedoms. Slavery, Intimacy, and Legal Mobilization in Colonial Lima, 1600–1700* (Cambridge: Cambridge University Press, 2016), 2–4; André Holenstein, "Introduction: Empowering Interactions: Looking at Statebuilding from Below," in *Empowering Interactions: Political Cultures and the Emergence of the State in Europe 1300–1900*, eds. Wim Blockmans, André Holenstein, and Jon Mathieu (Farnham, UK: Ashgate. 2009), 23.

[14] Maryvonne Génaux, "Social Sciences and the Evolving Concept of Corruption," *Crime, Law & Social Change* 42, no. 1 (2004): 21; Antonio Feros, *Kingship and Favoritism in the Spain of Philip III, 1598–1621* (Cambridge: Cambridge University Press, 2000), 140, 163–188; Daniel Bellingradt, "Organizing Public Opinion in a Resonating Box: The Gülich Rebellion in Early Modern Cologne, 1680–1686," *Urban History* 39, no. 4 (2012); Kris Lane, "From Corrupt to Criminal: Reflections on the Great Potosí Mint Fraud of 1649," in *Corruption in the Iberian Empires. Greed, Custom, and Colonial Networks*, ed. Christoph Rosenmüller (Albuquerque, NM: University of New Mexico Press, 2017), 33–62; Marc Eagle, "Portraits of

The chief aim of this book is tracing the concept of corruption between 1650 and 1755. By doing so, I do not explore all forms of government malfeasance, because that would require spilling a lot more ink on this subject. Instead, I have proceeded in the following way: I lay out the nature of the colonial justice system in the first chapter. Latin Americanists know much about social practices, customs, and networks, but they are less aware of the rich judicial underpinnings. Meanwhile, legal scholars have cast light on the interpretations of canon and Roman law that circulated among the empires. These concepts mattered in colonial Mexico, Spain, the Holy Roman Empire and beyond. I have drawn on published and archival sources to show that judges in Mexico City, for example, weighed these sources against local practices, royal mandates, and natural law to arrive at just verdicts. Sketching the legal pluralism of the time casts the foundation for understanding the crime of corruption. The second chapter analyzes the meaning of early modern or judicial corruption, which scholars have mostly ignored. By exploring manifold discourses, I propose that the concept of judicial corruption segued into the broader idea of administrative corruption in the eighteenth century. The third chapter then provides a view from below, reinterpreting the Native trade with their *alcaldes mayores*. While historians have amply discussed this subject, I argue that Natives used early modern legal concepts to challenge the unfair exchanges. These concepts have changed or lost their meaning in subsequent centuries,

---

Bad Officials: Malfeasance in *Visita* Sentences from Seventeenth-Century Santo-Domingo," ibid., 87–110; Mary Lindemann, "Dirty Politics or 'Harmonie'? Defining Corruption in Early Modern Amsterdam and Hamburg," *Journal of Social History* 45, no. 3 (2012): 582–604; for a long-term study on Peru, see Alfonso W. Quiroz, *Corrupt Circles. A History of Unbound Graft in Peru* (Washington: Woodrow Wilson Center Press; Baltimore: The Johns Hopkins Press, 2008), 2–6, 9, 36–37, 59–81; Jean Claude Waquet, *Corruption. Ethics and Power in Florence, 1600–1770*, trans. Linda McCall (University Park, PA: Pennsylvania State University Press, 1992), 12; three Spanish pioneers are Pilar Ponce-Leiva, "Percepciones sobre la corrupción," 193–211; Francisco Andújar Castillo, "Cuando el rey delegaba la gracia. Las comisiones de ventas de oficios en la Castilla del siglo XVII," in Andújar Castillo and Ponce-Leiva, *Mérito, venalidad y corrupción*, 135–156; and Carlos Garriga, "Crimen corruptionis. Justicia y corrupción en la cultura del ius commune (Corona de Castilla, siglos XVI–XVII)," *Revista Complutense de Historia de América* 43 (2017), 22–25; important are also Jens Ivo Engels, "Politische Korruption und Modernisierungsprozesse: Thesen zur Signifikanz der Korruptionskommunikation in der westlichen Moderne," in *Korruption: Historische Annäherungen an eine Grundfigur politischer Kommunikation*, eds. Niels Grüne and Simona Slanička (Göttingen, Germany: Vanderhoek & Ruprecht. 2010), 38–41; Andreas Suter, "Korruption oder Patronage? Außenbeziehungen zwischen Frankreich und der Alten Eidgenossenschaft als Beispiel (16. bis 18. Jahrhundert)," *Zeitschrift für Historische Forschung* 37, no. 2 (2010): 200.

and they are largely ignored except by scholars of the law. Deciphering these concepts throws light on Native strategies and the larger backdrop to the conflict over the trade. Natives sued their *alcaldes mayores* to halt declining agricultural prices, and they often succeeded in convincing the courts.

The fourth chapter reassesses the sale of office appointments, a classical topic for historians. The traditional elites of Spain attacked the purchasers of appointments as corrupt because of their flawed social origins, which differed starkly from our modern idea of abusive activities on the job. Yet the social origins in this sense had little bearing on the performance at work. This insight explains why the sale of appointments did not undercut the judiciary or hamper the empire as a whole, as most scholars have claimed. Instead, the sale, if anything, strengthened the monarchy. The fifth chapter illuminates Garzarón's methods in uncovering bribery and extortion, giving voice once again to Native lords, women, and commoners. Many colonial commoners knew the key ideas of corruption and sought redress for their injuries. Their collaboration explains Garzarón's success to a large degree. The sixth chapter explores the legal foundations of verdicts handed down by Garzarón and the Council of the Indies. The judges distinguished serious offenses such as corruption, fraud, and theft, from lesser ones such as charging excessive fees and sloppy record keeping. The ministers assessed corruption by drawing on sophisticated legal doctrines that circulated in the Atlantic world and beyond. These ministers also took into account the malicious intent and negligence of the suspects when punishing them. Finally, the last chapter explores the social and political background of Garzarón's *visita*. Historians have made great strides in unearthing the impact of social networks on judicial process. While politics played an important role, its impact should not be exaggerated for Garzarón's *visita*. Garzarón also followed established judicial guidelines to convict each offender according to their individual culpability, and not only according to political expediency.

This book begins in the middle of the seventeenth century. Historians have traditionally neglected this period, although they are currently mending this deficit, and they have overlooked important changes in the intellectual and imperial framework. These transformations had a bearing on the concept of corruption too. In the 1650s, many Spaniards debated the sale of appointments in the royal treasury that originated in 1633. In 1675, the crown began offering appointments of the *alcaldes mayores* in the Americas, unleashing yet another round of attacks. This period also witnessed a growing number of legal complaints against the trade with

Natives. The book then straddles the transition from Habsburg to Bourbon rule in 1700 and includes Garzarón's remarkable *visita*, which recorded plenty of conversations over corruption and other offenses. In addition, the crown phased out the sale of judicial appointments in 1750, while ministers, priests, and *alcaldes mayores* once again discussed reforming the trade of the *alcaldes mayores* with the Natives. A new government appeared in Madrid and a new viceroy arrived in Mexico City in 1754 and 1755. They were more interested in preserving rather than reforming the status quo, offering a good point to end the analysis.[15]

Few days pass in the Mexican news cycle without discussing a corruption scandal. Next to these revelations, the European economic crisis also triggered an uproar over opaque politics. Corruption cases abound in the USA too. Transparency International, a global watchdog, defines these breaches as "the abuse of entrusted power for private gain," adding that "it can cost people their freedom, health, money – and sometimes their lives."[16] This view is useful for understanding the magnitude of our present problems, but it cannot be transferred back to the period 1650–1755. The aim of this book is to understand how colonial Mexicans understood corruption in their period.

---

[15] On the dates, see J. H. Parry, *The Sale of Public Office in the Spanish Indies under the Habsburgs* (Berkeley, Los Angeles: University of California Press, 1953), 49–58; José Luis Gómez Urdáñez, *Fernando VI* (Madrid: Arlanza, 2001), 105–106, 111; Antonio del Valle Menéndez, *Juan Francisco de Güemes y Horcasitas: Primer conde de Revillagigedo, Virrey de México: La historia de un soldado (1681–1766)* (Santander, Spain: Librería Estudio, 1998), 335–337, 630.

[16] www.transparency.org/what-is-corruption. An excellent overview is provided by Arnold J. Heidenheimer and Michael Johnston, eds., *Political Corruption: Concepts and Contexts*, 3rd ed. (New Brunswick, NJ: Transaction Publishers, 2002).

1

Empire of Justice

INTRODUCTION

Corruption today is a crucial concern for Latin America, and many nations have relatively clear definitions of the crime on the books. Yet corruption in the Spanish empire from roughly 1492 to the early 1800s differed. Theologians, legal experts, and laypeople debated the meaning and boundaries of corruption, and the limits of gift giving and bribery were malleable to some degree. Jurists weighed various judicial sources to assess the crime, as the crown was not the only authority producing rules. Instead, Spaniards appreciated the Roman and the canon (Church) law and their manifold interpreters. Their doctrines had to conform to natural law, which was essentially reason, as past generations understood that notion. In addition, the maxims revealed in the Bible coexisted with the royal mandates, such as the *Law of the Indies* (law for Spanish America), and the local customs, including the indigenous traditions.

Latin American historians have always paid attention to canon and royal law and local customs, though English-speaking Latin Americanists have preferred focusing on social practices. Scholars, largely outside the United States, have also analyzed the actions of social networks composed of patrons and clients. Their contributions have greatly advanced our knowledge about justice in New Spain (colonial Mexico), although they have often overlooked the working of the law. Meanwhile, legal scholars have skillfully traced changing judicial concepts but often neglected their application in trials "on the ground."[1] This chapter focuses on the shifting

---

[1] According to Herzog, *Upholding Justice*, 9, 19, justice "was a communal rather than a state-run enterprise ... and the dominating rules in Quito were social and theological, not legal ... and these rules proceeded from a source other than the king," and she affirms that "law embodied a system of thought that was expressed in royal and local decrees." Much then depends on the

meaning of the law between 1650 and 1755 by drawing on the scholarship, published discourse, and archival sources. Legal concepts from a variety of sources mattered deeply for *novohispanos* (those from New Spain), especially when assessing corruption. Judges of various standing

definition of legality, because the Roman and canon laws (*leges*) constituted a crucial part of justice and were not strictly speaking theology. In *Frontiers of Possession: Spain and Portugal in Europe and the Americas* (Cambridge, MA: Harvard University Press, 2015), 262, Herzog modifies this view in that in "all these dynamics, law mattered to an enormous degree." According to Yannakakis, *The Art of Being*, 118, "decisions of individual local magistrates rather than judicial precedent and previous case decisions determined the enactment of justice," and "justices ruled based on specific enactment or codified clause." Owensby, *Empire of Law*, 45, maintains that there were three main aspects of justice, the "*derecho* ... the legal order ensuring 'good government,' the published *ley*, and the customs"; while Bianca Premo, "Custom Today: Temporality, Customary Law, and Indigenous Enlightenment," *HAHR* 94, no. 3 (2014): 355–380, traces innovations among the customs. Legal scholarship on the European *ius commune* is vast and often high quality; just to cite a few examples, O. F. Robinson, T. D. Fergus, and W. M. Gordon, *European Legal History: Sources and Institutions* (Oxford: Oxford University Press, 2000); Bartolomé Clavero Salvador, *Historia del derecho: derecho común* (Salamanca: Ediciones Universidad de Salamanca, 1994); Stephan Meder, *Rechtsgeschichte: Eine Einführung*, 5th amended ed. (Cologne: Böhlau, 2014); Hans Schlosser, *Neuere europäische Rechtsgeschichte: Privat- und Strafrecht vom Mittelalter bis zur Moderne*, 2nd ed. (Munich: C. H. Beck, 2014); Wim Decock, *Theologians and Contract Law: The Moral Transformation of the Ius Commune (ca. 1500–1650)* (Leiden, Boston: Martinus Nijhoff Publishers, 2013). Scholars also analyze legal ideas as they applied to indigenous people, see, e.g., Thomas Duve, *Sonderrecht in der Frühen Neuzeit: Studien zum ius singulare und den privilegia miserabilium personarum, senum und indorum in Alter und Neuer Welt* (Frankfurt: Vittorio Klostermann, 2008); Orazio Condorelli, "Diego de Covarrubias e i diritti degli Indiani," *Rivista Internazionale di Diritto Comune* 25 (2014): 207–267; Kenneth Pennington, "Bartolomé de las Casas," in *Great Christian Jurists in Spanish History*, eds. Rafael Domingo and Javier Martínez-Torrón (Cambridge: Cambridge University Press, 2018), 98–115. On government, see, e.g., Carlos Garriga, "Sobre el gobierno de la justicia en Indias (siglos xvi–xii)," *Revista de Historia del Derecho* 34 (2006): 67–160. Canon law is, for example, studied by Osvaldo Rodolfo Moutin, *Legislar en la América hispánica en la temprana edad moderna. Procesos y características de la producción de los Decretos del Tercer Concilio Provincial Mexicano (1585)* (Frankfurt: Max Planck Institute for European Legal History, 2016); McKinley, *Fractional Freedoms*; Jorge Eugenio Traslosheros Hernández, *La reforma de la iglesia del antiguo Michoacán. La gestión episcopal de fray Marcos Ramírez de Prado (1640–1666)* (Morelia: Universidad Michoacana de San Nicolás de Hidalgo, 1995); Jorge Eugenio Traslosheros Hernández and Ana de Zaballa Beascoechea, eds., *Los indios ante los foros de justicia religiosa en la Hispanoamérica virreinal* (Mexico City: UNAM, 2010). How these combined laws and customs actually played out in *novohispano* courts is less known; some examples are Jaime del Arenal Fenochio, "La Justicia civil ordinaria en la ciudad de México durante el primer tercio del siglo xviii," in *Memoria del X Congreso del Instituto Internacional de Historia del Derecho Indiano* (Mexico City: Escuela Libre de Derecho, UNAM, 1995); Victor Gayol, *Las reglas del juego*: vol. 1 of *Laberintos de justicia. Procuradores, escribanos y oficiales de la Real Audiencia de México (1750–1812)* (Zamora: El Colegio de Michoacán, 2007), 37–39; Manuel Torres Aguilar, *Corruption in the Administration of Justice in Colonial Mexico: A Special Case* (Madrid: Dykinson, 2015).

ruled on conflicts, while the crown sent *visitas* (judicial investigations) to enforce rules, uncover malfeasance, and gather information about the realms. At the same time, social networks glued together the colonial society, supported or defied the crown, and shaped the *visitas*. In addition, social bodies with their own jurisdictions, such the Jesuit order, determined the lives of *novohispanos*. These social bodies often had great autonomy, lived by their own norms, and mediated royal rule. This chapter sets the stage for this book by sketching the importance of the six key sources of the law (there were more) which defined the view of corruption. Moreover, the chapter outlines the influence of social networks and social bodies on judges and *visitas*, while casting an eye on the changing nature of the empire as a whole.

1.1 THE SIX PILLARS OF JUSTICE

Justice in the Spanish empire drew on a multitude of norms among them the Roman law. The classical lawyers, for example, had defined justice as "the continuous and unimpaired will of giving to each their due." Spaniards generally agreed with this dictum, yet the multitude of early modern norms made it difficult to ascertain what each person was actually due. Judges therefore ideally balanced the various legal and theological sources against one another, heard all involved parties in the conflicts, and applied the accepted ways of litigation. They also decided on a case-by-case basis and therefore every sentence differed from another. By adhering to this process, the judges resolved conflicts in a just manner. In the late seventeenth century, however, the judicial plurality began to dissolve. The Roman and canon laws lost influence, while the importance of the royal law and its interpreters rose. Later, some jurists even demanded to cast out the entire plurality and write an entirely new and systematic code.[2]

---

[2] According to *Institutes* 1.1.1, "*Iustitia est constans et perpetua voluntas ius suum cuique tribuens.*" Thomas Aquinas, *Justice*, vol. 37 of *Summa Theologiae*, ed. Thomas Gilby (Cambridge: Blackfriars, 1975), IIa–IIae, Q. 58, art. 11, obj. 3, understood justice as "dispensing to each their own (*reddere unicuique quod suum est*)"; see also Q. 61, art. 1, obj. 2. See also Juan de Azcargorta, *Manual de Confesores ad Mentem Scoti*, reprint from probably 1718, 273; Herzog, *Upholding Justice*, 9; António Manuel Hespanha, "Porque é que existe e em que é que consiste um direito colonial brasileiro," in *Brasil-Portugal: Sociedades, culturas e formas de governar no mundo português (séculos XVI–XVIII)*, ed. Eduardo França Paiva (São Paulo: Annablume. 2006), 29; Hespanha, "Paradigmes de légitimation, aires de gouvernement, traitement administratif et agents de l'administration," in *Les figures de l'administrateur. Institutions, réseaux, pouvoirs en*

Yet before these changes began, Roman law permeated legal thinking. Emperor Justinian (527–565) had cast an important foundation when he ordered his jurists to compile the vast judicial knowledge of the time. Between 533 and 534, the jurists produced four books, including the *Institutes* that were designed as a teaching tool and contained the phrase "giving to each their due." The jurists also devised the *Digest*, which assembled the interpretations of the important lawyers, while the *Code* comprised the emperors' orders. Finally, the *Novels* added Justinian's most recent mandates. Publishing the four books was an enormous achievement. Yet while Rome straddled Asia and Africa at that time, its rule in Europe had diminished. Many schools that taught the requisite skills to understand the four books had shut their doors. As a result, only some isolated pockets on the Italian peninsula adopted Justinian's collection.[3]

A revival blossomed in eleventh-century Bologna (Italy), deeply influencing Iberia and most of Europe. The scholars in that city were among the first to gather Justinian's scattered texts and revere them as sacred. They richly interspersed notes or glosses at the margins of the laws to explain the concepts, and they became known as the *glossators* for their style. In the later medieval period, the school of the *commentators* penned separate and longer treatises and superseded the glossators. Both schools set themselves apart from lay judges by studying in Latin at colleges and universities. They used the dialectical method of scholasticism to flesh out the principles and harmonize the apparent contradictions in Justinian's collection. This revival rubbed off on Spain's juridical culture. For example, the words for consultation of a Council, a decree, an edict to the public, or a legal opinion descended directly from the Roman model. Spanish literati also extolled Roman law and its interpreters as bulwarks of virtue and liberty. For the poet Francisco de Quevedo (1580–1645), the Roman norms "did not allow passion, anger, or bribery, and with sure method and due and universal process" they punished sins.[4]

Espagne, en France et au Portugal 16e–19e siècle, eds. Robert Descimon, Jean-Frédéric Schaub, and Bernard Vincent (Paris: EHESS, 1997), 20.

[3] James Arthur Brundage, *The Medieval Origins of the Legal Profession: Canonists, Civilians, and Courts* (Chicago: University of Chicago Press, 2008), 57–59; Petri Murillo Velarde, *Cursus Iuris Canonici [...]* (Matritum [Madrid]: Ex typographia Emmanuelis Fernández, 1743), preámbulo, paras. 10–12; Pennington, "Bartolomé de las Casas," 107–108; Meder, *Rechtsgeschichte*, 109–111.

[4] Francisco de Villegas Quevedo, *Fortuna con seso*, in *Obras de D. Francisco de Quevedo Villegas, Caballero del Habito de Santiago, Secretario de S. M. y Señor de la Villa de la Torre de Juan Abad* (Madrid: Joachín Ibarra, 1772), 2: 525–531, quote on 527. In addition, compare *consulta, decreto, edicto,* and *respuesta* to a Roman *Senatus*

Canon (Church) law joined Iberian judicial culture as the second pillar in the medieval period. Following the example set by the glossators, clergymen collected important Church decisions in the first half of the twelfth century. The popes later recognized the collection as the official Church Decree, and other priests gathered additional council resolutions, papal decisions (decretals), and the writings of the Church fathers. This body of norms evolved into its own discipline over time and separated from theology. Yet canon law also remained deeply intertwined with Roman law as jurists of the two fields continually conversed with one another. These two combined sources and their interpretations eventually became known as the *ius commune* (or the general law).[5]

Some interpreters of the *ius commune* rose to great renown, and their doctrines became law themselves. The Italian commentator Bartolus de Sassoferrato (1313/14–1357), for example, left a mark on the universities of the early Spanish empire, although his influence declined much in the seventeenth century. Many attorneys originally claimed that they "were not jurists unless they were Bartolists."[6] The sixteenth-century jurist Jerónimo Castillo de Bobadilla, for instance, cited Bartolus amply. Castillo de Bobadilla argued that the good *corregidor* (a district judge akin to an *alcalde mayor*), who usually had no academic training, should rule according to the law and the common opinion of the recognized jurists. Castillo de Bobadilla continued that it would be better in any case for the judge to consult his legal

---

consulta, an imperial *decretum* or *edictum*, and an attorney's *responsa prudentium*; see Brundage, *Medieval Origins*, 75–94; Robinson, Fergus, and Gordon, *European*, 2–3; Decock, *Theologians*, 28–55; Meder, *Rechtsgeschichte*, 21, 89, 197–212.

[5] Brundage, *Medieval Origins*, 1, 42–45, 96–107; Meder, *Rechtsgeschichte*, 153.

[6] Clavero, *Historia*, 27, quotes the dictum "*Nemo jurista nisi bartolista.*" See also Meder, *Rechtsgeschichte*, 199, note 30, 204–206. Peter Weimar, "Bartolus of Saxoferrato," in *The Oxford International Encyclopedia of Legal History*, ed. Stanley N. Katz (Oxford: Oxford University Press, 2009). See also Robinson, Fergus, and Gordon, *European*, 65–66; Schlosser, *Neuere europäische*, 75. According to Paul Koschaker, *Europa und das römische Recht* (Munich: C. H. Beck, 1966), 104–105 (admittedly dated), the Castilian *Pragmática* of 1449 determined that when the laws were silent, Bartolus and Baldus decided the issue. According to Pennington, "Bartolomé de las Casas," 100–101; and Condorelli, "Diego de Covarrubias," 210, Bartolomé de las Casas and Diego de Covarrubias (1512–1577) extensively discussed Bartolus. See also Susanne Lepsius, "Bartolus de Saxoferrato (1313/14–1357)," in *Handwörterbuch der deutschen Rechtsgeschichte (HRG)*, eds. Albrecht Cordes, Hans-Peter Haferkamp, Heiner Lück, Dieter Werkmüller, and Ruth Schmidt-Wiegand, 2nd ed., (Berlin: Erich Schmidt Verlag, 2008), 1: 450–453. www.hrgdigital.de/HRG.bartolus_de_saxoferrato_1313_14_1357.

adviser, who fully understood the interplay of scholarly arguments, including Bartolus's view, with the Roman, canon, and royal laws.[7]

Legal practitioners often also called on the Bible, the Church fathers, or other theological principles, and the divine law became the third pillar of legality. "Christ is justice himself," one early modern jurist held, and the faith commanded the king to safeguard that sacred underpinning of society. Many therefore cited the divine law in their arguments.[8] When the *visitador general* (investigative judge) Francisco Garzarón inspected the *audiencia* (high court) of Mexico City between 1716 and 1727, for instance, he insisted that a corrupt judge report to jail. Yet the delinquent ran off and pleaded with the king for mercy. He declared that his escape was "a natural defense, because Christ himself as a child escaped from Herod's slaughter and taught his disciples to flee elsewhere when persecuted by a city ... and Saint Paul practiced the same by descending from the Roman walls in a basket ... while Saint Peter fled from most heinous chains and prison when an angel saved him." The judge used that theological narrative for his defense, which the crown prosecutor in Madrid accepted without any astonishment. The prosecutor even suggested absolving the defendant from the charge of disobeying Garzarón's orders.[9]

While theological arguments ran strong, sixteenth-century secular ideas increasingly challenged the late medieval consensus. Humanists favored logic over ancient authority to explain natural phenomena. Especially French jurists began attacking the prevailing interpretations. They perceived Justinian's collection as a historical source that had developed over centuries with often opposing aims. Their insight vitiated the medieval enterprise of harmonizing the inherent contradictions of the collection. As a result, the sacred and immutable status of the Roman law took a blow. The humanist jurists derided their Bartolist colleagues as "ignorant donkeys" for ruminating profusely on each separate law. Instead, these modern jurists favored elegant treatises on a subject matter for which they assembled all applicable rules to assist the practicing attorneys.[10]

---

[7] Castillo de Bobadilla, *Política*, book 1, chap. 12, paras. 11–15. The *Política* was republished several times until 1775. Note that some *alcaldes mayores* had academic training in law, such as the mid-eighteenth-century *alcalde mayor* of Puebla; see Miguel Manuel Davila Galindo to Revillagigedo, Puebla, 14 Jan. 1754, AGN, Subdelegados 34, fol. 368v.

[8] Castillo de Bobadilla, *Política*, book 2, chap. 11, para. 21.

[9] Pedro Sanchez Morcillo to king, Mexico City, 28 July 1724; *parecer* (legal opinion) of the prosecutor of the Council of the Indies, Madrid, 16 Feb. 1727, AGI, Escribanía 287 B, *pieza* 38, fols. 14–14v, 18.

[10] Manlio Bellomo, *The Common Legal Past of Europe, 1000–1800*, trans. Lydia G. Cochrane (Washington, DC: Catholic University of America Press, 1995), 206–208;

André Tiraqueau (1488–1558), for example, marked a milestone by proposing to avert crime rather than punishing ruthlessly. He opposed defining a cruel penalty for each offense as had been the norm, and instead "sought to prevent others from sinning."[11] Tiraqueau suggested taking into account the seriousness of the committed crime and the personal qualities of the offenders including their age, sex, and mental condition. To this end, the jurist expanded the judge's *arbitrio* (judgment) to tailor the sentence to the circumstances of the crime. Tiraqueau and the humanists made an impression on the Spanish empire. The *arbitrio* unfolded and buttressed court rulings that even most commoners in Mexico City found appropriate well into the eighteenth century.[12]

Jurists reconciled these developing interpretations with natural law, the fourth pillar of justice. Natural law virtually meant reason as the cosmic order revealed it. The idea that the law had to be reasonable went back to the Romans, who compared human life to nature when ascertaining the principles that shaped the law. Cicero, for instance, espoused "the true

---

the quote on ignorant donkeys appears in Schlosser, *Neuere europäische*, 109, see also 108–21; Robinson, Fergus, and Gordon, *European*, 173–175. According to Michael Stolleis, *Histoire du droit public en Allemagne. La théorie du droit public impérial et la science de la police 1600–1800*, trans. Michel Senellart (Paris: Presse Universitaire de France, 1998), 132, Machiavelli (1469–1527) and his peers abandoned viewing history as the unfolding of salvation during which the all-knowing God avenged evil deeds and awarded the righteous. Instead, history followed a secular and cyclical logic according to fortune, necessity, or facts.

[11] Tiraqueau (Andreas Tiraquellus) cited here the philosopher Seneca, *De Ira*, in *Moral Essays*, ed. John W. Basore, vol. 1 (London and New York: Heinemann, 1928), book 1, chap. 16, www.perseus.tufts.edu/hopper/collections.

[12] Michael C. Scardaville, "Justice by Paperwork: A Day in the Life of a Court Scribe in Bourbon Mexico City," *Journal of Social History* 36, no. 4 (2003): 979–990; Jonathan Otto, "Tiraquellus, Andreas (André Tiraqueau)," in *The Oxford International Encyclopedia of Legal History*. According to Alejandro Agüero, "La tortura judicial en el antiguo régimen. Orden procesal y cultura," *Direito e Democracia* 5, no. 1 (2004): 207, the sixteenth-century jurist Angelo Gambiglioni defined "*arbitrio* of a judge as no other thing than jurisdiction." See also Massimo Meccarelli, "Dimensions of Justice and Ordering Factors in Criminal Law from the Middle Ages till Juridical Modernity," in *From the Judge's Arbitrium to the Legality Principle. Legislation as a Source of Law in Criminal Trials*. Comparative Studies in Continental and Anglo-American Legal History, vol. 31, eds. Georges Martyn, Anthony Musson, and Heikki Pihlajamäki (Berlin: Duncker & Humblot, 2013), 54, 57–59; Bernardino Bravo Lira, *El juez entre el derecho y la ley. Estado de derecho y derecho del Estado en el mundo hispánico, siglos xvi a xxi* (Santiago, Chile: Lexis Nexis, 2006), 334–336; Schlosser, *Neuere europäische*, 92, 119–123. The debate over appropriate sentencing raged also over the question of whether judges should choose the most probable or just any probable ruling for a conflict as part of the theological problem of probabiliorism; see Azcargorta, *Manual de Confesores*, 170–172.

reason that correlates with nature."[13] Justinian's collection also recognized that humans and animals showed similarities in matrimony and child rearing. Later, reason breathed new life into Spanish scholasticism at Salamanca.[14] During Garzarón's investigation, officials used natural law to ward off unwanted royal limitations on their fees, for example. An *audiencia* usher, who guarded the doors and carried documents among the offices, held that "natural law ... allowed demanding more than what is assigned, because there is much work to do and no salary." It was therefore reasonable that he charged Indians higher fees for his services so that he could make a living.[15] *Novohispano* judges stated a similar point. In their view, reason justified accepting gifts because of the considerable costs of living in Mexico City.[16]

When such practices became ingrained, they joined the customs, the fifth pillar of justice. In the early modern societies, many customs had the force of law and shaped judicial sentencing. Customs arranged much of the indigenous land ownership, for instance. Indian *alcaldes* (magistrates) usually observed the communal traditions in this regard, alleging that they had done so since immemorial times. The *Law of the Indies* explicitly recognized those "norms and customs that the Indians have had since old times for their good government and order, and those customs and usages, which they have obeyed and practiced since becoming Christians."[17]

---

[13] Cicero, *De legibus*, 1, para. 43, cited in Meder, *Rechtsgeschichte*, 261.

[14] *Digest* 1.1.1.3; *Institutes* 1.2. in Krueger and Mommsen, *Corpus Iuris Civilis*. The *Digest* included the definition of the late classical jurist Domitius Ulpianus. According to José Mariano Beristáin de Souza, Fortino Hipólito Vera, and José Rafael Enríquez Trespalacios, *Biblioteca Hispano Americana Septentrional o catalogo y noticias de los literatos* [...], 2nd ed. (Amecameca, Tipografía del Colegio Católico, 1883), 2: 60, *visitador* José de Gálvez called the *novohispano* jurist Baltasar Ladrón de Guevara the "American Ulpianus," indicating the lasting prestige of the classical lawyer. See also Borah, *Justice by Insurance*, 6–7; Meder, *Rechtsgeschichte*, 261–62; Schlosser, *Neuere europäische*, 149.

[15] Defense of Francisco de Castro, AGI, Escribanía 289 A, *Relazion*, fol. 383v. According to Linda Levy Peck, *Court, Patronage, and Corruption in Early Stuart England* (London: Routledge, 1993), 195, the Duke of Buckingham (1628–1687) also used natural law to ward off corruption accusations.

[16] According to Castillo de Bobadilla, *Política*, book 2, chapter 11, para. 45, esp. note f, the fourteenth-century commentator Angelus Ubaldus, based on Saint Paul's 1 Tim. 5:18, approved of judges who accepted food provided they did not draw a salary.

[17] *Recopilación de leyes de los reynos de las Indias mandada imprimir y publicar por la Magestad Católica del Rey Don Carlos II. Nuestro Señor* [...]. 1741, facsimile (Madrid: Consejo de la Hispanidad, 1953), www.leyes.congreso.gob.pe/leyes_indias.aspx, henceforth noted as *Law of the Indies*, book 2, title 1, law 4; similar were the *Institutes* 1.2.9. See also Murillo Velarde, *Cursus Iuris Canonici*, book 1, title 4, para. 114; de la Puente Luna and Honores, "Guardianes de la real justicia," 25, 31–32, 36; Renzo Honores, "El

In addition, for example, no explicit written code governed the conduct of people who moved to other places in the Spanish empire. The king occasionally intervened to award new citizenship to migrants, but in most cases, newcomers to towns performed along unwritten guidelines. When they showed their commitment to the faith, the community tacitly included them in the citizenry. At the same time, the towns usually denied the same rights to Romany (gypsies), Jews, or blacks and frowned upon them as rule breakers.[18]

Finally, the royal law of the land issued by kings and queens formed the sixth pillar of justice. In the 1260s, the king of Castile set an important milestone in this regard by publishing the *Siete Partidas* (Seven Parts). This collection comprised ample royal communications and Spanish translations of the Roman law. King Philip II (1556–1598) later ordered his jurists to draft a new compilation, incorporating the *Siete Partidas* and other Castilian collections. These jurists also selected suitable *reales cédulas* (royal provisions) from an immensity of the king's communications. When they completed the process, the king published the *Law of Castile* in 1567.[19] In a similar move, the crown assembled the *Law of the Indies*. By the middle of the sixteenth century, the crown had issued about 10,000 provisions for the Americas, filling 200 books. Legal experts began compiling them, but *reales cédulas* kept pouring out until 500 books could not hold them anymore. Finally, the American-born jurist Antonio de León Pinelo and his colleague, Juan de Solórzano y Pereyra, concluded the work in 1636. They arranged the rules according to subject matter, creating an authoritative guideline for the Indies.[20]

---

licenciado Polo Ondegardo y el debate sobre el Derecho Consuetudinario en los Andes del siglo XVI," unpublished manuscript. On the intertwining of customary law and *ius commune*, Yanna Yannakakis and Martina Schrader-Kniffki, "Between the 'Old Law' and the New: Christian Translation, Indian Jurisdiction, and Criminal Justice in Colonial Oaxaca," *HAHR* 96, no. 3 (2016): 517–548.

[18] Herzog, *Defining Nations. Immigrants and Citizens in Early Modern Spain and Spanish America* (New Haven: Yale University Press, 2003), 6–9, 201–208. Robinson, Fergus, Gordon, *European*, 108, on sentences confirming customs.

[19] *Recopilación de las leyes destos reynos hecha por mandado de la Magestad Catholica del Rey don Philipe Segundo nuestro señor* [...] (Alcalá de Henares: Juan Iñiguez de Liquerica, 1581), henceforth cited as the *Law of Castile*; Xavier Gil, "Spain and Portugal," in *European Political Thought, 1450–1700: Religion, Law, and Philosophy*, eds. Howell A. Lloyd, Glenn Burgess, and Simon Hodson (New Haven, CT: Yale University Press, 2007), 432; Decock, *Theologians*, 33–36.

[20] Arndt Brendecke, *Imperio e información: funciones del saber en el dominio colonial español* (Madrid, Frankfurt: Iberoamericana/Vervuert, 2012), 350–351; Bravo Lira, *Derecho común y derecho propio en el Nuevo Mundo* (Santiago de Chile: Ed. Jurídica

The *Law of the Indies* gave the Americas their own legal collection akin to the special *fueros* (rules) of the peninsular kingdoms. The collection described the Indies as "great kingdoms and seignories" in the empire instead of lesser provinces.[21] The aim of this phrase was to appease the American elites and increase their loyalty to Madrid. This mattered, because King Charles II (reigned 1665–1700) of Spain remained childless. The other European powers at that time discussed partitioning the Spanish empire among themselves. As a response, Madrid sought to tie the Americans firmly to the crown by publishing the new collection in 1680 and enshrining the status of the overseas kingdoms.[22]

The *Law of the Indies* generally superseded older collections and *reales cédulas* in the Americas. Its rules and its interpreters increasingly served as guidepost for judges and the Council of the Indies (the appeals court for American affairs), and reform-minded jurists tended to draw on other sources less frequently.[23] For instance, in 1719, Garzarón suspended a judge for buying a house in Mexico City, among other charges. The crown opposed such acquisitions, because they indicated that the ministers joined society and became corruptible. The judge showed in his defense a *real cédula* from 1663 allowing such a purchase. Yet the prosecutor of the Council of the Indies rebutted this argument in 1724 by maintaining that the *Law of the Indies* nullified the older *reales cédulas*. The prosecutor convinced the king and the Council, who convicted the judge.[24]

At the same time, locals on occasion suspended those newly arriving orders that they found undesirable. *Novohispano* judges and officials

---

de Chile, 1989), 30. See also James Muldoon, "Solórzano's *De indiarum iure*: Applying a Medieval Theory of World Order in the Seventeenth Century," *Journal of World History* 2, no. 1 (1991): 29–45.

[21] *Law of the Indies*, book 2, title 2, law 1.

[22] Pietschmann, "Antecedentes políticos de México, 1808: Estado territorial, estado novohispano, crisis política y desorganización constitucional," in *México, 1808–1821. Las ideas y los hombres*, eds. Pilar Gonzalbo Aizpuru and Andrés Lira González (Mexico City: El Colegio de México, 2014), 31, 34; Rodríguez O., "We Are Now," 20; Víctor Tau Anzoátegui, "Entre leyes, glosas y comentos. El episodio de la recopilación de Indias," in *Homenaje al Profesor Alfonso García-Gallo* (Madrid: Editorial Complutense, 1996), 4: 279–81.

[23] *Law of the Indies*, book 2, title 1, law 1; Tau Anzoátegui, "Entre leyes, glosas y comentos," 270–81; Bernd Hausberger and Óscar Mazín, "Nueva España: Los años de autonomía," in *Nueva Historia general de México*, eds. Erik Velásquez García et al. (Mexico City: Colegio de México, 2010), 269; Yannakakis, *The Art of Being*, 115–127.

[24] *Parecer* of José de Laysequilla, Madrid, 14 Aug. 1724, AGI, Escribanía 287 B, *pieza* 39, fols. 132–135. See also *Law of the Indies*, book 2, title 16, law 55.

returned the provisions to Spain when they collided with local experience or breached other rules. They requested additional instructions addressing these concerns. The functionaries also maintained that the "unjust law does not oblige the conscience" to act and preferred to "obey but not to execute" the royal mandate. In this way, colonials vowed loyalty to the crown while stalling the particular measure. Such maneuvering pervaded the Atlantic world. In the Austrian-Hungarian empire, for example, the ministers on occasion respectfully tabled the orders and sent them back to Vienna. They and their Spanish colleagues ultimately built on Roman traditions of forging a consensus to implement change.[25]

These evolving ideas circulated in the Atlantic world. The Spanish empire acknowledged the *ius commune*, and so did the Holy Roman Empire (Germany), France, and Italy. Even the English common law, which struck a different course than continental European law, conversed with canon and Roman law. Jurists advanced new legal solutions in response to the expanding economies and vibrant intellectual life. They avidly read their colleagues' works beyond any political or linguistic boundaries. For example, legal experts in the Holy Roman Empire cited the Spanish attorney Diego Covarrubias. *Novohispano* teachers and students alike read Italian, French, Dutch, or German scholars writing in Latin or as synthesized by others. The eighteenth-century rector of the University of Guatemala prepared his lectures by studying the Bavarian canonist Johann Georg Reiffenstuel. Another striking example are the eighteenth-century *Recitations*, a Latin comment on the Roman laws written by a lawyer from Saxony (Holy Roman Empire). The text was later translated into Spanish and freely adapted to the Americas. The Atlantic legal culture fused the *ius commune* with its own traditions.[26]

---

[25] Garriga, "Sobre el gobierno," 108. According to Antonio Annino, "El primer constitucionalismo Mexicano, 1810–1830," in *Para una Historia de América III. Los nudos 2*, eds. Marcello Carmagnani, Alicia Hernández Chávez, and Ruggiero Romano (Mexico City: Fondo de Cultura Económica, El Colegio de México, Fideicomiso Historia de las Américas, 1999), 155, "I obey but do not execute (*obedezco pero no cumplo)*" adapted the Roman principle that "what concerns all, needs to be approved by all." See also Decock, *Theologians*, 28; Hespanha, "Porque é que existe," 23–26; Pennington, "Bartolomé de las Casas," 103–104; Reinhard, *Geschichte der Staatsgewalt: Eine vergleichende Verfassungsgeschichte*, 3rd ed. (Munich: C. H. Beck, 2003), 80. Azcargorta, *Manual de Confesores*, 182, knew that "it is debatable whether binding laws – even papal ones – depend on the consent of the inferiors."

[26] Robinson, Fergus, and Gordon, *European*, 72–89; Tau Anzoátegui, *El Jurista en el Nuevo Mundo. Pensamiento. Doctrina. Mentalidad* (Frankfurt: Max Planck Institute for European Legal History, 2016), 42; Bravo Lira, *El juez*, 338; Clavero, *Historia*, 18–20; Herzog, *Frontiers*, 260. According to Decock, *Theologians*, 54, the Spanish

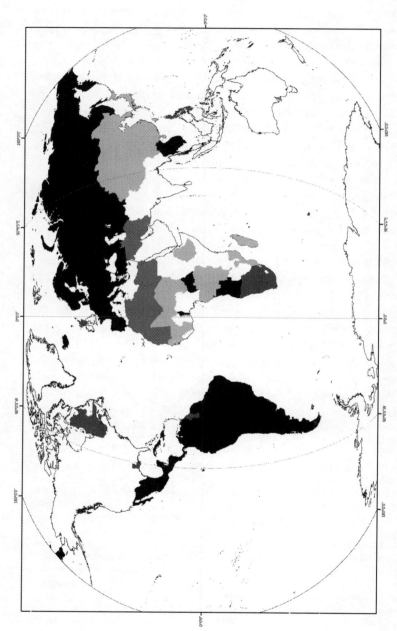

MAP 2 The Global *Ius Commune*. Today's legal systems that build directly on the *ius commune* are marked in black, while the regions colored in gray have mixed legal systems with heavy infusions of *ius commune* concepts. Map drawn by Ana Gabriela Arreola Meneses, based on *JuriGlobe*, University of Ottawa, www.juriglobe.ca/eng/rep-geo/index.php. and Maximilian Dörrbecker, *Map of the Legal Systems of the World*, https://en.wikipedia.org/wiki/Common_law#/media/File:Map_of_the_Legal_systems_of_the_world_(en).png.

In New Spain, many scholars were familiar with the legal culture. Theologians wrote manuals to prepare priests for administering the sacraments, especially for the confession. The clergymen drew on the *ius commune* and widely disseminated its concepts in relatable ways. In addition, professors at the University of Mexico City owned parts of Justinian's collection and its interpreters. The first professor of rhetoric in the sixteenth century, for instance, owned eleven books written by Bartolus, while early eighteenth-century booksellers sold humanists such as André Tiraqueau. The university professors in Mexico City cited these legal scholars when discussing the Roman and royal law.[27]

When law students graduated from the university, they often joined the *colegio de abogados* (college of attorneys) to practice, or they became salaried *relatores*. The *relatores* worked for the *audiencia* and assessed whether litigation had the standing to go to trial. They also summarized the documents submitted to court and greatly simplified the work for the judges. Most other lawyers spent four years in residence with an experienced attorney. When they completed that phase, they took an exam at the *audiencia*, at least in theory. The *audiencia* then admitted them to represent clients. Many, if not all, of these lawyers became lesser nobles or

---

scholastic Juan de Medina, for example, cited the German Conrad Summenhart von Calw; Samuel Pufendorff was also cited. Thomas Duve, "Von der Europäischen Rechtsgeschichte einer Rechtsgeschichte Europas in globalhistorischer Perspektive," *Rechtsgeschichte – Legal History* 20 (2012): 36–39; Olivia Moreno Gamboa, "Comercio y comerciantes de libros entre Cádiz y Veracruz en el tránsito hacia un nuevo orden (1702–1749)," in *Resonancias imperiales: América y la Paz de Utrecht de 1713*, eds. Iván Escamilla González, Matilde Souto Mantecón, and Guadalupe Pinzón Ríos (Mexico City: Instituto Mora, UNAM, 2015), 296.

[27] Decock, *Theologians*, 46. According to Enrique González González and Víctor Gutiérrez Rodríguez, "Los cadedráticos novohispanos y sus libros. Tres bibliotecas del siglo xvi," in *Dalla lectura all'e-learning*, ed. Andrea Romano (Bologna: Clueb, 2015), 91–93, 96, the admittedly sixteenth-century libraries contained publications by Andrea Alciato (1492–1550) and Guillaume Budé (1467–1540). Moreno Gamboa "Historia de una librería novohispana del siglo xviii" (MA thesis, UNAM, 2006), 132–133, and Moreno Gamboa, "Comercio y comerciantes de libros," 295–296, shows that a bookseller sold sections of the *corpus iuris civilis* in 1730 and Tiraqueau's books in 1732, but did not offer anything written by Bartolus. Judging by Jesús Yhmoff Cabrera, *Catálogo de obras manuscritas en Latín de la Biblioteca Nacional de México* (Mexico City: UNAM, Instituto de Investigaciones Bibliográficas, 1975), e.g. 8, 54, few jurídical manuscripts in Latin survive in the National Library of Mexico, although María Fernanda González Gallardo, *Las tesis de licenciados y doctores en leyes de la Real Universidad de México en el siglo XVII: Código* (Mexico City: Instituto de Investigaciones Jurídicas / UNAM, 2017) points to the body of theses written in Latin and kept in that library.

confirmed their status upon graduating from the university.[28] Most of them also joined the college of attorneys. This must have been some kind of a social body, perhaps a confraternity associated with a church. In 1724, the Council of the Indies chided the "college of attorneys for having charged excessive fees and gifts." Subsequently, the college became more formalized in 1760 as an independent social body.[29]

In addition, the legal agents without university training played much larger roles than historians have thought before. *Procuradores* (procurators) especially represented Natives and other commoners in matters of process. They submitted briefs, moved paperwork through the legal machinery, and contracted attorneys when necessary. Procurators often acquired substantial knowledge and successfully acted akin to lawyers. They even crafted their own judicial arguments for the courts, although the crown forbade them to do so. This is why I refer to both academically trained jurists and procurators as legal practitioners or experts in this book. In addition, notaries investigated crimes, questioned suspects, and copied or summarized papers. That may seem like a straightforward task, but the slant of their summaries and the aim of their interrogations deeply influenced the judicial verdicts.[30]

When legal experts went to work, they continuously weighed the royal law and local custom against Roman, canon, and biblical principles, and

---

[28] Rodolfo Aguirre Salvador, *Por el camino de las letras: el ascenso profesional de los catedráticos juristas de la Nueva España, siglo XVIII* (Mexico City: UNAM, 1998), 104–105; Enrique González González, ed., *Proyecto de estatutos ordenados por el virrey Cerralvo (1626)* (Mexico City: UNAM, 1991), 77–82; on New Grenada, Victor M. Uribe-Uran, *Honorable Lives: Lawyers, Family, and Politics in Colombia, 1780–1850* (Pittsburgh: University of Pittsburgh Press, 2000), 20–22. Garzarón generally did not call lawyers officials, because they dealt with matters of justice, but for the sake of clarity, I include them in this group to distinguish them from the judges. On acquiring nobility, see Mazín, "La nobleza ibérica," 64–72.

[29] Sentence of the Council of the Indies, Madrid, 10 Feb. 1724, AGI, Escribanía 1183 folder *1721–1730 Francisco Garzarón*. Óscar Cruz Barney, "Prólogo," in *Los abogados y la formación del Estado mexicano*, eds. Óscar Cruz Barney, Héctor Felipe Fix-Fierro, and Elisa Speckmann (Mexico City: UNAM, Instituto de Investigaciones Jurídicas, 2013), xiii; Mayagoitia, "Las últimas generaciones de abogados virreinales," ibid., 5; Christian Hillebrand, *Die Real Audiencia in Mexiko* (Baden-Baden: Nomos, 2016), 125, and others maintain that the college was formally founded in or near 1760, but apparently there existed a precursor during Garzarón's *visita*.

[30] McKinley, *Fractional Freedoms*, 5; Kathryn Burns, *Into the Archive: Writing and Power in Colonial Peru* (Durham, NC: Duke University Press, 2010), 14, 24; Gayol, *Laberintos de justicia*, I: 141–145, see also 172–194; Herzog, *Upholding Justice*, 53; de la Puente Luna and Honores, "Guardianes de la real justicia," 25. On earlier practices, Brundage, *Medieval Origins*, 353–364; Hillebrand, *Real Audiencia*, 117–133.

no clear boundary separated the law from social practices. Historians describe that complexity as "judicial pluralism," which differed markedly from modern ideas of a (relatively) unequivocal, systematic, and hierarchical legality.[31] The indigenous community of Meztitlan (Hgo.), for instance, complained in 1724 that a local resident had bought the appointment as *alcalde mayor*. The viceroy and the *audiencia* heard the case and agreed that a *real cédula* from 1691 permitted purchasing the appointment.[32] The viceroy's adviser then cited the contrary opinion of Roman emperor Severus Alexander (222–235) and noted that several theologians condemned selling offices as tantamount to selling justice. He balanced these points against the *Law of Castile* and the "*Law of the Indies* which did not hold that offices with jurisdiction were unsellable." The adviser finally emphasized that Charles de Borromeo, a sixteenth-century saint, had also sold his principality with his judicial duties, which was "licit and honest because his pious aim was giving alms to the poor." The adviser pondered the mandates of these different normative sources and concurred with the viceroy and the *audiencia* that the *alcalde mayor* could serve his post.[33]

The precise relationship among the six pillars of justice was often contested, although Spaniards generally preferred the specific over the general rule. Typically, the *Law of the Indies* reigned supreme in the Americas, followed by the *Law of Castile* and the *Siete Partidas*. Meanwhile, the Roman law and its interpreters did not have direct validity in the Spanish empire, but their concepts deeply infused

---

[31] Tau Anzoátegui, "El poder de la costumbre. Estudios sobre el Derecho Consuetudinario en América hispana hasta la Emancipación," in *Nuevas aportaciones a la historia jurídica de Iberoamérica*, ed. José Andrés-Gallego (Madrid: Fundación Histórica Tavera, Hernando de Larramendi/ Mapfre, 2000); Hespanha, "Porque é que existe," 22–23; Duve, *Sonderrecht*, 196–198; Hillard von Thiessen, "Korruption und Normenkonkurrenz: Zur Funktion und Wirkung von Korruptionsvorwürfen gegen die Günstling-Minister Lerma und Buckingham in Spanien und England im frühen 17. Jahrhundert," in *Geld–Geschenke–Politik: Korruption im neuzeitlichen Europa*, eds. Jens Ivo Engels, Andreas Fahrmeir, and Alexander Nützenadel (Munich: Oldenbourg, 2009), 93.

[32] Governor, *alcaldes*, and officials to viceroy, Meztitlan, n. d., AGI, México 492, *cuaderno* 8, fols. 35v–36v; Toribio Fernández de Rivera for the *alcalde mayor* Francio de Herrera Beltrán to viceroy, probably Atotonilco el Grande, ibid., fol. 36v; José Franciso de Landa for the governor and *común y naturales* of Meztitlan to viceroy, n. d., ibid., fols. 37v–40v; *real acuerdo*, Mexico City, 11 Feb. 1724, ibid., fols. 41–43; royal order, Buen Retiro, 7 June 1691, ibid., 77v–89v.

[33] *Parecer* of Dr. José Meléndez, Mexico City, 22 Jan. 1725, AGI, México 492, *cuaderno* 8, fols. 101–107; *Law of Castile*, book 7, title 3, law 7; similar exhortations against selling offices in *Novels*, 8, preface and 1.

jurisprudence.[34] Yet jurists and procurators did not always strictly observe that hierarchy. Juan de Hevia Bolaños, a brilliant legal agent working in Lima, exemplified this uncertainty in his discussion of Church protections for offenders. "Although imperial civil law," he explained, referring to the Roman collection, and the "royal law of the *Siete Partidas* order that adulterers, rapists of virgins, murderers, and debtors ... cannot seek asylum in the church ... Church law corrects this case, which is applicable since this is an ecclesiastical issue ... according to the common opinion of the doctors ... and the customs which have affirmed Church law." For Hevia Bolaños, the important jurists and customs concurred that canon law displaced both royal and Roman rules in this matter.[35]

Moreover, at least some *novohispano* ministers held that customs and process were more specific than royal law, especially when justifying their own actions. A civil judge claimed, for example, that a "particular custom is a law that nullifies other written ones," including the royal and Roman law.[36]

---

[34] Murillo Velarde, *Cursus Iuris Canonici*, book 1, title 32, para. 344. The hierarchy is debated; see Decock, *Theologians*, 34–35; Jesús Vallejo, "El cáliz de plata. Articulación de órdenes jurídicos en la jurisprudencia del ius commune," *Revista de Historia del Derecho* 38 (2009): 7–13, http://www.scielo.org.ar/scielo.php?script=sci_arttext&pid=S1853-17842009000200 002&lng=es&nrm=iso; Bravo Lira, *Derecho común*, 7–8; Alejandro Guzmán Brito, "Prólogo," in Bravo Lira, *Derecho común*, 7–8; Alejandro Agüero, "Local Law and Localization of Law. Hispanic Legal Tradition and Colonial Culture (16th–18th Centuries)," in *Spatial and Temporal Dimensions for Legal History. Research Experiences and Itineraries*, ed. Massimo Meccarelli and María Julia Solla Sastre (Frankfurt: Max Planck Institute for European Legal History, 2016), 116–122, www.rg.mpg.de/1091047/gplh_6_a guero.pdf; Carlos Garriga, "Concepción y aparatos de la justicia: las Reales Audiencias de Indias," in *Convergencias y divergencias: México y Perú, siglos xvi–xix*, ed. Lilia Oliver (Mexico City: University of Guadalajara, El Colegio de Michoacán, 2006), 35–36; Pennington, "Bartolomé de las Casas," 107; Meder, *Rechtsgeschichte*, 22, 253–254.

[35] Juan de Hevia Bolaños, *Curia Filipica, primero, y segundo tomo. El primero dividido en cinco partes, donde se trata breve y compendiosamente de los juicios, mayormente forenses, eclesiasticos y c ... el segundo tomo en tres libros distribuido, donde se trata de la mercancia, y contratación de tierra y mar*, with an index by Nicolás de la Cueva (Madrid: Francisco de Hierro, 1725), vol. 1, part 3, para. 12, no. 49. According to Alejandro Agüero and Francisco Javier Andrés Santos, "Republicanismo y tradición jurídica en los albores de la independencia: la significación americana del Tratado de los Oficiales de la República de Antonio Fernández de Otero," in *Actas del XIX Congreso del Instituto Internacional de Historia del Derecho Indiano*, ed. Thomas Duve (Madrid: Dykinson, 2017), vol. 1, 344, the *Curia Filipica* was the "most published book in the history of Spanish juridical literature."

[36] Defense of Juan Díaz de Bracamonte, AGI, México 670 B, *Relación*, fol. 142. Miguel de San Antonio, *Resumen de la theologia moral de el Crisol arreglado al exercicio prudente de las operaciones humanas, y practica de los Confesores* (Madrid: en la imprenta de Ángel Pascual Rubio, 1719), 7, suggested that attorneys could levy fees according to customs; drawing on Aquinas, *Summa*, IIa–IIae, Q. 71, a. 4 co. Felipe Castro Gutiérrez, "La fuerza de la ley y el asilo de la costumbre. Un proceso por fraudes y abusos en la real

One attorney added that "just and reasonable custom predominates and is preferable to the official fee in those locales" where the schedule did not adequately provide for the attorneys.[37] Another lawyer maintained in 1722 that the "municipal law is no other thing than the fee schedule," meaning that the customs of a town allowed him to ignore the official fee schedule imposed by a crown minister.[38] For many, the word *estilo* also referred to judicial process at a court of justice and resembled custom. An attorney argued that his client "never demanded or took more than *estilo* allows ... and if others gave him one peso then because this was *estilo*, and ... ruling against *estilo* is legally void ... it should remain in force because of its tradition and age."[39]

Many legal experts agreed with these officials that customs remained valid as long as the courts applied or the king tacitly approved them. Lawyers often cited a judicial precedent to demonstrate that a particular custom was still in use. When such direct evidence was lacking, implicit tolerance often sufficed. In this line of thinking, a *novohispano* attorney insisted in 1724, that "the custom that the agents receive some amounts ... is in force and vigor" and existed within plain "view, knowledge, and sufferance of that Senate and therefore the Prince ... and with their tacit consent." The lawyer compared here the *audiencia* of Mexico City to the Roman legislature and showed that no "prohibitive law, statute, constitution ... and law of the Indies" indicated that the king had withdrawn his tolerance of this particular custom.[40]

---

casa de Moneda de México," *Revista de Indias* 77, no. 271 (2017): 786–787, notes similar claims about the role of custom.

[37] Print *por Don Miguel Truxillo*, AGI, México 670 A, fol. 17v. Simon de Carragal on behalf of Juan José Aguilera, AGI, Escribanía 289 B, *Relazion*, fol. 41, argued that the *Siete Partidas* justified breaking the fee schedule, although *partida* 1, title 2, law 6 probably did not permit customs to displace the written royal law.

[38] Defense of Fernando de Quiroga, AGI, Escribanía 289 A, *Relazion*, fol. 1549. See the *Law of the Indies*, book 2, title 1, law 1, which recognized the "municipal laws of each city"; *Siete Partidas*, part 1, title 2, laws 4–9. The *audiencia* to king, Mexico City, 27 Feb. 1719, AGI, Escribanía 281 A, *cuaderno* 14, fols. 56–66, recognized both the "law of the Indies ... and other municipal laws of these kingdoms."

[39] Testimony of don Manuel de Rivas for scribe Francisco de Castro, AGI, Escribanía 289 A, *Relazion*, fols. 380v–382v. Murillo Velarde, *Cursus Iuris Canonici*, book 1, title 4, paras. 114–118, distinguished *estilo* as judicial process from the unwritten custom, and so did Quevedo, *Fortuna con seso*, 527; while the *RAE* (1732) p. 635 defined *estilo* as both "legal procedure" and "custom." See also Inés Gómez, "Entre la corrupción y la venalidad: Don Pedro Valle de la Cerda y la visita al Consejo de Hacienda de 1643," in Andújar Castillo and Ponce-Leiva, *Mérito, venalidad y corrupción*, 239.

[40] Print *por Don Miguel Truxillo*, AGI, México 670 A, fols. 17v–18. Similarly, Manuel de Rivas on behalf of Francisco de Castro, AGI, Escribanía 289 A, *Relazion*, fols. 380v–381, declared that "custom ... has the force of law according to common consent," while defense of Francisco de Alexo de Luna, AGI, Escribanía 289 A, fol. 352–352v, explained that charging inmates presentation fees was "just and not undue, because there is no law prohibiting

The defense of custom was no mere self-serving and cynical strategy because even the councilors of the Indies accepted the importance of customs to a point. For example, the Council meted out fairly lenient punishments to those officials charged with overcharging their clients. The officials stated in their defense that these excessive fees were customary to remedy their low income. The Council ordered these lower functionaries to pay their share of *visita* (special investigation) costs and perhaps minor penalties, and the officials then returned to their posts. Nonetheless, the doctrine on the tacit consent also slowly dissolved in the eighteenth century. This explains, in part, why Francisco Garzarón had tacked a harder line in suspending these officials.[41]

Next to the doctrine on tacit consent, the full legal plurality and perhaps many aspects of diversity declined when strands of the Enlightenment dawned on the empire in the late seventeenth century. As a consequence, the royal law gained strength over other normative sources in the courts and the colleges. Many professors shifted their focus to the royal law and their interpreters, and even academic chairs were renamed. They dropped references to Justinian's *Institutes*, for example, replacing them with sections of the royal law.[42] In part for these reasons, judges who based their defense on the *Law of the Indies* during Garzarón's *visita* usually fared better. A criminal judge, for instance,

---

them ... and these presentations are not expressly prohibited," although the *Law of the Indies*, book 2, title 23, law 44; title 30, laws 1–6, only allowed ushers and notaries to charge presentation fees for documents. On the doctrine of the *consensus universorum* (universal consent), see Vallejo, "El cáliz de plata," 11; on the tacit consent, Duve, "Global Legal History: A Methodological Approach," in *Max Planck Institute for European Legal History Research Paper Series* 4 (2016): 14, http://ssrn.com/abstract=2781104; Meder, *Rechtsgeschichte*, 255; Agüero, "Local Law," 108–110. According to Jean Bodin, *The Six Books of the Commonwealth*, trans. M. J. Tooley (New York: Barnes & Noble, 1967), book 1, chap. 10, "Custom only has binding force by the sufferance and good pleasure of the sovereign prince, and as far as he is willing to authorize it." According to Garriga, "Concepción," 31, Francisco Carrasco del Saz argued in his 1630 treatise that certain judicial rights of the prince also extended to the Senate/high court.

[41] Vallejo, "El cáliz de plata," 7–13; Meder, *Rechtsgeschichte*, 255. For a full discussion of the verdicts against officials, see Chapter six.

[42] Tau Anzoátegui, *El Jurista en el Nuevo Mundo*, 8–13. Scholars now contest the nature of the Enlightenment. Jorge Cañizares-Esguerra, *How to Write the History of the New World. Histories, Epistemologies, and Identities in the Eighteenth-Century Atlantic World* (Stanford, CA: Stanford University Press, 2001), 7, 9, separates this current from the "aggressively modern movement" called Baroque. While this is a good point, we also need to clarify further how to distinguish the two periods from one another. See also Matthew C. Mirow, *Latin American Law: A History of Private Law and Institutions in Spanish America* (University of Texas Press, 2004), 36–37.

acknowledged that he and his colleagues had to sign off jointly on prisoner release. Nevertheless, the criminal judge admitted that he had single-handedly set free a handful of inmates who owed small amounts of money, because the *Law of the Indies* forbade litigation under twenty pesos. Therefore he did not have to seek his colleagues' consent in these cases. It is likely that the judge's defense held, because Garzarón charged three other criminal judges with the same offense and acquitted them.[43]

Royal agents often legitimized this shift toward the royal law as a return to the good old order, because innovation was harder to justify. An exchange from 1721 illustrates this matter. The king deplored the general disregard for the royal law, and the civil judge José Joaquín Uribe seconded this point. He emphasized that the "due observance of the law" would restore the *audiencia* "to its ancient luster and dignity."[44] Rather than returning to the splendor of the past, however, the crown demanded from the ministers "the exact compliance with the law and ordinances" as a way of asserting royal control. The crown increasingly demanded obedience from its ministers.[45]

As the royal law grew in stature, jurists called for a new systematic code encapsulating all doctrines. A growing number of legal practitioners discarded the vast multitude of rules from the past. Instead, they distilled general principles of justice and derived from them subordinate clauses. Jurists also envisioned a precise language that lay people could understand without falling prey to pettifoggers. Consequently, they demanded curbing the *arbitrio* of judges to obtain more predictable rulings determined by the new code. The judge was to be no other than "the mouth that pronounced the words of the law."[46] Despite these innovations, many still recognized that the judge

---

[43] Defense of Juan Francisco de la Peña, AGI, México 670 B, fol. 492–492v, referring to *law of Castile*, book 2, title 6, law 6, and *law of the Indies*, book 5, title 10, law 1. De la Peña lost his post, but Garzarón absolved Nicolás Chirino Vandeval, Juan de la Beguellina y Sandoval, and Francisco Barbadillo Victoria (see table 6 in the Appendix). According to *Law of Castile*, book 3, title 9, laws 14, 18, and 19, judges could not delay punishing convicts and had to curb paperwork in small-claims trials.

[44] Vote of José Joaquín Uribe, AGN, Historia 102, exp. 10, fol. 134; Garzarón to king, Mexico City, 16 May 1717, AGI, México 670 A, also favored restoring "the practice of the royal ordinances and forgotten laws." See also Marquis of Casafuerte to king, Mexico City, 15 May 1724, referenced in *consulta* of the Council of the Indies, Madrid, 18 Jan. 1726, AGI, México 381.

[45] King to president and civil judges of the *audiencia*, Lerma, 13 Dec. 1721, AGN, Historia 102, fol. 82–82v; Rodrigo de Zepeda to king, n. d., attached to the *consulta* of the Council of the Indies, 5 Dec. 1721, AGI, México 670 A. Note that Garriga, "Concepción," 60, argues that Bourbon Reforms primarily aimed at restoring good justice, while I maintain that this was in part a rhetorical trope to legitimize reforms.

[46] Montesquieu, cited in Schlosser, *Neuere europäische*, 182.

had an important role to play in unforeseen conflicts. Legal experts also appreciated the wisdom of existing doctrines, which they incorporated into the developing codes. As a result, ministers in Prussia (Germany) began drafting a Civil Code in 1746. The French Civil Code followed soon, pioneering a lasting foundation for the emerging bourgeois society, which also influenced many other regions in a lasting way. A revised form of that code remains in force today in the state of Louisiana, for instance.[47]

The reformers in the early eighteenth-century Spanish empire jumped on the bandwagon. They began to distance themselves from the ancient compilations and lambasted wily and obfuscating jurists. The jurist Melchor de Macanaz stated in 1722 that "the multitude of our laws confound more than they guide equity and justice." For him, the Roman law "twists the process of justice, stupefying the understanding of the judges, who perhaps choose among the infinity of legal opinions the one that is least reconcilable with reason." Macanaz instead suggested one "code as pattern and rule for judges and lawyers."[48] About twenty-five years later, another jurist labeled even the *Law of Castile* as a bewildering source of litigation and derided the "compilation of laws and vague conclusions."[49]

Not everyone agreed. In New Spain, many stood by the *Law of the Indies* that guaranteed the autonomies of the kingdom. In addition, a late seventeenth-century Spanish judge maintained that "changing old process of government upsets the vassals, and one should always avoid innovations."[50] In 1700, the aristocrat Pedro de Portocarrero y Guzmán

---

[47] Bravo Lira, *El juez*, 325–328, 334–340; Franz Wieacker, *A History of Private Law in Europe with Particular Reference to Germany*, trans. Tony Weir (Oxford: Clarendon Press, 1995), 249–255; Meder, *Rechtsgeschichte*, 270–280; Schlosser, *Neuere europäische*, 175–184, 212–214.

[48] Melchor de Macanaz, *Los veinte y dos auxilios para el buen gobierno*, Paris, 29 Aug. 1722, Biblioteca Nacional de España (hereinafter cited as BNE), Ms. 5671, fol. 21–21v.

[49] Antonio Valero, "Ciencia de Estado y Politica exterior de España," n. d., about 1748, BNE, Ms. 10512, fols. 16, 239. According to José Antonio Escudero, *Los orígenes del consejo de ministros en España* (Madrid: Editorial Complutense, 2001), 1: 256, Pablo de Mora y Jaraba (ca. 1716–1790) wrote during the reign of Ferdinand VI under the pseudonym Valero. See also I. A. A. Thompson, "Absolutism, Legalism, and the Law in Castile, 1500–1700," in *Der Absolutismus – ein Mythos? Strukturwandel monarchischer Herrschaft in West- und Mitteleuropa (ca. 1550–1700)*, eds. Ronald G. Asch and Heinz Duchhardt (Cologne: Böhlau, 1996), 224–226; Bravo Lira, *El juez*, 325–344; María Paz Alonso Romero, *Orden procesal y garantías entre Antiguo Régimen y constitucionalismo gaditano* (Madrid: Centro de Estudios Políticos y Constitucionales, 2008), 160–168.

[50] Lancina, *Commentarios*, 19.

thundered against the "multiplicity of laws which is evident proof of the corruption of customs." Portocarrero y Guzmán directed his ire not against the *ius commune*, but against the pragmatics, the broad legal innovations of kings that undermined justice of the past. From his perspective, he had a point. As the privileges of the old order crumbled, new types of judges ascended to the courts. They downplayed the old judicial plurality and concentrated on royal compilations, their interpreters, and recent mandates from above. For Portocarrero y Guzmán, these innovations violated justice as he knew it. For others, they heralded a new epoch of justice.[51]

1.2 JUDGES, VISITAS, AND SOCIAL NETWORKS

Commoners and nobles had relatively easy access to legal representation and the courts in the sixteenth and seventeenth centuries. Civil and criminal trials were on the rise in most Atlantic empires, and this "popular legalism" marked New Spain too.[52] In addition, social networks pervaded the empire and local intermediaries played a crucial role in exchanging resources and making decisions. Yet when networks skewed the judicial and political deliberations excessively or when a revolt threatened the established order, the king appointed *visitadores*. These investigative judges sidestepped the cumbersome course of justice, suggested remedies, and often punished malefactors more quickly and harshly.

Judges assured that accusers, defendants, and witnesses had their say in lawsuits. For this reason, Natives, slaves, widows, and the elderly frequently turned to the courts for redress. The judges sometimes bemoaned litigious Indians who caused heavy workloads but often ruled in favor of the Natives and against the *alcaldes mayores* or other social superiors. The king or the

---

[51] Pedro Portocarrero y Guzmán, *Theatro monarchico de España: Que contiene las mas puras, como catholicas, maximas de estado, por las quales, assi los principes, como las republicas* ... (Madrid: Juan Garcia Infançon, 1700), 172–73. According to Rafael Diego-Fernández Sotelo, *El proyecto de José de Gálvez de 1774 en las ordenanzas de intendentes de Río de la Plata y Nueva España* (Zamora: El Colegio de Michoacán, 2016), 22, 137–143; and Moreno Gamboa, "La imprenta y los autores novohispanos. La transformación de una cultura impresa colonial bajo el régimen borbónico (1701–1821)" (PhD diss., UNAM, 2013), 200–201, Charles III ordered the gathering of recent *reales cédulas* to design a new law book for the entire empire. This may well have been an attempt to draft a systematic code. In response, a client of José de Gálvez's family, Eusebio Bentura Beleña, published a collection of Mexican *audiencia* verdicts, the *Recopilación sumaria de todos los autos acordados de la Real Audiencia y Sala del Crimen de esta Nueva España*. The king ultimately abandoned the law book, while Bentura Beleña crafted a new foundation for *novohispano* justice.

[52] Steven Hindle's term "popular legalism," is cited in Holenstein, "Introduction," 23.

queen upheld this system. They heard the appeals coming from the Americas, acted as the supreme arbiters, and showed good care for their vassals by listening to their concerns. In fact, the words for *audiencia* and *oidor* (civil judge) were both derived from hearing. Consequently, most *novohispanos* stated their viewpoint in the courts of justice when called upon, and most believed that the justice system of the Spanish empire sentenced appropriately.[53]

Even some "miserable widowed *Indias* [Native women]" successfully appealed to the courts for help against their *alcalde mayor*. In the early eighteenth century, the *Indias* sued Pedro Hernández, the Native governor of Santa María Nativitas Atlacomulco (state of Mexico). They alleged that Hernández had charged them three pesos tribute every year to release them from the labor draft for the silver mines of Tlalpujahua (Michoacan), although only men went to work there. When they took the case to the special Indian court, Hernández "attempted to cheat the widows with soft words offering compensation." He also asked a public notary to certify that the widows had paid three pesos in tribute every ten years instead of every year.[54] The *Indias*, however, complained to the *audiencia* in 1712 that the governor set a bad example. He had allegedly lived with a woman, "pretending that he would marry her ... and then the governor deceived and left her and married another." In addition, the "pregnant widows went to the mountains to give birth and leave their offspring to the cruelty of the animals that eat them, and they die without baptism," because Hernández threatened to imprison the widows.[55] The *audiencia* also noted that Hernández had hidden over 500 Indians from the tribute rolls and the labor draft. On August 14, 1713, the *audiencia* prosecutor recommended arresting the governor for holding the Indian widows "in notable slavery."[56] The *audiencia* imprisoned Hernández until the special Indian court released him on August 9, 1715. The widows obtained relief from the courts of justice in this case.[57]

---

[53] Brendecke, *Imperio*, 87, 92; Cutter, "The Legal System," 57–70; Cutter, "Community and the Law in Northern New Spain," *The Americas* 50, no. 4 (April 1994): 477–480; Scardaville, "Justice," 979–989; Owensby, *Empire of Law*; Yannakakis, *The Art of Being*; McKinley, *Fractional Freedoms*, 2–4; Borah, *Justice by Insurance*; Kagan, *Lawsuits and Litigants*.

[54] Widows to Viceroy Duke of Linares, n. d. (1712), no place, and *parecer* of prosecutor Espinosa, Mexico City, 4 May 1713, AGI, Escribanía 280 A, *Quaderno de comprovasiones*, fols. 171–173.

[55] Widows to Linares, n. d., ibid., fol. 174–174v.

[56] *Parecer* of prosecutor, Mexico City, 20 Nov. 1714; ibid., fol. 179.

[57] Decree of Linares, 23 Nov. 1712; decree of *real acuerdo*, 9 Feb. 1712, petition of governor, n. d.; reply of prosecutor, 4 May 1713; decree of [probably] *real acuerdo*, 3 Nov. 1713; *parecer* of prosecutor, 14 Aug.; *parecer* of prosecutor, Mexico City, 20

Various judges offered redress to commoners such as the *Indias*. The indigenous *pueblos* (polities) elected *alcaldes* (magistrates) for one-year terms to resolve conflicts within their communities. The *alcaldes* meted out six to eight lashes or a day in jail for missing mass, public drunkenness, or other minor offenses. They could not mutilate or execute culprits, however. The *alcaldes ordinarios* (magistrates) of the Spanish-speaking towns were also selected annually by the municipal council. Most of these magistrates had little formal education in the law and ruled by drawing on local customs. Separate from them were the district judges, usually called *alcaldes mayores* in New Spain. They heard trials of the first instance and the appeals against the sentences of the lower magistrates. Natives could also sue their *alcaldes mayores* and other Spaniards in the special Indian court in Mexico City, while all others turned for relief to the *audiencia*, composed of civil and criminal judges and prosecutors.[58]

Nov. 1714; sentences of viceroy, 9 Aug. 1715 and 7 Feb. 1717, all documents copied by *visita* notary José de los Ríos, Mexico City, 25 June 1718, AGI, Escribanía 280 A, *Quaderno de comprovasiones*, fols. 175–180v. On communal labor, James Lockhart, *The Nahuas after the Conquest: A Social and Cultural History of the Indians of Central Mexico, Sixteenth through Eighteenth Centuries* (Stanford, CA: Stanford University Press, 1992), 431.

[58] *Law of the Indies*, book 6, title 3, law 16 and title 7, law 13; Murillo Velarde, *Cursus Iuris Canonici*, book 1, title 32, para. 343. See also Lockhart, *Nahuas*, 38–40; Herzog, *Upholding Justice*, 22–23; Susan Schroeder, introduction to *The Conquest All Over Again: Nahuas and Zapotecs Thinking, Writing, and Painting Spanish Colonialism*, ed. Susan Schroeder (Brighton, UK: Sussex Academic Press, 2010), 2; Matthew Restall, *The Maya World. Yucatec Culture and Society, 1550–1850* (Stanford, CA: Stanford University Press, 1997), 53–55; Alonso Romero, *Orden procesal*, 63; John F. Schwaller, "*Alcalde* vs. Mayor: Translating the Colonial World," *The Americas* 69, no. 3 (2013): 391–400; Jeremy Mumford, "Litigation as Ethnography in Sixteenth-Century Peru," *HAHR* 88, no. 1 (2008): 12; Borah, *Justice by Insurance*, 91–97. According to Jeremy Baskes, *Indians, Merchants, and Markets: A Reinterpretation of the Repartimiento and Spanish-Indian Economic Relations in Colonial Oaxaca, 1750–1821* (Stanford, CA: Stanford University Press, 2000), 1, 37–38; Celina G. Becerra Jiménez, "Redes sociales y oficios de justicia en Indias. Los vínculos de dos alcaldes mayores neogallegos," *Relaciones* 132 bis (2012): 110; and Peter Gerhard, *México en 1742* (Mexico City: Porrúa, 1962), 19, the distinction between *alcaldes mayores* and *corregidores* faded after mid-sixteenth-century reforms, and *novohispanos* began to use the words interchangeably. William F. Connell, *After Moctezuma: Indigenous Politics and Self-Government in Mexico City, 1524–1730* (University of Oklahoma Press, 2011), 18–19, argues that Native annual elections were pre-contact customs, while Joseph Plescia, "Judicial Accountability and Immunity in Roman Law," *American Journal of Legal History* 45, no. 1 (2001): 51, shows that this was also Roman heritage.

Litigants could also request the Council of the Indies in Madrid to reexamine rulings. The Council usually read up on a petition or an appeal and then issued a *consulta* (consultation). The king, queen, or their senior ministers saw the *consulta* and agreed or ordered changes. Their notaries scribbled a royal decree on the margins of the *consulta* and passed them back to the Council. The Council then issued a *real cédula* (royal provision) to the litigants, communicating the decree and attaching the king's name and seal. Sometimes the Council or the king confirmed the request of one party, and the notaries merely copied the original petition into the *real cédula*. The Native city of Tlaxcala, for example, complained about two lackadaisical attorneys at the Indian court and asked for a greater role for its procurators. The *real cédula* from 1685 cited the complaint and settled the issue.[59]

Novohispanos generally expected to a point that these councilors and judges acted as impartial public persons. They should maintain their independence in court and ideally behave "without personal interests and zealous in the service of God, king, and the public."[60] For this reason, the crown prohibited *audiencia* judges from marrying local women or owning property in their districts. At the same time, the boundaries of good conduct depended on the perspective, and most people knew that royal ministers also served their own interests and those of their powerful social networks.[61]

---

[59] Borah, *Justice by Insurance*, 284; Brendecke, *Imperio*, 87, 349. Hevia Bolaños, *Curia Filipica*, vol. 1, part 5, paras. 1–5, provides a detailed analysis of appeals; Alonso de la Lama y Noriega on behalf of Sánchez Morcillo to king, Madrid, 1 Apr. 1727, AGI, Escribanía 287 B, *pieza* 38, fols. 30–43, argues for allowing his client's appeal.

[60] *Parecer* of prosecutor of the Council of the Indies, cited in *consulta*, Madrid, 29 May 1748, AGI, México 440; the *consulta* of the Council of the Indies, Madrid, 18 Jan. 1726, AGI, México 670 A, demanded that judges be "independent and freer."

[61] Gayol, *Laberintos de justicia*, 1: 204, refers to the eighteenth-century jurist Francisco de Alfaro, who cited Bartolus's dictum that "office is what man owes others in kind." According to Parry, *Sale of Public Office*, 3; Robert Descimon, "La venalité des offices et la construction de l'État dans la France moderne: Des problèmes de la représentation symbolique aux problèmes du coût social du pouvoir," in Descimon, Schaub, and Vincent, *Les figures*, 78; and Roland Mousnier, *La venalité des offices sous Henri IV et Louis XIII*, 2nd ed. (Paris: Presses Universitaires de France, 1971), 7, the French jurist Charles Loyseau emphasized in 1609 that an office was a "dignity with public function," serving both the people and the owner. The *Institutes* 1.1.4. separated private from public law; Aquinas, *Summa*, IIa–IIae, Q. 67, art. 2, co. separated private persons from public authority; see also Antunez Portugal, *Tractatus*, book 2, chap. 14, para. 1. According to Miguel de Cervantes Saavedra, *Licenciado Vidriera* (Barcelona: Imprenta de A. Bergnes y Comp., 1832), 57, "the notary is a public person." Antonio Valero, "Ciencia de Estado," fol. 7, separated the "public good" from the "private jurisdiction." Jerónimo Moreno, *Reglas ciertas y precisamente necesarias para juezes, y ministros de justicia de las Indias y para su confesores* (Puebla: Viuda de Miguel Ortega y Bonilla, 1732. Facsimile, Mexico City: Suprema Corte de Justicia de la Nación, 2005), 34, argued

Empire of Justice

The networks composed of intermediaries negotiated power and stitched together the empire. They also often skewed trials and shaped the information flowing to Madrid.[62] Analyzing these actors in Oaxaca, Yanna Yannakakis maintains that "the Bourbons harbored significant antagonism toward Native intermediary figures (and intermediary figures of all sorts) whom they perceived as corrupt and inimical to the efficient functioning of Empire."[63] This may well be the case in the largely Native region of Oaxaca, yet such a claim will be more difficult to prove for the whole empire. The first Bourbon king arrived in Spain in 1701 and his descendants ruled New Spain until its independence in 1821. The dynasty and their changing ministers seldom pursued a consistent policy toward any social group during this long century, and instead altered their aims according to expediency and convictions.[64]

In fact, the royal governments usually leaned heavily on local and regional power brokers. Loyal service usually mattered more than ethnic identity, although some minorities often faced harsher treatment. In fact, the Bourbons frequently preferred Basque and Navarrese intermediaries over Castilians from central Spain. In the eighteenth century, the crown

---

that any *alcalde mayor* who "assigned work for his own estate" had to pay the Indians appropriately. See also William Doyle, *Venality: The Sale of Offices in Eighteenth-Century France* (Oxford: Clarendon Press, 1996), 322; Paolo Prodi, *Settimo non rubare. Furto e mercato nella storia dell'Occidente* (Bologna: Società editrice Il Mulino, 2009), 243; Bravo Lira, *El Juez*, 133–134, 146; Garriga, "Sobre el gobierno," 81. Michel Bertrand, *Grandeur et misères de l'office: Les officiers de finances de Nouvelle-Espagne, XVIIe–XVIIIe siècles* (Paris: Publications de la Sorbonne, 1999), 31, points to the actual practices when claiming that the notion of public service was absent in the early eighteenth century; Herzog, *Upholding Justice*, 8, argues that "[o]fficers made no distinction between private and public behavior or between private and public ends."

[62] On the foundational literature on networks, see Mark S. Granovetter, "The Strength of Weak Ties," *American Journal of Sociology* 78, no. 6 (1973): 1360–1380; John F. Padgett and Christopher K. Ansell, "Robust Action and the Rise of the Medici," *American Journal of Sociology* 98, no. 6 (1993): 1259–1319; Stanley Wasserman and Katheryne Faust, *Social Network Analysis: Methods and Applications* (Cambridge, New York: Cambridge University Press, 1994); Dorothea Jansen, *Einführung in die Netzwerkanalyse. Grundlagen, Methoden, Forschungsbeispiele*, 2nd ed. (Opladen: Leske and Budrich, 2003).

[63] Yannakakis, *The Art of Being*, 165. Yannakakis wrote an excellent book, although I differ somewhat on this point.

[64] Bourbons also ruled France, Naples, and other principalities, see, for example, Allan J. Kuethe and Kenneth J. Andrien, *The Spanish Atlantic World in the Eighteenth Century: War and the Bourbon Reforms, 1713–1796* (Cambridge: Cambridge University Press, 2014), 3, 143.

also needed indigenous partners to wrest away parishes from the regular orders or relied on elites in provincial cities to bypass the powerful social bodies in Mexico City.[65] For these reasons, ministers forged alliances with suitable patrons, brokers, and clients to advance or to stall reforms. Historians have chiseled out the importance of these go-betweens during the historiographical turn toward social networks starting in the early 1970s. The local connections played a key role in achieving political goals, and both reformers and the opposition used them.[66]

[65] I have tried to show Native collaboration in Rosenmüller, "'The Indians ... long for change:' The Secularization of Regular Parishes in New Spain, 1749–1755," in *Early Bourbon Spanish America. Politics and Society in a Forgotten Era*, eds. Francisco A. Eissa-Barroso and Ainara Vázquez Varela (Leiden: Brill, 2013), 143–163; Pietschmann, "Antecedentes políticos," 50–62.

[66] Among the first in Latin American history was Stuart Schwartz, *Sovereignty and Society*; see also Sharon Kettering, *Patrons, Brokers, and Clients in Seventeenth-Century France* (Oxford: Oxford University Press, 1986); Wolfgang Reinhard, *Freunde und Kreaturen. "Verflechtung" als Konzept zur Erforschung historischer Führungsgruppen. Römische Oligarchie um 1600* (Munich: Ernst Vögel, 1979), based on his 1973 Habilitation. Path breaking are Bertrand, *Grandeur et misères*; and Herzog, *Upholding Justice*, 8–11. Michael Harsgor noted loyalty to two patrons, cited in Kettering, *Patrons, Brokers*, 21. On the outpouring of scholarship on network, François-Xavier Guerra, "Pour une nouvelle histoire politique: Acteurs sociaux et acteurs politiques," in *Structures et Cultures des Sociétés Ibéro-Américaines. Au-delà du Modèle-Économique: Coloque international en hommage au professeur Francois Chevalier, 29–30 avril 1988*, Maison des Pays Ibériques, Groupe Interdisciplinaire de Recherche et de Documentation sur l'Amérique Latine (Paris: CNRS, 1990), 250–258; Zacarias Moutoukias, "Negocios y redes sociales: modelo interpretativo a partir de un caso rioplatense (siglo XVIII)," *Caravelle* 67 (1997): 37–55; Christian Windler, "Bureaucracy and Patronage in Bourbon Spain," in *Observation and Communication: The Construction of Realities in the Hispanic World*, eds. Johannes-Michael Scholz, and Tamar Herzog (Frankfurt: Vittorio Klostermann, 1997), 299–320; Renate Pieper and Philipp Lesiak, "Redes mercantiles entre el Atlántico y el Mediterráneo en los inicios de la guerra de los treinta años," in *El Crédito en Nueva España*, eds. María del Pilar Martínez López-Cano, and Guillermina del Valle Pavón (Mexico City: Instituto Mora, 1998), 19–39; Michel Bertrand, "Del actor a la red: análisis de redes e interdisciplinariedad," in *Los actores locales de la nación en la América Latina: Análisis estratégicos*, ed. Evelyne Sanchez (Puebla: Benemérita Universidad Autónoma de Puebla; Tlaxcala: El Colegio de Tlaxcala, 2011), 39, see also 23–41; Jean Pierre Dedieu, "Procesos y redes. La historia de las instituciones administrativas de la época moderna, hoy," in *La pluma, la mitra y la espada: estudios de historia institucional en la Edad Moderna*, eds. Jean-Pierre Dedieu, Juan Luis Castellano, and María Victoria López-Cordón Cortezo (Madrid: Marcial Pons, 2000), 13–30. Juan Luis Castellano and Jean-Pierre Dedieu, eds., *Réseaux, familles et pouvoirs dans le monde ibérique à la fin de l'Ancien Régime* (Paris: CNRS, D. L. 1998); Dedieu, Castellano, and López-Cordón Cortezo and others collaborated in the group *Personal administrativo y político de España (PAPE)* at the CNRS to produce the massive FICHOZ database on social relations in the imperial bureaucracy. See also Alfredo Moreno Cebrián and Núria Sala i Vila, *El "Premio" de Ser Virrey. Los intereses públicos y privados del gobierno virreinal en el Perú de Felipe V* (Madrid: CSIC, 2004);

Audiencia judges frequently belonged to differing networks, and their varied interests and perspectives often defied a direct translation of a social desire into a sentence. Tamar Herzog maintains in this regard that any "distinction between institution and society was virtually inexistent" in Quito.[67] Some *audiencia* judges undeniably married or befriended locals and carried the conflicts riddling the communities into the courts. Yet the law, opposing allegiances, the need to forge compromises, and the threat of informants mattered too in New Spain. The crown knew of the antagonisms among ministers and packed the *audiencia* with several judges and prosecutors. These ministers could well belong to opposing camps and happily reported the failings of their adversaries to Madrid. In addition, the *audiencia* judges distinguished themselves from the rest of society. Their legal knowledge gave them great prestige, and they insisted on their elevated role at public events. In addition, men of "cloak and sword," that is, people of non-judicial training, often governed the courts, assisted by a slew of notaries and other officials. They frequently brought differing perspectives to the table. Madrid acted as an arbiter among the competing interests, reducing the ability of small groups to hijack the courts.[68]

As conflicts unfolded, notaries, judges, and other vassals readily gave the crown important information about the far-flung realms. For example, court notaries occasionally wrote down the prosecutor's legal opinions, the majority vote of the judges, and the dissenting viewpoints in lawsuits. Vassals also sent streams of petitions to Madrid. By doing so, they provided the kings with the best available information about local circumstances. "Knowledge is power," the English jurist Francis Bacon

---

Bernd Hausberger, "La conquista del empleo público en la Nueva España. El comerciante gaditano Tomás Ruiz de Apodaca y sus amigos, siglo xviii," *Historia Mexicana* 56, no. 3 (2007): 725–778; Bartolomé Yun Casalilla, ed., *Las redes del imperio. Élites sociales en la articulación de la Monarquía Hispánica, 1492–1714* (Madrid, Seville: Marcial Pons, Universidad Pablo Olavide, 2009); Becerra Jiménez, "Redes sociales y oficios."

[67] Herzog, *Upholding Justice*, 160.
[68] See, for example, Revillagigedo to Ensenada, Mexico City, 24 Oct. 1753, AGI, México 1350; Wim Blockmans, Jean-Philippe Genert, and Christoph Mühlberg, "Annexe 1: The Origin of the Modern State (Activité additionelle de la European Science Foundation)," in *L'état moderne: genèse. Bilans et perspective. Actes du colloque tenu au CNRS à Paris les 19–20 septembre 1989*, ed. Jean-Philippe Genet (Paris: CNRS, 1990), 295; Brendecke, *Imperio*, 35, 486–489. On officials *de capa y espada*, Francisco Andújar Castillo, "Prólogo," in Guillermo Burgos Lejonagoitia, *Gobernar las Indias: Venalidad y méritos en la provisión de cargos americanos, 1701–1746* (Almería: Universidad de Almería, 2014), 17.

(1561–1626) argued earlier, and the Spanish queens and kings relied on competing stories rising up from below to discern loyal from disloyal servants. Far from having absolute control, the kings and queens used their knowledge to curb powerful elites, rein in abuse, advance their clients, and implement reforms that slowly transformed the empire.[69]

In addition, "soft steering" promoted a sense of duty among the ministers. This cultural manipulation consisted of discursive methods, symbols, and rational arguments. The crown exhorted ministers to comply with the norms of good conduct, and these exhortations reverberated among the public. Over time, social values changed and the talk about the ministers' usefulness to the public good sank in. This does not mean that all functionaries followed suit right away or that the crown expected them to do so. Yet soft steering incrementally altered the behavior of ministers, because a broad audience in New Spain agreed with these changes.[70]

The kings claimed absolute power to pursue such policies. *Absolute power*, in this sense, meant that the kings could change or ignore the law of the kingdom when necessary, which was not the same as controlling the minutiae of everyday lives. The cities of the empire, for example, continued to issue their own statutes and live by their own customs. Nonetheless, the Roman *Digest* posited that any decision of the emperor became law. The *Siete Partidas* incorporated this rule, assigning absolute power to the kings of Castile who served akin to the emperor in their realm.[71] The cities of

---

[69] Brendecke, *Imperio*, 21, 481–487, quote of Bacon on p. 35, note 29. See also Mumford, "Litigation as Ethnography," 6–8.

[70] Gerhard Göhler, Ulrike Höppner, Sybille de la Rosa, and Stefan Skupien, "Steuerung jenseits von Hierarchie. Wie diskursive Praktiken, Argumente und Symbole steuern können," *Politische Vierteljahresschrift* 51, no. 4 (2010): 691–693; Holenstein, "'Gute Policey' und lokale Gesellschaft. Erfahrung als Kategorie im Verwaltungshandeln des 18. Jahrhunderts," *Historische Zeitschrift*, New Series 31 (2001): 433, 444–450.

[71] For example, *Digest* 1.3.31 stated that "the prince is absolved from the laws," and *Digest* 1.4.1 claimed that "[w]hatever pleases the prince has the force of law." Domingo de Soto, *De iustitia et iure, libri decem: De la justicia y del derecho, en diez libros* (Madrid: Instituto de Estudios Políticos, 1968), 2: 269, cited *Digest* 1.4.1. See also the late eighteenth-century *Discurso en que se demostra que o Poder dos Reys nao depende dos Povos e mormente o dos Senhores Reys de Portugal*, Biblioteca de Ajuda, 54-XI-16, although Rodríguez O., "We Are Now," 19, argues that the "concept of absolute royal power ... was never accepted in the Hispanic world," see also 20, 24–33. Ernst-Wolfgang Böckenförde, *Geschichte der Rechts- und Staatsphilosophie. Antike und Mittelalter* (Tübingen: Mohr Siebeck, 2002), 294, shows that William of Ockham (1280/85–1347/49) already used *Digest* 1.3.31 in the conflict between emperor and pope. For François-Xavier Guerra, "De la política antigua a la política moderna. La revolución de la soberanía," in Guerra and Lempérière, *Los espacios públicos en Iberoamérica*, 124–131, Jean Bodin (1529/30–1596) reinterpreted the *Digest*'s law as

Castile agreed, at least sometimes. A representative of the *Cortes* (parliament of estates) of 1523 held that "laws and customs are subject to the kings who can make and unmake them at their will."[72] In practice, the kings issued edicts without the consent of the *Cortes*, and for this reason, an attorney in Mexico City agreed that the king was "prince and legislator" of the empire.[73]

In addition, the idea of jurisprudence differed from today and included royal governance. The Spanish kings were the senior judges of the empire. They issued laws, levied taxes, defended the realm, and wielded "the force of the sword to punish evil-doing people."[74] Other kings claimed similar authority. The Portuguese jurist Antonio Sousa de Macedo ably summed up this point in 1651. For him, jurisprudence consisted not only of adjudicating complaints "as the incompetent believe," but referred to the entire political organization of the empire.[75]

The expanding royal authority, meanwhile, often encountered robust resistance from the great Councils, power elites, or popular groups. In 1693, during a period of bitter feuding, the Council of the Indies reminded King Charles II that "absolute power does not reside in the Catholic character, only ordinary justice governed by reason."[76] The Council at that point attempted to protect its own prerogatives by demanding that the king end the sale of office appointments. Earlier, the theologian Francisco Suárez (1548–1617) had devised a contract theory according to which the kings depended on the will of the people. Other scholars praised the mixed sovereignty shared among the people, the nobility, and the crown, which also countered the idea of absolute royal power.[77]

---

the "highest power over citizens and subjects that is unfettered by the laws." According to Lempérière, *Entre Dieu et le roi, la république: México, XVIe–XIXe siècle* (Paris: Belles lettres, 2004), 63, King Jean II of Castile (1406–1452) and his jurists at the latest insisted on the absolute power of the king; see also Gil, "Spain and Portugal," 432–433; Reinhard, *Geschichte der Staatsgewalt*, 37; Agüero, "Local Law," 104–105.

[72] I. A. A. Thompson, "Absolutism, Legalism," 219–220.

[73] Print *por Don Miguel Truxillo*, AGI, México 670 A, fol. 17v. See also Murillo Velarde, *Cursus Iuris Canonici*, book 1, title 32, paras. 343–344; according to Tau Anzoátegui, *El Jurista en el Nuevo Mundo*, 24, the eighteenth-century state was widely accepted as the exclusive legislator.

[74] *Digest* 2.1.3.

[75] Hespanha, "Paradigmes de légitimation," 20–22; for Reinhard, *Geschichte der Staatsgewalt*, 139, jurisprudence excluded warfare. See also Stolleis, *Histoire du droit public*, 66–67, 108;

[76] *Consulta* of the Council of the Indies, Madrid, 9 Nov. 1693, in Richard Konetzke, *Colección de documentos para la historia de la formación social de Hispanoamérica, 1493–1810* (Madrid: CSIC, 1953–1962), vol. 3, tome 1, p. 36.

[77] Rodríguez O., "We Are Now," 9–10; Reinhard, *Geschichte der Staatsgewalt*, 112.

Trust among ministers buttressed resistance against undesirable reforms or punishments, but it could also be betrayed. Judges and notaries, for example, had rehearsed passing on bribes and other favors for generations. They confided that all participating parties continued the profitable practices. Trust ran deep and it glued together the ministers, often encumbering meaningful prosecutions of malfeasance. Nonetheless, Francisco Garzarón obtained valuable testimony by threatening effective punishments for recalcitrant ministers. When the suspects saw that Garzarón succeeded, at least some changed their tune to save their skin. Garzarón, for example, charged a criminal judge with seizing confiscated assets from jailed suspects. The criminal judge blamed his notary for the malpractice, giving Garzarón's *visita* the necessary testimony to discipline the wayward official.[78]

In many cases, the crown tried to compromise with groups that disregarded royal rules or expressed their dissatisfaction, instead of penalizing them. When the moral economy of communities was violated and the channels of communications with the authorities blocked, for example, anger could boil over into revolts. Natives on these occasions threatened, evicted, or even killed their *alcaldes mayores* and their assistants. The state typically sought to appease the involved parties during these conflicts. The crown sent ministers to hear the Native complaints, and they pardoned most participants. They also sternly warned the Indians to return to peace and harmony or face the rigor of justice.[79]

---

[78] Defense of Pedro Sánchez Morcillo, AGI, México 670 B, *Relación*, fol. 731v. Notary Pedro Robledo to Garzarón, Mexico City, 2 June 1719, AGI, Escribanía 280 C, fol. 451, rejected the testimonies of his superiors as "biased." Speaking with Niklas Luhmann, the stimulus of Garzarón's *visita* irritated the *audiencia* and it adapted to survive, although not as king or society had desired. Niklas Luhmann, "Familiarity, Confidence, Trust: Problems and Alternatives," in *Trust: Making and Breaking Cooperative Relations*, ed. Diego Gambetta (Department of Sociology, University of Oxford), 97–103, distinguishes between trust and confidence. On structural coupling and *autopoiesis*, Luhmann, *Introduction to Systems Theory*, ed. Dirk Baecker (Cambridge: Polity, 2013), 7, 63, 70–90, 183,187; Luhmann, "Operational Closure and Structural Coupling: The Differentiation of the Legal System," *Cardozo Law Review* 13, no. 5 (1992): 72–78, 86–90; Anders La Cour and Holger Højlund, "Organizations, Institutions and Semantics: Systems Theory Meets Institutionalism," in *Luhmann Observed: Radical Theoretical Encounters*, eds. Anders La Cour and Andreas Philippopoulos-Mihalopoulos (Basingstoke: Palgrave Macmillan, 2013), 188–202; Reinhard, *Geschichte der Staatsgewalt*, 131; Armin Nassehi, *Wie weiter mit Niklas Luhmann?* (Hamburg: Hamburger Edition, 2008).

[79] Based on Stefan Brakensiek, "Ergebene Diener ihrer Herren? Herrschaftsvermittlung im alten Europa. Praktiken lokaler Justiz, Politik und Verwaltung im internationalen Vergleich," in *Ergebene Diener ihrer Herren? Herrschaftsvermittlung im alten Europa*, eds. Stefan Brakensiek and Heide Wunder (Cologne: Böhlau, 2005), 1–12;

Yet the crown could also call on *visitadores* to hand down harsh punishments, and these *visitadores* often drew on significant political support for their aims. The early modern state relied on collaboration to some extent, and the *visitadores* succeeded mostly when they counted on imperial and local acquiescence or agreement.[80] A *visitador* adjudicated the Indians of Tehuantepec who rebelled in 1660, for instance. The *visitador* denied the appeals and executed five death sentences. The scholarship has decried this process as a "mockery of justice."[81] Similarly, culprits later impugned the verdicts of Garzarón's *visita*, because his "rigor and harshness," was "exorbitant and opposed to the dispositions of the law."[82] Yet many early modern Spaniards saw these *visitas* as the king's duty to correct wrongs. An entire genre of literature affirmed that the king served as the spouse of the republic and "shepherd and father" of his vassals. These works described the republic as a body and the king as its head who closely observed any disorder. According to the Jesuit Andrés Mendo, for instance, the "most noble sense of the head are the eyes, and the prince has to be all eyes, vigilantly watching the appropriate behavior of his subjects. Nothing can flee from his gaze." The king named *visitadores* – whose title referred to seeing – to "defend the law and the flock." Many *novohispanos* agreed.[83]

The king wielded the economic power to appoint the *visitadores* who bypassed the courts of justice. In the early modern view, the term

---

E. P. Thompson, "The Moral Economy of the English Crowd in the Eighteenth Century," *Past and Present* 50 (1971): 76–136.

[80] Holenstein, "Introduction," 5, 25–27; Herzog, "Ritos de control," 11–12

[81] Owensby, *Empire of Law*, 284, see also 268–285, argues in his solid book that the *visita* sentences were "in direct contravention of recognized legal principle." Garriga, "Sobre el gobierno," 88, maintains that *visita* verdicts always needed royal approval.

[82] Defense of Juan Díaz de Bracamonte, AGI, México 670 B, *Relación*, fol. 128; Alonso de la Lama y Noriega on behalf of Pedro Sánchez Morcillo to king, Madrid, 1 Apr. 1727, AGI, Escribanía 287 B, *pieza* 38, fol. 32. The civil judge Félix Suárez de Figueroa, for example, denied the *visita's* jurisdiction to review his land grant commission. The *parecer* of prosecutor of the Council of the Indies, José de Laysequilla, Madrid, 14 Aug. 1724, AGI, Escribanía 287 B, *pieza* 39, fol. 133v, found that "this intent alone ... justifies the imposed punishment."

[83] Andrés Mendo, *Príncipe perfecto y Ministros Aiustados, Documentos Políticos y Morales. En Emblemas* (Lyon: Horacio Boissat y George Remeus, 1662), 54, 48, 61. The law justified frequent *visitas*. According to *Law of Castile*, book 3, title 8, laws 1–2, a *visita* could occur every year in every province, while for the *Law of the Indies*, book 2, title 34, laws 1 and 7, a *visita* should occur "when it is appropriate." The Latin word *visito* (I visit) derives from both *viso* and *video* (I see), and therefore *visitadores* were also called *veedores* or *visidores*; see, e.g., *consulta* of the Council of the Indies, Madrid, 18 Jan. 1726, AGI, México 670 A.

economic frequently referred to matters of the home. The king had the duty to keep his house in order, and this task extended to the entire kingdom. The *visitadores* served this end. A *real cédula* from 1750, for example, underlined the necessity of the "economic and political power ... for the public tranquility of my vassals."[84] This authority was separate from the ordinary course of justice, and the *visitadores* usually operated on their own to mend disorders. They resembled the king's favorite ministers and the *juntas* (committees) that convened for special purposes. They resolved challenges quickly, because they did not wait out the lengthy deliberations of the courts or Councils. For this reason, historians have traditionally interpreted the *visitas* as tools of reforming the nascent states.[85]

Next to the economic power and justice, the king's grace was the third domain of power. The king assuaged harsh judicial rulings and modified human fate by his acts of grace. He awarded vassals for loyal conduct and elevated commoners into the nobility. The king also voided the illegitimacy of birth of others and pardoned culprits. Early modern people mostly considered grace a necessary complement to justice and not as an arbitrary abuse of royal power. Andrés Mendo, for instance, praised the king of Portugal for commuting death sentences into banishments to overseas realms. The king, in this way, combined the utility of settlers in the territories with the grace of easing tough punishments.[86]

---

[84] *Real cédula*, San Lorenzo, 18 Oct. 1750, AGN, Indiferente Virreinal 3263, exp. 28.
[85] See Feros, *Kingship and Favoritism*, 4–5, 128–132; Hespanha, "Paradigmes de légitimation," 23–25; Andújar Castillo, "Prólogo," 15; Bertrand, *Grandeur et misères*, 34–40. According to Richard Bonney, "France, 1494–1815," in *Rise of the Fiscal State in Europe, c. 1200–1815*, ed. Richard Bonney (Oxford: Oxford University Press, 1999), 130, the French crown reintroduced the intendants in 1653 as "commissioners sent to execute the orders of His Majesty." Murillo Velarde, *Cursus Iuris Canonici*, book 1, title 32, para. 342, argues that the authority "which the father has over the son, the lord over the servant, and the husband over his wife ... is not public but private power, and it is called economic." Still readable, Otto Hintze, "Der Commissarius und seine Bedeutung in der allgemeinen Verwaltungsgeschichte," in *Staat und Verfassung. Gesammelte Abhandlungen zur allgemeinen Verfassungsgeschichte*, ed. Gerhard Oestreich (Göttingen: Vandenhoek und Rupprecht, 1962), 242–274.
[86] Mendo, *Príncipe Perfecto*, 165. See also Hespanha, "Porque que é existe," 32–35; Reinhard, *Geschichte der Staatsgewalt*, 139. Herzog, *Upholding Justice*, 41, argues that banishments were utilitarian and not part of Antonio Manuel Hespanha's economy of grace, according to which the king alternated between his roles as justiciary and father, but Mendo suggests otherwise.

1.3 EMPIRE IN TRANSITION

The Spanish empire comprised a string of kingdoms, principalities, and provinces. While the court in Madrid was the ultimate arbiter of conflicts, the empire did not merely consist of one great center from where political and social importance cascaded toward the fringes. In fact, several core kingdoms, among them New Spain and Peru, rivaled Castile in economics, population, and patronage in varying degrees. These core kingdoms also mattered, because other realms or territories attached to them in different ways. These realms or territories tended to be less densely settled and they often depended economically or politically on the core kingdom. Nevertheless, even these realms cherished their own rights and customs and preserved their local governance.

In the period 1650–1755, the crown tightened supervision over these kingdoms and territories with varying degrees of success. This process

MAP 3 The Iberian Peninsula in 1700.
Map adapted by Gabriela Chávez from William D. Phillips, and Carla Rahn Phillips, *A Concise History of Spain*, 2nd. ed. (Cambridge: Cambridge University Press, 2016), 178.

advanced in part, because Spain had to fend off the other great powers, including England, France, Habsburg Austria, and the Netherlands. These rivals tried to seize territories, fortresses, or trade from the empire. The crown mobilized ever larger resources to counter the threat. Madrid attempted to increase tax revenue from privileged groups or social bodies and channel more funds to the military. The queens and kings intensified their rule by incrementally curbing the autonomies of the kingdoms and limiting the jurisdictions of the social bodies. By and large, the process defined the boundaries of the provinces more clearly and advanced universal principles that applied to all individuals. These changes did not occur on a linear trajectory and many reforms remained piecemeal. Rulers rarely followed a master plan, and, instead, they usually responded to particular challenges with specific solutions.

New Spain traveled on a similar pathway. Colonial Mexico originally integrated into the polycentric Spanish empire after the conquest of the Aztec (Mexica) empire in 1521. Agriculture and silver mining expanded, and New Spain grew into an economic power house. The regions north of the old Aztec empire gravitated into the *novohispano* orbit. The viceroys in Mexico City, for example, monitored the military and the finances in New Galicia and its capital Guadalajara, located north of the Mexico City *audiencia* limits. In addition, the viceroys sent funds to the Caribbean isles and the Philippines to sustain fortresses and the missions of the religious orders. These regions did not formally belong to the viceroyalty – despite what textbook maps show – because the viceroy, the *audiencia*, or the tax collectors had no formal say there. Yet social networks, personal communications, and trade thrived. By sending money, merchants, mercenaries, and mendicants, New Spain gained informal leverage in these regions.[87]

---

[87] On the cascading structure, Heribert Münkler, *Empires. The Logic of World Domination from Ancient Rome to the United States*, trans. Patrick Camiller (Cambridge: Polity, 2007), viii, 4–11. Jane Burbank and Frederick Cooper, *Empires in World History: Power and the Politics of Difference* (Princeton: Princeton University Press, 2010), 16–17, suggest a nuanced relation of overlapping and shared sovereignty with the periphery. On the "fiscal submetropolis," Carlos Marichal, *Bankruptcy of Empire: Mexican Silver and the Wars between Spain, Britain, and France, 1760–1810* (New York: Cambridge University Press, 2007), 5, see also 1–12. Oscar Mazín Gómez, "Introducción," in *México en el mundo hispánico*, ed. Oscar Mazín Gómez (Zamora: El Colegio de Michoacán, 2000), 1: 15, see also 16–18, envisions a "political nucleus." On "informal empire," Pietschmann, "Diego García Panés y Joaquín Antonio de Rivadeneira Barrientos, pasajeros en un mismo barco: Reflexiones en torno al México 'imperial' entre 1755 y 1808," in *Un hombre de libros: homenaje a Ernesto de la Torre Villar*, eds. Alicia Mayer and Amaya Garritz (Mexico City: UNAM, 2012), 207. See also

In addition, New Spain consisted of social bodies that enjoyed great autonomy, lived by their own rules, and mediated royal power. These social bodies comprised the guilds of shoemakers and goldsmiths, African confraternities associated with churches, or municipal councils, for instance. These social bodies shaped the lives of their members, who were usually born into a hierarchical group and rarely left their community without severing most ties to other members. The social bodies frequently had jurisdiction over their members, who tended to have a "porous" identity, because they usually made decisions in conjunction with their social bodies.[88]

The social bodies competed to some degree with the ordinary justice system represented by *alcaldes mayores* and *audiencias*. The judges of the various social bodies applied norms of different provenance and therefore a "jurisdictional pluralism" reigned at that time. Ecclesiastical courts, for instance, offered conflict resolution on a broad swath of issues to clergy

---

Francisco Comín Comín and Bartolomé Yun-Casalilla, "Spain: From Composite Monarchy to Nation-State, 1492–1914. An Exceptional State?" in *The Rise of Fiscal States: A Global History 1500–1914*, eds. Francisco Comín Comín, Bartolomé Yun-Casalilla, and Patrick K. O'Brien (Cambridge: Cambridge University Press, 2012), 234; Marichal and Matilde Souto Mantecón, "La Nueva España y el financiamiento del imperio español en América: Los situados para el Caribe en el siglo XVIII," in *El secreto del imperio español: Los situados coloniales en el siglo XVIIII*, eds. Carlos Marichal and Johanna von Grafenstein (Mexico City: El Colegio de México, Instituto Mora, 2012), 61–93; Pedro Cardim, Tamar Herzog, José Javier Ruis Ibáñez, and Gaetano Sabatini, Introduction to *Polycentric Monarchies: How did Early Modern Spain and Portugal Achieve and Maintain a Global Hegemony?* (Brighton, UK: Sussex Academic Press, 2012), 5. Francisco Eissa-Barroso, *The Spanish Monarchy and the Creation of the Viceroyalty of New Granada (1717–1739): The Politics of Early Bourbon Reform in Spain and Spanish America* (Leiden: Brill, 2016), 13–14, argues for multi-layered yet hierarchical connections. John J. TePaske and Herbert S. Klein, *Ingresos y egresos de la Real Hacienda de Nueva España* (Mexico City: Instituto Nacional de Antropología e Historia, 1986–1988), vol. 2, p. 14, note 5, maintain that Florida and Louisiana and other regions belonged to the viceroyalty, yet this was only true in the sense that two secretariats labored at the Council of the Indies, one for a region called New Spain and one for Peru. According to Concepción de Castro Monsalve, "Las secretarías de los consejos, las de estado y del despacho y sus oficiales durante la primera mitad del siglo xviii" *Hispania* 59, no. 201 (1999): 203, each secretariat consisted in 1717 of six or seven officials. All incoming correspondence was divided between the secretariat of New Spain or Peru. According to *Law of the Indies*, book 5, title 2, law 1, Yucatan did not appeal lawsuits to the *audiencia* of Mexico City, but to the Council of the Indies, while the viceroy served as superior governor. Over the years, however, the governors of Yucatan claimed superior status themselves, attaining more autonomy from the viceroy.

[88] Brian Larkin, *The Very Nature of God. Baroque Catholicism and Religious Reform in Bourbon Mexico City* (Albuquerque, NM: University of New Mexico Press, 2010), 13, 222; on the term "social bodies," Meccarelli, "Dimensions of Justice," 50.

and even non-clergy, while soldiers, postal clerks, and merchants often litigated in their own separate courts. Similarly, the indigenous *pueblo* (polity) exemplified a social body. The *pueblo* largely lived by its own unwritten customs, and the indigenous *alcaldes* settled the conflicts of their community according to their values. Most social bodies had also forged their own explicit or implicit contracts with the king, and these agreements safeguarded privileges and internal organization. The central government in Madrid had limited say in their affairs and often cared less about the details.[89]

The variety of arrangements and competing jurisdictions declined, as the cycles of reforms accelerated in the seventeenth century. Some royal governments attempted to intensify – not necessarily centralize – authority. They often viewed the autonomy of the social bodies with some suspicion and preferred ruling individuals instead of negotiating with the social bodies. In addition, the kings and their reformist ministers aimed at undercutting the role of the core kingdoms and integrating them more fully into the state. While this was not a predictable process,

---

[89] Lauren Benton and Richard Ross, "Empires and Legal Pluralism. Jurisdiction, Sovereignty, and Political Imagination in the Early Modern World," in *Legal Pluralism and Empires, 1500–1850*, eds. Lauren Benton and Richard Ross (New York: New York University Press, 2013), 5–6; Guerra, "De la política antigua" 110–129. I use the term social bodies instead of corporations, which encompasses *cabildos*, confraternities, and courts, while the sources often speak of *universidad/universitas* or *cuerpo*. Ethno-historians have discarded the word *corporation* and favor *altepetl* (ethnic polity) and *calpolli* (a sub-unit of an *altepetl*) when analyzing Native social structures. Perhaps we should reconsider the term, however, not in the definition of Eric Wolf but in the meaning of François-Xavier Guerra or other Atlantic historians, who use the term *corporation* to describe basic social organizations of the old regime. These scholars have aimed to flesh out differences and parallels of the early modern societies. They share that aim with the Nahua annalist Chimalpahin, who found the similarities between New Spain and Courland on the other side of the Atlantic striking. Chimalpahin apparently gathered some information from the professor of mathematics in Hamburg, Henrico Martínez (Heinrich Martin) who lived in Mexico City in the 1620s to design the water drainage system. Martínez and Chimalpahin knew that the Baltic-speaking Curonian majority lived by their own traditions in the countryside, while most people in the cities spoke Swedish and German and were governed by Hanseatic laws and the *ius commune*. Similarly, analyzing corporations, when carefully cleared from older notions, can provide insights within an Atlantic perspective; see Schroeder, introduction to *The Conquest All Over Again*, 2–3; and Schroeder, "Chimalpahin Rewrites the Conquest. Yet Another Epic History?," in ibid., 115–116; Walther L. Bernecker, Horst Pietschmann, and Hans Werner Tobler, *Eine kleine Geschichte Mexikos* (Frankfurt: Suhrkamp, 2007), 91. Nancy M. Farriss, *Maya Society under Colonial Rule. The Collective Enterprise of Survival* (Princeton: Princeton University Press, 1984), 138–139, views Yucatan as a "corporate and hierarchical society." Corporate forms of society have not disappeared in modern Mexico. Taxi drivers, trash collectors, or teachers have often negotiated their labor terms en bloc and their leaders have served as congresspersons.

the crown took a step into that direction between 1707 and 1716. The crown removed four viceroys from the Spanish peninsula, abolished most provincial institutions, and introduced Castilian public law in the kingdoms of the crown of Aragon.[90]

These changes could encourage economic initiatives, create wealth, and provide for greater individual self-determination. For this reason, the kingdoms even favored reform under circumstances. New Spain, Peru, and Catalonia, for example, had long called for opening up the sclerotic Atlantic trade system. The trade fleets left Seville in southern Spain every year and traveled to New Spain and Panama/Peru to deliver European merchandise. The commercial oligopoly allowed merchants in Seville to charge excessive mark ups from the Americans. In the early eighteenth century, several governing coalitions in Madrid confronted the commercial oligopoly and successively eased up trade restrictions. The fleets declined in importance, while nimble registered ships sailed from various peninsular ports directly to the Americas.[91]

Yet much remained a "stubbornly incomplete process" during which imperial patterns prevailed. Conservative governments and their alliances backtracked on reforms. For example, the king's first minister fell in 1754, and the commercial oligopoly flexed its muscles once more. In the following year, the new government suppressed the registered ships going to New Spain and restored the fleet on this route.[92] This shows

---

[90] Based on Eissa-Barroso, *The Spanish Monarchy*, 1–4; Guerra, *Modernidad e Independencias. Ensayos sobre las revoluciones hispánicas* (Mexico City: Fondo de Cultura Económica, MAPFRE, 1992), 13, 22–23.

[91] Kuethe and Andrien, *Spanish Atlantic World*, 4, 45, 145, 203–206, 213; Kuethe, "Imperativos militares en la política comercial de Carlos III," in *Soldados del Rey. El ejército borbónico en América colonial en vísperas de la Independencia*, eds. Alan Kuethe and Juan Marchena (Castelló de la Plana: Universitat Jaume Primer, 2005), 153–154. Recent discussions of oceanic trade and corruption include Catherine Tracy Goode, "Merchant-Bureaucrats, Unwritten Contracts, and Fraud in the Manila Galleon Trade," in Rosenmüller, *Corruption in the Iberian Empires*, 171–197; Fabricio Prado, "Addicted to Smuggling: Contraband Trade in Eighteenth-Century Brazil and Rio de la Plata," ibid., 197–214.

[92] Benton, *A Search for Sovereignty. Law and Geography in European Empires, 1400–1900* (Cambridge: Cambridge University Press, 2010), 1–31, 280; Benton and Ross, "Empires and Legal Pluralism," 1–7; Rodríguez O., "We Are Now," 24, 33, see also 1–33, 335–345, argues that "Americans everywhere either objected to or opposed these innovations and modified many to suit their interests," while the "crown eventually would have reached accommodations with its American subjects who retained a significant degree of autonomy." Kuethe and Andrien, *Spanish Atlantic World*, 25, maintain that various social groups "attempted to shape the reform process," see also p. 213. On participation from below, see Eric Van Young, *The Other Rebellion: Popular*

that a king or his dynasty rarely pursued grand designs leading "inexorably from empire to nation-state" and the process was far from a smooth and steady process.[93] The king's ministers and their local allies considered their options when challenges arose, and they chose specific solutions rather than crafting a consistent policy. Sometimes, the kings even curbed the autonomy of one entrenched social body by creating competing institutions. In 1717, for example, the crown established a new viceroyalty in New Granada (modern Colombia, Venezuela, and Ecuador) to heighten control and dampen the influence of the powerful viceroy, *audiencia*, and oligarchy of Lima (Peru). In the second half of the eighteenth century, Manila in the Philippines, Guadalajara, and Veracruz also obtained *consulados* (merchant guilds) to rival the guild of Mexico City. Privileges and immunities of social bodies dissolved slowly and unevenly. Lasting change came only by enlisting local and imperial support, or at least acquiescence.[94]

At other times, the goals were oppressive, striking at indigenous self-administration, eradicating linguistic diversity, or raising taxation to new levels. Many historians of indigenous communities consider these changes as destructive to Native culture. Nancy Farriss, for example, argues that the Bourbon dynasty assaulted the traditional social order of Yucatan, and some scholars emphasize the exploitation of New Spain as a whole.[95]

Violence, Ideology, and the Mexican Struggle for Independence, 1810–1821 (Stanford, CA: Stanford University Press, 2001); see also Holenstein, "Introduction," 5, 11–31; Jon Mathieu, "Statebuilding from Below: Towards a Balanced View," in Blockmans, Holenstein, and Mathieu, *Empowering Interactions*, 305–311.

[93] Burbank and Cooper, *Empires in World History*, 2–3; Benton, *A Search for Sovereignty*, 10.

[94] Based largely on Guerra, "De la política antigua," 110–129; Kuethe and Andrien, *Spanish Atlantic World*, 25, 70; Bernecker, Pietschmann, and Tobler, *Kleine Geschichte*. According to del Valle Pavón, *Donativos, préstamos y privilegios: los mercaderes y mineros de la Ciudad de México durante la guerra anglo-española de 1779–1783* (Mexico City: Instituto Mora, 2016), 7, Buenos Aires and Guatemala also received *consulados*. See also Guerra, "Pour une nouvelle histoire politique," 250–258; Jorge Cañizares-Esguerra, *Puritan Conquistadors: Iberianizing the Atlantic, 1550–1700* (Stanford, CA: Stanford University Press, 2006), 5–9; Antonio Annino, "Soberanías en lucha," in *De los imperios a las naciones: Iberoamérica*, eds. Antonio Annino, Luis Castro Leiva, and François-Xavier Guerra (Zaragoza: Ibercaja, Obra cultural, 1994), 229–253. On the transition from the State of Associations to territorial state, Gerd Althoff, *Political and Social Bonds in Early Medieval Europe* (Cambridge: Cambridge University Press, 2004), 4–8.

[95] Farriss, *Maya Society*, 375–378. Notable is Yannakakis, *The Art of Being*, 223, which argues that the "imperial objective of cultural and ethnic homogenization" sought to "flatten the native social hierarchy" and turn "native peoples into pale imitations of Spaniards" while maintaining the hierarchy between Natives and Spaniards "on which colonialism was based." Owensby, *Empire of Law*, 297, views the seventeenth century as "relentless disintegration in the face of self-centered individual action," marked by

These are all excellent contributions, but these changes also had a different meaning.

Dismantling social bodies and curbing the privileges of old noble families could well benefit other groups that vied for community influence. For example, the elections for Native *alcaldes* and governors continued from pre-contact times, although they became incrementally more competitive. Tenochtitlan, the leading indigenous *parcialidad* (neighborhood) in Mexico City, demonstrates this shift. Its governors traditionally grew up in the *parcialidad* and descended from the Aztec royal lineage. In 1573, however, a well-educated non-noble from out of town won the election for governor. Social origin as selection criteria weakened further and direct appeals to the constituency mattered more. Candidates offered "entertainments, banquets, gifts, and extravagant election promises" to gain the vote by the 1650s. By this time, commoners began serving the indigenous municipal offices in greater numbers.[96] Competitive elections could well be popular among some middling and popular sectors.

In addition, the Enlightenment increasingly frowned upon treating social groups differently. Consequently, the separate laws for Natives were more and more seen as discriminatory and withered in the eighteenth century. The position of the protector of Indians disappeared in 1735, for example, and the incumbent joined the *audiencia* as a criminal judge.

"*aprovechamiento*" or exploitation. John Tutino, *Making a New World. Founding Capitalism in the Bajío and Spanish North America* (Durham, NC: Duke University Press, 2011), argues that "entrepreneurs took rising profits by assaulting the ways and welfare of the producing majority. Deepening inequities were sustained for decades." See also Dorothy Tanck de Estrada and Carlos Marichal, "Reino o Colonia? Nueva España, 1750–1804," in Velásquez García, *Nueva Historia general*, 307–353; Marichal, *Bankruptcy of Empire*, 1–12. In "Rethinking Negotiation and Coercion in an Imperial State," *HAHR* 88, no. 2 (2008): 217, Marichal argues that the colonies had to "adhere to the rules of an absolutist government that severely limited political autonomy ... despite the harshness of the regime ... [there] existed a certain degree of consensus in New Spain with regard to the legitimacy and functionality of the colonial tax system." Felipe Castro Gutiérrez, *Nueva ley y nuevo rey. Reformas borbónicas y rebelión popular en Nueva España* (Zamora: El Colegio de Michoacán; Mexico City: UNAM, 1996), 96–97, 262–275, argues that the populace revolted against specific aspects of the late Bourbon recolonization project to control and tax matters that previously had not been regulated by the state.

[96] Connell, *After Moctezuma*, 138, see also 70–75, 119–120, 154–155, 181–187. On lineages until 1610, Lockhart, *Nahuas*, 30–35; or 1650s, Hausberger and Mazín, "Nueva España," 291. Wiebke von Deylen, *Ländliches Wirtschaftsleben im spätkolonialen Mexiko. Eine mikrohistorische Studie in einem multiethnischem Distrikt: Cholula 1750–1810* (Hamburg: Hamburg University Press, 2003), 250–261, shows pre-Conquest nobles lost to competing families, communal landholdings declined, and private ownership expanded.

The Indian court also dissolved in the 1790s. Defense lawyers for Indians obtained better salaries to improve judicial standards and moved their trials into the *audiencia*.[97]

Indigenous peoples did not necessarily resent these changes if they did not conflict with their own interests. They often assimilated elements of the prestigious Hispanic culture – just as Hispanic urban culture borrowed heavily from Indians. Even the state's aim of spreading the Spanish language and mores among all inhabitants of the empire could be attractive for many when also offering full citizenship. Although this change strikes us now as innocuous to cultural diversity, a similar process was at play throughout Europe. For these reasons, the assessment of eighteenth-century empire should not be too somber. While not denying that groups suffered, reforms also came about with prodding from below. The analysis of corruption in this book bears this out.[98]

CONCLUSION

The law and social practices both mattered and evolved in the Spanish empire. Six pillars of law contributed to the legal pluralism in broad strokes. These were the combined Roman and canon law and their evolving interpretations, known as the *ius commune*. Spanish legal practitioners directly or indirectly drew on the *ius commune* for many years until the eighteenth century. Notaries or attorneys, for example, sometimes cited *ius commune* doctrines such as the tacit consent to defend the

---

[97] Owensby, *Empire of Law*, 37, 301–302; Annino, "El primer constitucionalismo Mexicano," 152–154; see also William Taylor, *Drinking, Homicide, and Rebellion in Colonial Mexican Villages* (Stanford, CA: Stanford University Press, 1979), 76.

[98] According to Lockhart, *Nahuas*, 443, "the Nahuas had no doctrinal distaste for Spanish introductions as such but related to them pragmatically," see also 2–5, 427–436, 442–446. On the religious change as part of the same trend, see Larkin, *The Very Nature of God*; while for Pamela Voekel, *Alone before God. The Religious Origins of Modernity in Mexico* (Durham, NC: Duke University Press, 2002), 12, elite projects "floated like large reefs atop an indifferent or hostile ocean." See also Duve, *Sonderrecht*, 274. On negotiated absolutism comparable to the British model, Alejandra Irigoin and Regina Grafe, "Bargaining for Absolutism: A Spanish Path to Nation-State and Empire Building," *HAHR* 88, no. 2 (2008): 173–209; Grafe, *Distant Tyranny: Markets, Power, and Backwardness in Spain, 1650–1800* (Princeton, NJ: Princeton University Press, 2012). On colonialism, "Para seguir con el debate en torno al colonialismo," *Nuevo Mundo Mundos Nuevos*, February 8, 2005, http://nuevomundo.revues.org/430; Philippe Castejón, "Colonia, entre appropriation et rejet: La naissance d'un concept (de la fin des années 1750 aux révolutions hispaniques)," *Mélanges de la Casa de Velázquez*. Nouvelle série, vol. 43, no. 1 (2013): 268–269.

excessive fees they had charged from litigants. Judges reconciled these concepts with biblical tenets and natural law, understood as the reasonable principles of ordering justice. The local customs and the royal law also played major roles. In addition, the judicial plurality engendered legal populism. *Novohispano* commoners and elites had relatively easy access to the courts and representation. The courts heard the involved parties in conflicts and ideally meted out sentences following general principles of justice. The king reviewed the process as the supreme arbiter, and the justice system was generally believed to be legitimate.

In the sixteenth century, humanist lawyers began challenging that matrix. They critically assessed the history of the Roman collection and furthered the judges' *arbitrio* to adjudicate criminal trials. In the late seventeenth century, inklings of enlightened thinking appeared on the intellectual horizon and the royal law gained further influence in the courts. Proponents of natural law suggested abandoning the legal pluralism in favor of an entirely new code built on systematic and unequivocal principles. Some experts even proposed discarding the *ius commune* and the royal law collections. Yet writing a full-fledged code for the entire empire failed, and the royal *Law of Castile* and the *Law of the Indies* continued to enshrine justice until the independence of New Spain in 1821.

When the social networks excessively skewed decisions, the king sent *visitas* to restore the proper working of justice. The networks consisted of patron–client relationships that tied together the social and ethnic groups of the empire, and local intermediaries played a crucial role in exchanging resources. The kings and queens relied on power brokers to gain information and advance reforms. Sometimes, these networks became too influential and clogged communication. *Visitas* then reviewed the institutions, penalized miscreants, and helped reward meritorious vassals. The *visitas* usually handed down swifter verdicts, because they avoided the slow grind of the ordinary courts. The suspects in these investigations often deplored the harsh and extra-judicial rulings against them, and the *visitadores* could well abuse their vast powers for personal vendettas. Nonetheless, many *novohispanos* supported Francisco Garzarón's investigation, and he and other *visitadores* relied on local agreement or acquiescence for their advances.

In the period under consideration, the empire slowly segued toward a state organized around territorial principles and a stronger role for individuals rivaling the semi-autonomous social bodies. These social bodies, such as the indigenous *pueblo* and the municipal councils, had sustained society and adjudicated the conflicts among their members. The social bodies fiercely defended their privileges and traditions, yet the crown sought to undermine their great autonomy and that of the realms as a whole. This process advanced piecemeal and was marked by ad hoc responses to specific challenges. Sometimes the social bodies or conservative elites imposed competing solutions or forced a return to old practices. Many facets of empire survived and change came only when significant sections of society agreed on reforms.

2

From Judicial to Administrative Corruption

INTRODUCTION

Corruption has a long history in Hispanic thinking about justice. Yet corruption in the early modern period differed from our modern views of the offense. Corruption did not refer to breaching one or several laws of office for self-benefit. Instead, the concept meant impeding the process of establishing justice. This mattered greatly, because the fair solutions for judicial trials and other conflicts were not always immediately clear for early modern beholders. Justice unfolded only when judges carefully weighed the evidence, selected the appropriate legal arguments from a multitude of sources, and tailored their verdicts to each civil or criminal case. Corruption skewed that process of finding justice.

Early modern corruption principally included three ideas. First, it referred to those who directly bent justice. For instance, abusive judges who accepted bribes to alter sentences, extorted litigants, or traded with their subjects committed corruption. Defendants, witnesses, and officials who took or offered cash to produce false testimony also corroded rulings. In addition, the second idea of corruption included promoting people of lowly social or racial descent to judges. According to many theologians and jurists, the unsuited judges would likely fall prey to the temptations of their office and issue unjust verdicts. Finally, the nefarious customs also perverted justice when they replaced the just law. Judicial corruption, as I call the concept, consisted of these three ideas. The first idea in particular overlapped to some degree with our modern notion of corruption, while the second and third ideas differ significantly.

Latin American historians have amply discussed the ambiguity of corruption. Some argue that the values of early modern Spaniards contrasted starkly with those of today, and Spaniards did therefore not apply the concept of corruption.[1] Yet while it is true that the values have changed much since colonial days, that does not mean that corruption did not exist in that period. In fact, the *visitador general* (investigative judge) Francisco Garzarón (1716–1727) drew on a fairly common definition of that crime to suspend thirteen ministers of the *audiencia* (high court). Many *novohispanos* (the inhabitants of New Spain or colonial Mexico) supported him in his investigation, because they had at least some familiarity with the idea. Meanwhile, according to Spanish scholar Antonio García García, the Council of the Indies concocted the fictional account that selling appointments to *novohispanos* would corrupt the judiciary, because the Council tried to retain its patronage power over these appointments.[2]

The Council certainly tried to defend its influence, but I propose nonetheless that the view of the corrupt candidates was not an impromptu fiction, but a widely accepted argument deeply rooted in the values of that time. Many political authors maintained that candidates needed the proper merits to attain offices, which referred to a large degree to their pure, noble, and Christian descent. The candidates also revealed the notable military actions or the administrative services that they or their forebears had completed for the crown and community, while aptitude for the job mattered as one qualification among others. The traditional elites, which comprised the aristocracy, the upper clergy, and most council and *audiencia* jurists, attacked social newcomers of lowly descent as corrupt, because they lacked the necessary social origins. The traditional elites employed the trope about merit to exclude all competitors of lower social origins and not just *novohispanos*. Yet the high birth of candidates or the deeds of their forebears said little about the candidates' performance on the job, and objective exams rarely verified their skills. In addition, the concept of corruption changed in the period 1650 to 1755. The idea slowly shed its innate connotation and expanded beyond the judiciary. Judicial corruption evolved into administrative corruption, which included the violations of the royal rules in the bureaucracy for self-benefit.

---

[1] Herzog, *Upholding Justice*, 154–160.

[2] Antonio García García, "Corrupción y venalidad en la magistratura mexicana durante el siglo XVIII," *Illes i Imperis. Estudis d'història de les societats en el món colonial i postcolonial* (Barcelona) 16 (2014): 13–38, building on Mark A. Burkholder and D. S. Chandler, *From Impotence to Authority: The Spanish Crown and the American Audiencias, 1687–1808* (Columbia, MO: University of Missouri Press, 1977), 32, who perceptively argued that the *cámara* of the Council of the Indies argued against selling appointments to keep its patronage.

This chapter traces the three key elements of judicial corruption and separates them from the non-judicial offences that did not shape verdicts. Subsequently, I juxtapose the ideal merit of the good judge with the faulty descent of candidates for judicial office and its alleged ramifications. Finally, the chapter offers evidence that the idea of corruption changed incrementally in the early eighteenth century. Most scholars have affirmed that any meaningful shift occurred in the later eighteenth century or beyond.[3] Yet the analysis shows that the Spanish term corruption came to include administrative acts by the 1750s.

2.1 BRIBERY, EXTORTIONS, AND EVIL CUSTOMS

Historians have held that "corruption and modernity emerged jointly, because comprehensive rules of law developed during modernity and made corruption possible."[4] Yet corruption was not a sign of modernity. Greek and Roman philosophers already lambasted the decay of their political systems. For Polybius (ca. 205–123 BC), for instance, an immoral body politic declined from monarchy to tyranny, from an aristocracy to an oligarchy, or from democracy to mob rule.[5] The statesman Cicero (106–43 BC), widely cited in the Spanish empire, asserted "that in the courts of law as they now exist, no wealthy man, however guilty he may be, can possibly be convicted ... and nothing is so holy that it cannot be corrupted, or so strongly fortified that money cannot conquer it."[6] At the same time, Cicero himself demonstrated the ambiguity of the concept. He

---

[3] Maryvonne Géneaux, "Social sciences and the Evolving Concept of Corruption," *Crime, Law & Social Change* 42, no. 1 (2004): 17, separates the judicial corruption from the "political corruption" that emerged at the end of the eighteenth century; see also Engels, "Politische Korruption," 39.
[4] Werner Plumpe, "Korruption. Annäherung an ein historisches und gesellschaftliches Phänomen," in *Geld–Geschenke–Politik. Korruption im neuzeitlichen Europa*, eds. Ivo Engels, Andreas Fahrmeir, and Alexander Nützenadel (Munich: Oldenbourg, 2009), 29. Kettering, *Patrons, Brokers*, 193, argues similarly that the "development of the concept of corruption accompanied the growth of the early modern state." See also Bellingradt, "Organizing Public Opinion," 556.
[5] Jürgen Gebhardt, "Ursprünge und Elemente des 'Korruptionsdiskurses' im westlichen Ordnungsdenken," in *Korruption und Governance aus interdisziplinärer Sicht: Ergebnisse eines Workshops des Zentralinstituts für Regionalforschung vom Mai 2001*, ed. Oskar Kurer (Bad Windsheim: Degener, 2003), 25–26.
[6] Cicero, *Against Verres*, in *The Orations of Marcus Tullius Cicero*, vol 1, ed., and trans. Charles Duke Yonge (London: George Bell & Sons, 1903), 1, 1, 1, www.perseus.tufts.edu/hopper/text?doc=Cic.+Ver.+1.1.; quoted, for instance, by Castillo de Bobadilla, *Política*, book 2, chap. 11, para. 3, esp. note e; see also para. 10, note c.

defended doling out gifts for votes as necessary generosity to friends, and the courts rarely condemned anyone for illegal canvassing during the elections in republican Rome.[7] Subsequently, corruption often depended on the intent of giving gifts. According to one jurist in medieval France, "any judge should refrain from accepting a gift that may corrupt him." This jurist allowed giving presents to a judge as long as they did not manipulate the sentence. This opinion also remained influential in the Spanish empire well into the eighteenth century.[8]

In addition, theologians cast bribery as a mortal sin. The Bible exhorted judges to "do justice to the humble and the poor." They should not "take a gift: for a gift blinds the eyes of the wise and perverts the words of the righteous."[9] The sixteenth-century canonist Martín de Azpilcueta commented on this idea in more detail. He pointed out that bribery violated the seventh commandment against stealing, because bribery was an "usurpation of alien things."[10] An eighteenth-century theologian similarly

---

[7] Uwe Walter, "Patronale Wohltaten oder kriminelle Mobilisierung. Sanktion gegen unerlaubte Wahlwerbung im spätrepublikanischen Rom," in Grüne and Slanička, *Korruption*, 147–164.

[8] Philippe de Beaumanoir (1252/54–1296), quoted in Génaux, "Social Sciences," 19; see also Génaux, "Corruption in English and French Fields of Vision," in Heidenheimer and Johnston, *Political Corruption*, 111–113; Schlosser, *Neuere europäische*, 44. According to Suter, "Korruption," 190, Jean Bodin (1529–1596) used the term *corrompre*, and Gil, "Spain and Portugal," 439, 442, shows that Bodin was widely read in the Spanish empire. See also the entry on *corrutela ne' giudici* in Cesare Ripa Perugino, *Iconologia del cavaliere Cesare Ripa Perugino notabilmente accresciuta d'immagini, di annotazioni e di fatti dell'abate Cesare Orlandi Patrizio di Citta della pieve accademico augusto a sua excellenza D. Raimondo di Sangro [...]* (Perugia: Nella Stamperia di Piergovanni Constantini, 1765), vol. 2, 78–79. Niccolò Machiavelli (1469–1527) also frequently used the terms *corrompere* or *corruzione* (corrupt, corruption), for example, in "Discorsi sopra la prima deca di Tito Livio," in *Machiavelli, Tutte le opere*, ed. Mario Martelli (Sansoni: Florence, 1971), book 3, chap. 1. See also Grüne, "Und sie wissen nicht," 18; Gebhardt, "Ursprünge," 27, 30; José Antônio Martins, "Os fundamentos da república e sua corrupçao nos Discursos de Maquiavel" (PhD diss., Universidade de São Paulo, 2007), 181–183. According to Susanne Lepsius, *Von Zweifeln zur Überzeugung. Der Zeugenbeweis im gelehrten Recht ausgehend von der Abhandlung des Bartolus von Sassoferrato* (Frankfurt: Klostermann, 2003), 283–284, esp. note 245, the medieval glossators developed a nuanced theory of bribery and distinguished between corrupting with money and favors.

[9] Ps. 82: 3–4 (corresponding to Vulgate ps. 81: 3–4); Deuteronomy 16: 19–20. Castillo de Bobadilla, *Política*, book 2, chap. 11, para. 18, cited Deuteronomy 16. See also 1 Samuel 12:2. Within an Atlantic context, Ps. 82 adorns the municipal council of Lemgo, Lippe, Germany, www.inschriften.net/lemgo/inschrift/nr/dio59-0108.html#content

[10] Martín de Azpilcueta, *Manual de Confesores y penitentes, que clara y brevemente contiene, la universal y particular decision de quasi todas las dudas, que en las confesiones suelen ocurrir de los pecados, absoluciones, restituciones, censuras, & irregularidades* (Salamanca: Andrea de Portonarijs, 1557), 182. According to Berart y Gassol, *Speculum visitationis*, chap. 17, para 5, "*Baratería* is called theft," and para. 14, the person "who

defined illicitly seizing valuables as a mortal sin, which meant, in most cases, taking more than half a silver peso. The bribes given to judges in New Spain frequently exceeded this amount and were serious offenses in this perspective. Theologians also wrangled over the duty to return the dishonest gains from bribery. Some conceded that perpetrators could retain the wages for their services, while others opposed wrongful salaries. Yet most agreed that corruption was a sin.[11]

The theological condemnation reverberated in the *Law of Castile*. The judges

> do not accept in public or hidden by themselves or through others any gifts from anyone ... who will appear in court before the judges, and these gifts may be gold, silver, cloth, dress, food, or other goods, or any other thing. Anyone who will take this gift for himself or for others will lose his office and will never again serve this or any other office and will also repay double of what he accepted."[12]

The terms for corruption and bribery appeared in lexicons and in the legal context, because they mattered to Spaniards. Sebastián Covarrubias's famous dictionary from 1611 noted *corruptela* as a foreign word but this does not indicate that Spaniards did not grasp the idea of corruption. Instead, Covarrubias clarified that he preferred the Spanish form *corrupción* over the Latin term *corruptela* (corruption).[13]

---

accepts money to do justice sins mortally"; for Castillo de Bobadilla, *Política*, book 2, chap. 11, para. 21, "Bartolus [de Sassoferrato] says that the judge who receives something on account of his office can be accused of robbery." See also Josef Bordat, "Martín de Azpilcueta," in *Biographisch-Bibliographisches Kirchenlexikon*, ed. Traugott Bautz (Nordhausen: Bautz, 2009), vol. 30, pp. 76–78.

[11] Azcargorta, *Manual de Confesores*, 166, 177–179, 271–273, citing St. Paul's "sinning is any conduct outside the faith." Decock, *Theologians*, 435–440, shows that the discussion included prostitution, which was also a sin performed for money. Murillo Velarde, *Cursus Iuris Canonici*, book 2, title 20, para. 150, argued that witnesses who took money for giving faithful accounts should return the money, while those "who accepted for a false testimony do not, and although they gravely sinned, they nevertheless acquired possession" of the money; in ibid, para. 364, Murillo Velarde argued that a prostitute could similarly keep the money for performed sexual work.

[12] *Law of Castile*, book 3, title 9, law 5, originally issued by King Alonso of Castile in 1385. See also *Law of the Indies*, book 2, title 16, laws 68–70; Murillo Velarde, *Cursus iuris canonici*, book 1, title 32, para. 346, agreed with this stance, although also citing a more permissive view.

[13] Sebastián de Covarrubias Orozco, *Tesoro de la lengua castellana, o española* [...] (Madrid: Luis Sánchez, 1611), 242–243. Alberro, "Control," 41–45, views Covarrubias's entry as an indication that corruption was still alien to the Spanish empire. See also *corrupción* in *RAE* (1729), book 2, p. 622–623. Nicolas Mez de Braidenbach, *Diccionario muy copioso de la lengua española y alemana hasta agora nunca visto, sacado de diferentes autores con mucho trabajo y diligencia* [...] (Vienna: Juan Diego

In addition, another lexicon translated the Spanish word for bribery into Latin as *repentundarum*, which was the Roman ban on giving to judges that most legal practitioners instinctively recognized.[14] Jurists often conjoined the law on *repentundarum* with another one called *ambitus*, which prohibited politicians from handing out gifts during Roman election campaigns. The Council of Castile, for example, seized on this idea and warned King Charles V before 1517 about the dangers of *ambitus repentundarum*. The Council of the Indies referenced this legal opinion in 1693 when attacking the corrupting sale of judicial appointments. Similarly, in 1724, an attorney deplored the "offense so abominable as bribery or *repentundarum*."[15] His colleagues in the Holy Roman Empire equally chastised that crime, demonstrating once more the global reach of the Roman law. One doctoral dissertation, for instance, suggested that all incoming judges should swear an oath against committing the offense.[16]

Bribery was a pact between two or more parties to shape an illicit verdict. As in the case of many Hispanic legal concepts, pacts and contracts had their roots in the *ius commune*, that is, the intertwined interpretations of the Roman and the canon law. The medieval canon lawyers began to understand contracts as formless and voluntary promises of transactions. These agreements "were for the keeping," and the jurists considered breaking them

---

Kürner, 1670), 76, 1, http://buscon.rae.es/ntlle/SrvltGUIMenuNtlle?cmd=Lema&sec=1.0.0.0.0, translated *corrupción* into German with *Bestechung*, the equivalent of bribery, showing the close semantic overlap of the two terms. According to Rafael Bluteau, *Vocabulario Portuguez e latino* (Coimbra: Collegio das Artes da Companhia de Jesu, 1712), 2: 788, corruption (*corrupção*) affected "a judge or justice."

[14] Antonio de Nebrija, *Vocabulario español-latino* (Salamanca: Impresor de la Gramática castellana, 1495) http://buscon.rae.es/ntlle/SrvltGUIMenuNtlle?cmd=Lema&sec=1.1.0.0.0., pp. 181, 2 and 45, 2. Nebrija rendered the more precise *cohecho de juez* (bribery of a judge) as *repentundarum*. The RAE (1729), p. 401,1, and (1726), p. 551, 1, similarly defined *cohecho* as "donation, gift, or payment that the judge, minister, or witness accepted so that he does what is requested although this may be unreasonable ... Repentundarum crimen," while *baratería* was "the bribe accepted by the judge for his sentence ... *subornatio*."

[15] Print *por Don Miguel Truxillo*, AGI, México 670 A, fol. 4; see also Jerónimo de Quintana, *Historia de la antigüedad, nobleza y grandeza de la villa de Madrid* (Madrid: Imprenta del Reyno, 1629, edited by E. Varela Hervías (Madrid: Artes Gráficas Municipales, 1954), 738–740, and Konetzke, *Colección*, book 3, tome 1: 34. According to defense of Juan Díaz de Bracamonte, AGI, México 670 B, *Relación*, fol. 150, litigants "bribed the judge." Note that the *lex Iulia de pecuniis repetundis* dated from the year 59 BC and prohibited bribing judges, while the *lex Iulia de ambitu* (18 BC) disallowed electioneering. They can be found in *Digest* 48.11.0 and 48.14.0. Génaux, "Social Sciences," 17–18, argues that the *lex Cornelius de falsis* punished judicial corruption. See also Plescia, "Judicial Accountability," 59–67.

[16] Schwartz and Linck, *De iuramento*, 16.

FIGURE 1 *The Decree of the Unjust Judge.* An image of a corrupt judge from Italy. After cutting down justice, the judge held meatballs in his hands, which signified ill-gotten wealth. C. M. Jnuentor, *Decreto di Giudice Ingiusto*, engraving, 1765, Cesare Ripa Perugino, *Iconologia*, vol. 2, p. 152.

a sin.[17] For some early modern scholars, the term *pact* had a looser meaning than *contract* and included informal and non-enforceable agreements. Bribery was therefore a wrongful pact, which is why a *novohispano* notary denied that he had ever agreed on "a pact prohibited by law."[18]

---

[17] On contracts that have to be fulfilled (*pacta sunt servanda*), see Robinson, Fergus, and Gordon, *European*, 88–89, 104–105; Meder, *Rechtsgeschichte*, 73–75, 162; Schlosser, *Neuere europäische*, 99–100.

[18] Defense of Juan José Aguilera, AGI, Escribanía 289 B, *Relazion*, fol. 109. See also *RAE*, 1737, p. 72 on "pact." For Murillo Velarde, *Cursus iuris canonici*, book 1, title 35, para. 360, a "pact ... is the agreement of two or more who are consenting" which included contracts that produced "obligation and civil action ... and some pacts are in open or in tacit agreement," and according to book 1, title 35, para. 364, pacts "committed in evil ways are legally impossible." For Azcargorta, *Manual de Confesores*, 281, contracts were "agreements among those who mutually bind themselves ... without deceit, error, or falseness knowingly playing a role."

Garzarón punished such pacts of bribery, and *novohispanos* understood why. The jurist Jerónimo Castillo de Bobadilla accused the judges who accepted "gifts, offerings, or money" of a "crime and corruption."[19] In 1719, one notary similarly described "the abominable offense of bribery in which the giver contributes so that the judge issues an unjust ruling."[20] Garzarón largely agreed. He gathered evidence that a judge had accepted a sizable gift from litigants and then ruled in their favor. When he obtained sufficient proof, he suspended the suspect.[21] During his investigation, for example, Garzarón heard accusations that a landowner gave 200 pesos to a civil judge after winning a verdict against some Natives. Garzarón noted that the accused civil judge had in fact been "the judge in this trial, which ended in favor" of the landowner. This boded ill for the civil judge, and only his death saved him from condemnation.[22] In another case, a litigant sent a gift to a judge, but the court voted against the litigant. Garzarón and the Council of the Indies acquitted the judge.[23]

The suspects argued on occasion that, if anything, they may have committed a lesser offense called *baratería*, which did not bend the verdict itself. The notary Pedro Robledo explained in 1719 that "bribery and *baratería* are not synonymous," because "bribery is acting against justice," while most forms of *baratería* were not. Robledo pointed out that *baratería* had three distinct meanings, consisting of "achieving justice in substance, negotiating between individual parties, or referring to matters of grace." The first definition meant, for example, convincing the judge to sentence more rapidly without changing the sentence itself. The second and third definitions referred to non-judicial matters such as grace, which was the royal domain to favor individuals. Robledo maintained that he had never "issued a just or unjust ruling for any gift in matters of justice or a lawsuit that would have constituted the despicable bribery or *baratería*

---

[19] Castillo de Bobadilla, *Política*, book 2, chap. 11, paras. 3–4; para. 21, added that "no thieve is as greedy for someone else's goods as the bad judge," while according to para. 50, Castillo de Bobadilla denied that giving food to judges was licit, because "the demon would enter to achieve his effects." See also book 2, chap. 11, paras. 36–40; book 5, chap. 1, paras. 227–230. On Anglo-Spanish demonology, Cañizares-Esguerra, *Puritan Conquistadors*, 5–9. According to Alonso Romero, *Orden procesal*, 130, the *Consejo Real* stated in 1748 that the *juicios de residencia* were "maliciously corrupted."
[20] José Saenz de Escobar on behalf of Pedro Robledo to Garzarón, Mexico City, 15 Apr. 1719, AGI, Escribanía 280 C, fol. 454v.
[21] Defense of Juan Díaz de Bracamonte, AGI, México 670 B, *Relación*, fol. 142v.
[22] Charges against Miguel Calderón de la Barca, AGI, México 670 B, fol. 13–13v; on the verdict, *consulta* of the Council of the Indies, 2 Sept. 1721, AGI, México 380.
[23] Charge against Jerónimo de Soria, AGI, México 670 B, *Relación*, fols. 109v–110.

in the first sense" involving justice.[24] Robledo built on past authorities, who claimed that *baratería* was doing something improper without corrupting justice, such as when the judge charged fees before the sentencing or when the litigants paid to avoid the harassment of a judge.[25]

By the seventeenth century, however, many jurists rejected this distinction and lambasted the "crime of corruption or *baratería*."[26] Castillo de Bobadilla, for example, objected to separating corruption from *baratería*, because giving money to a judge always intended something illicit. Garzarón largely concurred, and the suspects in the *visita* doubted that they could easily sway Garzarón with this argument. They typically reverted to a double-pronged defense. They denied having committed the offense that Garzarón charged them with, while also insisting that the legal argument justified their acts if they had occurred.[27]

Other suspects separated licit gifting among friends and family from corrupt giving with malicious intent. One civil judge rejected Garzarón's charges by stating that the "*dolo* [malicious intent] could vitiate a gift, but this is not the case when receiving from a friend or giving for friendship or when receiving small appropriate goods, even as a loan or the customary

---

[24] Robledo to Garzarón, Mexico City, 15 Apr. 1719, AGI, Escribanía 280 C, *Q.no* 12, fols. 455–456.

[25] Castillo de Bobadilla, *Política*, book 2, chap. 11, paras. 36–40; book 5, chap. 1, paras. 227–230, noted these past authorities. Castillo de Bobadilla's view leaned on late medieval authorities such as Paris de Puteo (1413–1493), for whom *baratería* was comparable to high treason, and Egidio Bossi, who rejected distinguishing licit from illicit *baratería*. On Puteo, see Moritz Isenmann, "Rector est Raptor. Korruption und ihre Bekämpfung in den italienischen Kommunen des späten Mittelalters," in *Nützliche Netzwerke und korrupte Seilschaften*, eds. Arne Karsten and Hillard von Thiessen (Göttingen: Vandenhoeck & Ruprecht, 2006), 215, note 34; on Bossi, Garriga, "Crimen Corruptionis," 15–16, 21. In charges against Joseph Anaya, AGI, Escribanía 289 A, fol. 8–8v, Garzarón recognized both *baratería* and bribery. Berart y Gassol, *Speculum visitationis*, chap. 17, para. 17, distinguished various activities under *baratería*, including the offense to "quickly resolve a case," because "the impoverished & outsider & older litigants" had to be heard in first place. Azcargorta, *Manual de Confesores*, 172, denied that judges could accept money even when both litigants had an equally solid claim. Note that according to brief of García de Xismeros, Mexico City, 24 Nov. 1721, AGI, Escribanía 286 C, *Q.no* 30, no. 7, fol. 563v, one official allegedly called his colleagues *baratilleros* (those who peddled goods). See also Peck, *Court, Patronage*, 8; Dubet, "La moralidad de los mentirosos," 226–228.

[26] Berart y Gassol, *Speculum visitationis*, chap. 17, para. 5; see also paras. 2–95.

[27] Defense of Juan Díaz de Bracamonte, AGI, México 670 B, *Relación*, fol. 143. See also defense of Francisco de Alexo de Luna, AGI, Escribanía 289 A, fol. 324v, who was accused of shoddy bookkeeping. Alexo de Luna denied the charge, because "even if this were true, he rejects being guilty, as no documents were lost and this was the practiced *formalidad* (form) and therefore the charge is invalid."

food and drink, because they lack the *dolo*."[28] For this reason, exchanging proper gifts without an evil purpose was acceptable. In addition, one civil judge declared that he only ever received the polite attentions from a relative of a former fellow student. They had a special friendship and no litigation was pending in court. Garzarón noted the defense and acquitted the minister. Many *novohispanos* agreed that giving to family or friends was usually permissible, and these gifts were often given in public. The presents belonged to legitimate social practices and starkly differed from corrupt giving to alter justice. [29]

Moreover, the civil judge Juan Díaz de Bracamonte claimed that a good judge had the *arbitrio* (judgment) to discern appropriate from inappropriate gifts. For him, the value of gifts had to correspond to the "wealth of the person who gives and the social status of the recipient." Díaz de Bracamonte introduced here distributive justice, which stated that exchanges had to match the social preeminence of the participants. He averred that the prudent judge had the *arbitrio* to know when such gifts were appropriate.[30] Lawyers working at the *audiencia* similarly chiseled

---

[28] Defense of Valenzuela Venegas, AGI, México, 670 B, *Relación*, fol. 30v. According to Feros, *Kingship and Favoritism*, 181, the Duke of Lerma (1598–1618), similarly distinguished between virtuous giving as a social obligation and giving with the "intention of forcing me to commit unjust acts."

[29] Defense of José Joaquín Uribe, AGI, México 670 B, *Relación*, fols. 88v–90v, 95. The testimony of José Joaquín Uribe, AGI, México 670 B, *Relación*, fol. 89v, referred to gifts from Andrés de Berrio, a relative of Uribe's *paisano* (countryman) and *colegial* (fellow student) at Salamanca, Francisco Berrio y Marzana. According to Mark Burkholder's personal note, Berrio y Marzana studied in Salamanca from 1662 to 1676, then held the chairs to teach Justinian's *Institutes* and the *Code* before joining the Council of Orders in 1689. Defense of Juan de Oliván y Rebolledo, AGI, México 670 B, *Relación*, fol. 284v, made a similar point as Uribe, and Murillo Velarde, *Cursus iuris canonici*, book 1, title 32, para. 346, supported his view. Meanwhile, Herzog, *Upholding Justice*, 155, denies the corrupt character of giving gold to an *audiencia* president, because this belonged to "social practices that were considered both legitimate and advantageous." Yet Hespanha, "Les autre raisons de la politique. L'économie de la grâce," in *Recherche sur l'histoire de l'État dans le monde ibérique (15e–20e siècle)*, ed. Frédéric Schaub (Paris: Presses de l'École Normale Superieure, 1993), 69–70, differs on mutual obligations; see also Clavero, *Antidora, antropología católica de la economía moderna* (Milan: Giuffrè Editore, 1991), 64–71; Meder, *Rechtsgeschichte*, 163. *Law of Castile*, book 3, title 9, law 16, and book 3, title 10 (containing only one law) both fixed fees and prevented presents. Suter, "Korruption," 210–211, argues that seventeenth-century Swiss negotiators shrouded bribes as losing card games.

[30] Defense of Díaz de Bracamonte, AGI, México 670 B, *Relación*, fols. 142v–143. Similarly, defense of Judge Félix González de Agüero, AGI, México 670 B, *Relación*, fol. 205. According to testimony of Juan de la Riva, Mexico City, 12 Oct. 1717, AGI, Escribanía 278 A, *Quaderno* 6, fol. 106v, the witness gave a "voluntary reward ... without a general or particular promise ... and the gift was sent after executing the verdict." According to

out the *arbitrio*, which allowed them to receive gifts for "mere generosity or for the speediness and shortness in executing" paperwork. The litigants gave without striking any pacts, one attorney contended, and he used his good judgment to accept their licit gifts.[31]

Some suspects also denied a link between gift and verdict when sufficient time had passed between the two actions. One priest told Garzarón that he gave a present to a criminal judge in April 1718 for releasing his friend from jail in October 1717. Garzarón heard the priest's testimony in September 1718 and suspected that the priest artificially extended the period between gifting and the prisoner's release to dampen suspicions of a quid pro quo. Garzarón concluded that the priest had bribed the criminal judge at about the same time when the prisoner was released, and he suspended the criminal judge.[32]

Yet many witnesses also confirmed that it was "the way and practice of this land to give presents for all things."[33] Judges in Mexico City expected attentions "with the abusive title of royalty which in this realm legitimizes such offerings." In one notably high-powered case, doña Mariana de Cantabrana litigated over a large hacienda. Her attorney allegedly rode around the city in his "carriage loaded with bags of money and distributed them among the homes of the judges," where he spent more than 40,000 pesos.[34] *Novohispanos* also claimed that they gifted during the holidays to stay in the judges' favor without seeking an immediate gratification. One person gave a civil judge "twenty-one sackfuls of sugar, twelve loads of barley, and two loads of flour," as the gifts for Saint Michael's Day and Easter.[35] Similarly, doña Nicolasa Ramírez sent, on two or three occasions, "a dozen loads of flour with some small boxes of starch, and four or six pairs of hemp straps for the carriages," worth between 100 and 150

Aquinas, *Summa* IIa–IIae, Q. 71, art. 4, co., attorneys can "take a moderate fee with due consideration for the people, the matter in hand, the labor entailed, and for the custom of the country." This dictum was cited by the eighteenth-century theologian Miguel de San Antonio, *Resumen de la theologia moral*, 7. On the *arbitrio*, Scardaville, "Justice," 990; Schlosser, *Neuere europäische*, 122–123.

[31] Print *por Don Miguel Truxillo*, AGI, México 670 A, fol. 17v.

[32] *Prueba* against Diego de Castañeda, AGI, México 670 B, fols. 552v–553v; see also defense of Díaz de Bracamonte, AGI, México 670 B, *Relación*, fol. 143.

[33] Testimony of Lucas de Careaga, AGI, México 670 B, *Relación*, fol. 135v, see also fols. 138–139v.

[34] Testimony of José Uribe, Mexico City, 6 Nov. 1716, AGI, Escribanía 278 A, fol. 166–166v; testimony of Uribe, AGI, México 670 B, *Relación*, fol. 20; see also defense of Uribe, AGI, México 670 B, *Relación*, fol. 5–5v; testimony of the Marquis of Buenavista, Mexico City, 2 Oct. 1717, AGI, Escribanía 278 A, *Quaderno* 6, fol. 35.

[35] Charge against Miguel Calderón de la Barca, AGI, México 670 B, *Relación*, fol. 13v.

silver pesos. She aimed at conserving the friendship with a judge who had just voted in her favor. Yet judges also rejected gifts, such as the judge who returned six chickens to indigenous litigants.[36]

Clients or family often took care of the details. For instance, Guillermo Flores claimed that he was a "*chino* [Asian] and resident of Manila in the Philippines" and served a merchant in Mexico City. Flores said that his master gave him a silver bowl filled with cloth from Brittany (France) worth about 200 pesos and told him to bring the gifts to the prosecutor's wife. She received Flores in "her ante-chamber where she was in the presence of her husband," and they thanked his master.[37] In addition, one attorney sent his servant to frequent the homes of the litigating parties. The servant "bartered over the pay ... as though he was selling fine cloth from Brittany." If the party did not pay the required fees, he left the documents at their homes and the case stalled. When the attorney negotiated with a judge to attain a favorable ruling, the litigants had to pay more. Witnesses claimed that the attorney received forty-eight pesos and a black sombrero with silk lining for arranging a good reply from a judge in one instance.[38]

The term corruption covered more ground than bribes. The idea included a variety of extortions, because judges who illicitly exacted cash from litigants or petitioners sabotaged justice.[39] A procurator (legal

---

[36] *Prueba* against Miguel Calderón de la Barca, AGI, México 670 B, *Relación*, fols. 20v–21; see also reputation of Juan Francisco de la Peña y Flores, AGI, México 670 B, *Relación*, fol. 496.

[37] Testimony of Guillermo Flores, Mexico City, 6 Oct. 1717, AGI, Escribanía 278 A, Quaderno 6, fols. 54v–55v.

[38] Print *por Don Miguel Truxillo*, AGI, México 670 A, fols. 10v–11, 14–14v. The servant was called a *zángano*, which Alexander von Humboldt, *Mexico-Werk. Politische Ideen zu Mexico; mexicanische Landeskunde*, ed. Hanno Beck, rev ed. (Darmstadt: Wissenschaftliche Buchgesellschaft, 2008), 414, explains as forger.

[39] For many legal experts, extortion meant that a judge denied a legitimate service as long as they did not receive a reward. Jurists often separated this offense from *concusión*, which referred to threatening or using violence to extract money, see Berart y Gassol, *Speculum visitationis*, chap. 17, para. 8, see also paras. 9, 36–37. Castillo de Bobadilla, *Politica*, book 2, chap. 11, para. 69, letter l, and book 5, chap. 1, para. 207, distinguishes *concusión* from bribery. See also *RAE* 1869, p. 195, 2. Bluteau, *Vocabulario Portuguez*, 2: 668, explained *concussão* as "violence or fraud of a judge or other public minister who embezzles money." According to Génaux, "Social Sciences," 19, Joss de Damhouder understood corruption in 1554 as the receiving and concussion as the active role of the judge. Note, however, that concussion meant violent extortion for Spaniards. See also Isenmann, "Rector est Raptor," 213; Plescia, "Judicial Accountability," 62. For a concussion case, see charge against Sánchez Morcillo, AGI, México 670 B, *Relación*, fol. 741v, discussed in Chapter 5. According to Viceroy Marquis of Casafuerte to king, Mexico City, 14 May 1725, AGI, México 492, concussion differed from "nuisances and ill-treatment."

agent) representing several indigenous communities near Metepec (state of Mexico), for instance, accused the *alcalde mayor* (district judge) in 1755 of "abuse and *corruptela*." This *alcalde mayor* levied twenty-six pesos and fourteen chickens for handing the staff of justice to the annually elected Indian magistrates. If the Natives did not pay, the *alcalde mayor* suspended the election. Both the prosecutor and the viceroy in Mexico City agreed with the procurator that the *alcalde mayor* charged too much.[40] Similarly, a civil judge rumbled about the *corruptela* of his colleague who demanded an annual pension of 1,800 pesos for awarding the contract to sell *pulque* (an alcoholic agave drink) in Mexico City. The *pulque* seller refused the terms, and the judge harassed him with judicial orders to extort the money.[41] In addition, judicial ministers who fabricated papers or simply lacked the skills to serve their office could act in corrupt ways. Even gross negligence (acting very carelessly) could be "a mortal sin and similar to malicious intent and punishable as a crime."[42] Finally, legal experts also objected to the bribers and to the witnesses who gave wrong testimony, as they contributed to skewing justice.[43]

Aside from these practices, reprehensible customs permanently displaced the just law. Customs played an important role in the early modern

---

[40] Procurator Joaquín María de Udaburu on behalf of the *repúblicas* San Mateo Mexicaltzinco, San Andrés Ocotlan, Santa María Nativitas, and la Concepción to captain general, n. d.; *parecer* of the Marquis of Aranda, Mexico City, 12 June 1758; viceregal decree, San Ángel, 17 June 1758, all three documents in AGN, Indios 59, exp. 72, fol. 66–66v. Viceroy Count of Revillagigedo originally ordered to investigate this case before 1755.

[41] Testimony of José Uribe, Mexico City, 11 Nov. 1716, AGI, Escribanía 278 C, fols. 146–148. Similarly, charge against Miguel Calderón de la Barca, AGI, México 670 B, *Relación*, fol. 26v.

[42] Berart y Gassol, *Speculum visitationis*, chap. 17, paras. 46–47, quote in para. 94.

[43] Murillo Velarde, *Cursus Iuris canonici*, book 2, title 20, paras. 150, 160. See also Juan Solórzano y Pereyra, *Política Indiana* [...] *Dividia en seis libros en los quales con gran distinción, y estudio se trata, y resuelve todo lo tocante al Descubrimiento, Descripcion, Adquisicion, y Retencion de las mesmas Indias* [...] *Sale en esta tercera impresión ilustrada por el Licenc. D. Francisco Ramiro de Valenzuela* [...] (Madrid, Gabriel Ramírez, 1739), book 5, chap. 8, para. 8, discussing "false and corrupted witnesses." See also Pierre Grégoire de Toulouse, *De republica libri sex et viginti: Antea en duos distincti tomos, nunc vno concise & artificiose comprehensi*, 3rd ed. (Frankfurt: Typis Matthæi Kempfferi, sumpt[i]bus Philippi Jacobi Fischeri, 1642), book 2, chap. 6, para. 17. Castillo de Bobadilla, *Política*, 1: 456, held that "the corrupted judge and the one who bribes are connected ... and the person selling justice is guilty and wicked, and so is the person buying it"; *Law of Castile*, book 3, title 9, law 6. The *audiencia* decree signed by Luis de Ortega, Mexico City, 25 Jan. 1717, AGI, Escribanía 281 D, fol. 984, indicates that Garzarón searched for fraudulent papers to prove corruption.

society, and sometimes they contradicted the written law. Legal practitioners for a long time discussed how to reconcile such conflicts between the customs and the law. The resolution often hinged on the perspective. One eighteenth-century canon lawyer affirmed, for example, that "no custom can attain the force of law over divine and natural law, and if the custom is unreasonable, it is not called custom but *corruptela* and should be rooted out." This argument dated back to the standard commentary on the thirteenth-century *Siete Partidas* (Seven Parts). The commentary, in turn, built in this regard on the Decretals, the medieval papal letters that belonged to canon law.[44]

The older view of evil customs that replaced the just law mattered. In 1721, the king chastised "all abuses established and practiced with the word process, which in truth is corruption." The term *process* was akin to custom when describing the local way of conducting trials.[45] The thinking

---

[44] Pedro Murillo Velarde, *Cursus iuris canonici*, book 1, title 4, para. 118; see also book 3, title 5, para. 42. Murillo Velarde built on Gregorio López's commentary, see Ignacio Sanponts y Barba, Ramon Marti de Eixalá, and José Ferrer y Subirana, eds., *Las Siete Partidas del sabio rey Don Alfonso el IX* [...] (Barcelona: Bergnes, 1843), vol. 1, *partida* 1, title 2, law 9, that "the *fuero* or custom which begins to be corruption needs to be destroyed, and the longer it has existed, the worse it is." López himself drew on the medieval papal *Decretals*, see Gregorius IX, *Decretales D. Gregorij Papae IX. suae integritati una cum glossis restitutae ad exemplar Romanum. Nunc recens perutilibus additionibus praeclariss. iurisc. D. Andreae Alciati illustratae* (Venetiis: Apud Socios Aquilae Renouantis, 1605), book 1, title 4, chap. 11, www.mdz-nbn-resolving.de/urn/resolver.pl?urn=urn:nbn:de:bvb:12-bsb10506589-3, that the "sins may be heavier when they have longer tied down the unhappy soul, and no one of clear mind can approve that natural law, whose transgression endangers salvation, can be abrogated to some extent through any custom that in this regard is better called corruption." Miguel de San Antonio, *Resúmen de la theologia moral*, 44, maintained that a custom which ignored a papal brief was "abuse and corruption, upheld by the tenacity of those who defend it." Similarly, prosecutor Pedro Malo de Villavicencio to king, Mexico City, 25 June 1722, AGN, Historia 102, exp. 10, fol. 93v, lamented "the appalling path of abuse, corruption, or error, which are the true names for any action that departs from the disposition or legal precept," and he demanded "banishing any corruptions of" the law of the Indies and Castile. Aquinas, *Summa* Ia–IIae, Q. 97. art. 3. ad 1, eschewed the term *corruptela* when arguing that "law and reason vanquish wicked customs." Premo, "Custom Today," 356–363, argues perceptively for an Enlightenment "turning point" comprised of new customs based on recent precedent and sentencing focused on the present rather than on the past. Her argument calls for further research, though, because casuistic ruling according to changing contemporary standards had also marked early modern justice. Note also that Berart y Gassol, *Speculum visitationis*, chap. 17, para. 59, asserted that the judge who "judges against it [the custom] would no less rule against the law."

[45] *Real cédula* to president and civil judges, Lerma, 13 Dec. 1721, AGN, Historia 102, fol. 82–82v; Rodrigo de Zepeda to king, n. d., attached to the *consulta* of the Council of the Indies, 5 Dec. 1721, AGI, México 670 A. According to Iván Escamilla, "La memoria de gobierno del virrey duque de Alburquerque, 1710," *Estudios de Historia Novohispana*

about customs even suffused to the grassroots level. The procurator representing the indigenous communities near Metepec added to his complaint that the *alcalde mayor* abused his clients with the "title of custom," which was nothing but "corruption."[46] This shows that the ideas of evil customs and abusive judges intersected occasionally. Similarly, the trade of the *alcaldes mayores* with their Native subjects corroded justice, because the *alcaldes mayores* ruled on their own business matters, broke the royal law, and perpetuated evil customs.[47]

Finally, the term corruption had a wider meaning outside the juridical context, indicating decay in general. Humans who excessively sought their personal advantage succumbed to vice, for example. Food, waters, and nature could be contaminated. This also applied generally to defiling purity, which is why the colonial society especially censored unmarried women for having sex outside marriage. Similarly, one clergyman in the mid 1750s praised the viceroy for covering the drainage canal of Mexico City, preventing the corrupted waters from infesting the neighborhoods.[48]

At the same time, non-judicial staff did not typically commit corruption, because they merely executed sentences without influencing justice. Scribes, ushers, and constables comprised these officials, among others.[49] The notary Pedro Robledo, for example, rejected the charge of corruption, because he did not work in a judicial office. Robledo worked for the land-grant commission, which regularized private acquisitions of unclaimed land. The commission judge and Robledo appointed deputy commissioners in the provinces of New Spain, often in exchange for bribes up

---

25 (2001): 161, the Duke of Linares needled his predecessor, the tenth Duke of Alburquerque, for "having soaked up the process of the land."

[46] Joaquín María de Udaburu and Nicolás Francisco de Quero for San Mateo Mexicaltzinco, San Andrés Ocotlan, Santa María Nativitas, and la Concepción to the viceroy, before June 1758, AGN, Indios 59, exp. 72, fol. 66.

[47] Duke of Linares to king, Mexico City, 15 Dec. 1712, AGI, México 485, fol. 280–280v. For a full discussion of the subject, see Chapter three.

[48] Testimony of Nuño Nuñez de Villavicencio y Orozco, 12 Feb. 1757, AGI, Escribanía 246 B, fol. 470. On the "corrupted body" of a deceased person, Sebastián Vasquez on behalf of several Natives of San Andres Xomiltepec (Quautla de las Amilpas) to José de Sarmiento, AGN, Indios 34, exp. 132, fol. 177v; Castillo de Bobadilla, *Política*, book 2, chap 11, para. 2. See also *RAE* (1729), p. 623; and Mez de Braidenbach, *Diccionario*, 76,1, translating *corrompimiento* as *Verderbung*.

[49] Defense of Francisco de Fonseca Enríquez, AGI, Escribanía 288 A, fol. 4v. The officials also included notaries' assistants called *amanuenses*, *oficiales de autos*, and *firmantes*.

FIGURE 2 Unknown artist, *Mexican Biombo of the first half of the eighteenth century, representing the entry of a Spanish king* (detail). Private collection, courtesy of the *Fomento Cultural Banamex, A.C.* The painting portrays undue sexual desire, which was often seen as intertwined with greed. The text reads

> parum vitat perdere lucri / To lose your life for little gain
> De el mucho logro en el ancia / Greed will always abuse us
> siempre la codicia abusa / when we give in to our yearning
> y es conocida ignorancia / and well-known is our foolishness
> porque la poca ganancia / to justify our great losses
> la mucha perdida escusa / for the small gain

to 3,000 pesos.⁵⁰ Robledo insisted that these deputy commissioners did "in some way have jurisdiction, not to sentence but rather to elucidate" the land titles, whereas his own "office was ... a matter of grace ... and bare of any ... administration of justice." Robledo emphasized that grace was the royal domain to favor individuals and differed from the regular course of justice. Robledo, therefore, could not have acted corruptly even if he had accepted gifts.⁵¹

In addition, officials could well accept voluntary gifts for appointing subordinates, because a sign of gratitude differed from an illicit quid pro quo. The case against a senior *audiencia* notary, don José Antonio de Anaya, illustrates this case. Anaya obtained his position as a child in 1695. He never passed an examination himself, issued no papers, and in "twenty years entered the palace only twice." In fact, he claimed to have "no knowledge or notice of the bad or good conduct of the ... officials" at all. According to a hostile witness, in 1714, Anaya named a scribe called Miguel Solís, and they agreed on a "pact that awarded him 500 pesos, ... a gold lamé coat for himself, and an embroidered skirt of fine wool for his wife."⁵² In his defense, Anaya claimed that Solís's brother, a Jesuit priest, had implored the Viceroy Duke of Linares (1710–1716) for the post. The viceroy then arranged for the appointment of Solís, and the Jesuit voluntarily gave Anaya a reward. This expression of appreciation differed from a pact. Garzarón largely concurred. In his own words, Garzarón could not prove that the "office was tied to the administration of justice

---

⁵⁰ Testimony of Gil de la Sierpe, Mexico City, 7 Oct. 1717, AGI, Escribanía 278 A, Quaderno 6, fol. 62v. See also testimony of Francisco de Mier, Mexico City, 7 Oct. 1717, AGI, Escribanía 278 A, fols. 58–59v; charges against Pedro Robledo, AGI, Escribanía 280 C, Q.no 12, fol. 416–416v. The commission was known as the *comisión de tierras baldías* or *juzgado privativo de tierras*.

⁵¹ José Saenz de Escobar on behalf of Pedro Robledo to Garzarón, Mexico City, 15 Apr. 1719, AGI, Escribanía 280 C, Q.no 12, fols. 453–454, in which Robledo admitted to paying 4,000 pesos to the land-grant commission judge but denied that they "assumed or agreed on" a payment, "because I was forced to join the office." See also defense of Félix Suárez de Figueroa, AGI, México 670 B, *Relación*, fol. 352v. On grace, see Hespanha, "Porque é que existe," 32.

⁵² Charges against Anaya, AGI, Escribanía 289 A, fols. 1–2v, 5v, 11v, 12. The full name of the *oficial de autos* was Miguel de Solís Alcazar. According to Garzarón's commentary on brief by Juan García de Xismeros, Mexico City, 24 Nov. 1721, AGI, Escribanía 286 C, Q. no 30, no. 7, fol. 554, Anaya (spelled Anaia in the source), was the nephew of the former civil judge Juan de Valdés. Berart y Gassol, *Speculum visitationis*, chapter 5, paras. 20–21, condemned selling offices to officials. See also Herzog, *Upholding Justice*, 51.

including a form of *baratería* or bribery ... and the only thing sold with this office were the scribe's fees that surpassed 1,000 pesos ... and it was not immoral, even if there had been a pact, a fulfilled contract, or a sale."[53]

Garzarón agreed that Anaya

"did not know or see Miguel Solís before appointing him or even afterwards ... and he voluntarily offered him the office ... without any pact and through the efforts of the Viceroy Duke of Linares, who after awarding the office freely and graciously gave this notary [Anaya] a quantity of pesos and cloth ... and the Jesuit also gave freely and spontaneously what he thought was right, and this merits acquittal, as Solís did not give the gift ... because it was his brother who has no access to the documents, papers, and fees of the office ... and the only charge could be accepting a gift that an interceding and disinterested party gave freely and spontaneously."[54]

Garzarón absolved Anaya, because the senior notary did not negotiate a price to sell an appointment, the post had no jurisdiction, and giving voluntary presents was legitimate. Anaya's simple life also demonstrated that he did not abuse the public, although he was entitled to the *don* in his name showing his nobility. Anaya lived in "the poverty of a humble home with a rough, inappropriate, and worn dress and on very narrow rations, and his offense was that fortune offered him a small benefit without damages, risk, or injury, helping to relieve many of his continual difficulties."[55] Garzarón suspended both Anaya and Solís on other charges, and, in the end, the Council of the Indies restored them both to their offices. A councilor of the Indies suggested ominously that "the owners serve their offices personally," referring to Anaya among others, or else the crown would "consider them vacant and for the treasury." In addition, Miguel Solís had to pay a fine of 200 pesos. Yet both Anaya and Solís returned to their stations, mainly because they had not committed serious crimes.[56]

---

[53] Defense of Anaya, AGI, Escribanía 289 A, fol. 6.
[54] *Prueba* against Anaya, AGI, Escribanía 289 A, fols. 7v–9v.
[55] *Prueba* against Anaya, AGI, Escribanía 289 A, fol. 10. Moreno, *Reglas ciertas*, 119–120, argued similarly that priests could accept presents as long as the Indians gave them freely; see also Clavero, *Antidora*, 8–9, 15–16, 67, 71. One deputy notary only accepted whatever "little the Indians wanted to give," according to brief of Juan García de Xismeros, Mexico City, 24 Nov. 1721, AGI, Escribanía 286 C, *Q.no* 30, no. 7, fol. 557.
[56] Rodrigo de Zepeda to king, n. d., attached to *consulta* of the Council of the Indies, 5 Dec. 1721, AGI, México 670 A.

2.2 "CORRUPTED BY AVARICE": MERIT AND THE INNATE BLEMISHES OF JUDGES

Let us focus now on the innate idea of corruption that favored judges with the proper merit and disqualified people of lowly descent. In the medieval period, the Christian idea of the vile nature of humans eclipsed the classical model of failing constitutions proposed by Polybius. Theologians argued that evil had entered the world through original sin and corrupted mankind. God expelled Adam and Eve from paradise, and corruption became an innate feature of all humans.[57] Subsequently, classical ideas returned and merged with new ones during the Renaissance. The concept of innate corruption survived in a different garb. Many jurists and theologians held that unworthy people tended to be greedy and corrupt the judiciary. This concept thrived and remained influential until at least the eighteenth century.

In this line of thinking, the aristocratic canon Pedro de Portocarrero y Guzmán affirmed in 1700 that the "tribunals ... sink in esteem by appointing undignified subjects who are incapable of government because of their inexperience or inability." Choosing these individuals was "the cause of the corruption that the courts suffer today."[58] When deploring this condition, Portocarrero y Guzmán did not principally worry about underperforming judges who broke the royal law. Instead, he believed that judges with insufficient merit tended to act corruptly. Yet what was this merit that Portocarrero y Guzmán so desired? According to widely held view, the combination of the proper social origins, the aptitude for a position, and the services to the king and the political community enabled virtuous service. These faculties were tightly interwoven. Literati sometimes spoke of merit and sometimes of merit and services, while services could also mean plain cash payments to the crown. Yet no doubt remained that obtaining an appropriate position hinged, for a long time, on the applicant's social origins.[59]

---

[57] According to Cross and Livingstone, "Original Sin," in *The Oxford Dictionary of the Christian Church*, rev. ed. (Oxford: Oxford University Press, 2005, online ed. 2009), www.oxfordreference.com, Saint Augustine (c. 354–430 A. D.) saw humanity as *massa damnata*; see also Grüne, "'Und sie wissen nicht, was es ist:' Ansätze und Blickpunkte historischer Korruptionsforschung," in Grüne and Slanička, *Korruption*, 18.

[58] Portocarrero y Guzmán, *Theatro*, 374, 337.

[59] The *relaciones de mérito* – résumés fashioned to the old society – usually listed aptitude, innate qualifications, and achievements; see, e.g., *relación de méritos* of Francisco Garzarón Vidarte, Madrid, 12 March 1706, AGI, Indiferente General 214, N. 90, fols.

For Portocarrero y Guzmán and his peers, the judges' origins secured sound jurisprudence. Many noble commentators confirmed that office seekers should descend from old Spanish families of Catholic faith who had never intermarried with people of other faiths or races, though this was often a fictional account. They emphasized their nobility and the purity of their bloodline – the famous *limpieza de sangre* – that instilled virtue. The nobles also showed their status by using the honorific *don* or *doña* in their names. In addition, the crown recognized the pure indigenous nobility to be on par with the *hidalgos*. For this reason, doña María Montezuma, "granddaughter of emperor Montezuma of the Indies of New Spain," asked the queen of Spain for an important magistracy and its proceeds, so that she could marry with a "person of her blood and responsibilities." Noble Indian lineage qualified her for an important judicial reward.[60]

Spaniards also obtained merit by performing valuable services to the community, the king, or the Church, but they differed from examined skills and professional qualifications in today's sense. The candidates for positions proved their valor on the battlefield and they completed a university degree. Or they might enter a military order, such as the Knights of Santiago, and serve in municipal councils, which also ennobled people.[61] Yet the skills that office holders needed were usually not well

---

427–429v. Even a *relación de servicios del Br. D.n Miguel Calderón de la Barca*, n. d., AGI, Indiferente 134, N. 4, fols. 1–3, was not strictly about service.

[60] Queen Mariana to Count of Medellín, Madrid, 29 Apr. 1673, AGI México 14. In New Spain, applicants for positions frequently pointed to their descent as part of their merit. According to examination, AGI, Escribanía 283 A, *cuaderno* 1, fol. 23, the lawyer Antonio Zesati asked witnesses to confirm that his mother was "doña Beata Lozano y Capela." See also Max S. Hering Torres, "Limpieza de sangre en España. Un modelo de interpretación," in *El peso de la sangre. Limpios, mestizos y nobles en el mundo hispánico*, eds. Nikolaus Böttcher, Bernd Hausberger, and Max S. Hering Torres (Mexico City: El Colegio de México, 2011), 30, 38; Hausberger, "Limpieza de sangre y construcción étnica de los vascos en el imperio español," ibid., 86, 94–96, 102; Mazín, "La nobleza ibérica y su impacto en la América española: tendencias historiográficas recientes," ibid., 64–65, 72; María Paz Alonso Romero and Carlos Garriga Acosta, *El régimen jurídico de la abogacía en Castilla (siglos XIII–XVIII)* (Madrid: Dykinson, 2013), 94–95. For Herzog, *Upholding Justice*, 93, the notaries' trust was largely an inherited quality.

[61] I. A. A. Thompson, "Do ut des: La economía política del 'servicio' en la Castilla moderna," in *Servir al rey en la monarquía de los Austrias: Medios, fines y logros del servicio al soberano en los siglos XVI y XVII*, ed. Alicia Esteban Estríngana (Madrid: Sílex, 2012), 285–286; see also Cristóbal de Moscoso y Córdoba, "Discurso [...] en cuanto si es licito [...]," Biblioteca del Palacio Real (hereinafter cited as BPR), Madrid, Ms. II/2843, fol. 34v.

defined. Notaries had to pass examinations to show their knowledge, but not all of them did. Francisco Garzarón also expected maturity, for example, and censored excessive youth. In addition, allegations emerged that one senior notary was "without any understanding, because his occupation was selling iron on the main square."[62] Another scribe reportedly "was a wicked man of the worst habits committing excesses and fraud for which he had been tried and declared unfit to serve an office of justice or of a scribe." These accusations disqualified the bad character of the officials and their insufficient experience, but they differed from the modern understanding of competence.[63]

In the early modern period, most learned on the job, although priests and *audiencia* judges studied at formal schools. The theologian Domingo de Soto, whose work was widely cited in the eighteenth century, accorded an elevated position to some trade skills, such as "singing sweetly to the sound of the lyre or painting."[64] Contemporaries also lionized soldiers who understood the art of war and delivered victories. Yet most musicians, painters, and soldiers did not study in formal academies until the eighteenth century. The majority of indigenous, municipal, and district judges never set foot in a university either. Nonetheless, the *audiencia* judges of the Spanish empire differed. They had to be at least twenty-six years old and have ten years of schooling, including in Roman or canon law. De Soto insisted that judges had "need of knowledge, prudence, and suitability, and above all fortitude of mind and good conduct."[65]

---

[62] Charges against Anaya, AGI, Escribanía 289 A, *Relazion*, fol. 199; see also charge against Juan José Aguilera, AGI, Escribanía 289 B, fol. 112v.

[63] Testimony of José Manuel de Paz, AGI, Escribanía 289 A, *Relazion*, fol. 200. See also charge against Anaya, AGI, Escribanía 289 A, *Relazion*, fol. 2; the brief of Juan García de Xismeros, Mexico City, 24 Nov. 1721, AGI, Escribanía 286 C, *Q.no* 30, no. 7, fol. 553, affirmed that he was "suitable, able, and capable," without naming his skills.

[64] Domingo de Soto, *De iustitia*, 2: 267. De Soto lived 1494–1560, but his work was republished into the early seventeenth century, and eighteenth-century authors, such as Valentín de la Madre de Dios, *Fuero de la conciencia: obra utilissima para los ministros, y ministerio del Santo Sacramento de la Penitencia* [...] *contiene seis tratados* (Madrid: Francisco Laso, mercader de libros, enfrente de S. Felipe, 1707), 120, 135, 177, cited de Soto. See also *Law of Castile*, book 3, title 9, laws 2–3.

[65] De Soto, *De iustitia*, 2: 268. Similarly, according to Castillo de Bobadilla, *Política*, book 1, chap. 12, para. 16, the *corregidores*' legal advisers had to have "experience of papers and good understanding." See also Burns, *Into the Archive*, 27–29. Antonio Jiménez Estrella, "Servicio y mérito en el ejército de Felipe IV: la quiebra de la meritocracia en época de Olivares," in Andújar Castillo and Ponce-Leiva, *Mérito, venalidad y corrupción*, 92–95, clarifies that "seniority, experience, services, and feats of arms" played a subordinate role in Spain's border forces. Yet *novohispanos* did recognize quality. Connell, *After Moctezuma*, 70–75, shows that clergy and functionaries praised the

These were the four cardinal virtues that guided the conduct of the ideal judge – justice, prudence, fortitude, and moderation – joined in the Christian tradition by the three divine virtues of faith, hope, and charity. Living up to these qualities prevented corruption in office, the thinking went. To this end, the jurist Juan Solórzano y Pereyra stressed the importance of "Christianity and goodness" as criteria for selecting magistrates in the Americas.[66] Since about the 1650s, *novohispanos* also clad these values increasingly in the language of the Roman stoics, who proposed controlling one's emotions to show a reasonable and serene conduct even during adversity. *Novohispanos* seeking appointments at least ostensibly complied with this ethical compass.[67]

Selecting meritorious judges who lived by these norms was vital, because the judge served as the vicar of the king in the court. Only the candidates with irreproachable reputation should ascend to the judicature.[68] The archetype of this judge was a prosperous nobleman of established lineage who had attended an important university. This judge had the necessary autonomy to ward off undue influence from the litigating parties and the powerful. In 1654 the Portuguese writer Luis Torres de Lima eulogized the king of Judas who "did not suffer injustices in his realm, administering justice most vigilantly and seeking ministers who are honorable and not partisan, rich and not poor, graduates and not idiots, free and pure, and not bound or dependents." These were the desirable qualifications for the good judge.[69]

---

mastery of Latin and Nahuatl of Antonio Valeriano, governor of Mexico-Tenochtitlan (1573–1599).

[66] Solórzano, *Política Indiana*, book 5, chap. 2 and 3. The anonymous author (probably Melchor de Macanaz, 1670–1760), "El deseado gobierno," n. d., BNE, Ms. 5671, fol. 25–25v, held that "faith ... is what affirms these four virtues." See also Miriam T. Griffin, *Seneca on Society. A Guide to De Beneficiis* (Oxford: Oxford University Press, 2013), 7–8.

[67] According to Salvador Cárdenas Gutiérrez, "La lucha contra la corrupción en la Nueva España según la visión de los neoestoicos," *Historia Méxicana* 55, no. 3 (2006): 722–725, *novohispanos* particularly admired Seneca (c. 4 BC–65).

[68] Print *por Don Miguel Truxillo*, AGI, México 670 A, fol. 17v.

[69] Luis Torres de Lima, *Compendio das mais notaveis cousas* [...] (Coimbra: Officina de Manoel Dias, 1654), 71, referring to King Hezekiel (c. 725–697 BC); similarly, Castillo de Bobadilla, *Politica*, book 5, chap. 1, para. 199. On the ideal of a judge, Garriga "Sobre el gobierno," 81–87, 158; Decock, *Theologians*, 28; Jesús Vallejo, "Acerca del fruto del árbol de los jueces. Escenarios de la justicia en la cultura del ius commune," in *La justicia en el derecho privado y en el derecho público. Series Anuario de la Facultad de Derecho de la Universidad Autónoma de Madrid* 2, eds. Liborio L. Hierro and Francisco J. Laporta (Madrid: Universidad Autónoma de Madrid, 1998), 26–31.

Next to fear and favor, greed and passion beset the unsuitable judge. The ministers who surrendered to these vices had corrupted minds and evinced bad reputations. They could not work as impartial and public arbiters of equity. Theologians especially derided the undue desire for riches as a cardinal vice. They drew on the apostle Saint Paul, for whom "the love of money is the mother and root of all evil,"[70] which the Roman law echoed as "avarice is the mother of all evil."[71] The *Law of Castile* agreed that "avarice blinds the hearts of some judges, and the good judges should flee from vile profit ... while avarice is very ugly, particularly when affecting those who govern the republic."[72] In addition, passion disqualified judges. While in today's language passion is a rather positive (albeit trite) word, in the early eighteenth century it usually meant the opposite. Derived from the Latin word for suffering, passion meant being tormented by pain and surrendering to vile inclinations, such as hate, envy, or malice. Passion was a vice that opposed moderation – one of the cardinal virtues. Consequently, suspects in the *visita* tried to disqualify Garzarón as a person riven by passion.[73]

On the other hand, harking back to the concept of innate corruption, many believed that inherited flaws predisposed judges to bribery and other judicial abuses. Persons of socially inferior descent lacked the suitable quality to serve virtuously. Non-Christians, converts, non-whites, and even rich but common people who exchanged money or worked with their hands should not attain judicial offices. The same was true for their descendants. In 1682, the jurist Antonio Fernández de Otero repeated

---

[70] 1 Tim. 6: 10; see the Vulgate, Eccles. 10: 10, "There is not a more wicked thing than to love money: for such a one setteth even his own soul to sale." See also Aquinas, *Summa* IIa–IIae, Q. 118, art. 4, obj. 1, and ad. [reply] 1–3; Q. 118, art. 7, ad. According to Berart y Gassol, *Speculum visitationis*, chap. 5, para. 19, "avarice is the root of all evil." On avarice as one of the seven deadly or cardinal sins next to pride, envy, wrath, sloth, lust, and gluttony, Andrés Lira, "Dimension jurídica de la justicia. Pecadores y pecados en tres confesionarios de la Nueva España, 1545–1732," *Historia Mexicana* 55, no. 4 (2006): 1141; or among the most sinful next to pride, Prodi, *Settimo non rubare*, 106–107. See also José de la Puente Brunke, "Codicia y bien público: los ministros de la Audiencia en la Lima seiscentista," *Revista de Indias* 236, no. 66 (2006): 136–138; Garriga, "Sobre el gobierno," 96–97; Castillo de Bobadilla, *Política*, book 1, chap 3, para. 65; Jesús Vallejo, "Acerca del fruto del árbol de los jueces," 26–32. On corrupted minds, de Soto, *De iustitia*, 2: 267.

[71] *Novels* 8, praef.

[72] *Law of Castile*, book 3, title 9, law 5.

[73] *Consulta* of the Council of the Indies, Madrid, 13 Nov. 1721, including attached dictamen of the prosecutor of the Council of the Indies, Madrid, n. d., AGI México 670 A. Passion is derived from Latin *pati*; see *RAE* (1737), p. 72,1 and 507,1; *RAE* (1780), p. 695, 3.

FIGURE 3 An unknown artist, *Refugium Peccatorum/Virgen del Refugio de los Pecadores* (detail), visualized the consequences of greed. Mid-eighteenth century, oil on canvas, courtesy of Museo de El Carmen, INAH, Mexico City, and Photographic Archive "Manuel Toussaint" of the Instituto de Investigaciones Estéticas, UNAM.

older exclusions of Jews and neophytes "who in Castile are called *marranos*," a word for both pigs and the descendants of non-Christians, reflecting the discriminatory values of the old regime.[74] Neither could those

[74] Antonio Fernández de Otero, *Tractatus de Oficialibus Reipublicae, necnon oppidorum utriusque Castellae* [...] (Colonia [Geneva]: Fratres de Fonties, 1732), part 1, chap. 3, para. 1, no. 1. Agüero and Andrés Santos, "Republicanismo y tradición jurídica," show that Fernández de Otero's book was widely read in eighteenth-century New Spain. The author – comparable to Castillo de Bobadilla – graduated from the university of Valladolid and served as prosecutor of the Valladolid chancellery. See also Benjamín González Alonso, "Estudio preliminar," in *Política para corregidores*

punished by the Inquisition, or the offspring of those burned at the stake obtain posts of justice. These families had betrayed the faith and its values, and they could not be trusted with important affairs.[75]

The view of defective descent extended to the mixed children of Indians, whites, and Africans in New Spain, although the boundaries were contested. Garzarón accused the *alguacil mayor de corte* (senior constable) of appointing "*mulatos, coyotes,* and *mestizos* who for their bad inclinations have been tried for various offenses," such as fraud and selling prohibited drinks.[76] In a comparable case from 1750 in Lima (Peru), the university resisted admitting "*mestizos, zambos,* and *mulatos*" for being "subjects without merit," who suffered "infamy" and "defects of birth."[77] Historians have amply documented discrimination against people of multi-racial descent, and many in the old society considered these people likely to abuse important responsibilities. Yet not everybody agreed in New Spain. The senior constable cared little about racial etiquette when choosing his assistants. In addition, pure Indians suffered less from the exclusionary rhetoric. One clergyman sustained, for instance, that the Indians had all the rights of full citizens.[78]

y señores de vassallos, en tiempo de paz, y de guerra, y para juezes eclesiásticos y seglares [...] by Jerónimo Castillo de Bobadilla, ed. Sebastián Martín-Retortillo (Madrid: Instituto de Estudios de Administración Local, 1978), 7–34. On Palafox, Carlos Garriga, "Sobre el gobierno," 102.

[75] Castillo de Bobadilla, *Política,* book 1, chap. 12, para. 16.

[76] Charge against Francisco de Fonseca Enríquez, AGI, Escribanía 288 A, *legajo (leg.)* 18, fols. 4–5v. See also Alonso de la Lama y Noriega for Pedro Sánchez Morcillo to king, Madrid, 1 Apr. 1727, AGI, Escribanía 287 B, *pieza* 38, fol. 43. See also *consulta* of the Council of the Indies, Madrid, 13 Nov. 1721, AGI, México 380, while in charges against Feliciano Ulloa y Sevilla, AGI, Escribanía 289 B, *Relazion,* fol. 865, one witnesses labeled a notary as "*mulato* or *mestizo.*"

[77] *Real cédula* to Lima's medical board, Buen Retiro, 27 Sept. 1752, in Konetzke, *Colección,* vol. 3, tome 1, pp. 265–266; see also *Law of the Indies,* book 1, title 22, law 57. According to *real cédula,* Casa Tejada, 15 Mar. 1704, AGN, Reales Cédulas Originales (hereinafter cited as RCO) 32, exp. 14, fol. 2, the *cabildo* of Veracruz excluded notaries of "Indian and *mulato*" origin. Cervantes, *Licenciado Vidriera,* 58, demanded that notaries were "free and not slaves, of legitimate birth and neither bastards or of bad race." In the racial construction of castes, *mulatos* were of mixed African descent, *coyotes* were considered offspring of *mestizos* and Natives, while *zambos* were children of blacks and Natives.

[78] Defense of Francisco de Fonseca Enríquez, AGI, Escribanía 288 A, *leg.* 18, fol. 6v. On pure Natives, Juan Zapata y Sandoval, *Disceptación sobre justicia distributiva y sobre la acepción de personas a ella opuesta,* trans. Arturo Ramírez Trejo, eds. Paula López Cruz and Mauricio Beuchot Puente (Mexico City: UNAM, 1994–1995), part 2, chap. 9, para 4–16, esp. 14; see also *consulta* of the Council of the Indies, Madrid, 12 July 1691, in Konetzke, *Colección,* vol. 3, tome 1, pp. 14–16. Coping with discrimination is the subject of Ann Twinam, *Purchasing Whiteness: Pardos, Mulattos, and the Quest for Social Mobility*

Meanwhile, working in vile occupations besmirched people and made them unsuitable for important offices. Besides blacksmiths and carpenters,[79] the jurist Antonio Fernández de Otero excluded "taverners, mule drivers, shoemakers, inn keepers ... meat pie makers, and those who [serve] ... in mechanical offices." In addition to these individuals who worked with their hands, Fernández de Otero added merchants and peddlers, in fact, all people who frequently exchanged money for a living. According to him, the fourteenth-century jurist "Bartolus de Sassoferrato claims that the merchants, the servile arts ... are excluded even from the humble dignities and honors ... and not because they serve their offices criminally, or because they are infamous, but because by serving ... they become decayed through vile offices and money."[80] In this line of thinking, another jurist had added in the early seventeenth century that "the life of merchants is vile and contrary to virtue ... and it is deplorable when those who hoard money through usury, deceit, and fraud, direct and govern the republic." Here was the foundation for denying middling groups access to judicial office.[81]

The idea of merchants corrupted by money and unfit for offices of justice survived until the eighteenth century, and even indigenous communities used it as a legal argument. The largely Native *cabecera* (district head town) of Meztitlan (Hidalgo) and its procurator attacked the

---

in the Spanish Indies (Stanford, CA: Stanford University Press, 2015). See also Burns, *Into the Archive*, 27; Frédérique Langue, "Los pardos venezolanos, ¿heterodoxos o defensores del orden social? Una revisión necesaria en el contexto de las conmemoraciones de la Independencia," in Sanchez, *Los actores locales de la nación*, 77–98.

[79] Böttcher, "Inquisición y limpieza de sangre en Nueva España," in Böttcher, Hausberger, and Hering Torres, *El peso de la sangre*, 188–189. The *Law of Castile*, book 3, title 9, law 8, also excluded servants.

[80] Fernández de Otero, *Tractatus*, part 1, chap. 3, para. 1, no. 37. Note that Bartoli ab Saxoferrato [Bartolus de Sassoferrato], *Omnium iuris interpretum antesignani comentaria nunc recens, praeter alias additiones ad hanc diem editas* [...]. *Tomus octavus in secundam, atque tertiam codici partem* (Venetiis [Venice]: Apud Iuntas, 1590), *ad duodecimum Librum Codicis*, title *de dignitatibus*, law 6 (fol. 48v), excepted swineherds and oil vendors from the ignoble occupations, rejecting the thirteenth-century *Glossa magna* (Great Gloss or standard commentary) on *Code* 12.1.6; on Bartolus, see Lepsius, "Bartolus de Saxoferrato," 450–453.

[81] Castillo de Bobadilla, *Politica*, book 2, chap. 12, no. 34. Jeronymo de Zeballos, *Arte Real para el buen govierno de los Reyes, y Principes, y de sus vassallos* [...] (Toledo: A costa de su Autor, 1623), 177v, argued "that nobody could be peddler or a merchant." The prosecutor's *parecer*, attached to the *consulta* of the Council of the Indies, Madrid, 19 Jul. 1675, AGI, Indiferente General 784, rejected selling titles of nobility to Americans, because they only possessed "the enclosure of a hacienda in the fields ... with no other vassalage over towns or dominion save for their Indians and slaves."

incoming *alcalde mayor* as unsuitable in 1724. The procurator proclaimed that the *alcalde mayor* was "a merchant with great quantities of money" who had "served an office so manual as a druggist," and was "married to the daughter of a publicly known midwife." Whether the procurator and the Natives truly rejected the *alcalde mayor* for his lowly social origins rather than their previous conflicts is open to speculation. In any case, the procurator used the accepted precept on vileness to strengthen his hand. Money, questionable occupations, and lowly origin disqualified this *alcalde mayor*, while his performance in office was only one consideration among others.[82]

Many early modern observers compared the commoners' ambition to excess and greed – most unlike our twenty-first century praise of aspiration and the will to succeed. The archbishop of Mexico, for example, opposed lowly regular clergymen who attempted to climb the social ladder. He lamented that these clergymen had "few objections to the defects of birth or the mixing of blood, which means that the regulars with these qualities do not sufficiently respect the estate that they have been given."[83] For the archbishop and many others, greed and ambition marked the non-noble groups who rose unduly from their questionable origins and occupations. Their financial success opened the door to offices that had long been reserved for the traditional elites and their clients. In 1673, a notable Portuguese jurist maintained on that ground that it was "indecent and indecorous" for princes to sell offices, since that occupied the magistracies with "men corrupted by ambition and avarice and shamed by their blood." With these words, he expressed his concern about admitting candidates of dubious origin to the judiciary.[84]

Early modern people also discussed the offspring of illegitimate unions and the mentally unstable. Fernández de Otero, for example, barred from

---

[82] José Franciso de Landa for the governor and community of Meztitlan to viceroy, n. d., AGI, México 492, *cuaderno* 8, fols. 38–39v. On Landa, Amanda de la Riva Fernández, *Guía de las actas del cabildo de la ciudad de México, 1731–1740* (Mexico City: UIA, DDF, 1988), 110.

[83] *Relación de mando* of Juan de Ortega y Montañes, Mexico City, 4 Mar. 1697, in Ernesto de la Torre Villar, ed., *Instrucciones y memorias de los virreyes novohispanos* (Mexico City: Editorial Porrúa, 1991), 1: 679; see also Diego Jiménez Arias, *Lexicon ecclesiasticum latino-hispanicum: Ex sacris Bibliis, conciliis, pontificum decretis, ac theologorum placitis* [...] (Girona, Spain: Narcissum Oliva, 1792), 30; Bobadilla, *Política*, book 1, chap. 3, para. 65.

[84] Antunez Portugal, *Tractatus*, second part, book 1, chap. 14, para. 6, 7. Portocarrero y Guzmán, *Theatro*, 372–377, for example, extensively cited Antunez Portugal. See also Pierre Grégoire, *De republica*, book 2, chap. 6, para. 17. According to Cárdenas Gutiérrez, "La lucha contra la corrupción," 735–738, the attack on the "inordinate appetite for honors and dignities" was part of the neo-stoic discourse.

office the blind, the deaf, "the mute and the violently deranged."[85] According to one legal opinion, the king should also exclude the children of illegitimate unions for having been "born in an unworthy place." Yet Fernández de Otero acknowledged that many of them had well served the empire. In addition, the restrictions placed on these children were to an extent negotiable. The upper echelon of the American societies often fully accepted the children born out of wedlock who belonged to wealthy families. The king also sometimes granted them legitimacy in exchange for cash, especially in the eighteenth century.[86]

The situation was similar for a woman, and she could not rule on justice in most cases. The *Law of Castile* stated that it "would be dishonest and unreasonable if she were in the council of men ruling on trials." This did not apply, however, to the queen or another noblewoman, provided there was "council of wise men who correct and amend her if she erred."[87] At the same time, practical experience showed that many women outperformed men. One writer rejected the maxim that the "rule of women is usually unbearable, as they are in all things extreme," because "in Spain this is not true ... and the Marianas have given law to many realms." The author referred to Mariana of Austria (1634–1696), the able ruler of Spain and mother of King Charles II, among other queens.[88] There are also examples from the eighteenth century. The French ambassador quipped in 1746 that the queen consorts rather than the kings succeeded to the Spanish throne. They overshadowed the political acumen of their husbands in many ways.[89]

---

[85] Fernández de Otero, *Tractatus*, part 1, chap. 3, paras. 28–29; *Law of Castile*, book 3, title 9, laws 1 and 7; Castillo de Bobadilla, *Política*, book 1, chap. 12, para. 16.

[86] Quotes in Fernández de Otero, *Tractatus*, part 1, chap. 3, paras. 30–32; on the Americas, Ann Twinam, *Public Lives, Private Secrets: Gender, Honor, Sexuality and Illegitimacy in Colonial Spanish America* (Stanford, CA: Stanford University Press, 1999), 336–341.

[87] *Law of Castile*, book 3, title 9, law 7.

[88] Lancina, *Commentarios*, 30, also referring also to Queen Berenguela of Castile (1180–1246). On queens, see Janna Bianchini, *Queen's Hand: Power and Authority in the Reign of Berenguela of Castile* (Philadelphia: University of Pennsylvania Press, 2012); Mercedes Llorente, "Mariana of Austria's Portraits as Ruler-Governor and Curadora by Juan Carreño de Miranda and Claudio Coello," in *Early Modern Habsburg Women: Transnational Contexts, Cultural Conflicts, Dynastic Continuities*, eds. Anne J. Cruz and Maria Galli Stampino (Brookfield, VT: Ashgate, 2013), 197–198.

[89] "It was rather Barbara who succeeded Elizabeth than Ferdinand succeeding Philip," quoted in Gómez Urdáñez, "Carvajal y Ensenada, un binomio político," in *Ministros de Fernando VI*, eds. José Luis Gómez Urdáñez and José Miguel Delgado Barrado (Córdoba, Spain: Universidad de Córdoba, 2002), 68, who referred to Queens Elizabeth Farnese (1714–1746) and Barbara de Bragança (1746–1758).

The discourse on flawed gender, race, and origin sought to limit social mobility. The traditional elites including the upper clergy, the aristocracy, and the jurists who proceeded from the municipal oligarchies of Castile advanced this point. The aristocracy was the most privileged group in Spain, and the jurists enjoyed preferred access to the six elite *colegios mayores* (study halls) at the preeminent universities of Salamanca, Valladolid, and Alcalá de Henares in Spain. The graduates of the schools stood a good chance of joining the great councils and *audiencias*, because their members came from a similar background and often helped their peers. The traditional elites often resented the competition from social newcomers of lower descent, such as merchants, bankers, lower-level bureaucrats, and the graduates from other universities.[90] Some of the humbler candidates for judicial positions descended from convert or mixed-blood families. They acquired money or influence through their capable work in business, banking, or administration. When the crown began selling appointments for posts of justice, these social groups seized the opportunity and joined the judiciary. Meanwhile, the traditional elites considered appointing these candidates as corrupt for lacking merit. For that reason, the aristocrat Pedro de Portocarrero y Guzmán opposed judges of unworthy descent.

2.3 FROM JUDICIAL TO ADMINISTRATIVE CORRUPTION

The idea of corruption changed in the Spanish empire as various currents of enlightened thinking infiltrated justice. As a result, the selection criteria for judges shifted and the idea of innate corruption withered. A person's education, performance on the job, and obedience to authority had always mattered to a degree, but these criteria grew in importance in the later seventeenth century. In the meantime, social origin as the primary selection standard declined, despite Portocarrero's rear guard argument in 1700. The older

---

[90] Dedieu, "La haute administration espagnole au XVIIIe siècle: Un projet," in Descimon, Schaub, and Vincent, *Les figures*, 170–171. Similarly, Twinam, *Public Lives*, 13, 208–215, holds that American elites reinforced boundaries to ward off social climbers. According to Gutiérrez Rodríguez, "El colegio novohispano de Santa María de Todos los Santos: alcances y límites de una institución colonial," in *Estudios de Historia Social y Económica de América*, no. 9 (Alcalá de Henares, Spain, 1992), 23, the four *colegios mayores* at the University of Salamanca were called San Bartolomé, Cuenca, Oviedo, and of the Archbishop. Valladolid had the *colegio* of Santa Cruz and Alcalá de Henares the *colegio* of San Ildefonso. On Portocarrero, Antonio Ramón Peña Izquierdo, *La casa de Palma: La familia Portocarrero en el gobierno de la Monarquía Hispánica (1665–1700)* (Córdoba, Spain: Universidad de Córdoba, 2004), 155–156, 207–210, 290–316.

precepts of the distributive justice and the economy of favor gave way as political friendship and clientage "were devalued, de-heroized, and banalized."[91] A more rational exchange through the market and the bureaucracy emerged. At roughly the same time, the validity of the *ius commune* and local customs slowly dissolved, dooming many norms that had long defended donations to judges. The prestige of the royal law increased and the idea of corruption expanded slowly to include the breaches of treasury officials by the middle of the eighteenth century. Corruption evolved to refer to all wayward ministers breaching the law for excessive self-interest.[92]

As part of this process, scholars cited the medieval authorities less frequently. For instance, the bishop of Jaca (Spain) published the famous *Dialogue against the Innovators, or Thomists against Non-Thomists* in 1714. He shored up the teachings of Thomas Aquinas, the principal exegete of Aristotle (384–322 BC) and thrashed innovations such as rigorous deductive arguments.[93] Yet these were the convulsions of a dying age. The intellectual prestige of Aquinas declined in the early eighteenth century. Jurists neglected the doctrines of the ancient authorities and attacked the "vanity of the Aristotelian philosophy." Intellectuals instead preferred empirical observation and systematic analysis of new subjects.[94]

---

[91] On France, Ronald G. Asch, Birgit Emich, and Jens Ivo Engels, "Einleitung," in *Integration, Legitimation, Korruption: Politische Patronage in Früher Neuzeit und Moderne*, eds. Asch, Emich, and Engels (Frankfurt: Peter Lang, 2011), 29. On Spain, Thompson, "Do ut des," 293. Kettering, *Patrons, Brokers*, 237, argues that clientelism in sixteenth-century France neutralized provincial lords and then declined.

[92] According to Paolo Prodi, *Settimo non rubare*, 109, theft originally broke with biblical justice but slowly gave way to a violation of concrete rules of contracts and property as the market emerged.

[93] Francisco Palanco (1657–1720), *Dialogus physico-theologicus contra philosophiae novatores, sive thomista contra atomistas* (Madrid: Blasii de Villa-Nueva, 1714).

[94] Quote in Antonio Valero, "Ciencia de Estado," fol. 16. See also Benito Jerónimo Feijóo y Montenegro, *Teatro crítico universal o Discursos varios en todo género de materias, para desengaño de errores comunes: escrito por el muy ilustre señor [...]* (Madrid: Pantaleón Aznar, 1777), vol. 3, tenth discourse, para. 26, praising the "critical spirit" of the French. See also Rodríguez O., "*We Are Now*," 11; Vicent Llombard Rosa, "El pensamiento económico," in *La Ilustración*, vol. 3 of *Economía y economistas españoles*, ed. Enrique Fuentes Quintana (Barcelona: Galaxia Gutenberg, 2000), 8; Jonathan I. Israel, *Radical Enlightenment: Philosophy and the Making of Modernity, 1650–1750* (Oxford: Oxford University Press, 2001), 528–540; Thompson, "Absolutism, Legalism," 224–226; Thompson, "Do ut des," 293–295; Reinhard, *Geschiche der Staatsgewalt*, 338; Pedro Ruiz Torres, *Reformismo e Ilustración*, vol. 5 of *Historia de España* (Barcelona: Crítica, Marcial Pons, 2008), 212–214. Years ago, John Leddy Phelan, *Kingdom of Quito in the Seventeenth Century: Bureaucratic Politics in the Spanish Empire* (Madison: University of Wisconsin Press, 1967), 145, insightfully perceived the competing value systems as a "dualism of attitude toward the holding of public office."

That is not to say that conduct and capacity had not played a role in the second half of the seventeenth century. For example, a Jesuit argued in 1662 that appropriate behavior trumped descent. In his view, "the inherited nobility which lacks generous deeds is not commendable. Praising a person for his nobility is lauding his forebears, while applauding his wealth is pointing to fortune's favor; acclaiming their education and conduct is elevating the person."[95] In 1687 Juan Alfonso de Lancina added that "combined nobility and merit should be preferable for offices, and when they do not go together, merit should play the more important role."[96] Lancina more clearly separated social origin from merit, which he understood as acquired knowledge and performance. Other literati of that time also joined in describing the good functionary as obedient, skilled, and diligent.[97]

Performance mattered even more in the eighteenth century. The Viceroy Marquis of Casafuerte (1722–1734) reinforced the ideal of the good minister, when praising Francisco Garzarón's "integrity, education, and prudence." In Casafuerte's opinion, Garzarón led "an exemplary life, notably aloof from inclinations and social bonds, and ... of well-known moderation and indifference to vanity and personal advantage." Garzarón was inclined to live up to this image; so much that one friend called on him to moderate his conduct.[98] Later the Marquis of la Ensenada, the chief minister of the monarchy, rose to the leadership position (1743–1754) from rather obscure origins. Ensenada's reform-minded predecessor had patronized him for his aptitude and loyalty rather than his select descent, as the aristocracy demanded. Ensenada also commissioned the naval officers Jorge Juan and Antonio de Ulloa to frame their experiences in America in a suitable way. They advocated for selecting judges on the "basis of merit by their performance in some previous

---

[95] Mendo, *Príncipe Perfecto*, 17.
[96] Lancina, *Comentarios*, 10.
[97] Thompson, "Do ut des," 294; Eissa-Barroso, "Of Experience, Zeal, and Selflessness: Military Officers as Viceroys in Early Eighteenth Century Spanish America," *The Americas* 68, no. 3 (2012): 318–345; Schwartz, *Sovereignty*, 355, notes an exemplary late seventeenth-century judge. On the process in the Holy Roman Empire, Plumpe, "Korruption," 39–40; Michael Stolleis, "Grundzüge der Beamtenethik (1550–1650)," in Michael Stolleis, *Ausgewählte Aufsätze und Beiträge*, eds. Stefan Ruppert and Miloš Vec (Frankfurt: Vittorio Klostermann, 2011), 41–72.
[98] Casafuerte to king, Mexico City, 15 May 1724, referenced in *consulta* of the Council of the Indies, Madrid, 18 Jan. 1726, AGI, México 670 A. See also José González de Jate to Garzarón, Madrid, 13 Feb. 1719, AGN, Inquisición 1543, exp. 3, fol. 96v.

post."[99] Application on the job now often surpassed descent. In the second half of the eighteenth century, skills, experience, and obedience – not mere fealty – more directly shaped the career path of governors and district judges in New Spain. The performance pattern prevailed over older notions of merit.[100]

The tradition that candidates pointed to the achievements of their predecessors also succumbed to the emerging bourgeois standards. Melchor de Macanaz, a proponent of a powerful monarchy, stated in the early eighteenth century that "the authority of justice and government cannot be given as a dowry to a woman ... and it is ignominious that the services of the father in various offices are considered merit so that the daughter can give away a post." Discussing unqualified noble candidates, the author affirmed that "if they are incompetent and do not pass rigorous examinations, the king will award their services with lay offices that do not require skills."[101] By the late eighteenth century, performance rode high. In 1783, King Charles III of Spain (reigned 1755–1789) legally ended the categorization of manual labor as vile, thrashing innate corruption and opening high office to commoners. He declared that

---

[99] Jorge Juan and Antonio de Ulloa, *Discourse and Political Reflections on the Kingdoms of Peru, Their Government, Special Regimen of Their Inhabitants* [...], ed. John J. TePaske, trans. John J. TePaske and Besse A. Clement (Norman: University of Oklahoma Press, 1978), 95, see also 51–54, 61, 65, 73–79, 94–100, 138–142. See also McFarlane, "Political Corruption," 46–47. According to Gómez Urdáñez, *Fernando VI*, 198–200; Gómez Urdáñez, *El proyecto reformista de Ensenada* (Lleida: Milenio, 1996), 60–66, Ensenada invented his *hidalguía* origins in Valdeosera, because he descended from impoverished *hidalgos* in Alesanco. The first minister José de Patiño (1726–1736) protected Ensenada.

[100] Referring to governors of important cities or provinces and to the subdelegates who replaced the *alcaldes mayores* in 1786, but not to indigenous governors; Philippe Loupès and Jean-Pierre Dedieu, "Pouvoir et vénalité des offices en Espagne: Corregidores et échevins, un groupe médian?" in *Les officiers "moyens" à l'époque moderne: France, Angleterre, Espagne*, ed. Michel Cassan (Limoges, France: Presses Universitaires de Limoges. 1998), 174; Dedieu, "La haute administration," 179. Pietschmann, "Alcaldes Mayores, Corregidores und Subdelegados: Zum Problem der Distriktsbeamtenschaft im Vizekönigreich Neuspanien," *Jahrbuch für Geschichte von Staat, Wirtschaft und Gesellschaft Lateinamerikas* 9 (1972): 229–230, and others doubted the subdelegates' quality, but Rafael Diego-Fernández Sotelo and María Pilar Gutiérrez Lorenzo, "Genealogía del proyecto borbónico. Reflexiones en torno al tema de las subdelegaciones," in *De reinos y subdelegaciones. Nuevos escenarios para un nuevo orden en la América borbónica*, eds. Rafael Diego-Fernández Sotelo, María Pilar Gutiérrez Lorenzo, and Luis Alberto Arrioja Díaz Viruell (Zamora: El Colegio de Michoacán, Universidad de Guadalajara, El Colegio Mexiquense, 2014), 17–48, now emphasize the subdelegates' improvements.

[101] Anonymous, "El deseado gobierno," fols. 111–112.

the office of tanner and the crafts of blacksmith, tailor, shoemaker, carpenter, and others of this sort are honest and honorable ... and they do not debase the family or the person serving the craft or exclude them from municipal posts ... nor does working in these offices diminish the prerogatives and privileges of the lower nobility.[102]

As these ideas gained traction, military officers and jurists squabbled with one another over their qualifications rather than highlighting their social descent. In the early eighteenth century, career officers began serving as governors of Veracruz, and, by mid-century, they appeared in the city of Puebla and the province of Sinaloa. Several chief ministers preferred the effective and obedient soldiers over other candidates.[103] The jurists meanwhile opposed the onslaught. One of them asked, in the early eighteenth century, "for which reason the posts of justice regularly go to those who do not claim any knowledge or understand it. What good would be an attorney charged with the command of the army? ... Unprepared men disproportionately obtain posts of justice and government, causing the disorder that the people bewail." The jurist did not lament the violation of distributive justice or the corrosive effect of lowly social station, as previous generations had; instead, he maintained that jurists possessed superior skills to foment justice, while officers should focus on the military.[104]

At that time, the concept of corruption began extending beyond the judiciary, signaling a decisive change. New words also entered the language (some from France) to condemn specific financial and administrative offenses. In the 1720s, Viceroy Marquis of Casafuerte chastised *malversación* (embezzlement), rather than speaking of abuse or excess. He lambasted the officials of the tribunal of accounts and the treasury who "through their failure and avarice doubtlessly embezzled ... large quan-

---

[102] *Real cédula*, El Pardo, 18 Mar. 1783, Madrid: Imprenta de Don Pedro Marín, 1783, http://bvpb.mcu.es/es/consulta/registro.cmd?id=447433#infoejemplares. The *real cédula*, San Ildefonso, 2 Sept. 1784, in Konetzke, *Colección*, vol. 3: tome 2, pp. 539–540, prohibited the exclusion of illegitimate children from offices; see also Twinam, *Public Lives*, 18–19.

[103] On Puebla and Sinaloa, Revillagigedo to Julián de Arriaga, Mexico City, 10 Mar. 1755, Archive of the Counts of Revillagigedo, Department of Special and Area Collections, University of Florida Library (hereafter cited as ACR, reel no.) 455; on Veracruz, Francisco A. Eissa-Barroso, "De corregimiento a gobierno político-militar: el gobierno de Veracruz y la 'militarización' de cargos de gobierno en España e Indias durante los reinados de Felipe V," *Relaciones* 147 (2016): 13–49.

[104] Antonio Valero, "Ciencia de Estado," fols. 233–233v.

tities" of money.[105] Twenty years later, Viceroy Count of Revillagigedo (1746–1755) was among the first to label the abusive conduct of financial officials as corruption. He suggested auditing "the integrity and application of the participating ministers to discover if their corruption reveals reprehensible acts."[106] In a similar instance, Revillagigedo lamented having "to leave uncorrected the matters constituting abuse and *corruptela*" in the treasury. Again, he did not refer to judges.[107] Most scholars agree that such a shift in the idea of corruption occurred in the late eighteenth century or even later, but this cannot be applied to the Spanish empire.[108] By the mid-eighteenth century, corruption came to include the misconduct of financial officials and, in all probability, began to extend to the administration as a whole. Several factors contributed to the change, although further research is needed to clarify the process.

The judges lost powers in shaping the verdicts and the locus of justice moved further to the king. The judicial pluralism declined in the eighteenth century, as legal experts discarded the great variety of legal sources, including the commentaries of past experts. Many jurists, for example, considered the once-revered lawyer Bartolus de Sassoferrato and his commentaries as decayed by this time. The legal experts also suggested curbing the vast *arbitrio* of the judges that marked sentencing for a long time. The king should instead issue a new codification that provided clear and predictable answers to all imaginable conflicts. When the judges encountered unforeseen cases, they had to refer to the king for the best decision. While that theory proved excessively optimistic in daily practice, the judicial bandwidth of the courts shrank.[109] The locus of justice moved further to the lawgivers, that is, the king and his senior ministers. They took on more responsibility for issuing the law but also for its abuses, and the term corruption probably expanded concomitantly.

---

[105] "malversado," Marquis of Casafuerte to king, Mexico, 14 May 1725, AGI, México 670 A. See also "mala versacion," Revillagigedo to king, Mexico City, 21 Sept. 1754, AGI, Guadalajara 89; "malversion," Revillagigedo to king, 15 Jan. 1754, AGI, México 2093. Castillo de Bobadilla, *Politica*, did not include *malversación*, which appears for the first time in a dictionary in Esteban de Terreros y Pando, *Diccionario castellano con las voces de ciencias y artes y sus correspondientes en las tres lenguas francesa, latina e italiana* [...], vol. 2 (Madrid, Viuda de Ibarra, 1787), 504, noting the French *malversation*.

[106] Revillagigedo to Ensenada, Mexico City, 2 Feb. 1748, ACR 412. With title, Buen Retiro, AGI, México, 384, Juan Francisco de Güemes y Horcasitas became the first Count of Revillagigedo on 12 Aug. 1749, but for simplicity's sake, I call him Revillagigedo throughout this book.

[107] Revillagigedo to José Banfi, Mexico City, 12 May 1751, ACR 404.

[108] Génaux, "Social sciences," 17; Engels, "Politische Korruption," 39.

[109] Bernardino Bravo Lira, *El juez*, 325–344.

In addition, the number of senior officials who were not primarily judges grew over time, and that bureaucratic expansion abetted the changing idea of corruption. In early New Spain, most mid- and upper-level ministers had been judges in some fashion, such as the *alcaldes mayores* and the *audiencia* judges. Meanwhile, there were few senior ministers who did not fully serve as judges. Among them were the royal officials of the financial administration, because they only wielded jurisdiction over their own staff. These royal officials operated the six treasuries of Mexico City, Guadalajara, Zacatecas, and elsewhere in the sixteenth century. Yet the crown set up additional treasuries subsequently, and, by 1800, twenty-three of them dotted the viceroyalty. In addition, the number of royal officials and their staff grew, because they began collecting the taxes that had previously been farmed out to private entrepreneurs. The crown also established the tribunal of accounts in 1605 to review the treasuries' receipts, and royal officials began administering the Mexico City mint in 1731. The breaches of these royal officials became a growing concern for many *novohispanos* and for the crown, which explains, in part, the changing idea of corruption.[110]

Ultimately, the idea of corruption expanded from judicial corruption to administrative corruption and then evolved into a political offense. At least in late eighteenth-century France, the term *corruption* took on the sense of undermining the state. Embezzling money became the equivalent of treason, and ministers avoided using the term corruption so as not to endanger the social fabric.[111] In addition, the concept expanded once again after the independence of Latin America (roughly 1821), taking on political overtones. Deputies of the newly created congresses, for example, attacked one other with charges of corruption for committing electoral fraud. These accusations would have been irreconcilable with the older

[110] On treasury and mail, *real cédula* to Casafuerte, Madrid, 9 Apr. 1731, AGN, RCO 50, exp. 29, fols. 85–86; *real cédula* to Casafuerte, Sevilla, 14 July 1732, AGN, RCO 51, exp. 61, fols. 264–266v; *real cédula* to Valero, San Lorenzo, 11 June 1717, AGN, RCO 38, exp. 29, fols. 72–73v. Kuethe and Andrien, *Spanish Atlantic World*, 145, 208–209; TePaske and Klein, *Ingresos y egresos*, 1: 16–18; Bertrand, *Grandeur et misères*, 325–336, 345. See also Renate Pieper, *Die spanischen Kronfinanzen in der zweiten Hälfte des 18. Jahrhunderts (1753–1788). Ökonomische und soziale Auswirkungen* (Stuttgart: Franz Steiner, 1988), 54, 72–74.

[111] Génaux, "Fields of Vision," 111–113, 116–117. Note, however, that Grüne, "Anfechtung und Legitimation. Beobachtungen zum Vergleich politischer Korruptionsdebatten in der Frühen Neuzeit," in Grüne and Slanička, *Korruption*, 423, argues that the corruption discourse allowed elites to settle political conflicts without questioning the system as a whole. Plumpe, "Korruption," 34, holds perspicaciously that critics accused absolutist kings of changing the order by appointing non-nobles at the expense of the nobility.

FIGURE 4 Unknown artist, *The King Reforms Justice*, 1764. Copper engraving from Berlin/Prussia in Iselin Gundermann, ed., *Allgemeines Landrecht für die Preußischen Staaten 1794. Ausstellung des Geheimen Staatsarchivs Preußischer Kulturbesitz, 1994* (Mainz: Hase & Koehler, 1994), 31. An Atlantic perspective shows the decline of the *ius commune*, although the trends varied much in detail in the different empires. In this image from Prussia, a boy holds the new comprehensive law code to the judge's eyes. The judge's hands are bound, and the boy holds a whip in his other hand, forcing the judge to read the text enshrining legal concepts and verdicts. The page also reads *refere*, which alludes to the *référé législatif*, the requirement that judges ask the legislator/ king to resolve a conflict when the code does not provide an answer. The boy symbolizes the coming of a better judicial system, yet bags of money, a writhing serpent, and ancient law books sit next to the judge and allude to the past. The name of Bartolus de Sassoferrato is engraved in the book. While Bartolus was formerly the champion of justice, he epitomized corruption and confusion by the 1760s. I owe Thomas Duve knowledge of the image. According to Ernst H. Gombrich, *The Uses of Images. Studies in the Social Function of Art and Visual Communication* (London:

idea of judicial corruption. The idea of corruption altered significantly from 1650 to the post-independence period.[112]

CONCLUSION

During the period from 1650 to 1755, a shift in the understanding of corruption was underway. Changing legal ideas, new views on probity, tighter supervision, and the growth of the early modern state contributed to this changing perception – in contrast to what many scholars of Latin America have claimed. Alfonso Quiroz, for example, proposed in his noteworthy study that abuses in Peru increased to "new levels" between 1750 and 1770, while "military graft and favoritism reached new heights" in the early nineteenth century. Some scholars of Brazil agree with that trend.[113] Nonetheless, considering the changing values of justice shows that contemporaries criticized what had once been tolerated. If anything,

---

CAPTION FOR FIGURE 4 (cont.)

Phaidon Press, 1999), 6–8; and Daniela Bleichmar, "Painting as Exploration: Visualizing Nature in Eighteenth-Century Colonial Science," in *Empires of Vision: A Reader*, eds. Martin Jay and Sumathi Ramaswamy (Durham, NC: Duke University Press, 2014), 64–90, imagery mirrored innovations in public taste, while Serge Gruzinski, "The Walls of Images," ibid., 47–63, sees images as impositions.

[112] Stephan Ruderer, "Corrupción y violencia. Una relación ambivalente en Argentina y Uruguay en el siglo xix," in *'Dádivas, dones y dineros.' Aportes a una nueva historia de la corrupción en América Latina desde el imperio español hasta la modernidad*, eds. Rosenmüller and Ruderer (Frankfurt, Madrid: Iberoamericana / Vervuert, 2016), 150–161, shows that nineteenth-century politicians characterized abusive government, illicit enrichment of opponents, and electoral fraud as corruption. See also Pablo Whipple, "Guerra a los abogados. La defensa libre y los debates sobre el monopolio de los abogados y la corrupción de la justicia peruana, 1841–1862," ibid., 127–146; Inés Rojkind, "'El triunfo moral del pueblo.' Denuncias de corrupción y movilización política en Buenos Aires, a fines del siglo xix," ibid., 169–187; see also Silke Hensel, "Symbolic Meaning of Electoral Processes in Mexico in the Early 19th Century," in Hensel, *Constitutional Cultures*, 385–389.
[113] Quiroz, *Corrupt Circles*, 63, 78, see also 60–80, who especially faults viceroys Manuel de Amat y Junyent (1761–1776) and Joaquín de la Pezuela (1816–1821). See also Schwartz, *Sovereignty*, 327; Paulo Cavalcante de Oliveira Junior, "Negócios de Trapaça: Caminhos y descaminhos na América portuguesa (1700–1750)" (PhD diss., Universidade de São Paulo, 2002), xi.

an altering awareness triggered renewed complaints about corruption, and possibly, a decline in the corruption of the judiciary as defined by royal law.

Literati claimed that appointing judges of unworthy background corrupted the judicature, because distributive justice demanded that candidates had the proper merit to obtain the corresponding posts. Merit in the old society did not primarily envelop examined qualifications and performance on the job, as historians have argued.[114] Instead, merit primarily combined social origin, aptitude, and services of the candidates and their forebears. Lack of nobility or *limpieza de sangre* disqualified judicial applicants. People seen as of non-Christian or otherwise impure descent, such as *mestizos*, lacked the prerequisites to be good judges. This also applied to those who served in mean and manual occupations such as mule drivers and merchants who regularly handled money. In this characterization, social groups of lowly origins lacked the necessary innate qualities. They were greedy and likely yielded to the manifold temptations offered by judicial power. Nominating them to office was corruption. The traditional elites, including the upper nobility, the senior clergy, and the jurists of the great councils who usually hailed from the municipal elites of Castile, sustained this legal argument. This concept also pervaded colonial thinking. Even the procurator representing Meztitlan maintained, in 1724, that the lowly origins of their *alcalde mayor* precluded him from serving in their district.

Judicial corruption referred to illicitly hampering the finding of justice. This chapter has offered evidence for a broad consensus that judges had to abstain from abusing justice for their own self-enrichment. When judges extorted cash by threatening violence, tampered with papers, traded with the Natives, and, most importantly, accepted bribes, they acted corruptly. The same applied to judges who acted very negligently or lacked the requisite skills. In addition, deceiving witnesses, forging notaries, and the bribers themselves could be corrupt when they skewed the judicial process. According to these standards, Garzarón vigorously prosecuted wayward ministers during his *visita*. He convicted judges for bribery when he proved that a litigating party had struck a pact to alter a sentence in exchange for a significant gift. At the same time, the officials of the *audiencia* did not

---

[114] José Luis Caño Ortigosa, "La real hacienda en venta: los oficiales reales de Guanajuato (1665–1775)," in *La venta de cargos y el ejercicio del poder en indias*, eds. Julián Bautista Ruiz Rivera and Ángel Sanz Tapia (León, Spain: Universidad de León, Secretariado de Publicaciones, 2007), 140, explains merit as "demonstrated efficiency."

From Judicial to Administrative Corruption

wield judicial powers and pointed out that they may have overcharged clients or accepted gifts. But they were rarely charged with corruption.

The precise boundaries between graft and licit giving were contested. Some defendants, for example, contended that some forms of *baratería* did not corrode justice. Others stated that customs justified appropriate gifts from friends and family to judges as long as they lacked the malicious intent to alter a ruling. Yet others claimed that distributive justice permitted presents that matched the social importance of givers and recipients. The judges also insisted on their sound *arbitrio* to distinguish between an innocuous and a malicious donation, even when such argument contravened the laws of Castile or the Indies. Yet Garzarón mostly rejected these defenses, showing that the boundaries of tolerating bribery had narrowed. The Council of the Indies also confirmed Garzarón's removal of thirteen corrupt judges, signaling that Garzarón had not convicted merely on a whim or for personal vengeance.[115]

In addition, the law, values, and the idea of corruption changed. The *Law of Castile* and the *Law of the Indies* increasingly overshadowed customs, the *ius commune*, and distributive justice as the predominant foundation to assess corrupt acts. The royal law clarified the boundaries between licit conduct and graft and curtailed discussions over the legitimacy of gift giving to judges. Furthermore, the social origin played a lesser role in the selection process for judges, while education, examined skills, and performance in office moved further to the foreground.[116] From the mid-eighteenth century at the latest, the idea of corruption also expanded beyond the realm of justice. From then on, all officials, bureaucrats, and judges in the empire could become corrupt. Judicial corruption gave way to administrative corruption. Finally, the term segued into political corruption in the early nineteenth century, when congressmen charged one another with the crime. Corruption has had a long and changing history in Hispanic thinking about justice.

---

[115] According to Engels, "Politische Korruption," 38–42, 47, a growing discourse demanded a better political system and opposed the nefarious practices of the "old" corruption. See also Doyle, *Venality*, 322–323.

[116] Max Weber, *Economy and Society. An Outline of Interpretive Sociology*, eds. Günther Roth and Claus Wittich (Berkeley, Los Angeles: University of California Press, 1978), 217–223, https://archive.org/stream/MaxWeberEconomyAndSociety#page/n325, proposed the ideal type of rational legal authority based on the modern salaried functionary, which he clarifies never existed in history.

3

"This Custom or Better Said Corruption": Legal Strategies and the Native Trade with the *Alcaldes Mayores*

INTRODUCTION

In 1719 some Indians from Milpa Alta (southern Mexico City) complained about the "wrongs and *repartimientos*" (illicit trade) that their *alcalde mayor* (district judge) committed against them. The *audiencia* sent the official Juan Raymundo de Paz to investigate, and Paz took full advantage of the situation for himself. He accepted thirty pesos from the *alcalde mayor* to soften any possible verdict.[1] Paz also brought a sizable entourage, consisting of a "scribe ... and another fellow with the title of senior constable, along with two women, and they all lived at the expense of the Indians." One indigenous witness, don Diego Juan, reported that during this time Paz merely released some *Indias* (Native women) imprisoned "on account of the *repartimiento*."[2] Yet a Franciscan friar reported that Paz had notified the deputy *alcalde mayor* "to stop disturbing the Indians with the *repartimiento* ... and such a number of Indians appeared who produced so much noise that they could not understand anything ... and everyone told them about the abuse they had suffered at the hands of the deputy *alcalde mayor* for charging them the *repartimiento*."

---

[1] Charge and defense of Juan Raymundo de Paz, AGI, Escribanía 289 B, fols. 1149v, 1154. According to reply of prosecutor José Antonio Espinosa Ocampo, Mexico City, 20 Nov. 1714, AGI, Escribanía 280 A, *Quaderno de comprovasiones*, fol. 176, Paz also traveled to Santa María Nativitas Atlacomulco and overcharged the Natives there. According to *Memoria de los asesores criados y allegados* by Francisco Alonso Rosales, Mexico City, 1 Oct. 1726, AGI, Escribanía 238 B, pieza 5, fol. 2–2v, the *alcalde mayor* Juan Ventura Moscoso was a gentleman-in-waiting of Viceroy Marquis of Valero (1716–1722).

[2] Charge against Juan Raymundo de Paz, AGI, Escribanía 289 B, fols. 1149v–1150; testimony of don Diego Juan, AGI, Escribanía 289 B, fol. 1155–1155v.

The episode shows three things: a number of Natives complained about the *repartimiento* and its terms, and the *audiencia* could find these complaints plausible. In addition, even the investigation of the *repartimiento* was fraught, because Paz cared more about lining his own pockets than correcting the wrongs.[3]

Under the circumstances of the time, the pervasive commerce between the Indians and the *alcaldes mayores* in New Spain could well be corrupt. The *repartimiento de mercancías*, or just *repartimiento*, provided Indians with loans and merchandise and delivered their goods to urban markets and beyond. Yet royal and other provisions prohibited *alcaldes mayores* from trading with their subjects, charging excessive prices, and advancing loans with interest. Many theologians and jurists argued that the judges who broke these rules were corrupt, and they held this view long before the so-called Bourbon Reforms during the time of Charles III (reigned 1755–1789).[4] The Viceroy Duke of Linares (1710–1716), for example, was an aristocrat, and people of his social background rarely sympathized with radical reforms. Yet he observed in 1712 that the *alcaldes mayores* "all trade and exchange, and they have always done so, and they obtain the positions for this purpose, and neither the laws of Your Majesty ... nor the oath they swear not to trade make them abstain from the excess ... and there are just reasons to punish that custom or better said *corruptela* (corruption) with lawful penalties." Linares merged here two key ideas of corruption in the early modern period: the judges who bent justice and the bad customs that replaced the just law as they both distorted justice.[5]

---

[3] Testimony of fray [brother] José Carianco, AGI, Escribanía 289 B, fol. 1153.

[4] According to Castillo de Bobadilla, *Política*, book 2, chap. 12, para. 34, "evil greed" prevailed if judges traded in their districts. According to *real cédula*, Madrid, 10 Feb. 1716, in Konetzke, *Colección*, vol. 3, tome 1, p. 123, the bishop of Puebla, Manuel Fernández de Santa Cruz (1677–99), agreed; see also the *relación* of the archbishop viceroy of New Spain, Juan de Ortega y Montañes's, in de la Torre Villar, *Instrucciones*, 1: 662. According to Cayetana Álvarez de Toledo, *Politics and Reform in Spain and Viceregal Mexico: The Life and Thought of Juan de Palafox, 1600–1659* (Oxford: Clarendon Press, 2004), 145, the bishop of Puebla, Juan de Palafox (1640–1653), also attacked the *alcaldes mayores'* trade with Indians.

[5] Linares to king, Mexico City, 15 Dec. 1712, AGI, México 485, fol. 280–280v, almost literally copied Juan Solórzano, *Política*, book 5, chap. 2, para. 17, who condemned the "custom or better said *corruptela*" of *alcaldes mayores* who demanded food and drink from the miserable Indians. Gaspar de Villarroel, *Govierno eclesiastico-pacifico, y union de los dos cuchillos pontificio, y regio* (Madrid: Antonio Marín, 1738), 2: 274–281, condemned public persons involved in trade. See also Berart y Gassol, *Speculum visitationis*, chap. 17, para. 32. For Linares' appointment, see queen to Alburquerque, Madrid, 8 June 1710, AGN, RCO 34, exp. 125, fols. 324–325.

The judges of the Indian court or the *audiencia* in Mexico City heard comparable complaints. They listened to Native litigants who often sued the *alcaldes mayores* for forced trade. That did not necessarily mean that the *alcaldes mayores* used physical violence against the Natives, especially as *alcaldes mayores* did not have the power to coerce entire regions to work against their will. Instead, the claim meant that the ministers paid the Natives unfair prices. Several theologians agreed and considered such forms of underpaying as involuntary and forced. Many judges of colonial Mexico knew the legal precepts and frequently ruled in favor of the Natives. A verdict for the complainants could significantly damage an *alcalde mayor*. The court could order him to restore all agricultural goods to the Natives while forfeiting any loans he had given them.

Native lawsuits against the *repartimiento* multiplied as a result. In part, this was owed to the changing views on justice and the higher standards for probity for the *alcaldes mayores*, which made Native litigation easier. In addition, the real prices for the coveted indigenous dyestuff cochineal dropped because of the growing competition from abroad and supply from within New Spain. Consequently, the *alcaldes mayores* offered less for agricultural products, which riled many Native communities. Conflicts erupted over the appropriate prices and carried over into the courts. The legal venues allowed Natives to challenge those *alcaldes mayores* who took excessive advantage of the *repartimiento*, whereas competition also provided alternatives. Admittedly, the sample base here is relatively small and focused on the region of Oaxaca and its fringes, and the conclusions cannot be generalized to all of New Spain. Nonetheless, the sources show that the *repartimiento* was not always more manipulative, coercive, or violent than other practices of early modern societies.

In the mid-eighteenth century, the viceroy of New Spain and the government in Madrid attempted to reform the *repartimiento*. The idea of *alcaldes mayores* trading with subjects remained noxious, but reformers now favored ample credits (lending money with interest) for producers and unfettered commerce, while downplaying older scholastic ideas about sinful usury and innately corrupt merchants who served as judges. The crown promoted more obedient functionaries and attempted to increase revenue, preferably by taxing all inhabitants according to wealth and income rather than exempting those of high birth or special privilege. The Marquis of la Ensenada, the king's chief minister in Madrid (1743–1754), even suggested seizing the profitable business for the state, comparable to the expanding tobacco monopoly of the time. The Viceroy Count of Revillagigedo (1746–1755) meanwhile proposed that merchants should compete with the *alcaldes mayores* on a level playing field. As a consequence, Ensenada ordered legalizing the trade while setting price limits. Revillagigedo inquired about the *repartimiento* in the 1750s to set the price caps, assess tax revenue, and provide a threshold for Native lawsuits against manipulations. The price caps failed nonetheless, but tax revenue probably rose as a result.

This argument adds some nuance to the historiographical position that the late eighteenth-century Bourbon reformers embarked on radical innovations, casting the *repartimiento* as manipulative, whereas the Natives relied on the much-needed loans of the trade. This insightful reinterpretation emerged in the 1970s, to which Jeremy Baskes has added that the *alcaldes mayores* used force mostly when collecting debt from the trade.[6] Meanwhile, several other scholars view the *repartimiento* as a "coercive mechanism imposed by Spaniards to extract additional work from the indigenous communities."[7] According to this thinking, the *repartimiento*

---

[6] Pietschmann, "*Alcaldes Mayores*," 198–212; Pietschmann, "El comercio de repartimientos de los alcaldes mayores y corregidores en la región de Puebla-Tlaxcala en el siglo XVIII," in *Estudios sobre política indigenista española en América. Simposio Hispanoamericano de Indigenismo Histórico. Terceras Jornadas Americanistas de la Universidad de Valladolid*, ed. Demetrio Ramos Pérez (Valladolid: Universidad de Valladolid, 1977), 3: 152–153, amply documented that the eighteenth-century *repartimiento de mercancías* was no longer manipulative or coercive, as the *visitador general* José de Gálvez claimed and instead provided credit to Indians and integrated them into the market. This thesis has proven influential: see Arij Ouweneel, *Shadows over Anáhuac. An Ecological Interpretation of Crisis and Development in Central Mexico, 1730–1880* (Albuquerque, NM: University of New Mexico Press, 1996), 160–169, 174. Danièle Dehouve, "El crédito de repartimiento por los alcaldes mayores, entre la teoría y la práctica," in Martínez López-Cano and del Valle Pavón, *El Crédito en Nueva España*, 152–174, combined the two views as mandatory credit; Baskes, *Indians, Merchants*, 76–79, provides a clever economic analysis.

[7] Margarita Menegus Bornemann, "La economía indígena y su articulación al mercado en Nueva España. El repartimiento forzoso de mercancías," in *Repartimiento forzoso de mercancías en México, Perú y Filipinas*, ed. Margarita Menegus (Mexico City: Instituto Mora, UNAM, 2000), 16. For Yannakakis, *The Art of Being*, 19, the "*repartimiento* represented a system of forced production and consumption," built on the "underlying coerciveness that defined Spanish-indigenous relations in Oaxaca." Zeitlin, *Cultural Politics*, 133–34, emphasizes the "obligatory purchase of manufactured commodities." Owensby, *Empire of Law*, 251, sees the *repartimiento* not as an imposition but as a credit line forcing the Natives to purchase goods. For Rodolfo Pastor, "El repartimiento de mercancías y los alcaldes mayores novohispanos. Un sistema de explotación, de sus orígenes a la crisis de 1810," in *El gobierno provincial en la Nueva España 1570–1787*, 2nd ed., ed. Woodrow Borah (Mexico City: UNAM, 2002), 219–258, the exchange combined credit, force, and exploitation. See also Stanley J. Stein, "Bureaucracy and Business in the Spanish Empire, 1759–1804: Failure of a Bourbon Reform in Mexico and Peru," *HAHR* 61, no. 1 (1981): 4–10; Laura Machuca, "El impacto del repartimiento

originally forced the declining indigenous population into consuming and delivering goods, which caused "pernicious effects" and unrest.[8] Some historians add that the proliferation of the *repartimiento* reflected the declining moral standards of the seventeenth century, during which "every moral principle was severely compromised by personal greed."[9] Yet instead of growing greed, I assert that the standards of justice changed at that time and what had once been acceptable came under increasing scrutiny. Native sued in greater numbers and claimed the use of force as a successful legal strategy.

3.1 NATIVE LEGAL STRATEGIES, NETWORKS, AND THE MARKET

The *alcaldes mayores* in New Spain administered districts that usually contained several indigenous *pueblos*. The larger *pueblos* elected their own *alcaldes* (magistrates), who adjudicated the trials of the first instance, and their governors, who gathered the tribute and administrated community resources. These indigenous ministers were usually drawn from among the local *caciques* (ethnic lords) or *principales* (lesser nobles). The *alcaldes mayores* meanwhile were almost invariably peninsular Spaniards or Spanish-speaking *novohispanos* (residents of New Spain). They paid for their appointments in some fashion, be it in cash, by fighting for the crown, or by serving a patron, and they held their position for about two to five years. To make do, the *alcaldes mayores* of the populous districts frequently

---

de mercancías en la provincia de Tehuantepec durante el siglo xviii: los pueblos de la grana," in Menegus, *Repartimiento forzoso*, 127; David Brading, *Miners and Merchants in Bourbon Mexico, 1763–1810* (Cambridge: Cambridge University Press, 1971), 48–51; Brian Hamnett, *Politics and Trade in Southern Mexico, 1750–1821* (Cambridge: Cambridge University Press, 1971), 4–8.

[8] Kenneth J. Andrien, *Andean Worlds. Indigenous History, Culture, and Consciousness under Spanish Rule, 1532–1825* (Albuquerque, NM: University of New Mexico Press, 2001), 98, see also 96–98, 202–208. Other important Peruvianists agree: see Moreno Cebrián, *El Corregidor de Indios y la economía peruana del siglo xviii (los repartos forzosos de mercancías)* (Madrid: CSIC, 1977), 739; Adrian J. Pearce, *The Origins of Bourbon Reforms in Spanish South America, 1700–1763* (New York: Palgrave Macmillan, 2014), 11, 151–153, defines the trade as "forced distribution of goods to Native population," although his focus is clearly elsewhere. The thesis of Pastor, "El repartimiento de mercancías," 201–236; and Owensby, *Empire of Law*, 251, that the *repartimiento* was constructed to force Natives into participating in the market is not fully proven, however. Note that Lockhart, *Nahuas*, 180, denies that the tribute aimed at coercing Natives to use money and instead suggests the opposite "causal flow."

[9] Zeitlin, *Cultural Politics*, 131–132. Owensby, *Empire of Law*, 292, argues that abuses exacerbated after 1660.

forged ties with the influential *consulado* (merchant guild) in Mexico City. *Consulado* merchants advanced cash to buy the appointments and *alcaldes mayores* frequently acted as their straw men. For this reason, the *alcaldes mayores* were rarely impartial arbiters when it came to the *repartimiento*.[10]

The Marquis of Buenavista, a wealthy aristocrat of New Spain, clarified in 1717 that the *alcaldes mayores* were in fact merchants themselves. According to Buenavista, "it is impossible for any of the *alcaldes mayores* to comply with their duty in correcting public sins ... and judge independently, because they have to look after their own *repartimiento* ... and they dare not to improve anything, and even if they tried, they would lose their money in lawsuits."[11] In addition, deputies with their own agenda represented the *alcaldes mayores* in the *pueblos* outside the main *cabecera* (district head town). These deputies were often local *hacendados* (owners of haciendas) or merchants with their own particular interests.[12]

The word *repartimiento* as it was used in the sources meant distribution, and it principally referred to two practices in the colonial period (roughly 1521–1821). In the early years of New Spain, *repartimiento* usually described the mandatory work assignment below market wages for a group of Indians to assist the crown, private entrepreneurs, or their own communities. The number of these *repartimientos* shrunk when the crown prohibited them for individual purposes in 1633. In the late sixteenth century, *repartimiento* appeared in the sense of the *alcaldes mayores* trading with Natives, although the sources are not always consistent, and *repartimiento* could also refer to any merchants who traded with Natives. Nevertheless, the term *repartimiento* is used in this chapter as the exchange of the *alcaldes mayores* with the Natives.[13]

This *repartimiento* was profitable in the mountains of Oaxaca, where Indians harvested the cochineal insects that produce a brilliant crimson

---

[10] Yannakakis, *The Art of Being*, 43–44; Baskes, *Indians, Merchants*, 1–4.
[11] Testimony of the Count of Buenavista, Mexico City, 2 Oct. 1717, AGI, Escribanía 278 A, Quaderno 6, fol. 33–33v.
[12] Lockhart, *Nahuas*, 46–47, 608; Baskes, *Indians, Merchants*, 1, 37–38.
[13] According to Lorenzo Gutiérrez de Colombres to Revillagigedo, Cholula, 11 Aug. 1752, AGN, Subdelegados 34, fol. 47; Bernardo de Huala, Huejotzingo to Revillagigedo, 7 July 1752, AGN, Subdelegados 34, fol. 64; Revillagigedo to Ensenada, Mexico City, 14 Sept. 1748, ACR 399, the word *repartimiento, repartir* or *repartidor* sometimes merely referred to trade or traders in general. Owensby, *Empire of Justice*, 59–61, notes an early complaint from 1619 against the *repartimiento* in Guanajuato. See also Lockhart, *Nahuas*, 55, 132, 430–432; Laura Machuca, "Los pueblos indios de Tehuantepec y el repartimiento de mercancías durante el siglo XVIII" (MA thesis, UNAM, 2000), 21.

color. Natives often purchased the animals when they reached maturity in the hotter lowlands of Tehuantepec. They planted them on the more productive cactus fields in the cooler highlands and protected them from predators. At the end of the season, the Indians brushed the grown insects off the cactus, killed, dried, and sold them. The Natives also marketed other products through the *repartimiento*, such as indigo, the basis for a blue vat dye; the jalapa root, a popular medication for purging; and cotton mantas.[14] On their side, the *alcaldes mayores* typically provided Indians with credit and collected their tribute. The ministers advanced cash, tools, draft animals such as oxen and horses, and even valuable silk textiles from China. The indigenous people later repaid the goods, principal, and interest with their own agricultural products. In many cases, the *alcaldes mayores* gathered these products in lieu of the tribute. They delivered the products to merchants in Oaxaca, Puebla, or Mexico City, who entered cash into the royal treasuries to settle the Native tribute dues. The boundaries between the theoretically distinct cash flows of *repartimiento* and tribute were often fluid.[15]

Many jurists and theologians opposed the *repartimiento* and maintained that unsuited judges should not trade with their subjects. They feared that merchants paid money to become *alcaldes mayores* and then sold judicial rulings just as they had plied their trade before. Especially people of questionable origins were unfit for these positions. Those who lacked purity of bloodline and worked in manual and mercantile occupations tended to be innately flawed and corrupt the judiciary. This concept also shaped the discussion over the *repartimiento*. The jurist Juan de Solórzano y Pereyra (1575–1655), for example, suggested denying the offices of *alcaldes mayores* to "those who seek them eagerly and especially to those who trade and buy for money and follow other wicked ways, because they usually turn into

---

[14] Baskes, *Indians, Merchants*, 10–11; Menegus, "Economía indígena," 34; see also Humboldt, *Mexico-Werk*, 406–414; *informe* of fray Joaquín Vasco, Santa María Ecatepec, 28 May 1776, in *Nocheztli, economía de una región. La grana cochinilla*, ed. Barbro Dahlgren de Jordán (Mexico City: Porrúa, 1963), 47, 53; reporting about his experiences since 1739. More details on *repartimiento* in Revillagigedo to Ensenada, Mexico City, 10 Apr. 1752, ACR 354; viceregal order to *alcalde mayor* of Chicomosuchil and *ruego y encargo* (request) to priest, both documents Mexico City, 9 Mar. 1752, AGN, Subdelegados 34, fols. 6–7; Juan Francisco de Apezechea to Revillagigedo, Tehuacan, 10 May 1752, AGN, Subdelegados 34, fol. 178.
[15] Danièle Dehouve, "El crédito de repartimiento," 162–168; Baskes, *Indians, Merchants*, 34–37.

"This Custom or Better Said Corruption" 99

FIGURE 5 José Antonio de Alzate, *Indian Who Gathers Cochineal with a Deer Tail*, Mexico City, 1777. AGN, Correspondencia de Virreyes, 1a. serie, vol. 90, exp. 56, fol. 262. Appears as Plancha 7, fig. 1. (126). 00126 F MAPILU. Courtesy of the Archivo General de la Nación, Mexico City.

tyrants and robbers."[16] In 1712, Viceroy Linares struck a similar note when lamenting that the *repartimiento* expanded when the crown began selling appointments in the Indies. The crown gave "the offices of justice to merchants, and because all merchants generally are blindly holding on to and advancing their interests and gains, they are turning the trade into a monopoly and set the prices at their whim." A key problem of the *repartimiento*, therefore, was the innate deficiencies of merchants who became *alcaldes mayores*.[17]

The *repartimiento* defied various other rules safeguarding justice. According to the canonist (Church jurist) Pedro Murillo Velarde, *alcaldes mayores* and other judges served a noble office and acted as impartial arbiters between plaintiffs and defendants. They should not imperil their duty by peddling goods or hearing the litigation against their own business. Another jurist added that neither should these judges participate in a veiled form of bribery, such as "buying something cheap in the district and selling it expensively elsewhere."[18] The Dominican friar Jerónimo Moreno concluded that "all those who advise the judges that they can trade in their districts commit a deadly sin."[19]

In addition, the Church provisions against charging interests on loans applied to *alcaldes mayores* too. Many theologians still viewed making a profit by lending money or other goods as sinful usury, although the condemnations tapered off as the economies developed. Civil lawyers had long recognized that loans were not given "for the salvation of the souls ... but because life without money is impossible." For this reason, the secular authorities tended to protect credit.[20] Yet for the Augustinian Martín Azpilcueta, also known as the Doctor Navarro (1491/3–1586), usury violated the seventh commandment against stealing. For Azpilcueta, "usury is of its type a mortal sin and saying the opposite is heresy."[21] Because of these

---

[16] Solórzano, *Política*, book 5, chap. 2, para. 4.
[17] The Duke of Linares, summarized by the prosecutor of the Council of the Indies, Madrid, 27 Feb. 1716, AGI, México 485, fol. 281–281v.
[18] Castillo de Bobadilla, *Política*, book 2, chap. 11, para. 53; see also Berart y Gassol, *Speculum visitationis*, chap. 17, para. 32. See also Murillo Velarde, *Cursus Iuris Canonici* (1743), book 1, title 32, chap. 347, drawing on the *Digest*; Jesús Vallejo, "Acerca del fruto del árbol de los jueces," 32.
[19] Moreno, *Reglas ciertas*, 4, 31, see also 1–51; Moreno's seventeenth-century work was reprinted in 1732. See also Zeitlin, *Cultural Politics*, 133–135; Lira, "Dimensión jurídica," 1167–1168; Mayagoitia, "Notas sobre las Reglas ciertas," 320–336.
[20] Prodi, *Settimo non rubare*, 99–100, quoting the jurist Baldus de Ubaldis (1327–1400).
[21] Martín de Azpilcueta, *Comentario resolutorio de usuras* [...] (Salamanca: Andrea de Portonarijs, 1556), 9, see also 6–16.

condemnations, notaries in the seventeenth century often cloaked loans as purchases, drawing up counter-contracts to return the objects later at a higher price. The offense of usury also included "lending wheat in August when it is cheap, and returning it at the price of May when it is usually pricier," as a theologian posited in the early eighteenth century.[22] That exchange resembled the *repartimiento* with its credit function, and Moreno implied that the *repartimiento* was usury. Not every *alcalde mayor* who sold oxen and obtained cochineal in return committed the offense, however, which hinged on the intent to garner a profit by lending.[23]

In addition, *alcaldes mayores* could not undercut the "just price" for any good by more than fifty percent. The "just price" was not some moral entity, according to Moreno, but the going rate at which the Indians sold to any stranger. Variations were acceptable, provided "the fraud did not exceed roughly half of the price" paid locally.[24] Moreno drew here on the Roman concept called the *laesio enormis* (enormous damages) that set the threshold at fifty percent of market prices. The classical jurists had originally allowed driving hard bargains in negotiations as this was the nature of business. Yet Aristotelian and Christian ideas on equity later infused contract law with an ethical dimension. The *laesio enormis* rule appeared in Emperor Justinian's legal collection, which was published between 533 and 534 AD. According to this rule, anyone who had sold goods or real estate for less than half of the legitimate amount could sue to undo the contract.[25]

---

[22] According to Azcargorta, *Manual de Confesores*, 281–290, contracts selling consumable items such as "money, wheat, wine, or oil," were known as *mutuos*, and usury was one form of these *mutuos*. Selling goods with the intent to recover them at a higher price was usury. According to Burns, *Into the Archive*, 83, 97–104, the sixteenth-century authors of notary manuals felt obliged to criticize usurious contracts while detailing how to draft documents to dodge the charge. See also the *parecer* of the prosecutor of the Council of the Indies, Madrid, 27 Feb. 1716, AGI, México 485, fol. 280v, observing that the sale of a hacienda was challenged in court for "some unjust conditions including interest and the promise to sell back." 284. On usury, Aquinas, *Summa* IIa–IIae, Q. 78; Clavero, *Antidora*, 7–9; Meder, *Rechtsgeschichte*, 166.

[23] Moreno, *Reglas ciertas*, 23, noted the credit character of the *repartimiento*; see also Baskes, *Indians, Merchants*, 74.

[24] Moreno, *Reglas ciertas*, 22–23, 27, 31.

[25] According to Decock, *Theologians*, 529–530; Raymond Westbrook, "The origin of 'Laesio Enormis,'" *Revue internationale des droits de l'antiquité* 55 (2008): 39–52; Meder, *Rechtsgeschichte*, 75, 104, 166; Christoph Becker, "Laesio enormis," in Cordes, *HRG*, 2nd ed., (2016), 3: 400–402. www.hrgdigital.de/HRG.laesio_enormis, the Roman jurist Paulus (2nd–3rd century) appeared in *Digest* 19.2.22.3, and endorsed seeking advantages in contract negotiations, whereas *Code* 4.44.2 defined the *laesio enormis*; see also Elisabeth Koch, "Gerechter Preis," in Cordes, *HRG*, 2nd ed., (2012), 2: 123–127. www.hrgdigital.de/HRG.gerechter_preis; Schlosser, *Neuere europäische*, 101.

The *laesio enormis* did not float like a cloud over a disjointed *novohispano* landscape. In fact, Natives and jurists in New Spain at least occasionally applied the legal principle in lawsuits. Several nobles from two small *pueblos* north of Xalapa (Veracruz), for example, complained that the *alcaldes mayores* colluded with "the local *hacendados* to sell corrupted and questionable species of young bulls, mares, mules, and pigs that are damaging to the health, particularly to the Indians at half over the just price."[26] In 1677, the prosecutor of the Mexico City *audiencia* agreed with the complaint, because he recognized the *laesio enormis*. The viceroy subsequently decreed an end to the *repartimiento* in the jurisdiction. Queen Mariana of Austria (1634–1696) even threatened the *alcalde mayor* with exemplary punishment if he continued to trade with the Natives.[27]

Natives could litigate these matters in the courts relatively easily, because the crown, jurists, and theologians viewed them as miserable persons. These miserables formed a discreet group of people originally comprising minors, widows, the poor, and the old. After the conquest of the Americas, the crown included most Indians among the miserable persons and applied special provisions for them. Judges had to protect them and temper the rigor of their criminal and civil verdicts, for example. Natives did not have to deposit any money when suing their *alcalde mayor*, unlike Spaniards and *mestizos*, and they presumably acted "free of *dolo* [malicious intent] or deceit." In addition, indigenous nobles enjoyed preferential treatment in court, such as foregoing torture in criminal cases. It fell to the judges to resolve the tension simmering between the general legal principles and the special provisions for miserable persons and Native nobles.[28]

---

[26] *Real cédula* of Queen Mariana to Marquis of Mancera, referenced by viceroy Payo Enriquez de Rivera referring to San Pedro Tonayan and San Pablo Coapan, Madrid, 28 Oct. 1678, AGN, Indios 25, exp. 259, fols. 194v–195.

[27] *Parecer* of prosecutor Gonzalo Suárez de San Martín, Mexico City, 27 Oct. 1677; decree of Viceroy Payo Enríquez de Rivera, Mexico City, 3 Nov. 1677, both in AGN, Indios 25, exp. 259, fol. 195v.

[28] Solórzano, *Política*, book 2, chap. 28, para. 25; Solórzano, *Disputationem de Indiarum iure sive De Iusta Indiarum Occidentalium inquisitione, acquisitione et retentione: tribus libris comprehensam* (Matriti: Ex typographia Francisci Martinez, 1629), book 1, chap. 27, para. 1, no. 44; see also book 1, chap. 27, paras. 17–18; *Law of the Indies*, book 2, title 1, law 5, on the "law in favor of the Indians." On *miserables*, see Duve, *Sonderrecht*, 202–203, 273–274; Owensby, *Empire of Law*, 56; Macarena Cordero Fernández, *Institucionalizar y desarraigar. Las visitas de idolatrías en la diócesis de Lima, siglo XVII* (Lima: Pontificia Universidad Católica del Perú, Instituto Riva-Agüero, 2016), 229–232. On the authorship of these trials, see Premo, "Custom Today," 359.

Under the terms for the *miserables*, Indians could dissolve sales contracts by alleging that the other party had injured them, a concept known as the *restitutio in integrum* (restitution to the previous condition). The restitution originally protected minors under twenty-five years. When a court ruled that a contract damaged a minor, all goods reverted to the original owners. The minor was not even "obliged to return to the lender the money he had received as a loan, if the minor had spent it without gain."[29] Juan de Solórzano y Pereyra recognized this principle and argued that Indians similarly enjoyed the restitution.[30]

Merchants had to think twice about any trade agreements with Indians given the circumstances, which explains, in part, the ascendancy of the *alcaldes mayores*. Merchants knew that some Natives would use the legal protections to avoid repaying loans. The elevated risk of doing business must have raised interest rates for Indians. To keep a lid on the interest, a protector of the Indians, a judge, or a priest could vouch for the contract and waive the right to sue under the restitution. Yet according to Solórzano y Pereyra, even if a protector had vouched for the contract, the Indians could still demand a restitution as long as the closing of the contract "did not surpass the space of thirty days after the sale of real estate or nine days for moveable things."[31] This uncertainty was probably one reason why *alcaldes mayores* stepped in to trade with Natives. They were judges in their own right and had better tools at their disposal to enforce contracts and ward off litigation.[32] If that was not enough, *alcaldes mayores* actively tilted business in their favor. Moreno affirmed, for instance, that preventing other merchants from selling in the districts caused "sterility of the market which raised the prices." Moreno objected to these practices as only the king had the right to set up monopolies. Manipulating prices was a real concern.[33]

Natives also claimed that the *alcalde mayor* had used force against them, but force did not necessarily mean physical violence. The theologian

---

[29] Murillo Velarde, *Cursus iuris canonici*, book 1, title 41, para. 394.
[30] Solórzano, *Política*, book 2, chap. 28, para. 25.
[31] Solórzano, *Disputationem de Indiarum*, book 1, chap. 27, para. 1, no. 65.
[32] For an insightful discussion of restitution, see Jakob Stagl, "Restitutio in integrum," forthcoming in *Diccionario Histórico de Derecho Canónico en Hispanoamérica y Filipinas. Siglos XVI–XVIII*, eds. Thomas Duve, Osvaldo R. Moutin, and María del Pilar Mejía Quiroga (Frankfurt: Max Planck Institute of European Legal History); on defaults, Baskes, *Indians, Merchants*, 7.
[33] Moreno, *Reglas ciertas*, 34–35. According to Prodi, *Settimo non rubare*, 231–232, Moreno's coreligionist Domingo de Soto (1494–1560) condemned monopolies as fraud, whereas commercial competition resolved the challenges of the *laesio enormis*; see also Plumpe, "Korruption," 31; Decock, *Theologians*, 3–4.

Moreno considered any contract as forced that was not voluntary, because contracts rested on mutual consent. In his opinion, distorted prices were forcible. When, for example, the going rate for eight vanilla beans was one *real* (an eighth of a *peso*), then "taking thirty-three or thirty-four beans for a *real* is unjust and forcible," according to Moreno. In addition, Natives usually feared the *alcaldes mayores* anyway, and trade with the *alcaldes mayores* was, hence, rarely voluntary. In Moreno's view, Indians could rescind their contracts with the *alcaldes mayores* and "should be restituted," when the Natives had a solid reason to disagree over the *repartimiento* payments. This explains, in part, the frequent allegations of violence against the *alcaldes mayores*.[34]

Indians took advantage of the restitution in their commercial matters. A 1682 case from the Oaxacan highlands near Tehuantepec illustrates this point. The nobles of San Juan Bautista Guichicovi lamented that the *alcalde mayor* did "distribute every year 275 pesos in goods for which we had no need ... which he gave married couples at very elevated prices and by force."[35] Their complaint was part of a larger initiative. The procurator (legal agent) speaking for the governors, *alcaldes*, council members, and other residents of twelve indigenous *pueblos* in the region complained that the *alcalde mayor* "did many *repartimientos* every year amounting to 416 pesos, for which we receive colored cloth, linen from Rouen [France], silk, buttons, fine silk cloth, and other things at elevated prices." The *pueblos* underlined "the many wrongs that Captain don Luis de Medina del Castillo inflicts upon us every year distributing by force 309 pesos and seven *reales* in cloth." The terms *force* and *many wrongs* meant unfair prices in this case, as the *alcalde mayor* would not have hauled fine textiles from France or silk from China into the mountains of Oaxaca if

---

[34] According to Moreno, *Reglas ciertas*, 23, 26–28, this was "injusto y forzado." As examples of Native complaints, don Manuel Juárez and Juan Juárez to (probably) the marquisate's administrator, Santos Reyes, n. d., AGN, Indiferente Virreinal 1477, exp. 9, were "demanding that the *alcalde mayor* abstain from treating us badly during the *repartimiento* of bulls and money." On "extortions that the naturals of ... Yucatan suffer through the *repartimientos*," see *real cédula* to Viceroy Casafuerte, Madrid, 2 Jan. 1725, AGN, RCO 45, exp. 1, fol. 1–1v.

[35] According to petition of governor don Augustín López, *alcaldes* don Augustín Marín and don Clemente, and don Martín Gregorio, don Juan Domingo, Diego Martín, Pedro Martín, Matías Domingo, Augustín de Mendoza, Juan Jerónimo, and the republic of San Juan Bautista Guichicovi, AGI, Escribanía 228 A, *leg.* 8, *pieza* 2, fols. 676v–677, "les da por fuersa." The *pueblos* of San Jerónimo, Ixtepec, Santiago Huixtepec, Magdalena de Tlacotepec, San Pedro Mártir Quiechapa, Santa María Guienagati, and others wrote similar petitions on roughly 11 May 1682, AGI, Escribanía 228 A, *leg.* 8, *pieza* 2, fols. 677v–681.

the Natives truly had no desire for the merchandise. In fact, the *alcaldes mayores* peddled these goods because the Natives demanded them. The Indians sued for contract dissolution, because they disagreed over the prices at which they had to repay their loans from the *alcalde mayor*.[36]

The prosecutor of the *audiencia* and other crown ministers found such complaints credible. The authorities worried about renewed rural unrest in the region anyway, following the Tehuantepec rebellion of 1660. As a result, the prosecutor suggested ending the "*repartimientos* by force and at elevated prices" and threatened the *alcalde mayor* with a fine of 2,000 pesos. The Natives could also seek redress from any municipal magistrate of Antequera (now the city of Oaxaca).[37] Similar complaints about excessive charges came from other regions. In 1701, the Indians of Tabasco complained that their *alcaldes mayores* "were doing *repartimiento* of clothes for their dress, such as mantas, Indian *huipiles* (sleeveless blouses), skirts, and iron tools at excessive prices."[38] A royal *cédula* (provision) from 1721 probably referred to the restitution as well. The king chided the negligent officials who received a fixed salary from the indigenous legal tax. Despite their income, the officials had conspired with the *alcaldes mayores* in the *repartimiento* and often brushed aside Native concerns. The king ordered the officials to "hear the Indians right away, nullifying all and any debt that Indians may have as a result of the *repartimientos*."[39] The restitution at least offers a plausible explanation why the king ordered to cancel these Native debts.

With several legal arguments against the *alcaldes mayores* on their side, Indians often succeeded in court.[40] The Indians of Tochimilco – a *pueblo*

---

[36] According to charges in the *juicio de residencia* of *alcalde mayor* Luis Medina Castillo, AGI, Escribanía 228 A, *leg.* 8, *pieza* 2, fol. 675v, "nos reparte por fuerza ... y ... por subidos precios."

[37] According to *parecer* of the prosecutor-civil judge, Mexico City, 28 May 1682, AGI, Escribanía 228 A, *leg.* 8, *pieza* 2, fol. 694, "por fuerça, y a subidos presios, repartimientos." For a comparable ruling on Coyotepec, *mandamiento* (order) of the Count of Paredes, Mexico City, 29 Nov. 1681, AGN, Indios 27, exp. 199, fols. 102v–103.

[38] *Real cédula* to Viceroy Duke of Alburquerque, Madrid, 12 Dec. 1703, AGN, RCO 31, exp. 165, fol. 450.

[39] *Real cédula* to president and civil judges of Mexico City, Lerma, 13 Dec. 1721, AGN, Historia, vol. 102, exp. 10, fols. 85–86. Ouweneel, *Shadows*, 207, argues – perhaps too strongly – that when abuses occurred, "in each of these cases firm measures were taken." Ouweneel, "El gobernador de Indios, el repartimiento de comercios y la caja de comunidad en los pueblos de Indios del México central (siglo xviii)," in Menegus, *Repartimiento forzoso*, 66, maintains that the "merchants and Indian chiefs" were not interested in the debate about the forcible nature of the *repartimiento*.

[40] Owensby, *Empire of Law*, 1; Borah, *Justice by Insurance*, 91–97. According to Juan García de Xismeros and José Romero on behalf of Tanzitaro and Pinzandaro to Viceroy Valero; viceregal decree, Mexico City, 13 Sept. 1719, both in AGN, Indios 42, exp. 150,

nestled in the foothills of the Popocatepetl volcano – opposed the *residencia* verdict acquitting their former *alcalde mayor*, for instance. Their procurator took the matter to the *audiencia* in the viceregal palace. There the *alcalde mayor* was debating his "charges, and ... he showed his revulsion and hatred towards the officials of the royal palace, and he boisterously disputed with me [the procurator] and the attorney regardless of the place, and he was detained, charged, and sentenced to a fine of 1,000 pesos ... paying for two bells for the Texan" missions. The *audiencia* punished the *alcalde mayor* for his lack of decorum and vociferous opposition to the indigenous lawsuit.[41]

In the later seventeenth century, Indians began suing over the *repartimiento* in greater numbers. Rather than seeing this as a period of moral decline, I argue that the standards of justice evolved, enabling Indians to challenge what had once been tolerated. Several factors contributed to this shift. The royal law gained greater weight and the influence of scholastic thinking dwindled, as various strands of the Enlightenment dawned on the empire. The Natives and other commoners also had fairly easy access to the courts and representation. The courts were often sympathetic to the Natives and applied the legal doctrines in their favor. In addition, the idea that people of social importance such as the *alcaldes mayores* were entitled to a larger piece of the pie also crumbled slowly. These were some of the causes for the rise in Native litigation.[42]

Equally importantly, prices for cochineal fell notably from the late seventeenth to the late eighteenth century. Several factors drove these changes. The Native population began recovering from the epidemics caused by Old World pathogens and the work force grew after the 1650s. More people raised cochineal and labor became cheaper. Production expanded, even on marginal lands.[43] With rising supply,

---

fols. 181–182; viceregal decree, Mexico City, 18 Aug. 1723, AGN, Indios 47, exp. 102, fol. 192v, for example, viceroys Valero and Casafuerte ordered the deputy *alcalde mayor* to end his abuse of Natives.

[41] Brief of Juan García de Xismeros, Mexico City, 24 Nov. 1721, AGI, Escribanía 286 C, *Quaderno* 30, no. 7, fol. 561v.

[42] In the last quarter of the seventeenth century, lawsuits over *repartimiento de mercancías* multiplied in the sections *Indios*, *Tierras*, *Civil*, and *General de Parte* of the AGN. Previously, most litigation under the title *repartimiento* dealt with forced labor assignments.

[43] On growing output until 1783, Baskes, *Indians, Merchants*, 40–44; see also Burkholder, "An Empire beyond Compare," in *The Oxford History of Mexico*, eds. Michael C. Meyer and William H. Beezley (Oxford: Oxford University Press, 2000), 127; Hausberger and Mazín, "Nueva España," 270. According to Tutino, *Making a New World*, 19–21, "population pressures allow capitalist predators to deny customary remunerations" beginning in the 1770s, while John J. TePaske, "General Tendencies

export prices for the dyestuff in the port of Veracruz declined. As the century advanced, cochineal competed increasingly with common madder (a red dyestuff) and Turkish dye (a processed form of common madder), South American brazilwood, and cochineal production in Guatemala and elsewhere. In addition, British cotton products emerged victorious and gained market share from wool textiles. Yet cotton was less suited for cochineal dying, which lowered demand for the product.[44] Cochineal prices dropped notably as a result. According to Viceroy Revillagigedo, the fleet merchants in Veracruz paid 90 pesos per *arroba* (25 pounds) of cochineal in 1729, while the product garnered 85 pesos in 1733. In 1752, the *arroba* sold for 70 pesos. Later, in the 1770s, merchants paid an average of 51 pesos for the *arroba* in Antequera.[45]

The dramatic decline of cochineal value is even clearer when eliminating inflation. Cochineal lost more than half its value between the mid-seventeenth and mid-eighteenth centuries on the other side of the Atlantic. A price index of various goods traded at the exchange in Amsterdam (Netherlands) traces the real value of cochineal and controls for inflation. According to this index, one *arroba* of cochineal sold for a mean of 188 pesos in the early seventeenth century. After 1645, the price declined to 115 pesos and dropped to 78 pesos by 1741. At the end of the century, the real price even collapsed to 63 pesos per *arroba*. These approximate numbers illustrate a trend. Surely, climate and infestations shaped the annual output, which fluctuated considerably. Wars also temporarily curbed exports, depressing prices in New Spain and driving them up in

---

and Secular Trends in the Economies of Mexico and Peru, 1750–1810: The View from the cajas of Mexico and Lima," in *The Economies of Mexico and Peru During the Late Colonial Period 1760–1810*, eds. Nils Jacobsen and Hans-Jörg Puhle (Berlin: Colloquium, 1986), 320–326, argues that population growth contributed to economic expansion in the period 1740–1775.

[44] According to Carmagnani, "Una institución económica colonial: repartimiento de mercancías y libertad de comercio," *Historia Mexicana* 54, no. 1 (2004): 258–59; Dahlgren de Jordán, "Prólogo," in *Nocheztli*, 28–29, prices declined more rapidly in the period 1775 to 1798. Humboldt, *Mexico-Werk*, 406, points to declining prices. See also Elena Phipps, *Cochineal Red: The Art History of a Color* (New York: Metropolitan Museum of Art, 2010), 5–46; *informe* of fray Vicente Magán, parish priest of Santa María Lachixio, n. d., probably 1776, in Dahlgren de Jordán, *Nocheztli*, 73–74. Ouweneel, *Shadows*, 175–176, sees price fluctuations as the origin of conflict over the *repartimiento*.

[45] Revillagigedo to Ensenada, Mexico City, 10 Apr. 1752, ACR 354; Dahlgren de Jordán, "Prólogo," in *Nocheztli*, 28–29. As a comparison, Jerónimo de la Maza Alvarado to Revillagigedo, Cádiz, 25 Jan. 1763, ACR 347, Revillagigedo's agent in Cádiz "sold four bags of cochineal at 87 ducats per *arroba*."

Europe. Nonetheless, the long-term trend of cochineal prices pointed downward.[46] Given these pressures, the *alcaldes mayores* in New Spain offered less for the dyestuff. Historian Arij Ouweneel asserts in this respect that the Natives considered the price alterations as a violation of good government and reciprocity. This may well be true, but the *alcaldes mayores* and the indigenous people could do little to reverse the falling value of cochineal.[47]

Collaboration with locals was paramount under this circumstance. Because Indians could sue relatively easily, *alcaldes mayores* relied on the assistance of indigenous nobles and their networks to operate the *repartimiento*. The parish priest of Ecatepec (Oaxaca) reported that "during the collection, republics, governors, *alcaldes*, and other officials are always near the royal buildings to bring forth debtors, meting out prison or other penalties if they are guilty of not paying."[48] The *alcaldes mayores* garnered sufficient support to sentence opponents to fines, prison, or lashes.

---

[46] Nicolaas Wilhelmus Posthumus, *Nederlandsche Prijsgeschiedenis*, vol. 1 (Leiden: Brill, 1943), in *Medieval and Early Modern Databank*, www2.scc.rutgers.edu/memdb/. According to the source, the mean nominal or non-indexed price of cochineal stood at 13 guilders per Amsterdam pound during the second half of the seventeenth century. After 1740, mean nominal prices declined to 8 guilders. The indexed price per *arroba* was 418.5 guilders up to 1645, 256 guilders after 1645, 174 guilders after 1741, and 139.5 guilders after 1774. In addition, Huemac Escalona Lüttig, "Rojo profundo: grana cochinilla y conflicto en la jurisdicción de Nexapa, Nueva España, siglo XVIII" (PhD diss., Pablo de Olavide University, Seville, Spain, 2015), 103–108, notes the declining price of the *arroba* of cochineal at 130–140 pesos in 1634, 75 pesos in 1655, 70 pesos in 1681, and 50 pesos in 1717 outside cultivation zones in New Spain, while he has almost 69 pesos per *arroba* in 1681, 53 in 1728, and 62.5 in April of 1730 in the city of Antequera. For a comparison, Dahlgren de Jordán, "Prólogo," in *Nocheztli*, 28–29 provides prices for *arroba* of cochineal in Antequera as 55 pesos in 1774, 50 pesos in 1775, 53 pesos in 1776, and 47 pesos in 1777. The freer commerce within the Spanish empire may have lowered prices in Amsterdam according to Victor Peralta Ruiz, *Patrones, clientes y amigos. El poder burocrático indiano en la España del siglo XVIII* (Madrid: Consejo Superior de Investigaciones Científicas, 2006), 132–145. For Baskes, *Indians, Markets*, 269, note 5, one Dutch guilder equalled 0.45 pesos in the late eighteenth century; see also his cochineal prices on p. 203, which are not inflation adjusted. Note that I converted Amsterdam pounds at 494 grams to Castilian pound at 460 grams according to *Just before the metre, the gram, the litre*, www.nuff.ox.ac.uk/users/murphy/measures/before_metre.htm; see also Brading, *Miners and Merchants*, xiv.

[47] Ouweneel, *Shadows*, 169. For example, Manuel Juárez and Juan Juárez of Santos Reyes to captain general, n. d., *Cuatro Villas* of the marquisate of Oaxaca, AGN, Indiferente Virreinal 1477, exp. 9, pointed out that that *repartimiento* violated "the usual use." Lockhart, *Nahuas*, 177–181; Farriss, *Maya Society*, 8; Menegus, "Economía indígena," 59, debate the extent of Native integration into the economy.

[48] *Informe* of fray Joaquín Vasco, Santa María Ecatepec, 28 May 1776, in Dahlgren de Jordán, *Nocheztli*, 63.

"This Custom or Better Said Corruption"

TABLE 1 *Absolute Cochineal Export Prices in the Harbor of Veracruz*

Year	Prices in pesos per *arroba* (25 pounds)
1729	90
1733	85
1752	70

Source: Revillagigedo to Ensenada, Mexico City, 10 April 1752, ACR 354

TABLE 2 *Mean Inflation-Adjusted Cochineal Prices in Amsterdam*

Years	Price in pesos per *arroba*
To 1645	188
After 1645	115
After 1741	78
After 1774	63

Source: Posthumus, *Nederlandsche Prijsgeschiedenis*, vol. 1, www2.scc.rutgers.edu/memdb/. Table 2 converts Posthumus' prices of cochineal in Dutch guilders per pound to pesos per *arroba* for a better comparison. I thank Renate Pieper, Graz, for computing the index. For the conversion of units, see footnote 46.

In 1681, the procurator for several Native noblemen from Coyotepec (Oaxaca) charged the indigenous "governors and magistrates of this *pueblo* ... backed by the *alcalde mayor* of Oaxaca" with committing "various *repartimientos* to my parties at excessive prices." In the procurator's view, the *alcalde mayor* manipulated the trade with Native support.[49]

Many *alcaldes mayores*, therefore, sought to take advantage of their position. The Zapotecs on the Isthmus of Tehuantepec revolted in 1660, for instance, because the *alcalde mayor* was well connected to the viceregal court in Mexico City. He tightened the screws on tribute collection, clamped down on commercial competitors, and whipped several Indians

---

[49] Petition of Juan Alexo Verdugo on behalf of the *caciques principales* of Coyotepec to Viceroy Count of Paredes, n. d., close to 24 Nov. 1681, AGN, Indios 27, exp. 199, fols. 102v–103.

for delivering mantas of poor quality to repay their loans. The Indians were also suffering from a drought. A crowd gathered on March 22, 1660, to protest against the *alcalde mayor*. Stones flew and the *alcalde mayor* ran for refuge. The Natives ultimately killed him, his black slave, a collaborating Zapotec nobleman, and a Spanish assistant. Soon after, the Natives of San Mateo de Capuluapa pelted a tribute collector out of town, while the *alcalde mayor* of Nexapa hunkered down in the church to hold off irate Indians.[50]

Yet Native oppression should not be overemphasized, because the authorities responded to the complaints. While an *audiencia* judge and his constables investigated the uprisings and hanged five people, the councilors of the Indies in Madrid also suggested ending the *repartimiento*. Subsequently, the crown published the *Law of the Indies* in 1680, which repeated the prohibition of the trade and gave Natives an additional base to challenge any excesses.[51] The prosecutor of the *audiencia* afterwards also demanded ending the unpaid personal services in Tehuantepec. According to a 1682 complaint, the *alcalde mayor* demanded cash and mantas for his deputy, the interpreter, and the constable, and levied "a peso for wine, one for chocolate, one for saffron spice, four *tomines* [*reales*] for bread and four *tomines* for meats."[52] In addition, in 1721, the king acerbically criticized the *audiencia* officials who did not "prevent *alcaldes mayores* and governors from exacting *repartimientos* of merchandise, personal services, and other burdens prohibited by law."[53] In 1725, Viceroy Marquis of Casafuerte (1722–1734) also homed in on the *alcaldes mayores* for extorting the "miserable Indians through bribes ... *repartimientos*, deals, nuisances, ill-treatments, and undue services." Many in Madrid and Mexico City took the issue seriously.[54]

---

[50] Owensby, *Empire of Law*, 252–255, 282–285; Zeitlin, *Cultural Politics*, 169; Hamnett, *Politics and Trade*, 9–15.

[51] *Law of the Indies*, book 5, title 2, *Formulario general* following law 7; and book 4, title 21, law 1; Owensby, *Empire of Law*, 268–273.

[52] The charges of *alcaldes* and officials of San Juan Bautista Guichicovi, n. d., roughly 11 May 1682, AGI, Escribanía 228 A, *leg.* 8, *pieza* 2, fol. 675–675v; *parecer* of the prosecutor, Mexico City, 28 May 1682, AGI, Escribanía 228 A, *leg.* 8, *pieza* 2, fol. 694–694v.

[53] *Real cédula*, Lerma, 13 Dec. 1721, AGN, Historia, vol. 102, exp. 10; fol. 85v.

[54] Casafuerte to king, Mexico City, 14 May 1725, AGI, México 492. See also Sebastián Vasquez on behalf of several Natives of San Andres Xomiltepec (Quautla de las Amilpas) to Viceroy José de Sarmiento; and viceregal decree, Mexico City, 10 Dec. 1699, both documents in AGN, Indios 34, exp. 132, fols. 176v–177v; don Gabriel Chimalpopoca to Duke of Alburquerque, probably Istlahuaca, n. d.; and viceregal decree, 9 Jan. 1703, both documents in AGN, Indios 36, exp. 3, fols. 2–3.

At least in some parts of New Spain, brewing discontent convinced the *alcaldes mayores* to make concessions. In September 1715, for example, a group of angry Indians gathered once more in Tehuantepec. During a shuffle, an Indian hit the deputy *alcalde mayor* who ran off to hide in the Dominican monastery. The Natives then deposed their governor and *alcaldes* and instead elected Juan Martín as their governor. Martín had earlier "spent, eaten, and consumed the royal tribute," for which he had gone to jail. The *alcalde mayor* appeared and meekly accepted the election to end the standoff. The *alcalde mayor* also dismissed his own deputy and appointed "one whom they liked." The *alcalde mayor* later secretly dispatched a report about the unrest to Mexico City, which he sent from the neighboring jurisdiction to avoid antagonizing the Indians. In 1719, the next *alcalde mayor* again warned of a rebellion, but the *audiencia* prosecutor merely suggested reviewing the militia to make an impression and restore order without taking any additional measures.[55]

Conflicts also transcended any dichotomous Spanish-indigenous relations, if they still existed. Since the 1990s, scholars of Latin American history emphasize that most inhabitants of the Spanish empire integrated into social networks as the default mode of their lives. The reciprocity among members of the networks varied according to local circumstances, yet the ties of *alcaldes mayores* crossed ethnic boundaries too. In addition, the boundary itself blurred over time as indigenous communities assimilated many elements of the Hispanic culture, just as the Hispanic *novohispanos* absorbed Native traditions and languages. Native nobles occasionally even joined the Spanish military orders, which emphasized pure bloodline. A *cacique* of Tula, for example, became a member of the Knights of Santiago in 1722.[56]

---

[55] Cosme de Mier y Estrada to Duke of Linares, Xalapa (Oaxaca), 12 Sept. 1715; and viceregal decree, Mexico City, 10 Oct. 1715, both documents in AGN, Indios 39, exp. 169, fols. 259–262v; fray Alonso de Vargas Machuca to Duke of Linares, Tehuantepec, 14 Sept. 1715; viceregal decree, Mexico City, 21 Oct. 1715, both in AGN, Indios 39, exp. 167, fols. 256–258; Pedro de Sarabia Cortes to Valero, Tehuantepec, 9 Apr. 1719, *parecer* of Francisco de Oyanguren, Mexico City, 2 May 1719; viceregal decree, Mexico City, 5 May 1719, these three documents in AGN, Indios 42, exp. 108, fols. 139v–140.

[56] The *Historia Mexicana, Redes sociales e instituciones* (Jan.–Mar. 2007) vol. 56, No. 3, devoted a volume to social networks; see also Chapter 1 in this volume. Ouweneel, "El gobernador," 93, rejects the dichotomy between Spaniards and Indians. On "interethnic intimacy" in Yucatan, see Mark Lentz, *Murder in Mérida, 1792. Violence, Factions, and the Law* (Albuquerque, NM: University of New Mexico Press, 2018), 13–15; von Deylen, *Ländliches Wirtschaftsleben*, 248, focuses on interethnic relations. See also Lockhart, *Nahuas*, 179–180; Hausberger and Mazín, "Nueva España," 291–294. Yannakakis, *The Art of Being*, 2, argues that the "the Spaniards did not count on … the limiting

Alcaldes mayores sometimes jailed or whipped Natives, showing that the *repartimiento* could well be violent. At the same time, violence pervaded conflict resolution more heavily than today. Murders occurred more often. Nobles dueled over sleights to their honor, and the lower class pulled knives in brawls. Systemic violence beyond the customary was not the norm in the *repartimiento*, however, as the *alcaldes mayores* could not force entire districts to produce and exchange goods against their will. The *alcaldes mayores* never closely supervised the work or made Indians toil in sweatshops. Instead, they needed some consent of the Natives to produce roughly 360,000 pounds of cochineal per year.[57]

Negotiations over prices were widespread in early modern times, bound by conventions, and discriminatory according to today's standards. Agricultural workers often received loans to work on haciendas, for example, and when better opportunities hailed elsewhere, they walked off without repaying the loans. *Hacendados* countered by paying in tokens redeemable only at the hacienda store. In addition, early modern individuals rarely made fully free and voluntary decisions. Indigenous nobles, the *alcaldes mayores*, and the priests shaped the actions of *novohispano* Natives. The *repartimiento* did not play out in a market of fully autonomous individuals who offered and bought merchandise according to their own wishes. To call this exploitation, as some scholars do, at least raises the question of what the standards for exploitation were in the seventeenth and eighteenth century. Economists have great difficulties in pinpointing the concept today, and it is even more challenging to apply this idea to the past.[58]

The *alcaldes mayores* attempted to skew prices but they could not dictate them as they saw fit, because other merchants competed with

---

effects of the strong bonds of reciprocity between nobility and commoners," in which the nobility "had to answer not only to their Spanish overlords but also to the people who legitimated their authority in Native society." While Yannakakis makes a good point (as always), my impression is that Spaniards expected some form of reciprocity, because it was an important part of their own social values.

[57] Taylor, *Drinking, Homicide*, 74, 109–112; Ouweneel, *Shadows*, 183. On the cochineal quantity, Revillagigedo to Ensenada, Mexico City, 10 Apr. 1752, ACR 354; while Menegus, "Economía indígena," 34, notes production of between 500,000 and 1,000,000 pounds.

[58] Eric Van Young, *Hacienda and Market in Eighteenth-Century Mexico: The Rural Economy of the Guadalajara Region, 1675–1820*, 2nd ed. (Lanham: Rowman & Littlefield Publishers, 2006), 245–272. Note that at least *A Dictionary of Economics*, 3rd ed., eds. John Black, Nigar Hashimzade, and Gareth Myles (Oxford: Oxford University Press, 2009), does not even define the term exploitation.

them. Between 1684 and 1702, two Native nobles crisscrossed the Villa Alta district in the Oaxacan highlands to sell goods. The nobles and dozens of other towns petitioned the *audiencia* to stop the *alcalde mayor* from overcharging Natives and meddling with their elections. The *alcalde mayor* struck back, equally with local help. Indigenous witnesses came forward against the two nobles, and the *alcalde mayor* sentenced them to lashes and hard labor for sedition and stealing mules. Subsequently, the *audiencia* in Mexico City lent an ear to the nobles. This conflict bears the marks of feuding networks across ethnic lines. Similarly, during a conflict over the *repartimiento*, the *alcalde mayor* of Tehuantepec worked with a Native governor to tear down the local guesthouse. The town council objected to the action, lamenting that the mercantile competitors now had a harder time plying their trade.[59]

In addition, Natives actively participated in the market, limiting the potential of *alcaldes mayores* to curb prices. Indians traded in their *pueblos* and in Antequera. Merchants exchanged goods, while the *alcalde mayor* of Puebla reported that "*macehuales* [Indian commoners] walk about the *pueblos* and sold clothes of the country in small amounts and quantities."[60] Indigenous governors retailed "digging sticks, clothes, cloth, towel, *huipiles*, and wax." In addition, according to another *alcalde mayor*, the Natives of San Pablo Zoquistlan (Puebla) sold on the regional market any cochineal that remained after satisfying the *repartimiento* terms.[61] Other Indians bought "rope and machetes" to produce "mescal wine and threads" or hauled ore, fire wood, and charcoal to the silver mines. Under these circumstances, competition often limited the gains of the *repartimiento*.[62]

---

[59] Based on Yannakakis, *The Art of Being*, 43–45; Zeitlin, *Cultural Politics*, 225.

[60] Miguel Manuel Dávila Galindo, *alcalde mayor* of Puebla, to Revillagigedo, Puebla, 14 Jan. 1754, AGN, Subdelegados 34, fol. 370v. See also *alcalde mayor* of Ixtepeji to Revillagigedo, n. d., AGN, Subdelegados 34, fol. 8v; *alcalde mayor* of Xalapa to Revillagigedo, 31 May 1752, AGN, Subdelegados 34, fol. 228; *alcalde mayor* of Cholula to Revillagigedo, Cholula, 11 Aug. 1752, AGN, Subdelegados 34, fols. 46–47; on "roaming merchants," Revillagigedo to Ensenada, Mexico City, 10 Apr. 1752, ACR 354.

[61] Juan Francisco de Apezechea, *alcalde mayor* of Tehuacan, to Revillagigedo, Tehuacan, 10 May 1752, AGN, Subdelegados 34, fol. 178.

[62] José Angula Vega, deputy *alcalde mayor*, to Revillagigedo, Sayula, AGN, Subdelegados 34, fol. 81–81v. See also Ignacio Rodríguez, *alcalde mayor* of Temascaltepec, to Revillagigedo, Temascaltepec, 9 Oct. 1752, AGN, Subdelegados 34, fol. 51; fray Pedro Parrales to Revillagigedo, Tuxcacuesco (Jalisco), 2 Sept. 1752, AGN, Subdelegados 34, fol. 93. Ouweneel, *Shadows*, 191, argues that the *repartimiento* was feeble in economically integrated regions; see also Lockhart, *Nahuas*, 185–190.

3.2 REFORMING THE REPARTIMIENTO AT MID-CENTURY

By the mid-eighteenth century, reformers in Mexico City and Madrid continued to view the *repartimiento* as corrupt. Nevertheless, the thinking had changed. The ministers worried less about vile merchants buying into the judicature or the dangers of usurious money lending. Instead, they favored leveling the playing field for merchants and *alcaldes mayores*. The Marquis of la Ensenada and a clique of like-minded ministers were also concerned about the low tax yield, the continuity of unlawful labor obligations, and the potential for unrest. Ensenada himself inclined more toward a state monopoly to raise revenue and oust the *alcaldes mayores* from the trade.[63] Viceroy Revillagigedo, meanwhile, drew on proto-liberal ideas to favor freer commerce rather than monopolies. Others espoused physiocratic notions supporting productive farmers over idle landholders and sterile commerce. All these ministers affirmed the Natives' potential to work and suggested curbing abusive *alcaldes mayores*, clergymen, and *hacendados*. In 1749, the naval officers Jorge Juan and Antonio de Ulloa, for example, assailed "the criminal corruption" of Peruvian *alcaldes mayores* in this context.[64]

Ensenada's team must have discussed legalizing the *repartimiento* in the early 1740s. The viceroy in Lima fathomed Peruvian views shortly after taking office in 1745. He suggested capping the prices for a range of goods that Indians traded, while also levying the *alcabala* (sales tax) for the crown. Soon after, Viceroy Revillagigedo rejected the *repartimiento* in New Spain, just as he opposed unpaid personal services. Only if the *alcaldes mayores* "did not use force ... or alter the going rates ... or obstruct the freedom to trade, and charge payments for their goods in the same way as any other, then there would be no grievance to the Indians." Revillagigedo, moreover, objected to the "mercantile spirit kindled by profit that is inappropriate for the good administration of justice, and it is irreconcilable with reason that a judge has the authority, order, and jurisdiction over his own business." Ministers of past generations would have agreed with this opinion. Yet Revillagigedo cared little

---

[63] On Ensenada's clique, Gómez Urdáñez, *El proyecto reformista de Ensenada*, 87–100, 229–230; on the intellectual background, Richard Bonney, "Early Modern Theories of State Finance," in *Economic Systems and State Finance*, ed. Richard Bonney (Oxford: Clarendon Press, 1995), 173–176; Annino, "El primer constitucionalismo Mexicano," 163.
[64] Juan and Ulloa, *Discourse*, 73, see also 78–79, 84, 99–100, 108, 148–153.

about the vile occupations of people who became *alcaldes mayores*, which had been a thorny issue for previous generations.[65]

Instead, he suggested a compromise. He declared that "commerce is the fountain giving life to all settlements: it is the principle from which the products of nature and labor spring, and it is the tool that makes people strive." That would be the proto-liberal ideal, but Revillagigedo was also aware that many of the roughly 137 *alcaldes mayores* in New Spain lived off the *repartimiento*, because the crown did not pay them appropriate salaries. In his view, legalizing and monitoring the trade would attract wealthier residents to serve as *alcaldes mayores*, ease the harassment of Indians, and reduce the embezzlement of tribute and taxes.[66] The commercial interests of Revillagigedo and his allies may have played a role in this view too. A client of Revillagigedo shipped the dyestuff and other goods from Veracruz to Santander and Cádiz in Spain and sold the merchandise. After Revillagigedo had returned to Madrid, for example, the client reported in 1762 that the "cochineal produced the largest part of the 21,000 pesos" that he gained on behalf of Revillagigedo. The viceroy was no enemy of a good deal.[67]

Meanwhile, Ensenada floated the idea of seizing the whole cochineal distribution for the state, but Revillagigedo demurred. Ensenada suggested cutting out the *alcaldes mayores* and the powerful merchants of the annual Spanish fleet and their *consulado* in Cádiz. Royal officials should instead pay for and gather the dyestuff in the *pueblos* of Oaxaca and ship it to Spain, where the crown would sell it at a handsome profit. This scheme resembled the tobacco monopoly that Ensenada successfully expanded in Peru. Yet Revillagigedo argued that employing officials to provide easy loans to Indians would reduce the incentives to produce dyestuff. As an alternative, the crown could establish a royal factory in

---

[65] Revillagigedo to Ensenada, Mexico City, 14 Sep. 1748, ACR, 399; see also Revillagigedo to Arriaga, Mexico City, 12 Apr. 1755, AGI, Guadalajara 89, calling the labor draft in the mining town Bolaños an "extreme to which it should not come." On the Peruvian viceroy José Antonio Manso de Velasco, see Pearce, *Origins of Bourbon Reforms*, 145, 151–152.

[66] Revillagigedo to Ensenada, Mexico City, 14 Sep. 1748, ACR, 399; see also Revillagigedo's *relación* to Amarillas, Mexico City, 8 Oct. 1755, in de la Torre Villar, *Instrucciones*, 2: 805. According to Brading, *Miners and Merchants*, 47, Viceroy Bucareli estimated later that replacing *alcaldes mayores* with officials on an annual salary of 2,000 pesos would accrue to 300,000 pesos per year.

[67] Jerónimo de la Maza Alvarado to Revillagigedo, Cádiz, 1 June 1762, ACR 347; see also de la Maza Alvarado to Revillagigedo, Cádiz, 28 May 1762, ACR 346; Manuel de Barroeta to Revillagigedo before Lic. Juan Manuel de Vargas, n. d. [1750], no place, AGI, Escribanía 217 A, *cuaderno* 1, fols. 1–4.

Antequera or purchase the cochineal in Veracruz, but this approach would undermine the vital loans for the growers. Revillagigedo added that "when the price of cochineal rose in these kingdoms [New Spain], consumption could diminish, as we have experienced in all goods." Observing the relationship between supply and demand, Revillagigedo noted that the crown would have to absorb the shortfall. In short, he repudiated Ensenada's vision of a state monopoly and proposed better credits and more competition.[68]

On July 17, 1751, Ensenada fell in line with Revillagigedo and the Peruvian viceroy and ordered them and their colleague in New Granada to legalize the trade with limitations. The viceroys should convene committees to draw up price schedules for the most important goods traded in each jurisdiction. The aim of these schedules was to estimate the tax revenue. Moreover, the schedules provided a basis for the Native lawsuits against their commercial partners. Once the local priest, the *alcalde mayor*, and some merchants had established a fair threshold, the Natives could challenge serious differences in court by citing the *laesio enormis* and other norms. The crown believed that the *alcaldes mayores* who complied with the schedule could "remain free of serious compunctions."[69]

According to the royal communications, the "laziness of those Indians to all type of work" and their "indolence, drunkenness, and other vices" made that solution necessary. [70] Usually, the proponents of the *repartimiento* subscribed to the trope of the inactive Natives to justify the exchange. Ensenada probably used the word "laziness" here to palliate the opposition to the reform, although several of his ministers rejected the idea. Revillagigedo maintained that "the Indians are generally industrious." [71] Juan and Ulloa similarly found the trope "wholly unfounded." They asserted in 1749 that the *hacendados* maligned the indigenous people to keep labor obligations in place. In their view, the Indians declined to work harder, because the *alcaldes mayores* seized any

---

[68] Revillagigedo to Ensenada, Mexico City, 10 Apr. 1752, ACR 354. On Peru, see Pearce, *Origins of Bourbon Reforms*, 154.

[69] *Real Cédula* to viceroys of Peru, New Spain, and New Granada, 17 July 1751, Buen Retiro, AGN, RCO 71, exp. 147, fols. 540–543. Price caps were also a matter of just price theory, which, according to Elisabeth Koch, "Gerechter Preis," in Cordes, *HRG*, 2nd ed., (2012), 2: 123–127, declined at least in the late eighteenth-century Holy Roman Empire.

[70] *Real cédula* to viceroys of Peru, New Spain, and New Granada, 17 July 1751, Buen Retiro, AGN, RCO 71, exp. 147, fol. 540v. See also *real cédula*, Ensenada to Revillagigedo, 15 Mar. 1751, Madrid, AGN, RCO 71, exp. 72.

[71] Revillagigedo to Ensenada, Mexico City, 14 Sept. 1748, ACR 399.

additional gains. Juan and Ulloa also pointed out that ending the *repartimiento* in Quito had not resulted in any commercial decline.[72]

On March 7, 1752, Revillagigedo met with five *audiencia* ministers and a senior accountant, and they ordered the *alcaldes mayores* and the priests to inform about the *repartimiento* in their jurisdictions. The recipients probably had a good idea about the underlying political motives. Their reports trickled in half a year later and have to be taken with a grain of salt. The Natives of Xalapa, for example, underlined the collusion between the priests and *alcaldes mayores*, while Revillagigedo also knew that "*alcaldes mayores*, priests, and their deputies" frequently collaborated. At least some *alcaldes mayores* skewed their replies because they lived off the *repartimiento*.[73]

Many *alcaldes mayores* denied that they participated in the exchange. Some of them called a council of the important residents of the jurisdiction to discuss the matter, showing their zeal for the monarchy. The *alcalde mayor* of Michoacan, for example, replied that "until now his predecessors had not practiced the *repartimiento* of goods and products," and the merchants in his jurisdiction advised him "to draw up the schedule according to the regular prices" paid in the region.[74] That would have contributed little to improving the free trade of goods. Another *alcalde mayor* contended that the real problem were the *hacendados*, who ran stores where the workers' wages "lost more than a third of their value, because the *hacendado* charged high prices." Such attacks on abusive landholders deflected the reform's aim, but they found ready ears among the physiocrats in Madrid and Mexico City.[75]

---

[72] Juan and Ulloa, *Discourse*, 96, 141–143, quote on p. 141.
[73] Revillagigedo to Ensenada, Mexico City, 10 Apr. 1752, ACR 354; see also petition of Natives of Xalapa summarized in *real cédula* of Queen Mariana to Viceroy Marquis of Mancera, Madrid, 28 Oct. 1678, AGN, Indios 25, exp. 259, fols. 194v–195; according viceregal decree to *alcalde mayor* of Chicomosuchil and *ruego y encargo* to local priest, Mexico City, 9 March 1752, AGN, Subdelegados 34, fols. 6–7, the civil judges Domingo Valcárcel, Marquis of Altamira, Fernando Dávila, Domingo Trespalacios, the prosecutor Antonio Andreu, and the accountant José Rafael Rodríguez Gallardo composed the junta. See also *real cédula*, Ensenada to Revillagigedo, San Lorenzo, 18 Oct. 1752, AGN, RCO 72, exp. 155, fols. 426–427; *real cédula* signed by José Ignacio de Goyeneche to Revillagigedo, Madrid, 7 May 1753, AGN, RCO 73, exp. 42, fol. 427.
[74] Diego Antonio de Heira Ponce de León, *alcalde mayor* of Tancitaro y Pinzandaro, to Revillagigedo, Tancitaro, 15 June 1752, AGN, Subdelegados 34, fols. 28–29v; Manuel Vicente de la Barrera, parish priest in Xalapa, to Revillagigedo, Xalapa, 1 July 1752, AGN, Subdelegados 34, fol. 231.
[75] Ambrosio Merino, *alcalde mayor* of Huejotzingo, to Revillagigedo, Huejotzingo, 14 Dec. 1752, AGN, Subdelegados 34, fols. 60–63v.

Nevertheless, several *alcaldes mayores* forthrightly detailed their *repartimientos*. The *alcalde mayor* of Cholula claimed "that these *repartimiento* merchants obtained a ruling from the *audiencia* that allowed a 25% gain for the terms under which they sell and their work to recover the credit" from the Natives. This limitation stood at half the *laesio enormis* standard, and all *alcaldes mayores* stated that they did not exceed it.[76] Most *alcaldes mayores* reported more modest gains. The *alcalde mayor* of Santa Catarina Ixtepeji in the Oaxacan Sierra stated that he gave credit to the Indians every October or November. Between May and August, the locals repaid him with cochineal for twelve *reales* per pound. He sold the dyestuff in Antequera for fourteen to eighteen *reales*. Another *alcalde mayor* reported a return of fifteen to sixteen percent on the principal, which he recovered after about eighteen months. One priest added, not surprisingly, that assessing prices and profits was difficult, because they fluctuated according to the "variety of the weather."[77] Some ministers confessed to gaining more. The *alcalde mayor* of Teotitlan del Camino (Oaxaca) maintained, for example, that he sold mules with a 70 percent markup. The priest in Huejotzingo, a district southeast of the Popcatépetl volcano, averred that the *alcalde mayor* of his jurisdiction garnered even higher margins: "A bull cost six peso, and he sold them for twelve ... and according to custom, the locals give two *reales* a week so that at the end of the year they paid off twelve pesos." According to the priest, the *alcaldes mayor* occasionally garnered a markup of 100 percent.[78]

---

[76] Lorenzo Gutiérrez de Colombres, *alcalde mayor* de Cholula, 11 Aug. 1752, AGN, Subdelegados 34, fols. 46v–47; similar, José Manuel de las Peñas Montalbo, *alcalde mayor* of Huaxhuapan, to Revillagigedo, n. d., AGN, Subdelegados 34, fols. 97–103v; Miguel Manuel Dávila Galindo, *alcalde mayor* of Puebla, to Revillagigedo, Puebla, 14 Jan. 1754, AGN, Subdelegados 34, fol. 370v; Andrés Antonio Rodriguez Moreno, *alcalde mayor* of Huatulco, to Revillagigedo, 22 May 1752, AGN, Subdelegados 34, fols. 111–114v; Juan Antonio Arrazola, *alcalde mayor* of Nexapa, to Revillagigedo, Quiechapan, 5 July 1752, fols. 119–122v; Juan Francisco de Apezechea, *alcalde mayor* of Tehuacan, Tehuacan, 10 May 1752, AGN, Subdelegados 34, fol. 177.

[77] Matías Lorenzo Misangos, Santa Catarina Ixtepeji, 12 June 1752, AGN, Subdelegados 34, fols. 11–12; see also *alcalde mayor* of Santa Catarina Ixtepeji (Oaxaca) to Revillagigedo, n. d., AGN, Subdelegados 34, fols. 8–9; José Manuel de las Peñas Montalbo, *alcalde mayor* of Huaxhuapan, to Revillagigedo, Huaxhuapan, 19 July 1752, AGN, Subdelegados 34, fols. 97v–103v.

[78] Bernardo de Huala to Revillagigedo, Huejotzingo, 7 July 1752, AGN, Subdelegados 34, fol. 64; Joaquín de Lazarte, *alcalde mayor* of Teotitlan del Camino Real, to Revillagigedo, Teotitlan, 6 Oct. 1752, AGN, Subdelegados 34, fols. 160–162.

Yet these *repartimiento* prices were not net profits, as the business came with expenses and risks. Hail, heavy rain, or infestations ravaged the cochineal. Especially *aguja* worms feasted on cochineal insects and annihilated entire fields. When the harvest fell short, both producers and *alcaldes mayores* still had to pay back their creditors. Some Native farmers also fell sick, passed away, or were otherwise unwilling to repay the principal and interest. Absconding debtors was a favorite and feared topic for *alcaldes mayores*. Those who drove mules from Puebla to the Oaxacan Sierra also dealt with animals running off, suffering from diseases, or dying during transport. In addition, the money lenders in Antequera levied 8 to 10 percent annual interest on the cash which they advanced to *alcaldes mayores*.[79]

There were other costs. According to some accounts, packaging and transporting one pound of cochineal from the highlands to Antequera amounted to about a third of a *real*. One *alcalde mayor* also paid his deputy 300 pesos a year, which was a common salary. In addition, *alcaldes mayores* had personal expenses. A Peruvian district judge calculated in 1741 that he spent 59,720 pesos for five years of service. He paid 16,000 pesos to purchase his appointment, 4,000 pesos to travel to the Indies, and 5,000 pesos to obtain his appointment papers from the viceroy, among other expenses. Yet he only drew an annual salary of 1,250 pesos. This district judge claimed higher expenses than most of his colleagues in New Spain, but many could not make ends meet without the *repartimiento*.[80] Revillagigedo also observed that too many went bankrupt, while the governor of New Galicia (north of New Spain) lamented in the mid-eighteenth century, that most *alcaldes mayores* in his province lived in "poverty and misery."[81]

---

[79] *Informe* of fray Joaquín Vasco, Santa María Ecatepec, 28 May 1776, in Dahlgren de Jordán, *Nocheztli*, 53; Ignacio Rodríguez, *alcalde mayor* of Temascaltepec (state of Mexico), to Revillagigedo, Temascaltepec, 9 Oct. 1752, AGN, Subdelegados 34, fol. 51; on interest, *alcalde mayor* of Santa Catarina Ixtepeji to Revillagigedo, AGN, Subdelegados 34, fols. 8–9. Hamnett, "The Appropriation of Mexican Church Wealth by the Spanish Bourbon Government: The 'Consolidación de Vales Reales,' 1805–1809," *Journal of Latin American Studies* 1 (1969): 86, shows that wealthier *novohispanos* secured credit from the pious funds of the Church for 5 percent interest per year, although these loans tended to be backed by collateral.

[80] *Alcalde mayor* of Santa Catarina Ixtepeji to Revillagigedo, AGN, Subdelegados 34, fols. 8–9; see also Juan Antonio Arrazola, *alcalde mayor* of Nejapa, to Revillagigedo, Quijechiapa, 15 July 1752, AGN, Subdelegados 34, fols. 119–122v; Baskes, *Indians, Merchants*, 22; Moreno Cebrián, *Corregidor de Indios*, 106, see also 109–110.

[81] José de Basarte to king, Guadalajara, 29 July 1755, AGI, Guadalajara 107; Revillagigedo to Ensenada, Mexico City, 14 Sept. 1748, ACR, 399; Revillagigedo to king, Mexico City, 20 Feb. 1747, AGI, México 1341.

Revillagigedo and the special committee discussed the responses from the *alcaldes mayores* and priests on August 17, 1753, but "did not decide anything for finding abundant inappropriateness in the reports."[82] Shortly afterwards the folder containing the responses vanished. Probably one of the notaries working for the viceregal government seized the folder, because at least some of these officials were tied to the Mexico City *consulado*. Many *consulado* merchants profited from the *repartimiento* and opposed the fee schedule, a more stringent collection of sales taxes, and opening the markets to additional competitors. Years later, the documents resurfaced under the secret of the confessional. Revillagigedo's committee never agreed on price limits in New Spain, while the *alcaldes mayores* continued "tyrannizing the neighbors with injustices," as he saw it.[83]

The crown probably collected more tax revenue as a result of the reform. Revillagigedo claimed that the *alcabala* gathered outside Mexico City and its surroundings rose by 116,445 pesos annually during his tenure. Although other factors clearly played a role too, legalizing the *repartimiento* helped the tax collection. This meant that the Natives had to shoulder higher tax payments while facing declining cochineal prices. The combined factors explain the smoldering discontent among the Natives in the highlands and the continuing debate over the issue.[34]

---

[82] José Manuel de Castro Santa-Anna, *Diario de Sucesos Notables. Documentos para la historia de Méjico* (Mexico City: Imprenta de Juan R. Navarro, 1854), 4: 148.

[83] Revillagigedo's *relación* to Amarillas, in de la Torre Villar, *Instrucciones*, 2: 805; see also Pietschmann, "Justicia, discurso político y reformismo borbónico en la Nueva España del siglo xviii," in *Dinámicas del antiguo régimen y orden constitucional. Representación, justicia, y administración en Iberoamérica. Siglos xviii–xix*, ed. Marco Bellingeri (Turin: Otto, 2000), 47–49.

[84] The sentence of the Council of the Indies, Madrid, 13 Mar. 1758, AGI, Escribanía 1194, agreed with Revillagigedo's claim on the growing *alcabala* receipts in Mexico City. Pearce, *Origins of Bourbon Reforms*, 152–153, convincingly ties the growth of *alcabala* receipts to the *repartimiento* reform in Peru, while in New Spain, the amount of *alcabala* revenue from cochineal trade is difficult to trace. According to TePaske and Klein, *Ingresos y egresos*, vol. 1, 134–138, and vol. 2, n. p., entries under "Oaxaca," the *alcabala* receipts in the Mexico City treasury rose in the period 1751 to 1755 from 766,362 to 1,209,034 pesos, but there was significant fluctuation, and, in 1757, the entries dropped again to 766,362 pesos. More reliable tax data for Oaxaca is available only since 1790, when a treasury was set up in the city. For a comparison, according to Fabian de Fonseca and Carlos de Urrutia, *Historia general de real hacienda* [...] (Mexico City: V. G. Torres, 1845–53), vii, the treasury of Mexico City collected 41,387 pesos per year in taxes on cochineal, indigo, and vanilla between 1785 and 1789. See also Baskes, *Indians, Merchants*, 150–154.

CONCLUSION

The changing values of corruption better explain the debate over the *repartimiento*. Juan de Solórzano y Pereyra and other jurists of his time still opposed vile merchants who became judges and violated their noble duty of imparting justice impartially. The Duke of Linares similarly reproached greedy traders and lambasted the *repartimiento* as corruption breaching the royal law. *Alcaldes mayores* also violated a number of provisions that regulated commerce in general. Some theologians, for example, chastised lending money with interest as usury. In addition, they and some jurists also considered Indians as miserable persons who needed special protections and easy access to the courts. Natives capitalized on these opportunities. They frequently argued that the *alcalde mayor* had used force against them. This claim often indicated a disagreement over the price, because the theologian Moreno maintained that exacting an unjust price for merchandise was forcible. The Indians held, therefore, that they had suffered this injury in their contracts. As a result, the courts could apply the *restitutio in integrum* and require the *alcalde mayor* to restore all goods to the original owners. The *alcalde mayor* could even forfeit any cash he had loaned to the Indians, which was a painful reversal. Legal representatives for Natives also maintained that the *alcaldes mayores* caused enormous damages by paying less than half the just prices for merchandise. This doctrine was known as the *laesio enormis*. When the judges of the *audiencia* or the Indian court agreed, they invalidated the agreements and ordered to end the *repartimiento* in the jurisdiction.

Alcaldes mayores called on support in their jurisdiction as prices declined and conflicts exacerbated. The *alcaldes mayores* could not coerce entire regions to work against their will and instead had to reach some accommodation with indigenous nobles and other local leaders. Most Indians also voluntarily requested the goods and credit offered by the *alcaldes mayores*. Sometimes, an alliance manipulated prices or oppressed individuals excessively, which triggered additional conflicts. Moreover, the indigenous population grew again since the late seventeenth century. Labor became cheaper and cochineal output grew, while global competition increased as well. Nominal prices for cochineal eroded in Veracruz for these reasons, and real prices declined significantly in Amsterdam. The *alcaldes mayores* had to pass on the changes to the producers. These conflicts often ended up in court and occasionally turned violent.

That background explains why the Marquis of la Ensenada and Viceroy Revillagigedo attempted to overhaul the exchange. Ensenada and the viceroy did not worry anymore about usurious or vile merchants. Instead, Ensenada suggested a state monopoly to collect cochineal and sell it to European merchants at steep profit for the crown. But Revillagigedo opposed the idea and favored untethering markets to create abundant loans for producers. Ensenada yielded, to an extent, ordering to legalize the trade with the *alcaldes mayores*. He also mandated to create a price schedule for local goods so that Natives could better challenge excessive manipulations and rapid price declines. The schedule should also help in collecting the sales tax and perhaps even provide transparency for any interest charged on the *repartimiento*. Revillagigedo subsequently inquired about local conditions and priests and *alcaldes mayores* responded, but the price caps failed. When later generations protested against the *repartimiento*, they did so because of increasing tax pressure, declining real value of cochineal, and continuing manipulation of local markets by alliances of *alcaldes mayores* and Native nobles.[85]

---

[85] On the Túpac Amaru rebellion of 1780–81, see Pearce, *Origins of Bourbon Reforms*, 153; Kuethe and Andrien, *Spanish Atlantic World*, 209.

4

"Vile and Abominable Pacts": The Sale of Judicial Appointments and the Great Decline of Viceregal Patronage

INTRODUCTION

The rising sales of *alcalde mayor* (district judge) appointments marked the end of Habsburg and the beginning of Bourbon rule in the Spanish empire. This expansion of sales decisively curbed the patronage power of the viceroys of New Spain (colonial Mexico). Historians have generally suggested that the *beneficio* (royal sale of appointments) corrupted the administration and undermined the king's control over the American realms, but a close examination suggests otherwise.[1] The *beneficio* of *alcaldes mayores*, if anything, buttressed the monarchy, because the viceroys had sold the appointments for money or given them to their clients. In 1675, the crown began awarding the important appointments, routing the money into royal coffers and gaining oversight over the *alcaldes mayores* in distant realms. The move also weakened the viceroys, who almost exclusively belonged to the aristocracy, a group that was often at loggerheads with the king.

The *beneficio* of *alcaldes mayores* paralleled the *beneficio* of *audiencia* (high court) judges (1687–1750) in the empire. The sale of *audiencia* appointments came largely at the expense of the great Councils and their patronage committees in Madrid. The councilors were historically tied to the municipal oligarchies of Castile, another traditional elite that often defied the crown. The councilors, many *audiencia* jurists, and the aristocracy usually claimed that awarding offices should comply with distributive justice. That meant giving entitlements to people of

---

[1] Ruiz Rivera and Sanz Tapia, "Presentación," in Ruiz Rivera and Sanz Tapia, *La venta de cargos*, 13.

corresponding merit, which included a heavy dose of social origins. The councilors and the aristocracy rejected purchasers of appointments, because they lacked the proper descent and corrupted the judiciary. This view allowed the traditional elites to prefer their peers for the important positions. Yet the idea that lacking merit corrupted justice declined during the period 1675–1755, while performance in office mattered more. In addition, the social sectors less tied to the traditional elites, including in the Americas, gained ground and tended to favor *beneficio*. Accepting money rather than considering the candidates' merit was therefore a utilitarian consideration for the crown, and "reformist" or "executive" governments expanded *beneficio*.[2]

Historians originally assumed that the sale of appointments to offices with jurisdiction played a minor role in the empire.[3] Then, years ago, Mark A. Burkholder and D. S. Chandler masterfully fleshed out the widespread character of such sales, which created "susceptibility of influence" that "heralded an age of royal impotence."[4] While this solid interpretive *basso continuo* plays on, Tamar Herzog has posited that wealthy purchasers on the Quito *audiencia* primarily sought social recognition rather

---

[2] The term *executive* is found in Christopher Storrs, *The Resilience of the Spanish Monarchy, 1665–1700* (Oxford: Oxford University Press, 2006), 188, replacing the controversial term *absolutism*, which according to Thompson, "Absolutism, Legalism," 225, is used to signify the intent to change the "ethos of government from a judicialist to an administrative mode."

[3] Francisco Tomás y Valiente, "Les ventes des offices publics en Castille aux XVIIe et XVIIIe siècles," in *Ämterkäuflichkeit: Aspekte sozialer Mobilität im europäischen Vergleich (17. und 18. Jahrhundert)*, ed. Klaus Malettke (Berlin: Colloquium Verlag, 1980), 100–101; Tomás y Valiente, *La venta de oficios en Indias (1492–1606)* (Madrid: Instituto de Estudios Administrativos, 1972), 46–51, 111–115; José Antonio Maravall, *Estado moderno y mentalidad social (siglos XV a XVII)* (Madrid: Ediciones de la Revista de Occidente, 1972), 2: 482–487.

[4] Burkholder and Chandler, *From Impotence to Authority*, 17, 20, see also 9–41; Burkholder and Chandler, "Creole Appointments and the Sale of Audiencia Positions in the Spanish Empire under the Early Bourbons, 1701–1750," *Journal of Latin American Studies* 4, no. 2 (1972): 189–190; Burkholder, "Honest Judges Leave Destitute Heirs: The Price of Integrity in Eighteenth-Century Spain," in Matthews, *Virtue, Corruption, and Self-Interest*, 247–248, 251, 254–258, 263. Burkholder, *Spaniards in the Colonial Empire: Creoles vs. Peninsulars?* (Chichester, UK: Wiley-Blackwell, 2013), esp. 74, 83, 97, stresses creole influence; Andrien, "The Sale of Fiscal Offices and the Decline of Royal Authority in the Viceroyalty of Peru, 1633–1700," *HAHR* 62, no. 1 (1982): 50, agreed that selling appointments allowed "untrained, inefficient, and even dishonest officials to exercise power." Andrien, *The Kingdom of Quito, 1690–1830: The State and Regional Development* (Cambridge: Cambridge University Press, 1995), 165–180, emphasizes socioeconomic factors; see also Parry, *Sale of Public Office*, 51–54, 60–63.

than riches and were therefore less corrupt.[5] In her view, conflicts erupted mainly when local social networks sought to hinder their enemies from taking office.[6] I argue that, if anything, the sale enhanced royal power by considering able applicants of lower origins that lacked the necessary ties of patronage to attain positions. My argument on the *beneficio* therefore also feeds into the ongoing scholarly reevaluation of imperial decline in the later seventeenth century.[7]

---

[5] Andújar Castillo, *El sonido del dinero: Monarquía, ejército y venalidad en la España del siglo XVIII* (Madrid: Marcial Pons, 2004), 7, see also 18–23, 26, meticulously shows the "scandalous" venality of officers extending into Charles III's reign. See also Andújar Castillo, *Necesidad y venalidad: España e Indias, 1704–1711* (Madrid: Centro de Estudios Políticos y Constitucionales, 2008), 9; Andújar Castillo, "Prólogo," 14; Andújar Castillo, "Cuando el rey delegaba la gracia," 154–156, also cautions against "idyllical" views, because the councilors themselves sold the posts. Ponce-Leiva and Andújar Castillo, "Introducción," 8, argue that selling offices or honors, "was never understood as comparable to corruption." See also Burgos Lejonagoitia, *Gobernar las Indias*, 457, 470; Moreno Cebrián, "La Confusión entre lo público y lo privado en el reinado de Felipe V," *Boletin de Historia y Antigüedades* 93, no. 835 (2006): 854; see also the thoughtful analysis by Roberta Stumpf, "Formas de venalidade de ofícios na monarquia portuguesa de século xviii," in *Cargos e ofícios nas monarquias ibéricas: Provimento, controlo e venalidade (séculos XVII–XVIII)*, eds. Roberta Stumpf and Nandini Chaturvedula (Lisbon: Centro de História de Além-Mar, 2012), 293–295; Chaturvedula, "Entre particulares: venalidade na Índia portuguesa no século xvii," ibid., 267–277. Inés Gómez, "Entre la corrupción y la venalidad," 246, argues that the councilor of Finance, Pedro Valle de la Cerda, committed "innumerable frauds" because of his "corrupt and venal trajectory." Burns, *Into the Archive*, 12–13, 63 cites this view, although her focus is clearly elsewhere.

[6] Herzog, *Upholding Justice*, 77–83, 89–90. Cañeque, *Living Image*, 177, even avers that contemporaries overwhelmingly did not see "the sale of offices ... as a corrupt practice whatsoever," provided that the offices "were sold to capable and suitable persons, at moderate prices." Bertrand, "La élite colonial en la Nueva España del siglo XVIII: un planteamiento en términos de redes sociales," in *Beneméritos, aristócratas y empresarios: Identidades y estructuras sociales de las capas altas urbanas en América hispánica*, eds. Bernd Schröter and Christian Büschges (Frankfurt: Vervuert, 1999), 39–41, argues that venal and meritorious officials shared similar biographies. Henry Kamen, *Spain in the Later Seventeenth Century, 1665–1700* (London: Longman, 1980), 33; Reinhard, *Geschichte*, 190–195; Doyle, *Venality*, 7–9, 238–272; García García, "Corrupción y venalidad, 13–38, contend that venality did not corrupt the monarchies. These works build on Mousnier, *La vénalité*, 85–89, 594–603, 665–668; and Mousnier, *The Organs of State and Society*, vol. 2 of *The Institutions of France under the Absolute Monarchy, 1598–1789*, trans. Arthur Goldhammer (Chicago: University of Chicago Press, 1984), 27–59, esp. 57–59.

[7] Kamen, *Spain*, vii; John Lynch, *The Hispanic World in Crisis and Change, 1598–1700* (Oxford: Blackwell, 1992), 249–251, 276; Christian Hermann and Jacques Marcadé, *Les royaumes ibériques au XVIIe siècle* (Paris: SEDES, 2000), 14–16; Storrs, *Resilience*, 10–14.

This chapter begins by tracing the evolving stances on selling offices since about the mid-seventeenth century, which laid the foundation for the first *beneficio* of *alcaldes mayores* of New Spain in 1675. The chapter explores the bitter infighting at the Spanish court and shows that the changing governments expanded or cut back the *beneficio* in tune with their political aims. In addition, I compare the appointments of the first Count of Revillagigedo, viceroy of New Spain (1746–1755), with that of his predecessors to demonstrate the dramatic erosion of viceregal patronage and the strengthening of royal power. The analysis ends in 1750/51, when the sales of appointments for positions in New Spain terminated.[8]

4.1 SELLING APPOINTMENTS CONFLICTED WITH JUSTICE

Many early modern theologians and jurists insisted that offices should be awarded according to distributive justice, that is, taking into account the social station of the recipients. These scholars maintained that the king should select candidates for their merits and not for passion or friendship. By the mid-seventeenth century, most jurists of the great Councils or the *audiencias* agreed with this view and rejected *beneficio* as a violation of the distributive justice. The Augustinian Martín de Azpilcueta (1491/93–1586) meanwhile justified the expanding sales as long as the appointees were suitable. By the early eighteenth century, Azpilcueta's view influenced those who were less tied to the Council jurists and aristocracy. They accepted the pervasive use of *beneficio*, which opened doors for social newcomers to join the judiciary.

The discussion over the sale of appointments had deep historical roots. Many Romans condemned the sale, and some medieval scholars stigmatized selling judicial offices as simony, that is, the sale of spiritual things or even Jesus Christ himself. Jurists and theologians hammered out a distinction between offices with and without judicial authority. Consequently, the Spanish crown could legally only sell offices without jurisdiction, such as notaries. The purchasers of these positions acquired the right to bequeath inheritable offices to their children, among other privileges. Yet the crown also began selling the appointments to offices without relinquishing these privileges and expanded the practice during financial emergencies, such as in 1591 after the defeat of the great Armada fleet. In 1633, the crown began offering treasury office appointments through *beneficio*. By the mid-seventeenth century, *beneficio* still angered

---

[8] Valle Menéndez, *Juan Francisco de Güemes*, 337, 366–67, 630.

many literati, who discussed the practice in similar terms as previous authorities had debated venality, that is, the royal sale of offices.[9]

Awarding an office was, in most cases, a matter of justice. For the Dominican Thomas Aquinas (1224/25–1274), justice balanced the relations of humans with each other, and its two main aspects consisted of commutative and distributive justice. Commutative justice concerned people who interacted on an equal level, such as when trading goods or receiving payments for services to the community. A scribe, for example, should charge all his customers the same fees for performing the same paperwork. Meanwhile, distributive justice assigned burdens and entitlements to the individuals according to their social rank. Distributive justice stipulated that "so much the more is given from the common stock as the recipient holds more prominence in the community." As a consequence, a person of higher standing received more of the available rewards. The distributive justice reflected the values of the early modern society and differed starkly from our modern notion of giving to the less privileged to mitigate social injustice.[10]

---

[9] *Law of the Indies*, book 8, title 20, law 1; Castillo de Bobadilla, *Política*, book 2, chap. 11, no. 21. *Beneficio* was the sale of revocable appointments to noninheritable offices, probably named after the similar Church positions called *beneficia*. On this issue, see Ángel Sanz Tapia, "Aproximación al beneficio de cargos políticos americanos en la primera mitad del siglo XVIII," *Revista Complutense de Historia de América*, no. 24 (1998): 155–156, 161; Sanz Tapia, *¿Corrupción o necesidad? La venta de cargos de Gobierno americanos bajo Carlos II (1674–1700)* (Madrid: CSIC, 2009), 30–31, 53–56; Andújar Castillo, *Necesidad*, 9; Andújar Castillo, *El sonido*, 18; Reinhard, "Staatsmacht als Kreditproblem: Zur Struktur und Funktion des frühneuzeitlichen Ämterhandels," in *Absolutismus*, ed. Ernst Hinrichs (Frankfurt: Suhrkamp, 1986), 216–224; Reinhard, *Geschichte der Staatsgewalt*, 190–191; Herzog, *Upholding Justice*, 71; Pietschmann, "Alcaldes Mayores," 186; Teresa Nava Rodríguez and Gloria Franco Rubio, "Vénalité et futuras dans l'administration espagnole au XVIIIe siècle," in Descimon, Schaub, and Vincent, *Les figures*, 98–99. The term *venal* often conveys a sense of abuse, and I mostly use the more neutral phrases of selling of appointments, tenures, or offices. Burkholder and Chandler, *From Impotence to Authority*, 19, include *beneficio* of *audiencia* positions in the term *venal*, while according to Reinhard, "Staatsmacht," 214, Mousnier distinguished royal venality from private "commerce of offices."

[10] Aquinas, *Summa* IIa–IIae, Q. 61, art. 2, ad.; art. 3, arg. 2, see also arts. 1–3; Q. 21, art. 1, drawing on Aristotle, *Nicomachean Ethics*, trans. W. D. Ross (1908), book 5, secs. 2–4, http://classics.mit.edu/Aristotle/nicomachaen.5.v.html. Note that the third aspect of justice was the *iustitia legalis*, the duty of the individual toward the community. Juan de Azcargorta, *Manual de Confesores*, 273–275, fully explains the two concepts in the early eighteenth century. See also John Finnis, "Aquinas' Moral, Political, and Legal Philosophy," in *The Stanford Encyclopedia of Philosophy*, ed. Edward N. Zalta (Fall 2011 Edition), http://plato.stanford.edu/entries/aquinas-moral-political/; Brendecke, *Imperio*, 78–82. On distributive justice as an "argument of social estates," Ponce-Leiva, "El valor de los méritos. Teoría y práctica política en la provisión de oficios (Quito, 1675–1700)," *Revista de Indias* 73, no. 258 (2013): 351; Werner Veith, "Gerechtigkeit,"

Aquinas favored considering both aspects of justice when appointing someone to an office, because offices were a reward for the deserving and a service to the public. Selling appointments conflicted with distributive justice, because money replaced merit. Under commutative justice, the sale of non-ecclesiastical offices may have been permissible, Aquinas averred, as long as able people did not pay more than what the office yielded in fees. Nonetheless, Aquinas held that selling was not useful, because it excluded the suitable and benevolent. Those who bought were "ambitious and lovers of money" who would exploit the public and poorly serve the government. Aquinas did not really discuss professional qualifications of candidates, because they hardly existed in the medieval period; instead, he cared for merit in the sense of character, social standing, and distinguished extraction.[11]

Thomas Aquinas remained a guiding authority in Iberian scholasticism until the early eighteenth century, and distributive justice formed the touchstone for discussing *beneficio*. The councilor of Castile, Cristóbal de Moscoso y Córdoba, even titled his mid-seventeenth-century treatise the "Discourse ... on Whether It is Licit for Kings to Sell Offices ... and What Saint Thomas Felt about This Issue."[12] Distributive justice, for example, explains why the crown traditionally named aristocrats as the viceroys of New Spain. Their social group deserved the prestigious rewards. In turn, the viceroys themselves should appoint the most deserving offspring of the conquistadors by considering "distributive justice," the jurist Juan de Solórzano y Pereyra suggested.[13]

---

in *Christliche Sozialethik. Ein Lehrbuch. Band 1: Grundlagen*, ed. Marianne Heimbach-Steins (Regensburg: Pustet, 2004), 316–319; Böckenförde, *Geschichte*, 246–247.

[11] According to Aquinas, "Letter," 235–238, not useful (*non expediens*), cited by, for one, Solórzano, *Política*, book 6, chap. 13, no. 5.

[12] Cristóbal de Moscoso y Córdoba, "Discurso," BPR, Ms. II/2843, fols. 32r–53; Génaux, "Fields of Vision," 113, argues that selling offices was rejected because of "changes in the nature of *service* for the king, once money had replaced merit in the selection process."

[13] Solórzano, *Política*, book v, chap. xii, paras. 35–39, 45, 47, 48, quote in para. 39. According to Burkholder, *Spaniards*, 63; Hespanha, "Paradigmes de légitimation," 22, distributive justice also called for sharing desirable posts among Americans, peninsular Spaniards, and the clients of the viceroys. The Portuguese statesman Torres de Lima, *Compendio*, 130–131, held that "ministers, governors, generals, and councilors who distributively work for the general good, the increase and conservation of the vassals and the realm, serve just government." Jean Bodin, *Los seis libros de la republica* [...] *traducidos de lengua Francesa, y enmendados Catholicamente: por Gaspar de Añastro y Sunza* (Turin: Herederos de Bevilacqua, 1590), book 6, chap. 6, meanwhile opposed distributive justice, which, according to Aristotle's usage, he called geometric justice: "[G]eometric justice which is giving weight to the wealth and the offense, has no need for laws ... and the variety of people, of the cases, of time, of space is infinite and

Azpilcueta later reinterpreted Aquinas to justify the royal sale of office under some conditions. Azpilcueta agreed that it would be better not to sell office, yet he opposed censoring the kings for "giving them [the offices] for money, as dowry, or in reward for their services." The king did have to exclude those "ignorant or of bad conscience" and instead confer the posts "for an honest price to suitable persons." In Azpilcueta's opinion, only the king of a realm wielded the *dominium* (power akin to private property) to sell offices, which excluded aristocrats and courtiers from giving out positions. This restriction applied to the viceroys in the Americas, too.[14]

Aquinas and Azpilcueta staked out the central arguments discussed in the Iberian empire.[15] Later, Councilor Cristóbal de Moscoso y Córdoba rejected Azpilcueta by reinterpreting Aquinas. Moscoso y Córdoba contended that Aquinas had only theoretically allowed the sale of offices. On a practical level, however, Aquinas advised never to sell jurisdictional offices because it meant "sinning mortally."[16] Following in his footsteps, Pedro de Portocarrero y Guzmán, an aristocratic canon of the cathedral of

---

incomprehensible." According to Gil, "Spain and Portugal," 435, the Church put Bodin on the index in 1612, and Spaniards could not easily cite his views directly anymore.

[14] Azpilcueta, *Manual de confesores y penitentes que contiene casi todas las dudas que en las Confesiones suelen occurrir los peccados*, 2nd ed. (Valladolid: Francisco Fernández Córdoba, 1570), chap. 25, para. 7 (note that all citations in this chapter stem from this edition). Antunez Portugal, *Tractatus*, part 2, book 1, chap. 14, para. 2, agreed; see also part 2, book 1, chap. 14, para. 16. Portocarrero y Guzmán, *Theatro*, 373, cited Antunez Portugal. Nonetheless, Zeballos, *Arte Real*, fol. 76v, held that the kings "are not the absolute lords to give but prudent administrators." On *dominium*, see Gil, "Spain and Portugal," 426.

[15] For example, Antunez Portugal, *Tractatus*, part. 2, book 1, chap. 14, para. 2, cited Domingo de Soto and Cajetan, who elaborated on the key arguments made by Aquinas. See Soto, *De iustitia*, 2: 266–271; Thomas Cajetan, *De peccatis summula* (Antwerp: Petrus Bellerus, 1575), 433.

[16] Moscoso y Córdoba, "Discurso," BPR, Ms. II/2843 fol. 48, see also fols. 38v–49. See also Castillo de Bobadilla, *Politica*, book 3, chap. 8, paras. 285–289. On Moscoso y Córdoba, see Javier Barrientos Grandon, "Guía prosopográfica de la judicatura letrada indiana (1503–1898)," in *Nuevas aportaciones a la historia jurídica de Iberoamérica*, ed. José Andrés-Gallego (Madrid: Fundación Histórica Tavera, 2000. CD-ROM), 985–986. Solórzano, *Politica*, book 5, chap. 2, no. 17, see also nos. 3, 4, 6, acknowledged that common opinion allowed selling appointments according to the counsel of Saint Thomas as explained by Azpilcueta. According to Miguel Ángel Ochoa Brun, "Vida, obra y doctrina de Juan de Solórzano y Pereyra," in *Politica Indiana*, ed. Miguel Ángel Ochoa Brun (Madrid: Atlas, 1972), vol. 1, xvii–xxv; Phelan, *Kingdom*, 160, Solórzano was the Count-Duke of Olivares' protégé. That explains why Solórzano condemned venality in milder terms than his fellow jurists did. He insisted nonetheless that those who purchased *alcalde mayor* tenures would become "tyrants and robbers" and succumb to *corruptela* (corruption). Solórzano's *Politica Indiana* was published in Latin in 1629 and in Spanish in 1648, and republished between 1736 and 1739.

Toledo, acerbically attacked selling offices. Portocarrero y Guzmán finished his treatise in or before March 1700, during the decline of the childless Habsburg king Charles II (r. 1665–1700). At that point, the succession to the crown was still up in the air.[17] Portocarrero y Guzmán exhorted any future king to guard the privileges of the aristocracy and the upper clergy. In the *sic et non* (yes and no) fashion of late scholasticism, Portocarrero y Guzmán first refuted Azpilcueta's stance. Then he suggested that the next king should deny the accession of unworthy candidates to the judiciary, because the "incapable and ambitious friends of money obtain the offices and seriously injure you and your vassals."[18]

Most aristocrats, and the jurists who sat on the great Councils or the *audiencias*, agreed. They rejected selling appointments, because they were the beneficiaries of distributive justice. These jurists often hailed from the municipal oligarchies of Castile. Most gained their coveted positions because they had belonged to one of the six exclusive *colegios mayores* (study halls) at the three preeminent universities of Spain – Salamanca, Valladolid, and Alcalá de Henares. These jurists largely opposed *beneficio*, because it diminished the patronage power of the great Councils and its committees and undermined the privileged access of their own social group to the posts.[19]

---

[17] Censor's review on 21 Mar. 1700, in Portocarrero y Guzmán, *Theatro*, n. p. On the background of the author, see Gil, "Spain and Portugal," 456–457; Peña Izquierdo, "La crisis sucesoria de la monarquía española: El cardenal Portocarrero y el primer gobierno de Felipe V (1698–1705)," (PhD diss., Universidad Autónoma de Barcelona. 2005), 1: 463; Peña Izquierdo, *La casa*, 155–156, 207–210, 290–316; Joaquim E. López i Camps, "La embajada española del conde Ferdinand von Harrach y la formación del austracismo," in *Hispania-Austria III: Der Spanische Erbfolgekrieg: La Guerra de Sucesión española*, eds. Friedrich Edelmayer, Virginia León Sanz, and José Ignacio Ruiz Rodríguez (Munich: Oldenbourg, 2008), 20–25. According to Andújar Castillo, *Necesidad*, 33, Pedro de Portocarrero argued for not condemning princes who sold appointments; see also Cañeque, *Living Image*, 178.

[18] Portocarrero y Guzmán, *Theatro*, 377, see also 372–377, citing Pierre Grégoire of Toulouse (1540–1617), *De republica*, book 2, chap. 6, para. 17; Antunez Portugal, *Tractatus*, part. 2, book 1, chap. 14, esp. paras. 6–7. According to Gil, "Spain and Portugal," 435, 451–452, Grégoire transmitted much of Jean Bodin's teachings to the peninsula. Bodin, *Six Books*, chap. 2, and chap. 4, para. 10, argued that "the sale of honors, offices, and benefices is the most pernicious and sordid," because "those who put honors, offices, and benefices up for sale, thereby sell the most precious thing in this world, and that is justice."

[19] Dedieu, "La haute administration," 170–171; Burkholder and Chandler, *From Impotence to Authority*, 32; Herzog, *Upholding Justice*, 78–79. María del Mar Felices de la Fuente, "Hacia la nobleza titulada: Los "méritos" para titular en el siglo XVII," in Andújar Castillo and Ponce-Leiva, *Mérito, venalidad y corrupción*, 25, adds that the Inquisition opposed selling titles of nobility.

Nevertheless, the political authors less tied to this social group differed. Francisco de Seijas y Lobera, who lived an extended period in America, largely accepted the sale of appointments. Seijas y Lobera served as *alcalde mayor* of Tacuba in New Spain from 1692 to 1695 and quarreled with the viceroy and the *audiencia*. When the *audiencia* sentenced him to forced service in an African fortress, Seijas y Lobera fled to Peru, where he again clashed with the viceroy. Seijas y Lobera then returned to Europe and settled in Versailles (France). At that point, a French clique largely conducted the politics of the young king Philip V in Spain. Seijas y Lobera's view reflected, to an extent, these new policies. For example, he excoriated the *audiencia* ministers who were promoted because they had married a relative of a councilor of the Indies rather than the ministers who obtained their posts through *beneficio*.[20] In addition, the legal adviser of the viceroy of New Spain, José Meléndez, agreed with Seijas y Lobera on *beneficio* in 1725. Meléndez first cited the Roman emperor Severus Alexander (222–235), who had suggested that the person "who buys has to resell." Yet Meléndez observed that other scholars allowed *beneficio*, because the kings were the lords of the offices. Even if the kings were only their dispensers, they could still sell the posts, because they were supreme judges. Meléndez reframed the prevalent arguments to tolerate *beneficio*, which had become widespread and often served American interests.[21]

[20] Francisco de Seija y Lobera to Viceroy Galve, Mexico City, 25 Jan. 1695, AGI, México 627, *cuaderno* 5, fol. 12; *Informe* of Francisco de Seija y Lobera to king, n. d., before 1704, AGI, México 628; *parecer* of the prosecutor of the Council of the Indies, Madrid, 17 May 1704, AGI, México 628; *consulta* of the Council of the Indies, Madrid, 29 Apr. 1704, AGI, México 628. See also Francisco de Seijas y Lobera, *Gobierno militar y político del reino imperial de la Nueva España (1702)*, ed. Pablo Emilio Pérez-Mallaína Bueno (Mexico City: UNAM, 1986), 202–203. On *arbitrismo*, the literature to improve the empire, see, Eagle, "Restoring Spanish Hispaniola," the First of the Indies: Local Advocacy and Transatlantic *Arbitrismo* in the Late Seventeenth Century," *Colonial Latin American Review* 23, no.3 (2014): 387–412; Christian Herrmann, "L'Arbitrisme: Un autre état pour un autre Espagne, in *Le premier âge de l'état en Espagne (1450–1700)*, ed. Christian Hermann (Paris: Editions du Centre National de la Recherche Scientifique, 1989), 239–356.

[21] *Parecer* of Dr. José Meléndez, Mexico City, 22 Jan. 1725, AGI, México 492, *cuaderno* 8, fol. 105, see also fols. 101–105, reinterpreting Pierre Grégoire, *De republica*, book 2, chap. 6, para. 17, who attributed this doctrine to Severus Alexander. According to Aelius Lampridius, *The Life of Severus Alexander*, trans. David Magie (Loeb Classical Library, 1921), part 2, para. 49, 1, http://penelope.uchicago.edu/Thayer/E/Roman/Texts/Historia_Augusta/Severus_Alexander/2*.html, Severus Alexander argued that "it is necessary that he who buys also sells, and I will not allow that merchants have authority, for if I allow that, then I cannot punish them." See also "Imperator Caesar M. Aurelius Severus Alexander Augustus," in *Brill's Encyclopedia of the Ancient World*, eds. Hubert Cancik and Helmuth Schneider (Leiden: Brill, 2008), 13: 360–361.

While the sale of appointments expanded, early modern scholars also discussed how to reconcile distributive justice with the ubiquitous patronage. Candidates for office ritually emphasized their and their forebears' "feudal" – that is, direct and personal – contract with the king. They had provided their services at risk, cost, or with toil, and they had not received a commensurate gratification that they deserved according to distributive justice, especially for their age or lack of means. Yet Spaniards were also keenly aware that the "economy of favor," that is, the recommendation of a patron and the influence of a client network, profoundly shaped their biographies.[22] Non-elite families typically stretched their resources so that a noble house groomed their sons and daughters to attain merit. The clients endured long years working without wages to acquire the necessary "cultural capital." These applicants deserved a reward that corresponded to their merit, and they hoped that aristocrats and ministers interceded for them for jobs. The prospect of the patron's recommendation and the actual appointment to an office justified the long unpaid service.[23]

Early modern contemporaries well perceived the latent tension between bountifully providing for clients and justly choosing good ministers. Clients usually applauded generosity in distributing rewards and offices.[24] They often drew on the Roman philosopher Seneca (c. 4 BC–65), for whom it was "less dishonorable to be vanquished by arms than in liberality."[25] Seneca's work was reedited in 1605 and became popular in Spain and in New Spain after 1650. Yet Seneca also cautioned against lavish rewards as a means in itself. Instead, he endorsed giving on equal terms among social peers, adding that "we must also consider the character and position of the person to whom we give, for some men are too great to give small gifts, while others are too small to receive great ones."[26] Such ideas rang of distributive justice,

---

[22] Antonio Manuel Hespanha, "Les autre raisons de la politique. L'économie de la grâce," 67–86 (span. transl. "La economía de la gracia"), coined the term "economy of favor."
[23] Based on Pierre Bourdieu, "The Forms of Capital," in *Handbook of Theory and Research for the Sociology of Education*, ed. John G. Richardson (New York: Greenwood, 1986), 47–51; Thompson, "Do ut des," 285–286, 294; Heiko Droste, "Patronage in der frühen Neuzeit: Institutionen und Kulturformen," *Zeitschrift für Historische Forschung* 30 (2003): 578, 583–584, 588.
[24] Cañeque, *Living Image*, 157–162.
[25] Seneca, *De consolatione ad Polybium*, in *Moral Essays*, ed. John W. Basore, vol. 2 (London and New York: Heinemann, 1932), chap. 12, para. 3, www.perseus.tufts.edu/hopper/collections, cited literally by Mendo, *Príncipe Perfecto*, 172.
[26] Seneca, *On Benefits*, trans. Aubrey Stewart (London, 1887), book 2, chap. 15, www.gutenberg.org/3/7/9/3794/; see also Cárdenas Gutiérrez, "La lucha contra la corrupción," 723–724. According to R. V. Young, "Introduction," in Justus Lipsius, *Concerning Constancy* (Tempe, AZ: ACMRS, 2011), xx–xxi, early modern observers attacked

which, in part, explains Seneca's popularity. Many agreed with Seneca on balancing generosity against distributive justice. The Jesuit Andrés Mendo, for instance, maintained that "when the prince is too liberal in giving, he will make the vassals greedy in asking." Mendo suggested that the king abstain from being "extreme in generosity" and adjust favors to the quality of the people.[27]

The king could show some partiality in appointing ministers but naming for other criteria than merit meant committing a crime. Many commentators observed that patrons should not give offices to friends and partisans only for paying court or giving illicit favors. In 1609, the Augustinian Juan Zapata y Sandoval, for example, characterized selecting someone for "kinship or blood relationship" rather than merit as "a sin which opposes distributive justice."[28] Spaniards often called promoting a less dignified person for friendship, favor, or passion the "inhuman crime" of acceptation. The intercession of a patron with the king was only then appropriate, they said, when the applicant was worthy of the post. Worthy, of course, did not mean examined performance on the job, but merit in the traditional sense, including a heavy dose of social origin.[29]

Seneca for preaching water while drinking the insane emperor Nero's wine. Yet according to Griffin, *Seneca*, 2–14, 188, Seneca insisted on the strict mores of the Roman nobility, fell out with Nero after Rome burned in 64 AD, and committed suicide in 65.

[27] Mendo, *Príncipe Perfecto*, 172 (republished in 1662), citing Seneca, *On Benefits*, book 2, chap. 15; see also Portocarrero y Guzmán, *Theatro*, 128, 174, 343, 367; Zeballos, *Arte Real*, fols. 75–76v. According to Aquinas, *Summa* II–IIae, Q. 61, art. 1, ad. 1; *Summa*, IIa–IIae, Q. 188, art. 7, ad. 1, see also Q. 117, art. 6, "moderation be showed in dispensing community goods," because "liberality is not a principal virtue," and "a prodigal man is a fool rather than a knave," citing Aristotle, *Ethics*, iv, 1. Machiavelli, *The Prince*, eds. Quentin Skinner and Russel Price (Cambridge: Cambridge University Press, 1988), 57–58, often viewed critically in Spain, suggested that "therefore, it is shrewder to cultivate a reputation for meanness ... than ... through wanting to be considered generous, to incur a reputation for rapacity." Machiavelli, "Discorsi," book 1, chap. 18, added that "the Roman people no longer valued virtue but favor in bestowing the consulship, drawing to that dignity those who better knew how to court men than those who better knew how to conquer their enemies." www.classicitaliani.it/machiav/mac32.htm#18. The *Law of the Indies*, book 2, title 15, laws 24, 31; book 3, title 2, law 27, also circumscribed patronage.

[28] Zapata y Sandoval, *Disceptación*, part 1, chap. 4, para. 9; chap. 5, para. 7.

[29] On *crimen acceptionis personarum*, Fernández de Otero, *Tractatus*, part 1, chap. 3, paras. 1 and 24; de Soto, *De iustitia*, 2: 250–251, 271; J. F. Niermeyer, C. Van de Kieft, and G. S. M. M. Lake Schoonebeek, *Mediae Latinintatis Lexicon Minus* (Leiden: Brill, 1976), 10. There seems to be some overlap between *acepción* and *excepción*; consider Portocarrero y Guzmán, *Theatro*, 337, for whom the "distribution of an award ... which does not correspond to merit without excepting anyone, disturbs the minds and is perhaps oppression"; similarly, Berart y Gassol, *Speculum visitationis*, chap. 9, para. 8, favored administering justice "*sine personarum exceptione* (without excepting people)."

4.2 SEIZING POWER FOR THE CROWN

The debate over *beneficio* spilled over to the court in Madrid. At that time, Queen Mariana of Austria (1634–1696) and her favorite ministers seized the opportunity to cut back on the patronage power of the viceroys. In 1675, the queen and her favorite began selling several appointments through *beneficio*. While historians originally criticized spineless favorites for this decadent practice, they now accept that the favorites led successful governments and initiated important reforms. In this new view, the favorites often opposed the aims of the aristocracy, the upper clergy, and the jurists of the great councils.[30] When the queen and her favorite curtailed viceregal patronage, they also curbed the quantity of cash and gifts that *novohispano* (colonial Mexican) candidates for offices showered on the viceroys. The queen's move diminished the viceroys' ability to place their retainers in lush positions. This change made the long unpaid service in aristocratic houses less attractive.

By the mid-seventeenth century, many clergymen and ministers criticized the vast patronage of the viceroys, who used their faculties to sell numerous appointments of *alcaldes mayores*. The candidates paid considerable sums for appointments in the wealthy regions where Indians produced the precious dyestuff cochineal. While the *alcaldes mayores* received only a meager salary from the crown, they traded with the locals

---

Ponce-Leiva, "El valor de los méritos," 352; Ponce-Leiva, "Percepciones sobre la corrupción," 204; points to the conflict between intercession and the crime of aceptación.

[30] Tomás y Valiente, *Los validos en la monarquía española del siglo XVII: Estudio institucional* (Madrid: Siglo Veintiuno, 1982), reinterpreted the favorites or chief ministers. Feros, *Kingship and Favoritism*, 1–5, 129–140, 173–182, 186, views the Duke of Lerma as a genuine precursor of the chief ministers for expanding King Philip III's (1598–1621) autonomy from the councils. Lerma also expelled some of the queen's ladies-in-waiting from the court and cut out parts of the aristocracy from coveted posts. Political enemies attacked this form of patronage for excluding them from the spoils. The Council of Castile convicted a client of Lerma for selling offices and accepting bribes from foreign princes; see also Thiessen, "Korruption," 99–111; for Phelan, *Kingdom of Quito*, 157, and Burkholder, "Honest Judges," 249, Lerma was the pinnacle of corrupt patronage. James M. Boyden, *The Courtier and the King: Ruy Gómez de Silva, Philip II, and the Court of Spain* (Berkeley, Los Angeles: University of California Press, 1995), 63–66, shows that the declining *privanza* of Ruy Gómez de Silva inversely mirrored the growing self-confidence of King Philip II; see also Christian Büschges, "Del criado al valido. El padronazgo de los virreyes de Nápoles y Nueva España (primera mitad del siglo XVII)," in *Las cortes virreinales de la Monarquía española: América e Italia. Actas del Coloquio Internacional, Sevilla, 1–4 Junio 2005*, ed. Francesca Cantú (Rome: Viella, 2008), 165–173. On patronage of these chief ministers in general, Asch and Birke, eds., *Princes, Patronage and the Nobility: The Court at the Beginning of the Modern Age, c. 1450–1650* (Oxford: Oxford University Press, 1991), 21.

and took a cut from the tribute collection to make a living and pay back the viceroy. Many in Madrid knew about this practice. Bishop Juan de Palafox, the *visitador general* (investigative judge) of New Spain (1639–1647), had lambasted the custom in his reports.[31]

The criticism of the viceroys exacerbated after the 1660 revolt in Tehuantepec, when Natives killed their *alcalde mayor* for deteriorating prices and ruthless methods to recover credits. Discontent also erupted in Nexapa and the highlands of Villa Alta.[32] These incidents were bad news for the court in Madrid, which worried about large-scale Indian unrest. In 1663, the prosecutor of the Council of the Indies blamed the guilt squarely on the Viceroy Marquis of Leyva. Leyva had sold the appointments for the *alcaldes mayores* at excessive prices, forcing the *alcaldes mayores* to gouge the locals to recover their expenses. The prosecutor recommended that, in future, the Council of the Indies' patronage committee or "*cámara* should appoint to the *alcaldías mayores* [offices of the *alcaldes mayores*] of greater value," while the municipal magistrates of the Spanish towns should administer the remaining districts.[33] In the next year, the bishop of Michoacan blamed the greedy retainers of the viceroy for the problems. He suggested that the Spanish town halls and the trade guilds should elect magistrates to govern their districts. The solution to the excessive viceregal patronage was therefore to move control from the viceroys to Madrid or to devolve it to the local social bodies.[34]

Queen Mariana and her favorite capitalized on the Tehuantepec revolt to bring about larger changes in the imperial framework. Her first attempt to curtail viceregal patronage derailed in 1669, however, when the opposition orchestrated the downfall of her favorite. Yet soon a successor emerged. Fernando Valenzuela, the son of a tax farmer, rose to power by 1673. He tackled social problems with a populist approach, financing public works, attempting to rein in inflation, and cutting the number of councilors. Valenzuela confronted the aristocracy, which accused him of selling even the prestigious court offices traditionally reserved for their

---

[31] Álvarez de Toledo, *Politics and Reform*, 145; Pietschmann, "Alcaldes Mayores," 188, esp. note 37a; Alberto Yalí Román, "Sobre alcaldías mayores y corregimientos en Indias: Un ensayo de interpretación," *Jahrbuch für Geschichte von Staat, Wirtschaft und Gesellschaft Lateinamerikas* 9 (1972): 28–29.

[32] Owensby, *Empire of Law*, 252–290; Yannakakis, *The Art of Being*, 33–34.

[33] *Parecer* of the prosecutor, Madrid, 24 Nov. 1663, AGI, México 600.

[34] Marcos Ramírez de Prado to king, Valladolid, 16 July 1664, AGI, México 600. On the prelate, see Traslosheros, *La reforma de la iglesia*, 2–7.

kin. Rather than changing course, the government took on the viceroys, who, until 1722, usually hailed from aristocratic families.[35]

The queen and Valenzuela legitimized the shift in patronage. In December 1674, Mariana wrote to fray Payo Enríquez de Ribera, the archbishop of Mexico City and interim viceroy (1673–1680). She ordered him to verify rumors that the *alcaldes mayores* of the cochineal-producing Villa Alta district in Oaxaca paid large bribes for their appointments. She also demanded information whether the *cámara* should in the future propose the candidates for these important districts. Enríquez de Ribera was the son of an aristocrat and probably no fan of transferring patronage to Madrid.[36] When he replied to Mariana in the following year, he avoided denying or confirming bribes for the appointments, which most jurists considered illegal. Enríquez de Ribera reported that according to "common opinion" and "people of truth and reputation," the *alcalde mayor* of Villa Alta paid the viceroys 24,000 pesos for the first year of tenure and subsequently 1,500 pesos each month thereafter. The *alcaldes mayores* also gave the viceroys merchandise, probably cochineal. When the letter reached Madrid, the Council of the Indies concluded that it would be better for the queen rather than the viceroys to choose the candidates. This also implied that the *cámara* would in future suggest many suitable people.[37]

---

[35] Peña Izquierdo, *La casa de Palma*, 172–174, 180–182; Storrs, *Resilience*, 123; Lynch, *Hispanic World*, 366–370. On viceroys, José Ignacio Rubio Mañé, *Introducción al estudio de los virreyes de Nueva España, 1535–1746* (Mexico City: UNAM, 1959), 1: 251–284, esp. 215, 266. According to Rafaella Pilo, *Juan Everardo Nithard y sus "causas no causas": Razones y pretextos para el fin de un valimiento* (Madrid: Silex, 2010), 79, a similar constellation of social groups opposed the former favorite Juan Everado Nithard (Johann Eberhard Nithard), claiming that "justice and distribution of awards are sold publicly." Felices de la Fuente, "Hacia la nobleza titulada," 24–29, observes that the aristocracy opposed Olivares for titling new nobles who supported his agenda.

[36] *Real cédula* to fray Payo Enríquez de Ribera (referring to *cédula* from 31 Dec. 1674), Madrid, 13 Feb. 1676, AGN, RCO 15, exp. 2. In addition, the Council presided over by the Count of Medellín recommended confirming Enríquez de Ribera as viceroy, but the queen rejected this. While somewhat speculative, this could point to the traditional view of Enríquez de Ribera, *consulta* of the Council of the Indies, Madrid, 1 Aug. 1675, AGI, México 7. On the dates of Payo Enríquez de Ribera's tenure, Rubio Mañé, *Introducción*, 1: 295. According to Pietschmann, "Alcaldes Mayores," 184, the Duke of Peralta, viceroy of Peru, defended appointing his clients to *alcaldías mayores* because they would otherwise not accompany him across the Atlantic.

[37] Payo Enríquez de Ribera probably to queen, 7 Nov. 1675; and *consulta* of the Council of the Indies, 27 Apr. 1676, summarized in *consulta* signed by Count of Medellín, Tomás de Valdes, Antonio de Castro, Juan de Santelices, and Bernabé de Ochoa, Madrid, 30 Apr. 1676, all of which appear in AGI, México 7.

Yet on April 3, 1675, the queen ordered the Count of Medellín, an aristocrat and president of the Council, to estimate the proceeds from selling appointments to all offices in the Indies. The queen assured Medellín that these sales "would not conflict directly with justice and conscience."[38] At the same time, the queen sought the moral high ground in the fight against corruption, and she declared that the public good required mending the defects in New Spain. She reissued *reales cédulas* (royal communications) prohibiting the crown-appointed *alcaldes mayores* from marrying within their districts and abusing the native population.[39] In 1676, the queen also assembled a *junta* (an ad hoc committee) of ministers and theologians to address the moral and legal hazards of *beneficio*. The *junta* concluded that the appointees "have to be suitable, the price proportionate and moderate, and that the proceeds go to public defense," echoing the views of Azpilcueta.[40] The *junta* cleared the way for the *beneficio* of the *alcaldías mayores* in Madrid, although the opposition was not idle. Pedro de Portocarrero y Guzmán later mocked these "courtier theologians" and challenged them to consider whether *beneficio* "is useful for maintaining the monarchy or if it is ruining it." The controversy over the *beneficio* grew bitter.[41]

One of the first *beneficio* cases demonstrates the struggle. A candidate requested appointment as the general of the fleet sailing to New Spain and as governor of Yucatan. He had served the crown for twenty-three years, and his father had sat on the Council of Orders. The *cámara*, presided over by the Count of Medellín, confirmed that the candidate was "a renowned subject." Nonetheless, the *cámara* protested sharply against the arrangement that the candidate would lend 100,000 pesos to the treasury, pointing out the "grief that this would cause the meritorious vassals of these kingdoms and the Indies, seeing themselves deprived of the reward that they could have expected for their services and risk of their life ... as it is a very dubious matter to ignore the distributive justice, upon which

---

[38] *Consulta* of the *cámara* of the Indies, Madrid, 21 Oct. 1676, AGI, México 362, R., N. 8, fol. 2.

[39] Royal decree, Madrid, 30 Apr. 1676, AGI, México 7. See also royal order, Madrid, 24 Mar. 1676, AGN, RCO 15, exp. 35; *real cédula*, Madrid, 11 Aug. 1676, Archivo Histórico Nacional, Madrid (hereinafter cited as AHN), Códices y Cartularios 684 B, fols. 2v–3v. With the *real cédula*, Madrid, 14 Feb. 1675, AGN, RCO 14, exp. 104, the queen had previously ordered the sale of all vacant renounceable offices.

[40] *Consulta* of the *cámara* of the Indies composed of Count of Medellín, Tomás de Valdes, and the Marquis of Santillán, Madrid, 21 Oct. 1676, AGI, México 362, R., N. 8, fols. 1–2r; Azpilcueta, *Manual de confesores*, chap. 25, para. 7.

[41] Portocarrero y Guzmán, *Theatro*, 374, 376.

depends everything of the universal government."[42] Distributive justice was alive for the *cámara*, whose chief concern was not that *beneficio* hampered performance in the modern sense. Instead, a wealthy subject set a precedent replacing merit in the traditional sense with cash. Yet despite the *cámara's* remonstrance, the queen appointed the candidate and cleared the way for further *beneficio*.

The Council of the Indies subsequently attacked the governor of Yucatan, but with little success, because he served the office well. In 1680, the Council recommended to investigate the governor's malfeasance and confiscate his estate. Yet the viceroy of New Spain, a partisan of the queen's former favorite, praised the governor for driving English settlers from the western shore of Yucatan. The queen titled the governor as a nobleman and assigned him an annual pension of 500 pesos. The governor exemplified that *beneficio* did not necessarily worsen the administration of justice or the military capability of the Americas.[43]

The controversy at the court also shows that the *beneficio* expanded not only in times of military conflict for financial reasons, as most historians argue.[44] Instead, governing coalitions expanded or cut back on *beneficio* in correspondence with their larger political aims. Don Juan (José) de Austria's coup against Valenzuela in 1676–1677 demonstrates this fact. Don Juan de Austria was the illegitimate son of King Philip IV and standard-bearer for the opposition. The aristocracy and the upper Church – that is, largely the traditional elites – supported don Juan de Austria. He marched on Madrid, entered the city without notable resistance, and ousted Valenzuela. Don Juan de Austria then ended the sale of *alcalde mayores* appointments, as he had promised during his campaign. As a result, the crown made no provision by *beneficio* between 1678 and 1681.[45]

---

[42] The candidate was Antonio de Layseca Alvarado, *consulta* of the *cámara* composed of Medellín, Valdes, and Santillán, Madrid, 21 Oct. 1676, AGI, México 362 R., N. 8, fols. 1–2v. According to Queen to Count of Medellín, Aranjuez, 20 May 1675, AGI, México 15, the first *beneficio* appointee was the alcalde mayor of Metepec, Captain Diego de Ableta y Moreda. The *consulta* of the *cámara*, Madrid, 21 Aug. 1674, AGI, Guadalajara 2, shows that the crown had rejected an earlier offer for the *alcaldía mayor* of either Xochitepec or Zacatecas for 1,000 dobloons and a loan of 12,000 pesos.

[43] According to *consultas* of the Council of the Indies, Madrid, 14 May 1680, and Madrid, 3 Sept. 1681, both in AGI, México 8, the governor fought the English at the *Laguna de Términos*. See also Governor Antonio de Layseca Alvarado to king, Madrid, 27 Sep. 1686, AGI, México 15. On the Viceroy Count of Paredes, Pilo, *Juan Everardo Nithard*, 101.

[44] Sanz Tapia, *¿Corrupción?*, 30–31, 60–61, 71; Burkholder, *Spaniards*, 100, 110.

[45] The *reales cédulas* from 28 Feb. 1678 and 24 May 1678 ended patronage of viceroys and presidents, referenced in *real cédula*, Madrid, 29 Feb. 1680, in Antonio Muro Orejón, ed. *Cedulario americano del siglo XVIII: Colección de disposiciones legales indianas desde*

When he died on September 17, 1679, the policy changed again. King Charles II had become of age by this time and ruled the empire advised by Queen Mariana. The Duke of Medinaceli took the reins of government on February 21, 1680, and presided over the Council of the Indies. Medinaceli restored a balance between the feuding factions at court, because he was a grandee (upper aristocrat), who had also supported Mariana and Valenzuela. In particular, Medinaceli sought to reduce foreign influence in American commerce. Gradually shifting course, Medinaceli ignored or changed the king's wishes against selling appointments, and he heeded the protests against the termination of viceregal patronage.[46] His government decided to reserve the most profitable districts in New Spain for the crown but wavered on allowing the viceroys to name six or twelve *alcaldes mayores*. Medinaceli and his government then decided that twelve viceregal retainers could serve *alcaldías mayores* at the same time. The Council of the Indies suggested that the viceroys appoint their retainers to two of the most profitable districts, five of the second class, and five of the third-class, corresponding to the estimated value of the districts. This compromise eased the way for a renewed expansion of *beneficio*. In addition to this change, the government also decreed selling *audiencia* appointments in 1680.[47]

Table 3 visualizes the connection between fluctuating numbers of *beneficios* for New Spain and Spanish America and the political changes in Madrid. The crown sold fifty appointments to *alcaldes mayores* in New Spain in the period 1675–1686.[48] After a wobbly start, the sale rose to include ten districts in 1677. When don Juan de Austria seized the government, the practice sharply fell for all of the Americas and ended completely for New Spain. The table registers this drop with a slight lag. The crown used other channels for the appointments during this period, including the

---

1680 a 1800, contenidas en los cedularios del Archivo General de Indias (Seville: Escuela de Estudios Hispano-Americanos, 1956), 1: 77–78; Sanz Tapia, *¿Corrupción?*, 72; Peña Izquierdo, *La Casa de Palma*, 66–67, 177–188, 229–234; Lynch, *Hispanic World*, 355, 371–382, holds that the aristocracy and don Juan de Austria manipulated the weak king.

[46] Storrs, *Resilience*, 123–124, 156–159; Lynch, *Hispanic World*, 374–376; Kamen, *Spain*, 27–28. The eighth Duke of Medinaceli was called Juan Tomás de la Cerda.

[47] *Consultas* of the Council of the Indies, Madrid, 8 Oct. and 7 Nov. 1680; *real cédula*, Madrid, 19 Nov. 1680, in Konetzke, *Colección*, vol. 2, tome 2: 716–717; superseded *real cédula*, Madrid, 29 Feb. 1680, in Muro Orejón, *Cedulario americano*, 1: 77–79, which restored full patronage to the viceroys and presidents of New Spain and Peru and was issued eight days after Medinaceli took the helm.

[48] According to folder AGI, México 15.

TABLE 3 *The Beginnings of the* beneficio *of* Alcaldías Mayores

Year	New Spain including Yucatán	Spanish America including presidencies
1675	3	14
1676	2	4
1677	10	29
1678–1681	0	4
1682	4	26
1683	5	30
1684	2	8
1685	10	12
1686	14	50

Sources: AGI, México 15 (for New Spain); Sanz Tapia, ¿Corrupción?, 70 (for Spanish America)

customary provision list that the *cámara* prepared for the queen and the king. The sale resumed in 1682 when Medinaceli took the helm.[49]

The Count of Oropesa replaced Medinaceli to serve as chief minister in 1685 and largely stayed the political course amid larger social changes in the empire. Oropesa tightened the tax collection by introducing the Superintendency of Finance and adding an "element of social justice" to his policies.[50] The aspiring bourgeoisie and lower nobility supported the new direction. These groups gained ground on the traditional pillars of the monarchy – the aristocracy, the upper church, and the conciliar jurists educated in the *colegios mayores* – in the last three decades of the century. The rising groups successfully traded, banked, or worked in the lower bureaucracy, and many of their members boasted university degrees. Juan Alfonso de Lancina claimed in 1687, for example, that the lower nobility buttressed the monarchy, which was threatened by the titled nobles.[51]

---

[49] The fifty appointments in AGN, México 15 usually occurred by royal decree of the queen or by king to the *cámara* president, served at that time by the Count of Medellín or the Marquis of Vélez. See also Payo Enríquez de Ribera to king, Mexico City, 6 June 1679, AGI, México 471, R.1, N. 1.
[50] Lynch, *Hispanic World*, 378.
[51] Peña Izquierdo, *La Casa de Palma*, 153, see also 234–237. According to Lynch, *Hispanic World*, 376–379; Hermann and Marcadé, *Les royaumes ibériques*, 102–103, able ministers like José de Veytia y Linaje, secretary of the Council of the Indies and then of the

"Vile and Abominable Pacts"

The rise of these aspiring groups encouraged Oropesa to expand *beneficio* as it eased their entry into the administration. Oropesa and his ministers sold fifty appointments in 1686. In the following year, the crown conferred thirty-two appointments of *alcaldías mayores* and presidencies in all of Spanish America solely by *beneficio*, while giving out an additional fifty-two appointments for combined *beneficio* and "services and merits." In addition, Oropesa ushered in the sweeping sales of American *audiencia* appointments from 1687 to 1712.[52]

Nonetheless, Oropesa's grip weakened when King Charles married the German princess Mariana of Neuburg (not to be confused with Charles' mother, Mariana of Austria). The crown issued a decree on June 6, 1689, to end the sale of judicial and treasury offices to defend the "correct administration of justice."[53] This remained a mere declaration of intent, however, and few things changed. In the following year, the Viceroy Count of Galve (1688–1696) complained to his brother about the "very bad consequences" of "selling all offices in the Indies."[54] Aristocrats such as Galve often objected to *beneficio*, and the viceroys in particular deplored their loss of patronage. In the same year, Galve and the civil judges of the *audiencia* refused seating a judge who had purchased his appointment. Galve and the judges claimed to preserve justice "peace, rectitude, and zeal" of the bench. In response, Madrid fined the body 6,000 ducats.[55]

Court politics continued to determine the extent of *beneficio*. Oropesa fell in 1691 and subsequently an aristocratic triumvirate wrangled with

---

despacho universal (central secretariat among the councils), exemplified this shift. Note that Macanaz, "Los veinte y dos auxilios [...]," Paris, 29 Aug. 1722, Biblioteca de Aragón, Miscelánea, Ms. 141, fol. 24, thrashed the "tyranny of the magnates," and in "Testamento de España," Biblioteca de Huesca, Miscelánea, Ms. 141, fol. 109r, http://bibliotecavirtual.aragon.es, the "hydra of all the grandees." David Ringrose, *Spain, Europe, and the 'Spanish Miracle,' 1700–1900* (Cambridge: Cambridge University Press, 1996), 366–368, argues that elite constellation changed substantially in the early eighteenth century.

[52] According to Burkholder, *Spaniards*, 94–97, 100–101; Burkholder and Chandler, "Creole Appointments," 191–192, the second period of sales of *audiencia* appointments was from 1740 to 1750. See also Sanz Tapia, *¿Corrupción?*, 70; Kamen, *Spain*, 386.

[53] Konetzke, *Colección*, vol. 3, tome 1, pp. 34–35.

[54] Gaspar de la Cerda Sandoval, seventh Count of Galve, to Gregorio de Silva Mendoza, ninth Duke of el Infantado and Marquis of Cenete, Mexico City, 30 June 1690, Archivo Histórico Nacional, Sección Nobleza (Toledo, Spain), Archivo de los Duques de Osuna, carpeta 55, D. 52. Both Galve and Infantado belonged to the Osuna family.

[55] *Real acuerdo* to king, Mexico City, 30 June 1690, AGI, México 10. See the *cámara's* rebuke of the *real acuerdo*, Madrid, 28 Mar. 1691, AGI, México 10.

Queen Mariana of Neuburg's German clique over influence. Beginning on October 26, 1692, the crown formally resumed selling appointments, but now awarding them overwhelmingly on account of both merit and services. What difference that really entailed is unclear. The conservative Council of the Indies protested on November 9, 1693, that "justice and its staff of authority are sold in public auction ... at excessive prices."[56] Attached was a copy of the Council of Castile's sixteenth-century call for "virtuous people, educated, and of righteous conscience" for these positions.[57] The Council of the Indies thus refuted the special *junta* of 1676 by arguing that *beneficio* "produced a difficulty which is morally impossible." *Beneficio* needed to satisfy all the criteria of the appropriate administration of royal finances, extreme urgency, and suitable candidates purchasing at a limited price. Otherwise, *beneficio* was illegal. The king asserted in 1693 that he would end the sale as soon as the financial urgency lessened, but the protests of the Council did not bear fruit yet.[58]

In 1698, the Count of Oropesa returned as chief minister and struck a temporary pact with Cardinal Luis Manuel Fernández de Portocarrero. Fernández de Portocarrero had helped engineer don Juan de Austria's coup in 1676/77. The queen removed him later from the court, yet his fortunes rose after 1696. Fernández de Portocarrero gathered strength and finally ousted the Count of Oropesa for a second time on April 28, 1699. Subsequently, appointments for *beneficio*, as well as *beneficio* combined with service and merit, dropped precipitously in the Spanish empire.[59]

---

[56] Konetzke, *Colección*, vol. 3, tome 1, p. 35. According to Joaquim E. López i Camps, "La embajada española," 19–25, Mariana of Neuburg counted among her allies her secretary, Heinrich von Wiser, whom his critics derided as "*el cojo* (the cripple)," the friar Gabriel Pontiferser, a.k.a Gabriel Chiusa or "closed for business," the *camarera mayor* Countess of Berlepsch alias "*la perdiz* (the porridge)," and the Count of Melgarejo. Hermann and Marcadé, *Les royaumes ibériques*, 103, argue that both Medinaceli and Oropesa encountered stiff aristocratic resistance. Medinaceli demitted because of the diplomatic defeat in 1684, whereas the aristocratic memorandum of May 1691 brought down Oropesa.

[57] Council of Castile to King Charles V written before 1517, cited in Quintana, *Historia de la antigüedad*, 738–740.

[58] Konetzke, *Colección*, vol. 3, tome 1, p. 36; royal decree attached to *consulta* of the Council of the Indies, n. d., ibid., vol. 3, tome 1, p. 39.

[59] According to Sanz Tapia, *Corrupción*, 70, 80, 367–368, the crown sold 658 of the 1,026 appointments from 1675 to the passing of Charles II in 1700. After Oropesa, 64.1 percent of all nominations were given for *beneficio* or combined *beneficio* and merit. See Storrs, *Resilience*, 124, 187–188; Peña Izquierdo, "La crisis sucesoria," 1: 463; Peña Izquierdo, *La casa de Palma*, 155–156, 207–210, 290–316, argues that the death on Feb. 3, 1699, of the presumptive heir Joseph Ferdinand, son of the Bavarian elector, strengthened Portocarrero's hand, and Oropesa fell in the *motín de los gatos* (Cat Riot). Virginia León Sanz, "La nobleza austracista. Entre Austrias y Borbones," in *Nobleza*

The *beneficio* politics continued to alter between conservative and reformist governments after the transition from Habsburg to Bourbon rule. When Charles II died, Philip V acceded to the throne in 1700 and initially suspended *beneficio* to appease the traditional elites. The War of the Spanish Succession (1701–1714) forced the government yet again to seek additional funds. At the same time, the aristocracy and the great councils were rapidly losing influence. The French clique had the ear of the queen and the king, and they dismissed many Habsburg-era politicians, including Cardinal Fernández de Portocarrero. Ministers at court again discussed the Villa Alta uprising and the sale of appointments in New Spain during the early stages of this transition in 1702. The crown resumed *beneficio* in 1704 in unparalleled measure, offering judiciary, military, financial, and administrative positions in New Spain. In 1705, the king ordered the viceroys to sell "all honorific things that are not offices of justice" because those latter appointments were sold in Madrid.[60]

The sale intensified after Philip replaced a number of councilors of the Indies in 1706 for siding with the Habsburg cause. The Council had so far been a paragon of resistance against *beneficio*, but it performed a stunning reversal as a result. The Council reinterpreted the Azpilcuetan stipulation in 1707, stating that it was not the king but the candidates who sinned

---

y Sociedad en la España Moderna II, ed. María del Carmen Iglesias (Madrid, Oviedo: Nobel, Fundación Banco Santander Central Hispano, 1997), 54–59; and León Sanz, "La llegada de los Borbones al trono," in *Historia de España: Siglo XVIII: La España de los Borbones*, ed. Ricardo García Cárcel (Madrid: Cátedra, 2002), 54, holds that Cardinal Portocarrero's cousin, Pedro de Portocarrero y Guzmán, later adhered to the Habsburg cause. According to Adalberto de Baviera and Gabriel Maura Gamazo, eds., *Documentos inéditos referentes a las postrimerías de la casa de Austria en España* (Madrid: Tipografía de Archivos, 1927–35), 5: 151–152, the Austrian ambassador reported on Dec. 30, 1699, that the *castrato* musician Mateo Mateucci sold court offices. On the cardinal as an "energetic character ... of scarce intelligence," Germán Bleiberg, ed., *Diccionario de Historia de España*, 2nd ed. (Madrid: Revista de Occidente, 1969), 3: 298.

[60] *Real cédula*, Madrid, 31 Mar. 1705, BNE, Fondo Reservado, Ms. 437, fols. 55–56; see also royal decree, Madrid, 19 Feb. 1705, AGI, México 376; see summary of Villa Alta case to Manuel Aperregui, Madrid, 5 Feb. 1702, AGI, México 7; León Sanz, "La llegada," 45–46, 50, 54; Antonio García García, "La reforma de la plantilla de los tribunales americanos de 1701: El primer intento reformista del siglo XVIII," in Ruiz Rivera and Sanz Tapia, *La venta de cargos*, 61–63, 69–70; Carlos Martínez Shaw and Marina Alonso Mola, *Felipe V* (Madrid: Arlanza Ediciones, 2001), 210–213. Luis Navarro García "Los Oficios vendibles en Nueva España durante la Guerra de Sucesión," *Anuario de Estudios Americanos* 32 (1975): 133–152, argues that removing officials from the Mexican tribunal of accounts in 1701 had created additional openings. Felices de la Fuente, "Hacia la nobleza titulada," 40, draws on Francisco Andújar Castillo to emphasize the continuity of sales from the Habsburgs to the Bourbons.

when acquiring a post for which they were unsuitable. Two years later, the Council maintained that "in cases of evident necessity, the law permits selling even the chalices for succor and defense of the state."[61]

The sale of appointments fluctuated during the subsequent governments. In 1714, Philip's second wife, Elizabeth Farnese, removed large parts of the French clique and replaced them with Giulio Alberoni, her de facto chief minister (1715–1719). Alberoni expanded *beneficio* once again as part of a larger reform of the state. He reintroduced the provincial intendants in Spain, largely bypassed the great councils, and communicated directly with the king and the secretaries of state. When he fell from power, José Grimaldo succeeded him and steered a more conservative course (1719–1724). *Beneficio* declined. Between 1720 and 1727, the crown sold only a handful of appointments for *alcaldías mayores* and the presidencies of the *audiencias*.[62] The prosecutor of the Council of the Indies in 1721 concurred with the policy shift. He argued that judges suspected of corruption have "*beneficio* working against them, since he who buys also sells, according to common doctrines, and the king therefore justly ended the *beneficio* of offices with jurisdiction." Emperor Severus Alexander's censure still reverberated in the early eighteenth century.[63]

In 1725, the Marquis of Casafuerte, viceroy of New Spain (1722–1734), helped shift the discussion from the legitimacy of *beneficio* to the problem of reselling office appointments. Casafuerte came from the lower nobility and rose because of his military service, whereas most of his

---

[61] Quoted in Andújar Castillo, *Necesidad*, before pagination. On the background, Henry Kamen, *Philip V: The King Who Reigned Twice* (New Haven, CT: Yale University Press, 2001), 56. The *real cédula* to presidents and *audiencias*, Madrid, 31 Dec. 1708, AGN, RCO 33, exp. 177, fol. 491–491v, ordered ensuring that *alcaldes mayores* passed the end-of-tenure reviews before obtaining new appointments.

[62] *Real cédula*, Madrid, 10 Feb. 1716, in Konetzke, *Colección*, vol. 3, tome 1, p. 123. The *real cédula*, Madrid, 23 Feb. 1716, AGN, RCO 37, exp. 87, fol. 228–228v, inquired about salaries of the *alcaldes mayores*. On the king's marriage, see *real cédula*, Buen Retiro, 23 Feb. 1716, AGN, RCO 37, exp. 16, fol. 42. Burgos Lejanogoitia, *Gobernar las Indias*, 316, 325, 342, 373, confirms the stark decline of *beneficio* between 1719 and 1727/28, whereas sale of treasury posts ceased from 1713 to 1728. Sanz Tapia, "Aproximación," 155–156, notes two "political" appointments during 1720–1727. On the backdrop, see Kuethe, "La política colonial de Felipe V y el proyecto de 1720," in *Orbis Incognitus: Avisos y legajos del Nuevo Mundo: Homenaje al Profesor Luis Navarro García*, ed. Fernando Navarro Antolín (Huelva, Spain: Universidad de Huelva. 2007), 1: 233–239; León Sanz, "La llegada," 61–70; Kamen, *Philip V*, 97, 117–118, 124.

[63] *Parecer* of the prosecutor, n. d., attached to *consulta* of the Council of the Indies, Madrid, 13 Nov. 1721, AGI, México 670 A.

predecessors had belonged to the aristocracy.[64] His background explains, in part, his commitment to strengthening royal power. Casafuerte noted that a peninsular Spaniard attained an *alcaldía mayor* for 2,800 pesos. The Spaniard then sold the tenure for 8,000 pesos, despite all prohibitions against doing so. Casafuerte chastised the "abominable agreements by which the recipient of a royal reward makes an office of the administration of justice and jurisdiction venal and sellable."[65] The viceroy mainly criticized the private trade with judicial offices rather than the advent of unsuitable people. He also echoed Azpilcueta's view that only the king could offer these assets. At that point – the tail end of Grimaldo's tenure – the prosecutor of the Council of the Indies agreed. He replied that *beneficio* had ceased in any case, because the king was aware of its "inappropriateness." The prosecutor blamed the secretary of the Indies of the previous government for the sale.[66]

Beneficio expanded again when José Patiño became secretary of the treasury in 1726. He pieced Alberoni's project back together, and, in 1728, the sale rebounded to sixty appointments in all the empire. In 1736, Patiño died, yet, in 1740, the crown expanded the *beneficio* of all posts in the Indies, including *audiencia* ministers. The rise of José Campillo y Cosío, who, in 1741, became secretary of the treasury, and the War of Jenkins' Ear (1740–1748), triggered this growth. Responding to the military effort, the Council of the Indies suggested on July 18, 1740, to exclude the port and frontier posts from *beneficio* during the war. Yet the Council's initiative failed, and the sale of appointments continued until 1750.[67]

---

[64] Eissa-Barroso, "Politics, Political Culture, and Policy Making: The Reform of Viceregal Rule in the Spanish World under Philip V (1700–1746)," (PhD diss., University of Warwick, 2010), 185–202, 221–250; Eissa-Barroso, "Of Experience, Zeal," 318, 338–344; Rubio Mañé, *Introducción*, 1: 264–270.

[65] Marquis of Casafuerte to king, Mexico City, 14 May 1725, AGI, México 492, referring to the *alcaldía mayor* of Meztitlan de la Sierra (Hidalgo). See also the earlier prohibitions to reassign offices, king to Duke of Alburquerque, Buen Retiro, 28 Apr. 1705, AGN, RCO 32, exp. 122, fol. 5; *consulta* of the Council of the Indies, 13 Nov. 1705, AGI, México 376; Alburquerque to king, Mexico City, 20 Sept. 1706, AGI, México 479.

[66] *Parecer* of the prosecutor, Madrid, 28 Oct. 1725, AGI, México 492. On the indigenous community objecting to the purchaser, see *oficiales de república* to viceroy, n. d.; *real acuerdo*, Mexico City, 11 Feb. 1724; *royal order* serving as precedent, Buen Retiro, 7 Jun. 1691; *parecer* of Dr. José Meléndez, Mexico City, 22 Jan. 1725, all of which can be found in AGI, México 492, *cuaderno* 8, fols. 35v–36v, 37v–40v, 42–43, 77v–89v, 101–105.

[67] José de la Quintana to Count of Montijo, Buen Retiro, 13 Apr. 1740, AGI, México 383; *consulta* of the *cámara* of the Indies, 18 July 1740, in Konetzke, *Colección*, vol. 3, tome 1, pp. 227–228. The War of Jenkins' Ear segued into the War of the Austrian Succession (1740–1748). See León Sanz, "La llegada," 73, 79–80, 85; Kamen, *Philip V*, 207, 211, 245, 250.

The heyday of *beneficio* ended when the Marquis of la Ensenada became chief minister in 1743. Beginning in 1745, the viceroys of New Spain could bar ill-suited purchasers of appointments from taking office. Viceroy Count of Revillagigedo argued in 1748 that many newly minted *alcaldes mayores* resold appointments to local purchasers, whom they cloaked as their deputies. The exchange shortchanged the treasury and gave the posts to "subjects without character or experience in administering justice."[68] Instead, the Indies needed "mature" and experienced ministers, language that reflected the changing selection criteria.[69] In addition, Revillagigedo favored paying the *alcaldes mayores* the prescribed salaries as an incentive for better compliance.[70]

Consequently, Ensenada phased out the sale of appointments to both *alcaldías mayores* and *audiencias* between 1750 and 1751. This was part of a larger overhaul of the district judiciary, which also responded to American complaints. Revillagigedo ordered drafting a fixed-price schedule to regulate the *alcaldes mayores*' trade with the Indians. Ensenada also discussed the establishment of intendants akin to those in Spain, and salaried military governors supplanted the *alcaldes mayores* in two important districts of New Spain. These governors, just like the viceroy, were career officers with a convincing record of accomplishment.[71] Ensenada

---

[68] Count of Revillagigedo to king, Mexico City, 20 Feb. 1747, AGI, México 1341.
[69] Revillagigedo to Ensenada, Mexico City, 26 June 1748, AGI, México 1506, no. 45.
[70] An old request, since, for example, Pierre Grégoire, *De republica*, book 2, chap. 6, para. 18, suggested curbing the judges' arbitrary exactions, "although it is difficult to do, unless sufficient salaries are established to counter greed and excessive fees." On Ensenada, see also Felipe Abad León, *El Marqués de la Ensenada, su vida y su obra* (Madrid: Editorial Naval, 1985), 2: 53.
[71] *Relacion se ha formado de orden de S.M.*, n. d., after Mar. 1746, AGI, Indiferente General 1847; Revillagigedo to Ensenada, Mexico City, 10 July 1746, AGI, México 1506, no. 7; Revillagigedo to king, Mexico City, 20 Feb. 1747, AGI, México 1342; Revillagigedo to Ensenada, Mexico City, 2 Feb. 1748, ACR 412; *real cédula*, Madrid, 1 Apr. 1748, AGN, RCO 68, exp. 81, fols. 309–310; Revillagigedo to king, Mexico City, 6 Apr. 1748, AGI, México 1506, no. 41; Ensenada to Revillagigedo, Madrid, 18 Sept. 1752, AGI, México 1506, no. 122; *real cédula*, Madrid, 15 Mar. 1751, AGN, RCO 71, exp. 72, fols. 247–248; *real cédula*, Buen Retiro, 17 July 1751, AGN, RCO 71, exp. 147, fols. 540–543; Revillagigedo to king, Mexico City, 4 June 1752, ACR 347; Ensenada to Revillagigedo, 2 Sept. 1751, ACR 347; Ensenada to Count of Superunda, Madrid, 2 Sept. 1751, ACR 347. See also Revillagigedo to Ensenada, Mexico City, 14 Sept. 1748, ACR 399; royal order, Madrid, 5 Feb. 1754, AGI, México 1352. On the background and the importance of José de Carvajal y Lancaster, secretary of state (1746–1754), see Andújar Castillo, *El sonido*, 31, 415–418; Valle Menéndez, *Juan Francisco de Güemes*, 337, 366–367, 630; Pietschmann, "Alcaldes Mayores," 209; Burkholder, *Spaniards*, 100–101. Bertrand, "Clientélisme et pouvoir en Nouvelle-Espagne (1680–1770)," in *Cultures et sociétés, Andes et Méso-Amérique, Mélanges en hommage à Pierre Duviols*,

and Revillagigedo also agreed that the performance model should more heavily influence appointments to the judiciary, with the aim of better serving their and the state's interests. While considerations of clientage continued to matter significantly, the coalition preferred more obedient officials to the funds received from *beneficio*.

4.3 THE DRAMATIC DECLINE OF VICEREGAL PATRONAGE IN NEW SPAIN

Between 1704 and 1750/51, the crown sold 1,399 appointments to *alcaldías mayores* and *audiencia* presidencies in the Americas in fluctuating patterns. Madrid gave out 1,139 of these appointments in exchange for money, and 244 as reward for money, merit, and services. The growing sale of appointments in Madrid significantly diminished viceregal patronage in New Spain. The scope of this loss has so far been unclear or even considered "hesitant."[72] Yet the archival data shows that the crown curbed viceregal patronage by at least half and possibly more, a much deeper cut than previously assumed.

Before 1673, the viceroys appointed almost all *alcaldes mayores* and several of their deputies, including for important cities such as Puebla and the cochineal trading districts in Oaxaca. The viceroys also named the governors and fortress soldiers on the northern frontier, such as in New Mexico. In addition, the viceroys assigned dozens of other posts, among them the attorneys at the Indian court, a "barber-surgeon" of the College of Christ, and the warden of Chapultepec Forest.[73] The crown merely named the district judge of Mexico City and, after 1628, the *alcalde mayor* of Acapulco. Subsequently the crown appointed some additional ministers. When the discussion over transferring patronage intensified, the archbishop viceroy Payo Enríquez de Ribera reported the quantity of his appointments to the crown. He still wielded vast patronage and named on

---

ed. Raquel Thiercelin (Aix-en-Provence: Publications de l'Université de Provence, 1991), 1: 144, argues that ending the sale of treasury positions strengthened viceregal influence.

[72] Quote in Cañeque, *Living Image*, 175. On the unclear scope, see Andújar Castillo, *Necesidad*, 61; Rubio Mañé, *Introducción*, 1: 102–104; Pietschmann, "Alcaldes Mayores," 188; Yalí Román, "Sobre alcaldías mayores," 30; Phelan, *Kingdom*, 168; Burgos Lejonagoitia, *Gobernar las Indias*, 458–459, documents the "hard hit" for the viceroys. For the numbers, Sanz Tapia, "Aproximación," 150, who includes sixteen reassignments for ministers who had purchased appointments to occupied positions.

[73] *Relacion de las Alcaidias Mayores y corregimientos*, n. d., after 1628, BNE, Ms. 18684/8.

average of 11.25 *alcaldes mayores* per month, at least for short periods between 1673 and 1679.[74]

Studying the patronage power of two subsequent viceroys demonstrates that Enríquez de Ribera's high numbers declined strikingly in the following years. By 1680, the viceroys only kept the right to name twelve retainers simultaneously to the better districts of New Spain. The viceroys nonetheless also appointed candidates for the lesser districts that the crown did not fill.[75] Later reports comparable to those written by Enríquez de Ribera are not available, yet the tax paid by incoming *alcaldes mayores* provides additional data on appointment patterns. This record illuminates the change from Enríquez de Ribera to his successors. The tenth Duke of Alburquerque, viceroy of New Spain (1702–1710), for example, epitomized excess, and he had to pay an unheard-of penalty of roughly 700,000 pesos for his malfeasance. His successor during the mid-century, the first Count of Revillagigedo, meanwhile, loyally served Ensenada's reform agenda.[76]

The crown succeeded in notably curbing viceregal patronage during this period, weakening the viceregal prestige and appropriating resources for Madrid. The Duke of Alburquerque exemplified this shift. According to the record, he appointed about 2.8 *alcaldes mayores* per month,

---

[74] According to Payo Enríquez de Ribera to king, Mexico City, 6 June 1679, AGI, México 471, R. 1, N. 1, Payo Enríquez de Ribera named 73 *alcaldes mayores* between Dec. 13, 1673, and May 8, 1674, and 62 *alcaldes mayores* between Dec. 22, 1678, and May 22, 1679. See also *relación* of Santiago de Cue Calday, Mexico City, 16 June 1679, AGI, México 471, R.1, N.1. According to note of criminal prosecutor Juan Francisco Esquivel, 17 May 1676, AGI, México 600, fols. 694–696, the viceroys did not assign the Querétaro district judge. See also *Memoria de todos los oficios*, AGI, México 600, fols. 698–700. Gerhard, *A Guide to the Historical Geography of New Spain*, rev. ed. (Norman: University of Oklahoma Press, 1993), 40, 361, holds that the king began appointing Acapulco in 1628 and Veracruz in 1629, whereas the certification of royal officials, Mexico City, 5 June 1679, AGI, México 471, R.1, N.1, fol. 4, included Veracruz for the viceroy.

[75] *Consulta* of the Council of the Indies, Madrid, 7 Nov. 1680, AGI, México 8. This included Oaxaca and Tepeaca, ranked as first class or wealthiest district; Tehuacan, Miahuatlan, Chalco, Guanajuato, and Xochimilco, ranked as second class; and Meztitlan, Veracruz Vieja, Huatulco, Tonala, and Sultepec, which ranked as third class.

[76] Juan Antonio Valenciano to Ensenada, 23 May 1749; Francisco de Varas to Ensenada, Cádiz, 13 Oct. 1750, AGI, México 1505, discuss the fine for Alburquerque. On the dates of the viceregal tenures, Rosenmüller, *Patrons, Partisans, and Palace Intrigues: The Court Society of Colonial Mexico, 1702–1710* (Calgary: Calgary University Press, 2008), 143–162; Valle Menéndez, *Juan Francisco de Güemes*, 335–337, 630. The *consulta* of the Council of the Indies, Madrid, 13 Mar. 1758, AGI, Escribanía 1158, considered that Revillagigedo's tenure lasted from July 9, 1746, until Nov. 9, 1755. These varying dates refer to the royal appointment itself, the arrival in Veracruz, the exchange of the baton in Otumba, or the entry in Mexico City.

TABLE 4 *Viceregal Appointments to* Alcaldías Mayores *of New Spain*

Value of district	Payo Enríquez de Ribera (December 13, 1673–November 7, 1680)	Duke of Alburquerque (November 27, 1702, to November 13, 1710)	Count of Revillagigedo (July 7, 1746 to November 8, 1755)
1	–	40	19
2	–	54	49
3	–	62	41
4	–	20	20
5	–	13	8
6	–	8	2
7	–	0	0
8	–	5	3
Ínfima (small)	–	13	2
No assigned value	–	50	11
Appointments per month on average	11.25	2.8	1.4
Total		265	155

Sources: On Revillagigedo, AGN, Archivo Histórico de la Hacienda (hereinafter cited as AHH) 1056, 1058, 1614, 1615, 1653; AGN, Media Anata 20, 42, 50, 205; certification of Juan José de Zarascua, Mexico City, n. d., 1757, AGI, Escribanía 246 A, fols. 151v–161v; certification of Zarascua, Mexico City, 28 Jan. 1757, AGI, Escribanía 246 A, fols. 162v–170; certification of Juan José de Paz, Mexico City, 25 Feb. 1757, AGI, Escribanía 246 A, fols. 181v–194; *auto* titled *Los Alcaldes Mayores y Corregidores que ... Revillagigedo proveió*, n. d., 1757, AGI, Escribanía 246 A, fols. 194–209; *Indice extractado de todos los Goviernos, Correximientos*, by an anonymous author, 1784, Biblioteca Nacional de México, Fondo Reservado (hereinafter cited as BNM, FR) 455, fols. 210–212. The district values are provided by *Yndize Comprehensibo de todos los Goviernos corregimientos y Alcaldias mayores que contienen la Governacion del Virreynato de Mexico ... Año de [1]777*, manuscript in the New York Public Library, printed in Pietschmann, "Alcaldes Mayores," 239–257. On Alburquerque, see Rosenmüller, *Patrons, Partisans*, 66–78, 191–217 (I slightly amended the appointment data from my prior publication).
Note: Enríquez de Ribera reported his total appointment numbers, but he did not mention the districts. Meanwhile, the *media anata* tax receipts of appointees provide the data for the periods 1702–1710 and 1746–1755.

a significant drop in comparison with Enríquez de Ribera. Yet Alburquerque was canny enough to name a number of interim officeholders to the lucrative districts, and most of his nominees still served the better districts, including Oaxaca. Subsequently, the crown further reined in the viceroys. Between 1746 and 1755, Revillagigedo merely appointed 1.4 ministers per month on average. That is half of Alburquerque's average and a little bit over a tenth (12.44 percent) of Enríquez de Ribera's patronage.

CONCLUSION

Most of the aristocracy, the upper echelons of the Church, and the conciliar jurists educated in the *colegios mayores* and hailing from the Castilian municipal oligarchies considered *beneficio* as corrupt. These traditional elites viewed the purchasers of judicial appointments as innately flawed, because the buyers lacked the social origins that bequeathed the qualities needed to act virtuously. The elites called for returning to Thomas Aquinas's distributive justice to end corruption. That also meant reserving for themselves the best offices and the ability to appoint their clients. Their retainers often clamored for generous patronage to compensate for long years of unpaid service. Yet political authors also warned of the dangers of excess. The Jesuit Andrés Mendo, for example, drew on Seneca when he suggested to balance rewards against distributive justice. Handing out too many rewards weakened the crown, he and other commentators contended.

Meanwhile, reformist governments expanded *beneficio* of the *alcaldes mayores*, which replaced the older model of selecting ministers. Azpilcueta laid the foundation for allowing the royal sale of appointments under some circumstances while excluding vassals from selling the posts. In the late seventeenth century, lower nobles, bourgeois groups, and other social newcomers increasingly competed with the traditional elites for posts and political influence. These rising groups benefited from *beneficio*, and that also applied to ministers in the Indies. The *novohispano* attorney José Meléndez, for example, defended selling royal appointments as this practice often benefitted the *novohispanos*. The newcomers also downplayed the notable origins of candidates as selection criteria in favor of performance, education, and experience. Thus the idea of merit shifted in the period from 1650 to 1755 and the innate character of corruption declined. This changing concept of merit, along with the crown's financial urgency, triggered the expansion of *beneficio*.

The governing coalitions of reformist inclination, such as those of Fernando Valenzuela, the Count of Oropesa, and José Patiño, sold appointments in larger numbers in Madrid. They gained oversight over *alcaldes mayores* in distant realms, appropriated resources, and reduced viceregal power. They also attempted to weaken the traditional elites as a whole and co-opt bourgeois groups, depending on the circumstances. As a consequence, the viceroys of New Spain shed more than half of their patronage and a major, although illicit, source of revenue. Contrary to the prevailing historiographical argument, there is little evidence that the purchasers of these appointments were more corrupt than their predecessors, if this is understood as violating the royal law of their occupation. Nonetheless, by the 1750s, the Count of Revillagigedo and the Marquis of la Ensenada acknowledged that *beneficio* came with its own challenges. Purchasers illicitly resold their appointments to others, creating a thriving market. Ensenada and his allies at this time phased out *beneficio*, further emphasizing performance in office as a criterion.

This chapter provides evidence that the sale of *alcaldes mayores* tenures from 1675 to 1751 did not destabilize the empire but, instead, belonged to a cycle of reforms to strengthen royal authority. My argument, therefore, contributes to the ongoing historiographical reevaluation of the decline of monarchic power or of the Spanish Empire as a whole in the later seventeenth century.[77] This insight also casts doubt onto the radical innovation of the Bourbon Reforms, traditionally understood as the *visita* of José de Gálvez in New Spain (1765–1771) and his subsequent term as Secretary of the Indies (1776–1787). Scholars now emphasize that meaningful reforms began with the first Bourbon kings and their ministers in the early eighteenth century, yet they have largely ignored the imperial history of the later seventeenth century (though this is now changing). For this reason, they have tended to overlook significant changes in this period, which cast the foundation for Philip V's advances. This chapter highlights an important example of these cycles of reform that continued from the Habsburg into the Bourbon period.

There are still caveats needed for this revision. Much of this chapter has been devoted to sketching the fragmented nature of the early modern state, in which various networks jockeyed for influence in public discourses, in the councils, and with the king. I have only addressed the patronage mechanism itself within this complexity. How the purchasers of appointments, be they judges, financial officials, or *alcaldes mayores*, differed in their service on the ground from those named by the viceroys or the *cámara* still needs further examination. Regional differences between the realms mattered too. Getting to the bottom of this matter will be an

---

[77] See note 7.

intriguing challenge, especially when considering the changing nature of corruption during this period.

Some forty years ago, Mark Burkholder and D. S. Chandler published the standard work on the *beneficio* of *audiencia* ministers. I have attempted to add nuance to these scholars' claim that purchasers of appointments tended to be corrupt, ushering in an age of royal impotence. The main aim of Burkholder and Chandler, however, was not to analyze the period before 1675. They demonstrated through rigorous research that the crown increasingly selected a new kind of *audiencia* ministers who arrived after 1712 and again after 1750/51, when the last phase of *audiencia beneficio* ended. The crown drew on the performance model to strengthen oversight in comparison to the purchasers. Their conclusion stands, in my view. Further research on corruption, a topic that scholars have only recently rediscovered, will cast additional light on this issue.[78]

---

[78] Burkholder and Chandler, *From Impotence to Authority*, 17–18.

5

Criminal Process and the "Judge Who Is Corrupted by Money"

INTRODUCTION: CRIME AND PROCESS IN THE
SPANISH EMPIRE

In 1716, the *alcalde de crimen* (criminal judge) Pedro Sánchez Morcillo set out to prosecute criminals near Puebla – colonial Mexico's second largest city. Instead of adhering to process, however, he took advantage of the opportunity and shook down merchants and lowly suspects. In one instance, Sánchez Morcillo "seized Benito Martín from the justice of Tlaxcala for murder, and he ruled for and carried out torture without signing any order, and despite the delinquent's appeal, whose confession on the torture rack was not properly recorded, he condemned him to 200 lashes and ten years of forced labor."[1] Two hundred lashes most likely meant death for Benito Martín, but rather than executing the gruesome verdict, Sánchez Morcillo settled for cash. The sordid affair shows that corruption was a concern even for humble *novohispanos*, among them Indians and blacks. When the *visitador general* (investigative judge) Francisco Garzarón (1716–1727) later traced Sánchez Morcillo's actions, some *novohispanos* testified voluntarily, while Garzarón probably nudged others. The witnesses may not all have known the legal details of corruption, but they largely agreed that a judge who tortured suspects to obtain cash acted wrongfully.[2]

The *visitadores* enjoyed wide discretion in prosecuting corruption, while they followed, to an extent, the pattern of ordinary criminal

---

[1] Charge against Sánchez Morcillo, AGI, México 670 B, *Relación*, fol. 741v. The quote of the chapter title is in Berart y Gassol, *Speculum visitationis*, chap. 7, para 3.
[2] Reputation of Sánchez Morcillo, AGI, México 670 B, *Relación*, fol. 778.

investigations. For example, Garzarón based a guilty verdict on the concurring testimonies of two reputable witnesses. Yet unlike in ordinary criminal trials, the *visitadores* also accepted the testimonies of three witnesses who had participated in or perceived separate corrupt acts as long as they did not contradict one another. This special provision made convicting suspects easier. The *visitas* also withheld from the defendants the names of the witnesses who had testified against them. While the cards were often stacked against the suspects, Garzarón afforded them some protections. The defendants debunked evidence, called on attorneys and witnesses for support, and appealed guilty verdicts.

The *visitas* then had much power to prosecute crime, but they could also serve political ends or satisfy an individual thirst for vengeance when they were in the wrong hands. Scholars of social networks have for this reason analyzed the *visitas* as part of scheming alliances or political machinations.[3] Nevertheless, social and cultural historians have affirmed that the colonial justice system tended to resolve crimes and conflicts legitimately according to the standards of the time.[4] In addition, legal scholars have predominantly cared about developing judicial principles, but they have seldom mined the archival bedrock to unearth the daily life of the past. As a consequence, we still know relatively little about the actual functioning of complex law in the courts and conflicts of New Spain.[5] This chapter, therefore, seeks to combine the approaches and add a perspective from below. There is no doubt that the scheming social networks skewed *visitas*, but they did not determine Garzarón's verdicts alone. Garzarón proved that, according to accepted standards, several judges had accepted bribes or extorted suspects, while officials had committed fraud, theft, or lesser offenses. In part, Garzarón secured the support from many *novohispanos* for his prosecution precisely because he followed the recognized process of the time. Jousting over corruption occurred within the context of shared cultural values about justice.

---

[3] Pioneering are Bertrand, *Grandeur et misère*; Herzog, *Upholding Justice*; Dedieu, "Procesos y redes," 13–30. See also Rosenmüller, *Patrons, Partisans*.

[4] Kagan, *Lawsuits and Litigants*; Borah, *Justice by Insurance*; Cutter, "The Legal System," 57–70; Owensby, *Empire of Law*; McKinley, *Fractional Freedoms*; Holenstein, "Introduction," 23.

[5] María Paz Alonso Romero's outstanding books, for example, have focused on legal ideas; see *El proceso penal en Castilla siglo XIII–XVIII* (Salamanca: Universidad de Salamanca, 1982), and *Orden procesal*; see also Decock, *Theologians*. A few scholars have also combined these approaches; see Alejandro Agüero, "La tortura judicial en el antiguo regimen," 187–221.

Three cases studies analyze the methods of Spanish crime investigations and *visitas*. They detail Garzarón's ways of unearthing offenses and sentencing suspects and the interaction of *visitador*, suspects, and witnesses. The first case study throws light on Garzarón's reexamination of Sánchez Morcillo's infamous tour near Puebla, while also fleshing out the principles of ordinary criminal trials and the *visitas*. The second case study traces a criminal judge who jailed a shopkeeper for allegedly showing his private parts to some soldiers. Finally, the last case study follows Garzarón as he walked through the palace jail to gain his own impressions of malfeasance. Garzarón largely applied the *visita* principles and suspended dozens of ministers as a result.

5.1 THE DEATH OF JOSÉ MIGUEL NIETO IN HUEJOTZINGO

In early 1714, Diego García de Guesca killed the Native peon José Miguel Nieto in the district of Huejotzingo. Diego's brother, the *hacendado* José García de Guesca, and don Miguel Pérez, an indigenous governor, both witnessed the killing. The *alcalde mayor* (district judge), Juan Antonio de Cos y Cevallos, scurried to the crime scene and absolved the García de Guesca brothers and Pérez. Two years later, Pedro Sánchez Morcillo came to town, jailed the García de Guesca brothers and Pérez, and demanded money for their release. Francisco Garzarón began studying the trial in the following year, and from that point on, Sánchez Morcillo fought an uphill battle to defend himself against the charge of corruption.

Pedro Sánchez Morcillo had a fairly successful career as a lawyer. He originally hailed from Michoacan in western New Spain and married the *novohispana* doña María Teresa de Aramburu y Vilches. Sánchez Morcillo worked as an attorney at the *audiencia* (high court) from 1704, and became a criminal judge on December 6, 1711, after donating 9,000 silver pesos to the crown. As we have seen, judges who bought their positions were, on average, not more corruptible than those who obtained them for their merits. In fact, the viceroy praised Sánchez Morcillo in the following year for his efforts in levying 18,500 pesos from contraband traders of the Manila galleon. His success laid the groundwork for additional assignments.[6]

---

[6] The full name of the *alcalde de crimen* (criminal judge) was Pedro Sánchez Manuel Alcaraz Morcillo, although he usually went by Pedro Sánchez Morcillo. According to certification by Juan de Oribay, Mexico City, 18 Dec. 1710, AGI, México 658, fol. 336v; Viceroy Duke of Linares to king, Mexico City, 15 Dec. 1712, AGI, México 557, Sánchez Morcillo also served a commission to investigate adultery in Tinquindin in 1704.

In late 1715, the viceroy ordered Sánchez Morcillo to "destroy the thieves, highwaymen, and delinquents ... that infest the roads between Puebla and Veracruz."[7] These roads formed the arteries connecting Mexico City to Puebla and the important port of Veracruz on the Gulf of Mexico. Crime was rampant and Sánchez Morcillo obtained an *acordada*, which was an extraordinary commission to sentence criminals quickly and without appeals to the *audiencia*. This *acordada* was a precursor of the notorious summary court, but at this time, the crown frowned upon such commissions.[8] In fact, the king later chastised Sánchez Morcillo for drawing excessive daily expense allowances. The lack of collegial control of the *acordada* had also exacerbated corruption, because interested *novohispanos* often curried favor with the judge to attain favorable verdicts.[9]

During his tour, Sánchez Morcillo spent some time in Tlaxcala and its vicinity. He and the constable of the Tlaxcala jail bilked a number of criminal suspects. According to "Pablo Mateo, Juan Salvador, and Juan Pascal, Indians of the *pueblo* of Magdalena, and inmates in Tlaxcala, [the constable Antonio Ruiz de] Santiago seized eighty-one pesos and demanded another 400 pesos, saying that if they did not give them to him, he would whip them. After they spent two months in prison, he ordered their release in the presence of the criminal judge" Sánchez Morcillo.[10] After the incident, Sánchez Morcillo traveled to the near-by *pueblo* of San Martín Texmelucan, where he heard of the killing of the Indian peon. In early 1714, the García de Guesca brothers, their "slave, and their Indian servant Miguel Antonio"[11] "whipped and beat José Miguel Nieto for catching him stealing some corn," and Nieto died as a result. The *alcalde mayor* Cos

---

[7] Decree of Sánchez Morcillo, Puebla, 30 May 1716, AGI, Escribanía 281 D, fol. 983v.
[8] The *audiencia* then reversed itself and insisted on allowing appeals; *Real Probicion de la comicion acorda*, Mexico City, 31 Dec. 1715, AGI, Escribanía 281 D, fols. 1014–1015v. See also *Law of the Indies*, book 2, title 16, laws 31, 40–41, and book 7, title 1, laws 1–6. According to the *Law of Castile*, book 3, title 9, law 10, a royal council had to approve such commissions. Colin M. MacLachlan, *Criminal Justice in Eighteenth-Century Mexico. A Study of the Tribunal of the Acordada* (Berkeley and Los Angeles: University of California Press, 1974): 32–34, argued that the *acordada* grew out of the Querétaro *hermandad* (summary court) in 1710 and was fully established by 1722, deriving its title from the *audiencia's acuerdo* (approval).
[9] *Real cédula* to president and civil judges, Lerma, 13 Dec. 1721, AGN, Historia 102, exp. 10, fol. 83–83v.
[10] Charge 83 against Sánchez Morcillo, AGI, México 670 B, *Relación*, fols. 758v–759; on the entourage, decree of Sánchez Morcillo, Puebla, 10 June 1716, AGI, México 670 B, *Relación*, fols. 589v–590.
[11] *Prueba*, AGI, México 670 B, *Relación*, fol. 734.

Criminal Process and the "Judge Who Is Corrupted by Money" 157

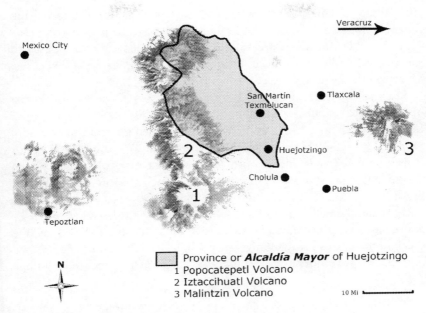

MAP 4 The Jurisdiction or *Alcaldía Mayor* of Huejotzingo.
Based on Peter Gerhard, *A Guide to the Historical Geography of New Spain*, rev. ed. (Norman: University of Oklahoma Press, 1993), 141–142.

y Cevallos appeared on the scene and ruled that the García de Guesca brothers had acted in self-defense. They got off lightly. Diego García de Guesca was exiled from the Huejotzingo district for a year but allowed to go about his business elsewhere, while José García de Guesca paid for Nieto's burial and for saying masses.[12]

However, Micaela de Cervantes, Nieto's mother, reported to Sánchez Morcillo that her son had only stolen "a little bit of corn" from the hacienda, and that "she had not been awarded justice."[13] Sánchez Morcillo also noted some irregularities when questioning the suspects. For instance, José García de Guesca stated on February 7, 1716, that he had "tried to recompense" Cervantes, although his brother had not committed any crimes, and that he had given "another person more than 600 pesos ... which were for the *alcalde mayor*, don Juan Antonio de Cos

---

[12] Decree of Sánchez Morcillo, Tlaxcala, 23 Feb. 1716, AGI, Escribanía 281 D, fol. 979v; testimony of José García de Guesca, AGI, México 670 B, *Relación*, fol. 729.
[13] Defense of Sánchez Morcillo, AGI, México 670 B, *Relación*, fol. 731; decree of Sánchez Morcillo, Tlaxcala, 23 Feb. 1716, AGI, Escribanía 281 D, fol. 979v.

y Cevallos."[14] That testimony sufficed for Sánchez Morcillo to jail the García de Guesca brothers. Soon after, he released them on a 100-pesos bond. In addition, José García de Guesca paid a fine of 412.5 pesos to Sánchez Morcillo and faced another 300 pesos in legal expenses. Moreover, he never recovered the bond.[15]

Sánchez Morcillo also sharply criticized Cos y Cevallos and Pérez. According to Sánchez Morcillo, Cos y Cevallos had accepted José García de Guesca's bribe and improperly recorded the trial. In addition, Sánchez Morcillo noted that Cos y Cevallos was the godfather of Governor Pérez and failed to prosecute him for his gross negligence in the killing. That was an offense of office, Sánchez Morcillo asserted.[16] Furthermore, Sánchez Morcillo denied that Pérez was a *cacique* (ethnic lord) as he claimed but a *mestizo* who spoke Spanish. When *mestizos* participated in abusing Indians, they violated the usual laws and the special protections for the indigenous people. The accession of a *mestizo* to an Indian governorship also smacked of illegitimacy. Since many Indian

---

[14] Declaration of José Garcia de Guesca, San Martín Texmelucan, 7 Feb. 1716, AGI, Escribanía 281 D, fol. 980v.
[15] Charge and defense of Sánchez Morcillo, AGI, México 670 B, *Relación*, fols. 728v–737v.
[16] "Gravemente culpado" or grossly negligent according to decree of Sánchez Morcillo, Tlaxcala, 23 Feb. 1716, AGI, Escribanía 281 D, fol. 979v; decree of Sánchez Morcillo, Puebla, 30 May 1716, AGI, Escribanía 281 D, fol. 983v. According to defense of Sánchez Morcillo, AGI, México 670 B, *Relación*, fols. 666, 668v; and decree of Sánchez Morcillo, Tlaxcala, 24 Feb. 1716, AGI, Escribanía 281 D, fol. 981v, Sánchez Morcillo labeled the governor as the *alcalde mayor's* "ahijado [godson]" and "parcial y paniaguado [dependant]." Lidia Gómez Garcia, "La conformación de los ayuntamientos constitucionales en los pueblos indios de la jurisdicción de San Juan de los Llanos, Puebla, 1765–1824," in Sanchez, *Los actores locales de la nación*, 109–110, observes the close relationship among *alcaldes mayores*, their deputies, and the governors in Native jurisdictions. According to petition of Juan Antonio de Cos y Zevallos, n.d.; presentation, Mexico City, 22 Jan. 1719; information of Alonzo de Arce y Velarde, Mexico City, 20 Jan. 1719; information of Félix González de Agüero, Mexico City, 21 Jan. 1719, all documents in AGN, Matrimonios 189, exp. 27; Viceroy Alburquerque to king, 16 Feb. 1709, AGI, México 482, Cos y Cevallos hailed from the mountains north of Burgos (Spain) and served as *alcalde mayor* of Pánuco in the Huasteca region. In 1719 Cos y Cevallos married Augustina de la Canal y Baeza, daughter of silver merchant Domingo de la Canal and Augustina de Baeza. Cos y Cevallos' *paisanos* (countrymen) Alonzo de Arce y Velarde, owner of a "public store" in San Martín Texmelucan, and *audiencia* judge Félix González de Agüero served as witnesses for the marriage banns. The session of the Mexico City municipal council, 19 July 1724, Archivo Histórico de la Ciudad de México, Mexico City (hereinafter cited as AHCM), Ayuntamiento, Actas del Cabildo 50A, fol. 65v, shows that Juan Antonio Cos y Cevallos served as municipal councilman (*regidor*) of Mexico City in 1724. On de la Canal's wealth, see king to Alburquerque, Madrid, 25 Feb. 1709, AGI, México, 403; Ricardo Magdaleno Redondo, ed., *Títulos de Indias. Catálogo XX del AGS* (Valladolid: Archivo General de Simancas, 1954): 158, 199.

nobles in the region spoke Spanish and had adopted Spanish customs, Sánchez Morcillo could doubt Pérez's status, even though the locals generally accepted the preeminence of these families.[17]

Sánchez Morcillo jailed Pérez in Tlaxcala and demanded money for his release. Antonio Pérez, the governor's son, visited his father in the city during Lent of 1716. Subsequently, "don Antonio sent the criminal judge 400 silver pesos and 100 chickens and he accepted" the gift. The son also delivered about 200 pesos to the *escribano* (notary). At that point, the "criminal judge told his father don Miguel not to worry." Yet Sánchez Morcillo kept Pérez in jail until June when he returned to Mexico City. Pérez asked for a written verdict, but Sánchez Morcillo shrugged off the request and departed.[18] In the meantime, complaints about his extortions reached Mexico City. Viceroy Marquis of Valero (1716–1722) cut short the commission and recalled Sánchez Morcillo to the *audiencia*.[19]

Later, in October 1716, Francisco Garzarón called on all residents of New Spain to register their complaints against the *audiencia* ministers. He also appointed a commissioner to gather testimony against Sánchez Morcillo by retracing his steps in the Puebla and Tlaxcala region. Governor Pérez and the García de Guesca brothers heard the call and made detailed statements to the commissioner. Four witnesses, among them Cos y Cevallos and his deputy, corroborated their account. At the same time, the commissioner collected few exonerating details, which the victim's mother could have provided.[20] The whole affair took an ill turn

---

[17] According to Solórzano, *Política*, book 2, chap. 28 (p. 120), punishments against perpetrators "would be even more justified if Native *caciques* or nobles were injured." This applied to Sánchez Morcillo's *acordada* too. See also Peter B. Villella, "Indian Lords, Hispanic Gentlemen: The Salazars of Colonial Tlaxcala," *The Americas* 69, no.1 (2012): 27–28; Duve, *Sonderrecht*, 202–203, 273–275. Complaints against indigenous governors who abused their positions were common, although they were probably not cases of judicial corruption; see, e.g., viceregal decree, Mexico City, 20 Nov. 1712, and response of prosecutor, no place, 14 Aug. 1713, AGI, Escribanía 280 A, Q[uader]no 10, fols. 175–176v; an in-depth discussion provides Connell, "Clients, Patrons, and Tribute: The Indigenous Aguilar Family in Mexico Tenochtitlan," in Rosenmüller, *Corruption in the Iberian Empires*, 63–85; see also Tanck de Estrada and Marichal, "¿Reino o colonia?," 333.

[18] *Prueba*, AGI, México 670 B, *Relación*, fol. 664v.

[19] "Extorsiones y estafas," according to *auto* of Marquis of Valero, n. d., AGI, México 670 B, *Relación*, fol. 610v. According to the reputation of Sánchez Morcillo, AGI, México 670 B, *Relación*, fol. 778, various witnesses knew of "complaints against his commission."

[20] Edict of Garzarón, Mexico City, 17 Oct. 1716, AGI, Escribanía 278 A, *legajo* 8; *prueba*, AGI, México 670 B, *Relación*, fols. 664v–665v. The third witness was Antonio Pérez, and the fourth witness was Francisco de Ortega, the deputy *alcalde mayor* of Tlaxcala.

for Sánchez Morcillo, and he shifted the blame back to his accusers. He argued that José García de Guesca had attempted to give him "a bribe of over 600 pesos."[21] In addition, Cos y Cevallos had tried "to corrupt" him through the "crime of attempted bribery" with 400 pesos and 100 chickens. Sánchez Morcillo claimed that he had accepted cash and chickens only because the miscreants deserved a punishment.[22]

Sánchez Morcillo also pointed out that he had distributed 500 pesos and 100 chickens among Nieto's family members and charitable institutions. According to him, Cervantes obtained 100 pesos. Josefa Nicolasa, Nieto's widow, also came to Tlaxcala on March 8 and received 200 pesos for a shroud, interment, and Mass. Three witnesses confirmed this account. At that time, 200 pesos equaled roughly thirty to sixty months of wages for an Indian agricultural worker, so this was a sizable settlement. Sánchez Morcillo stated, moreover, that he paid an additional 100 pesos to say masses for the deceased and assigned another 100 pesos to feed poor prisoners in Tlaxcala. In February 1716, his constable also distributed fifty chickens each to sick houses in Tlaxcala and San Martín Texmelucan. In line with colonial practices, Sánchez Morcillo kept 100 pesos as a commission fee for himself.[23]

The conduct of Sánchez Morcillo and the *alcalde mayor* could have been acceptable, because compensations for the aggrieved parties often settled violent crimes in the early modern period. The courts usually found it hard to prove premeditation in a killing, and they considered that male offenders defended their honor, acted rashly, or in self-defense. Under these circumstances, the courts frequently ruled that the perpetrators paid private compensations, called *compositions*, to the victims' family. Matters often differed for religious minorities or marginal groups, such as Jews, vagabonds, or bandits. They often received harsh sentences to set an example of deterrence. Many commoners also resented the sentences

---

[21] Defense of Sánchez Morcillo, AGI, México 670 B, *Relación*, fol. 731v.

[22] The original reads that the *alcalde mayor* "con nombre de su Ahijado el cazique me quiso corromper," which Sánchez Morcillo prosecuted as the "crimen de atentado soborno," *presentación* of Sánchez Morcillo, Mexico City, 24 July 1719, AGI, Escribanía 287 A, *pieza* 33, fol. 298; see also decree of Sánchez Morcillo, Tlaxcala, 24 Feb. 1716, AGI, Escribanía 281 D, fol. 981v; defense of Sánchez Morcillo, AGI, México 670 B, *Relación*, fol. 666.

[23] Defense of Sánchez Morcillo, n. d., AGI, Escribanía 287 A, *pieza* 33, fol. 298–298v; decree of Sánchez Morcillo, Tlaxcala, 24 Feb. 1716; inquiries of García de Xismeros, Tlaxcala, 8 Mar. 1716, AGI, Escribanía 281 D, fols. 981–982; defense of Sánchez Morcillo, AGI, México 670 B, *Relación*, fols. 728v–737v; see also Murillo Velarde, *Cursus Iuris Canonici*, book 1, title 32, para. 346.

that privileged the elite. The law, they said, were like "the webs of spiders that catch the small flies with forceful rigor, while any strong power breaks the web." Yet Diego García de Guesca stood to gain from such a system, as he was a man of local prominence, if not a nobleman himself. He claimed to have acted in self-defense and Cos y Cevallos could well have believed this. Sánchez Morcillo's compensations for Nieto's widow and mother were also a plausible resolution of a violent conflict.[24]

But Garzarón did not principally review the content of Sánchez Morcillo's verdicts and instead analyzed the discrepancies between his paper trail and the oral testimony. Judges rarely gave reasons for their verdicts and were hardly ever tried for flawed sentences themselves. In fact, an attorney representing a judge in 1719 contended that his client "cannot be reproached for or charged with wrong sentencing, according to the trial law and the law of the Indies."[25] Garzarón, for this reason, never assessed how Nieto died or if the brothers had truly bribed the *alcalde mayor*. Some informal bookkeeping was also usual and would have been excusable. What was worse, several signs indicated that Sánchez Morcillo had fabricated the papers. Some numbered pages were missing from the record. Others appeared to have been added later, because the paper and the ink had a fresher look. Garzarón also noted that Sánchez Morcillo had stored the trial record with the *audiencia* on January 25, 1717, just after Garzarón interviewed him about this issue for the first time. Garzarón found this remarkable in itself, as it pointed to fraud.[26]

Garzarón became convinced that Sánchez Morcillo had falsified the papers to make it appear that he had arrested Cos y Cevallos. According to the record, Cos y Cevallos had sent fowl and funds on the governor's behalf, but Garzarón could not believe that he would be so generous as to

---

[24] Mendo, *Príncipe Perfecto*, 117–118; see also Karl Härter, "Violent Crimes and Retaliation in the European Criminal Justice System between the Seventeenth and Nineteenth Century," in *Max Planck Institute for European Legal History Research Paper Series* 1 (2013): 6–8, http://dx.doi.org/ 10.2139/ssrn.2218350; Meccarelli, "Dimensions of Justice," 54, 59, argues that judges sought to deter crimes while compensating victims. See, e.g., the *declaración* of José Garcia de Guesca, Huejotzingo, 23 Feb. 1716, AGI, Escribanía 281 D, fol. 980v; charge and defense of Sánchez Morcillo, AGI, México 670 B, *Relación*, fols. 675–677v.

[25] Juan Francisco de Córdoba on behalf of Juan de Oliván y Rebolledo to Garzarón, Mexico City, 21 Aug. 1719, AGI, Escribanía 280 C, fol. 9.

[26] *Prueba*, AGI, México 670 B, *Relación*, fols. 670–671v; decree of *audiencia* signed by Deputy Notary Luis de Ortega, Mexico City, 25 Jan. 1717, AGI, Escribanía 281 D, fol. 984; Murillo Velarde, *Cursus Iuris Canonici*, book 2, title 20, para. 152, no. 4, pointed out that "the actor or accuser in a trial cannot be a witness."

"run the risk that his pesos and chickens be applied to the purpose of don Miguel Pérez." It seemed more likely that Sánchez Morcillo attempted to discredit Cos y Cevallos as a witness by casting him as a perpetrator.[27] Garzarón also doubted that Sánchez Morcillo had ordered house arrest for Cos y Cevallos, who would have claimed that the viceroy, as his senior officer, had sole military jurisdiction in the case. According to the notes scribbled by Sánchez Morcillo's notary, a servant rode on horseback to Mexico City to seek permission for arresting Cos y Cevallos, but the viceroy never provided a receipt or responded in any other way to that or two subsequent requests. Sánchez Morcillo told Garzarón that he had arrived in Puebla by May 30, 1716, where he ended his inquiry and lifted Cos y Cevallos's arrest. Yet Garzarón concluded that Sánchez Morcillo had invented this entire tale about Cos y Cevallos.[28]

The *visitador* noted additional problems. Garzarón inferred that Sánchez Morcillo had given Josefa Nicolasa cash to instigate the process. With this move, Sánchez Morcillo avoided investigating the case ex officio, which would have raised further suspicions against him. Nevertheless, he failed to provide any credible documentation showing that the widow had actually received the compensation. Garzarón also read an improbable story of Sánchez Morcillo's physically active notary. According to the record, the notary dispatched papers in Tlaxcala on February 23. On the same day, he walked about twenty miles, or six hours, over hilly terrain to Huejotzingo, where he continued his work. The next day the notary returned to Tlaxcala to draft documents for Sánchez Morcillo and then once more journeyed to Huejotzingo to take the widow's testimony and confiscate Cos y Cevallos's estate. Garzarón doubted that the notary walked back and forth between the two cities, when a single trip would have sufficed. Finally, there was no record documenting the release of the García de Guesca brothers from jail or for charging them a deposit. In short, something was awry in the record.[29]

At this point, Sánchez Morcillo took recourse to tarnishing the reputation of the *provisor* (vicar-general) of Puebla, who had gathered evidence against him. Sánchez Morcillo began by recounting that his notary had been in the Saint Joseph church in Puebla "where he saw a beautifully

---

[27] Prueba, AGI, México 670 B, *Relación*, fol. 666–666v.
[28] Decree of Sánchez Morcillo, Tlaxcala, 24 Feb. 1716; *diligencia*, Tlaxcala, 24 Feb. 1716; decree, Tlaxcala, 16 Mar. 1716; *diligencia*, 17 Mar. 1716; decree, Puebla, 20 Apr. and 30 May 1716, AGI, Escribanía 281 D, fols. 980v–983v; *prueba*, AGI, México 670 B, *Relación*, fols. 671v–672.
[29] Prueba, AGI, México 670 B, *Relación*, fols. 669–671v, 733.

adorned woman seated at the foot of one altar ... and a footman in livery came in, who appeared to serve the vicar-general, and she immediately left and the notary rushed after her," witnessing that the woman entered the vicar-general's coach.[30] Sánchez Morcillo had declined charging "doña María Barbero, who had been accused ... of being in an illicit and scandalous friendship with the vicar-general." Yet the episode showed clearly that "while the vicar-general may be a clergyman, he is still subject to the passions of love and hate."[31] Sánchez Morcillo demanded, therefore, that "everything the vicar-general had gathered against him be declared void." Yet Garzarón repulsed that argument by denying that Sánchez Morcillo's *acordada* in Puebla had ever included the vicar-general's conduct.[32]

Sánchez Morcillo also questioned the vicar-general's impartiality, because he had prosecuted the vicar-general's *compadre* (close friend) in 1716 for selling stolen merchandise. The *compadre* admitted trading with dubious goods and therefore "voluntarily gave his Grace [Sánchez Morcillo] twenty yards of fine cloth and some stockings that he sent with an old *mulato* called Francisco, who is the vicar-general's usher ... because he feared the jail that the criminal judge threatened him with."[33] The usher Francisco de Santa María confirmed the story, but Sánchez Morcillo claimed that the vicar-general had instead attempted to bribe him to absolve the *compadre*. Yet Garzarón threw out this defense too, because the vicar-general had recused himself from investigating that case. Instead the *alcalde mayor* of Puebla confirmed that the *compadre* had in fact given Sánchez Morcillo 800 pesos.[34]

---

[30] Sánchez Morcillo's testimony, Mexico City, 4 July 1719, AGI, México 670 B, fol. 601. According to *relación de méritos*, AGI, Indiferente, 217, N. 79, the commissioner was Diego Felipe Gómez de Ángulo, *provisor* of the bishop of Puebla.
[31] *Presentación* of Sánchez Morcillo's, Mexico City, 24 July 1719, AGI, Escribanía 287 A, fol. 293.
[32] Defense of Sánchez Morcillo, AGI, México 670 B, *Relación*, fols. 591v, 593; Garzarón's commentary on Sánchez Morcillo's defense, AGI, México 670 B, fol. 591.
[33] Testimony of Juan de San Martín, n. d., AGI, México 670 B, fols. 582v–583.
[34] Testimony of Francisco de Santa María, n. d., AGI, México 670 B, fols. 557v–558; *auto* of Sánchez Morcillo, Puebla, 10 June 1716, AGI, Escribanía 281 D, fol. 915; Sánchez Morcillo, *Probansa dada en la Visita general*, Mexico City, 2 June 1719, AGI, Escribanía 281 D, fols. 918v–920; Sánchez Morcillo's testimony, Mexico City, 4 July 1719, AGI, México 670 B, fol. 601v; *prueba*, AGI, México 670 B, fol. 616v; Juan José Veytia Linage to (probably) Valero, 12 Sep. 1716, AGI, México 670 B, fol. 588v; see also *relación de méritos* of Diego Felipe Gómez de Ángulo, AGI, Indiferente General, 217, N. 79.

Sánchez Morcillo was out of luck, as he lacked support to buoy him through the tempest. He could not show that he had properly distributed the fines among the monasteries and the Native family. Garzarón therefore concluded that Sánchez Morcillo had demanded money to release the García de Guesca brothers and Governor Perez from jail, committing crimes that jurists often called *concusión* (violent extortion). Moreover, Sánchez Morcillo had tampered with the papers to hide his trail. Importantly, the Marquis of Valero, the *alcalde mayor* of Puebla, and even some clerics of the Puebla Cathedral confirmed Sánchez Morcillo's corruption. This evidence sufficed for Garzarón to suspend the judge. The Council of the Indies and the king later removed the judge for this and other crimes. The Council also dismissed the notary, who had to return all fees and deposits that he had gained by fleecing the litigants in Huejotzingo.[35]

5.2 THE STANDARDS OF JUSTICE IN THE VISITA

The Huejotzingo affair illustrates how a *visita* operated in practice. These *visitas* were criminal trials that ultimately descended from the late medieval Inquisition processes. The Holy Office had early on eschewed practices such as purging oaths and ordeals of battle and supplanted them with the judge who carefully analyzed the evidence to establish the guilt of individual suspects. The judge acted simultaneously as prosecutor and detective who contended with the defendant. This method became known as the inquisitorial method, which, over time, evolved into the Castilian standard of criminal trials. *Visitas* largely built on the framework, although they also included additional provisions on the number, quality, and secrecy of testimony giving the investigating judges wider rein. These special rules made it easier to convict suspects, and *visitas* were efficient in uncovering malfeasance and corruption.[36]

---

[35] *Consulta* of the Council of the Indies, Madrid, 2 Sept. 1721, AGI, México 380; sentence of the Council of the Indies, Madrid, 18 Mar. 1727, AGI, Escribanía 1183, folder 1721–1730 Francisco Garzarón. On *concusión*, see Castillo de Bobadilla, *Politica*, book 2, chap. 11, para. 69, letter l, and book 5, chap. 1, para. 20; Berart y Gassol, *Speculum visitationis*, chap. 17, paras. 8–9.

[36] On inquisitorial trials, see Kimberly Lynn, *Between Court and Confessional. The Politics of Spanish Inquisitors* (Cambridge: Cambridge University Press, 2013), 19–29; Michel Foucault, *The History of Sexuality: An Introduction*, trans. Robert Hurley (New York: Vintage Books, 1978), 58; Burns, *Into the Archive*, 33; Francisco Bethencourt, *The Inquisition. A Global History, 1478–1834* (Cambridge: Cambridge University Press, 2009), 6, 215. Mireille Peytavin argues that *visitas* never

Meanwhile, the adversarial process declined in the Spanish world. Adversarial (also known as accusatorial) trials consisted of judges who supervised the charges that an aggrieved victim brought against the alleged perpetrator of a crime, while juries decided the outcomes. Most modern Anglo-Saxon judicial systems adhere to this framework. We tend to think of the inquisitorial process as the embodiment of cruelty, shaped by Edgar Allan Poe's terrifying account in *The Pit and the Pendulum*. The inquisitorial process did convict the innocent more easily and could be a terrifying tool in the wrong hands. Yet the process also reduced the chances of dangerous criminals walking free. It also lowered the risks for victims, because accusers who lost a trial had earlier suffered the same punishment that they had sought for the perpetrators. In addition, the investigative judges did not need an individual to denounce a crime. Public rumors, clandestine denunciations, or royal communications about alleged offenses sufficed for judges to investigate ex officio. What is more, historians now downplay the sharp distinctions between the accusatorial and inquisitorial processes. Both early modern trial forms frequently coerced defendants into involuntary confessions and negotiated rulings against the suspects even when the evidence was questionable.[37]

The criminal judges in the Spanish empire typically uncovered the facts in several stages while observing limited guarantees for the defendants. During the *sumaria* (initial inquiry), the judges interviewed witnesses, searched for a written record, and frequently gained first-hand insights by observing the crime scene. They also consulted with physicians about the victims' injuries or heard the expertise of notaries and printers about forgeries. While doing so, judges hunted primarily for inculpatory rather than exculpatory evidence, and they often proceeded in secrecy and without the suspects' knowledge, at least during this early stage. The judges then compressed their information into lengthy questionnaires that the witnesses

---

followed the same pattern, cited in Herzog, "Ritos de Control," 12. A case study is Edgar Iván Mondragón Aguilera, "Atrapados por el procedimiento. Un proceso inquisitorial como espacio para el juego de estrategias," in Sanchez, *Los actores locales de la nación*, 41–77.

[37] Meccarelli, "Dimensions of Justice," 53–63; Máximo Langer, "The Long Shadow of the Adversarial and Inquisitorial Categories," in *The Oxford Handbook of Criminal Law*, eds. Markus D. Dubber and Tatjana Hörnle (Oxford: Oxford University Press, 2015), 4–5, 8. On Castilian trials as "at once adversarial and inquisitorial," see Mumford, "Litigation as Ethnography," 37. According to Lepsius, *Von Zweifeln*, 11–12, most inquisitorial trials were initially considered extraordinary, because the essential third person next to judge and suspect disappeared, but the trial form became the norm in Castile over time.

and the suspects had to answer. The judges and their notaries took detailed notes of the interrogations to aid them mnemonically. Taking notes ensured that the judges heard all involved parties in a similar fashion without ruling arbitrarily. The suspects, in turn, attempted to disprove the charges. When the judge had gathered enough evidence against a suspect, the *sumaria* ended and the *plenaria* (main phase) began. The judges defined the substantiated charges against the defendants, who presented additional exonerating evidence and could demand that unsuited judges recuse themselves. Once the *plenaria* ended, the attorneys argued their case, orally in the lower courts and with written briefs in the higher courts.[38]

Then the judges ruled. In trials of the first instance, the magistrates issued a verdict. *Visitadores* similarly ruled after pondering the evidence. Meanwhile, the judges of the appellate courts such as the Mexico City *audiencia* convened behind closed doors. The criminal chamber ideally consisted of four criminal judges who had read the motions and each voted on the sentence without any discussion. The junior judges went first so that the senior colleagues would not intimidate them. At least two judges had to agree on a criminal sentence and three to punish physically or by death. The judges then signed off on the verdict, regardless of how they had voted, and pronounced the sentence. A notary published the verdict, and the trial ended by carrying out the punishment.[39]

---

[38] For a standard interrogatory for the *juicios de residencia* of *alcaldes mayores,* jailers, and notaries, see Castillo de Bobadilla, *Política*, book 5, chap. 1; see also Brendecke, *Imperio*, 382–385; Alonso Romero, *Orden procesal*, 35–40, 44; Cordero Fernández, *Institucionalizar*, 348–349; and Javier Villa-Flores, "Archivos y falsarios: producción y circulación de documentos apócrifos en el México borbónico," *Jahrbuch für Geschichte Lateinamerikas* 46, no. 1 (2009): 25, 34–35; Andreas Deutsch, "Beweis," in Cordes, *HRG*, 2nd ed., (2008), 1: 559–566. www.hrgdigital.de/HRG.beweis. For examples of recusations in the *visita*, see defense of Jerónimo Soria, AGI, México 670 B, *Relación*, fols. 110–111, in accordance with the *Law of the Indies*, book 2, title 15, law 31; testimony of don Miguel Pérez de Santa Cruz, Marquis of Buenavista, 2 Oct. 1717, AGI, Escribanía 278 A, *legajo* 8, fols. 17–18. See also the petition to recuse a *visitador* in Gómez, "Entre la corrupción y la venalidad," 240. According to Robinson, Fergus, and Gordon, *European*, 199, and Schlosser, *Neuere europäische*, 85–89, Justinian's *Code* contained the two *Terrible Books* on criminal prosecution, which formed the basis for the developing standards. The right of *nemo tenetur se ipsum accusare* (the right to remain silent) is a twelfth-century brocard, whereas *in dubio pro reo* (rule for the suspect when in doubt) appeared in Egidio Bossio's treatise of 1562. Castillo de Bobadilla, *Política*, book 2, chap. 11, para. 25 and 64, fn. h, for example, frequently cited the humanists Bossio and André Tiraqueau.

[39] Solórzano, *Política Indiana*, book 5, chap. 8, paras. 5–8; *Law of Castile*, book 2, title 6, law 5; Garriga, "Sobre el gobierno," 140–144; Mirow, *Latin American Law*, 27; Hillebrand, *Real Audiencia*, 113.

Draconian rulings and authoritarian practices could mark these trials to deter crimes, although critics also insisted on trial guarantees and attacked opaque and unreasonable process in the seventeenth and eighteenth centuries. Many demanded that "crimes must not remain unpunished," and this desire often outweighed the concerns over wrongful convictions.[40] King Philip V fretted about theft, for example, and, in 1734, he ordered that anyone caught stealing from the royal court or its slaughterhouse be put to death. Early modern judges also lowered the burden of proof to convict suspects of heinous crimes and adjusted the punishment to fit the evidence rather than the crime. They handed down extraordinary punishments, for example, when only circumstantial evidence was available. Yet clemency often assuaged harsh rulings. Jurists also insisted on trial guarantees such as not sentencing defendants twice for the same offense. In addition, criminal prosecutors increasingly joined the courts, adding a voice to the process and relieving the judges from building the case against suspects.[41]

Garzarón molded his *visita* on these Spanish criminal trials. He received the *real cédula* (royal communication) appointing him *visitador general* of New Spain on October 13, 1716. The next day he started the *sumaria*, inquiring secretly about the *audiencia* judges. On October 17, he publicly announced the investigation and sent messages to the *alcaldes mayores* of the *audiencia* district, encouraging all residents to report the misconduct of the president, judges, and the *audiencia* staff. Criminal convicts, Native governors, *hacendados*, and a few *novohispanas*, such as doña Úrsula de Salazar, answered the call. We do not know to which degree Garzarón coerced or nudged the witnesses, though others rendered testimony voluntarily. He concluded the first round of interviews in early November and began interrogating the judges afterwards.[42]

---

[40] Hevia Bolaños, *Curia Filipica*, vol. 1, part 3, para. 16, no. 1, citing Pope Innocent III's dictum "ne crimine remaneant impunita"; see also nos. 11, 14, 15, 18; Lepsius, *Von Zweifeln*, 11.
[41] Alonso Romero, *Orden Procesal*, 40–44, 103–107; Cordero Fernández, *Institucionalizar*, 364; Schlosser, *Neuere europäische*, 89–91.
[42] Edict of Garzarón, Mexico City, 17 Oct. 1716, AGI, Escribanía 278 A, *legajo* 8; Garzarón to king, Mexico City, 21 Dec. 1716, AGI, México 670 A; the *sumaria* was also called *pesquisa secreta* (secret inquiry). On witnesses, see, e.g., testimonies of don Miguel Pérez and don Antonio Pérez, AGI, México 670 B, *Relación*, fol. 664–664v; Alonso de la Lama y Noriega for Sánchez Morcillo to king, Madrid, 1 Apr. 1727, AGI, Escribanía 287 B, *pieza* 38, fols. 42v–43. On unknown selection criteria for testimony, Herzog, "Ritos de control," 8.

Garzarón questioned hundreds of witnesses, while eschewing great public gestures of power. He forewent the inaugural Mass and peripatetic inspections of the provinces that had marked earlier *visitas*. Instead, he questioned about 700 witnesses, when, in comparison, previous *visitadores* had interrogated about thirty witnesses. Garzarón and his notaries then produced a massive paper trail of thirty-five folders of nearly 2,000 pages each in addition to two summarized volumes. By recording the evidence in detail, Garzarón aimed at curbing doubts about the fairness of his prosecution. In addition, Garzarón remained in Mexico City, where he interrogated the suspects and witnesses in his room in the Inquisition palace. He sent out commissioners in his stead to gather evidence in Puebla and other parts of the viceroyalty. By using this methodical approach, Garzarón gained access to important information and guarded himself against accusations of excessively partisan rulings.[43]

He also hunted for written evidence to convict ministers, just as he did in the Huejotzingo case. Garzarón and his assistants ferreted out business or personal papers to demonstrate nefarious bribes to judges or fraud. For instance, Garzarón saw the detailed daily entries in the "first record book of don Manuel Francisco Garces ... who recognized his own writing and signature," according to which he had given 200 pesos to a civil judge.[44] Such strong proof boded ill for the suspect. In a comparable case, a merchant complained that a senior constable and a notary working for another investigative judge "entered my study ... and without any judicial formality that may have mattered, seized my account books and debt papers and brought them to the home of the judge."[45]

Garzarón then distilled the information into questionnaires. Initially he interviewed people who belonged to his social alliance or else were

---

[43] Armando Guevara-Gil and Frank Solomon, "A 'Personal Visit' Colonial Political Ritual and the Making of Indians in the Andes," *Colonial Latin American Review* 3, nos. 1–2 (1994): 8–10, 24; Herzog, "Ritos de control," 23–24, 26; Brendecke, *Imperio*, 92; Luhmann, *Legitimation durch Verfahren*, 6th ed. (Frankfurt: Suhrkamp, 2001). On the number of 700 witnesses, *consulta* of the Council of the Indies, Madrid, 13 Nov. 1721, AGI, México 670 A. Garzarón's colleague, Francisco Pagabe, first interviewed the witnesses in the Inquisition palace but later rented a home for that purpose, see *consulta* of the Council of the Indies, Madrid, 20 Apr. 1718, AGI, México 379.

[44] *Prueba*, México 670 B, *Relación*, fol. 13v. The earlier *Compendio y breue instruction por tener libros de cuentas, deudas y de mercaduria: muy prouechoso para mercaderes y toda gente de negocio: traduzido de Frances en Castellano*, by an anonymous author (Barcelona: en casa de Claudio Bornat al Aguila fuerte, 1565), no page, gives an indication of the three typical record-keeping methods of merchants.

[45] Testimony of Antonio de Zavaleta, Veracruz, 20 Oct. 1717, AGI, Escribanía 278 A, Quaderno 6, fol. 738.

reasonably friendly with him. He took this preliminary evidence and condensed it to confront further witnesses with his knowledge. Garzarón asked questions and the witnesses replied, first, answering the so-called general questions about the witness's identity and relationship to the suspect. Garzarón then asked whether they were family members or enemies? Had anyone persuaded them to alter their statements? Afterwards, Garzarón got to the heart of the case, assembling 241 questions about the conduct of the jail officials, for instance. He questioned whether the witnesses knew that "the constables arrested some people without court order, although they were not committing crimes"? Were they aware that the jailers had "carnal excess with a female prisoner" or even "forced any married or unmarried woman"? Garzarón asked about the time and place of an offense and about additional witnesses of the crime.[46]

After listening to or reading the depositions, the *visitador* evaluated their credibility. He discerned whether the witnesses had participated in or seen malfeasance or heard about it from somebody else. Or where they were merely reporting a rumor? Meanwhile, according to one of Garzarón's commissioners, the witnesses had no "duty to justify or prove their statements ... but only to say the truth about what they knew or had heard."[47] It fell to the *visitador* to draw the proper conclusions from the answers. For example, several witnesses defended a scribe by denying that he levied the same fees from Indians and Spaniards, although the law required that Indians paid less. Yet Garzarón dismissed the exonerating statements as inconclusive and suspended the scribe.[48]

The *visita* also accepted other testimony than ordinary criminal trials to root out the "ugliness and vileness" of corruption.[49] In the ordinary trial and the *visita*, the testimonies of two reputable witnesses who had not

---

[46] *Ynterrogatorio*, AGI, Escribanía 281 C, *pesquisa secreta* Q.o 19, fols. 1–6v, quotes on fols. 2, 3v; Burns, *Into the Archive*, 33, observes that the notaries in Peru did not typically record the answers to the general questions. In addition, while the sources say little about forced testimony, McKinley, *Fractional Freedoms*, 6, shows that *censuras* (notes) were publicly posted or read to force parishioners to alter their conduct short of a trial. Garzarón may have used similar tools.

[47] Gregorio de Salinas, Veracruz, 27 Sept. 1717, *Quaderno 6*, AGI, Escribanía 278 A, fols. 699–700. See also Hevia Bolaños, *Curia Filípica*, vol. 1, part 3, para. 10, no. 8–10; and vol. 1, part 3, para. 15, no. 12–13.

[48] Defense of Francisco de Castro and *prueba*, AGI, Escribanía 289 A, *Relazion*, fols. 383v–389.

[49] Castillo de Bobadilla, *Politica*, book 5, chap. 1, para. 229; see also para. 220, "the Romans found corrupting justice by money hateful."

participated in the crime sufficed for a conviction. In the Americas, one Indian did not always count as much as a Spaniard, and six Indians had to testify to equal a full testimony. Yet the *visitas* also recognized three full testimonies that described separate accounts of corruption as long as they did not contradict one another. These witnesses could even have participated in the crime. Jurists called this standard the irregular evidence of three singular witnesses, and it eased convictions in the *visita*. Those who testified did not have to fear any punishments for their past sin, although they could not recover their gifts either, "so that greed does not move people to give false testimony."[50]

The defendants criticized Garzarón for convictions based on either the regular or irregular standard. One judge contended that the "irregular evidence only proved bribery and *baratería* (corruption)," and that neither applied to him because he had only ever received appropriate attentions.[51] Garzarón nonetheless hewed to the law, allowing three witnesses to prove corruption. For example, don Bernabé Ximénez, a *cacique* from Tlacotla (Veracruz) served two months in the jail of Tlaxcala for being an accomplice in a robbery. One day, the jail constable entered the dungeon and threatened to flog Ximénez unless he paid 120

---

[50] *Law of Castile*, book 3, title 9, law 6; this law denied restitution to witnesses "unless they can fully provide evidence for" their claims. Note that the Roman jurist known simply as Paul argued that bribes given to judges could not be recovered, and his comment appeared in Justinian's *Digest* 12.5.3; see also Decock, *Theologians*, 440. In addition, the *Law of Castile*, book 3, title 9, law 6, did not specifically restrict the irregular testimony to bribery and instead stated that the *visitador* can hear "those who give something to the judges in whose court they are litigating," and the *visitador* "can prove the offense when three witnesses or more testify under oath that they gave the judge" something. The print *por Don Miguel Truxillo*, AGI, México 670 A, fols. 5, 9, refers to this law. Castillo de Bobadilla, *Politica*, book 5, chap. 1, para. 220, see also paras. 204–209, 221–223, 230, separated the "two concurring witnesses that saw an incident" from the "three irregular witnesses" for cases of bribery and *baratería*. Yet for Castillo de Bobadilla, a higher standard should apply to judges and he argued in book 5, chap. 1, para. 135, that "one should not scrupulously investigate a judge who has clean hands," citing the fourteenth-century commentator Angelo de Ubaldo; similar, Berart y Gassol, *Speculum visitationis*, chap. 5, paras. 1–5, 37–38, 56–62, 76. On the witness standard, Hevia Bolaños, *Curia Filipica*, vol. 1, part 3, para. 15, no. 11, 14, 15. On Indians, Murillo Velarde, *Cursus Iuris Canonici*, book 2, title 20, para. 157; see also para. 165, that "adversative" testimonies contradicted one another and had less value in court, "accumulative" testimonies provided different yet supporting accounts which counted as half or even as full testimony, and "diversificative" testimony did not directly support or debunk other testimony and counted for more than half a testimony. See also Alonso Romero, *Orden Procesal*, 40.

[51] Defense of González de Agüero, AGI, México 670 B, *Relación*, fol. 205; see also defense of Díaz de Bracamonte, AGI, México 670 B, *Relación*, fol. 128, opposing the "irregular proof" of three witnesses.

pesos. Ximénez's brother and the *mulato* shoemaker José de Sicilia, a *compadre* of Bernabé Ximénez, handed over cash to the constable. When questioned about the incident, the constable stated that "a tall, young, Chinese-looking boy from Puebla" had given him money, of which he retained a jail fee of twenty pesos while the remainder went to Pedro Sánchez Morcillo and his notary. Sánchez Morcillo then sentenced Ximénez to six months' exile from Tlaxcala. Sánchez Morcillo subsequently played down the incident. In his view, the indigenous municipal council of Tlaxcala "demanded that the Indian *cacique* be brought from the public jail to the building of the council." Sánchez Morcillo implied that at that point he lost jurisdiction over Ximénez. Yet Sánchez Morcillo presented a dubious record of his actions, especially as he could not show what happened to the 100 pesos he had received from the constable. Garzarón put more faith in the three incriminating testimonies of the witnesses who had participated in the incident: Ximénez, his *compadre*, and the constable.[52]

The *visitador* relied on two legitimate witnesses who had not participated in the offense when convicting for other offenses than corruption. In one case, a witness stated that "the *mulata* [a woman of mixed African descent] Juana de San Cayetano was in jail for theft in 1716 or 1717," when a notary charged her sixteen pesos for drafting a motion and conducting some interviews. The court then fined her four pesos for her crime. According to the witness, the notary subsequently pressed San Cayetano for more money, even though he had already overcharged her. A clergyman confirmed this account. Garzarón later examined a woman called María Josefa at the notary's behest. She claimed to be the delinquent's sister and presented three witnesses stating that the notary did not take anything more than the four pesos. Yet Garzarón did not believe her witnesses and suspended the notary on the two accusing testimonies, among other charges. The Council of the Indies later found the notary guilty on all 127 counts against him and removed him from his post.[53]

Suspects attempted to discredit hostile testimony against them. One attorney, for instance, demanded a copy of all charges against him so he could point out his enemies. This was common practice in ordinary

---

[52] Testimony as summarized by Garzarón in *prueba*, AGI, México 670 B, fols. 685–687v. That case was probably *concusión* rather than bribery, although both acts were understood as *baratería* or corruption.

[53] Testimony of Cristina Josefa and María Josefa, AGI, Escribanía 289 B, *Relazion*, fols. 742–743; sentence of the Council of the Indies, Madrid, 18 Mar. 1727, AGI, Escribanía 1183, folder *1721–1730 Francisco Garzarón*.

criminal processes, and, according to the attorney, the *visita's* "rigor has to be limited to the secrecy of the process itself, and it cannot break other rules of justice," including the right to challenge unsuited witnesses.[54] One *receptor* (an agent receiving money and documents) added that most "litigants hate the ministers even if they attain justice. They believe they unduly had to pay the official, and those who lose a trial commonly blame all those who participate, saying that the judge is wicked, the receptor and the notary are forging thieves, the agent is negligent, and the attorney ignorant."[55] Others claimed that the witnesses were malicious, driven by personal gain, or had been previously punished elsewhere. They should be excluded, because only testimony "as clear as the light at midday" should be admitted. This argument echoed the thirteenth-century legal collection *Siete Partidas* (Seven Parts). The defendants also pointed to scholars who favored acquitting suspects rather than convicting potentially innocent people when evidence was shaky.[56]

Garzarón instead promised confidentiality for all witnesses to assuage fears of retribution. As a solution to the defendants' complaints about hostile testimony, he suggested that they provide him with the names of all their enemies, which they never did. At the same time, Garzarón and his commissioners told the witnesses to keep quiet about their interviews and

---

[54] Alonso de la Lama y Noriega on behalf of Pedro Sánchez Morcillo to king, Madrid, 1 Apr. 1727, AGI, Escribanía 287 B, *pieza* 38, fol. 32; Pedro Robledo to Garzarón, Mexico City, 2 June 1719, AGI, Escribanía 280 C, *Q.no* 12, fols. 449–450; see also Juan Francisco de Córdoba on behalf of Juan de Oliván y Rebolledo to Garzarón, Mexico City, 21 Aug. 1719, AGI Escribanía 280 C, fol. 7.

[55] Defense of Feliciano de Ulloa y Sevilla, n. d., AGI, Escribanía 289 B, *Relazion*, fol. 732.

[56] Petition of Juan José de Sevilla to Garzarón, Mexico City, 29 Oct. 1721, AGI, Escribanía 285 B, *Q.no* 26, fol. 249; the *Siete Partidas* are cited in Alonso Romero, *Orden Procesal*, 40. Hevia Bolaños, *Curia Filipica*, vol. 1, part 3, para. 17, no. 1, argued that without "certain, full, and clear evidence like the midday light," the judge could not convict criminal suspects. For a discussion whether to reveal the witness names, ibid., vol. 1, part 3, para. 13, no. 5, and para. 14, no. 8. For Berart y Gassol, *Speculum visitationis*, chap. 5, para. 38, witnesses had to be "above any exception." On witnesses, see also Castillo de Bobadilla, *Política*, book 5, chap. 1, para. 202; *presentación* of Sánchez Morcillo, Mexico City, 24 July 1719, AGI, Escribanía 287 A, fol. 293; print *por Don Miguel Truxillo*, AGI, México 670 A, fol. 4v; Juan José Veytia Linage to Miguel Fernández Durán, Puebla, 17 Oct. 1719, AGI, México 670 A; *consulta* of the Council of the Indies, Madrid, 13 Nov. 1721, AGI, México 380; defense of Juan Díaz de Bracamonte, AGI, México 670 B, *Relación*, fol. 128. Garzarón to king, Mexico City, 3 Aug. 1720, AGI, México 670 A, denied that his witnesses showed "hate or other passion." According to *Law of Castile*, book 4, title 8, laws 1–3, litigants could not reject all witnesses. According to Cordero Fernández, *Institucionalizar*, 325, 349, even the infamous and excommunicated testified in idolatry *visitas*. On acquittals, Murillo Velarde, *Cursus Iuris Canonici*, book 1, title 32, para. 344.

inform no one. They had good reason to do so. Several witnesses worried that the Marquis of Valero would order them to the palace to report about their accusations. Other witnesses were threatened not to speak out against the suspects.[57]

Garzarón himself took great strides to corral any disclosures, yet at least two officials leaked the names of *visita* witnesses. In one instance, Garzarón's notary was on the threshold of death and desired salvation. He gave the criminal judge Sánchez Morcillo the names of the witnesses against him, including those of the Native Governor Miguel Pérez and his son. Soon after, on February 21, 1724, at three o'clock in the afternoon, the notary lay "on a mat with four candles lighted, dressed in the habit of Our Father Saint Francis, appearing to be dead."[58] This story underlines once more the power of notaries to skew judicial decisions, though this could also have been a ruse to blame Garzarón's trusted notary and cloak the true source of the leak. In a similar case, Garzarón suspected that a lawyer had copied the court record in 1724. The lawyer printed his defense and included the names of witnesses. One print wandered from desk to desk at the tribunal of accounts in Mexico City. Some broadsheets crossed the Atlantic and circulated in Madrid. Garzarón seized several copies and ordered the viceroy's legal adviser to surrender his print or pay a 500-peso fine. The adviser balked at the order, and Garzarón raised the penalty to 1,000 pesos. The adviser finally buckled and submitted the print. There were surprisingly few leaks of this kind in the *visita*.[59]

In addition, Garzarón sent friendly clergymen to question witnesses or suspects in other towns. The *Law of the Indies* mostly confined *visitadores* to their residences, and for this reason, an Inquisition commissioner prowled around Veracruz in 1717. He hunted for evidence that an *audiencia* judge had extorted cash to absolve merchants and officials from the

---

[57] Gregorio de Salinas, Veracruz, 27 Sept. 1717, AGI, Escribanía 278 A, *Quaderno* 6, fol. 699; while interrogatory of Garzarón, Mexico City, 1 Oct. 1717, AGI, Escribanía 278 A, *Quaderno* 6, fol. 1, assured confidentiality to the Marquis of Buenavista. *Law of the Indies*, book 2, title 34, law 24 ordered the secrecy of *visitas*; on secrecy, see Garriga, "Sobre el gobierno," 88. On threats, Garzarón to king, 7 Aug. 1724, as summarized in *consulta* of the Council of the Indies, Madrid, 18 Jan. 1726, AGI, México 670 A; see also Garzarón to king, Mexico City, 2 May 1725, AHN, Inquisición 1740, exp. 18.

[58] Lama y Noriega for Sánchez Morcillo to king, Madrid, 1 Apr. 1727, AGI, Escribanía 287 B, *pieza* 38, fols. 42v–43. On the notary's death, see *certificación* of Antonio de los Rios, Mexico City, 27 Feb. 1724, AGI, Escribanía 287 A, Q.no 31, fol. 80v.

[59] Garzarón to king, Mexico City, 7 Aug. 1724, AGI, México 670 A. On Juan Pacheco Picado, Valero's adviser, see Table 6 in the Appendix.

charge of dealing with foreign merchants during the War of the Succession (1702–1714). In addition, the dean of the cathedral chapter of Antequera (now Oaxaca) verified information in his city, and Puebla's vicar-general sniffed out Sánchez Morcillo's infamous trail.[60]

Garzarón also elicited information on the ministers' reputation and personal life, which influenced his ruling. Almost all witnesses attested that the civil judge Jerónimo Soria was known to return gifts, and Garzarón absolved him. A deputy notary also pointed out that an earlier investigation had confirmed him as a trustworthy minister. In his view, this good reputation itself dispelled at least minor charges against him. On the other hand, a judge with bad report could lose the presumption of innocence. In the case of a prosecutor, nobody "excepted him from the bad reputation of ... receiving donations and gifts."[61] Garzarón also inquired about rumors of an immoral life – such as playing cards, having extramarital affairs, or skipping Mass. In the colonial thinking, the judges' official and private lives were intertwined, and private misconduct indicated that suspects did not act impartially on the bench either. A notary, for example, allegedly acted as the *alcahuete* (procurer) for a criminal judge, setting up trysts in brothels. The judge also caused a scandal when he entered the confessional smoking cigars.[62]

Similar charges were leveled against the prosecutor Juan Francisco de la Peña. His wife hosted card games with people of various social stations, and even her servants commented about them. De la Peña downplayed the accusations, since the *Law of the Indies* prohibited gambling and

---

[60] Gregorio de Salinas, and testimony of Manuel de Soto Guerrero against Felix de Agüero, Veracruz, 27 Sept. 1717, AGI, Escribanía 278 A, *Quaderno* 6, fols. 699, 700v; *Probansa dada en la Visita general*, Mexico City, 2 June 1719, AGI, Escribanía 281 D, fols. 918v–920. The *Law of the Indies*, book 2, title 34, laws 18–20, allowed *visitadores* to leave their residences only in important instances. This rule mostly ended the peripatetic visitations.

[61] Charges against José Antonio de Espinosa Ocampo y Cornejo, AGI, México 670 B, *Relación*, fol. 462. See also reputation of Soria, AGI, México 670 B, *Relación*, fols. 112–115v; "good reputation," in defense of Nicolás Moreno, n. d., AGI, Escribanía 289 A, fols. 1480v–1481. Also tarnished was the reputation of Sánchez Morcillo, AGI, México 670 B, *Relación*, fol. 778. Similarly, according to individual reputation of Calderón de la Barca, AGI, México 670 B, *Relación*, fols. 23, 25, Miguel Calderón de la Barca allegedly "traded and contracted with various people, and he brought great wealth to Spain." On losing the presumption of innocence, Castillo de Bobadilla, *Politica*, book 5, chap. 1, para. 208.

[62] Reputation of Diego Francisco Castañeda, AGI, México 670 B, *Relación*, fol. 581v; according to Berart y Gassol, *Speculum visitationis*, chap. 5, para. 16, and chap. 3, para. 75, "the *visitadores* should ... inquire about the officials' life, customs, virtues, and doctrine." On accusations of immorality, see Herzog, *Upholding Justice*, 157–158.

socializing with locals. He pointed out that his wife had only modestly entertained "people of her quality, estate, and sex." He had attempted to end the gatherings, but it was "difficult to temper all actions of another individual, even of the spouse and children, and even more so when they do not breach decency." Playing cards in de la Peña's home continued until Garzarón read him the charges. Then de la Peña ended the reunions, but it was too late, and Garzarón suspended him.[63]

A life of excess and luxury signaled ill-gotten gains. For instance, a court agent traveled to Xochimilco to inquire about an *alcalde mayor's* malfeasance. The agent, though married, brought female companions, and the Indians fed and housed them until a public outcry ensued. The agent returned to Mexico City only after the dust had settled. There the agent "donned mask and dress and went about the streets and the homes of some ministers dancing, mocking them, and trifling with this *visita* during the carnival of 1720 ... and he misses no festivity, which he attends with various hooded suits in pursuit of his lechery." Garzarón heard the incriminating testimony and suspended the notary on April 6, 1724. The Council of the Indies added six additional years of suspension for him to chasten this and other offenses.[64] In a similar instance, another agent bought a grand coach at the expense of the "miserable litigants." These miserable people included the elderly, unmarried women, slaves, and Indians, who were entitled to special protections. Overcharging them aggravated any accusation. The agent, however, maintained that the dowry of his wife doña Ana Ventura de Aguilera supported their modest lifestyle. The Council of the Indies later dismissed the agent.[65]

Notoriety also eased convictions. Merely claiming that an incident was notorious did not usually suffice as evidence. At least several people from a community had to have witnessed a crime or a court must have had

---

[63] Charge, defense, and *prueba* of de la Peña, AGI, México 670 B, fols. 483–484v; testimony of Martín Lusón Andrade, Mexico City, 30 Mar. 1718, AGI, Escribanía 279 B, fol. 61–61v. *Law of the Indies*, book 2, title 16, laws 49, 50, 53, and 75, prohibited *audiencia* judges from socializing with the people of their districts. Juan José de Sevilla to Garzarón, Mexico City, 29 Oct. 1721, AGI, Escribanía 285 B, Q.no 26, fol. 249, for example, stressed his exemplary life with "regular visits to the holy shrines, and sharing in the holy sacraments and communion ... which are the appropriate customs of a Christian."

[64] Charge against Juan Raymundo de Paz, AGI, Escribanía 289 B, fols. 1150, 1210–12; certification of Antonio de los Ríos, Mexico City, 6 Apr. 1724, AGI, Escribanía 287 B, *pieza* 55, fol. 1; sentence of the Council of the Indies, Madrid, 18 Mar. 1727, AGI, Escribanía 1183, folder *1721–1730 Francisco Garzarón*.

[65] Brief of Juan García de Xismeros, Mexico City, 24 Nov. 1721, AGI, Escribanía 286 C, Q.no 30, no. 7, fol. 562.

established the offense in another ruling. In that case, a judge could abridge the trial and sentence the delinquent. For this reason, participants in the *visita* occasionally claimed that their knowledge was notorious. For instance, it was "very notorious, common knowledge, and most scandalous" that the notary of the land-grant commission attempted to make a fortune, according to a witness.[66] This claim alone was not enough to convict the official, however. In another case, the prosecutor of the Council of the Indies rejected an appeal for "trying to dispel what exists with obvious notoriety."[67]

During the *visita*, one defendant, who was also an ordained priest, insisted on the legal presumption of innocence that favored judges and clergymen. Early modern law recognized the presumption without direct evidence, which undid minor indications of guilt or required a higher standard of proof. In addition, the deputy notary Nicolás Moreno underlined the presumption of innocence in his case, for instance, as any suspicion falling on him "is against the great faith that should support his record according to the doctors" of the law.[68] In addition, the king had ideally chosen good ministers who faithfully served their office, and this doctrine buttressed their innocence. Yet Garzarón gathered much incriminating evidence to undermine the presumption of innocence and justify the suspension of ministers.[69]

Moreover, Garzarón observed other protections for the suspects. He tortured no one and jailed delinquents only when they failed to provide bond or pay penalties. Nor did Garzarón seize the suspects' property during the *sumaria*'s onset to encumber the defense as some judges did. Instead, he waited until he had collected sufficient evidence to begin the *plenaria*.[70] He did not force anyone to confess either. According to one

---

[66] Testimony of Gil de la Sierpe, AGI, Escribanía 278 A, *Quaderno* 6, fol. 62v.

[67] José de Laysequilla to king, Madrid, 14 Aug. 1724, AGI, Escribanía 287 B, *pieza* 39, fol. 133. "Notoriously false were the litigating parties," according to Juan Francisco de Córdoba on behalf of Juan de Oliván Rebolledo to Garzarón, Mexico City, 21 Aug. 1719, AGI, Escribanía 280 C, *Quad*. 12, fol. 8. See also Hevia Bolaños, *Curia Filipica*, vol. 1, part 3, para. 14, no. 1; Alonso Romero, *El proceso penal*, 25–26, 310–315; Mathias Schmoeckel, "Notorietät," in Cordes, *HRG*, 2nd ed., (2016), 3: 1985–1987. www.hrgdigital.de/HRG.notorietaet.

[68] Defense of Nicolás Moreno, AGI, Escribanía 28 9 A, fol. 1480v; see also defense of Juan Díaz de Bracamonte, AGI, México 670 B, *Relación*, fol. 128v.

[69] Hevia Bolaños, *Curia Filipica*, vol. 1, part 3, para. 15, no. 19. Note that Castillo de Bobadilla, *Política*, book 5, chap. 1, para. 223, denied that a conviction required three witnesses instead of two because of the presumption of a judges' innocence. See also Bravo Lira, *El juez*, 150; and Lepsius, *Von Zweifeln*, 284.

[70] In accordance with the *Law of the Indies*, book 2, title 34, law 22; and Hevia Bolaños, *Curia Filipica*, vol. 1, part 3, para. 11, no. 1.

early modern scholarly opinion, witnesses and suspects had to state their full, self-incriminating knowledge, even in death-penalty cases. Remaining silent was equal to admitting guilt. Viceroy Valero, however, insisted that suspects were innocent until proven guilty. He complained about "despoiling honors, liberties, and property and injuring some vassals which His Majesty wishes to see unharmed until justice condemns them."[71] Garzarón also deliberated whether witnesses actually had the obligation "to say the truth that could damage others."[72] He, furthermore, gave the defendants the chance to rebut allegations and to enlist help from attorneys and supportive witnesses. A criminal judge, for instance, called on three witnesses who had heard about and three witnesses who had seen an incident exonerating him. A scribe and an attorney brought friends who attested to their good character, and four witnesses denied that an attorney employed a servant to barter over bribes.[73]

Garzarón pondered these concepts when he questioned the judges in early November 1716. He concluded the process by July 5, 1717, and continued gathering evidence until April 1719. Then he segued from the *sumaria* to the *plenaria*, singling out the real suspects and presenting well-defined charges against them. At this point, Garzarón seized their property to pay for the expected penalties and the *visita* expenses. The indicted judges and the prosecutors had eighty days to refute the charges, and Garzarón heard their defenses until early August 1719. In late September or early October 1719, he suspended thirteen judges and prosecutors.[74]

---

[71] Valero as summarized in *consulta* of the Council of the Indies, Madrid, 20 Apr. 1718, AGI, México 379. On this doctrine, see Hevia Bolaños, *Curia Filipica*, vol. 1, part 3, para. 13, no. 3, 6; Pennington, "Sovereignty and Rights in Medieval and Early Modern Jurisprudence: Law and Norms without a State," in *Roman Law as Formative of Modern Legal Systems: Studies in Honour of Wiesław Litewski*, eds. J. Sondel, J. Reszczyński, and P. Ściślicki (Krakow: Jagiellonian University Press, 2003), 2: 28–29.

[72] Garzarón to king, Mexico City, 7 Aug. 1724, AGI, México 670 A.

[73] Charge against Juan José Aguilera, AGI, Escribanía 289 B, fol. 96; *interrogatorio* of Juan José Aguilera, AGI, Escribanía 289 B, Relazion, fols. 39–43v; defense of Francisco de Castro, AGI, Escribanía 289 A, *Relazion*, fols. 379–382v; *prueba*, AGI, Escribanía 288 A, *legajo* 18, fol. 52v.

[74] *Real cédula* signed by Miguel Fernández Durán to Marquis of Valero, Madrid, 26 Dec. 1717, AGN, RCO 38, exp. 61, fol. 164. The precise date of the suspension varies, though Garzarón issued several verdicts on 16 Aug. 1719; see, e.g., sentence against Pedro Sánchez Morcillo, Mexico City, 16 Aug. 1719, AGI, Escribanía 287 A, fol. 347v; sentence against Juan Francisco de la Peña y Flores, Mexico City, 16 Aug. 1719, AGI, México 670 B, fol. 496v; sentence against Diego Castañeda, Mexico City, 16 Aug. 1719, AGI, México 670 B, fol. 582. According to *Actas Antiguas del Cabildo. Libros 48 al 50. Años 1714 a 1719* (Mexico City: Impresa particular G. Oropeza Velasco, 1912), vol. 1, p. 212, Díaz de Bracamonte still dispatched business on 20 Sep. 1719. Valero to king, Mexico City, 12

Afterwards, Garzarón began investigating the officials of the *audiencia*, and he followed the same pattern. Garzarón heard scores of witnesses before September 1719, and, in 1722, informed the officials of the charges against them. They tried to exonerate themselves within eighty days. Garzarón then suspended the officials, seized their property, and banished them from Mexico City in 1723. The king reserved the final verdicts for himself.[75]

5.3 THE TRIALS OF DOÑA ANDREA CERDÁN

Let us look at *visita* process again by focusing on the case of the shopkeeper Ignacio Negrete, who exposed himself indecently to some soldiers in 1717. The soldiers went to Diego Castañeda, a criminal judge of the *audiencia*, and reported the incident. Castañeda jailed Negrete, and doña Andrea Cerdán, Negrete's wife, negotiated a bribe to release her husband. A few months later, Garzarón heard about the affair and reviewed the case according to *visita* standards. Garzarón unearthed and scrutinized documentation, while questioning and refuting witnesses and suspects. Finally, Garzarón sentenced the judge and his assisting notary.

Ignacio Negrete went to jail after fighting with his neighbors and some viceregal guards. Negrete complained that his neighbors "did not let him sell freely, damaged him, and stuck their noses into his business."[76] Yet he may have been part of the problem himself, because two viceregal guards stated "that he provoked them with words and lewd actions, showing them his dishonest parts, in which they saw female nature." Four witnesses attested to this account. Diego Castañeda presided over the case, because he served at that time on the provincial court, which adjudicated many first-instance trials in Mexico City. Castañeda took the depositions of Negrete's neighbors on August 8, sent Negrete to jail, and heard his defense on October 26, 1717. Subsequently, the *protomedicato* (medical board) of Mexico City convened. Three barber-surgeons and two midwives examined Negrete and concluded that "he did not have two sexes, and there were

---

Oct. 1719, AGI, México 487; Garzarón to king, Mexico City, 3 Aug. 1720, AGI, México 670 A; memorandum of suspended ministers, no place, 3 Aug. 1722, seen in Council of the Indies, Madrid, 22 Mar. 1723, AGI, Escribanía 287 B, *pieza* 35, fols. 8v–9, registered the suspensions.
[75] Trial order based on *auto* of 8 Oct. 1719, AGI, Escribanía 288 A, *legajo* 18, fol. 2–2v; Garzarón to king, Mexico City, 3 Aug. 1720, AGI, México 670 A; see also Berart y Gassol, *Speculum visitationis*, chap. 7, paras. 1, 6.
[76] Testimony in the second trial, AGI, México 670 B, *Relación*, fol. 552.

no signs of nefarious use of his person." Although Negrete paid each of the medical inspectors 100 pesos for their services, he remained in jail.[77]

At this point, Cerdán sought help from friends and family to negotiate her husband's release. The clergyman Juan Bravo de Laguna and a Carmelite friar began communicating with the receptor Juan José Sevilla, who conferred with Castañeda. Sevilla then told Bravo de Laguna that "the *sumaria* was still ongoing and it would end in the prisoner's favor" if they paid 1,000 pesos to Castañeda. Sevilla also requested fifty pesos for himself to pay for drafting papers. On October 28, 1717, the Carmelite friar "called Sevilla to his house where he had a long and secret conversation with him." They decided "to leave everything at the disposition of the criminal judge [Castañeda] who was the director of the negotiations while the receptor Sevilla arranged them." A witness then saw the "the judge's black servant next door discussing what had been said," and Castañeda released Negrete from jail on October 30, 1717.[78]

In this case, as in many others, reputation and family ties helped to build trust, since both parties had to fulfill their end of the deal. Castañeda was known to accept gifts, in exchange for verdicts, which gave Cerdán reason to believe that he would also receive her presents, keep the bargain, and release her husband. On the other hand, Castañeda had the leverage to send Negrete back to jail if she did not act as agreed. The fact that Garzarón was in town complicated matters. This was one reason why doña Andrea sent her relative Bravo de Laguna to handle the delicate negotiations over the bribe. Other *novohispanas* acted similarly. The wives of *audiencia* judges, for example, often spoke with intermediaries to shield their husbands from suspicion of corruption.[79]

---

[77] *Prueba* against Diego de Castañeda, AGI, México 670 B, *Relación*, fols. 541–542v; testimony of Tomás Ximénez, Mexico City, c. 25 May 1719, AGI, Escribanía 289 B, *Relazion*, fols. 102v–103. According to Arenal Fenochio, "La Justicia civil ordinaria," 45–47; Hillebrand, *Real Audiencia*, 60, the provincial court had jurisdiction over the city and surrounding territory within five leagues (about thirteen miles).

[78] Testimony of fray Jerónimo de Ureña, Nicolás Gómez Burgueño, and José Barrasa, AGI, México 670 B, fols. 538v–541v.

[79] Reputation of Castañeda, AGI, México 670 B, fol. 581. According to the testimony of Juan de la Riva, Mexico City, 12 Oct. 1717, AGI, Escribanía 278 A, *Quaderno 6*, fol. 105, "doña Micaela de Alarcón, the wife of Miguel González del Pinal, has family connection [*conecion de deuda*] with her ladyship, the wife of don Félix de Agüero," a criminal judge, whom doña Micaela gave 650 pesos. According to charge against Miguel Calderón de la Barca, AGI, México 670 B, *Relación*, fols. 14v–15v, José de Pliego, a landowner in Amozoque, gave the *Poblano* presbyter Roque del Valle 100 pesos to pass the money to Alonso de Acinas, who finally handed the cash in an envelope to doña Ana de Pividal, the wife of civil judge Miguel Calderón de la Barca.

According to rumors swirling in November 1717, Cerdán sent Castañeda a sizable bribe fifteen to twenty days after Negrete emerged from prison. She asked Bravo de Laguna to give Castañeda 1,000 pesos, six boxes of candy, and six bundles of tobacco, recognizing the "kindness and affection" that the judge had shown to her husband. Castañeda refused the gifts. Yet according to testimony, Bravo de Laguna and an Indian carrier returned to the judge's home later that night. Bravo de Laguna intimated that only he, the Indian carrier, and Cerdán knew about the presents, so Castañeda could accept without trepidation. They left the gift with Castañeda and departed.[80] The chatter in the cathedral of Mexico City grew excited about the exchange. Some hostile observers knew for certain that Castañeda had accepted the bribe that night. Others speculated whether Bravo de Laguna had offered 1,000 pesos, 8,000 pesos, or even two pearl wristbands belonging to Cerdán. These observers must have noted something fishy about Negrete's release from jail without punishment, and perhaps Cerdán or one of her confidants had even leaked some information.[81]

The day after Bravo de Laguna and the Indian had delivered the gift, Castañeda staged a small ceremony at his home. At six in the morning, Castañeda sent a servant to call on two people and a notary to witness the event. Shortly afterwards, an Indian woman also stopped by at Castañeda's home on her own business. She and the others were ushered into the judge's study, where they saw him at his desk. In front of him sat a small bag allegedly containing gold. As the four witnesses watched, Castañeda wrote the following letter:

My dear lady doña Andrea, yesterday night the Licenciate Juan Bravo de Laguna brought me a parcel that I am now sending you, and which I have returned to you twice before. This must be sufficient for you to cease in your intent and to understand that I cannot accept this gift for the reasons that I have given. Even if it were licit for me to accept, there could not be a worse occasion than the present one, for there is no lack of subjects who attempt to falsely smear my good reputation, which thank God is well-known everywhere. My lady, please accept what is yours and cannot be mine, and if you insist again, I will do in this matter what suits me. May God protect you many years."[82]

---

[80] Testimony of Nicolás Gómez Burgueño, AGI, México 670 B, *Relación*, fols. 538v–539v.
[81] Testimony of José de Movellán and other witnesses, AGI, México 670 B, *Relación*, fols. 543v–544. On the possible leak, see testimony of Bernardo de Aysa, Mexico City, 25 May 1719, AGI, Escribanía 289 B, *Relazion*, fol. 101v.
[82] Charge against Juan José Aguilera, AGI, Escribanía 289 B, *Relazion*, fol. 97.

The notary recorded this act on sealed paper, and the judge ordered his *mulato* servant Agustín Silvestre Pinto to walk to Cerdán's home in Santa Clara Street and return the gift.[83]

When Garzarón got wind of the affair, Castañeda worried that Negrete and Cerdán would confess the whole affair to the *visitador*. Castañeda once again charged Negrete on December 23, 1717, with committing an "unspeakable sin."[84] He renewed the imprisonment for Negrete and confiscated both the store and Cerdán's property. She sought refuge in the convent of St. Claire, while her husband scurried to the hospital of St. Hippolytus. Although they escaped, some of her friends were arrested. On January 24, 1718, Bravo de Laguna came to see Garzarón and expressed his regrets that he had earlier cleared Castañeda from the accusations of bribery. Bravo de Laguna showed Garzarón the letter that Castañeda had written to Cerdán, which Garzarón kept for further analysis. Garzarón responded that Bravo de Laguna's "compunctions were most easily absolved," and admonished him "not to talk about its content with doña Andrea or don Diego Castañeda."[85]

Garzarón heard Andrea Cerdán and other witnesses until May 24, 1719, and then pointed out the inconsistencies of Castañeda's defense. According to Garzarón, Bravo de Laguna had originally stated that he handed Castañeda the gift in May 1718. But according to the rumors in the cathedral, Bravo de Laguna had already delivered the present in November 1717, shortly after Negrete's release. That seemed more plausible. In addition, Garzarón summarized Cerdán's testimony that "her husband was in jail for false slander, and the criminal judge Castañeda prosecuted him, and when he left jail ... she tried to give the criminal judge 1000 pesos ... but the next day, when she was in her own room, the *mulato* came with a bundle and a letter" to return the gift. She claimed that Pinto handed her the parcel, and she did not send it to Castañeda again.[86] Castañeda, however, insisted that he returned the gift twice, while Bravo de Laguna reported that he left the gift in the judge's home three times. These differences indicated to Garzarón that

---

[83] Charge and testimonies against Juan José Aguilera, Mexico City, 25 May 1719, AGI, Escribanía 289 B, *Relazion*, fols. 97–99v.

[84] Testimony of Negrete in the second trial, AGI, México 670 B, *Relación*, fol. 552–552v.

[85] Testimony of Juan Bravo de Laguna, AGI, México 670 B, *Relación*, fols. 544–545v. See also *prueba*, AGI, México 670 B, *Relación*, fol. 556; testimony of Jerónimo de Ureña, AGI, México 670 B, *Relación*, fols. 541v–542; testimony of José Carrillo de Viezma, AGI, México 670 B, *Relación*, fol. 542.

[86] Testimony of Andrea Cerdán, AGI, Escribanía 289 B, fols. 100v–101.

the bag with money "did not go to his house more than once" and stayed there right away.[87]

Nor did Pinto's word match other testimony about the ceremony at Castañeda's home. Some witnesses reported that they entered Castañeda's study at 7:30 am, and the gold was still in the bundle lying on the table. Yet Pinto contradicted that view when telling Garzarón that he had seen the notary arrive in the study at 6:30 am. Pinto averred that he took the bundle and delivered it to Cerdán at 7:30 am. Garzarón doubted Pinto's word in this regard, in part, because some canon lawyers argued that blacks and *mulatos* such as Pinto easily fell prey to evil temptations. In their view, slaves should not testify in court at all. That was probably one reason why Pinto claimed to be a free and "white *mulato* who had served his lord for ten years."[88]

Garzarón found additional problems on January 24, 1719, when he closely examined the notarial record and Castañeda's letter. According to Garzarón, the notary had failed to record the presence of Pinto and another witness who "was a Spaniard and not *mulato* like Agustín," and none of them had signed the document. In addition, the notary did not write down the contents of the bag, whereas Pinto claimed that it "weighed a lot when he received it wrapped and tied." Garzarón concluded that it was impossible to discern whether the bag contained "pesos and not horseshoes." Moreover, the two copies of the letter provided by Castañeda and Bravo de Laguna did not coincide. The content of the two letters "was in substance the same, but the letter brought by the clergyman ... ended with 'May God protect you' and a signature, while the other ended with 'May God protect you many years'" without the signature. In addition, Garzarón observed that the "first letter was longer; the writing surpassed half a page and the handwriting was tighter than the other, while it contained more reasons for not receiving the 1,000 pesos." Garzarón noted that the copies were not faithful and not written at the same time by the same person. It seemed more likely that Castañeda conceived a copy at a later point when Garzarón began inquiring about the issue. This confirmed the suspicion that the judge only pretended to return the gift.[89]

---

[87] *Prueba* against Diego de Castañeda, AGI, México 670 B, *Relación*, fols. 553v–554.

[88] Testimony of Agustín Silvestre Pinto, Mexico City, 24 May 1719, AGI, Escribanía 289 B, *Relazion*, fols. 98v–100, quote on fol. 99. On these minorities, see Murillo Velarde, *Cursus Iuris Canonici*, book 2, title 20, para. 149. McKinley, *Fractional Freedoms*, 2–6, 11–12, argues for a "contingent liberty" of manumitted people, who mostly successfully sued on "family unification and ecclesiastical immunity."

[89] *Prueba* against Diego de Castañeda, AGI, México 670 B, *Relación*, fols. 553v–555.

Garzarón proved to his satisfaction that Castañeda had pulled strings in the matter and convicted him for corruption. Castañeda had been too confident about his abilities to cloak the whole matter when Garzarón was in town hunting for corruption. In addition, Garzarón determined that the notary had signed a blank document after the faux ceremony in Castañeda's home. For these reasons, the *visitador* also suspended the notary. The Council of the Indies later reviewed the sentences and removed Castañeda from the *audiencia*. The Council also suspended the notary for roughly five years for other violations of office, but it cleared him from the charge of forgery in this instance.[90]

5.4 TORTURE CHAMBER AND JAIL, WHERE THE "NOTARY IS JUDGE"

In April 1717, Francisco Garzarón personally descended to the lower floor of the viceregal palace to inspect the jail. Gaining his own observations about the abuses in the jail was an important part of his investigation. He knew that according to the *Siete Partidas* and the *Law of Castile*, the criminal judges were the ones who imprisoned, convicted, and released suspects. Notaries assisted the judges and jailers executed the judicial orders. Yet Garzarón heard a different tale from officials, inmates, and their spouses. The jailers in Mexico City, as elsewhere in the empire, preferred their customs over the law. The silver peso reigned supreme, while prisoners of lower status suffered on meager rations in filthy and narrow cells. The informality declined somewhat when the officials noted that Garzarón severely punished wayward ministers. Garzarón's evidence and the verdicts of the Council of the Indies offer a rare snapshot of everyday practices in the palace jail.

Extended jail terms to correct and reintegrate offenders to society did not generally exist in colonial society. The judges of the *audiencia* or the provincial court often detained criminal suspects and confiscated their property when they saw indications of guilt. According to law, the prosecuting judge had to release on bond anyone accused of a lesser crime once the *sumaria* ended. Those charged with serious offenses such as murder

---

[90] *Consulta* of the Council of the Indies, Madrid, 2 Sept. 1721, AGI, México 380; sentence of the Council of the Indies, Madrid, 15 Mar. 1727, AGI, Escribanía 1183, folder *1721–1730 Francisco Garzarón*; Manuel Salazar on behalf of Juan José Aguilera to Council of the Indies, Madrid, n. d. (1727), AGI, Escribanía 1183, folder *1726–1733 Francisco Garzarón*.

remained in custody until the judges ruled. The judges then ordered culprits to pay a fine or a compensation, sent them to sweat shops or grueling military fortresses, and sometimes proclaimed a death sentence. Nonetheless, some judges kept in jail even the patently innocent and those suspected of lesser violations, coercing them to accept fines and relinquish appeals so that they could leave the dungeons quickly. Sometimes inmates remained in limbo for extended periods while the judges pondered their fate. One prisoner in Antequera complained that for "four years and more, I have been suffering intolerable pains in this jail, and I was mortified by shackles for two years and a month, and by double chains for all of the four years, and I was suffering great need and hunger, and being naked in a dark dungeon."[91] Only occasionally was prison the penance itself, when "the jail time sufficiently purged the guilt," as a prosecutor held after an *audiencia* trial.[92]

Garzarón entered the jail and observed its woeful condition. He interviewed the usher, who watched the prison doors from seven in the morning until nine at night. The usher claimed that he had the "immense work of opening and closing every day for friends and servants." He added that he shut the doors for half an hour at two every afternoon, after the relatives of the prisoners had brought them food. People were driving bulls over the main square at that time and there was a lot of commotion that made escaping easier. Yet Garzarón suspected that the usher locked the doors at two for the remainder of the day and did not return to work.[93] Garzarón also found the building dilapidated, when he walked past the entrance. He saw the jailer's small abode and passed through the main hall, where the prisoners were usually lined up for roll calls. Connecting to this hall was the pharmacy and the infirmary that threatened to fall apart. Garzarón noted the constant traffic of inmates and officials through the infirmary. Wooden screens divided the hall to protect the prisoners' beds from the "draft ... which is very uncomfortable." The *visitador* also saw another poorly maintained hall, where the criminal judges and notaries took the inmates' depositions. In addition, there was a chapel and a kitchen with a connection to an underground water pipe.[94]

---

[91] Sebastián María Garzón to Garzarón, Antequera, 4 Jan. 1724, AGN, Historia 102, exp. 20, fol. 494–494v, 503; see also Alonso Romero, *Proceso penal*, 197.
[92] Response of José Antonio Espinosa Ocampo, Mexico City, 20 Nov. 1714, AGI, Escribanía 280 A, *Q.no* 10, fol. 179v.
[93] Defense of *portero* Alonso de Guzmán, AGI, Escribanía 288 A, *legajo* 18, fol. 137.
[94] *Reconocimiento* of Garzarón, Mexico City, 14 Apr. 1717, AGI, Escribanía 278 A, *legajo* 8, fols. 165–167.

Immediately adjacent and without any separation was the torture chamber, which judges used infrequently. When they did, they employed force to attain an admission of guilt, which was known as the "queen of evidence." The judges could speedily solve the puzzle of any crime by hearing a full confession, and this worthy goal justified appropriate violence. The culprits purged guilt during the torment, repented, and eventually reconciled with Christendom. Rules circumscribed the agony. At least one fully reputable witness had to incriminate the suspect under oath. Nobles, legal minors, old people, pregnant women, and those recovering from childbirth for forty days were exempt from torture. Most academic jurists were also skeptical of the practice, and more importantly, the goal to purge past sins through suffering declined over time. Judges increasingly convicted on the basis of evidence rather than confessions. As a result, torture dwindled in the eighteenth-century Spanish empire.[95]

Nonetheless, the *Siete Partidas* permitted employing water, ropes, and pulleys. That included a form of waterboarding or a leverage to painfully crush, twist, or stretch the body. Many judges also developed their own techniques and chose when, how long, and how painfully to torture, sometimes in "exquisite ways," as representatives of the Castilian Cortes (parliament) lamented in the late sixteenth century.[96] The Mexico City jail in the early eighteenth century featured a solid "*potro* [rack] and the iron rings to torment." For the procedure, the constables strapped suspects to the rack, ran ropes through the rings protruding from the wall, and then hauled them tight to hang or contort the suspect's body. These measures convinced most prisoners to admit what the judges wanted to hear.[97] The king's portrait covered by a withered damask canopy watched over the ordeal. Below sat an iron chest with two locks to secure the torture instruments. The *audiencia* ordered renovations to the chamber after the criminal judges had

---

[95] Hevia Bolaños, *Curia Filipica*, vol. 1, part 3, para. 16, nos. 5, 13; para. 17, no. 1; Murillo Velarde, *Cursus Iuris Canonici*, book 2, title 20, para. 155, 158; *Law of Castile*, book 4, title 23, law 9, prohibited officials from torturing without judicial order. Alejandro Agüero, "La tortura judicial en el antiguo régimen," 202–216; Alonso Romero, *Orden Procesal*, 103–107; Lynn, *Between Court and Confessional*, 20; Herzog, *Upholding Justice*, 26–28; Lepsius, *Von Zweifeln*, 12–13; Richard van Dülmen, *Theater des Schreckens: Gerichtspraxis und Strafrituale in der frühen Neuzeit* (Munich: C. H. Beck, 2014): 25–32, holds that suspects in the Holy Roman Empire suffered whipping, burning the skin with sulfurous wood, or driving splinters below the fingernails on the Spanish rack.

[96] Alonso Romero, *Orden procesal*, 104.

[97] *Reconocimiento* of Garzarón, Mexico City, 14 Apr. 1717, AGI, Escribanía 278 A, *legajo* 8, fol. 165–165v.

inspected the room on June 28, 1707. On that day, "in the same space in the hall where the ministers usually sat, two large bricks came crashing down, and they would have endangered the ministers' lives." The judges took this as a sign from heaven and ordered improvements to the structures.[98]

Leaving the gruesome chamber, Garzarón inspected the dungeons. He first observed the men's cells. He saw that the straw dispersed in the cells was supposed to be swept out twice a week, but this did not always happen. Garzarón then walked down a wooden hallway that connected to the women's cells. Legally, judges could only jail women of dubious reputation or those suspected of serious crimes. This was one reason why there were fewer women than men in the palace jail, when Garzarón inspected the premises.[99]

Status also mattered in the dungeons. According to the *Siete Partidas*, nobles and suspects of minor violations enjoyed better conditions than serious criminals of common descent, yet cash reigned supreme in Mexico City. The jailer stated that "inmates of lower station and serious offenses" were crammed into narrow dungeons with thick walls.[100] Prisoners also paid cash to avoid the shackles. The coachbuilder Manuel Hernández Bravo testified that he was standing in the upper hall when the jailer fastened the shackles so tight that he could not move. The jailer "wanted to beat him, making him go downstairs bent and dragging." The jailer took off the shackles only after the coachbuilder gave him fifty pesos. By adding fifteen pesos he could sometimes go home for the night to see after his work.[101] A former inmate concurred that pesos opened prison gates, regardless of the crime. He testified that he was in custody during "Lent of 1721 for hitting an Indian with a club, from which the Indian died, and for being able to sleep at home," the inmate gave the *alguacil mayor de corte* (the senior constable who supervised the jail) twenty-five pesos.[102] Most inmates of Spanish descent who were in jail for minor civil and criminal lawsuits slept at home anyway. They had to be back at "the

---

[98] Report of Miguel Calderón de la Barca, Mexico City, 29 Mar. 1719, AGI, Escribanía 280 A, fols. 509–511.
[99] *Reconocimiento* of Garzarón, Mexico City, 14 Apr. 1717, AGI, Escribanía 278 A, *legajo* 8, fol. 166; Hevia Bolaños, *Curia Filipica*, vol. 1, part 3, para. 11, no. 11.
[100] Defense of Juan Martín Moreno, AGI, Escribanía 288 A, *legajo* 18, fol. 79v. See also Hevia Bolaños, *Curia Filipica*, vol. 1, part 3, para. 11, no. 11; Alonso Romero, *Proceso penal*, 199–200; van Dülmen, *Theater*, 21–22.
[101] Testimony of Manuel Hernández Bravo, AGI, Escribanía 288 A, *legajo* 18, fol. 93–93v.
[102] Testimony of Román Pérez de la Varrena, Mexico City, AGI, Escribanía 288 A, *legajo* 18, fol. 10v.

jail at six o'clock in the morning and be visible there all day," the senior constable explained and denied that there had ever been a problem with this arrangement. If it was true that the jail doors closed at two o'clock in the afternoon, then these inmates spent about eight hours in jail per day.[103]

Cash solved most additional hardships and sometimes paved the way for an escape. The inmates often paid to bring their own mattresses for their comfort or they even slept upstairs. The price for such a privilege fluctuated between ten and twenty-four pesos. In 1718, one prisoner paid pesos to rest in the upper hall right next to the prison chapel. At some point, he saw the priest leaving to administer the last rites for an inmate. When the priest returned, the prisoner "embraced him, imploring him for church asylum, and while outside the senior constable was calling for the guards ... the inmate pleaded to go to the chapel." Many jurists of the time agreed that suspects could obtain asylum by fleeing to a church, but not by holding on to a priest's oil for the last unction. This is why Garzarón lambasted the officials' carelessness that allowed the suspect to escape from jail.[104]

Yet, the jail officials denied most allegations that they were derelict in their duty or that they sold food and water in jail. Clean water should have been available at no extra charge but Garzarón had his doubts. He also heard complaints that poor people starved, but the jailer insisted that he always provided "beef, *atole* [a hot maize drink], and tortillas" to the needy. In addition, the arch-confraternity of the knights of the Vera Cruz Church collected money to feed the poor on Thursdays.[105] Furthermore, the senior constable served brandy to the inmates and allowed them to play cards in exchange for cash. Gambling was both illegal and popular throughout the realm and in the jail. Moreover, the same official charged the visitors a fee for letting them bring fresh clothes to the inmates. The officials alleviated the jail time for the better off and enhanced their income.[106]

---

[103] Defense of Francisco de Fonseca Enríquez, AGI, Escribanía 288 A, *legajo* 18, fol. 11–11v.

[104] Charge, defense, and *prueba* of Fonseca Enríquez, Mexico City, AGI, Escribanía 288 A, *legajo* 18, fols. 10, 19–19v; Hevia Bolaños, *Curia Filipica*, vol. 1, part 3, para. 12, nos. 8–9, argued that the prisoner who "touches or goes for the Holy Sacrament when it is being carried to the ill" did not enjoy asylum.

[105] Defense of Juan Martín Moreno, AGI, Escribanía 288 A, *Relacion*, fols. 52, 85–86.

[106] Defense and reputation of Fonseca Enríquez, AGI, Escribanía 288 A, *Relacion*, fols. 10, 51–52v.

There were additional ways of pillaging prisoners. The usher at the entry demanded an arbitrary presentation fee of up to one peso from arriving inmates. The jailer also charged the *décima*, a fee for every ten days spent in custody, and the *carcelaje*, a fee paid for releasing inmates from jail. The senior constable did not draw a salary but pocketed 10 percent of the jailing fees and received twelve *reales* per day from the jailer who rented his position. The senior constable also overcharged most inmates for their release, the wealthy more than the poor. A canon of the cathedral, for instance, gave him 100 pesos for his discharge. Meanwhile, blacks, *mulatos, mestizos*, and Indians paid twelve *reales* for recovering their freedom, although legally they only had to pay four. If the inmates did not give cash, the jail officials kept them confined or even tortured them. Such practices were widespread, illegal, and rarely punished.[107]

Furthermore, the officials allowed unmarried men and women to be together in the cells – a scandal for the time – and sometimes solicited sexual favors for themselves. The jailer Juan Martín Moreno and the usher Alonso de Guzmán accused each other of these offenses. For instance, an inmate named María Romero allegedly spent time with Andrés de la Cruz alias the Eyebrow and became pregnant. According to Guzmán, "she gave birth twice in jail, once with a pregnancy that she brought from the street and another time acquired in jail ... and having entered poor, she left decent and well clothed at the expense of prisoner" de la Cruz. Yet Juan Martín Moreno averred that he reported de la Cruz's illicit friendship to a criminal judge, who locked up de la Cruz and María Romero in separate cells.[108] Garzarón probed deeper and questioned an inmate's wife called Juana María de Medina about Romero. Medina stated that "the delinquent was pregnant when she came to jail, and

---

[107] Defense of Francisco Alejo de Luna, AGI, Escribanía 289 A, fols. 352–353; defense of Fonseca Enríquez, AGI, Escribanía 288 A, *legajo* 18, fol. 3v. According to José Sánchez and Francisco Leri, 1716, AGI, Escribanía 278 A, Fonseca did not draw a salary. See also sentence of the Council of the Indies, Madrid, 2 Mar. 1724, AGI, Escribanía 1183, folder *1721–1730 Francisco Garzarón*; testimony of José Perez de Santos, Mexico City, 19 Oct. 1719, AGI, Escribanía 281 C, *Quaderno* 19, fols. 43–44; Garzarón's *interrogatorio*, AGI, Escribanía 281 C, *Quaderno* 19, fol. 6. For Cervantes, *Licenciado Vidriera*, 58–59, a "few *alguaciles* have enemies, because their job is to arrest you, seize your belongings, and jail you while they eat at your expense."

[108] Charge and defense of Juan Martín Moreno, AGI, Escribanía 288 A, fols. 55–56. Andrés de la Cruz's nickname was *la pestaña*, which translates as the eyebrow or the stare. The *carcelero* (jailer) José Martín Moreno also appeared as *alcayde de entradas*, see defense of Feliciano Ulloa y Sevilla, AGI, Escribanía 289 B, *Relazion*, fol. 773.

Moreno baptized the first, and then the usher Alonso de Guzmán baptized the second" child of Romero. Five prisoners confirmed the story, indicating that both the jailer and the usher had fathered a child out of wedlock with the same woman.[109]

Usher Alonso de Guzmán hurled another charge against Martín Moreno, but he could not convince the Council of the Indies of its truthfulness. In the usher's words, Juan Martín Moreno himself behaved in a way that was "lewd and lascivious with the women of the prisoners, just as he did with an Indian woman called Juana whose husband was in jail for a crime." When Juana's husband was sent to the sweatshops, she began visiting Martín Moreno during the nights. In addition, the jailer had seduced another inmate called Teresa de Artiaga. Yet Moreno dismissed the accusations, because Artiaga's "husband was quarrelsome and jealous, and he stayed on the patio at night, so he could see his wife sleeping, although his cell is at a distance from the women, and it is wrong that he [Moreno] solicited her, because her husband saw her" all the time. Other witnesses also cleared Moreno, and the Council of the Indies dropped the charges against him.[110]

Informal arrangements extended to record keeping, as elsewhere at the *audiencia*. Before the *visita*, jail officials often simply memorized the names of the inmates and rarely kept a written record. According to Moreno, "every day there was a ruckus when the guards called up the inmates who had disappeared." When the *visita* loomed, he began writing down the names of arriving prisoners. Moreno used four large scarlet-covered record books for incoming prisoners and smaller tomes for departing prisoners. These books were bound with unstamped paper. The senior constable and a notary occasionally jotted down entries, and sometimes the prisoners themselves signed in because some deputy constables were illiterate. By November 1718, the jail notary had noted that the *visita* meant business and came every day two to three times to the jail, where he remained at the gate for extended periods.[111]

Generally, the notaries greatly shaped the trials, because they acted as detectives and faithfully recorded legal proceedings, but they also took liberties. *Novohispanos* solicited notarial services when finalizing dowry

---

[109] Testimony of Juana María de Medina, AGI, Escribanía 288 A, fol. 56.
[110] Charge, defense, and *prueba* of Juan Martín Moreno, AGI, Escribanía 288 A, fols. 56–57v; sentence of the Council of the Indies, Madrid, 2 Mar. 1724, AGI, Escribanía 1183, folder *1721–1730 Francisco Garzarón*.
[111] *Prueba* against de la Peña, AGI, México 670 B, *Relación*, fols. 489–491v.

agreements, recording important sales, or making their wills.[112] In addition, the officials investigated crime, captured suspects, and took their depositions in the presence of judges. The notaries were supposed to show their skills in an exam administered by the *audiencia*. Some studied the techniques of interrogation, but others never took the exam or lacked a royal title appointing them. A few notaries never came to work. The contemporaries observed and criticized the self-serving conduct of notaries. Castillo de Bobadilla lamented earlier that the "notary is judge ... and the popular saying goes 'take care of the trial, my friend, and rule however you wish.'"[113]

The notaries and, more importantly, criminal judges often booked and released suspects informally. The *Law of Castile* prescribed that all criminal judges of the *audiencia* had to sign off on discharging prisoners. Yet between February and October 1718, one prosecutor set free thirty-five inmates without his colleagues' consent, including an Indian who had mistreated his wife. Prosecutors also frequently scribbled mere slips without signing them to release a suspect. To prove this point, the jailer showed Garzarón an abundance of "paper scraps glued onto forty pages and additional forty-three scraps," ordering to jail or free suspects. Judges sometimes sent the receptors to the jail, who then "came in a hurry and forcefully demanded the prisoners on orders from the criminal chamber, the judge, or by their own word."[114] A few notaries even jailed and

---

[112] See, e.g., will of the Duchess of Alburquerque, Mexico City, 27 June 1711, Acervo Histórico del Archivo General de Notarias, Mexico City (hereinafter cited as AHAGN), Fondo Antiguo, Sección Notarías (Siglos XVII–XIX), Escribano José de Ledesma, notaría 340, vol. 2247.

[113] Quoted in Alonso Romero, *El proceso penal*, 194–195. Burns, *Into the Archive*, 13–14, 19–27, 32, quote on 22, cites Francisco Quevedo's dictum that "nothing grows as fast as your guilt when you are in the hands of a notary." Herzog, *Upholding Justice*, 53, agrees that the officials translated "the truth in legal terms – indeed the most important part of the process"; while Moreno Gamboa, "Historia de una librería novohispana," 133, notes the abundant study books for notaries. See also de la Puente Luna and Honores, "Guardianes de la real justicia," 25; Scardaville, "Justice," 980–983. Gayol, *Laberintos de justicia*, 1: 143–145, analyzes the *audiencia* lawsuit promoted by a Tlaxcalan *cacique*, a procurator for Indians, and a *picapleitos* (legal agent) during 1789–1803. See also Lockhart, *Nahuas*, 40–41. According to Cervantes, *Licenciado Vidriera*, 57–58, the notaries "charge excessive fees, and they fudge with papers, and these two extremes could meet in the middle, having them look after the proper ways." In addition, Cervantes misquotes *Eccles.* 10:5, writing that the power (instead of prosperity) of man is in the hands of God, who "stamps his authority on the scribe's brow." Cervantes's irony is thrown into relief when the protagonist recovers his senses and chooses death in battle over life at the royal court.

[114] *Prueba* against de la Peña, AGI, México 670 B, *Relación*, fols. 491v–492.

released suspects without judicial mandate, perhaps because some judges trusted them enough to give them free rein. Nonetheless, this usurpation of justice particularly riled Garzarón, and all notaries vigorously denied the practice.[115]

For example, in 1717, a notary inquired about the death of an Indian bricklayer near the tavern belonging to Gregorio Montiel and his Indian wife, doña Juana de los Ángeles. The notary found little evidence tying the tavern to the homicide, yet he decided to stay around until eight o'clock at night, after which it was forbidden to sell *pulque* (an alcoholic agave brew). Fearing some mishap to his tavern, Montiel gave the notary fifty pesos in boxed tobacco, and the notary withdrew.[116] Two years later, pearls were stolen in Mexico City, and the criminal judges ordered the same notary, the senior constable, and two guards to search various taverns. The officials searched Montiel's premises at midnight and found four strands of large pearls. According to the notary, they apprehended Juana de los Ángeles and her husband and duly reported the arrest to the criminal chamber.[117]

Nonetheless, Garzarón perceived serious irregularities in the notary's defense and found the taverners' testimony more trustworthy. Montiel claimed that he had been shackled and waiting when the notary took him "out of the line and let him go," and then the notary "recorded an order of the criminal chamber but without the signatures of the judges." Meanwhile, Juana de los Ángeles stayed at home under guard, and the notary demanded twenty-six pesos for her husband's release. In addition, the notary never returned the pearls. Juana de los Ángeles and her husband feared repercussions, so they never lodged an official complaint about their loss. Yet they trusted Garzarón enough to tell him about the notary's wrongdoing.[118] Garzarón then questioned the notary's scribe, who admitted that it was the "process to let the prisoners go with only the notary's decree and without the signatures of the criminal judges." The notary insisted, however, that the judges had approved the release.

---

[115] The sentence of the Council of the Indies, Madrid, 18 Mar. 1727, AGI, Escribanía 1183, folder *1721–1730 Francisco Garzarón*, fined Antonio de Catillexa 100 pesos for releasing prisoners without orders and for committing forgery, see also charge against Feliciano Ulloa y Sevilla, AGI, Escribanía 289 B, *Relazion*, fols. 804–808; charge against de la Peña, AGI, México 670 B, *Relación*, fols. 488–490. *Law of Castile*, book 2, title 6, law 6, prescribed that detentions needed judicial orders; see also Hevia Bolaños, *Curia Filipica*, vol. 1, part 3, para. 11, no. 2.
[116] Testimony of Gregorio Montiel, AGI, Escribanía 289 B, *Relazion*, fols. 776v–777.
[117] Charge and defense of Ulloa y Sevilla, AGI, Escribanía 289 B, *Relazion*, fols. 770–771v.
[118] Testimony of Montiel, AGI, Escribanía 289 B, *Relazion*, fols. 768v–770.

Nonetheless, Garzarón found yet another inconsistency. One Bernardo González claimed that he had witnessed a part of that episode. He was in the notary's home at three o'clock on a holiday, when Juana de los Ángeles entered and said her name. González, who described himself as *mulato*, "laughed at the Indian woman calling herself doña" and saw that the notary gave her two or three strands of small pearls.[119] While this story should have exonerated the notary, Garzarón inferred that the testimonies diverged on the size and quality of the pearls and discarded the notary's explanations. Garzarón suspended him for forgery and releasing inmates without judicial orders. The Council of the Indies agreed and removed the official from his post.[120]

In addition, the senior constable appointed jail officials in exchange for a sign of gratitude. The appointment to senior constable itself had not been free, because his grandfather had purchased the office in an auction for the considerable sum of 70,000 pesos. The grandfather later gave his daughter two-thirds of the office as her dowry. In 1691, she and her husband passed on the position to their son, don Francisco de Fonseca Enríquez. One perquisite of the office was appointing jail officials. Fonseca Enríquez insisted that he always named them for free, although a few later showed their appreciation by giving him twenty-five or fifty pesos. His deputy confirmed the practice. He had himself given the senior constable "a small amount of 40 or 50 pesos" for awarding him the position.[121] Since only the king could sell appointments, all deputies insisted on the spontaneous and voluntary nature of their gifts. Garzarón saw no fault in these arrangements, because he mainly objected to officials who offered occupations in exchange for cash.[122]

More complicated was the fact that too many ad hoc enforcers served the senior constable and the *audiencia*. The law allowed a maximum of six constables and three deputies to chase suspects and patrol the city. Yet the *audiencia* and the senior constable customarily named thirty-eight additional constables. The practice caused some confusion, because the senior

---

[119] Testimony of Bernardo González, AGI, Escribanía 289 B, *Relazion*, fols. 775–776.
[120] Defense of Ulloa y Sevilla, AGI, Escribanía 289 B, *Relazion*, fol. 782; sentence of the Council of the Indies, Madrid, 18 March 1727, AGI, Escribanía 1183, folder *1721–1730 Francisco Garzarón*. There is a possibility that Ulloa y Sevilla was removed as receptor but stayed on as notary.
[121] Testimony of Sebastián Guerrero, AGI, Escribanía 288 A, *legajo* 18, fols. 6v–7.
[122] Defense of Francisco de Fonseca Enríquez, AGI, Escribanía 288 A, *legajo* 18, fol. 3–3v, 5v. Bequeathing offices was common. The notary of the intestate office, Carlos Romero de la Vega, for instance, inherited his post from his father Isidro, see *auto*, n. d. (1711), AGI, México 658, fol. 856v. See also discussion in Chapter two.

constable did not always know the constables appointed by the *audiencia*. In addition, these officials did not usually draw a salary, so they too leeched onto the defendants to provide for themselves and pay off the senior constable.[123]

Garzarón concluded the investigation on August 3, 1722. He suspended the senior constable, the jailer, four deputies, the usher, and a notary for informalities, charging excessive fees, and extortions. The fate of the thirty-eight constables is unknown, although Garzarón probably dismissed them too as they did not have a royal title. The Council of the Indies reviewed the cases in March 1724 and absolved the senior constable from the charge of appointing the officials but convicted him on all other counts. The Council also reprimanded the other jail officials except for two deputies. At the same time, the Council denied that the charges were sufficiently egregious to warrant dismissals, especially since the senior constable owned his office. In addition, King Louis I had just acceded to the throne at that time, and he and his entourage favored a more lenient outcome of the *visita*. The Council consequently sentenced the officials to pay their share of the *visita* expenses according to their offenses. Then they returned to their posts in the jail.[124]

CONCLUSION

While politics and clientelism shaped Garzarón's *visita*, they did not determine the entire outcome. Instead, Garzarón largely followed the process prescribed by *visitas* and criminal trials. Garzarón acted as detective, prosecutor, and judge at the same time, and he sought to attain the full picture about the offenses committed by *audiencia* ministers. He privileged incriminating over exculpatory evidence and heard an abundance of testimony, gathered written evidence, and inspected the premises to gain his impressions. Garzarón had previously presided over the criminal trials of the Church, so he combined the experience and the judgment

---

[123] Charge and defense of Fonseca Enríquez, AGI, Escribanía 288 A, *legajo* 18, fols. 4–5, reports on the additional *alguaciles* or *comisarios de calles y barrios*.

[124] Garzarón's *auto*, 3 Aug. 1722, AGI, Escribanía 288 A, *legajo* 18, fol. 52. According to *provisión executoria* to Garzarón, Madrid, 5 Mar. 1724, AGN, Indiferente Virreinal 5249, exp. 8, fols. 1–3; and sentences of the Council of the Indies, Madrid, 2 Mar. 1724, AGI, Escribanía 1183, folder *1721–1730 Francisco Garzarón*, the Council of the Indies reprimanded Fonseca Enríquez and his deputies Sebastián Guerrero and Francisco de Deza, while absolving deputy Sebastián Vello. The Council also reprimanded jailer Juan Martín Moreno, usher Alonso de Guzmán, and notary Francisco Alonso Cortés but acquitted the deputy jailer Miguel de Samano.

to assess the claims and gauge the reputation of witnesses and suspects. Garzarón accepted the usual two witnesses who agreed on the same criminal incident for the conviction of a judge. In addition, the *visita* recognized three witnesses describing separate corrupt acts, as long as the testimonies did not contradict one another. This included the witnesses who had bribed judges or suffered extortions. Garzarón also kept the names of witness secret to protect them from revenge, which curbed the suspects' ability to challenge the testimony. Yet defendants also had the opportunity to debunk evidence, call on attorneys and supporting witnesses, and impugn rulings. Moreover, Garzarón did not jail or torture anyone to attain a confession, because that practice was falling into disuse, and he had assembled sufficient evidence for the suspensions in any case. Garzarón then confiscated the property of the guilty ministers and banned them from the city. The king issued the final judgment on the culprits.

Corruption and fraud were, therefore, an important concern for *novohispanos*. Seven hundred witnesses testified in the *visita*, and many of them agreed with at least some *visita* objectives. Some at the lower and middle rungs of society deplored the crimes, whereas others took advantage of them for their own ends. Two case studies provide evidence for these arguments. Several Natives in Huejotzingo, for example, sought to redress corrupt sentences. The brother of an *hacendado* killed the Indian worker José Miguel Nieto but received a light verdict. Nieto's mother deplored the injustice and Sánchez Morcillo reexamined the case. Later, Garzarón's commissioner retraced Sánchez Morcillo's steps, and Garzarón contrasted the testimonies, the written evidence, and Sánchez Morcillo's deposition. Garzarón ruled that Sánchez Morcillo had extorted the suspects and forged much of the record and suspended him. In addition, Garzarón revisited the verdict of the criminal judge Diego Castañeda who had jailed the shopkeeper Ignacio Negrete for committing uncouth acts. Andrea Cerdán negotiated her husband's freedom in exchange for 1,000 pesos. Garzarón used similar methods as in the Huejotzingo affair. He uncovered the contradictions among Castañeda's record and the testimony of Andrea Cerdán, Agustín Silvestre Pinto, and others. The evidence convinced Garzarón to suspend the judge for corruption as well.

Finally, Garzarón cast his gaze onto the gruesome dungeons and the torture rack that tormented poorer *novohispanos*, while status and cash saved many others. The *Siete Partidas* and the *Law of Castile* detailed the jail operations, but the officials preferred their own rules, offering food and brandy to the inmates. Prisoners rested more comfortably on a mattress or stayed at home in exchange for money. When they could not pay, however, the jailers tightened the shackles and crammed prisoners into the dungeons on short rations. In addition, the record keeping was shoddy. Garzarón saw dozens of paper snippets scribbled by judges and receptors to release prisoners, and frequently verbal orders of the officials sufficed. Notaries even virtually acted as judges, jailing and releasing delinquents. As a result of his investigation, Garzarón suspended eight jail officials. The Council of the Indies largely agreed with his assessments but nonetheless restored all officials to their posts. The councilors found that the officials had sufficiently atoned for their offenses after living for years without any income and by paying their share of the *visita* costs.

6

Guilt and Punishments for Fraud, Theft, and the "Grave Offense of Bribery or Corruption"

INTRODUCTION

Between 1719 and 1723, Garzarón suspended several judges and dozens of officials from the *audiencia* and banished them from Mexico City. The Council of the Indies in Madrid later reviewed his verdicts and also handed down tough sentences against many judges and officials. Yet neither Garzarón nor the Council of the Indies ever reasoned which laws or doctrines the miscreants had violated. Garzarón and the Council usually gave only pithy rulings, in line with most jurists who held that it fell to the defendants and the prosecutors to lay out their arguments. On that ground, we have to mine the legal opinions of prosecutors, the briefs prepared by attorneys or procurators (procedural agents without academic training), and the manifold learned treatises to reveal the sophisticated knowledge about criminal justice. These sources show that eighteenth-century practitioners such as Garzarón distinguished bribery and extortion from *falsedad* (fraud), overcharging fees, or mere sloppiness in drafting papers. Jurists and procurators also separated ordinary and gross negligence from malicious intent. These concepts mattered greatly in the *visita*, because, by and large, Garzarón and the Council assigned the punishments in accordance with the proven offenses.[1]

This argument on Garzarón's *visita* differs substantially, therefore, from many historians who have downplayed the importance of the law and its interpretations. Latin Americanists such as Woodrow Borah and

---

[1] The chapter title is taken from *consulta* of the Council of the Indies, Madrid, 13 Nov. 1721, AGI, México 670 A. Similar, Berart y Gassol, *Speculum visitationis*, chap. 17, para. 3.

"Grave Offense of Bribery or Corruption"   197

Brian Owensby have successfully illuminated the daily practices and outcomes of lawsuits in the special Indian court in Mexico City, but much remains to be gleaned from the plurality of the laws and their impact on the litigation.[2] In addition, historian Anne Dubet has pointed out that in many cases "talk was loud and repression inefficient," during investigations of fraudulent tax collectors. Political or personal interests regularly tinged these inquiries that almost always ended by negotiating lower punishments for the defendants. Dubet provides valuable insights on financial embezzlements, but they do not apply to all instances of judicial corruption and forgery, which Garzarón punished with rigor.[3] This chapter is therefore a foray – at least within Anglophone scholarship – into the understudied operation of judicial concepts in criminal prosecutions such as the *visita*. While the previous chapter discussed Garzarón's method of uncovering miscreants, this chapter explores the legal foundation of his verdicts as suggested by published and archival sources.[4] Studying the combined officials and judges of the *audiencia* also sets into relief the differences and commonalities of their charges and convictions. By doing so, my aim is not to condemn the suspects of the past but to understand the values of justice and contribute to the growing research on legal history and notarial practices.[5] The chapter starts out by following the *visitador* Francisco Garzarón through the *audiencia* offices in 1717. Garzarón intended to gain a first-hand perspective on the lackadaisical application of the rules, and his personal impressions guided his sentencing of the ministers.

6.1 A PERSONAL VISIT TO THE AUDIENCIA

When Garzarón inspected the notarial offices, he lamented that incomplete documents abounded and inventories were lacking. Litigants often paid excessive fees for lengthy searches to find the record. Most officials

---

[2] Borah, *Justice by Insurance*, 91–97; Owensby, *Empire of Law*.
[3] Dubet, "La moralidad de los mentirosos," 213–234, 213–214, 219–220; on p. 230, she argues that corruption existed "when a judge, official, or a subject exchanged goods with venal intention," see also p. 213–234; see also her notable cultural approach in *La Hacienda real de la Nueva Planta (1713–1726), entre fraude y buen gobierno. El caso Verdes Montenegro* (Madrid: Fondo de Cultura Económica, 2015), 31–36; see also Cañeque, *Living Image*.
[4] Legal historians such as Tau Anzoátegui, "El poder de la costumbre"; Duve, "Global Legal History," 4–5, mostly illuminate the history of legal concepts.
[5] On notarial practices, see, for example, Burns, *Into the Archive*; Herzog, *Upholding Justice*, 49–53.

overcharged litigants and some stole or forged papers. Garzarón also admonished the lack of secrecy in the *real acuerdo*, the joint meeting of the *audiencia* civil judges and the viceroy. Historians have rarely observed the functioning and equipment of the *real acuerdo* and the *audiencia* offices, as the viceregal palace is largely understudied. Garzarón provided a detailed account of its daily practices.

Francisco Garzarón set out to examine the offices in the viceregal palace on April 13, 1717. He left his room in the Inquisition palace at 7:30 AM, and passed the square in front of the Dominican monastery. He then walked toward the main plaza and entered the palace when "the clock in the Holy Cathedral struck three quarters ... to eight." Garzarón walked up the central flight and down the corridor and stepped into the *audiencia* hall. Civil judge José Joaquín Uribe, Garzarón's friend, was waiting there. Before eight o'clock, the dean of the *audiencia* entered, while ministers joined them at the full hour. Two ministers were absent. One served on a commission outside the city, and the other was ill. One judge arrived late at quarter past eight. At that point, a secretary left the meeting and called on the viceroy to join the ministers.[6]

Garzarón then examined the books in the presence of the viceroy, the civil judges, and the civil prosecutor. Garzarón first admonished the lack of the book that recorded the merits of *novohispano* residents. A registry of the judicial reviews of outgoing officials was missing, and the list of people who had moved from Castile to New Spain was also out of date. In addition, Garzarón was particularly interested in the Secret Books that recorded the judges' votes on the trial sentences, because the books allowed him to verify allegations of bribery against individual ministers. Garzarón reviewed the volumes and found that one of them began in 1652, and it was bound in cowhide and secured by iron lock and key. Another book noted the votes since 1688 and contained an empty page crossed by a line. Neither of these met the standard. According to the *Law of Castile*, all judges had to record their votes when they split on important sentences. In Mexico City, however, there was only an entry when one or

---

[6] *Reconocimiento* of Garzarón, Mexico City, 13 Apr. 1717, AGI, Escribanía 278 A, *legajo* 8, fols. 150–151. According to this document, Uribe, the dean of the *audiencia* Francisco Valenzuela Venegas, the *oidores* (civil judges) Juan Díaz de Bracamonte, Jerónimo de Soria, Félix González de Agüero, Félix Suárez de Figueroa, and the *fiscal de lo civil* (civil prosecutor) José Antonio de Espinosa Ocampo arrived by eight o'clock, while *oidor* Juan de Oliván y Revolledo entered the hall at 8:15 (though the *visita* later absolved him). Both Agustín Franco de Toledo and Antonio Terreros y Ochoas missed the inspection on that day.

two votes differed from the majority opinion. That scarcity of information made it harder to trace who had actually been present during trials and voted with the majority. Garzarón implicitly rebuked the junior civil judge, who was responsible for the shortcomings.[7]

Garzarón then complained about the lack of privacy and appropriate working conditions in the *real acuerdo*. The civil judges and the viceroy deliberated important matters of government in the smallest room on the main floor, which also served as the ante-chamber of the viceregal bedroom. Few discussions in the *real acuerdo* remained confidential, according to Garzarón, since the entry to the room consisted of "two small doors made of iron and cloth with wooden frames ... so that even with the doors closed, one could hear what was being said inside the room." During the meetings of the ministers, the viceroy's retainers stood outside and pricked up their ears. Inside various chairs seated the ministers, but the room "lacked a table or a thing that indicated its purpose" for formal meetings. Such a table would have been in the way for the many guests who passed through the room to visit the viceroy. At least the king's portrait hung at the wall, adorned by a velvet canopy. A small adjacent room served as the office of the viceregal secretary.[8]

Garzarón and the ministers then exited the ante-chamber and entered a long corridor connecting to the *audiencia* hall. The procurators and other officials gathered in the corridor to submit written motions to the court notaries and waited on benches to be called for further services. A cheerful mood reigned there occasionally. A witness remarked, for instance, that a procurator sat there during court hours to meet "a woman called doña Manuela with whom he had publicly lived together, and it was a scandal that various unchaste women came there to drink and have lunch."[9]

---

[7] *Reconocimiento* of Garzarón, Mexico City, 13 Apr. 1717, AGI, Escribanía 278 A, *legajo* 8, fols. 151v–152v. See *Law of Castile*, book 2, title 5, law 42; *Law of the Indies*, book 2, title 15, laws 99–109; Solórzano, *Política*, book 5, chap. 8, para 8. Note that few detailed voting records are extant from an earlier period; for example, the vote of Dr. Quesada, 21 June 1604, and dissenting votes in the *real acuerdo*, 12 May 1605, The Latin American Library at Tulane University, Mexican Administration Records, Manuscripts Collection 16, box 3, vol. 1, no pagination.

[8] *Reconocimiento* of Garzarón, Mexico City, 13 Apr. 1717, AGI, Escribanía 278 A, *legajo* 8, fol. 156–156v; see also charges against ministers, AGI, México 670 B, *Relación*, fol. 821; *real cédula* to president and civil judges, Lerma, 13 Dec. 1721, AGN, Real Audiencia 4, exp. 33, fol. 174v.

[9] Testimony of Juan de Salazar, AGI, Escribanía 289 B, *Relazion*, fol. 865–865v. See also *reconocimiento* of Garzarón, Mexico City, 13 Apr. 1717, AGI, Escribanía 278 A, *legajo* 8, fol. 156v; Hillebrand, *Real Audiencia*, 121–133.

Leaving the hallway behind, Garzarón and the judges saw more informal customs in the notarial offices. Garzarón and the judges passed through a gallery and a horseshoe-shaped hallway to enter a room that had formerly served as the bedroom of the Viceroy Duke of Linares (1710–1716). By 1717, this room was being converted into the intestate office, where notaries searched for the heirs of people who had died without a will. Construction was underway in the room, "building a raised floor to place a canopy, table, seats, and other necessary things." Garzarón and his group also went over the papers in the office. Then they left and walked down a wooden staircase to arrive at the section of the old palace that survived the fire of 1692. A corridor took them to the office that archived court orders and collected the penalties assigned by the *audiencia*.[10]

Afterwards, Garzarón and the ministers entered the office of a senior notary, where they saw "a great quantity of trial papers half scorched in the palace fire." Some papers were missing and others were decomposing. In addition, the record keeping was irregular. The notaries did not properly file the documents by year, but alphabetically and "not always by the first letter of the litigant's last name, since some begin with 'r' such as 'record of John Doe' ... while others begin with the title captain, doctor, bachelor ... and this makes searching under many letters necessary," as a notary put it.[11] He and his colleagues billed their clients for the extended work. Subsequently, Garzarón's group walked to the end of the old palace, where he criticized the great distance between the offices and the *audiencia* hall and the lack of cover during rainfall.[12]

At the end of the hallway, Garzarón stepped into the room of the senior notary don José Antonio de Anaya. Garzarón deplored that Anaya's inventory lacked the proper form noting dates and page numbers of the *audiencia* papers. Furthermore, the registry of an usher, who carried documents between Anaya's office and the *relatores* (salaried drafting attorneys), was out of order. The registry consisted only of loose papers in a shambles rather than a bound and paginated volume.[13] Other

---

[10] *Reconocimiento* of Garzarón, Mexico City, 13 Apr. 1717, AGI, Escribanía 278 A, *legajo* 8, fols. 156v–158.

[11] Brief of Juan García de Xismeros, Mexico City, 24 Nov. 1721, AGI, Escribanía 286 C, Q[uader]no 30, no. 7, fol. 556v.

[12] *Reconocimiento* of Garzarón, Mexico City, 13 Apr. 1717, AGI, Escribanía 278 A, *legajo* 8, fols. 158–159v. On excessive searches, *real cédula* to president and civil judges, Lerma, 13 Dec. 1721, AGN, Historia 102, exp. 10, fol. 84.

[13] *Reconocimiento* of Garzarón, Mexico City, 13 Apr. 1717, AGI, Escribanía 278 A, *legajo* 8, fol. 159; charge against Francisco de Alexo de Luna, AGI, Escribanía 289 A, fol. 324.

notaries did not even keep a record of documents. In addition, the official fee schedule was hardly legible, which encouraged the notaries to charge arbitrary amounts. According to the schedule, for instance, Indians and blacks paid lower fees than Spaniards for obtaining signed documents, but scribes and notaries usually ignored these rules.[14]

Finally, the palace chaplain told Garzarón that the viceroys and their families heard mass in their own chapel, where the *audiencia* ministers did not participate. Uribe explained that the chapel "was at the disposition of the viceroy's *mulatos*, and no service was offered at the beginning of the regular *audiencia* time." Nonetheless, Uribe claimed that he regularly arrived at the palace between 7:30 and 7:45 AM to study and hear mass.[15] One of his colleagues added that "what serves as a chapel is so far away that it greatly discomforts us to go there," except at the time of the lent sermons. For this reason, the ministers attended mass elsewhere before or after *audiencia* meetings. Garzarón took note and objected to the informality of these ways.[16]

6.2 NEGLIGENCE AND MALICIOUS INTENT

Concluding the visual inspection of the *audiencia* offices, Garzarón charged most judges with corruption and the officials with fraud, theft, or lesser offenses. Garzarón suspended these ministers between the fall of 1719 and April 1724. The suspensions demonstrated that the *visitador* found the ministers guilty of serious offenses and worthy of removal from their posts. The Council of the Indies subsequently reviewed the sentences and dismissed thirteen judges and eleven officials. The Council also fined dozens of officials between 50 and 2,000 pesos and sometimes ordered them to restore ill-gotten gains. At the same time, the Council absolved fourteen attorneys and a handful of other officials, among them Francisco Xuárez, an interpreter of the Native language Otomí. Almost all minister, including the absolved judges also paid their share of *visita* expenses.[17]

---

[14] Charge against Francisco de Castro, AGI, Escribanía 289 A, fol. 382v; charges against ministers, AGI, México 670 B, *Relación*, fols. 819–820; *real cédula*, Lerma, 13 Dec. 1721, AGN, Historia 102, exp. 10. fols. 82–86.

[15] Defense of José Uribe, AGI, México 670 B, *Relación*, fols. 808–808v, 874; see also *reconocimiento* of Garzarón, Mexico City, 13 Apr. 1717, AGI, Escribanía 278 A, *legajo* 8, fol. 160–160v.

[16] Defense of Juan Francisco de la Peña, AGI, México 670 B, *Relación*, fol. 942.

[17] For the sources and an overview, see Tables 6 and 7 in the Appendix. According to *Law of the Indies*, book 2, title 34, law 25, a *visitador* should suspend those ministers who merited dismissal. Note, for example, that according to sentence of the Council of the

During his investigation, Garzarón occasionally commented on the testimony, indicating which evidence he found convincing or flawed. He sometimes scribbled terse notes on the margins of the testimony. One notary who owned his office, for instance, explained that he had merely complied with orders when he overcharged litigants. Garzarón abbreviated that defense by noting that "the civil judge Valdés, tutor of the office owner, ordered him to do so," and "that he had to follow the rules that are kept in the office."[18] In addition, Garzarón condensed all proven charges against the judges into two separate folders. These volumes are heavily interpretive, as he engaged directly with the testimony, disqualifying unsuitable evidence or juxtaposing it with incriminating material. In these volumes, he only concluded in a few cases that "there is no sufficient evidence for this charge."[19]

Garzarón did not state which specific law or legal doctrine the culprits had violated or which testimony and evidence was sufficient to convict for corruption, fraud or other offenses. Early modern judges rarely laid out their reasoning or clarified the value of testimony. They typically never provided more than a few brief sentences for their verdicts. In part, the practitioners instinctively understood the references, and in part, judges maintained that their sentences were just, and it was the duty of the defendants or prosecutors to argue their case. Additional explanations merely opened venues for appeals, which the judges preferred to avoid. Judges had to explain their motivations only when they chose criminal punishments that differed from standard ones.[20]

The sources nonetheless demonstrate that Garzarón found the judges guilty of corruption, while he sentenced the officials for fraud and other offenses. Garzarón gathered ample evidence that the judges had accepted bribes to alter rulings, forged documents, and extorted money from suspects by threatening violence or by ignoring their just pleas until they paid up. In addition, the judges had also pandered to local interests and

---

Indies, Madrid, 27 Sept. 1725, AGI, Escribanía 1183, folder *1721–1730 Francisco Garzarón*, the *oficial de autos* (scribe) Matías de Araús, who served in José de Medina Saravia's *escribanía de cámara* (notary's office), was absolved. See also *consulta* of the Council of the Indies, Madrid, 22 Mar. 1723, AGI, Escribanía 287 B, *pieza* 35, fols. 8v–9.

[18] Brief of Juan García de Xismeros, Mexico City, 24 Nov. 1721, AGI, Escribanía 286 C, Q. no 30, no. 7, fol. 554.

[19] Charges against Valenzuela, AGI, México 670 B, *Relación*, fols. 30v, 34. Garzarón's volumes comprise AGI, Escribanía 278 A–289 B, and AGI, México 670 A–B.

[20] According to Alonso Romero, *Orden procesal*, 101–102, all judges' rulings were presumed to be just under *ius commune* precepts, while the *Rota* (papal court in Rome) was among the first to justify its rulings at length.

formed a "sacred league" of peninsular Spaniards to take on the *novohispanos* on the *audiencia*.[21] Moreover, they had neglected to guard silence before publishing the verdicts, oppressed Indians, acted as businessmen, and lived depraved lifestyles.[22] Later, the Council of the Indies in Madrid studied and confirmed Garzarón's verdicts against the judges. Yet the Council differed in sentencing the officials and dismissed fewer than a tenth of the suspended culprits. The Council issued separate sentences for each official, briefly pointing out which of Garzarón's charges it upheld or struck down. The Council also found some evidence more convincing than others, because it ruled differently on similar offenses, while never clarifying the reasoning.[23]

The prosecutor of the Council of the Indies provided one of the few solid arguments in 1724. He read up on the case of the civil judge Félix Suárez de Figueroa, who tried to appeal his dismissal from the bench. The prosecutor maintained that all of Garzarón's twenty-six charges against Suárez de Figueroa were fully proven. Garzarón provided a sales deed showing that Suárez de Figueroa had purchased a house in Mexico City, which violated the *Law of the Indies*. In addition, the judge had

---

[21] According to testimony of Suárez de Figueroa, AGI, México 670 B, *Relación*, fol. 11v, the "sacred league opposed those from these lands" who were led by Tristán de Rivadeneyra and Juan de Oliván y Rebolledo. According to reputation of Miguel Calderón de la Barca, AGI, México 670 B, *Relación*, fols. 23v–24v, Calderón de la Barca organized a voting bloc to increase bribes.

[22] Charges against Félix González de Agüero, AGI, México 670 B, *Relación*, fol. 203; Zepeda to king, n. d., attached to *consulta* of the Council of the Indies, 5 Dec. 1721, AGI, México 670 A; reputation of Calderón de la Barca, AGI, México 670 B, *Relación*, fols. 25v–26; see also charge 32 in *juicio de residencia* of Valenzuela against Calderón de la Barca, Mexico City, 1715, AGI, Escribanía 236 A, *pieza* 1a, fol. 102, which formed the basis of the *visita*. According to charges, AGI, México 670 B, *Relación*, fol. 114, Soria Velásquez "was living in a liaison" with a woman, while according to charges, AGI, México 670 B, *Relación*, fol. 158, Díaz de Bracamonte was "in a liaison."

[23] For example, the sentence of the Council of the Indies, Madrid, 15 Mar. 1727, AGI, Escribanía 1183, folder *1721–1730 Francisco Garzarón*, fined Miguel de Solís y Alcazar, a secretary in don José Antonio de Anaya's office, 200 pesos for charging excessive fees from *alcaldes mayores* who paid their deposits, while receptor Fernando de Gálvez was acquitted from a similar charge. Charges against José Romo de Vera, AGI, Escribanía 289 B, fol. 1889–1889v; sentence of the Council of the Indies, Madrid, 18 Mar. 1727, AGI, Escribanía 1183, folder *1721–1730 Francisco Garzarón*, show that Garzarón suspended the procurador José Romo de Vera for embezzling 7,200 pesos while acting as the warden of two minors. The Council of the Indies agreed, assigned a penalty of 500 pesos, and reinstated the procurator. While this may appear as a light penalty, it was heavier than most others for the officials. It may have helped that Romo de Vera did not seize the money in his function as procurator, although Berart y Gassol, *Speculum visitationis*, chap. 3, para. 23, argued that "the *visitadores* should know the crimes of the officials, even outside of their positions."

accepted "copious and repeated gifts" for appointing deputy commissioners to regularize landholdings in the provinces. Finally, the prosecutor noted ample evidence that the judge had received gifts from litigants in at least two cases. Suárez de Figueroa's "*baratería* (corruption)" undercut any doubt in the sentence, and the prosecutor recommended rebutting the appeal.[24]

When the prosecutor and other legal experts arrived at such conclusions, they typically assessed the carelessness or the intention to act of the ministers and the consequences. It mattered greatly whether somebody was merely sloppy in copying papers or deliberately forged papers. The theologian Miguel de San Antonio, for example, pointed out in 1719 that *culpa leve* (simple guilt) meant that a very diligent person had overlooked an issue and caused damages to someone else. That very diligent person incurred ordinary negligence. Meanwhile, being guilty of gross negligence was called the *grave culpa* (or serious guilt). For San Antonio, gross negligence indicated not "showing the diligence and care that all people regularly show in similar matters."[25] The theologian Valentín de la Madre de Dios offered a more complex theory. For him, gross negligence meant disregarding "the care that people of one estate or office usually show," referring to occupational groups such as the "physician, surgeon, judge, and attorney ... and the guard." These people acted grossly negligently, when they ignored the standards of their own occupations.[26]

In 1721, for example, the king explicitly told the *audiencia* judges that "you are grossly negligent" for failing to mend abuses in the notarial offices. The king censored the notaries for "continually cheating the litigants, delaying the processing of Native law suits, the indecency of

---

[24] *Parecer* of José de Laysequilla, prosecutor of the Council of the Indies, Madrid, 14 Aug. 1724, AGI, Escribanía 287 B, *pieza* 39, fols. 132–135; applying *Law of the Indies*, book 2, title, 34, law 23. For Berart y Gassol, *Speculum visitationis*, chap. 7, para. 16, "the punishment for the crime of *baratería* is loss of office and a financial penalty."

[25] San Antonio, *Resumen de la theologia moral*, 116–117; according to this source, gross negligence "always includes the *dolo*," as it comprises knowing the bad consequences and tacitly approving them. Below this standard were the *culpa leve* and *culpa levisima*, both simplified here as ordinary negligence. Separated from this were the theological venial and mortal *culpa* which were forms of sinning. This view parallels the definition in the *RAE* (1729), p. 696. See also the definitions in John Stevens, *A New Spanish and English Dictionary, Collected from the Best Spanish Authors Both Ancient and Modern* [...] *To which is added a Copious English and Spanish Dictionary* [...] (London: George Sawbridge, 1706), 156; *RAE* (1732), p. 330. On freedom to act, Azcargorta, *Manual de Confesores*, 163.

[26] De la Madre de Dios, *Fuero de la conciencia*, 168–169.

their clothes, ... misplacing papers without order or inventory by year, and instead charging the parties excessively for the difficulties in finding documents." In the king's view, the judges had not themselves committed these offenses but failed the standards of their profession by tolerating them. This verdict also explains, in part, why the absolved ministers had to pay considerable *visita* expenses, because most of them had turned a blind eye to the abuses.[27] Even before the *visita* in 1716, the criminal judge Pedro Sánchez Morcillo had jailed the Native governor of Huejotzingo for being "grossly negligent" in the homicide of an Indian. In Sánchez Morcillo's view, the governor had not killed the Indian himself but failed to care properly for his subject.[28]

Beyond these forms of recklessness, those who willfully wronged someone incurred the *gravísima culpa* (most serious guilt). When jurists and theologians assessed this level of guilt, they usually established that the defendant deliberately intended to commit an evil. This intent has been known as the *dolo*. For this reason, the jurist Jerónimo Castillo de Bobadilla pointed out that it "is bad but pardonable when someone sins because of ignorance or incompetence, but the *dolo* and the intent increase the guilt."[29] In this line of thinking, corrupt judges were not merely ignorant or ordinarily or grossly negligent. Instead, they had shown the manifest *dolo* to commit a crime when they accepted money in exchange for bending justice. Therefore, they knew that they faced stern penalties if convicted for the most serious guilt. One attorney even confirmed in 1719 that "the corrupted judge incurred the most serious guilt" when issuing unjust sentences for money. Garzarón agreed and suspended the corrupt judges, for he largely assigned punishments corresponding to the culpability of the ministers.[30]

The accused ministers also wrangled over their guilt, because it mattered in assessing their liability; that is, the duty to restore damages to aggrieved parties. "When there is gross negligence, there is always the obligation to restore damages," the theologian San Antonio argued.

---

[27] According to *real cédula*, Lerma, 13 Dec. 1721, AGN Historia 102, exp. 10, fol. 84, "Sois vosotros gravemente culpados."
[28] On "gravemente culpado," decree of Sánchez Morcillo, Tlaxcala, 23 Feb. 1716, AGI, Escribanía 281 D, fol. 979v.
[29] Castillo de Bobadilla, *Política*, book 2, chap 11, para. 2.
[30] José Saenz de Escobar on behalf of Pedro Robledo to Garzarón, Mexico City, 15 Apr. 1719, AGI, Escribanía 280 C, fol. 454v. According to Francisco Larraga, *Promptuario de la theologia moral: muy vtil para todos los que han de exponer de co[n]fessores [...]* (Madrid: Manuel Román, 1718), 343, the *dolo* included fraud or deception.

Meanwhile, in the case of "ordinary negligence, attorneys are not required to return their salaries or wages or the damages of a lost lawsuit," San Antonio continued. In other words, if the lawyers had acted very diligently and yet overlooked something that hampered their litigation, they did not have to reimburse their clients. Comparable standards existed for other officials. This was yet another reason why the suspects attempted to lower their level of culpability during the *visita* and denied incurring that of gross negligence or the most serious guilt.[31]

The fine-grained legal distinctions were part of the common Atlantic culture of the *ius commune*. The *ius commune* included the interpretations of canon (Church) and Roman law, which, to varying degrees, shaped justice in the Iberian empires, France, the Holy Roman Empire, and elsewhere. Theologians and jurists had developed these concepts over centuries and mutually influenced each other. For example, when some theologians defined gross negligence, they indirectly drew on the fourteenth-century Italian commentator Bartolus de Sassoferrato, who was among the first to conceptualize occupational groups to compare levels of negligence.[32]

6.3 FRAUD, OVERCHARGING, AND THEFT

While most *audiencia* officials evaded the serious charges of corruption, they could well have committed other crimes such as *falsedad* (fraud). The crime of fraud was broadly defined in the early modern period and usually included tampering with official documents, seals, coins, or artifacts, or deceiving and damaging individuals in other ways. The canonist Pedro Murillo Velarde gave three criteria for fraud, which consisted of changing the truth of a record, the *dolo* to do so, and potentially or

---

[31] San Antonio, *Resumen de la theologia moral*, 116–118. See also de la Madre de Dios, *Fuero de la conciencia*, 169–172.

[32] De la Madre de Dios, *Fuero de la conciencia*, 168–169. According to Lepsius, *Von Zweifeln*, 275–281, 290–291, 296, Bartolus de Sassoferrato both conceptualized comparative occupational groups and separated *culpa latisima* from *culpa latior*. Note that in 1718, Larraga, *Promptuario de la theologia*, 343, separated *culpa latisima* (Latin)/ *gravisima culpa* (Spanish) with the manifest *dolo* from *culpa latior* (more serious guilt) in the cases when judges could only assume that *dolo* had existed. See also Gerhard Lingelbach, "Arglist," in Cordes, *HRG*, 2nd ed., (2008), 1: 294–296, www.hrgdigital .de/HRG.arglist; Ina Ebert, "Fahrlässigkeit," ibid., 1470–1474, www.hrgdigital.de/HRG .fahrlaessigkeit; Ekkehard Kaufmann, "Schuldstrafrecht," in *Handwörterbuch zur deutschen Rechtsgeschichte,* eds. Adalbert Erler, Ekkehard Kaufmann, and Ruth Schmidt-Wiegand (Berlin: Erich Schmidt Verlag, 1990), 4: 1516–1517.

actually hurting others. Notaries who informally amended or loosely copied a record, for example, did not commit fraud as long as the content remained true. Similarly, a scribe who erred in drafting paperwork lacked *dolo* and therefore did not act fraudulently. Meanwhile, those convicted of deliberately defrauding others could face tough penalties, both in theory and in Garzarón's *visita*.[33]

Some separated forgery committed by officials from the errors of private individuals to lessen their guilt. For instance, a notary defended himself against Garzarón's charge by claiming that "jurists and theologians recognize fraud when a public person serving as notary or secretary certifies an act or record that did not exist." The notary implied that he had solely acted as a private person in the specific case and therefore "could only be charged ... with inexperience."[34] The notary built his argument on the early modern distinction between private and public acts. Garzarón suspended him nonetheless, and it is doubtful that the Council of the Indies fully accepted the defense. The Council handed down a tough penalty for the notary and also severely punished other officials who had committed "fraud or illegalities."[35]

Garzarón also hunted for evidence of fraud when prosecuting the notary and procurator Juan García de Xismeros. García de Xismeros was no stranger to trouble. In 1718 the *audiencia* convicted him for

---

[33] Murillo Velarde, *Cursus iuris canonici*, book 5, title 20, para. 245; according to the *Siete Partidas*, partida 7, title 7, law 1, "*falsedad* is altering the truth," which drew on the Roman jurist Paulus, *Sententiae Receptae* 5.25.3, who defined the *falsum* as "whatsoever is not truthful but is proclaimed to be true." See also the *Lex Cornelia de Falsis* in *Digest* 48.10 and the *Institutes* 4.18.7; Jeremy Ravi Mumford, "Forgery and *Tambos*: False Documents, Imagined Incas, and the Making of Andean Space," in Rosenmüller, *Corruption in the Iberian Empires*, 21–23; Villa-Flores, "Archivos y falsarios," 19–41.

[34] Defense of Juan José Aguilera, AGI, Escribanía 289 B, *Relazion*, fol. 108–108v. According to Luis Emilio Rojas Aguirre, "Historia dogmática de la falsedad documental," *Revista de Derecho de la Pontificia Universidad Católica de Valparaíso* 39 (2012): 548–553, 568, the Holy Roman Empire's penal code Carolina (*Constitutio Criminalis Carolina*) enumerated specific forgeries, while Andreas Deutsch, "Fälschungsdelikte," in Cordes, *HRG*, 2nd ed., (2008), 1: 1489–1496, www.hrgdigital.de/HRG.faelschungsdelikte, and Schlosser, *Neuere europäische*, 87, 90, show that the French penal code of 1810 departed from enumerating the manifold ways of deceiving and instead defined the protected legal goods. The code separated between fraud against public trust in a record (*escroquerie*) and fraud as deceitfully damaging the individual property (*faux*). This distinction spread to other European empires. Aguilera's argument reflected an older distinction between public and private actions.

[35] See, for example, the sentence of the Council of the Indies, Madrid, 18 Mar. 1727, AGI, Escribanía 1183, folder *1721–1730 Francisco Garzarón*.

"swindling and extortions" and suspended him for two years.[36] In 1719, Garzarón accused him of the same crimes. According to the charges, García de Xismeros had cheated litigants to the tune of 50 to 300 pesos in about fifty cases. García de Xismeros denied any "*dolo* or fraud,"[37] but Garzarón suspended him nevertheless. The Council of the Indies also found him guilty in 1727 of "fraud and replacing papers and other excesses." The Council ordered him to restore approximately 11,000 pesos to the aggrieved parties – an enormous amount of money.[38]

While officials rebutted the allegations of fraud, they occasionally justified overcharging litigants with biblical and other rules. The officials held that they were poor and their wages did not adequately reflect their work. For one lawyer, "the jurists concur that the fee has to correspond to the work done," echoing the apostle St. Paul for whom the laborer was "worthy of his reward."[39] García de Xismeros added that he did not receive any money for the "insurmountable work in the searches for old cases," while there was always "the danger causing the loss of health, and this happened to me hurting me so much that I would have been ... in serious risk of losing my life ... because the folders are full of greasy dust that stain and spoil the clothes."[40]

Officials also denied abusing the poor Indians, because they were underpaid themselves. One deputy notary emphasized that he always

---

[36] Charges against Juan Garcia de Xismeros, AGI, Escribanía 289 B, fols. 1596–1597; charges against Pedro Sánchez Morcillo, AGI, México 670 B, fols. 615–616v. According to these sources, García de Xismeros served as procurator since 1714, while according to García de Xismeros on behalf of Tanzitaro and Pinzandaro to Viceroy Valero, AGN, Indios 42, exp. 150, fol. 181–181v, he also served as procurator in the year 1719.

[37] Brief of Juan García de Xismeros, Mexico City, 24 Nov. 1721, AGI, Escribanía 286 C, Q. no 30, no. 7, fols. 561v–562.

[38] Sentence of the Council of the Indies, Madrid, 18 Mar. 1727, AGI, Escribanía 1183, folder 1721–1730 Francisco Garzarón, see also certification of Antonio de los Ríos, Mexico City, 6 Apr. 1724, AGI, Escribanía 287 B, *pieza* 55, fol. 1. Based on these sources, I estimate García de Xismeros' approximate restitution by multiplying by four the initial twenty of the eighty penalty fees. On fraudulent impostors, see Villa-Flores, "Wandering Swindlers: Imposture, Style, and the Inquisition's Pedagogy of Fear in Colonial Mexico," *Colonial Latin American Review* 17 (2008): 251–272.

[39] Testimony of Manuel de Rivas on behalf of Francisco de Castro, AGI, Escribanía 289 A, *Relazion*, fol. 381v; St. Paul, 1 Tim. 5:18, who was cited, e.g., by Castillo de Bobadilla, *Política*, book 2, chap. 11, para. 21.

[40] Brief of Juan García de Xismeros, Mexico City, 24 Nov. 1721, AGI, Escribanía 286 C, Q. no 30, no. 7, fol. 556v. The *Law of the Indies*, book 2, title 23, law 42, excluded charging fees for the work that Xismeros listed, while stating the permitted fees for notaries in laws 42–55.

took into account indigenous poverty when assessing fees.[41] Another official admitted to charging more than allowed for issuing court orders. The fee schedule capped the price for the service at one peso for Spaniards and four *reales* for Indians. The official maintained that "the royal law favors the Indians and charges them low fees because of their poverty," but he was himself so poor that "he had to overcome his shame many times and ask his friends to bring his family bread ... and it would be practicable if the prince or the republic assigned him fees that paid him sufficiently for his food and ordinary expenses, while providing for some additional and abounding savings for his old age and posterity."[42]

According to some defenses, the office owners were entitled to higher fees or had not posted the proper rules for charging the fees. García de Xismeros posited, for example, that a notarial office yielded an expected income from the fees, and a candidate purchased the office with the corresponding amount of money. The purchasers then recovered their expenses by receiving a third of the fees collected by their deputy notaries, who also paid three thousand pesos per year to serve their posts. Foregoing that customary income would defraud the owner of the office, García de Xismeros averred. The deputies would also cease working if they had to stop charging higher fees, because they would not be able to earn a living anymore.[43] In addition, a deputy fee assessor pointed out that the *audiencia* chancellor had failed to post the current fee schedule in their office. The deputy fee assessor therefore did not know the appropriate charges, and it was "common agreement and well-argued by moralists, theologians, and jurists that those are excused who unwittingly behave wrongly when they feel they are doing right, and they would sin if they did otherwise."[44]

Garzarón read the suspects' defenses and ruled on the merits of each individual. Some *visitadores* had in the past punished all members of a municipal council or another social body in the same way, regardless

---

[41] Brief of Juan García de Xismeros, Mexico City, 24 Nov. 1721, AGI, Escribanía 286 C, Q. no 30, no. 7, fol. 557.
[42] Testimony of don Manuel de Rivas and defense of Francisco de Castro, AGI, Escribanía 289 A, *Relazion*, fols. 381v–383v.
[43] Brief of Juan García de Xismeros, Mexico City, 24 Nov. 1721, AGI, Escribanía 286 C, Q. no 30, no. 7, fols. 553v–557, who also argued that an *audiencia* judge had ordered him to levy fees according to custom. See also defense of Francisco Antonio Casses, Mexico City, 6 Nov. 1721, AGI, Escribanía 285 C, Q.no 27, no. 5.
[44] Defense of *teniente de tasador* Francisco Antonio Casses, Mexico City, 6 Nov. 1721, AGI, Escribanía 285 C, Q.no 27, no. 5, fols. 725–735v, quote on fol. 724v.

of their individual guilt.[45] Garzarón initially proceeded in a similar way, simultaneously investigating all ministers of a particular office. He questioned and suspended all the members of the jail staff in close order, for instance. Yet Garzarón recorded the charges and the evidence against every single suspect. The Council of the Indies equally tailored the rulings to every minister, fining some, reprimanding others, and absolving a few judges and officials.[46]

In fact, the Council of the Indies issued verdicts according to the evidence, the seriousness of the offenses, and the positions of the officials. Fraud was a crime for which the Council meted out harsh punishments. The Council also punished other illegalities, such as jailing or releasing suspects without court orders or stealing money from confiscations. In addition, it mattered whether the officials had a life-term appointment with a royal title or served as deputies of others. The bar for removing officials with title was higher, while it was easier to terminate the deputies who often had no title to their post. As a result, the Council dismissed eleven officials. Five of them had titles of appointments. Among these, the Council removed García de Xismeros and three other officials for fraud and other illegalities. The Council also dismissed notary Pedro Robledo for bribing the land-grant commission judge with 4,000 pesos and selling numerous appointments for deputy commissioners. Garzarón had censored Robledo's sales, and the Council added a fine of 2,000 pesos. The removed officials also paid hefty penalties.[47]

Moreover, the Council dismissed six deputies and handed down serious penalties to others. The Council removed two deputy officials for committing illegalities during confiscations and dismissed three deputies for lesser offenses. Evidence suggests that these three officials did not have a title of appointment in the first place. In addition, one interim official had to go, because he never paid the annual rent on his office and improperly pocketed *audiencia* fines. The Council also handed down fines of between 50 and 1,000 pesos for sixteen other officials, who kept their positions. Furthermore, the Council extended the suspensions

---

[45] Herzog, "Ritos de control," 18–20, although she also notes that notaries received individual verdicts.

[46] See, for example, sentences of the Council of the Indies, Madrid, 23 Sept. 1721 or 14 Dec. 1726; all documents in AGI, Escribanía 1183, folder *1721–1730 Francisco Garzarón*.

[47] Sentences of the Council of the Indies, Madrid, 23 Sept. 1721; 14 Dec. 1726; 15 Mar. 1727; 18 Mar. 1727, all documents in AGI, Escribanía 1183, folder *1721–1730 Francisco Garzarón*.

without pay for nine officials. Garzarón had already banished them from Mexico City, and they had to endure additional periods of up to six years from the time they received the Council's verdicts. While some negotiated lower punishments, at least one official did not return to Mexico City before early 1729.[48]

Feliciano Ulloa y Sevilla, a notary of the provincial court, belonged to the eleven removed officials. He had committed fraud and jailed suspects without court orders. According to a testimony, the "*mulata* [a woman of mixed African ancestry] María Teresa found eleven small diamonds wrapped in paper in 1717 and sent an old man called *the captive* to sell them on San Francisco Street, and [Ulloa y Sevilla] came and seized them with the pretext that they could have been stolen from a woman of Xochimilco," a *pueblo* south of Mexico City. When the woman from Xochimilco looked at the confiscated jewels, she denied that they were hers, yet Ulloa y Sevilla kept them anyway. María Teresa subsequently went to the viceregal palace to find him and demand her diamonds. Ulloa y Sevilla detained María Teresa at that point and "put her into jail on his own authority and without a judicial order and kept her there for six days, demanding additional ten pesos to release her, which in effect she paid." The Council of the Indies reviewed the charges and dismissed Ulloa y Sevilla for committing "forgeries, fraud, and illegalities."[49] The Council also ordered him to restore to María Teresa the diamonds along with the ten pesos. The Council did not usually return funds to *visita* witnesses, yet María Teresa was eligible for recovery, because she had not bribed anyone and this was not a corruption case.[50]

In addition to these crimes, officials also deprived the treasury of revenue when they rented their positions to others without a royal permit. For instance, one notary of the provincial court took on additional work as deputy notary in the viceregal government. In 1715, the notary struck a "deal and accord" to sublet his post in the provincial court to Juan José Aguilera for a peso per day. This deal equaled more than 7,000 pesos,

---

[48] Sentences of the Council of the Indies, Madrid, 27 Sept. 1725, 24 July 1726, 14 Dec. 1726, 16 Dec. 1726, 18 Mar. 1727, 28 Mar. 1729, all documents in AGI, Escribanía 1183, folder *1721–1730 Francisco Garzarón*; Diego de Puerto on behalf of José Diego de Medina to king, n. d. (1729), Madrid, AGI, Escribanía 1183, folder *1726–1733 Francisco Garzarón*.

[49] "*falsificaciones ... falsedades e ylegalidades*," sentence of the Council of the Indies, Madrid, 18 Mar. 1727, AGI, Escribanía 1183, folder *1721–1730 Francisco Garzarón*.

[50] All quotes in this paragraph except note 49 in charge against and defense of Feliciano Ulloa y Sevilla, AGI, Escribanía 289 B, *Relazion*, fols. 780v–782.

although the notary had paid only 3,000 pesos to the treasury to obtain his post. In Garzarón's view, the notary abused his faculties, because he had no illness or other impediment to justify his actions.[51] In addition, Aguilera worked as interim fine collector of the *audiencia*. This position offered some potential, as the collectors sometimes took up to one tenth of the proceeds for themselves. Aguilera stated that he had made an offer during the 1713 auction to work in that position for one year. Yet another notary offered more. After the heat of the bidding subsided, the successful notary suffered buyer's remorse and requested a new auction. The viceroy demurred, but the remorseful notary insisted, and papers and petitions flew back and forth. Meanwhile, Aguilera began serving as interim fine collector and continued for four years without paying the crown the required rent for the office. Aguilera argued that the remorseful notary owed the rent "for being the motor of not re-auctioning" the position, but Garzarón suspended all three officials.[52]

Between 1726 and 1727, the Council of the Indies punished both the deputy notary who sublet his post and the remorseful bidder lightly, but severely chastised Aguilera, mainly for misappropriating cash. The Council assigned a 2,000 peso fine to Aguilera and dismissed him from the interim position. The precise offenses corresponding to the punishment are unclear, because Aguilera faced over 250 charges. The Council ordered him to reimburse 900 pesos to the crown for serving his office without paying rent. What was worse, he also had failed to record the court fines that he collected and embezzled these moneys.[53]

Removing the officials seems harsh, but the results were ultimately more lenient, because some officials also held other positions at the *audiencia*. Aguilera, for example, continued in his position as a notary

---

[51] Charge against Antonio de Avilés, Mexico City, 1721, AGI, Escribanía 285 B, *Q.no* 26, no. 8, fol. 678.

[52] Charge against Avilés, Mexico City, 1721, AGI, Escribanía 285 B, *Q.no* 26, no. 8, fol. 678–678v; defense of Juan José Aguilera, AGI, Escribanía 289 B, *Relazion*, fols. 3v–4; according to ibid., fols. 1–4, Aguilera served as *receptor de penas de cámara* (fine collector) of *the audiencia* and as *teniente de escribano de provincia* (deputy notary of the provincial court), where the remorseful bidder, Juan José de Sevilla, worked as a notary. Note that notary of the provincial court, Antonio de Avilés, also appears as Alonso de Avilés in the sources, probably confusing him with the notary of the criminal chamber, don Alonso de Fuenlabrada y Avilés, who was adjudicated by sentence of the Council of the Indies, Madrid, 24 July 1726, AGI, Escribanía 1183, folder *1721–1730 Francisco Garzarón*.

[53] Sentence of the Council of the Indies, Madrid, 16 Dec. 1726, AGI, Escribanía 1183, folder *1721–1730 Francisco Garzarón*; sentence of the Council of the Indies, Madrid, 15 Mar. 1727, ibid.

of the provincial court. The Council suspended him from that post for an additional period of roughly five years and fined him 200 pesos because of his slovenly paper work. According to the Council, his trial records were unbound and unpaginated and contained bits of papers sewn into a volume. Aguilera acknowledged that he used unstamped paper but claimed that he had worked more diligently than his predecessors. They "did not even have page numbers or keep the trial order," while he used even "greater care and formality than the senior notary."[54] Notary García de Xismeros similarly lost his work as notary but stayed on as a procurator. In addition, there are indications that some officials and even judges renegotiated their penalties. For instance, the Council of the Indies convicted one senior secretary on several charges, but the culprit's attorney declared in 1726 that the king allowed his client to return to work without any expenses.[55]

Francisco Garzarón also suspended ten *relatores* and twenty-eight attorneys. Some *relatores* had acted as go-betweens between clients and judges to negotiate bribes and this was clearly wrong. In addition, the crown noted that some lawyers serving at the *audiencia* did not finish their schooling, failed to pass the necessary examinations, or were "entirely ignorant" in the law.[56] Yet the Council of the Indies subsequently acquitted all *relatores* and fourteen attorneys, an unusually high number in one occupational group. Seven attorneys had to return between twenty and 970 pesos in excessive fees charged to former clients. Five attorneys received fines. One of them paid fifty pesos for drafting a will in 1715 that

[54] Charge and defense of Aguilera, AGI, Escribanía 289 B, *Relazion*, fols. 111v–112v; see also fols. 4v–25, according to which Aguilera charged incoming *alcaldes mayores* excessive fees. For a similar charge, see testimony of don Simón de Carragal, AGI, Escribanía 289 B, fol. 42. According to *auto* of Manuel Salazar, Madrid, 20 Dec. 1727, AGI, Escribanía 1183, folder *1726–1733 Francisco Garzarón*, the Council prematurely ended Aguilera's suspension in 1727. According to sentences of the Council of the Indies, Madrid, 16 Dec. 1726, and 15 Mar. 1727, both in AGI, Escribanía 1183, folder *1721–1730 Francisco Garzarón*, the Council of the Indies admonished the record keeping in the provincial court and fined six of the eight notaries between 50 and 200 pesos. On widespread informal drafting practices in Peru, Burns, *Into the Archive*, 76–93.

[55] Juan Baptista Munilla on behalf of *oficial mayor* José Antonio de Ariza to king, Madrid, 1727; decree, Madrid, 24 Nov. 1726, both documents in AGI, Escribanía 1183, folder *1726–1733 Francisco Garzarón*.

[56] *Real cédula*, Lerma, 13 Dec. 1721, AGN, Historia, 102, fol. 85; based on Rodrigo de Zepeda to king, n. d., attached to the *consulta* of the Council of the Indies, 5 Dec. 1721, AGI, México 670 A. According to *Law of the Indies*, book 2, title 22, laws 1–34, particularly 26, 31, and 32, *relatores* were prohibited from accepting gifts or relaying money to the ministers. On *relatores* and attorneys, Hillebrand, *Real Audiencia*, 119–126.

contained irritating clauses to disinherit the testator's grandchildren. No notary had been present to validate the record and the attorney signed as his own witness. He later wrote an addendum with "much nonsense" to salvage the document. Next to this delinquent, the salaried attorney for the poor had to serve for two years without any wages, because he had shelved petitions when his clients refused to pay him additional fees. He even hid occasionally in the palace when the ushers came calling for him to appear in the criminal chamber. Many prisoners suffered extended jail time because of his lackluster attitude. Moreover, the attorney for the Indians received an annual salary of 447 pesos, yet he often sent a substitute to represent the Natives at the criminal chamber. The Council fined him 200 pesos.[57]

The Council concluded that most other notaries and their deputies had largely complied with their essential duties. They overcharged the public but had not committed more serious offenses. The Council reprimanded and sternly warned the officials to abstain from further misconduct. The Council also acquitted several notaries, jailers, and Native interpreters. Some of them passed away during the *visita*, and the Council withheld a verdict on them. Subsequently, almost all officials paid their share of the *visita* expenses and perhaps minor penalties. Once they had entered the cash into the royal treasury, Garzarón allowed them to return to their posts.[58]

Among the acquitted interpreters was Francisco Xuárez, whom several *caciques* (ethnic lords) vouched for. Xuárez translated between the indigenous language Otomí and Spanish, and a few procurators complained about his self-serving attitude. One procurator accused Xuárez of charging fees according to his whim.[59] Three procurators also affirmed that Xuárez did "not appear on time during the *audiencia* hours, and although they search for him to interpret the proceedings, he meets up with Indians in reunions and speeches to take advantage of them, and he acts as their agent and collects papers instead of bringing them to the homes of the procurators and attorneys as he should have." These procurators mainly

---

[57] Sentences of the Council of the Indies, Madrid, 10 Feb. 1724 and 17 Dec. 1723, both in AGI, Escribanía 1183, folder *1721–1730 Francisco Garzarón*.

[58] It would require careful work to distinguish between those declared free (*libre*) of some or all charges, free because they died, and those who were absolved and admonished; see, e.g., the sentences of the Council of the Indies, 18 Mar. 1727 and 24 July 1726, AGI, Escribanía 1183, folder *1721–1730 Francisco Garzarón*.

[59] Charge against *intérprete* Xuárez, and testimony of José Francisco de Landa, Mexico City, 1719, AGI, Escribanía 288 A, *Relación*, fol. 366.

objected to Xuárez taking over their work and depriving them of their fees.⁶⁰

At the same time, over a dozen ethnic lords of Toluca, Querétaro, and other places denied seeing Xuárez in gatherings. One lord claimed that the interpreter did not take more than two *reales* for issuing a power of attorney. Another one painted an even rosier image. He testified that Xuárez had drawn up a power of attorney for the "Indians of Huichapan and he did not receive anything and rejected their gifts; he also lent them four pesos, and they still owe him three." Xuárez added that he had never drawn a salary from the *audiencia*, and for this reason, he changed to the ecclesiastical courts. In his view, the accusations "were against the truthful natural law that he had to maintain himself." The Council of the Indies declared Xuárez free; in part, because the Council did not trust the hostile testimony of a procurator and notary who was dismissed for fraud.⁶¹

How to explain the difference between Garzarón's great number of suspensions of officials and the Council of the Indies' milder rulings? In part, Garzarón had earned a reputation as stern inquisitor. He and other *visitadores* also often handed down tough sentences to demonstrate efficacy to the crown, frequently with an eye on their own social advancement. In addition, Garzarón tended to interpret the royal law more literally than others. Meanwhile, charging excessive fees was small fry for at least a few councilors of the Indies. They understood that many officials received low or no salaries and needed additional income. Some councilors probably also subscribed to more traditional notions of justice. They accepted the importance of customs and balanced clemency against the rigor of the law. In addition, the crown had a financial interest, as it could more easily collect fines from ministers who eagerly sought to return to their posts than from the dismissed functionaries. Furthermore, politics mattered. The Council early on opposed the *visita* and thrashed Garzarón's excessive zeal in 1726. The Council's stance explains its lenience in part. Finally, the social networks also shaped the rulings of

---

⁶⁰ On *tlatoles* (speeches), charge against Xuárez based on testimonies of Nicolás de Navia, Juan García de Xismeros, and Miguel de Vallecillo, Mexico City, 1719, AGI, Escribanía 288 A, *Relación*, fol. 369.

⁶¹ Charges against and defense of Xuárez, Mexico City, 1719, AGI, Escribanía 288 A, *Relacion*, fols. 365v–370; see also sentence of the Council of the Indies, Madrid, 14 Dec. 1726, AGI, Escribanía 1183, folder *1721–1730 Francisco Garzarón*. It is unclear whether the ethnic lords lived in Mexico City, were summoned by the *visita*, or were requested by Xuárez. The hostile witness was Juan García de Xismeros.

Garzarón and the Council, but the sources rarely reveal these details candidly.[62]

Garzarón ordered the suspended judges and officials to post bond and leave town, causing additional hardship. These ministers had to pay their share of the *visita* costs within three days or provide collateral. The ministers could deposit cash in the treasury, show that they owned property, or provide solid bondsmen, such as Cathedral canons or merchants.[63] When the ministers did not comply, Garzarón confiscated their possessions. He then banished judges and officials to any place twenty leagues (fifty-three miles) outside Mexico City. Abandoning town was not easy. A *relator*, for instance, lamented that he lacked the wherewithal to leave town with his family. He had no relatives to rely on and had to support "five children, two of them ladies, seventeen and twelve years old, and three boys, one of them is studying liberal arts, the other grammar, and the third is in school." If he left the city and his "daughters alone, he risked their destruction." The *relator* was on his knees pleading for clemency, but Garzarón shrugged off the request.[64] He nonetheless gave a two-month extension to another *relator* who feared that his pregnant wife would "miscarry during the agitation of the road."[65] When Garzarón suspended a scribe in 1721, the culprit sold his belongings to leave town with his wife and their eight children. At least he was able to secure another position that allowed him to provide for his family.[66]

---

[62] On Garzarón's "burning zeal," see the *consulta* of the Council of the Indies, Madrid, 18 Jan. 1726, AGI, México 670 A, while the *consulta* of the Council of the Indies, 22 Dec. 1736, AGI, México 383, favored applying "piety and sympathy in moderating the law this time and without setting a precedent." On clemency, Torres de Lima, *Compendio*, 103; Mendo, *Príncipe Perfecto*, 166.

[63] According to doña María Gertrudis Sánchez to Garzarón, Mexico City, 20 Sept. 1726, AGN, Historia 102, exp. 20, fol. 514–514v, and certification of royal officials, Mexico City, 7 July 1724, AGN, Indiferente Virreinal 5976, exp. 94, fol. 2v, the Count of Miravalle underwrote the deposits for notary José Sánchez and attorney Juan de Dios del Corral.

[64] Cristóbal González de Fonseca to Garzarón, Mexico City, 18 Aug. 1722; see also reply by Garzarón, n. d., AGI, Escribanía 283 A, *cuaderno* 19, fols. 1286–1287.

[65] Pedro Carrillo y Espinosa to Garzarón, Mexico City, 22 Aug. 1722; see also reply by Garzarón, n. d.; *auto de providencia* by Garzarón, Mexico City, 3 Aug. 1722, all documents in AGI, Escribanía 283 A, *cuaderno* 19, fols. 1252, 1255–1256v. On exiling José Sánchez and Feliciano Ulloa y Sevilla, *auto* of Garzarón, 18 Jan. 1723, AGI, Escribanía 289 A, fols. 201–202v; *auto* of Garzarón, AGI, Escribanía 289 B, *Relazion*, fol. 867.

[66] Carlos Marcelo de la Nuza to Garzarón, Mexico City, 7 Oct. 1727; Garzarón's reply, n. d., both documents in AGN, Historia 102, exp. 20, fol. 513.

Some officials posted insufficient bond, and the treasury sent armed commissioners to escort them to jail in Mexico City. The deputy jail constable, for instance, could not scratch together 624 pesos for his share of the *visita* expenses. The commissioners seized him in Huichapan (Hidalgo). He and three other officials shared in the "great humiliation and cruelty as though we were some criminals, taking us to prison with guards and causing a scandal in the city."[67] Following this walk of shame, the deputy jail constable experienced the dungeons from the other perspective. He suffered for seven months from the "greatest misery, insults, hunger, nakedness, and sickness." Although the crown reinstated the miscreant to his office, Garzarón demanded that he pay his share of *visita* expenses in full before his release. The deputy jail constable remained in jail "spending the four great feasts of the year waiting to be heard ... as though he was a convict worse than [Martin] Luther."[68]

Some of the dismissed judges played tug-of-war over fines, deposits, and even their robes with Garzarón. Several judges proclaimed in 1723 that the king had taken their jobs but not their cloaks which they kept donning in public. In response Garzarón threatened to lock them up in the municipal council building. The culprits rather suddenly dressed like ordinary people, Garzarón observed with some satisfaction. The recalcitrant ministers also averred that their poverty prevented them from paying their penalties, but Garzarón believed that the judges preferred jail time or exile over settling accounts. Garzarón seized as much as he could. In 1722, he ordered the heirs of one deceased judge to pay 2,000 pesos in addition to 130 pesos to pay for shipping the money to Spain. He also sold the stage coach and seized the heavily mortgaged real estate belonging to another judge. The judge ran off and hid with only "two *petacas* (baskets) containing his dress and white linen" in the Augustinian church of Saint Paul where Garzarón could not easily extract him. By 1723, one

---

[67] Antonio de Castilleja, José Ruiz Caval, Francisco Alejo de Luna, and Sebastián Guerrero to king, palace jail, Mexico City, 15 Aug. 1724, AGI, Escribanía 287 B, *pieza* 56, fols. 32–33; see also José Ruiz Cabal to Garzarón, Mexico City, 9 Feb. 1724, AGN, Historia 102, exp. 20, fol. 510.

[68] Petitions of *teniente de alguacil de corte* Sebastián Guerrero to viceroy, Garzarón, and the archbishop, seen in *real acuerdo*, Mexico City, 3 July 1724, AGI, Escribanía 287 B, fols. 2–5. According to Carlos Romero de la Vega to Garzarón, Mexico City, 7 Oct. 1726, AGN, Historia 102, exp. 20, fols. 511–512, the suspended notary of the intestate office, Juan de Valbuena, even pocketed 351 pesos and six *reales* from the estate of a deceased attorney who had to pay *visita* cost, but Valbuena never paid the treasury.

judge had paid 22,048 pesos, while another judge paid a similar amount.[69]

Garzarón succeeded, by and large, in defraying 50,216 pesos that he had spent in the course of the investigation. He was about 6,000 pesos shy of reaching that goal by May of 1724. For this end, a fee assessor calculated the amount payable by each suspect. One scribe had to contribute around 600 pesos to the *visita* costs, for example.[70] The attorney Juan de Dios del Corral relinquished 1,129 pesos, although the Council of the Indies threw out all twenty-one charges and reinstated him in the spring of 1724. When the royal communication ordering the reinstatement arrived in Mexico City, a friend of Dios del Corral paid his share of *visita* expenses on July 7, 1724. Garzarón received notice of the payment on July 12. He also saw the royal communication, "took it in his hands, kissed it, and put it on his head as a letter and provision of our King." Two days later, the *audiencia* lifted Dios del Corral's exile, and he returned to the capital to resume his work.[71]

---

[69] Garzarón to king, 24 May 1723, AGI, Escribanía 287 B, *pieza* 57, fols. 1–5, referring to civil judge Tristán de Rivadeneyra. According to Rivadeneyra to Casafuerte, n. d., no place; tribunal of accounts to royal officials, Mexico City, 3 Aug. 1723; and Gaspar Felipe de Rivadeneyra to tribunal of accounts, Mexico City, 16 May 1725, all three documents in AGN, Indiferente Virreinal 734, exp. 40, fols. 20–21v, 61, 81–81v, Rivadeneyra resisted paying, joined the Franciscan order, and passed away in 1725; see also Garzarón to king, Mexico City, 1 May 1724, AGI, Escribanía 287 B, *pieza* 57, fols. 9–10v; *parecer* of the prosecutor of the Council of the Indies, Madrid, 17 Sept. 1724, AGI, Escribanía 287 B, *pieza* 57, fol. 10v; Garzarón to king, Mexico City, 1 May 1724, AGI, Escribanía 287 B, *pieza* 51. According to these documents, Félix González Agüero paid 22,048 pesos, while royal officials confiscated almost the same amount from Rivadeneyra. On the heirs of judge Valenzuela, decree of Garzarón, Mexico City, 21 Oct. 1722, AGI, Escribanía 287 A, *Q.no* 31, *pieza* 33, fol. 47; Garzarón to king, Mexico City, 20 Feb. 1723, AGI, Escribanía 287 B, *pieza* 58, fols. 6–7; *consulta* of the Council of the Indies, Madrid, 28 July 1731, AGI, Escribanía 287 B, *pieza* 46, fol. 8v. Berart y Gassol, *Speculum visitationis*, chap. 3, paras. 21–22, affirmed that *visitadores* could proceed against the heirs of judges sentenced for "theft, bribery, and illicit extortions," while noting dissenting views. On the Augustinian Saint Paul's College as the seat of the "Creole monarchy" and center of contraband trade, Antonio Rubial García, *Una Monarquía Criolla (La provincia agustina en el siglo XVII)* (Mexico City: Consejo Nacional para la Cultura y las Artes, 1990), 54–60, 101–105. On the robes, Garzarón to king, Mexico City, 20 Feb. 1723, AGI, Escribanía 287 B, fols. 6–7.

[70] Garzarón to king, Mexico City, 1 May 1724, AGI, Escribanía 287 B, *pieza* 58, fols. 1–3v; Antonio de Castilleja, José Ruiz Caval, Francisco Alejo de Luna, and Sebastián Guerrero to king, palace jail, Mexico City, 15 Aug. 1724, AGI, Escribanía 287 B, *pieza* 56, fol. 32, claimed that they had to pay 600 pesos or more as their share.

[71] Obedience of Garzarón, Mexico City, 12 July 1724, AGN, Indiferente Virreinal 5976, exp. 94, fol. 3v; *real executoria* of the Council of the Indies, 1724; certification, Mexico

"Grave Offense of Bribery or Corruption" 219

The suspended ministers had atoned for their misdeeds with commensurate damages to their finances and reputation. Dios del Corral and his colleagues lived for years without pay, fees, tips, or bribes. The banishment from their homes in Mexico City caused additional expenses. They also paid fines and their shares of *visita* costs. In addition, the verdicts damaged their honor, a key concern for colonials. There were no popular fiestas unlike the staging of death sentences in criminal trials. Yet the *visita* allowed the public to witness the catharsis of ministers who left town with their families. Exiling them made "an impression on the principal people" of the realm.[72] The banned ministers lamented falling into the king's disgrace and deplored their "injury to honor and reputation."[73] Their prestige mattered deeply in New Spain, because *novohispanos* tended to perform their status, while the nobility in Spain relied more on its legal protections. This also explains why the ministers loathed surrendering their robes and other insignia of office.[74]

After the *visita*, the ingrained custom of overcharging litigants receded slowly. The Council of the Indies demanded that the *audiencia* post new fee schedules, although previous efforts to impose the official price lists had delivered tenuous results.[75] There had been a *visita* of the *audiencia* notaries shortly before Garzarón's inquiry. In 1714, the crown ordered the deputy notaries to end charging Indians for issuing documents, because the Natives paid for this work with the tax of the half *real*. Nevertheless, Garzarón observed five years later that many officials ignored the order. At roughly the same time, another investigative judge

---

City, 7 July 1724; *notoriedad* of the *audiencia*, Mexico City, 14 July 1724, all three documents in AGN, Indiferente Virreinal 5976, exp. 94, fols. 1-4.

[72] Valero to king, Mexico City, 12 Oct. 1719, AGI, México 670 A.

[73] Print *por Don Miguel Truxillo*, AGI, México 670 A, fol. 4; see also summary of Agustín Robles, Sánchez Morcillo and others to king, n. d., attached to *parecer* of the prosecutor of the Council of the Indies, Madrid, 11 Nov. 1721, AGI, México 670 A; see also king to Valero, Buen Retiro, 13 Mar. 1724, AGI, Escribanía 287 B, *pieza 36*, fol. 19.

[74] Herzog, *Upholding Justice*, 26; Bourdieu, "Forms," 51-53; Cutter, "The Legal System," 58-63; van Dülmen, *Theater*, 8-10; Büschges, "Don Quijote in Amerika. Der iberoamerikanische Adel von der Eroberung bis zur Unabhängigkeit," in *Lateinamerika 1492-1850/70*, eds. Friedrich Edelmayer, Bernd Hausberger, and Barbara Potthast (Vienna: ProMedia, 2005), 161-164.

[75] *Consultas* of the Council of the Indies, Madrid, 16 Dec. 1723, AGI, Escribanía 1183, folder *1726-1733 Francisco Garzarón*; and 27 Sept. 1725, AGI, Escribanía 1183, folder *1723-1727 Francisco Garzarón*; José Toribio Medina (1718-1744), vol. 4 of *La imprenta en México (1539-1821)* (Mexico City: UNAM, 1989. Facsimile of the first edition, Santiago de Chile, 1911), 96-117, registers fee schedules for notaries, receptors, jail wardens, and interpreters from the year 1723, conceived after Garzarón's *visita*.

audited the notaries of the ecclesiastical court. Yet the archbishop's vicar-general threatened to excommunicate any notary who complied with the audit for violating ecclesiastical immunity. Nonetheless, research shows that the notaries served as fairly reliable officials in the late eighteenth century. Reining in excessive fees and misconduct at the *audiencia* of Mexico City proceeded incrementally.[76]

CONCLUSION

Garzarón uncovered malfeasance during his personal inspection of the notarial offices in the viceregal palace. He observed that the officials followed customs rather than the royal law when haphazardly recording documents. Garzarón prosecuted these and other wayward ministers by using sophisticated legal tools. He hewed closely to the recommendation of the jurist Gabriel Berart y Gassol, who argued that *visitadores* should investigate "*dolo*, fraud, and corruption which comprises gross negligence, thefts and illicit appropriations through *baratería*," and other offenses.[77] Garzarón, the *novohispano* legal practitioners, and the Council of the Indies also distinguished several levels of the suspects' guilt, defined by various shades of negligence or the *dolo* to commit a crime. According to the legal doctrines, ordinary negligence meant that very diligent people had caused damages to others by omitting a precaution. Meanwhile, ministers acted with gross negligence when they lacked the typical care expected from their occupational group. Separate from these were the ministers who showed the palpable *dolo* to commit a crime, and they incurred the most serious guilt.

These standards of culpability mattered greatly when Garzarón and the Council of the Indies removed thirteen corrupt judges for corruption and levied significant penalties. These judges had shown the *dolo* to exchange justice for money. The remaining judges were cleared of that crime and returned to the bench. Nonetheless, the king sharply criticized them for gross negligence in tolerating continual abuses in the notarial offices. This rebuke explains, in part, why the absolved ministers paid considerable *visita* expenses. In addition, these criminal standards were not restricted to

---

[76] *Real cédula*, Madrid, 3 Dec. 1714, AGN, RCO 36, exp. 153, fol. 424–424v; *audiencia* to king, Mexico City, 27 Feb. 1719, AGI, Escribanía 281 A, *cuaderno* 14, fols. 56–66. Scardaville, "Justice by Paperwork," 980–990, considers late eighteenth-century notaries as fairly just and efficient "judicial officers."

[77] Berart y Gassol, *Speculum visitationis*, chap. 3, para. 72.

the *visita* or corruption cases, and they also played a role in other offenses. Sánchez Morcillo, for instance, determined the gross negligence of Governor Miguel Pérez in the killing of an Indian worker in 1714.

Garzarón also suspended 156 officials for a range of violations, and the Council of the Indies later dismissed eleven of them for fraud, theft, and other illegalities. Fraud comprised the *dolo* to potentially damage someone else by altering a record. Theft was also a serious offense, while the Council considered insufficient record keeping, charging excessive fees, and wearing inappropriate dress as lesser evils. For this reason, the Council removed five officials for fraud, theft, or other unlawfulness, while six lost their positions for the combination of offenses and lacking a royal title. Sixteen officials paid hefty fines up to 2,000 pesos and nine suffered extended suspensions after committing serious violations. Some also returned ill-gotten funds to former litigants. One notary in particular had to return roughly 11,000 pesos to former litigants, an unparalleled amount of money. In addition, the Council especially punished the notaries of the intestate office, where sizable portions of unclaimed inheritances disappeared over time. These officials paid their parts of the *visita* expenses, which ranged between 600 and 1,150 pesos. Almost all officials returned to their work after receiving their verdicts, except for the eleven dismissed. Yet even some of the culprits continued to serve other positions that they also held at the *audiencia*. Nonetheless, the early modern legal concepts discussed in this chapter played an important role for Garzarón and the Council of the Indies and, to a large extent, explain their sentences.

7

The Politics of Justice: Francisco Garzarón's *Visita* (1716–1727)

> And lastly, Garzarón does not pay me the respect that I am due.
> "Confession" of the Viceroy Duke of Alburquerque (1702–1710).[1]

INTRODUCTION

In 1715, Queen Elizabeth Farnese and King Philip V called on Inquisitor Francisco Garzarón to scrutinize judges and officials in Mexico City. Garzarón took his task seriously and suspended thirteen of the nineteen judges and prosecutors and 156 officials. Measured by the sheer number of people dismissed from a single institution, this multi-year *visita general* (comprehensive investigation) was the most radical in imperial Spanish history. In part, Garzarón owed this outcome to his backing in New Spain and Spain, although the opposition was not idle. The Viceroy Marquis of Valero (1716–1722) threw his weight behind several judges, and the young King Louis I and his advisers dealt a serious blow to the *visita* in 1724. Politics in New Spain and Spain veered like a weathervane in a storm. Yet in the end, Garzarón achieved far-reaching results because punishing corrupt judges and abusive officials enjoyed support in the empire.

The swirling machinations and the influence of social networks in Mexico City and Madrid shaped Garzarón's investigation. For example,

---

[1] *Confession, que haze, en los últimos días de su gobierno; el Excelentísimo Señor Duque de Alburquerque Don Francisco Fernández de la Cueva, virrey*, AGN, Inquisición 740, exp. 3, fol. 58. The *Confession* was in fact a satire at the expense of Alburquerque.

civil judge José Joaquín Uribe assisted his friend Garzarón in gathering testimony against other judges, and, in exchange, Garzarón probably downplayed some charges against Uribe.[2] In addition, Garzarón dismissed another civil judge, who traveled to Madrid to lobby for his reinstatement. The political currents shifted in the civil judge's favor in 1724, and a special committee reinstated him in 1725. These outcomes point to political activities and the clientelist relationships that pervaded the Spanish empire.

Scholars have affirmed that, in this vein, that well-organized social networks stymied investigations and demonstrated the limitations of royal control, or that *visitas* cleared communication channels and controlled the conduct of ministers in far-flung realms. Others posit that *visitas* ritually created new realities and showed the king's concern for justice.[3] These observations are insightful, but we should not forget that Garzarón and even the Council of the Indies also followed the law and the recognized *visita* process. The Council of the Indies opposed the *visita* politically, for example. Nonetheless, its councilors upheld Garzarón's verdicts against the judges in 1721, because they largely agreed with his legal interpretations. In addition, Uribe did befriend Garzarón, but he also

---

[2] The civil judge's full name was José Joaquín Uribe Castejón Medrano.
[3] Holenstein, "Introduction," 20–21; Guevara-Gil and Solomon, "A Personal Visit," 3–36; Herzog, "Ritos de Control," 11–15, 29; Herzog, *Upholding Justice*, 257, argues that the "most striking character of the administration was its absence: that is, it rarely intervened," and it was a sign of "failure" when the king became involved. While insightful, the same cannot be said of New Spain. Bertrand, "Clientélisme," 140–149, maintains that Pedro Domingo de Contreras's *visita* (1729–1733) miscarried because of the opposition of Viceroy Marquis of Casafuerte, the *audiencia* ministers, and the officials of the tribunal of accounts. On *visitas* in general, see the magisterial Bertrand, *Grandeur et misères*, 280–322. Amalia Gómez Gómez, *Las Visitas de la Real Hacienda novohispana en el reinado de Felipe V (1710–1733)* (Seville: Escuela de Estudios Hispano-Americanos, 1979), 3, 215–217, attributed a "qualitative betterment of the fiscal apparatus" to *visitas*. Pietschmann, "Alcaldes Mayores," 190–191, outlines Garzarón's verdicts against judges. Pilar Arregui Zamorano, *La Audiencia de México según los visitadores (xvi y xvii)* (Mexico City, Instituto de Investigaciones Jurídicas, UNAM, 1981), 271, holds that the *visita*'s "efficacy seems highly positive" for transmitting information to the crown and for the "respect and fear" that the inspectors instilled among ministers. Ligia Berbesí de Salazar and Belín Vázquez de Ferrer, "Juicios de residencia en el gobierno provincial de Maracaibo, 1765–1810," *Anuario de Estudios Americanos* 57, no. 2 (2000): 477, analyze *visitas* as control mechanisms revealing the influence of social networks. Carlos Garriga, cited in Alonso Romero, *Orden procesal*, 128, argues that peninsular *visitas* thrived in the sixteenth century and then declined markedly. That is not the case for New Spain, however, where *visitas* declined with the intendancy system.

married the rich *novoshipana* doña Micaela María de Sandoval y Caballero. Her wealth and social connections helped him to steer clear of accepting bribes, which was Garzarón's main concern. Furthermore, the special committee reinstated the other civil judge, in part, because Garzarón had only proven two solid corruption charges against him, considerably less than against the other judges. While politics mattered, Garzarón's *visita* was also a process rooted in the law.

Scholars have paid scant attention to his *visita*, despite its spectacular outcome. Spanish historian María Luz Alonso, for example, argued that Garzarón removed primarily the corrupt Creoles (those born and educated in the Americas) who had purchased their appointments, and justice improved when new judges arrived from Spain.[4] Alonso draws on the classical argument advanced by Mark A. Burkholder and D. S. Chandler. Nevertheless, these two scholars have already observed that the dismissed ministers were not disproportionately Creoles or purchasers, and the charges against them "did not arise from weighty issues of principles but rather from routine peculation and influence peddling."[5] Other scholars also speculate whether the *visita* removed those judges who remained loyal to the previous Habsburg dynasty.[6]

Yet the analysis provides little evidence that the crown or Garzarón targeted Creoles or Habsburg sympathizers. Garzarón ruled that the purchasers of posts were about as corrupt as those appointed for their merits and services, and any nostalgia for the House of Habsburg mattered little to him. If anything, Garzarón collaborated with Uribe and his friends, who quarreled by this time with a group of ministers formerly

---

[4] María Luz Alonso, "La visita de Garzarón a la Audiencia de México," in *Estudios jurídicos en homenaje al maestro Guillermo Floris Margadant* (Mexico City: UNAM, 1988), 13–15, 26–27; Teresa Sanciñena Asurmendi, *La Audiencia en México en el reinado de Carlos III* (Mexico City: UNAM, Instituto de Investigaciones Históricas, 1999), 14–15, cites Alonso's interpretation, although her focus lies elsewhere. García García, "Corrupción y venalidad," 26–28, agrees that Garzarón aimed at removing *novohispano* purchasers from the bench.

[5] Burkholder and Chandler, *From Impotence*, 6–21, 32–40, the quote on 40; Burkholder and Chandler, *Biographical Dictionary of Audiencia Ministers in the Americas, 1687–1821* (Westport, CT: Greenwood Press, 1982), 241; synthesized in Burkholder, *Spaniards*, 97; see also Francisco Andújar Castillo, "Cuando el rey delegaba la gracia," 154–156; Parry, *Sale of Public Office*, 73, interpreted venality as the "slow paralysis of the system." Herzog, *Upholding Justice*, 90, meanwhile argues that buyers and merit appointees were equally accused of corruption.

[6] Arenal Fenochio, "La Justicia civil ordinaria," 51, see also 39–64; reprised in Victor Gayol, *Laberintos de justicia*, 1: 125–126, though Gayol's impressive work concentrates on the lower echelons of officials.

The Politics of Justice: Francisco Garzarón's Visita (1716–1727)

allied with the Viceroy Duke of Alburquerque. Madrid did not particularly aim at suppressing that group or any Habsburg or Creole ministers. This chapter clarifies these matters by evaluating the impact of the social networks on the *visita* from both a local and an imperial perspective. The chapter sketches the political backdrop in Mexico City and Madrid, the coming of the *visita*, and Garzarón's social ties in New Spain. I then home in on the number of purchasers and merit appointees at the *audiencia* and their ratio of convictions. Finally, the chapter provides evidence that King Louis demoted Garzarón and strengthened his foes, but the subsequent government mostly undid these changes. The fierce fight probably sapped Garzarón's strength and contributed to his demise in 1727.

7.1 THE BEGINNINGS OF A PIVOTAL INVESTIGATION

The beguiling twists and turns of politics conditioned Garzarón's *visita*. Queen Elizabeth Farnese (r. since 1714) and Giulio Alberoni, her chief minister (1715–1719), aimed at reforming the judiciary of Spanish America. Several sitting judges of the *audiencia* of Mexico City had been embroiled in scandals, delivering a good pretext to launch a *visita general*. The queen and Alberoni named Garzarón for this task, and he relied on the Inquisition and local allies in New Spain for help. Yet the suspects found support in Valero, in addition to the powerful *alcalde mayor* (district judge) of Puebla and the Council of the Indies, making the investigation's outcome unpredictable.

Francisco de Garzarón Vidarte – Francisco Garzarón for short – hailed from a relatively modest background in Pamplona in Navarre, a small kingdom in northern Spain. He attended the university in Sigüenza, a city located south of Pamplona, where he studied the intertwined Roman and Church law – also known as the *ius commune*. In 1688, he graduated with a degree in canon law. Sigüenza was a humble school compared to the prestigious universities of Salamanca, Valladolid, or Alcalá de Henares. The six *colegios mayores* (study halls) at these universities were the most renowned in the empire, and their student body largely emanated from the offspring of judges and councilors, the municipal oligarchies of Castile, and sometimes the aristocracy. Sigüenza's students tended to be less privileged, yet Garzarón offset his lack of pedigree with loyal service to the Church and the dynasty.[7]

---

[7] Garzarón's will drafted by Antonio de los Ríos, Mexico City, 18 June 1727, AHAGN notaría 571, vol. 3937, fols. 158v–159; genealogy of Garzarón, Madrid, 22 Aug. 1705, AGN, Inquisición 729, fol. 529–529v; *relación de méritos*, Madrid, 12 Mar. 1706, AGI,

The crown and the Church appreciated Garzarón's qualities. After graduation, he worked for the Church in Navarre. He then moved to Ceuta in North Africa to serve as the bishop's vicar-general. When the bishop rose to the position of inquisitor-general of Spain, Garzarón followed him to Madrid in 1705. Soon after, the prelate recommended him to join the rank of the "bishops of the Indies," and the crown heeded this advice, to an extent.[8] Garzarón traveled to the Americas and arrived in Mexico City on February 25, 1708, not as a bishop, but as an inquisitor of New Spain appointed by the king. Garzarón moved into a room of the Inquisition palace next to the imperial Dominican monastery and began his work.[9]

The Holy Office had lost much of its late fifteenth-century fervor, and Garzarón primarily dedicated himself to prosecuting Protestant merchants, censoring books, and uncovering other forms of trespassing. There were casualties nonetheless. On Friday, May 17, 1709, a "dark *mulato*" broke through the ceiling of Garzarón's coach to steal the glass window. Later, the "*mulato* made himself suspicious, because he lived with the coachman and returned to his home on that night bleeding." The Inquisition constables seized the suspect the next day and threw him into the secret dungeons. Soon after, the assistant constable approached Garzarón on May 22 to report that the suspect had fallen ill. The surgeon bled him and he lost so much blood that he died.[10]

In 1715, Garzarón and his two fellow inquisitors showed their zeal by trying a Bethlehemite friar for heresy. The friar refused to recant his criticism of the official creed, and years spent in a monastic cell, the Inquisition's dungeons, or regular whippings did not cow him. At one flogging, he cursed the Church and demanded that the clergy "hang me ... right away." Ultimately the tribunal acceded, ordering the friar's death.

Indiferente General 214, N. 90, fols. 427–429v. On Castilian elites, Dedieu, "La haute administration," 170–171, 176–177. According to Lynn, *Between Court and Confessional*, 4; Meder, *Rechtsgeschichte*, 22, degrees were called *utriusque iuris* when students studied in-depth both Roman and canon law.

[8] Bishop Vidal Marín (1694–1709) to Domingo López Calo, Madrid, 16 May 1706, AGI, Indiferente General, 214, N. 90, fol. 431.

[9] According to Garzarón to bishop of Pamplona, Mexico City, 12 Aug. 1724, AGN, Inquisición 792, exp. 13, fol. 294; *relación de méritos*, Madrid, 12 Mar. 1706, AGI, Indiferente General 214, N. 90, fols. 427–429v; *consulta* of the Council of the Indies, Madrid, 30 Oct. 1706, AGI, México 403, Garzarón's parents were Miguel Garzarón and Mariana Vidarte, and he became Ceuta's vicar-general in 1700. In 1706 the Council of the Indies approved his embarkation in France for Veracruz.

[10] *Auto* of Garzarón, Mexico City, 22 May 1709, AGN, Inquisición 882, exp. 5, fol. 244.

On June 16, 1715, the inquisition staged an *auto de fé* in front of the main Dominican monastery. When the friar walked to the pyre in penitential garb, he begged for forgiveness and professed his faith, "much consoling the inquisitors who were with him until the last minute." The *corregidor* (district judge) of Mexico City then tied the Bethlehemite to the stake and set the pyre ablaze. The friar was the last person to suffer such gruesome death in colonial Mexico.[11]

Madrid took notice. On December 21, 1715, a reformist government ordered Garzarón to investigate all royal ministers of the viceroyalty, beginning with the *audiencia* in Mexico City. Such a sweeping *visita general* of the entire realm gave Garzarón more responsibility than an ordinary *visita* which usually focused on one particular crime or miscreant.[12] The crown often chose inquisitors for the *visitas generales*, because they mastered the criminal trials of the Church and knew how to gather evidence, question suspects, and assess testimony. Garzarón received his appointment on October 13, 1716, and the Holy Office welcomed the news, as this would shut the door to public "murmurs" about the Inquisition's recent failings.[13]

Garzarón's appointment followed on the heels of the treaties of Utrecht and Rastatt (1713/14), that angered many in Madrid. The treaties sealed the peace among the European powers warring over the succession to the Spanish throne (1701–1714). England and Habsburg Austria recognized Philip V, the grandson of the French King Louis XIV, as king of the

---

[11] Gabriel Torres Puga, "Fragmentos del proceso contra fray José de San Ignacio," unpublished transcription manuscript, p. 17, detailing the trial of friar Juan Fernández de León. On the Inquisition, see Ana E. Schaposchnik, *The Lima Inquisition: The Plight of Crypto-Jews in Seventeenth-Century Peru* (Madison: University of Wisconsin Press, 2015), 3–17. Van Dülmen, *Theater*, 124, points out that delinquents were last publicly burned in the Holy Roman Empire in 1786.

[12] Hevia Bolaños, *Curia Filípica*, vol. 1, part 3, para. 10, no. 1; Ismael Sánchez Bella, *Derecho Indiano: Estudios I. Las visitas generales en la América española (siglos XVI–XVII)* (Pamplona, Spain: Ediciones Universidad de Navarra, 1991), 127–158.

[13] José Cienfuegos and Francisco Antonio Palacio y del Hoyo to king, Mexico City, 14 July 1717, AHN, Inquisición 1738, exp. 6. See also Garzarón to king, Mexico City, 21 Dec. 1716, AGI, México 670 A; Garzarón continued to serve as inquisitor after his appointment as *visitador general*; see Toribio Medina, *Historia de la Inquisición*, 353–355; orders of restitution, Mexico City, 1720, in John Chuchiak, ed., *The Inquisition in New Spain 1536–1820: A Documentary History* (Baltimore: The Johns Hopkins University Press, 2012), 266–270; see also Garzarón interrogation of Francisco Álvarez, n. d. (after 1716), AGN, Indiferente Virreinal 2325, exp. 20; on inquisitors, Lynn, *Between Court and Confessional*, 3–4, 19–21, 43; Bethencourt, *The Inquisition*, 6, 35, 38, 285; Jaime Contreras, *Historia de la Inquisición Española (1478–1834). Herejías, delitos, y representación* (Madrid: Arco, 1997), 45–49.

Spanish monarchy. In exchange Spain yielded commercial privileges and territory, above all, in Italy. The concessions did not sit well with Farnese and Alberoni. Beginning in mid 1715, they plotted to regain the islands of Sardinia and Sicily, control commerce more tightly, raise the cash flow to Madrid, and improve the American *audiencias*.[14]

Farnese and Alberoni unleashed an energetic reform. Focusing on trade and taxes, Alberoni favored "applying the heavy hand, because the common good of Spain, the maxims of government, and the necessary funds for the reputation of both the arms and the nation depend on it."[15] He was true to his word. Armed guards searched merchant ships in Spanish ports and entered the warehouses of foreign traders. Alberoni also appointed a capable navy intendant on January 28, 1717, to rebuild the royal Armada. In the same year, the crown ordered the *casa de contratación* (Board of Trade) and the *consulado* (merchant guild) to move from the city of Seville to Cádiz. The crown kept a closer watch on contraband commerce and weakened the influence of the Sevillian oligarchy. In addition, Farnese and Alberoni established the viceroyalty in Bogotá (in present-day Colombia) in 1717 and dissolved the *audiencias* of Panama and Quito in the following year. They favored a nimbler executive government over lengthy judicial deliberations. As a consequence, they pruned the power of the Council of the Indies, the "historic instrument of the conservative aristocratic elite." Alberoni also ignored the Council when appointing Garzarón for the *visita*, and the Council deeply resented the slight.[16]

---

[14] Kuethe and Andrien, *The Spanish Atlantic World*, 38, 57–60, 69; Kuethe, "Política colonial," 233–238; Anthony McFarlane, "Hispanoamerika," in *Handbuch der Geschichte Lateinamerikas*, ed. Horst Pietschmann (Stuttgart: Klett-Cotta, 1994), 1: 757.

[15] *Real cédula* to Valero, Madrid, 11 Jan. 1718, AGN, RCO 39, exp. 25, fol. 59–59v, see also fols. 53–58v.

[16] Kuethe and Andrien, *The Spanish Atlantic World*, 48. On the navy intendant José de Patiño, Kuethe, "Política colonial," 233–239. Alan Kuethe has contributed most to reinterpreting Giulio Alberoni as an energetic reformer, see Kuethe "Cardinal Alberoni and Reform in the American Empire," in Eissa-Barroso and Vázquez Varela, eds., *Early Bourbon*. 23–38; Kuethe, "Decisiones estratégicas y las finanzas militares del XVIII," in *Por la fuerza de las armas. Ejercito e independencies en Iberoamerica*, eds. Juan Marchena and Manuel Chust (Castelló de la Plana: Universitat Jaume Primer, 2008), 84. The creation of the viceroyalty is now the subject of Eissa-Barroso, *The Spanish Monarchy*, 1–19, 125–140; Francisco A. Eissa-Barroso, "La Nueva Granada en el sistema de Utrecht: Condiciones locales, contexto internacional, y reforma institucional," in Escamilla, *Resonancias imperiales*, 58; Adrian Pearce, "Repercusiones comerciales del Tratado de Utrecht en Hispanoamérica," ibid., 221–446, emphasizes internal factors of trade reform, while Souto, "Tierra Adentro: los riesgos de permitir la internación de los flotistas gaditanos y los factores ingleses en Nueva España," ibid., 247–273, argues that the Xalapa fairs restrained the English

In Farnese and Alberoni's view, the viceroy of New Spain should help with the reform and contribute more to the royal coffers. They named a loyal partisan, the Marquis of Valero, to replace the ailing Duke of Linares as viceroy. In February 1716, Valero embarked in a small flotilla of war ships sailing straight to New Spain, rather than waiting for the merchant fleet that slowly gathered in Cádiz. On June 30, 1716, he took the helm of the kingdom of New Spain. Subsequently, Alberoni wrote to Valero that "Your Excellency has heard of the conquest of Sardinia, for which I am working tirelessly." A fleet would be ready in April to carry 30,000 soldiers to the island. Alberoni needed silver from New Spain to continue the mission, and Valero was the man to provide it.[17]

At the time, rumors about corrupt judges made their rounds and well served Farnese and Alberoni. They needed a solid cause for the *visita general*, since the *audiencia* of Mexico and even the Council of the Indies would trenchantly oppose the investigation. The Viceroy Duke of Linares buttressed the cause in 1711 by writing a scathing report on the criminal chamber.[18] More importantly, suspicion fell on the former civil judge of Mexico City, Miguel Calderón de la Barca, who by that time held a purchased appointment to the Council of the Indies in Madrid. He had previously invested more than 44,000 pesos into commercial venues, although judges were barred from such business in New Spain. In addition, he embezzled large quantities of money and worse, allowed a "subject to adorn him with pearls" in exchange for a favorable judicial

---

annual ship that regularly delivered merchandise and slaves to New Spain. Burgos Lejonagoitia, *Gobernar las Indias*, 455, shows that the royal decrees curtailing the Council were never fully implemented. My own impression is that conservative governments tended to give the great Councils more rein; see also Kamen, *Philip V*, 97; Stanley J. Stein and Barbara H. Stein, *Silver, Trade, and War: Spain and America in the Making of Early Modern Europe (Baltimore,* (London: Johns Hopkins Press, 2000), 137; Burkholder and Chandler, *From Impotence*, 38–40; Escudero, "El gobierno central de las Indias: el consejo y las secretaría del despacho," in *El gobierno de un mundo. Virreinatos y audiencias en la América Hispánica*, ed. Feliciano Barrios (Cuenca, Spain: Ediciones de la Universidad Castilla-La Mancha, Fundación Rafael del Pino, 2004), 103; León Sanz, "La llegada," 60–65, 108–109.

[17] *Real cédula*, Madrid, 11 Jan. 1718, AGN, RCO 39, exp. 25, fol. 58, see also fols. 53–58v; see also *real cédula* to Linares, Madrid, 29 Jan. 1716, AGN, RCO 37, exp. 73, fols. 199–200. On the date of taking office, José Sánchez, Francisco Leri, *Nomina de los Ex.mos S.res Presidentes*, 1716, AGI, Escribanía 278 A. See also Iván Escamilla, "Nueva España ante la diplomacia de la era de Utrecht, 1716–1720: El caso de la guerra de la cuádruple alianza," in Escamilla, *Resonancias Imperiales*, 28–41.

[18] Linares to king, 6 Jan. 1711, AGI, México 484; see also Arenal Fenochio, "La Justicia civil ordinaria," 50–51.

ruling.[19] His wife, doña Ana Pividal, allegedly helped negotiating bribes and operated a *pulqueria* (tavern) in Mexico City. The crown heard these rumors, delayed closing Calderón de la Barca's *residencia* (end-of-term review), and ordered Garzarón to investigate his conduct.[20]

Another judge in Mexico City faced charges of marital infidelity. Tristán Manuel de Rivadeneyra had visited doña Juana de Salazar in a convent in Mexico City, where she lived after separating from her husband. Rivadeneyra tried to convince his fellow ministers to set her free from cloistered life, because she belonged to his family. Her husband, however, opposed the release, being "much embarrassed by the infidelity of his wife." The archbishop sided with the husband. In July 1715, the king sent Rivadeneyra packing to the *audiencia* of Guadalajara, while the viceroy allowed Salazar to move to her sister's home.[21] Two years later, the president of the Guadalajaran *audiencia* accused Rivadeneyra of truancy and "being conspicuously involved with a married woman and publicly living his blind passion." This time the king banned Rivadeneyra from Guadalajara and cut his income by half.[22]

---

[19] Charge against Miguel Calderón de la Barca in *residencia*, Mexico City, 1715, AGI, Escribanía 236 A, *pieza* 1a, fol. 102; see also reputation and charges of Miguel Calderón de la Barca, AGI, México 670 B, *Relación*, fols. 9v, 15, 25v–27.

[20] Garzarón to king, Mexico City, 21 Dec. 1716, AGI, México 670 A; *consultas* of the Council of the Indies, Madrid, 19 Feb. 1717 and 12 July 1720, AGI, México 379. According to Ignacio Peces to king, n. d., and *consulta* of the Council of the Indies, Madrid, 11 Feb. 1717, both in AGI, Escribanía 236 A, *pieza* 5, the *residencia* cleared Calderón de la Barca of the charges, condemning José Joaquín Uribe to pay half the *residencia* costs for falsely smearing Calderón de la Barca. According to charges, AGI, México 670 B, *Relación*, fol. 115v, accusations also emerged against Félix Gónzalez de Agüero, Juan Díaz de Bracamonte, and Jerónimo Soria. With the *real cédula*, Madrid, 14 Mar. 1703, AGN, RCO 32, exp. 94, fols. 1–2, the crown reprehended clergyman Díaz de Bracamonte for purchasing a silver mine and yet sold him an appointment as *audiencia* judge in 1706.

[21] Quote in *real cédula* to Marquis of Valero, Madrid, 8 Feb. 1718, AGN, RCO 39, exp. 44, fol. 104; see also Rivadeneyra to Viceroy Duke of Linares, Mexico City, 22 July 1715, AGN, RCO 37, fols. 58v–59; Rivadeneyra to Linares, Querétaro, 12 Aug. 1715, AGN, RCO 37, fols. 64–65; Rivadeneyra to Linares, Mexico City, 23 July 1715, AGN, RCO 37, fol. 62v; four letters from Linares to Rivadeneyra, Mexico City, 21 and 23 July, 28 July, 3 Sept. 1715, AGN, RCO 37, fols. 58v–60, 64–65; Linares' receipt of *real cédula*, Mexico City, 3 Sept. 1715, AGN, RCO 37, fol. 65v; *real cédula*, Buen Retiro, 30 Mar. 1715, AGN, RCO 37, exp. 24, fols. 72–73. Doña Juana stayed at the convent of Our Lady of Balbanera in Mexico City.

[22] *Real cédula* to Valero, el Pardo, 15 Jan. 1719, AGN, RCO 40, exp. 6, fol. 13v, referencing letters of Tomás Terán de los Ríos, president of the Guadalajara *audiencia*, to king, 2 Dec. 1717 and 15 April 1718.

Garzarón also investigated the large indemnities payable to the crown and reexamined the conduct of the judges' servants. During the War of Succession, *novohispanos* had traded freely with French ships and even those belonging to enemy states. The king appointed an *audiencia* judge to trace the rampant contraband trade in Veracruz. In 1708, the judge ensnared several port officials and merchants, who confessed to their sins and paid considerable sums to be absolved. But much of the indemnities seeped away elsewhere, reportedly into the judge's pockets. Garzarón had to get to the bottom of these allegations.[23] In addition, he censored the *mulato* coachmen who served the *audiencia* judges. These servants had forced "Indian water carriers and others who passed by on the street to clean the coaches and horses, even when carrying loads," although they had no right to do so. Garzarón also found that the *mulatos* "shamelessly swindled" about the whereabouts of the ministers and demanded bribes from the litigants to gain access to the judges. Worse still, the judges abetted these practices.[24]

While conducting the *visita*, Garzarón demonstrated a notable modesty for the standards of the time, recommending him to Madrid. Garzarón refused the 6,000 ducats that *visitadores* received as annual salary and continued with the 2,000 pesos corresponding to an inquisitor of New Spain.[25] In addition, Garzarón communicated with his relatives in Spain and sent them money, but he kept them at arm's length. In at least one instance, he ordered that "none of the nephews come to these lands" to request a post from him. His conduct was one reason why the crown later expressed its satisfaction by naming him bishop of Oaxaca.[26]

---

[23] See, e.g., the interrogatories of Gregorio de Salinas in Veracruz, 27 Sept. 1717, AGI, Escribanía 278 A, *Quaderno* 6, fols. 699–739; Bernardo de Tinajero to king, Madrid, 5 Nov. 1709, AGI, México 377, on the appointment of Félix Gónzalez de Agüero as commissioner to investigate contraband trade.

[24] General charge 41 against all judges, AGI, Escribanía 281 A, *Q.no* 14, fols. 8v–9; see also king to president and *oidores* of Mexico City, Lerma, 13 Dec. 1721, AGN, Historia, vol. 102, exp. 10, fol. 85.

[25] Garzarón to king, Mexico City, 21 Dec. 1716, AGI, México 670 A. While *Law of the Indies*, book 2, title 34, law 37, assigned 2,000 *maravedís* for Garzarón's notary, according to the assessment, Mexico City, 14 Sept. 1722, AGI, Escribanía 287 B, *pieza* 35, fols. 2–3v, he received 94 pesos per year as salary and drew additional fees for every document that he produced. In 1722, for example, he received a lump sum of 653 pesos.

[26] Juan Miguel de Lizasoáin to Garzarón, Pamplona, 17 Mar. 1717, AGN, Inquisición 1543, exp. 3, fol. 60v, although Juan Garzarón to Garzarón, Havana, 21 Sept. 1717, AGN, Inquisición 1543, exp. 3, fols. 68v–69; and Garzarón's will drafted by Antonio de los Ríos, Mexico City, 18 June 1727, AHAGN, notaría 571, vol. 3937, fol. 159v, indicate that Juan Urros y Garzarón traveled to New Spain to seek favor and later served as one of Garzarón's

Despite limiting the favors toward his immediate family, Garzarón integrated into local society as was customary, and his social ties shaped the *visita*. Garzarón had arrived in New Spain eight years before the *visita* began. He befriended two other inquisitors, an *audiencia* prosecutor, and Uribe. At that time, this group fought the Viceroy Duke of Alburquerque, and later, according to the *alcalde mayor* of Puebla, they all became "intimate friends of the *visitador* and united in their cause for revenge, and all those who drink or do not drink with them have been made witnesses in the *visita*."[27] Uribe allegedly also met with another *visitador* who inspected the treasury, and they "meddled in the matter every night in one of the rooms of the Inquisition." In exchange, Garzarón probably cut Uribe some slack in the *visita*. Garzarón was clearly no social outsider when his investigation began.[28]

Neither was Uribe a saint, although he and Garzarón shared some basic ideas about corruption. For example, Uribe obtained a royal permit to

executors. On Garzarón's appointment as bishop, *real cédula* to Casafuerte, Madrid, 22 Dec. 1725, AGN, RCO 45, exp. 146; acknowledged by Casafuerte, Mexico City, 22 July 1726, AGN, RCO 45, exp. 146. The crown also advanced the other *visitadores* of New Spain, Francisco Pagabe, Prudencio Palacios, and Domingo Contreras, to the Council of the Treasury in Madrid, see *consulta* of the Council of the Indies, Madrid, 11 Aug. 1710, AGI, México 557; resolution of the king, attached to *consulta* of the Council of the Indies, Madrid, 21 Apr. 1728, AGI, México 381; *consulta* of the Council of the Indies, 8 Oct. 1734, AGI, México 382.

[27] Juan José Veytia Linage to Miguel Fernández Durán, Puebla, 17 Oct. 1719, AGI México 670 A, included "inquisitor Cienfuegos, José de Uribe, Gaspar de Zepeda, Canon Costela, and the Count del Fresno de la Fuente." Similarly, Juan Garzarón to Garzarón, Havana, 21 Sep. 1717, AGN, Inquisición 1543, exp. 3, requested that "Your Grace confer to me obedience to the lords [José] Zienfuegos, [Francisco Antonio de] Palazios [y del Hoyo], [José Joaquín] Uribe, [merchant Joaquín de?] Zabaleta, and lord don Prudenzio [Palacios, treasury *visitador*]." According to Alonso, "La visita de Garzarón," 14, the Duke of Linares faulted all *audiencia* judges except for Uribe and Francisco Barbadillo Victoria, while according to *real cédula*, Madrid, 25 Nov. 1719, AGN, RCO 40, exp. 139, fol. 317, Uribe assigned a 6,000-peso penalty to Linares in the *residencia*. In addition, according to testimony of Uribe, AGI, México 670 B, *Relación*, fol. 89v; and *consulta* of the Council of the Indies, 10 Aug. 1708, AGI, México 403, Uribe also counted on his *colegial* (study hall fellow), Francisco Berrio y Marzana, who sat on the Council of Orders, while the councilor of the Indies, Rodrigo Zepeda, was related to Uribe's friend, the former prosecutor Gaspar Zepeda. José Toribio Medina, *Historia de la Inquisición en México* (Mexico City: Ediciones Fuentes Cultural, 1905), 354, noted that inquisitor José Cienfuegos reported his strife with Viceroy Duke of Alburquerque to the Council of the Indies in Spain; see also Rosenmüller, *Patrons, Partisans*, 114–123. On the impossibility of ministers staying aloof from society, Brendecke, *Imperio*, 487–488.

[28] Valero referenced in *consulta* of the Council of the Indies, Madrid, 20 Apr. 1718, AGI, México 379. Nonetheless, there is no hard evidence that Garzarón cut a deal when absolving Uribe from the charges.

marry doña Micaela María de Sandoval y Caballero, a rich landholder in the Puebla region. Before August 1708, she observed that "she was five months pregnant."[29] Usually the crown frowned upon judges who married women from their jurisdictions. The law also prohibited judges from buying real estate within their districts, but this did not mean that their wives had to divest their property. Consequently, Uribe ferociously defended doña Micaela's dowry, even in *audiencia* meetings. Following the *visita*, the crown admonished Uribe and two colleagues for excessively favoring their family. Yet Uribe was wealthy enough to stay away from most forms of bribery, which was Garzarón's main focus of prosecution. At least some *novohispanos* agreed that Uribe remained clean. A merchant, for example, "understood that don José Uribe ... does not accept gifts."[30]

Nonetheless, Juan José Veytia Linage, the *alcalde mayor* of Puebla, accused Uribe of micro-managing the *visita*. Veytia Linage had befriended a civil judge on the Mexican bench and resented that Garzarón suspended the judge. Veytia Linage sharply criticized that "Garzarón's *visita* was under the direction and prompting of the ardent and vengeful temper of civil judge don José Joaquín Uribe, his close companion and friend."[31]

---

[29] Micaela María de Sandoval y Caballero to king, 18 Aug. 1708, AGI, México 1326. According to defense of Uribe, Mexico City, AGI, México 670 B, *Relación*, fols. 87–88, Alburquerque passed on the marriage permit on 19 June 1706. According to the exemplars, Madrid, 17 Dec. 1729, AGI, México 382, Uribe received the permit in 1715 in exchange for 2,000 pesos. See *Law of the Indies*, book 2, title 16, laws 55–67, 82–87. According to de la Torre Villar, *Instrucciones y memorias*, 2: 759, the king instructed Viceroy Count of Montezuma to enforce the marriage prohibitions on 10 May 1696, referring to the previous *real cédula* from 10 Feb. 1575.

[30] Testimony of Francisco de Mier, Mexico City, 6 Oct. 1717, AGI, Escribanía 278 A, *Quaderno* 6, fol. 44v. I cannot prove that Uribe never accepted bribes other than the information provided by Garzarón, but any claim to the opposite would need evidence too. See also draft of *consulta* of the Council of the Indies, Madrid, 2 Sept. 1712, AGI, México 670A, referring to Uribe, Juan de Oliván Rebolledo, and Jerónimo Soria. See also Valero to king, 20 Aug. 1724, AGI, México 490, fol. 690–690v. On the conflict over access to the water of the *Tres Ojos* hacienda that Uribe obtained from the Jesuit College of Saint Ignatius in Manila, see Casafuerte to king, Mexico City, 13 Nov. 1723, AGI, México 491, while Veytia Linage to Fernández Durán, Puebla, 17 Oct. 1719, AGI México 670 A, claimed that Uribe had "unjust lawsuits" with the landowners of the region.

[31] Veytia Linage to Fernández Durán, Puebla, 17 Oct. 1719, AGI, México 670 A. On friendship among investigating judges, Hevia Bolaños, *Curia Philipica*, vol. 1, part 3, para. 6, no. 12. According to bishop to viceroy, Puebla, 6 Oct. 1719, AGN, Real Audiencia 1, exp. 3, fols. 157–161; *real cédula* to Casafuerte, Aranjuez, 13 May 1723, AGN, RCO 44, exp. 21, fols. 49–51; *consultas* of the Council of the Indies, Madrid, 22 Mar. 1720 and 25 May 1723, AGI, México 379, Juan José Veytia Linage's group included his nephew, the municipal councilor José Fernández Veytia. Uribe's alliance

Garzarón, however, was not Uribe's stooge. Uribe, for instance, accused another judge of illicitly favoring his own *colegio mayor* in Mexico City, but Garzarón absolved that judge for lack of evidence.[32]

Viceroy Marquis of Valero clearly impinged more on Garzarón's independence. Valero and his predecessors had usually been titled nobles and did not kindly regard *visitadores* of humble origins meddling in their affairs. The Marquis of Valero's secretary proclaimed that Garzarón's *visita* remained "subject to the judgment of the marquis who could dispose of and direct it as he sees fit."[33] Valero even called Garzarón to the palace to name witnesses and disclose preliminary results to him and the civil judges, who were the very targets of the investigation. Many suspects also courted Valero to sabotage the *visita*, and he especially recommended four judges to the crown. Earlier, Valero had made a mark by sending "soldiers with muskets and fixed bayonets" to detain Garzarón's predecessor. Yet the viceroy was legally subject to the *visita*, because he presided over the *audiencia*. Garzarón resented Valero's conduct and eventually labeled him a declared opponent and demanded to fully exclude him from the *visita*.[34]

---

meanwhile consisted of Pedro de Mendoza y Escalante, the *alguacil mayor* (senior constable) of Puebla, and Diego Gómez de Angulo, the bishop's *provisor* (legal adviser). The *precentor* (chantre) and former criminal prosecutor of Mexico City, Gaspar Zepeda, had passed away earlier, harboring "mortal hate" toward Veytia Linage. On Veytia Linage advancing pre-Bourbon reforms in Puebla, see Ramos, *Identity, Ritual*, xxiii–xxiv, 8–12, 61; Ramos, "Custom, Corruption, and Reform in Early Eighteenth-Century Mexico: Puebla's Merchant Priests versus the Reformist Bureaucrat," in Rosenmüller, *Corruption in the Iberian Empires*, 151–170; and Bertrand, *Grandeur et misères*, 333–349. On civil judge Francisco Valenzuela Venegas, Javier Sanchiz and José I. Conde, *Títulos y dignidades nobiliarias en Nueva España* (in preparation).

[32] *Prueba* against Jerónimo Soria, AGI, México 670 B, *Relación*, fols. 101v–102.

[33] As referenced in Garzarón to king, Mexico City, 21 Dec. 1716, AGI, México 670 A, reporting on Valero's secretary, Bartolomé Crespo.

[34] As referenced in *consulta* of the Council of the Indies, Madrid, 20 Apr. 1718, AGI, México 379, referring to *visitador* Prudencio Palacios; José Rodrigo to Valero, Madrid, 8 January 1719, AGN, RCO 39, exp. 1; edict of Garzarón, Mexico City, 17 Oct. 1716, AGI, Escribanía 278 A, *legajo* 8. According to *consulta* of the Council of the Indies, Madrid, 20 Apr. 1718, AGI, México 379, Valero assembled a junta of civil judges to assess *visitador* Francisco Pagabe's verdicts. See also *Law of the Indies*, book 2, title 34, law 11; *consulta* of the Council of the Indies, Madrid, 20 Apr. 1718, AGI, México 379; Garzarón to king, Mexico City, 2 May 1725, AHN, Inquisición 1740, exp. 18; royal order of 13 Dec. 1722, referenced in *consulta* of the Council of the Indies, Madrid, 18 Jan. 1726, AGI, México 670 A; José Rodrigo to Valero, Madrid, 5 Apr. 1718, AGN, RCO 39, exp. 63, fol. 154; Valero to king, Mexico City, 12 Oct. 1719, 29 Aug. 1719, 30 Aug. 1719, and 15 Oct. 1719, all in AGI, México 670 A, specifically endorsed Francisco Valenzuela Venegas, Francisco de Oyanguren, Juan Díaz de Bracamonte, and Félix

As tensions grew, the *audiencia* and others appealed to the public sphere. They were not the first to do so. In Portugal, rumors were described as acting "without head, hands, feet, and with five tongues ... destroying the high and low, the rich and the poor."[35] The *audiencia* of Mexico City also published a royal decree that reprimanded an Inquisition official, hoping to discredit Garzarón by association.[36] Even one hundred "miserable soldiers" from New Mexico lamented in 1720 that treasury officials had cheated them out of their pay and asked the *visita* to investigate the fraud. According to their printed complaint, the officials "soak in liquids like sponges, and subsequently the royal hand enters and squeezes them to release their ill-gotten juice ... and Catholic rules require that they let go of the prey and suffer retribution like Tantalus burning at the sight of the water."[37] The mythological Tantalus had suffered eternal thirst while standing in water, and many *novohispanos* related to this story. Not everyone believed these campaigns for public opinion, however. One official noted that "at this court many things spread as facts although they are not, because of the passions and personal interests that create them."[38]

As the discussion over the *visita* raged in public, Garzarón severely punished the corrupted judges and prosecutors. Between August 16 and early October 1719, he suspended thirteen of the nineteen *audiencia*

Suárez de Figueroa. See also *parecer* of the prosecutor of the Council of the Indies, Madrid, 22 Sept. 1720, AGI, México, 670 A.

[35] Torres de Lima, *Compendio*, 147–148.

[36] José Cienfuegos and Francisco Antonio Palacio y del Hoyo to king, Mexico City, 14 July 1717, AHN, Inquisición 1738, exp. 6.

[37] José Méndez, *Breve Memorial extracto, y declamación, que hacen los cien soldados del Presidio de la Nueva-México*, Mexico City, 17 June 1720, AGI, Escribanía 282 D, fol. 458.

[38] Testimony of José Victoriano Delgado, AGI, Escribanía 280 C, fol. 492; see also testimony of Luis Fernández Batalla, 6 June AGI, Escribanía 280 C, fols. 494v–495. Rumors, even those with political aims, were often called *voces* (voices); see Francisco Pagave to king, Havana, 5 July 1715, AGI, México 588 on the circulating "voice in that kingdom"; or the "spreading voice" in Revillagigedo to Álvarez de Toledo Lobato, Mexico City, 4 July 1755, ACR 347. On the public sphere, see Gabriel Torres Puga, *Opinión pública y censura en Nueva España. Indicios de un silencio imposible. 1767–1794* (Mexico City: El Colegio de México, 2010), 21–24; Martin Bauer, "Die 'Gemein Sag' im Späteren Mittelalter. Studien zu einem Faktor mittelalterlicher Öffentlichkeit und seinem historischen Auskunftswert," (PhD diss., University of Erlangen, Germany, 1981), 1, 6, 13–15, 37, both rejecting much of Jürgen Habermas, *The Structural Transformation of the Public Sphere: an Inquiry into a Category of Bourgeois Society* (Cambridge: Polity Press, 1996).

ministers for corruption, finding them worthy of removal from the bench. Never before had a *visita* demoted so many judges from one institution, nor did this happen again in New Spain.[39]

At roughly that time, the political landscape in Madrid changed. Alberoni took the blame for the botched war against the Quadruple Alliance (1718–1720) and stepped down on December 5, 1719. The new strongman, José de Grimaldo, pursued a more cautious political approach, although this brought no relief for the judges in New Spain.[40] On September 2, 1721, the Council of the Indies reviewed Garzarón's proceedings and recommended confirming his rulings. The king – and most likely Grimaldo – agreed and rejected a stream of appeals from New Spain. The judges had to pay significant fines ranging from 2,000 to 8,000 pesos and lost their salaries, privileges, and prestige. The one judge who had investigated contraband trade in Veracruz even had to restore a stunning 22,048 pesos to the treasury. At the same time, the Council sentenced the six remaining judges to pay a significant share of the *visita* expenses but otherwise absolved them.[41]

The story of criminal judge Pedro Sánchez Morcillo took an almost histrionic turn as he was waiting for his verdict. Sánchez Morcillo got into a fist fight with a clergyman in 1718, while Garzarón still gathered evidence against him. The king ordered Sánchez Morcillo to continue his work and resume friendship with the priest. At that point, Valero attested to Sánchez Morcillo's "zeal, integrity, and impartiality," but

---

[39] See chapter 5, note 74.
[40] Kuethe, "Política colonial," 235–239. According to Roberto Fernández, *Carlos III* (Madrid: Alianza, 2001), 26, Alberoni objected to the war but succumbed to pressure at court; see also Kamen, *Philip V*, 97, 207, 211.
[41] *Consulta* of the Council of the Indies, 2 Sept. 1721, AGI, México 380; *dictamen* of the prosecutor and *consulta* of the Council of the Indies, resolution of the king, all three documents Madrid, 13 Nov. 1721, AGI, México 670 A; sentence of the Council of the Indies, Madrid, 23 Sept. 1721, AGI, Escribanía 1183, folder *1721–1730 Francisco Garzarón* (another copy in AGI, Escribanía, 287 B, *pieza* 36, fols. 14–15); on Agüero's payments to the treasury, Garzarón to king, Mexico City, 20 Feb. 1723, AGI, Escribanía, 287 B, *pieza* 58, fols. 6v–7; *real cédula* to Casafuerte, Buen Retiro, 25 Mar. 1726, AGN, RCO 45, exp. 61, fols. 191–193. See also *parecer* of prosecutor of the Council of the Indies, 22 Sept. 1720, AGI, México 670 A. Garzarón to king, Mexico City, 3 Aug. 1720, AGI, México 670 A, wrote that he absolved civil judges José Joaquín de Uribe, Jerónimo de Soria Velásquez Marquis of Villahermosa de Álfaro, and Juan de Oliván Rebolledo along with the criminal judges Nicolás Chirino Vandeval, Juan de la Beguellina y Sandoval, and Francisco Barbadillo Victoria. Castillo de Bobadilla, *Política*, book 1, chap. 11, no. 26–37, discussed the punishments for corrupt judges, including burning alive.

that helped little.⁴² Garzarón suspended Sánchez Morcillo on August 16, 1719, on over 100 charges of corruption. Sánchez Morcillo begged Garzarón to postpone his banishment from Mexico City because of his illness. Garzarón must have rejected the plea, because soon after, Sánchez Morcillo applied for a license to travel to Spain. He arrived with two colleagues at the court in Madrid in October 1721 at the latest, yet achieved no results. The Council of the Indies declared Sánchez Morcillo unfit to serve a post of justice again and fined him 8,000 silver pesos; just 1,000 pesos shy of three annual salaries.⁴³

After sentencing the judges, Garzarón punished the *audiencia*'s officials, and the Council of the Indies partially confirmed these rulings. Garzarón suspended 156 of these officials between August 1722 and 1723 and notified the crown. He suggested after each batch of suspensions that the viceroy appoint interim officials within eight days to keep the offices open. Valero agreed.⁴⁴ After the first suspensions, Garzarón tied up ten volumes containing the detailed proceedings of the investigation. In September 1722, his notary placed the heavy folders in a crate and handed them to the postal service that delivered them to an inquisition commissioner in Veracruz. The commissioner passed the crate to a fleet merchant who embarked for Havana. The documents crossed the Atlantic and finally arrived in Cádiz, Spain, from where they traveled to Madrid. The Council of the Indies began assessing the cases in December 1723.

---

⁴² Valero to king, Mexico City, 6 July 1718, AGI, México 486 A. According to Valero to king, Mexico City, 30 Mar. 1719, AGI, México 487, Sánchez Morcillo fought with clergyman Nicolás de Castañeda.

⁴³ Sentence of Garzarón, Mexico City, 16 Aug. 1719, AGI, Escribanía 287 A, fol. 347v; appeal by Sánchez Morcillo, Mexico City, 22 Aug. 1719, AGI, Escribanía 287 A, fol. 348; sentence of the Council of the Indies, Madrid, 23 Sept. 1721, AGI, Escribanía 1183, folder *1721–1730 Francisco Garzarón*; *consulta* of the Council of the Indies, Madrid, 13 Oct. 1721, *pieza* 52, fol. 1; *auto* of Garzarón, Mexico City, 24 July 1720, *pieza* 52, fols. 3v–4; Valero to Sánchez Morcillo, Mexico City, 2 May 1721, *pieza* 52, fol. 7, all three documents in AGI, Escribanía 287 B. According to *Informe* of the tribunal of accounts, Mexico City, after 1776, BNM, FR, 439 (1376), tomo 4, fol. 333v, a criminal judge earned 2,941 pesos per year plus emoluments in 1721, the same as a civil judge.

⁴⁴ See, e.g., Garzarón's *auto*, 18 Jan. 1723, AGI, Escribanía 289 A, fols. 201–202v; certification of Antonio de los Ríos, Mexico City, 6 Apr. 1724; AGI, Escribanía 287 B, *pieza* 55, fol. 1–1v; Garzarón to king, Mexico City, 1 May 1724, AGI, Escribanía 287 B, *pieza* 58, fols. 1–3v; the Council of the Indies' sentences are in AGI, Escribanía 1183, folder *1721–1730 Francisco Garzarón*.

In the following years, the Council removed eleven officials, assigned heavy fines, or extended the officials' suspensions.[45]

Shortly before, the political stage in Mexico City had changed to favor Garzarón. Viceroy Valero complained about the onset of dropsy in 1721, stepped down at the end of 1722, and returned to Spain.[46] His successor, the Marquis of Casafuerte arrived on or before December 16, 1722 (served until March 17, 1734). The permanent friction between Valero and Garzarón dissolved, and Casafuerte enthusiastically supported the *visitador*. The following year, the viceroy appointed Garzarón as his legal adviser, considering him to be "the only one who can help me with the goal of serving" the crown.[47]

7.2 PURCHASERS OF JUDICIAL APPOINTMENTS WERE NOT MORE CORRUPT THAN OTHERS

Garzarón's rulings against the judges were stringent, and the Council of the Indies punished the delinquents no less. Yet contrary to what historians have argued, the *visita* did not home in on judges who had bought their appointments. These judges may appear more corrupt to us at first sight, and the majority of the jurists and theologians in the Spanish empire condemned them for purchasing their appointments. In fact, however, the *visita* proportionally removed slightly more judges who had been named for their "merits and services" than those who had purchased their appointments. Why was that?[48]

---

[45] *Auto*, Mexico City, 18 Sept. 1722; Garzarón to king, Mexico City, 15 Sept. 1722, AGI, Escribanía 287 B, *pieza* 35, fols. 5–8v. The next shipment of documents occurred in early 1723, Garzarón to king, Mexico City, 20 Feb. 1723, AGI, México 547.

[46] *Real cédula*, Madrid, 24 May 1722, AGN, RCO 43, exp. 26, fol. 94–94v; Valero to king, San Cosme, 16 Dec. 1722, AGI, México 489; the crown had previously named Valero *mayordomo* of the princess of Asturias, *real cédula*, Madrid, 24 Dec. 1721, AGN, RCO 42, exp. 96, fol. 225–225v.

[47] Casafuerte to king, Mexico City, 13 Nov. 1723; *consulta* of the *Cámara* of the Indies, Madrid, 21 Feb. 1724, both documents in AGI México 491; Casafuerte to king, Mexico City, 14 May 1725, AGI, México 670 A; the *real cédula* to Casafuerte, Madrid, 17 Dec. 1725, AGN, RCO 45, exp. 37, fols. 134–135, showed that Casafuerte sharply criticized Valero. On Juan de Acuña y Bejarano, Marquis of Casafuerte, see Eissa-Barroso, "Of Experience, Zeal," 317–325, 334–345; Felices de la Fuente, *Condes, marqueses y duques. Biografías de nobles titulados durante el reinado de Felipe V* (Madrid: Doce Calles, Junta de Andalucía, 2013), 81–82.

[48] A few examples of scholarship include Burkholder and Chandler, "Creole Appointments," 187–206; Andrien, "Sale," 50–63; Andújar Castillo, *Necesidad*, 9; Caño Ortigosa, "La real hacienda en venta," 140. Zeballos, *Arte Real*, fol. 176–176v, for example, denounced the sale of offices.

The Politics of Justice: Francisco Garzarón's Visita (1716–1727) 239

When Garzarón began the investigation, nineteen judges and prosecutors sat on the *audiencia*. Six of them remained on the bench after Garzarón had issued his suspensions. Of the dismissed ministers, the crown had appointed ten ministers through *beneficio* (royal sale of appointments) and three for their "merits and services." Merit, as we recall, did not mean the same as today and referred to a great extent to the social origins of ministers rather than their convincing performance on the job. Meanwhile, five of the six absolved ministers had bought their appointments while one had obtained the position for his merits. In other words, one third of the fifteen purchasers and one quarter of the four merit appointees remained on the court. In addition, the *visita* did not significantly change the composition of *beneficio* and merit appointees. Before the *visita*, the *beneficio* judges dominated the merit appointees in a ratio of 79 percent to 21 percent, and after the *visita*, the ratio was 85 percent to 15 percent, at least until new judges arrived. This outcome largely confirms the argument made in this book. The purchasers tended to be about as corrupt as the merit appointees according to the standard of the time.[49]

Judge Jerónimo Soria illustrates the case. He was the type of civil judge that many branded as corrupt. He descended from a wealthy *novohispano* family, bought his appointment to the *audiencia*, and kept his manifold social ties to his "brothers and family" in his home town Pátzcuaro in Michoacan. Soria also acquired many other commitments while studying in Mexico City. He should have been a target for the prosecution. In fact, allegations surfaced that Soria had clandestinely favored Pátzcuaro in the lawsuit against the city of Valladolid (now Morelia) over preeminence in Michoacan. Yet Soria held that he never cloaked his origins, because he had served as attorney for his city before becoming a civil judge, and that his intentions were generally known.[50]

The *visitador* then questioned Soria about assigning parts of two unclaimed inheritances to the *colegio mayor* of All Saints in Mexico City. Soria had earmarked the money to support a chapel and

---

[49] See Table 5 below; for sources, see Table 6 in the Appendix.
[50] Defense of Soria, AGI, México 670 B, *Relación*, fol. 101–101v. According to Felices de la Fuente, *Condes, marqueses,* 290–291, Soria (1660–1740) obtained the title of Marquis of Villahermosa de Alfaro in 1711; Gutiérrez Rodríguez, "El colegio novohispano," 23–27, analyzes Soria's *colegio mayor* of Saint Mary of All Saints; according to Moreno Gamboa, "La imprenta y los autores novohispanos," 199–200, Soria's colleague, Juan de Oliván y Rebolledo (1676–1738), was a fellow *colegial* of Saint Mary of All Saints, although there is no further evidence of their relation. Garzarón absolved both Soria y Oliván y Rebolledo in the *visita*.

a chaplain. Soria replied that he had lived in the *colegio mayor* and sworn to "favor it and not to fail in this obligation."[51] Soria contended that the earmarking was not excessive or illicit, because a *real cédula* allowed using these funds for pious foundations such as the chapel. The *audiencia* later reversed much of the earmark, and the college never appointed a chaplain, lessening any possible culpability. Aside from these issues, there were few other complaints against Soria, and only a handful of witnesses testified against him. His social obligations were a lesser evil than accepting bribes or extorting prisoners, of which other judges were guilty. Garzarón largely accepted Soria's explanation and acquitted him. Historians can speculate whether Garzarón did so for political reasons, but they would have to prove such a claim too.[52]

Soria's case exemplifies that American-born judges were no more corruptible than their peninsular colleagues according to the colonial standards. Of the six absolved ministers, three were born in New Spain, one was from Havana (Cuba), and two from Spain. Meanwhile, eight of the culprits hailed from New Spain, one from elsewhere in the Americas, and five from Spain. In other words, Garzarón absolved a little bit more than a quarter (27 percent) of the judges born in New Spain, 33 percent of all Americans taken together, and 29 percent of those born in Spain. In addition, these percentages omit the role of civil judge Miguel Calderón de la Barca, who came from Spain to Mexico City. The serious accusations against him had originally triggered the *visita*. Garzarón collected ample evidence against Calderón de la Barca, and only his death in 1719 precluded his verdict. If we assume that Calderón de la Barca been found guilty, the outcome changes. The share of absolved Spaniards drops to 25 percent of all judges in this case, less than the percentage of absolved *novohispanos*. Admittedly, this is a small sample, which says little about all ministers serving in the empire. Yet it indicates that Garzarón did not target a specific group or find the *novohispano* judges more corrupt than the Spanish-born ones. In fact, he found them rather equally honest, as he understood the idea.

Some scholars speculate whether Garzarón and the Council of the Indies removed those judges sympathizing with the House of Habsburg, the former dynasty that ruled the Spanish empire until 1700. Yet there is not much evidence pointing in this direction either. Two judges appointed

---

[51] Defense of Soria, AGI, México 670 B, *Relación*, fol. 102.
[52] *Real cédula* from 22 Apr. 1700, cited in defense of Jerónimo de Soria, AGI, México 670 B, *Relación*, fols. 101v–102v.

by a Habsburg ruler remained on the *audiencia* when the *visita* began. Garzarón did not inquire about this issue and none of witnesses alluded to the matter. Garzarón ultimately suspended these two ministers because he found sufficient evidence of corruption. Nonetheless, Garzarón also removed eleven Bourbon appointees for the same reasons.[53]

After Garzarón and the Council of the Indies demoted the judges, the *audiencia* altered slowly and became less corrupt according to the colonial standards. Ministers from other *audiencias* in Spain and the Americas arrived in Mexico City. They encountered judges who had predominantly purchased their appointments and formed strong ties to local society. At the same time, Garzarón had sent a strong warning against corruption. These combined factors contributed to a slow change of *audiencia* culture, and widespread bribery and extortions probably declined. There is the possibility that judges found other sources of income, but the *visitador* José de Gálvez (1765–1771), at least, observed that the *audiencia* worked satisfactorily and opposed inspecting the court again.[54]

The changing social profile of the judges offers an opportunity to speculate about the stages of appointment patterns. Scholars have usually assumed that the crown selected qualified judges by their merit and replaced them in the late seventeenth century with less-qualified colleagues who bought their appointments. The crown then returned to the practice of appointing by merit. I suggest, however, that the graduates of the six *colegios mayores* in Spain originally tended to obtain the most desirable posts in the empire. Most of these jurists had studied in the privileged *colegios mayores*, came from the municipal oligarchies or the upper nobility, or had a family member sitting on the Councils or *audiencias*. Their social background and networks paved their way to the *audiencias*, although they often pursued other goals than the reformist

---

[53] Arenal Fenochio, "La Justicia civil ordinaria," 51, see also 39–64; Gayol, *Laberintos de justicia*, 1: 126.

[54] According to Diego Antonio de Oviedo y Baños to Mexico City *cabildo*, Guatemala, 15 Nov. 1719, AHCM, Fondo Ayuntamiento, Sección Actas del Cabildo, vol. 45 A, fol. 163; Valero to king, Mexico City, 12 Oct. 1719, AGI, México 487; and *consulta* of the Council of the Indies, Madrid, 25 Nov. 1720, AGI, México 670 A, the king appointed Diego Antonio de Oviedo Baños, a former judge of Guatemala, as civil judge, and Francisco del Barco from Santo Domingo as criminal prosecutor. The viceroy appointed attorney José Sáenz as interim civil and criminal prosecutor. According to *real cédula* to Valero, Madrid, 29 Oct. 1720, AGN, RCO 41, exp. 58, fols. 206–207, two ministers ascended from Guadalajara. One of them was Juan Picado Pacheco in 1721, according to Picado Pacheco to king, attached to *consulta* of the Council of the Indies, Madrid, 14 Jan. 1727, AGI, México 670 A. On Gálvez, see García García, "Corrupción y venalidad," 28.

ministers of the crown.⁵⁵ This was one reason why the crown began selling appointments to the *audiencias* in larger numbers during the second stage beginning in 1687. The changing policy opened a breach for economically successful social groups who were less tied to the *colegios mayores* or the upper nobility. Their representatives assailed the newcomers as corrupt, harkening back to the idea of innate corruption that tied the newcomers' insufficient social origin to the inability to serve justice. At the same time, the idea of corruption was changing and performance in office gained ground. This opened the door for the newcomers, who did not miscarry justice any more than previous generations of jurists had.⁵⁶

This process ultimately segued into the third or reformist model of selecting and promoting officials and judges by performance. The years 1712 and 1750/51 marked the beginnings of this period. Forging ties with local elites remained necessary and desirable, but somewhat less than before. The crown increasingly promoted functionaries on account of training and compliance rather than primarily considering lineage. The concept of innate corruption retreated and obedient ministers advanced. Judges born into lower social strata graduated from the lesser universities and capitalized on the opportunities to rise through the ranks. In addition, the crown set up pensions for the loyal ministers and their families, and newly created ministers such as secretaries of state and provincial intendants supervised the judiciary more closely. This observation is not to sing the praise of these reforms. These ministers served the crown more zealously, which could well come at the expense of protections for social bodies or individuals. Neither were the ministers the same as twenty-first century judges who ideally observe due process and civil rights. Yet the changes demonstrate that the crown slowly tightened its grip on the empire in the early eighteenth century by advancing more efficacious functionaries.⁵⁷

---

[55] Dedieu, "La haute administration," 170–171.
[56] Felices de la Fuente, "Hacia la nobleza titulada," 24–29, 38, makes a similar case for the sale of noble titles to fill royal coffers and dilute the old aristocracy. On scholars advancing the idea of merit appointees versus purchasers, see footnote 48.
[57] Burkholder and Chandler, *From Impotence*, 119–135, thoroughly analyze the reformist model.

TABLE 5 *Suspended and Absolved Ministers*

	Ministers	Beneficio	Merits and Services	From Spain	From New Spain incl. New Galicia	From the Americas other than New Spain
total	19	15	4	7	11	1 – received degree from the university of Mexico City
Suspended	13	10	3	5	8	
Absolved	6	5	1	2	3	1
According to Burkholder and Chandler, *From Impotence to Authority*.						
Total	18	11	7	5	11	2 – one unknown
Suspended	11	7	5	3	8	one unknown
Absolved	6	4	2	2	3	1

Sources: See Table 6 in the Appendix.

KING LOUIS, COMPENSATIONS FOR THE DISMISSED MINISTERS, AND GARZARÓN'S DEATH

Historians should reconsider the argument that colonial corruption cases ended with a "slap on the wrist." Instead, Garzarón's *visita* belonged to a long tradition of stringent royal investigations in the Spanish empire, and his rulings were in many ways even tougher. Yet his *visita* entered a period of turmoil when King Philip V abdicated in favor of his son Louis I in 1724. The young king downsized the *visita* as both the Council of the Indies and its *cámara* (patronage committee) opposed Garzarón. Louis died soon, however, and Philip returned to the palace.

Garzarón's *visita* followed in the footsteps of a number of consequential *visitas*. For example, Pedro Moya de Contreras, the *visitador* of New Spain between 1583 and 1589, suspended three of the five civil judges of the Mexico City *audiencia* and prosecuted roughly 200 royal officials and crown contractors. He tortured a tax collector to obtain a confession and hanged a ship builder who had defrauded the treasury. In this regard, Moya de Contreras was sterner than Garzarón, who did not torment or execute anyone. In addition, a total of roughly sixty *visitas* scrutinized the *audiencias* of Spanish America between 1524 and 1700. What's more, a torrent of investigations descended on the port of Veracruz in the second half of the seventeenth century. These *visitas* audited officials who embezzled import duties and merchants suspected of contraband trade. The Council of the Indies usually assessed the *visita* sentences, extended some suspensions, fined judges up to 12,000 ducats in penalties and demoted them to other courts. Yet the Council only once removed an *audiencia* minister, who served as *relator* and not as judge. In comparison, Garzarón issued harsher rulings, as he suspended more than a dozen judges and the Council of the Indies dismissed them.[58]

For this reason, the famous *visita general* of Gálvez belonged to a long tradition of stringent investigations, rather than representing a clean break with the past, as scholars have traditionally argued. Galvéz did not shy away from controversy, for example, by expelling the Jesuit order from New Spain. Yet he suspended fewer ministers from one royal institution than Garzarón had. Afterwards, Gálvez became secretary of the Indies and introduced the provincial intendants in New Spain in 1786. These provincial intendants controlled regional affairs more tightly and the *visitas* fell into disuse. Gálvez's *visita* therefore has to be seen as

---

[58] Stafford Poole, *Pedro Moya de Contreras. Catholic Reform and Royal Power in New Spain, 1571–1591* (Berkeley: University of California Press, 1987), 88–112; according to Arregui Zamorano, *La audiencia de México según los visitadores*, 53–68, 267–270, the principal *visitadores* of the Mexico City *audiencia* were Tello de Sandoval (1543–1547), Jerónimo de Valderrama (1563–1566), Diego Landeras de Velasco (1606–1612), Juan de Villela (1609–1612), Martín Carrillo y Alderete (1625–1627), Juan de Palafox (1639–1653), and Pedro de Gálvez (1650–1653). María Justina Sarabia Viejo, *Don Luís de Velasco, virrey de Nueva España, 1550–1564* (Sevilla, CSIC, EEHA, 1978), 47–48, maintains that Valderrama suspended six sitting judges and prosecutors. In 1571, the Council of the Indies transferred three judges to other *audiencias* and reinstated two, while one judge had passed away. On Juan de Ovando, *visitador general* of the Council of the Indies (1567–1571), see Brendecke, *Imperio*, 321–325. According to Phelan, *Kingdom of Quito*, 152–157, 170–174, 297–303, the *visita* of Quito (1624–1637) uncovered little judicial malfeasance but fined the president of the court 31,300 ducats for contraband trade, tax evasion, and excessive social ties. Two treasury officials ended up in jail. On *visitas* in Veracruz during the periods 1660–1680 and 1710–1730, Bertrand, *Grandeur et misères*, 35; Kris Lane, "From Corrupt to Criminal" 40–43; and Lane, "Corrupción y dominación colonial: el gran fraude a la Casa de la Moneda de Potosí en 1649," *Boletín del Instituto de Historia Argentina y Americana Dr. Emilio Ravignani* 43 (2015): 111–113 (including an insightful historiographical discussion on 121–128), shows that the *visitador* of Potosí, Francisco de Nestares Marín (1647–1660), executed two senior mint officials, while the treasurer died in jail. Castro Gutierrez, "La visita del virrey conde de Galve a la Real Casa de Moneda de México, 1693," in *Comercio y minería en la historia de América Latina*, eds. José Alfredo Uribe Salas and Eduardo Flores Clair (Mexico City: Universidad Michoacana de San Nicolás de Hidalgo, Instituto Nacional de Antropología e Historia, 2015), 135–137, emphasizes mild *visita* punishments of up to 200 pesos.

a conclusion of a long series of reviews, epitomized in many ways by Garzarón.[59]

This outcome was by no means clear when King Louis I took the reins on January 15, 1724, and demoted Garzarón's *visita*. The sixteen-year old "boy-king" and his councilors steered a more conservative course than Philip V. They dissolved the viceroyalty of New Granada and openly favored returning the Board of Trade from Cádiz to Seville. Louis also named the Marquis of Valero as governor of the Council of the Indies by late January 1724. Valero used the opportunity to discredit Garzarón and Viceroy Casafuerte. The following year, the king awarded Valero the title of Duke of Arión for his loyal services. In addition, the *cámara* of the Indies attacked Garzarón, claiming that "slanderers, frauds, and the malevolent" had prompted him to suspend the judges.[60] The Council of the Indies even called for dismissing Garzarón altogether. Louis agreed in part and ended the *visita general* with the provision that Garzarón first complete the review of all treasury officials and the *consulado* in Mexico City. The king added that the viceroy should correct any remaining abuses outside the capital. While plenty of work remained for Garzarón, Louis significantly reduced the prestige of the *visita*.[61]

In this favorable court climate, Félix Suárez de Figueroa, one of the convicted civil judges, challenged his sentence. He had traveled with Sánchez Morcillo and another judge to Madrid in 1721 to lobby against

---

[59] Bertrand, *Grandeur et misères*, 291–292, holds that Gálvez's *visita* belongs to an established tradition. Brading, *Miners and Merchants*, 39–44; Castro Gutierrez, "Del paternalismo autoritario al autoritarismo burocrático: Los éxitos y fracasos de José de Gálvez (1764–1767)," in *Mexico in the Age of Democratic Revolutions, 1750–1850*, ed. Jaime Rodríguez O. (Boulder, CO: Lynne Rienner Publications, 1994), 26; emphasize the importance of Gálvez's *visita*; see also Susan Deans-Smith, *Bureaucrats, Planters, and Workers. The Making of the Tobacco Monopoly in Bourbon Mexico* (Austin: University of Texas Press, 1992); Bethencourt, *Inquisition*, 213, argues that the *visitas* targeting the Spanish Inquisition declined in the late seventeenth century.

[60] *Consulta* of the *cámara* of the Indies composed of Valero, Rivas, Silva, Zúñiga, Machado, Madrid, 28 Feb. 1724, AGI, México 381; see also *consulta* of the *cámara* of the Indies, Madrid, 14 Nov. 1725, AGI, México 381.

[61] The *consulta* of the Council of the Indies, Madrid, 21 Apr. 1728, AGI, México 381, again suggested terminating the *visita*; king's resolution, attached to *consulta* of the Council of the Indies, Madrid, 10 May 1724, AGI, México 670 A; *consulta* of the *cámara* of the Indies, Madrid, 18 Jan. 1726, AGI, México 670 A. On Garzarón's plans to investigate the Guadalajara *audiencia*, Garzarón to king, Mexico City, 20 Feb. 1723, AGI, Mexico 547; see also letters of Juan Antonio de Urdangarin, *oficial mayor* of the treasury in Guadalajara, to Garzarón, Guadalajara, 20 Sept. 1719, AGN, Indiferente Virreinal, caja 5687, exp. 3, fols. 1–8; and Kuethe, "Política colonial," 239; on Valero, see Felices de la Fuente, *Condes, marqueses*, 50–51.

their removal. While unsuccessful, Suárez de Figueroa stayed in Madrid. In August 1724, the crown directed the prosecutor of the Council of the Indies to reappraise his sentence. The prosecutor struck down the plea for leniency, but Louis ordered three councilors of Castile to reevaluate the case.[62] There were several reasons for this change. Most importantly, Suárez de Figueroa had not accepted as many kickbacks as others. Garzarón fully proved only two charges of bribery against him, while convicting other judges on dozens of charges. In addition, Suárez de Figueroa had originally obtained his post in exchange for his family's services to the Bourbons during the War of Succession. That loyalty did not sway Garzarón, but it may have influenced some at the court in Madrid. Furthermore, the legal doctrine on appeals was an "impenetrable forest of exceptions." Defendants could demand a review, for example, when *visitadores* had committed notorious injustices or ignored due process. These combined factors convinced the crown to relent and hear Félix Suárez de Figueroa's defense once more in 1724.[63]

The appeal ended in a compensation. Suárez de Figueroa gained access to Garzarón's papers and laid out his arguments. The councilors of Castile then withdrew to a private residence on Saturday, November 4, 1724. After due deliberations, they split on the verdict. The king added two councilors to the committee, and the process dragged on. In late April 1725, doña Teresa Aranda, Suárez de Figueroa's wife, reported that her husband had passed away. The committee at that point only had to decide on a suitable indemnity for her. On July 7, 1725, the councilors recommended striking down Suárez de Figueroa's sentence and allowing Aranda to recover about 18,000 pesos in her husband's foregone salary. At the same time, the councilors upheld the 2,000 pesos fine for her husband and his share of *visita* expenses. The remaining compensation probably covered Aranda

---

[62] The *consulta* of the Council of the Indies, Madrid, 13 Oct. 1721, AGI, Escribanía 287 B, *pieza* 52, fol. 1, shows that Suárez de Figueroa and the criminal judges Agustín de Robles Lorenzana and Sánchez Morcillo had traveled to Spain; *parecer* of José de Laysequilla, Madrid, 14 Aug. 1724, AGI, Escribanía 287 B, *pieza* 39, fols. 132–135; Francisco Molano, Tomás Melgarejo, and Francisco de Aperregui to king, Madrid, 26 Jan. 1725, AGI, Escribanía 287 B, *pieza* 39, fol. 138–138v.

[63] Cited in Alonso Romero, *Orden procesal*, 118–119; see also Cordero Fernández, *Institucionalizar*, 371. Alonso de la Lama y Noriega on behalf of Sánchez Morcillo to king, Madrid, 1 Apr. 1727, AGI, Escribanía 287 B, *pieza* 38, fol. 38, see also fol. 32, advocated for an appeal, for example, because in the provinces of "Aragón and Catalonia ... the appeal goes forward for punishments against honor or life, and it is similar in Portugal."

and Suárez de Figueroa's significant expenses of moving their family to Spain and petitioning the crown.[64]

Criminal judge Pedro Sánchez Morcillo also benefitted. He returned empty-handed to New Spain in late 1722. Garzarón detained him soon after for failing to pay his penalty fees. Initially Garzarón confined Sánchez Morcillo in the building of the municipal council and then in the palace jail, where the former judge had previously held criminals. Sánchez Morcillo's health declined during his seven months of incarceration, or so he claimed. He convinced Garzarón to let him retire to his home and provided bondsmen willing to underwrite his release. Sánchez Morcillo left the jail in June 1723 and before long was walking about the streets of Mexico City. When Garzarón heard of these strolls, he ordered the bondsmen to return the delinquent to jail within three days or be fined. Garzarón ruled that to remain free, Sánchez Morcillo immediately would have to pay 2,000 pesos in addition to 480 pesos (6 percent of the total) to pay for shipping the cash to Spain. The remaining 6,000 pesos were due in installments when the next two fleets departed Veracruz.[65]

Sánchez Morcillo asserted his lack of means, refused to pay, and went back to jail on January 8, 1724. Garzarón threatened to move him from the more comfortable sections of the palace jail to the dungeons or send him off to some grueling military fortress. As a result, Sánchez Morcillo lamented Garzarón's cruelness for imposing on the dismissed judges "irregular banishments, leaving their wives and unmarried daughters to the necessities and insults of hunger, which so many times has forced them to eat human flesh and even that of their own children, because hunger is a stronger enemy than war."[66] Sánchez Morcillo underlined his poverty in this way, because he had not received a salary for years, and his wife resisted squandering her dowry. His family would have died of hunger, if

---

[64] Louis to Valero, Buen Retiro, 13 Mar. 1724, AGI, México 670 A; *autos*, Madrid, 12 and 20 May 1724, AGI, Escribanía 287 B, *pieza* 36, fols. 20, 22; *consulta* of the junta, Madrid, 4 May 1725, AGI, México 670 A; king to Valero, San Ildefonso, 5 July 1725, AGI, México 670 A; *auto*, Madrid, 31 Oct. 1724; Francisco Molano, Tomás Melgarejo, and Francisco de Aperregui to king, Madrid, 26 Jan. 1725; and definitive sentence, Madrid, 7 July 1725, these two documents in AGI, Escribanía 287 B, *pieza* 39, fols. 136v, 138, 142–144; sentence of the Council of the Indies, Madrid, 7 July 1725, AGI, Escribanía 1183, folder *1721–1730 Francisco Garzarón*; *consulta* of the Council of the Indies, Madrid, 19 June 1726, these two documents in AGI, México 381.

[65] Garzarón to king, Mexico City, 1 May 1724, AGI, Escribanía 287 B, *pieza* 45, fol. 1.

[66] Sánchez Morcillo to king, Mexico City, 28 July 1724, AGI, Escribanía 287 B, *pieza* 38, fol. 18, see also fol. 14–14v.

the archbishop had not provided alimony, according to Sánchez Morcillo's attorney.[67] Garzarón acknowledged that Sánchez Morcillo had "the archbishop's recognition as a pauper," but observed that the prelate paid very little, because Sánchez Morcillo and his family lived as comfortably as ever. Garzarón was convinced that his adversary possessed "jewelry, wrought silver in great quantity, and gems."[68]

After serving further time in the jail, Sánchez Morcillo solved his predicament. He convinced the jailer to let him spend the nights at home and return early in the mornings. Following the night of February 7, Sánchez Morcillo did not present himself at jail. Instead, he went to the church of the Hospital of the Holy Trinity and requested asylum. This complicated matters for Garzarón, because the priests usually insisted on ecclesiastical immunity and opposed the secular authorities from extracting culprits. The jailer also fled, because he had allowed the nightly relieve without the consent of the senior constable, who oversaw the jail. As a consequence, Garzarón confiscated the estate of both judge and jailer, but Sánchez Morcillo hid his funds well and Garzarón netted only 113 pesos from him. Garzarón then held the senior constable liable, because the jailer had worked without a formal appointment. Garzarón seized the senior constable's estate, garnished the proceeds of his office, and placed him under house arrest. The senior constable soon agreed to pay Sánchez Morcillo's fine, if Garzarón lifted his house arrest in exchange.[69]

In January 1724, the crown ordered Sánchez Morcillo's release from jail, while reiterating that he pay his penalty. The crown confined Sánchez Morcillo to Mexico City. Garzarón received the order and obeyed in general terms but decreed that Sánchez Morcillo first present himself at jail for the order to take effect. The former judge refused, expecting additional punishment or jail time. In July, he appealed the decree to the *audiencia*. When the *audiencia* deliberated the appeal, Garzarón

---

[67] José de Guibelondo on behalf of Sánchez Morcillo to king, AGI, Escribanía 287 B, *pieza* 40, fol. 75.
[68] Garzarón to king, Mexico City, 2 Aug. 1724, AGI, Escribanía 287 B, *pieza* 38, fols. 5v–6v.
[69] Garzarón to king, Mexico City, 1 May 1724, AGI, Escribanía 287 B, *pieza* 45, fols. 1–4; Garzarón to king, Mexico City, 2 Aug. 1724, AGI, Escribanía 287 B, *pieza* 38, fols. 5v–6v; Garzarón to king, Mexico City, 8 Oct. 1726, AGI, Escribanía 287 B, *pieza* 14, fols. 14–16v. On asylum, see Hevia Bolaños, *Curia Filipica*, vol. 1, part 3, para. 12, nos. 1, 54, 55, 61.

threatened to fine the court for "disturbing or usurping" his jurisdiction. Sánchez Morcillo remained in church asylum that time.[70]

At this point, Garzarón also resented the newfound strength of his opponents in Madrid. By 1724, he was investigating the tribunal of accounts and the royal treasury in Mexico City and suspended at least one official. Nevertheless, in early May 1725, Garzarón heard the king's decision to downgrade the *visita*. He felt slighted and lamented Valero's promotion to the governorship of the Council of the Indies. Garzarón claimed that the *audiencia* now had its "back well protected" by Valero and decided to step down.[71] In response, the majority of the councilors of the Indies suggested severely reprehending Garzarón and drafted a suitable *real cédula* in October 1725. The Council cast him as a "injurious libeler" who maligned Valero and called for Garzarón's removal from the *visita*, because the law prohibited any "minister from declaring himself someone's enemy and judging the same person."[72]

Yet politics in Madrid performed another somersault, and the reform forces returned. Louis died unexpectedly on August 31, 1724, and Philip V and his advisers moved back to the palace. Philip dismissed the president of the Council of Castile, a conservative protagonist who had probably supported Suárez de Figueroa's appeal. From November 27, 1725, until May 14, 1726, the Baron of Ripperda had the ear of the queen and the king, serving as chief minister and secretary of the Indies. On November 8, 1725, Ripperda ordered the Council of the Indies to reconsider its damning assessment of the *visita*. The crown also publicly expressed its pleasure with Garzarón by restoring the full *visita general*. In addition, the crown named him bishop of Oaxaca in December 1725, although he never wore the miter. The prosecutor and the councilors of the Indies held the line, however, adding that Viceroy Casafuerte was too "biased in favoring Garzarón." As a consequence, on February 4, 1726,

---

[70] Auto of Garzarón, Mexico City, 18 July 1724, AGI, Escribanía 287 B, *pieza* 41, fols. 14v–15.

[71] Garzarón to king, Mexico City, 2 May 1725, AHN, Inquisición 1740, exp. 18; according to *real cédula* to Valero, Madrid, 26 Dec. 1717, AGN, RCO 38, exp. 61, fol. 164; Ignacio José de Miranda to (probably) Casafuerte, Mexico City, 7 May 1727; and viceregal decree, Mexico City, 7 May 1727, both in AGN, Indiferente Virreinal, 6181, exp. 70, Garzarón heard the initial defense of the tribunal of accounts ministers in 1717.

[72] *Consulta* of the Council of the Indies, Madrid, 18 Jan. 1726, AGI, México 670 A; draft of *real cédula* to Garzarón, Madrid, attached to *consulta* of the Council of the Indies, Madrid, 18 Jan. 1726, AGI, México 670 A.

Ripperda excluded the Council from all future communications with Garzarón and the viceroy.[73] Madrid continued to abet the *visita* as the wheel of fortune kept turning. Ripperda fell from power and fled the court on May 14, 1726. Meanwhile, José de Patiño was riding high. Patiño had belonged to Alberoni's entourage and stitched his former patron's program back together. Patiño opposed clemency for the dismissed judges. He denied the requests of two former judges for appointments as cathedral prebendaries and turned down Teresa Aranda's pleas for a pension.[74]

Despite Patiño's harder line, Sánchez Morcillo slowly regained a respectable position in colonial society. The former judge slipped out of the hospital church in Mexico City and journeyed to Veracruz. He again embarked on a ship to Spain and resided in Madrid in February 1727, at the latest, lobbying the Council of the Indies to lower his fine.[75] In that year, the Council still upheld the verdict against him and prohibited him from leaving Madrid. Yet the Council also waived the collection of Sánchez Morcillo's fine and approved his voyage to Spain, although he had lacked permission to leave New Spain.[76] Sánchez Morcillo achieved the breakthrough three

---

[73] *Consulta* of the Council of the Indies, Madrid, 18 Jan. 1726, and attached king's resolution, Madrid, 4 Feb. 1726, both documents in AGI México 670 A. See also *real cédula* to Casafuerte, Madrid, 22 Dec. 1725; receipt confirmed by Casafuerte, Mexico City, 22 July 1726, AGN, RCO 45, exp. 146; king to Casafuerte, signed by the Duke of Ripperdá, Buen Retiro, 25 Mar. 1726, AGN, RCO 45, exp. 61, fols. 191–193. According to León Sanz, "La llegada de los Borbones," 69–73, the Council president was Luis Miraval y Espínola.

[74] On Juan Díaz de Bracamonte, who asked for a prebendary in Mexico City, and Agustín Robles Lorenzana, who asked for the position of school master at the Puebla cathedral, draft of a *consulta* of the *cámara* of the Indies, 29 July 1726, AGI, México 670 A. According to *consulta* of the Council of the Indies, Madrid, 19 June 1726, AGI, México 381, Teresa Aranda requested a half-salary pension, which the Council of the Indies supported.

[75] *Dictamen* of the prosecutor of the Council of the Indies, Madrid, 10 Dec. 1723; *consulta* of the Council of the Indies, Madrid, 15 Jan. 1724, AGI, Escribanía 287 B, *pieza* 40, fol. 75v; king Louis to Garzarón, Madrid, 3 Feb. 1724, AGI, Escribanía 287 B, *pieza* 41, fol. 1–1v; obedience of Garzarón, Mexico City, 26 June 1724, Escribanía 287 B, *pieza* 41, fols. 4, 12v–13; Garzarón to king, Mexico City, 2 Aug. 1724, AGI, Escribanía 287 B, *pieza* 38, fols. 5v–6v; *consulta* of the Council of the Indies, Madrid, 18 Jan. 1726, AGI, México 670 A. See also *parecer* of the prosecutor of the Council of the Indies, Madrid, 31 May 1727, AGI, Escribanía 287 B, *pieza* 14, fol. 17–17v. According to Hevia Bolaños, *Curia Filipica*, vol. 1, part 3, para. 11, no. 13, absconding from jail merited a punishment at the judge's discretion.

[76] Garzarón to king, Mexico City, 8 Oct. 1726; *parecer* of the prosecutor of the Council of the Indies, Madrid, 31 May 1727, AGI, Escribanía 287 B, *pieza* 14, fols. 14–17v; *parecer* of the prosecutor, Madrid, 16 Feb. 1727; *consulta* of the Council of the Indies, Madrid, 4 Mar. 1727, Alonso de la Lama y Noriega on behalf of Sánchez Morcillo to king, Madrid, 1 Apr. 1727; the last three documents are in AGI, Escribanía 287 B, *pieza* 38, fols. 23–25;

years later – eleven years after his suspension from the *audiencia*. He obtained a prebendary at the cathedral chapter of Guadalajara. Sánchez Morcillo's wife must have passed away by this time for him to be allowed to take the vows. While he was not a priest by training, his law degree was similar to a canon law degree and served as his formal qualification.[77]

Garzarón's end drew near when he felt his ailing health in 1727. In May, he left Mexico City and retired to the countryside for "better air."[78] Soon after, Garzarón returned to Mexico City, where he fell very ill. He drafted his will on June 18, setting apart twenty-five pesos each to his chambermaid, his cook, and his footman. Garzarón also bequeathed 100 pesos to his coachman José, "who had been at my side during all the time of my illness assisting with great care and watchfulness." He assigned the remainder of his belongings to the Holy Office in Mexico City. Garzarón died the next day. He was buried in the Dominican monastery adjacent to the Inquisition palace in Mexico City.[79]

The *visita's* rigor declined considerably at that point. The crown named a successor to prosecute the treasury officials and other social bodies, but the zeal for stern punishments tapered off. The *consulado* of Mexico City subsequently evaded the investigation by lending the crown one million pesos.[80] Half a year later, on December 26, 1727, Valero followed Garzarón into the grave. The suspended judges lamented losing a powerful voice on their behalf in Madrid. They were not the only ones. The indigenous noble nuns of the Corpus Christi convent in Mexico City also mourned Valero's death, honoring him as the founder

---

consulta of the Council of the Indies, Madrid, 13 May 1728, with royal decree on reverse, AGI, México 381.

[77] *Relación de méritos* of Sánchez Morcillo, Madrid, 21 May 1728; *consulta* of the *cámara* of the Indies, no place, 30 Mar. 1730, both in AGI, Indiferente General 144, N. 151. This appointment is confirmed in title, 7 June 1730, in Magdaleno Redondo, *Títulos de Indias*, 122.

[78] Casafuerte to king, Mexico City, 20 June 1727, AGI, México 670 A.

[79] Garzarón's will, Mexico City, 18 June 1727, AHAGN, fols. 159v–160v; Casafuerte to king, Mexico City, 20 June 1727, AGI, México 670 A; *consulta* of the Council of the Indies, Madrid, 17 Apr. 1728, AGI, México 670 A. Torribio Medina, *Historia de la Inquisición*, 355, notes that Garzarón left the considerable sum of 23,000 pesos to his heirs, but that point is at odds with his will.

[80] According to king to Andrés Elcorobarrutia, royal palace in Madrid, 13 Sept. 1728, AGI, México 670 A; *consulta* of the Council of the Indies, Madrid, 21 Apr. 1728, AGI, México 381, Garzarón's successor was Pedro Domingo Contreras. Bertrand, "Clientélisme," 140–149, argues that Contreras's *visita* (1729–1733) failed largely because Casafuerte and various ministers opposed his aims. On the *consulado*, see *real cédula*, Madrid, 4 Apr. 1727, AGN, RCO 46, exp. 37, fols. 65–66; José Patiño to *consulado* of Mexico City, Madrid, 8 Apr. 1727, AGN, AHH 213, exp. 3, fols. 99v–101; *real cédula*, El Pardo, 2 Feb. 1728, AGN, RCO 47, exp. 13.

of their community. The sermon was dedicated to Valero's successor Casafuerte, and the *audiencia* and all tribunals attended in full force. Garzarón's fight with Valero and the *audiencia* had ended.[81]

CONCLUSION

King Philip V, Queen Elizabeth Farnese, and their chief minister, Giulio Alberoni, ordered Inquisitor Francisco Garzarón to inspect the *audiencia* of Mexico City as part of a larger reform. Garzarón took his task seriously and suspended thirteen of the *audiencia*'s nineteen judges and prosecutors and 156 officials. Although largely forgotten, this *visita* was the most radical in imperial Spanish history in terms of ministers removed from a single institution. Politics, friendship, and the power of social networks undoubtedly shaped the *visita*. Garzarón, for example, befriended the civil judge José Joaquín Uribe and acquitted him from all charges, indicating (though not proving) favoritism. In addition, when King Philip stepped down in 1724, his son Louis tacked a more conservative course. The new king downsized the *visita* in that year, as the Council of the Indies called for Garzarón's removal. At that point, Judge Félix Suárez de Figueroa also succeeded in appealing his removal. A special committee soon after revoked his conviction and substantially compensated his widow, Teresa Aranda.

Yet these verdicts were not exclusively politically motivated. Garzarón also absolved five judges besides Uribe who were not particularly beholden to him or Uribe. Rather than following the prompts of Uribe or an assumed social network lurking in the back, Garzarón chiefly assessed the merits of their cases and ruled that there was scant evidence to convict them. In addition, Giulio Alberoni, one of the principal instigators of the *visita*, had fallen from power by the time of the sentences. The Council opposed the *visita* and nonetheless confirmed Garzarón's verdicts on the judges in 1721, because the councilors found Garzarón's rulings mostly convincing. Even King Louis largely stood by Garzarón's verdicts against the judges except for Suárez de Figueroa.

---

[81] *Sermón fúnebre que con término de tres días*, 1729, BNM, FR, La Fragua, ms. 1194, exp. 11. See Susan Migden Socolow, *The Women of Colonial Latin America*, 2nd ed. (Cambridge: Cambridge University Press, 2015), 112–113; Felices de la Fuente, *Condes, marqueses*, 51. According to *real cédula* to Casafuerte, Madrid, 24 June 1727, AGN, RCO 46, exp. 62, fol. 133–133v; *real cédula* to Casafuerte, Madrid, 31 May 1728, AGN, RCO 47, exp. 68, fol. 273, the crown extended Casafuerte's viceregal term for three years.

In addition, Garzarón's investigation belonged to a long line of harsh *visitas*. Pedro Moya de Contreras, for example, vetted roughly 200 royal officials and contractors, hanged or tortured suspects, and suspended three civil judges in the late sixteenth century. Notwithstanding these verdicts, no punishment ever rose to the level of Garzarón's. Even José de Gálvez's *visita* did not pummel one institution as stringently as Garzarón did. Garzarón's *visita* mattered for its tough sentences and the popular backing it received for its goals, despite the changing politics in Mexico City and Madrid. Such broad support existed, because corruption and fraud were a real concern for *novohispano* commoners, ministers, and the crown in Madrid.

Finally, Garzarón and the Council of the Indies did not particularly target Creole judges who had purchased their appointments or Habsburg sympathizers. Ten of the removed judges had attained their positions through *beneficio* and three for their "merits and services." Meanwhile, five of the six absolved ministers had bought their appointments and only one had obtained his post on account of merits. In other words, one third of the purchasers and one quarter of the merit appointees remained on the court. Very similar things can be said when comparing Creoles against Spaniards. Garzarón absolved just over a quarter of the judges born in New Spain, 33 percent of all Americans, and 29 percent of those born in Spain. The calculation changes when including Miguel Calderón de la Barca, and the share of absolved Spaniards drops to 25 percent. Overall, Garzarón found the *novohispano* and the Spanish-born judges similarly honest, as he understood the idea. This – admittedly small sample – shows that Garzarón did not seek to weed out a particular ethnic group during the *visita*.

Even so, the convicted judges had held life-time positions. Their offices were not fully patrimonial, such as the senior notaries, who could bequeath their offices or appoint deputies to serve in their stead.[82] But even the dismissed judges claimed some compensation for their loss; in part, because several of them had paid thousands of pesos to obtain their appointments. This explains why Pedro Sánchez Morcillo attained a comparable post after an odyssey of eleven years during which he

---

[82] See, for example, title for Juan Rodríguez Mediano issued by the Duke of Alburquerque, Mexico City, 22 Sept. 1710; certification of renouncing position in somebody else's favor, Villa de Carrión, 23 Aug. 1710, AGN, Real Acuerdo 7, fols. 8–11; *real cédula* to Alburquerque, Madrid, 20 Jan. 1705, AGN, RCO 32, exp. 89, fols. 185–186.

traversed the ocean multiple times. He pleaded at the courts of Mexico City and Madrid and languished in jail. Finally he received a coveted prebendary at the cathedral of Guadalajara. Many humble victims had accused him of extortions and torture, and Garzarón, the Council of the Indies, and the king agreed. Nevertheless, in 1730, Sánchez Morcillo returned to a position of respect in colonial society.

Conclusion: Approaching Historical Corruption

Corruption existed well before the Enlightenment and referred to any illicit obstacle to establishing justice. The process of finding justice mattered deeply, because early modern judges did not merely ascertain whether a crime met the definition of a specific law. The foundation for justice rested instead on a multitude of written and unwritten norms that often appended or contradicted one another. Justice anchored in the royal law, the *ius commune* (the combined Roman and Church law and their interpretations), the customs, and even theology. Judges had great leeway to select the appropriate rules, weigh the evidence, and tailor their sentences to the specific cases. Justice was therefore usually casuistic, and corruption impeded this process of finding justice.

Judicial corruption covered a wide swath. Corrupt judges accepted bribes to alter sentences, extorted litigants or suspects, tampered with documents, traded with their subjects, and sometimes acted very negligently. Defendants, witnesses, and officials who took or offered bribes to produce false testimony also corroded rulings. In addition, nefarious customs that replaced the just law perverted justice and were often also called corrupt. Furthermore, judicial corruption had an innate aspect, because candidates for judicial offices needed the proper merit to serve. Unlike today, this past idea of merit strongly pointed to the proper social origins of the candidates for office, to their and their forebears' services to crown and community, and to the aptitude for office. People of impure descent, and those who worked in debasing occupations or frequently handled money lacked the inner qualities to be good judges. They tended to be greedy and yield to evil temptations. Consequently, many early modern jurists and theologians considered appointing such people as corruption.

Early modern Spaniards contested the precise boundaries between corruption and tolerable conduct. Some defendants maintained that corruption was not identical with *baratería*, which, in their view, meant giving gifts to judges without distorting the sentence itself. Others added that gifts which corresponded to the social importance of the recipients were legitimate, and so was giving among friends and family. It fell to the judges and their good *arbitrio* (judgment) to distinguish between an innocuous present and offerings with evil design. Notaries also rebutted the most serious charges of corruption against them, because they served a manual position and never impeded the administration of justice. Although the suspects advanced these arguments, the ambiguity of corruption should not be pushed too far.

In fact, corruption could well be an actionable crime. Francisco Garzarón conducted the *visita general* (investigation) of the *audiencia* of Mexico City between 1716 and 1727, to uncover corruption and other crimes. He suspended thirteen of the nineteen judges, because they had accepted major gifts shortly before or after voting for the givers in the trials. The Council of the Indies confirmed his verdicts and removed the suspended judges. Garzarón or the Council of the Indies never clearly stated which concepts they considered breached, because early modern judges rarely did so. Yet they wielded sophisticated legal tools to assess corruption and fraud. They, and many other jurists, theologians, and procurators distinguished between various crimes and differing levels of guilt, and this mattered for the rulings. Ordinary negligence referred to ministers who did not act very diligently and caused damages to others. Meanwhile, ministers acted grossly negligently when they violated the typical standards of care of their occupation. For instance, the king reprimanded the judges' gross negligence in tolerating the manifold abuses of the officials in 1721. Yet showing the *dolo* (malicious intent) to accept cash for altering justice constituted the most serious guilt. When Garzarón established the judges' *dolo* to corrupt verdicts, he suspended them, and the Council confirmed the sentences.

In addition, officials committed *falsedad* (fraud), theft, and extortions; they jailed or released suspects without court orders, and they were guilty of lesser offenses. Garzarón gathered ample incriminating testimony and suspended 156 officials on these grounds, and the Council removed eleven of them. Four officials had demonstrated the *dolo* to falsify records and damage others, and two had committed other illegalities, such as theft. In

Conclusion: Approaching Historical Corruption

addition, two officials were removed for accepting considerable bribes or for embezzling royal moneys and failing to pay the crown the rent for an office. In addition, sixteen officials paid significant fines or returned cash to former litigants, while the Council extended the suspensions without pay for nine suspects. Meanwhile, the officials who merely overcharged litigants or kept poor records returned to their posts. While these officials had also acted deliberately or negligently, they had committed minor offenses. In addition, the local customs tolerated, to an extent, that unsalaried officials levied excessive fees to make a living. Moreover, the innate faults of ministers played a minor role in the *visita*. Garzarón and the witnesses occasionally attacked officials of *mestizo* or *mulato* descent as unsuited, and they frowned upon officials who displayed lewd behavior during and outside their occupational duties. These charges alone, however, were not enough for the Council of the Indies to remove the ministers.

Without any doubt, politics and the ubiquitous social networks deeply shaped early modern justice, but Garzarón's *visita* was not primarily a political process. Truly, the civil judge José Joaquín Uribe had befriended Garzarón and assisted him, and the *visitador* probably looked the other way on some incriminating evidence against Uribe. In addition, another civil judge successfully lobbied the court in Madrid to review his removal, just as the political currents shifted in his favor. As a result, his wife attained his posthumous reinstatement and a significant cash settlement in 1724. These incidents point to the workings of clientelist relationships, although they also had a legal basis. Uribe, for example, had become rich by marriage and had less need for accepting bribes, which was Garzarón's main aim of inquiry. What is more, Garzarón had proven only two corruption charges against the reinstated judge, whereas he had raised dozens of charges against the other culprits. Finally, the Council of the Indies upheld the verdicts against the other judges, although it fiercely opposed the *visita*, at least at times. This shows that the Council largely agreed with Garzarón's judicial conclusions about corruption.

Garzarón, by and large, followed the pattern of ordinary Castilian criminal trials, and the *visita* gave him additional leeway. The ordinary criminal trials usually stuck to the inquisitorial trial form, in which the judge acted as a detective, prosecutor, and judge at the same time, collecting incriminating over exonerating evidence against the suspects. These processes effectively repressed crimes, although they could also be misused to settle personal vendettas and punish the innocent. Yet Garzarón did not condemn on a whim as he gathered abundant testimony against the ministers. He accepted the word of two witnesses who concurred about a single criminal incident to convict a suspect. Unlike the ordinary criminal trials, he also recognized the testimonies of three witnesses who detailed their own participation in different corrupt acts as long as they did not contradict one another. This lowered the bar for convictions. In addition, Garzarón kept secret the names of witnesses to protect them from revenge while curbing the possibility to challenge their testimony. Meanwhile, the defendants had the chance to debunk evidence, call on attorneys and witnesses, and impugn rulings. They pointed to legal principles which justified their conduct and denied that they had committed the offenses they were charged with. Garzarón heard the defenses of the suspects. He assessed their credibility, weighed the additional evidence, and then issued a verdict for each suspect.

Corruption and other abuses in New Spain (colonial Mexico) were not exclusively elite affairs. Some at the lower and middle rungs of society deplored the offenses, while others committed them for their own advantage. For instance, an *hacendado*'s brother killed the Native worker José Miguel Nieto for stealing corn in 1714. The *alcalde mayor* (district judge) of Huejotzingo (near Puebla) acquitted the *hacendado* and his brother. Subsequently, Micaela de Cervantes, Nieto's mother, lamented that justice had not been done, because the *hacendado* had bribed the *alcalde mayor*. Pedro Sánchez Morcillo, a criminal judge of the *audiencia*, arrested the perpetrators along with don Miguel Pérez, the indigenous governor of Huejotzingo. The *hacendado* and the governor paid cash for their release, whereas the mother and widow of Nieto received compensations. Later, Francisco Garzarón retraced Sánchez Morcillo's steps, carefully comparing oral testimony against written evidence. The compensations for mother and widow were typical solutions for violent crimes at the time, but Sánchez Morcillo had also lined his pockets with the remaining funds and forged the record about the money's whereabouts. Garzarón suspended him.

Garzarón's concept of corruption rested on a plurality of legal sources, as justice in most Atlantic empires was a hybrid matter. Roman and canon law continually influenced one another, giving rise to the *ius commune*, the general law that spanned the globe (save for the English empire). The legal practitioners in both Spain and New Spain knew at least aspects of the *ius commune*, which they weighed against natural law and biblical tenets. In addition, local customs profoundly shaped justice, and so did the stream of royal communications pouring out of Madrid. Years ago, Michel Foucault claimed that the early modern French widely disregarded these royal ordinances and lived in a pervasive illegality which "was so deeply rooted and so necessary to the life of each social stratum."[1] Yet such a view is no longer tenable when taking into account the presence of the "judicial pluralism." Early modern people who downplayed royal provisions by no means lived in illegality, because they adhered to a series of other norms. In corruption cases, this variety of norms could buttress gift-giving to judges and provide the tools for their prosecution.

Further, a shift in the understanding of corruption was underway during the period from 1650 to 1755. The prestige of the royal law grew slowly, dimming the legal plurality, including those rules justifying dubious conduct. Performance and skills rivaled descent, dealing a blow to the idea of innate corruption. By the mid-eighteenth century, the idea of corruption began to refer to the violation of royal rules of public offices for self-benefit. Judicial corruption was expanding into administrative corruption that encompassed the entire bureaucracy.

This shift in justice explains the bitter fighting at the Spanish court about selling judicial appointments. The aristocracy, the senior clergy, and the jurists of the great Councils and *audiencias* lost political ground in the late seventeenth century. Reformers in Madrid and elsewhere struck alliances with social newcomers, including middling groups drawn from commerce, banking, and the lower bureaucracy. The privileged elites attacked these newcomers as unworthy, because they lacked the inherent qualities to resist judicial crimes. Selling appointments to these groups corrupted the judiciary, in their view. Yet that argument said little about the actual skills and performance of the purchasers. This was one reason why the widespread discourse on flawed social credentials lost credibility in the late seventeenth century. In 1675, the crown cracked open the doors to the judiciary by selling the appointments of the *alcaldes mayores* of New Spain. Queen Mariana of Austria and her ministers began offering these appointments in Madrid to increase supervision over the *alcaldes mayores* and appropriate funds. The policy also weakened the viceroys, who almost always hailed from the aristocracy and appointed most *alcaldes mayores* in exchange for cash or other services. The process was not linear, as conservative coalitions curbed the sale when they acceded to power. Yet the sale continued, and the crown clipped viceregal patronage power by over 50 percent, if not more.

---

[1] Foucault, *Discipline and Punish. The Birth of the Prison* (New York: Random House, 1995), 82–89. See also Cañeque, *Living Image*, 182. Foucault conceived his brilliant ideas in the 1970s by drawing predominantly on French or Western archives, and historians need to reassess his ideas critically.

This pervasive sale of judicial appointments in Madrid did not hamper justice or the empire as a whole, as historians have traditionally argued. There is little evidence that the purchasers were more corrupt than their predecessors, if understood as diverging from the royal law. Instead of crippling the empire, the sale of appointments was part of yet another reform cycle intensifying – not necessarily centralizing – royal power. Francisco Garzarón's 1719 verdict against the *audiencia* judges buttresses this view. He dismissed about as many purchasers as those who had obtained their posts for their merits and services to the community. The Council of the Indies confirmed his verdicts, because the king, the Council, or Garzarón never deliberately attempted to root out the purchasers. Neither did they take aim at those born in the Americas or the appointees from the previous Habsburg dynasty. My argument contributes therefore to the ongoing historiographical reevaluation of weakening royal power, or the Spanish empire as a whole, in the later seventeenth century. That period was neither staid nor stagnant and neither was the early eighteenth century. These two periods, in fact, laid the groundwork for later reforms, such the introduction of regional intendants by the secretary of the Indies, José de Gálvez, in 1786.

The drifting values of justice also contributed to a growing number of Native lawsuits over the *repartimiento* in the late seventeenth century. The *repartimiento* trade usually referred to the commerce of *alcaldes mayores* who loaned Natives cash, which the Indians repaid with agricultural goods. Indians often succeeded in the lawsuits, because they had relatively easy access to courts and representation. In addition, the judges of both the Indian court and the *audiencia* in Mexico City knew the legal precepts of corruption and applied them. Theologians, for example, still assailed loaning cash with interest as sinful usury. The complainants also claimed that they were miserable Indians whom the *alcalde mayor* had forced to buy goods at excessive prices. If the court agreed that the *alcalde mayor* had injured the Natives in the commercial contract, it could rule for the *restitutio in integrum* (restitution in its entirety) that protected the miserable people. Both parties then had to restore all goods to the original owners, while the *alcalde mayor* could even forfeit the loans he had given to the Natives. This could ruin an *alcalde mayor*. Claiming force under these circumstances did, therefore, not usually mean that the *alcaldes mayores* sold luxury goods from China or France at the barrel of a gun. Instead, litigation often indicated that the *alcalde mayor* and Natives could not agree on the terms of repaying the cash loans. The legal arsenal frequently gave the Indians the tools to ward off excessively unfavorable terms for the *repartimiento*.

The decreasing prices of the precious dyestuff cochineal contributed to the multiplying lawsuits against the *repartimiento*. The indigenous population grew again after the calamitous post-conquest collapse. Labor costs declined, and the production of cochineal rose. Global competition depressed the value of cochineal too. As a result, the inflation-adjusted price of cochineal dropped in the late seventeenth and throughout the eighteenth centuries. The Natives sought to stem the tide by challenging these losses in court. At the same time, the *alcaldes mayores* negotiated payments for agricultural goods to an extent, just as other power relations in the old regime. They built alliances with indigenous nobles and other leaders of the districts to operate the *repartimiento*, because the *alcaldes mayores* lacked the power to force entire regions to work against their will. An *alcalde mayor* and his alliance occasionally hampered competition and manipulated prices excessively. The unfair negotiation over local prices and the sinking value of cochineal caused conflicts that carried over into the courts.

By the mid-eighteenth century, the standards for assessing the *repartimiento* had shifted. The Viceroy Count of Revillagigedo (1746–1755) and the Marquis of la Ensenada (1743–1754), first minister of the monarchy, cared little about innately corrupt *alcaldes mayores* or the sinful nature of credit. Instead, Ensenada suggested a state monopoly to gather and ship all cochineal from New Spain to Spain, akin to the tobacco monopoly that he set up in Peru. Revillagigedo insisted on more competition to the *repartimiento* and fostering loans to raise cochineal production. He and Ensenada agreed on legalizing the *repartimiento* trade and creating local price schedules. Their aim was to assess the sales tax and help Natives to challenge excessive manipulations and curb price drops. The price caps failed, but their actions probably enhanced *alcabala* (sales tax) revenue and lowered gains for both *alcaldes mayores* and the indigenous producers, to an extent. When later generations of Indians objected to the *repartimiento*, they did so because of rising tax pressure, declining cochineal value, and below-market prices offered by the *alcaldes mayores*.

WRITING THE HISTORY OF CORRUPTION: METHODS, SOURCES, AND HISTORIOGRAPHY

This book seeks to fathom the change from judicial to administrative corruption by studying the ways early modern commoners, commentators, and ministers labeled bribery or giving presents to judges and officials. Where did these people draw the boundaries among licit and illicit practices? What were the consequences for suspects charged with breaching the limitations of corruption or fraud? What was the role of the rising bourgeois groups that gained on the aristocracy and the graduates of the prestigious *colegios mayores*? And finally, how did the law and the economy affect the discussion over the *repartimiento*?

Studying the arguments advanced by the queen, her ministers, and the great Councils in Madrid answers these questions. Jurists and theologians wrote treatises, and the judges and lower echelons of the *audiencia* also discussed corruption. Notaries or procurators often cast corruption, fraud, or theft in a way to deflect the charges against them. In addition, Garzarón's *visita* provided popular groups with a stage to discuss injuries they had committed or experienced themselves. Indians, *mulatas*, coach-builders, and others incriminated flawed ministers. Their combined expressions clarify the semantic bandwidth of the word corruption and helped to separate the crime from fraud, theft, and other illegalities. Admittedly, given the choice of primary sources, these discussions occurred predominantly in a juridical context. Procurators, notaries, or jurists often guided or shaped the questions and the testimonies to be useful for the judicial process. But these are often the best sources for studying colonial corruption from various perspectives, and this approach contributes to a growing research trend on popular justice and notarial culture. It is also a rare foray – at least within anglophone scholarship – into the operations of legal arguments in criminal prosecutions such as the *visita*. I have tried to flesh out the meaning of the early modern law – itself a vast research field – by exploring how judges and litigants employed the legal concepts in the courts and in the *visita* within the social and intellectual backdrop of the time.

This book covers roughly one century of corruption, beginning in the middle of the seventeenth century and ending just after 1750. In 1650, the debate about selling appointments still roiled in the empire following the first sales of treasury appointments by the chief minister Count-Duke of Olivares (in office 1621–1643). In 1675, the crown began offering appointments of the *alcaldes mayores* in the Americas, triggering yet another round of bitter recriminations. The book continues until the mid-eighteenth century, straddling the transition from the Habsburg to the Bourbon dynasty in 1700. The sale of appointments and the shifting values of justice transcended this transition, which adds nuance to the importance of the dynastic change. The period also includes Francisco Garzarón's remarkable *visita general* that produced dozens of volumes containing corruption and fraud charges and the suspects' defenses. Later

Conclusion: Approaching Historical Corruption 263

in 1750/51, the crown phased out the sale of judicial appointments. More obedient officials and judges appeared in the Americas, while Indians, *alcaldes mayores*, the viceroy, and the first minister yet again discussed reforming the *repartimiento*. For this reason, the end of the Count of Revillagigedo's viceroyalty in 1755 is a good point to conclude the analysis. A different government served in Madrid, and a new viceroy arrived in Mexico City. The debate shifted away, for a time, from curbing corruption.[2]

This project takes both a local and an imperial perspective. The aim is to elucidate the interconnections between the concerns of judges, officials, and popular groups in New Spain, the court in Madrid, and the judicial and theological discourses in Spain, and to a lesser degree in Portugal, France, and the Holy Roman Empire. The analysis places this book within Atlantic scholarship. At the same time, this book throws light on corruption outside of Mexico City. Pedro Sánchez Morcillo left the colonial capital to prosecute miscreants in Puebla, Tlaxcala, and Huejotzingo in 1715, for example. In addition, the conflict over the *repartimiento* played out mostly in the Oaxacan highlands, which adds a de-centered perspective to the book.

The sources for this study are as varied as the approaches, and they draw on fresh archival and bibliographical research in Mexico, Spain, Portugal, Germany, and the USA. The archival research homes in on four large fields: Garzaróns's *visita*, the *repartimento*, the sale of appointments of the *alcaldes mayores* in New Spain, and the published discourses on corruption and ideal judges. Garzarón's thirty-five trial volumes recorded the minutiae of the *visita general*, giving many insights into the abuses of jailers, notaries, and scribes, along with judges and prosecutors. Historians have not consulted these volumes before. Garzarón also compressed his annotated interrogations of the judges into two additional volumes, which scholars have reviewed. These volumes are located in the sections *Escribanía de Cámara* and *audiencia de México* of the Archive of the Indies, Seville, Spain (AGI). In addition, I traced the sales of judicial appointments, because I first needed to understand (and amend) the classical arguments on corruption before venturing on to new territories.

---

[2] On the dates, see J. H. Parry, *Sale of Public Office*, 49–58; Gómez Urdáñez, *Fernando VI*, 105–106, 111; Valle Menéndez, *Juan Francisco de Güemes*, 335–337, 630.

These papers are mostly in the section *audiencia de México* of the AGI. Some correspondence of the viceroys ended up in the Historical General Archive, Section Nobility in Toledo, Spain.[3]

Additional information, the long series of *reales cédulas* (royal communications), petitions to Garzarón, inquisition papers, some biographical information on officials and judges, and lawsuits over the judges' property are located in the General National Archive (AGN) in Mexico City. Its sections *Indios, Civil*, and *Indiferente Virreinal* also document the Native lawsuits over the *repartimiento*. The much-consulted folder *Subdelegados* 34 contains an abundance of mid-eighteenth-century reports on the *repartimiento* written by *alcaldes mayores*, their deputies, and priests. Furthermore, the family archive of the Counts of Revillagigedo provided valuable insights into the viceroy's informal communications. The Special Collections of the Library of the University of Florida, Gainesville, microfilmed the originals several years ago, although scholars have rarely studied them. Some correspondence is also scattered throughout archives in Guadalajara (Mexico) and the Latin American Library at Tulane.

Lastly, the archival record needed to be balanced against the legal and theological discourse. Many treatises are now online; others are dispersed in libraries in Mexico City, Madrid, Seville, Lisbon, Coimbra, New Orleans, Nashville, and Frankfurt (Germany). Early modern scholars wrote an abundance of texts in Latin, of which I have used a few. I originally started out by reading Pedro Portocarrero y Guzmán's *Theatro Monarchico* and scoured the sources that he quoted, which indicated their validity around 1700. These were Seneca, Cicero, Thomas Aquinas, Cajetan, Domingo de Soto, and Domingo Antunez Portugal, among others. Portocarrero y Guzmán and even some "miserable soldiers" from New Mexico also cited the French jurist Pierre Grégoire of Toulouse.[4] Pierre Grégoire, Antunez Portugal, Antonio Fernández de Otero, and others discussed the nature of corruption as well as the ideal and flawed judges and officials. Theologians such as Valentín de la Madre de Dios, Miguel de San Antonio, and Francisco Larraga explained the standards of negligence and guilt. In most questions of canon and civil law as it regards to court procedure, Juan de Hevia Bolaños's *Curia Filipica* and Pedro Murillo Velarde's *Cursus Iuris Canonici* proved indispensable.

---

[3] See AGI, Escribanía 278 A–289 B and AGI, México 670 A and B.
[4] Méndez, *Breve Memorial extracto*, Mexico City, 17 June 1720, AGI, Escribanía 282 D, fol. 458.

The challenges to demonstrate how *novohispanos* actually read these texts are formidable. Martín de Azpilcueta (1491/93–1586), for example, published his *Manual of Confessors* originally in Portuguese before it was translated into Spanish. Every subsequent edition featured new content, and this process continued even after his death. Multiple editions of his work traversed the Atlantic. The library of the Museum of Anthropology of Mexico City, for example, owns a few editions, among them Azpilcueta's *Manual* published in 1557. Azpilcueta claimed in this *Manual* that corruption violated the biblical seventh commandment against theft. It is a difficult task, however, to prove that *novohispanos* read this, or any other edition, in the same way in the late seventeenth and early eighteenth centuries, and few, if any, more recent editions of the book remain in Mexico to buttress this view. I also admit that Gabriel Berart y Gassol, a jurist from Barcelona, published his *Speculum visitationis secularis* (*Mirror of the Secular Visita*) in 1627, before the time frame of this book. Nonetheless, Berart y Gassol precisely defined the criminal offenses investigated by secular *visitas*. Garzarón did not mention him but never strayed far from his methods.[5]

Scholars have also long grappled with problems defining corruption. Political scientists, for instance, analyze self-interested violations of the public trust and the law of office, or they poll the public about these abuses. Corruption in these approaches consists of nepotism to provide jobs for less qualified friends and family, bribery of government employees, and other illicit forms of collusion with officials in exchange for benefits. More recently, the crime has come to include financial fraud in banking or other businesses.[6] Yet early modern ideas of malfeasance differed starkly from modern ones. Some scholars propose principal-agent models to avoid measuring the past against the yardstick of today. According to this model, an employer (principal) contracts officials (agents) to perform some work, while a third party (client) bribes the officials to bend the rules to his or her advantage. Such models lucidly

---

[5] Azpilcueta, *Manual de Confesores* (Salamanca: Andrea de Portonarijs, 1557).
[6] Steven David Morris and Charles H. Blake, eds., *Corruption and Politics in Latin America: National and Regional Dynamics* (Boulder, CO: Lynne Rienner Publications, 2010); Irma Eréndira Sandoval, ed., *Corrupción y Transparencia: Debatiendo las fronteras entre Estado, mercado y sociedad* (Mexico City: UNAM, 2009); John Gardiner, "Defining Corruption," in Heidenheimer and Johnston, *Political Corruption*, 25–38; James C. Scott, *Comparative Political Corruption* (Englewood Cliffs, NJ: Prentice-Hall, 1972), 3–4, 7–10; Michael Johnston, "The Search for Definitions: The Vitality of Politics and the Issue of Corruption," *International Social Science Journal* 48, no. 3 (1996): 321–335.

show the discrepancy between the official contracts and the actual results of bribery, but they run into their own problems. Early modern employers and officials, for example, did not always precisely hammer out the job expectations, and the multitude of norms did not clarify them either. In addition, the broad definition of principals and agents also includes fraud outside government or the judiciary, and this field lies beyond the scope of this book.[7]

The theoretical advances have also influenced historians, who have discussed the topic of corruption with great controversy. Among the first to insist on the contingency of corruption was the Dutch scholar Jacob van Klaveren. In the 1950s, he grasped that most participants in the Spanish transatlantic fleets regularly breached the royal law. Social groups such as the merchants only then complained about corruption when they felt excluded from the spoils. These two insights – the pervasive disregard for the royal law and the conflict among social groups over community benefits – has molded scholarship.[8] Subsequently, a "relativist" consensus

---

[7] Edward C. Banfield, "Corruption as a Feature of Governmental Organization," *Journal of Law and Economics* 18, no. 3 (1975): 587–605; Suter, "Korruption," 187–188; Peter Graeff, "Prinzipal-Agent-Klient-Modelle als Zugangsmöglichkeit zur Korruptionsforschung. Eine integrative und interdisziplinäre Perspektive," in Grüne and Slanička, *Korruption,* 55, 59, 68; Oskar Kurer, "Was ist Korruption? Der Stand der Diskussion um eine Definition von Korruption," in Kurer, *Korruption und Governance,* 49. Quiroz, *Corrupt Circles,* 9, 2–3, see also 6, argues that "corruption is not immutable and does not have the same effect in every temporal or spatial context," and defines the phenomenon as the "misuse of political-bureaucratic power by cliques of public officials, colluding with other self-serving interests, to obtain political and economic gain for purposes inimical to societal development purposes, through the misappropriation of public resources and the distortion of policies and institutions." Early modern historians will find clarifying these concepts challenging. Claudio Lomnitz, "Introducción," in Lomnitz, *Vicios públicos,* 15, also uses a broad definition that parallels fraud, since as "a cultural category corruption includes all the practices that seize on the contradictions or ambiguities of the normative system for personal profit."

[8] Jakob van Klaveren, "Corruption as a Historical Phenomenon," in Heidenheimer and Johnston, *Political Corruption,* 83–94; van Klaveren, "Die historische Erscheinung der Korruption, in ihrem Zusammenhang mit der Staats-und Gesellschaftsstruktur betrachtet," *Vierteljahresschrift für Sozial- und Wirtschaftsgeschichte* 45, no. 4 (1958): 292–294, 306–321; van Klaveren, "Die historische Erscheinung der Korruption. II. Die Korruption in den Kapitalgesellschaften, besonders in den Großen Handelskompanien, III. Die internationalen Aspekte der Korruption," *Vierteljahresschrift für Sozial- und Wirtschaftsgeschichte* 45, no. 4 (1958): 433–468, 469–504. Van Klaveren himself drew on James Scott, *Comparative Political Corruption,* 3–4, 7–10, 53, according to whom historians have been aware since the 1930s that corruption meant different things in different epochs, correlating with Marcel Maus's 1925 analysis of traditional gift-giving practices.

emerged, as historians of Latin America abandoned the straightforward institutionalist approaches in the late 1960s.[9] Scholars saw corruption increasingly as a matter of excess. In the 1970s, Stuart Schwartz held that community standards frequently refrained from censuring bribery or contraband trade, allowing local elites to gain a say in governance and justice. Other historians have insisted that corruption provided a flexible balance between local and crown interests.[10]

This view gained in influence as the awareness of powerful social networks grew in the 1970s and burgeoned in the 1990s. Academicians initially showed that historical actors did not always align with the assumed interests of their social groups, such as the aristocracy, the bureaucrats, or the commoners. Instead, the webs of patronage connected popular, middling, and elite classes. Historians conceived these webs as Procrustean frameworks that inexorably determined the actions of the embedded individuals. About ten years ago, scholars abandoned that rigidity when they realized the networks' substantial volatility. Historical actors, even in close-knit families, often pursued opposing goals, especially during contentious times such as the

---

[9] See Phelan, *Kingdom of Quito*; Burkholder and Chandler, "Creole Appointments," 187–206. Hespanha, *As vésperas de Leviathan. Instituções e Poder Político. Portugal Sec. XVII* (Lisbon: Hespanha, 1986), 8, proposed in 1986 departing from purely legal and institutionalist approaches to understand the "mechanisms of power as they were really lived," while in his 1993 chapter "Les autre raisons de la politique," 67, he argued that "the insufficiency of the official law and the formal judicial institutions to explain all means of power is now taken for granted."

[10] Schwartz, *Sovereignty and Society*, 181–182, 281, 325, 360–368. McFarlane, "Political Corruption," 46–47, see also 54–63, views corruption as a "scourge" for Indian communities and a way of co-opting elites to make government more tolerable. According to Jeremy Adelman, "Commerce and Corruption," in *Corrupt Histories. Studies in Comparative History*, eds. Emmanuel Kreike and William Chester Jordan (Rochester: University of Rochester Press, 2006), 452, "charges of monopoly and corruption were rhetorical means" to attack competitors. Bertrand, "Viejas preguntas, nuevos enfoques: la corrupción en la administración colonial española," in *El poder del dinero. Ventas de cargo y honores en el Antiguo Régimen*, eds. Andújar Castillo and Felices de la Fuente (Madrid: Biblioteca Nueva, 2011), 61–62, argues that corruption of the tax collection declined as negotiation ceded to authoritarianism. Noteworthy sixteenth-century studies include Luis Miguel Costa's Weberian analysis, "Patronage and Bribery in Sixteenth-Century Peru: The Government of Viceroy Conde del Villar and the Visita of Licentiate Alonso Fernández de Bonilla," (PhD diss., Florida International University, 2005), 1–22; Oswaldo Holguín Callo, *Poder, corrupción y tortura en el Perú de Felipe II. El Doctor Diego de Salinas (1558–1595)* (Lima: Fondo Editorial del Congreso del Perú, 2002). For Mary Lindemann, "Dirty Politics," 585, "corruption is situational." See also Linda Peck, *Court, Patronage*, 5, 195, 220. An overview of scholarship provide Alexandre Coello de la Rosa, Claudia Contente, and Martín Rodrigo y Alharilla, "Introducció: Corrupció, cobdícia i bé públic al món hispànic (segles XVIII–XX)," *Illes I Imperis* 16 (2014), 7–12. See also Introduction, note 11.

decades before independence. These early modern people sometimes shared competing patrons, and they joined, left, and straddled social networks.[11]

Scholars of this approach have tended to interpret corruption as excessive forms of legitimate small-scale politics, even to the point of denying the phenomenon altogether. Sharon Kettering argued in 1985, for example, that "corrupt activities were those that damaged the interests of the crown," including "embezzlement of state funds, forgery, and fraudulent accounting." Clientelism "was considered corrupt only when it resulted in the appointment of men of decidedly inferior ability because they were relatives, clients, or favorites."[12] Some recent scholars have pushed the argument further. Alejandro Cañeque has maintained that "most of the types of graft ... were not seen as illicit at the time," while Pierre Ragon holds that "contemporaries did not use the term 'corruption' when qualifying stigmatized practices." These three scholars have offered shrewd insights into clientelism, which is one facet of today's idea of corruption.[13] Yet clientelism did not yet typically form part of the early modern idea of corruption, because it rarely impinged on finding justice. Generalizing from the limited aspect of clientelism cannot fully elucidate historical corruption.

Colin MacLachlan has shaped the debate by arguing that corruption was a matter of excess, since people were only prosecuted for breaching accepted norms. Yet this view explains only so much, because it applies to many offenses, including modern ones, when corruption is the excess of a specific law. The argument does not completely illuminate the meaning of corruption charges and the thresholds for prosecution and punishment through the changing times. German scholar Jens Ivo Engels maintains that many dubious acts occurred in "a moral greyzone ..., which could be justified according to context."[14] This is certainly correct for many cases, but at least Garzarón used a fairly clear definition of corruption and fraud when punishing miscreants. Scholars approaching the subject have also relied too much on historical dictionaries, which are by nature

---

[11] See Chapter 1, note 66. Recent research on the individuals' leeway in these networks, see Bertrand, "Del actor a la red," 32–39; Evelyne Sanchez, "Introducción," in Sanchez, *Los actores locales de la nación*, 13–14. I myself stressed social networks in *Patrons, Partisans*.

[12] Kettering, *Patrons, Brokers*, 193, 203, see also 192–196, 203–205. Reinhard, *Freunde und Kreaturen*, separated corruption from clientelism in 1979. Reinhard, "Review" of *Geld–Geschenke–Politik*, eds. Engels, Fahrmeir, and Nützenadel, *Historische Zeitschrift* 290, no. 1 (2010): 141–142, argues that corruption was the excessive "variant of a ubiquitous and not a priori reproachable conduct that I call micro-politics."

[13] Ragon, "Abusivo o corrupto?," 277–278; Cañeque, *Living Image*, 177.

[14] Engels, "Politische Korruption," 39.

conservative and often shy away from tracking judicial or political developments.[15] The term *concusión* (violent extortion), for example, entered the dictionary of the Spanish Royal Academy in 1869. At first glance, the word seems an innovation to define a crime. Yet the jurist Castillo de Bobadilla discussed *concusión* much earlier, and he himself drew on the Roman term. In this case, and in others, the lack of lexical entries does not indicate that Spaniards had no knowledge of a crime or did not prosecute it.[16]

The absence of corruption in the early modern world would require that rules containing the conduct of judges or officials did not exist, or that these rules merely floated in space without relevance for the courts, *visitas*, judges, or Indians. But how can that be reconciled with Saint Bernard of Siena's 1425 sermon lambasting officials who exploited their subjects like locusts?[17] Similarly, in 1724, the Indians of Santiago Tecali (Puebla) accused their *alcalde mayor* of *baratería*, which their contemporaries understood as a close relative of corruption. What is more, by the time of the accusations, Garzarón and the Council of the Indies had removed thirteen judges for corruption. These instances demonstrate that doctrines of corruption and fraud existed, and the courts and commoners knew and applied at least parts of them.

For this reason, historians of early modern Europe now examine various aspects that we would call corruption today, such as nepotism and bribing politicians, and analyze how these facets played out in the past. They argue that court factions avenged their exclusion from patronage, and that popular classes toppled self-serving municipal authorities.[18] One scholar points out,

---

[15] To an extent, in Solange Alberro, "Control de la iglesia," 35, 41–45; on the problem of relying on dictionaries, Reinhart Koselleck, "Introduction and Prefaces to the *Geschichtliche Grundbegriffe*," trans. Michaela Richter, *Contributions to the History of Concepts* 6, no.1 (2011): 15.

[16] *Concusión* in Castillo de Bobadilla, *Politica*, book 2, chap. 11, para. 69, letter l, and book 5, chap. 1, para. 207; see also *Concusio* in Berart y Gassol, *Speculum visitationis*, chap. 17, para. 8. Another example is *peculado* or *peculato*, which does not appear in Castillo de Bobadilla's *Politica*, and only in the *RAE* (1737) p. 179, and in Domingo Valcárcel y Formento to Count of Revillagigedo, Mexico City, 22 Jan. 1753, AGI, México 1350; the term is older, notwithstanding, as the *lex Iulia de peculatu et pecunia residua* in Digest 48.13 defined the offense.

[17] Isenmann, "Rector est Raptor," 213.

[18] Feros, *Kingship and Favoritism*, 140, 163–188; Quiroz, *Corrupt Circles*, 2–6, 9, 36–37, 59–81, has rejected the "relativistic interpretation" of "extremely cautious historians." See also Bellingradt, "Organizing Public Opinion," 553–566; Waquet, *Corruption. Ethics*, 12; Engels, "Politische Korruption," 38–41; on the Spanish empire, Villa-Flores, "Archivos y falsarios," 38; Andújar Castillo, "Cuando el rey delegaba la gracia,"

for instance, that the popes in Rome often lived by high-minded virtues while they encouraged their nephews to ransack the state.[19] Judicial pluralism plausibly explains how people could live within this normative tension, although such juxtaposition rarely existed in early eighteenth-century New Spain. Instead, this book provides evidence that *novohispanos* were more concerned with fathoming the boundaries of corruption and fraud. In addition, a few historians have traced the historical meaning of the term *corruption*. Marivonne Génaux, for example, shows that early modern French literati understood corruption as the "set of unjust deeds committed by the holders of supreme public offices." In addition, Carlos Garriga studies published Latin treatises to add that corrupt judges usually took money or gifts to distort sentences.[20] Both historians have contributed decisively to the discussion, yet I nevertheless favor a wider understanding of historical corruption as obstructing the finding of justice, which also applied to lower judges and even non-judges under some circumstances.

This historiographical sketch also hints at the importance of interdisciplinary work. Cultural and intellectual historians have opened many paths to understanding the values of the past. Similarly, legal scholars have traced the history of judicial ideas and sometimes the quotidian operations of the courts. Yet these scholars often neglect communicating with the other schools of thought. Historians of Latin America working in the USA, Latin America, or Europe are not always fully aware what their colleagues abroad are working on. Similar things could be said for early modern Europeanists who tackle comparable phenomena. All of them have innovated ideas in the field, and I have drawn on their cultural, political, and legal perspectives to elucidate the speech and actions of popular and elite groups in various settings.

Scholars have, over various generations, also cautioned against adopting teleological perspectives and imposing our current views onto the past. This call has sharpened our perception, undermining, for example, the view of logical and invariable transitions from empires to nation-states.[21] Yet historians should equally guard against "downstreaming" phenomena from the

---

135–156; Ponce-Leiva, "Percepciones sobre la corrupción," 193–211; Andreas Suter, "Korruption," 187–214.

[19] Thiessen, "Korruption," 95–97.

[20] Génaux, "Social Sciences," 21; Génaux, "Fields of Vision," 107–121; Garriga, "Crimen corruptionis," 22–25.

[21] Ragnhild Marie Hatton, Robert Oresko, G. C. Gibbs, and Hamish M. Scott, introduction to *Royal and Republican Sovereignty in Early Modern Europe: Essays in Memory of Ragnhild Hatton*, eds. Ragnhild Marie Hatton, Robert Oresko, G. C. Gibbs, and

Conclusion: Approaching Historical Corruption   271

past by ignoring palpable change. Social networks, for example, governed the everyday lives of early modern humans. They often delayed or deflected verdicts against miscreants and impunity was rampant. Yet to assume that social networks exclusively shaped the human experience turns a blind eye to all other determining factors. The law, economy, faith, habits, rituals, personal convictions, and other cultural elements influenced human decisions, and the state played an ever-larger role. Competing ideas of corruption thrived within this complexity between 1650 and 1755, as the modern notion of violating rules of office for self-interest was just emerging.

Conceptual history has also been helpful. Starting in the 1970s, Reinhart Koselleck traced the changing key concepts of early modern European social and political organization. In his view, a concept is a word of significance that covers a field of meaning and contains various ideas. For example, the concept *corruption* referred to various forms of judicial abuse but also to sexual impurity and polluted nature in general. Unearthing these multiple meanings of a concept is called semasiology. Koselleck used that approach to track the concept's connotations over time and argued that some of its content went moribund, some persisted, and new ideas seeped in. Meanwhile, onomasiology grasps the various terms that contributed to an idea. Onomasiology asks which words Spaniards used to express the idea of judicial abuse? The sources reveal *cohecho* (bribery) or *concusión* (extortion), among others, and these terms vary over time, regions, and languages. Koselleck also posited that following a concept through the transition from the old regime of the mid-eighteenth century to the modern world casts light on a "threshold period" of human experience. The aristocracy, jurists, and the learned lost their almost exclusive monopoly on the political debate at that time. The lower social groups joined the conversation in droves, while an outpouring of publications coined new words in baffling numbers. Koselleck and his collaborators gleaned these semantic changes from state documents and everyday sources, such as pamphlets, diaries, and letters.[22]

Koselleck set a milestone, and combining semasiology and onomasiology has helped to flesh out the historical concept of corruption in this book.

Hamish M. Scott (Cambridge: Cambridge University Press, 1997), 5; Grafe, *Distant Tyranny*, 36; Burbank and Cooper, *Empires in World History*, 2–3, 9.

[22] Koselleck, "Introduction and Prefaces," 8–22. For Koselleck, "Historia de los conceptos y conceptos de historia" trans. Javier Fernández de Sebastián and Gonzalo Capellán de Miguel, *Ayer* 53, no. 1 (2004): 40–42, the Marxian view that reality shaped language and Haydn White's argument that language shaped reality have both stimulated the analysis. See also Koselleck, *Futures Past. On the Semantics of Historical Time*, trans. and ed.

Yet I stopped short of prolonging the analysis into the period beyond 1750, precisely with the aim to show that important changes were already underway in the social and legal culture. Latin Americanists also shift the focus away from Europe and probe untapped primary sources. They no longer believe that the popular classes contributed little to debates before 1750. The sources for this book, too, include ample judicial sources revealing the voices of commoners. Moreover, Quentin Skinner and others have suggested further contextualizing the strategic uses of concepts in discourse. In this sense, I have attempted to analyze how Spaniards employed and repudiated corruption charges in a variety of imperial and local settings. I have sketched a wide framework of justice and corruption, including the shifting intellectual background, the doctrines of crimes, fraud, and other malfeasance, the prosecutions, and the daily experiences of common people. I have also paid much attention to the underlying political conflicts and the economic underpinnings of the discussions over corruption.[23]

Hopefully, this book contributes to a renewed conversation over justice, corruption, and concepts. The mega-project *Iberconceptos*, for example, has set out to fathom the diverse meanings of key terms within the Iberian World. Scholars will also find vast and open fields of analysis on how criminal law in general, and corruption and fraud in particular, developed over time, and how the lower and upper courts of the Spanish and other Atlantic empires applied the doctrines. This project has thrown light on some aspects of these intriguing approaches. Much remains to be done.

Keith Tribe (New York: Columbia University Press, 2004), 81–92; Koselleck, *The Practice of Conceptual History: Timing History, Spacing Concepts* (Stanford, CA: Stanford University Press, 2002); and the original conceptual lexicon by Otto Brunner, Werner Conze, and Reinhart Koselleck, eds., *Geschichtliche Grundbegriffe. Historisches Lexikon zur politisch-sozialen Sprache in Deutschland* (Stuttgart: Klett-Cotta, 1978).

[23] Quentin Skinner, "On Intellectual History and the History of Books," *Contributions to the History of Concepts* 1, no 1 (2005): 29–36, 34; Quentin Skinner and Javier Fernández Sebastián, "Intellectual History, Liberty and Republicanism: An Interview with Quentin Skinner," *Contributions to the History of Concepts* 3, no. 1 (2007), critiqued that Koselleck traced the history of words rather than contextual ideas whose terminology even changed, while overestimating the French Revolution. In addition, according to Melvin Richter, "A Note on the Text of Reinhart Koselleck: 'Offene Fragen an die Geschichtlichen Grundbegriffe,'" *Archiv für Begriffsgeschichte* 54 (2012): 251–252, John Pockock suggested studying synchronic discourses instead of diachronic concepts. Practitioners of the Iberian world have pragmatically integrated both argumentative strands, see Javier Fernández Sebastián, ed., *Diccionario político y social del mundo iberoamericano: Conceptos políticos fundamentales, 1770–1870*, *Iberconceptos* 2 (Madrid: Universidad del País Vasco, 2014).

Appendix

TABLE 6 *Verdicts against Ministers in Garzarón's Visita Suspended Judges and Prosecutors*

	Name of judge or prosecutor	Dates of appointment and taking office	Charges	Penalty	Price of purchased appointment	Origins	University	Spouse/family
			Civil Chamber (*Sala civil*)					
1	Francisco Miguel Antonio Valenzuela Venegas y Esquivel*	Born 1660; since 1687 minister in Guatemala; since 7 May 1696 *oidor* (civil judge) in Mexico City; on 12 Dec. 1719 dean; died 14 Mar. 1721	Bribery	2,000 ps, barred from judicial service	No evidence of *beneficio* (purchased appointment)	Madrid, Spain		Estefanía de Ortega; his father was a councilor of the Indies; Juan José Veytia y Linage witnessed taking the habit
2	Dr. Juan Díaz de Bracamonte	Since 16 Aug. 1706 supernumerary (supern.); taking office on 16 Sept. 1707	Embezzlement of c. 390,000 ps; accepted bribes up to 8,000 ps	Barred	1,000 doubloons	New Spain	Mexico City	Priest, owner of the *Rayas* mine; bankruptcy in 1708; since 1724 precentor in Puebla
3	Félix González de Agüero	31 Aug. 1708	Embezzlement, bribery	4,000 ps, barred, owed 20,800 ps in indemnity	1,000 doubloons	Fuenmayor, Calahorra, España		License to marry in 1712 for 1,500 ps

(*continued*)

4	Antonio Terreros y Ochoas	14 Dec. 1710; died in 1721	Bribery	His death precluded a sentence of the Council of the Indies, but his estate had to pay the *visita* costs	Probably 2,000 ps	New Spain	Mexico City	
5	Dr. Agustín Franco de Toledo	23 Dec. 1710; was ill during the *visita*	Bribery	1,000 ps, barred	8,000 ps *escudos*	New Spain	Mexico City	Gertrudis de la Peña; he also loaned money to Rayas mine
6	Félix Suárez de Figueroa	20 July 1716 supern.; died in 1725	Bribery, accepted cash to appoint deputy commissioners of the land-grant commission	4,000 ps, barred; the crown lowered fine to 2,000 ps, and in 1724 allowed his appeal and reinstated him posthumously in 1725	Services of his family during War of the Succession	Spain	Spain	Teresa de Aranda
7	Tristán Manuel Rivadeneira Luna y Arellano	26 Apr. 1710; demoted to Guadalajara in 1715	"Head of the Creole party," embezzlements during commission in San Luis Potosí	500 ps penalty and 5,000 ps restitution of embezzled moneys	14,000 ps	Puebla	Mexico City	License to marry; owned entailed estate on San Francisco Street in Mexico City

(continued)

TABLE 6 (*continued*)

	Name of judge or prosecutor	Dates of appointment and taking office	Charges	Penalty	Price of purchased appointment	Origins	University	Spouse/family
8	José Antonio de Espinosa Ocampo y Cornejo	26 Nov. 1699 *fiscal del crimen* (criminal prosecutor); in Nov. 1701 *fiscal de lo civil* (civil prosecutor); then promoted to civil judge	Bribery, gifts from the *consulado*	6,000 ps, barred		Salamanca	Alcalá de Henares	Married
			Criminal Chamber (*sala del crimen*)					
9	Juan Francisco de la Peña y Flores	5 Sep. 1708	Bribery, illicit friendships, gambling	500 ps	3,000 doubloons	Mexico City		*Novohispana* wife
10	Agustín de Robles Lorenzana	In Dec. 1708 supern.		1,000 ps	9,000 ps	Canary Islands	San Marcos de Lima	Had license to marry
11	Diego Francisco de Castañeda	On 5 Mar. 1711 / 27 Apr. 1712 supern.	Bribery	1,000 ps	8,000 + 5,000 ps	Mexico City	Mexico City	
12	Pedro Sánchez Manuel Alcaraz (or Alcázar) Morcillo	6 Dec. 1711	Extortions, bribes, fraud	8,000 ps, jailed, barred	9,000 ps	Michoacan	Mexico City	María Teresa de Aramburu y Vilches, Mexico City; in 1730, he was appointed as prebendary in Guadalajara

(*continued*)

13	Francisco de Oyanguren	18 Aug. 1710 criminal prosecutor; interim civil judge		4 000 ps, barred	2,000 doubloons	Mexico City	Owner of the hacienda San Blas, Tlaxcala

Absolved Ministers

	Name of judge or prosecutor	Dates of appointment and taking office	Charges	Price of purchased appointment?	Origins	University	Spouse/family
1	José Joaquín de Uribe Castejón Medrano	29 Dec. 1702	Excessive family obligations in New Spain		Jerez de la Frontera	Salamanca	License in 1706/1715 to marry Micaela María de Sandoval y Caballero, heiress in Tlaxcala, for 2,000 ps
2	Jerónimo de Soria Velásquez, Marquis of Villahermosa de Alfaro	1 Sep. 1706; died in 1740	Ditto	*Beneficio* probable	Pátzcuaro	Mexico City	Son of landholders; license to marry in 1705
3	Juan de Oliván y Rebolledo	In 1710 supern.; on 19 Jun. 1715 full appointment; died in 1738	"Head of the Creole party"	1,000 doubloons + 9,000 ps	Coatepec, Veracruz	Mexico City	Son of landholders; married Rosaria Dosal Híjar of Madrid, then Juliana de la Campa Cos

(*continued*)

			Sala de crimen			
4	A. Nicolás Chirino Vandeval	Born in 1664; civil judge in Santo Domingo; on 6 Feb. 1710 supern. in Mexico City; on 23 Nov. 1716 full appointment; died 3 Oct. 1726	Released 29 prisoners	5,000 ps *escudos* or 7,000 silver ps	Havana	Mexico City	Clara María Palazián of Mexico City; Chirino's family allegedly lived in "extreme poverty"
5	Juan de la Beguellina y Sandoval	Supern. on 15 Oct. 1711; died 1736	Released 36 prisoners	8,000 ps *escudos*	Mexico City	Mexico City	Married Águeda María Martínez de Solís y Gatica of Mexico City; his parents owned entailed estate in Puebla
6	Francisco Barbadillo Victoria	Born 1675; on 5 Dec. 1712 supern.; died ca. 1727	Released prisoners	2,000 ps	Escaray, Burgos	Valladolid	License to marry in 1716 for 3,000 ps; in 1723 married Juana Bolio of Mérida (Yucatan), widow of ex-governor of Manila

(*continued*)

Ministers without sentence

Name	Dates of appointment and taking office	Charge	Penalty	Price of purchased appointment	Origins	University	Spouse/family
Miguel Calderón de la Barca	Born 27 Dec. 1652; in 1692 civil judge; in 1707 councilor of the Indies; took office in 1709; died in 1716	Bribes up to 2,000 ps, illegal commerce, head of the "sacred league" of peninsular Spaniards	Passed away before sentence	12,000 ps, and 14,000 ps for the Council seat	Spain	Spain	Ana Josefa de Pividal
Juan Picado Pacheco (or Montero)	In 1703 prosecutor in Guadalajara; legal adviser of Viceroy Marquis of Valero; in 1721 civil judge in Mexico City; died 1740	Excessive reimbursements	Had to restore 29,347 ps, which Council lowered to 8,760 ps		Hoyos, Spain	Salamanca/Ávila	

Abbreviations: ps: pesos; supern.: supernumerary; the * indicates that Burkholder and Chandler do not list this judge

Sources: Burkholder and Chandler, *Dictionary of Audiencia Ministers*, 21, 34–35, 77, 97, 101, 112, 141, 240–241, 257, 262, 286–287, 291, 325; Burkholder and Chandler, *From Impotence to Authority*, 29, note 49, 39–40, 210–217; Burkholder and Chandler excluded Valenzuela Venegas for having been appointed before the time span under consideration; Barrientos Grandon "Guía prosopográfica," 191–192, 289–90, 343–344, 444–445, 457, 496–497, 636–637, 1044–1045, 1087–1088, 1130–1131, 1267–1268, 1354–1355, 1421–1422, 1430, 1452–1455, 1484–1485, 1515, 1558; del Arenal Fenochio, "La Justicia civil ordinaria," 48–50; Jaime González Rodríguez, "La condición del intelectual en México. Los juristas mexicanos en las audiencias de Nueva España entre 1600 y 1711," *Revista Complutense de Historia de América* 34 (2008): 173–179; Escamilla, "Oliván Rebolledo," 118–120; Rosenmüller, *Patrons, Partisans*, 180–187; AGN, Indiferente Virreinal 734, exp. 40; razon de los Oydores, AGI, México 377; *consulta* of the Council of the Indies, Madrid, 12 July 1720, AGI, México 379; *consulta* of the Council of the Indies, 2 Sept. 1721, AGI, México 380; *real acuerdo*, Mexico City, 15 Nov. 1725; *consultas* of the Council of the Indies, Madrid, 14 Jan. 1727 and 13 May 1728, AGI, México 381; *consultas* of the Council of the Indies, Madrid, 18 Jan. 1730, and 2 Dec. 1734, AGI, México 382; *consulta* of the Council of the Indies, Madrid, 13 Nov. 1721; Alburquerque to king, Mexico City, 17 Sept. 1705, Mexico City, AGI, México 477, exp. 33, fols. 382–385; Casafuerte to king, Mexico City, 10 Nov. 1723, AGI, México 491; Garzarón to king, Mexico City, 3 Aug. 1720, Mexico City, 7 Aug. 1724; *consultas* of the Council of the Indies, 18 Jan. 1726 and 14 Jan. 1727, AGI, México 670 A; taking of office, AGI, México 670 B; individual charges against Uribe, AGI, México 670 B, fol. 87; nómina de los Ex.mos S.res Presidentes by José Sánchez and Francisco Leri, no place, 1716, AGI, Escribanía 278 A; sentences of the Council of the Indies, Madrid, 23 Sept. 1721, and 7 July 1725, AGI, Escribanía 1183; *relación* by order of Ensenada, Madrid, 31 Mar. 1746, AGI, Indiferente General 1847, fol. 122 v; see also Rosenmüller, "El grave delito de … corrupcion." La visita de la audiencia de México (1715–1727) y las repercusiones internas de Utrecht," in Escamilla, *Resonancias imperiales*, 105–113. Javier Sanchiz, UNAM, kindly provided the information on the spouse/ family rubric on judge Valenzuela Venegas.

TABLE.7 *The Eleven Dismissed* Audiencia *Officials*

	Name and office	Charges	Date of sentence
1	Procurator and notary Juan García de Xismeros	Fraud	18 Mar. 1727
2	Notary Manuel de la Torre	Fraud, ignored *audiencia* orders, failed to submit papers, released inmates without orders	18 Mar. 1727
3	Notary and deputy in the intestate office Nicolás Moreno	Fraud by forging the signature of a bondsman on a sales deed, which deprived the heirs of 1,602 ps	14 Dec. 1726; charges against Moreno, AGI, Escribanía 289 A, fols. 1458, 1478–1487
4	Notary Feliciano Ulloa y Sevilla	Fraud, illegalities, jailed people without orders, theft	18 Mar. 1727
5	Notary of the land-grant commission Pedro Robledo	Took bribes to sell appointments for deputy commissioners	23 Sep. 1721
6	Interim fine collector and deputy notary of the provincial court Juan José Aguilera	Served as interim fine collector without paying the crown rent, excessive fees, failed to record fines	15 Mar. 1727
7	Deputy receptor Juan Antonio de Alegría	"Unduly obtained 100 pesos for some work during confiscations" and other charges; he was ordered to cease working	18 Mar. 1727
8	Deputy notary Diego Ignacio de la Rocha	Confiscations and illegalities; excessive fees; he was ordered to cease working	18 Mar. 1727
9	Deputy receptor Diego Félix de Valdes	Confiscations and illegalities; excessive fees; he was ordered to cease working	18 Mar. 1727

(*continued*)

TABLE.7 (*continued*)

	Name and office	Charges	Date of sentence
10	Deputy receptor Francisco Arellano	Excessive fees, examined witnesses without a notary; he was ordered to cease working	18 Mar. 1727
11	Deputy notary and receptor Luis Ortega	He was ordered to cease working as deputy notary until examined by *audiencia*	18 Mar. 1727

Sources: unless otherwise noted, sentence of the Council of the Indies, Madrid, date given in column, all documents in AGI, Escribanía 1183. The crimes are translated as *falsedad/* fraud; *falsificación/* forgery; *ilegalidad/* illegality. The officials with the numbers 1–5 owned their positions and the Council ordered their *privación* (removal). The Council also ordered *privación* of the interim official with the number 6, while officials 7–11 served as deputies and had to cease working.

Glossary

Acordada. Special judicial commission.
aguja. insect that feeds on cochineal.
alcabala. A sales tax.
alcalde de crimen. A criminal judge of the *audiencia*.
alcalde mayor. A first-instance judge and administrator of a district; in some parts also known as a *corregidor*.
alcalde ordinario. A first-instance magistrate of a municipal council.
alcayde de entradas. The jailer or *carcelero*.
alguacil. A constable.
alguacil mayor de corte. The senior constable who supervised the palace jail.
altepetl. An ethnic polity.
ambitus. The Roman prohibition to dispense gifts during election campaigns.
Antequera. The colonial name for the city of Oaxaca.
arbitrio. The good judgment of a judge to rule fairly.
asesor letrado. Legal advisor of the viceroy.
atole. A drink made of corn and hot water.
audiencia. The high or appeals court that reviewed civil and criminal cases.
auditor de guerra. A viceregal lawyer for military jurisdiction, often an *audiencia* minister.
baratería. An offense similar to corruption.
beneficio. The royal appointment to an office in exchange for cash or credit.

benemérito. An important member of society.
Board of Trade. See *casa de contratación.*
cabecera. A principal *pueblo* of a district and sometimes the seat of an *alcalde mayor.*
cabildo. A council. The *cabildo civil* was a municipal council, whereas the *cabildo eclesiástico* (or in the archdiocese, the *cabildo metropolitano*) was the cathedral chapter.
cacique. An ethnic lord.
calpolli. A sub-unit of an *altepetl.*
cámara de Indias. A committee of the Council of the Indies that suggested candidates for office.
canon law. The law of the Church.
carcelero. Jailer.
casa de contratación. The Board of Trade in Seville, and since 1717 in Cádiz, Spain that supervised the trade with the Americas.
cédula. See *real cédula.*
chief minister. The first or prime minister who served the king or queen in Madrid; sometimes also called favorite.
china/o. A person of Asian descent.
cochineal. A precious red dyestuff.
cohecho. Bribery.
colegio mayor. A study hall. The six most prestigious *colegios mayores* in Castile were associated with the universities of Salamanca, Valladolid, and Alcalá in Spain. There was also the *colegio mayor* of Saint Mary of All Saints in Mexico City.
colegial mayor. A university student or graduate who belonged to a *colegio mayor.*
comadre or compadre. Co-parenthood, that is, the family bond established between parents and their children's godmother/father.
comisión or *juzgado de tierras baldías.* The land-grant commission.
composition. A private compensation paid to victims or their family in a criminal trial.
concusión. Often understood as violent extortion.
consulado. The merchant guild; one each was located in Mexico City, Lima, and Seville/Cádiz.
consulta. A judicial verdict submitted to the king or another authority.
Council of the Indies. The Council in Madrid acted as highest appeals court and advised the king on American affairs.
corregidor. A district judge akin to an *alcalde mayor.*
corrupción. Corruption.

corruptela. Another word for corruption.//
Cortes. The Castilian parliament of estates.//
coyote. An offspring of *mestizos* and Natives in the racial imaginary.//
Creoles. The long-time residents of Spanish descent in the Americas.//
culpa. Culpa leve can be translated as ordinary negligence, *culpa grave* as gross negligence, while *gravísima culpa* included the intention to commit a crime.//
dolo. Malicious intent.//
don/doña. The honorific address in the name indicated nobility.//
encomendero. A recipient of Indian tribute.//
escribano. A notary.//
falsedad. Fraud.//
fiscal. A prosecutor. *Fiscales de lo civil* of the *audiencia* handled civil matters, while the *fiscal del crimen* presented criminal cases. The Inquisition prosecutor was also known as *fiscal*.//
fray. Literally brother, a member of a regular order.//
fuero. A set of regional laws and privileges.//
futura. The title to serve an office once it vacated.//
Granada, new kingdom of. Viceroyalty from 1717 to 1723 and 1739 onward, comprising modern Colombia, Venezuela, and Ecuador.//
grande. A grandee or member of the highest echelon of the titled aristocrats.//
hacendado. An owner of an hacienda or landed estate.//
hidalgo. A member of the lower nobility or gentry.//
hidalguía. The lower nobility.//
huipil. A Native embroidered blouse or shift.//
intendant. An *intendente* or royal provincial governor established in 1786.//
informe. A report.//
Ius commune. The intertwined Roman and Church laws and their legal interpretations.//
juicio de residencia. The review of official conduct at the end of an official's tenure.//
junta. An ad hoc committee.//
laesio enormis. A legal doctrine that allowed dissolving sales contracts.//
land grant commission. See *comisión* or *juzgado de tierras baldías*.//
Law of Castile. The *Recopilación de las leyes de estos reynos* or the royal law of Castile published in 1567.//
Law of the Indies. The *Recopilación de leyes de los reynos de las Indias* or the royal law for the Americas published in 1680.

league. A Castilian league which measured about 2.6 miles/ 4.22 km.

limpieza de sangre. Purity of the blood, that is, the proof that a Christian family had allegedly not intermarried with people of other races or faiths.

macehual. An Indian commoner.

maravedí. A coin; 34 *maravedís* were the equivalent of one *real*.

marrano. A derogatory word for the descendants of non-Christians; also referring to pigs.

media anata. A tax of half of an annual salary payable by all those accepting a crown office.

mestizo. Offspring of Natives and Spaniards in the racial imaginary.

miserable person. A person who belonged to a group of people that were subject to special rights and restrictions, such as Natives, minors, or the poor.

mulata/o. A woman/ man of mixed African descent.

New Spain. Colonial Mexico.

nao. The galleon shuttling annually between Manila and Acapulco.

novohispana/o. Referring to New Spain (colonial Mexico) and its residents.

oidor. A civil judge on the *audiencia*.

ordenanza. Founding instructions.

paisano. Person who shares the same regional background as someone else.

parcialidad. A Native neighborhood.

parecer. A legal opinion, usually written by a prosecutor for a council or the king.

pesquisa. A criminal investigation.

peso (ps). A silver coin consisting of eight *reales* or *tomines* that each consisted of 34 *maravedís*.

petaca. A bag.

plaza mayor. The main square in Mexico City, also known as the *zócalo*.

plenaria. The main phase of a criminal trial.

portero. An usher who assisted others, guarded entry doors, or carried papers.

potro. Torture rack.

presidio. A fortress.

prince. A supreme ruler of a state.

principal. A lesser Native noble.

procurador. A procurator or legal agent who typically did not attend law school. Procurators were allowed to write procedural motions but frequently also made full legal arguments.

procurador de Indios. A procurator representing Natives.
procurador de pobres. A procurator representing the poor.
procurador general. A procurator of a social body.
procurator. See procurador.
promotor fiscal. Chief diocesan judge.
provisor. The bishop's vicar-general who also served as an ecclesiastical judge.
provincial court. The *juzgado de provincia* was a first-instance court for Mexico City and surrounding territory within five leagues (about thirteen miles)
prueba. The reasoning for a conviction in a trial.
pueblo. A polity, usually Native in this book.
pulque. A popular alcoholic agave brew.
pulquería. A tavern selling pulque.
real. Also called a *tomín*, which was the equivalent of one eighth of a silver peso.
real acuerdo. Joint conference of the viceroy and civil judges (*oidores*) of the *audiencia*.
real cédula. A royal provision settling a conflict, requiring some action, or bestowing a favor; often the result of a *consulta* approved by the king.
real hacienda. The king's financial administration.
receptor. An *audiencia* agent who collected documents and fees or ran errands for the judges.
regidor. A municipal councilman.
relación. An account.
relación de méritos. An account of merits and/or services, often conceived by candidates who solicited appointments from the crown.
relator. An *audiencia* lawyer who assessed the standing of appeals or prepared and summarized trial documents.
repartimiento de mercancías. The illegal but widespread trade of the *alcaldes mayores* with Indians, also known as *repartimiento*.
repentundarum. The Roman prohibition on giving gifts to judges.
residencia. See *juicio de residencia*.
restitutio in integrum. A legal doctrine dissolving a commercial contract when a miserable person was injured, restituting all goods to the previous owners.
ruego y encargo. "I request and require," a strong request of the king or the viceroy for the Church to execute something.
sala civil. The *audiencia* chamber dealing with civil cases.
sala del crimen. The criminal chamber of the *audiencia*.

sargento mayor. The equivalent of a major or third-in-command of a regiment.
secretary of the Indies. The senior minister in Madrid dealing with American affairs.
senior constable. See *alguacil mayor de corte*.
Siete Partidas. The Seven Parts, an important thirteenth-century legal collection from Castile.
sumaria. The initial phase of a criminal trial, which consisted of gathering testimony and other evidence.
tomín. One *real*.
tribunal de cuentas. The tribunal of accounts that audited the colonial treasuries.
tributo. Native tribute.
valido. The king's favorite; see also chief minister.
Valladolid. Now the city of Morelia in Michoacan. There is also the city of Valladolid in Spain with a famous university.
visita. An inspection of secular institutions or the Church.
visitador. An investigative judge; someone who conducts a *visita*.
visita general. A comprehensive *visita*, usually of an entire kingdom.
zambo. Offspring of blacks and Natives in the racial imaginary.
zángano. Lazy person or scammer; originally a drone.

Bibliography

I ARCHIVAL SOURCES

Mexico

Archivo General de la Nación (AGN) (*Ramo* and volumes)
Real Acuerdo 7
Real Audiencia 1, 4
Archivo Histórico de la Hacienda (AHH) 213, 1056, 1058, 1614, 1615, 1653
Civil 993
Correspondencia de Virreyes. 1a. serie, vol. 90
General de Parte (GdP) 41, 42
Historia 102
Indiferente Virreinal 734, 1477, 2325, 3263, 5249, 5687, 5976, 6181
Indios 25, 27, 34, 36, 39, 42, 47, 59
Inquisición 729, 740, 792, 882, 1543, 1738, 1740
Media Anata 20, 42, 50, 205
Matrimonios 189
Reales Cédulas Originales (RCO) 14, 15, 31–34, 36–47, 50, 51, 68, 71–73
Subdelegados 34
Archivo Histórico de la Ciudad de México (AHCM)
Fondo Ayuntamiento, Sección Actas del Cabildo, vols. 45 A, 50 A.
Biblioteca Nacional, Fondo Reservado (BNM, FR)
Manuscripts 439, 455
La Fragua, ms. 1194
Acervo Histórico del Archivo General de Notarias (AHAGN), Mexico City
Fondo Antiguo, Sección Notarías (Siglos XVII–XIX)
Notaría 340, Escribano José de Ledesma, vol. 2247
Notaría 571, Escribano Antonio de los Ríos, vol. 3937

Spain

Archivo General de Indias (AGI), Seville (*fondos* and *legajos*)
Audiencia de México (México) 7, 8, 10, 14, 15, 362, 376, 377, 379–383, 403, 440, 471, 479, 482, 485, 486 A, 487, 489–492, 547, 557, 588, 600, 627, 628, 658, 670 A, B; 879, 1326, 1341, 1342, 1350, 1352, 1505, 1506, 2093, 2712
Escribanía de Cámara (Escribanía) 217 A, 228 A, 236 A, 238 B, 246 A, B, 262 C, 278 A, B, C; 279 A, B, C; 280 A, B, C; 281 A, B, C, D; 282 A, B, C, D; 283 A, B, C; 284 A, B, C; 285 A, B, C; 286 A, B, C; 287 A, B; 288 A, B; 289 A, B; 1158, 1183, 1194
Guadalajara 2, 89, 107
Indiferente General 134, 144, 214, 217, 784, 1847
Archivo Histórico Nacional (AHN), Madrid
Códices y Cartularios 684 B
Inquisición 1738, 1740
Archivo Histórico Nacional, Sección Nobleza, Toledo
Archivo de los Duques de Osuna, carpeta 55
Biblioteca Nacional de España (BNE), Madrid
Ms. 5671, 10512, 18684/8
Fondo Reservado, ms. 437
Biblioteca del Palacio
Manuscript II/2842
Biblioteca de Aragón (http://bibliotecavirtual.aragon.es)
Miscelánea, ms. 141
Biblioteca de Huesca (http://bibliotecavirtual.aragon.es)
Miscelánea, ms. 141

Portugal

Biblioteca de Ajuda, Lisbon
Manuscript 54-XI-16

USA

Archivo de los Condes de Revillagigedo, Library of the University of Florida, Gainesville, Department of Special and Area Collections (ACR). In 1985 the University of Florida Library microfilmed the private archive of the Counts of Revillagigedo in Madrid.
Microfilm reels no. 346, 347, 352, 354, 399, 404, 412, 455
The Latin American Library at Tulane University (New Orleans).
The Mexican Administration Records, Manuscripts Collection 16, box. 3, vol. 1.

2   PUBLISHED PRIMARY SOURCES

Actas Antiguas del Cabildo, Libros 48 al 50. Años 1714 a 1719. Vol. 1. Mexico City: Impresa particular G. Oropeza Velasco, 1912.

Antunez Portugal, Domingo. *Tractatus de donationibus jurium et bonorum regiae coronae*. 2 vols. Lisbon: Ioannis a Costa, 1673.
Aquinas, Thomas. *Justice*. In *Summa Theologiae*, vol. 37, edited and translated by Thomas Gilby. Cambridge: Blackfriars, 1975.
Aquinas, Thomas. "The Letter to the Duchess of Brabant 'On the Government of Jews' (*Opusculum de regimine Iudaeorum ad Ducissam Brabantiae*)." In *Political Writings*, edited by R. W. Dyson, 233–238. Cambridge: Cambridge University Press, 2002.
Aristotle. *Nicomachean Ethics*. Translated by W. D. Ross. 1908. http://classics.mit.edu/Aristotle/nicomachaen.html.
Avendaño, Diego de. *Thesaurus Indicus sev generalis instructor pro regimine conscientiae in iis quae ad Indias spectant*. Antwerp: Jacob Meurs, 1668. Span Transl. *Thesaurus Indicus*, edited by Ángel Muñoz García. Pamplona: EUNSA, 2001.
Ayala, Manuel Josef de. *Dicionario de Gobierno y Legislación de Indias*. Edited by Marta Milagros del Vas Mingo. Madrid: Ediciones de Cultura Hispánica, 1995.
Azcargorta, Juan de. *Manual de Confesores ad Mentem Scoti*. Reprint from probably 1718, based on the edition Granada, 1713.
Azpilcueta, Martín de. *Comentario resolutorio de usuras, sobre el capitulo i de la question iii de la xiiii causa, compuesto por el Doctor Martín de Azpilcueta. Dirigido a uno con otros quatro sobre el principio del cap. fin. de usur. y el cap. fin de symo. y el cap. non inferenda. xxiii. quest. iiii. y el cap. fin. xiiii questi. final*. Salamanca: Andrea de Portonarijs, 1556.
Azpilcueta, Martín de. *Manual de Confesores y penitentes, que clara y brevemente contiene, la universal y particular decision de quasi todas las dudas, que en las confesiones suelen ocurrir de los pecados, absoluciones, restitutciones, censuras, & irregularidades*. Salamanca: Andrea de Portonarijs, 1557.
Azpilcueta, Martín de. *Manual de confessores y penitentes: Que contiene quasi todas las dudas que en las confessiones suelen occurrir delos peccados [. . .]*. 2nd ed. Valladolid, Spain: Francisco Fernández de Córdoba, 1570.
Baviera, Adalberto de, and Gabriel Maura Gamazo, eds. *Documentos inéditos referentes a las postrimerías de la casa de Austria en España*. Madrid: Tipografía de Archivos, 1927–1935.
Bentura Beleña, Eusebio, ed. *Recopilación sumaria de todos los autos acordados de la Real Audiencia y Sala del Crimen de esta Nueva España, y providencias de su superior gobierno; de varias reales cédulas y órdenes que después de publicada la Recopilacion de Indias han podido recogerse así de las dirigidas á la misma Audiencia ó gobierno, como de algunas otras que por sus notables decisiones convendrá no ignorar*. 2 vols. Mexico City: Felipe de Zúñiga y Ontiveros, 1787.
Berart y Gassol, Gabriel. *Speculum visitationis secularis omnium magistratum, iudicum, decurionum, aliorumque Reipublicae administratorum: in quo de necessitate visitationis, visitatoribus eligendis, illorumque qualitate, iurisdictione, et officio ordineque procedendi, et fulminandi processum in visitatione, de testibus officialumque suspensionibus et carcerationibus, visitatorumque recusationibus: De excessibus quoque, gravaminibus, et culpis omnium magistratuum: ipsorumque defensionibus et excusationibus, ac etiam*

bonorum Reipublicae erogationibus, sententiis denique, appellationibus, et poenis in eisdem, imponendis, deque falsis querelantibus puniendis [...]. Barcinone [Barcelona]: Ex Typographia Sebastiani Mathenat, 1627.

Beristáin de Souza, José Mariano, Fortino Hipólito Vera, and José Rafael Enríquez Trespalacios. *Biblioteca Hispano Americana Septentrional: o catalogo y noticias de los literatos [...].* 2nd ed. Amecameca: Tipografía del Colegio Católico, 1883.

Bodin, Jean. *Los seis libros de la republica [...] traducidos de lengua Francesa, y enmendados Catholicamente: por Gaspar de Añastro y Sunza.* Turin: Herederos de Bevilacqua, 1590.

Bodin, Jean. *Six Books of the Commonwealth.* Translated by M. J. Tooley. New York: Barnes & Noble, 1967.

Cajetan, Thomas. *De peccatis summula.* Antwerp: Petrus Bellerus, 1575.

Campillo y Cosío, José. *Nuevo sistema de gobierno económico para la América: Con los males y daños que le causa el que hoy tiene, de los que participa copiosamente España; y remedios universales para que la primera tenga considerables ventajas, y la segunda mayores intereses.* Madrid: Imprenta de Benito Cano, 1789.

Castillo de Bobadilla, Jerónimo. *Política para corregidores y señores de vasallos, en tiempo de paz, y de guerra [...].* 2 vols. Barcelona: Jerónimo Margarit, 1616.

Castro Santa-Anna, José Manuel de. *Diario de Sucesos Notables. Documentos para la historia de Méjico.* Vols. iv–vi. Mexico City: Imprenta de Juan R. Navarro, 1854.

Cervantes Saavedra, Miguel de. *Licenciado Vidriera.* Barcelona: Imprenta de A. Bergnes y Comp., 1832.

Cicero, Marcus Tullius. "Against Verres." In *The Orations of Marcus Tullius Cicero*, vol 1, edited and translated by Charles Duke Yonge. London: George Bell & Sons, 1903. www.perseus.tufts.edu/hopper/text?doc=Cic.+Ver.+1.1.

Code. See Krueger, Paul, and Theodor Mommsen, eds. *Corpus Iuris Civilis.*

Compendio y breue instruction por tener libros de cuentas, deudas y de mercaduria: muy prouechoso para mercaderes y toda gente de negocio: traduzido de Frances en Castellano, by an anonymous author. Barcelona: en casa de Claudio Bornat al Aguila fuerte, 1565.

Covarrubias Orozco, Sebastián de, *Tesoro de la lengua castellana, o española [...].* Madrid: Luis Sánchez, 1611.

Diccionario de la lengua castellana, en que se explica el verdadero sentido de las voces, su naturaleza y calidad, con las phrases o modos de hablar, los proverbios o refranes, y otras cosas convenientes al uso de la lengua. Edited by Real Academia Española. Madrid: Imprenta de Francisco del Hierro, 1726–1739. http://buscon.rae.es/ntlle/SrvltGUILoginNtlle.

Digest. See Krueger, Paul, and Theodor Mommsen, eds. *Corpus Iuris Civilis.*

Feijóo y Montenegro, Benito Jerónimo. *Teatro crítico universal o Discursos varios en todo género de materias, para desengaño de errores comunes: escrito por el muy ilustre señor [...].* Vol. 3. Originally published in 1729. Madrid: Pantaleón Aznar, 1777.

Fernández de Otero, Antonio. *Tractatus de Oficialibus Reipublicae, necnon oppidorum utriusque Castellae, tum de eorundem electione, usu, exercitio.*

Bibliography 293

Opus non solum tironibus, sed etiam magistris pernecessarium, duplici indice, capitum scilicet, & rerum locupletatum. Editio Tertia, auctior et accuratior. Colonia [Geneva]: Fratres de Fonties, 1732.

Fonseca, Fabian de, and Carlos de Urrutia. *Historia general de real hacienda, escrita por D. Fabian de Fonseca y D. Carlos de Urrutia, por orden del virey, conde de Revillagigedo. Obra hasta ahora inedita y que se imprime con permiso del supremo gobierno.* 6 vols. Mexico City: V. G. Torres, 1845–53.

Franciosini Florentín, Lorenzo. *Vocabulario español-italiano, ahora nuevamente sacado a luz [...]. Segunda parte.* Roma: Iuan Pablo Profilio, a costa de Iuan Ángel Rufineli y Ángel Manni, 1620. Reproducido a partir del ejemplar de la Biblioteca Nacional de Madrid.

Goethe, Johann Wolfgang von. *Faust: A Tragedy.* Translated by Charles T. Brooks. 7th ed. Boston: Ticknor and Fields, 1868. http://www.gutenberg.org/cache/epub/14460/pg14460.html.

Grégoire de Toulouse, Pierre (Tholosianus, Petrus Gregorius). *De republica libri sex et viginti: Antea en duos distincti tomos, nunc vno concise & artificiose comprehensi.* 3rd ed. Frankfurt: Typis Matthæi Kempfferi, sumpt[i]bus Philippi Jacobi Fischeri, 1642.

Gregorius IX. *Decretales D. Gregorij Papae IX. suae integritati una cum glossis restitutae ad exemplar Romanum. Nunc recens perutilibus additionibus praeclariss. iurisc. D. Andreae Alciati illustratae.* Venetiis [Venice]: Apud Socios Aquilae Renouantis, 1605. www.mdz-nbn-resolving.de/urn/resolver.pl?urn=urn:nbn:de:bvb:12-bsb10506589-3.

Hevia Bolaños, Juan de. *Curia Filipica, primero, y segundo tomo. El primero dividido en cinco partes, donde se trata breve y compendiosamente de los juicios, mayormente forenses, eclesiasticos y seculares, con lo sobre ello está dispuesto por derecho y resoluciones por doctores ... el segundo tomo en tres libros distribuido, donde se trata de la mercancia, y contratación de tierra y mar,* with an index by Nicolás de la Cueva Madrid: Francisco de Hierro, 1725.

Humboldt, Alexander von. [1809] *Mexico-Werk: Politische Ideen zu Mexico; mexicanische Landeskunde.* Edited by Hanno Beck. 2nd rev. ed. Darmstadt: Wissenschaftliche Buchgesellschaft, 2008.

Institutes. See Krueger, Paul, and Theodor Mommsen, eds. *Corpus Iuris Civilis.*

Jiménez Arias, Diego. *Lexicon ecclesiasticum latino-hispanicum: Ex sacris Bibliis, conciliis, pontificum decretis, ac theologorum placitis [...].* Girona, Spain: Narcissum Oliva, 1792.

Juan, Jorge, and Antonio de Ulloa. *Discourse and Political Reflections on the Kingdoms of Peru, Their Government, Special Regimen of Their Inhabitants [...].* Edited by John J. TePaske. Translated by John J. TePaske and Besse A. Clement. Norman: University of Oklahoma Press, 1978. A Spanish original is Jorge Juan and Antonio de Ulloa. [1749]. *Noticias secretas de America, sobre el estado naval, militar, y politico de los reynos del Perú y provincias de Quito, costas de Nueva Granada y Chile [...].* Edited by David Barry. London: R. Taylor, 1826.

Konetzke, Richard, ed. *Colección de documentos para la historia de la formación social de Hispanoamérica, 1493–1810.* 3 vols. Madrid: CSIC, 1953–1962.

Krueger, Paul, and Theodor Mommsen, eds. *Corpus Iuris Civilis*. Berlin: Apud Weidmannos. 1954. Accessed under Y. Lassard and A. Koptev (eds.), *The Roman Law Library*. webu2.upmf-grenoble.fr/DroitRomain.

Lampridius, Aelius. *The Life of Severus Alexander*. Translated by David Magie. Loeb Classical Library, 1921. http://penelope.uchicago.edu/Thayer/E/Roman/Texts/Historia_Augusta/Severus_Alexander/2*.html.

Lancina, Juan Alfonso de. *Commentarios politicos a los Annales de Cayo Vero Cornelio Tácito [...]*. Madrid: Oficina de Melchor Álvarez, 1687.

Larraga, Francisco. *Promptuario de la theologia moral: muy vtil para todos los que han de exponer de co[n]fessores, y para la debida administracion del Santo Sacramento de la Penitencia. Nuevamente reconocido, mejorado, corregido, y añadido por su autor en esta dezimaquarta edición*. Madrid: Manuel Román, 1718.

Lipsius, Justus. *Concerning Constancy*. Edited and translated by R. V. Young. Tempe, AZ: Arizona Center for Medieval and Renaissance Studies, 2011.

Machiavelli, Niccolò. "Discorsi sopra la prima deca di Tito Livio." In *Machiavelli, Tutte le opere*, edited by Mario Martelli. Sansoni: Florence, 1971. www.classicitaliani.it/index054.htm.

Machiavelli, Niccolò. *The Prince*. Edited by Quentin Skinner and Russel Price. Cambridge: Cambridge University Press, 1988.

Madre de Dios, Valentín de la. *Fuero de la conciencia: obra utilissima para los ministros, y ministerio del Santo Sacramento de la Penitencia, donde hallarán quanto necesitan para hazerle suficientes en la ciencia moral, y aplicarlo con acierto, y fruto a la practica. Contiene seis tratados*. Madrid: Francisco Laso, mercader de libros, enfrente de S. Felipe, 1707.

Mendo, Andrés. *Príncipe Perfecto y Ministros Aiustados, Documentos Políticos y Morales. En Emblemas*. Lyon: Horacio Boissat y George Remeus, 1662.

Mez de Braidenbach, Nicolas. *Diccionario muy copioso de la lengua española y alemana hasta agora nunca visto, sacado de diferentes autores con mucho trabajo y diligencia [...]*. Vienna: Juan Diego Kürner, 1670. http://buscon.rae.es/ntlle/SrvltGUIMenuNtlle?cmd=Lema&sec=1.0.0.0.0.

Moreno, Fray Jerónimo. *Reglas ciertas y precisamente necessarias para juezes, y ministros de justicia de las Indias y para sus confesores*. Puebla: Viuda de Miguel Ortega y Bonilla, 1732. Facsimile, Mexico City: Suprema Corte de Justicia de la Nación, 2005.

Murillo Velarde, Pedro. *Curso de derecho canónico hispano e indiano*. Translated by Alberto Carrillo Cázares, et al. Zamora: El Colegio de Michoacán, 2008, based on Murillo Velarde. *Cursus juris canonici, hispani, et indici in quo, juxta ordinem titulorum decretalium non solum canonicae decisiones [...]*. 3rd ed. Matriti, Typographia Ulloae a Romane Ruíz. 1791.

Murillo Velarde, Petri. *Cursus iuris canonici Hispani, et indici, in quo juxta ordinem titulorum decretalium non solum canonicae decissiones afferuntur, sed insuper additur, quod in nostro Hispaniae Regno, & in his Indiarum Provinciis Lege, consuetudine, privilegio, vel praxi statutum & admissum est [...]*. 2 vols. Matriti [Madrid]: Ex typographia Emmanuelis Fernández, 1743.

Muro Orejón, Antonio, ed. *Cedulario americano del siglo XVIII: Colección de disposiciones legales indianas desde 1680 a 1800, contenidas en los cedularios del Archivo General de Indias*. 2 vols. Seville: Escuela de Estudios Hispano-Americanos, 1956

Nebrija, Antonio de.*Vocabulario Español-Latino*. Salamanca: Impresor de la Gramática castellana, 1495. Facsimile. Madrid: Real Academia Española, 1989. http://buscon.rae.es/ntlle/SrvltGUIMenuNtlle?cmd=Lema&sec=1.1.0.0.0.

Novels. See Krueger, Paul, and Theodor Mommsen, eds. *Corpus Iuris Civilis*.

Palanco, Francisco. *Dialogus physico-theologicus contra philosophiae novatores, sive thomista contra atomistas*. Madrid: Blasii de Villa-Nueva, 1714.

Palet, Juan. *Diccionario muy copioso de la lengua española y francesa [...]. Dictionaire tres ample de la langue espagnole et françoise*. Paris: Matthieu Guillemot, 1604. http://buscon.rae.es/ntlle/SrvltGUILoginNtlle

Portocarrero y Guzmán, Pedro. *Theatro monarchico de España: Que contiene las mas puras, como catholicas, maximas de estado, por las quales, assi los principes, como las republicas [...]*. Madrid: Juan Garcia Infançon, 1700.

Quevedo, Francisco de Villegas. *Fortuna con seso*. In *Obras de D. Francisco de Quevedo Villegas, Caballero del Habito de Santiago, Secretario de S. M. y Señor de la Villa de la Torre de Juan Abad*. Vol. 2, 479–567. Madrid: Joachín Ibarra, 1772.

Quintana, Jerónimo de. *Historia de la antigüedad, nobleza y grandeza de la villa de Madrid*. Madrid: Imprenta del Reyno, 1629. Edited by E. Varela Hervías. Madrid: Artes Gráficas Municipales, 1954.

Real Academia Española. *Diccionario de la lengua castellana, en que se explica el verdadero sentido de las voces, su naturaleza y calidad, con las phrases o modos de hablar, los proverbios o refranes, y otras cosas convenientes al uso de la lengua [...]*. Madrid: Imprenta de la Real Academia Española, por los herederos de Francisco del Hierro, 1737. http://buscon.rae.es/ntlle/SrvltGUILoginNtlle.

Real Academia Española. *Diccionario de la lengua castellana [...]*. Madrid: Joachín Ibarra, 1780.

Recopilación de las leyes destos reynos hecha por mandado de la Magestad Catholica del Rey don Philipe Segundo nuestro señor. Contienese en este libro las leyes hechas hasta fin del año de mil y quinientos y ochenta y uno [...]. Alcalá de Henares: Juan Iñiguez de Liquerica, 1581.

Recopilación de leyes de los reynos de las Indias mandada imprimir y publicar por la Magestad Católica del Rey Don Carlos II. Nuestro Señor [...]. 1741. Facsimile. Madrid: Consejo de la Hispanidad, 1953. www.leyes.congreso.gob.pe/leyes_indias.aspx.

Ripa Perugino, Cesare. *Iconologia del cavaliere Cesare Ripa Perugino notabilmente accresciuta d'immagini, di annotazioni e di fatti dell'abate Cesare Orlandi Patrizio di Citta della pieve accademico augusto a sua excellenza D. Raimondo di Sangro [...]*. Tome 2. Perugia: Nella Stamperia di Piergovanni Constantini, 1765.

Robles, Antonio de. *Diario de sucesos notables (1665–1703)*. Edited by Antonio Castro Leal. 2nd ed. 3 vols. Mexico City: Editorial Porrúa, 1972.

San Antonio, Miguel de. *Resumen de la theologia moral de el Crisol arreglado al exercicio prudente de las operaciones humanas, y practica de los Confesores*. Madrid: en la imprenta de Ángel Pascual Rubio, 1719.

Sanponts y Barba, Ignacio, Ramon Marti de Eixalá, and José Ferrer y Subirana, eds. *Las Siete Partidas del sabio rey Don Alfonso el IX, con las variantes de mas interés, y con la glosa del Lic. Gregorio Lopez, vertida al castellano y estensamente adicionada con nuevas notas y comentarios y unas tablas sinópticas comparativas, sobre la legislacion española, antigua y moderna, hasta su actual estado.* Barcelona: Bergnes, vol. 1 (1843)–vol. 4 (1844).

Saxoferrato, Bartoli ab [Bartolo de Sassoferrato]. *Omnium iuris interpretum antesignani comentaria nunc recens, praeter alias additiones ad hanc diem editas, aureis adnotationibus Iacobi Anelli de Bottis & Petri Mangrellae [...]. Tomus octavus in secundam, atque tertiam codici partem.* Venetiis (Venice): Apud Iuntas, 1590.

Schwartz, Benjamin Heinrich, and Heinrich Linck. *De iuramento ambitus et repetundarum, ex l. fin. C. ad L. Jul. repetund. Sub Praesidio Dn. Henrici Linckens.* "PhD diss., University of Altdorf: Henricus Meyerus, 1695.

Seneca, Lucius Annaeus. *De Ira.* In *Moral Essays.* Edited by John W. Basore. Vol. 1. London and New York: Heinemann, 1928. www.perseus.tufts.edu/hopper/collections.

Seneca, Lucius Annaeus. *On Benefits.* Translated by Aubrey Stewart. London, 1887. www.gutenberg.org/3/7/9/3794/.

Seneca, Lucius Annaeus. *De consolatione ad Polybium.* In *Moral Essays.* Edited by John W. Basore. Vol. 2. London and New York. Heinemann, 1932. www.perseus.tufts.edu/hopper/collections.

Seijas y Lobera, Francisco de. *Gobierno militar y político del reino imperial de la Nueva España (1702).* Edited by Pablo Emilio Pérez-Mallaína Bueno. Mexico City: UNAM, 1986.

Sigüenza y Góngora, Carlos de. "Teatro de las virtudes políticas." In *Obras Históricas.* 2nd ed. Mexico City: Editorial Porrúa, 1960.

Solorzano Pereira, Ioannes (Juan) de. *Disputationem de Indiarum iure sive De Iusta Indiarum Occidentalium inquisitione, acquisitione et retentione: tribus libris comprehensam.* Matriti: Ex typographia Francisci Martinez, 1629.

Solórzano y Pereyra, Juan. *Politica Indiana [...] Dividia en seis libros en los quales con gran distinción, y estudio se trata, y resuelve todo lo tocante al Descubrimiento, Descripcion, Adquisicion, y Retencion de las mesmas Indias [...] Sale en esta tercera impresión ilustrada por el Licenc. D. Francisco Ramiro de Valenzuela [...].* 2 tomes. Tome 1 (libros 1–3): Madrid: Matheo Sacristán, 1736; tome 2 (libros 4–6): Madrid: Gabriel Ramírez, 1739.

Soto, Domingo de. *De iustitia et iure, libri decem: De la justicia y del derecho, en diez libros.* Madrid: Instituto de Estudios Políticos, 1968.

Stevens, John. *A New Spanish and English Dictionary. Collected from the Best Spanish Authors Both Ancient and Modern [...] To which is added a Copious English and Spanish Dictionary [...].* London: George Sawbridge, 1706. http://buscon.rae.es/ntlle/SrvltGUIMenuNtlle?cmd=Lema&sec=1.0.0.0.0.

Terreros y Pando, Esteban de. *Diccionario castellano con las voces de ciencias y artes y sus correspondientes en las tres lenguas francesa, latina e italiana [...].* Vol. 2. Madrid: Viuda de Ibarra, 1787.

Torres de Lima, Luis. *Compendio das mais notaveis cousas que no reyno de portugal acontecerão desde a perda del Rey D. Sebastião até o anno de 1627 com outras cousas tocantes ao bom governo, & diversidade d'Estados.* Coimbra: Officina de Manoel Dias, 1654.

Torre Villar, Ernesto de la, ed. *Instrucciones y memorias de los virreyes novohispanos.* 2 vols. Mexico City: Editorial Porrúa, 1991.

Uztáriz, Jerónimo de. *Theoria y practica de comercio y de marina en diferentes discursos [...].* 3rd ed. Madrid: Imprenta de Antonio Sanz, 1757.

Villarroel, Gaspar de. *Govierno eclesiastico-pacifico, y union de los dos cuchillos pontificio, y regio.* Vol. 2. Madrid: Antonio Marín, 1738.

Zapata y Sandoval, Juan. *Disceptación sobre justicia distributiva y sobre la acepción de personas a ella opuesta.* Vol. 1: *Sobre la justicia conforme a sí misma.* Vol. 2: *En qué cosas tiene lugar la acepción de personas y la injusta distribución de los bienes.* Valladolid: Lasso Vaca, 1609. Translated by Arturo Ramírez Trejo, edited by Paula López Cruz and Mauricio Beuchot Puente. Mexico City: UNAM, 1994–1995.

Zeballos, Jeronymo de. *Arte Real para el buen govierno de los Reyes, y Principes, y de sus vassallos, en el qual se referen las obligaciones de cada uno, con los principales documentos para el buen govierno. Con una tabla de las materias, reduzidas a trezientos Aforismos de Latin y Romance. Dirigido a la catolica magestad del Rey don Felipe IIII. N. S. Monarca y Emperador de las Españas, no reconiciente superior en lo temporal. Por el licenciado Geronymo de Zevallos, Regidor de la Imperial ciudad de Toledo en el vanco, y assiento de los Cavalleros, y unico Patron del Monasterio de los Descalços Franciscos de la dicha ciudad [...].* Toledo: A costa de su Autor, 1623.

3 SECONDARY LITERATURE

Abad León, Felipe. *El Marqués de la Ensenada, su vida y su obra.* 2 vols. Madrid: Editorial Naval, 1985.

Adelman, Jeremy. "Commerce and Corruption." In *Corrupt Histories. Studies in Comparative History*, edited by Emmanuel Kreike and William Chester Jordan, 428–460. Rochester: University of Rochester Press, 2006.

Agüero, Alejandro. "La tortura judicial en el antiguo régimen. Orden procesal y cultura." *Direito e Democracia* 5, no. 1 (2004): 187–221.

Agüero, Alejandro. "Local Law and Localization of Law. Hispanic Legal Tradition and Colonial Culture (16th–18th Centuries)." In *Spatial and Temporal Dimensions for Legal History. Research Experiences and Itineraries*, edited by Massimo Meccarelli and María Julia Solla Sastre, 101–129. Frankfurt: Max Planck Institute for European Legal History, 2016. www.rg.mpg.de/1091047/gplh_6_aguero.pdf.

Agüero, Alejandro, and Francisco Javier Andrés Santos. "Republicanismo y tradición jurídica en los albores de la independencia: la significación americana del Tratado de los Oficiales de la República de Antonio Fernández de Otero." In *Actas del XIX Congreso del Instituto Internacional de Historia del Derecho Indiano*, edited by Thomas Duve, vol. 1, 329–358. Madrid: Dykinson, 2017.

Aguirre Salvador, Rodolfo. *Por el camino de las letras: el ascenso profesional de los catedráticos juristas de la Nueva España, siglo XVIII*. Mexico City: UNAM, 1998.

Alberro, Solange. "Control de la iglesia y transgresiones eclesiásticas durante el periodo colonial." In *Vicios públicos, virtudes privadas: La corrupción en México*, edited by Claudio Lomnitz, 33–47. Mexico City: CIESAS, 2000.

Alonso, María Luz. "La visita de Garzarón a la Audiencia de México." In *Estudios jurídicos en homenaje al maestro Guillermo Floris Margadant*, 11–27. Mexico City: UNAM, 1988.

Alonso Romero, María Paz. *El proceso penal en Castilla siglo XIII–XVIII*. Salamanca: Universidad de Salamanca, 1982.

Alonso Romero, María Paz. *Orden procesal y garantías entre Antiguo Régimen y constitucionalismo gaditano*. Madrid: Centro de Estudios Políticos y Constitucionales, 2008.

Alonso Romero, María Paz, and Carlos Garriga Acosta. *El régimen jurídico de la abogacía en Castilla (siglos XIII–XVIII)*. Madrid: Dykinson, 2013.

Althoff, Gerd. *Political and Social Bonds in Early Medieval Europe*. Cambridge: Cambridge University Press, 2004.

Álvarez de Toledo, Cayetana. *Politics and Reform in Spain and Viceregal Mexico: The Life and Thought of Juan de Palafox, 1600–1659*. Oxford: Clarendon Press, 2004.

Andrien, Kenneth J. *Andean Worlds. Indigenous History, Culture, and Consciousness under Spanish Rule 1532–1825*. Albuquerque, NM: University of New Mexico Press, 2001.

Andrien, Kenneth J. "Corruption, Self-Interest, and the Political Culture of Eighteenth-Century Quito." In *Virtue, Corruption, and Self-Interest: Political Values in the Eighteenth Century*, edited by Richard K. Matthews, 270–296. Bethlehem, PA: Lehigh University Press, 1994.

Andrien, Kenneth J. *The Kingdom of Quito, 1690–1830: The State and Regional Development*. Cambridge: Cambridge University Press, 1995.

Andrien, Kenneth J. "The Sale of Fiscal Offices and the Decline of Royal Authority in the Viceroyalty of Peru, 1633–1700." *Hispanic American Historical Review (HAHR)* 62, no. 1 (1982): 49–71.

Andújar Castillo, Francisco. "Cuando el rey delegaba la gracia. Las comisiones de ventas de oficios en la Castilla del siglo XVII." In *Mérito, venalidad y corrupción*, edited by Francisco Andújar Castillo and Pilar Ponce-Leiva, 135–156.

Andújar Castillo, Francisco. *Necesidad y venalidad: España e Indias, 1704–1711*. Madrid: Centro de Estudios Políticos y Constitucionales, 2008.

Andújar Castillo, Francisco. "Prólogo." In *Gobernar las Indias: Venalidad y méritos en la provisión de cargos americanos, 1701–1746*, by Guillermo Burgos Lejonagoitia, 13–17. Almería: Universidad de Almería, 2014.

Andújar Castillo, Francisco. *El sonido del dinero: Monarquía, ejército y venalidad en la España del siglo XVIII*. Madrid: Marcial Pons, 2004.

Annino, Antonio. "El primer constitucionalismo Mexicano, 1810–1830." In *Para una Historia de América III. Los nudos 2*, edited by Marcello Carmagnani,

Bibliography

Alicia Hernández Chávez, and Ruggiero Romano, 140–189. Mexico City: Fondo de Cultura Económica, El Colegio de México, Fideicomiso Historia de las Américas, 1999.

Annino, Antonio. "Soberanías en lucha." In *De los imperios a las naciones: Iberoamérica*, edited by Antonio Annino, Luis Castro Leiva, and François-Xavier Guerra, 229–253. Zaragoza: Ibercaja, Obra Cultural, 1994.

Arenal Fenochio, Jaime del. "La Justicia civil ordinaria en la ciudad de México durante el primer tercio del siglo xviii." In *Memoria del X Congreso del Instituto Internacional de Historia del Derecho Indiano*, vol. 1, 39–64. Mexico City: Escuela Libre de Derecho, UNAM, 1995.

Arnold, Linda. *Bureaucracy and Bureaucrats in Mexico City 1742–1835*. Tucson: University of Arizona Press, 1988.

Arregui Zamorano, Pilar. *La audiencia de México según los visitadores (xvi y xvii)*. Mexico City: Instituto de Investigaciones Jurídicas, UNAM, 1981.

Asch, Ronald G. "Absolutismus." In *Lexikon zum aufgeklärten Absolutismus. Herrscher-Denker-Sachbegriffe*, edited by Helmut Reinalter, 15–21. Vienna: Böhlau, 2005.

Asch, Ronald G., and Adolf M. Birke, eds. *Princes, Patronage and the Nobility. The Court at the Beginning of the Modern Age, c. 1450–1650*. Oxford: Oxford University Press, 1991.

Asch, Ronald G., Birgit Emich, and Jens Ivo Engels. "Einleitung." In *Integration, Legitimation, Korruption: Politische Patronage in Früher Neuzeit und Moderne*, edited by Ronald G. Asch, Birgit Emich, and Jens Ivo Engels, 7–30. Frankfurt: Peter Lang, 2011.

Ballone, Angela. *The 1624 Tumult of Mexico in Perspective (c. 1620–1650): Authority and Conflict Resolution in the Iberian Atlantic*. Leiden/ Boston: Brill, 2018.

Banfield, Edward C. "Corruption as a Feature of Governmental Organization." *Journal of Law and Economics* 18, no. 3 (1975): 587–605.

Barrientos Grandon, Javier. "Guía prosopográfica de la judicatura letrada indiana (1503–1898)." In *Nuevas aportaciones a la historia jurídica de Iberoamérica*, edited by José Andrés-Gallego, 1–1640. Madrid: Fundación Histórica Tavera, Hernando de Larramendi / Mapfre, 2000. CD-ROM.

Baskes, Jeremy. *Indians, Merchants, and Markets: A Reinterpretation of the Repartimiento and Spanish-Indian Economic Relations in Colonial Oaxaca, 1750–1821*. Stanford, CA: Stanford University Press, 2000.

Bauer, Martin. "'Die Gemein Sag' im Späteren Mittelalter. Studien zu einem Faktor mittelalterlicher Öffentlichkeit und seinem historischen Auskunftswert." PhD diss., University of Erlangen, Germany, 1981.

Becerra Jiménez, Celina G. "Redes sociales y oficios de justicia en Indias. Los vínculos de dos alcaldes mayores neogallegos." *Relaciones* 132 bis (2012): 109–150.

Becker, Christoph. "Laesio enormis." In *Handwörterbuch der deutschen Rechtsgeschichte (HRG)*, edited by Albrecht Cordes, Heiner Lück, and Dieter Werkmüller. 2nd ed., vol. 3: 400–402. Berlin: Erich Schmidt Verlag, 2016. www.hrgdigital.de/HRG.laesio_enormis.

Bellingradt, Daniel. "Organizing Public Opinion in a Resonating Box: The Gülich Rebellion in Early Modern Cologne, 1680–1686." *Urban History* 39, no. 4 (2012): 553–570.

Bellomo, Manlio. *The Common Legal Past of Europe, 1000–1800*. Translated by Lydia G. Cochrane. Washington, DC: Catholic University of America Press, 1995.

Benton, Lauren, and Richard Ross. "Empires and Legal Pluralism. Jurisdiction, Sovereignty, and Political Imagination in the Early Modern World." In *Legal Pluralism and Empires, 1500–1850*, edited by Lauren Benton and Richard Ross, 1–7. New York: New York University Press, 2013.

Benton, Lauren. *A Search for Sovereignty. Law and Geography in European Empires, 1400–1900*. Cambridge: Cambridge University Press, 2010.

Berbesí de Salazar, Ligia, and Belin Vázquez de Ferrer. "Juicios de residencia en el gobierno provincial de Maracaibo, 1765–1810." *Anuario de Estudios Americanos* 57, no. 2 (2000): 475–499.

Berger, Adolf. *Encyclopedic Dictionary of Roman Law*. Philadelphia: The American Philosophical Society, 1953. Reprint, 1991.

Bernardo Ares, José Manuel de. *Corrupción política y centralización administrativa. La hacienda de propios en la Córdoba de Carlos II*. Córdoba, Spain: Universidad de Córdoba, Servicio de Publicaciones, 1993.

Bernecker, Walther L. *Schmuggel. Illegalität und Korruption im Mexiko des 19. Jahrhunderts*. Frankfurt: Vervuert, 1989.

Bernecker, Walther L., Horst Pietschmann, and Hans Werner Tobler. *Eine kleine Geschichte Mexikos*. Frankfurt: Suhrkamp, 2007.

Bertrand, Michel. "Del actor a la red: análisis de redes e interdisciplinariedad." In *Los actores locales de la nación en la América Latina: Análisis estratégicos*, edited by Evelyne Sanchez, 23–41. Puebla: Benemérita Universidad Autónoma de Puebla; Tlaxcala: El Colegio de Tlaxcala, 2011.

Bertrand, Michel. "Cliéntelisme et pouvoir en Nouvelle-Espagne (1680–1770)." In *Cultures et sociétés, Andes et Méso-Amérique, Mélanges en hommage à Pierre Duviols*, edited by Raquel Thiercelin, vol. 1, 140–152. Aix-en-Provence: Publications de l'Université de Provence, 1991.

Bertrand, Michel. "La élite colonial en la Nueva España del siglo XVIII: un planteamiento en términos de redes sociales." In *Beneméritos, aristócratas y empresarios: Identidades y estructuras sociales de las capas altas urbanas en América hispánica*, edited by Bernd Schröter and Christian Büschges, 35–51. Frankfurt: Vervuert, 1999.

Bertrand, Michel. *Grandeur et misères de l'office: Les officiers de finances de Nouvelle-Espagne, XVIIe–XVIIIe siècles*. Paris: Publications de la Sorbonne, 1999. Spanish edition translated by Mario Zamudio as *Grandeza y miseria del oficio: Los oficiales de la Real Hacienda de la Nueva España, siglos XVII y XVIII*. Mexico City: Fondo de Cultura Económica, 2011.

Bertrand, Michel. "Penser la corruption." *E-Spania: Revue interdisciplinaire d'études hispaniques médiévales et modernes* 16 (December 21, 2013). http://e-spania.revues.org/22807.

Bertrand, Michel. "Viejas preguntas, nuevos enfoques: la corrupción en la administración colonial española." In *El poder del dinero. Ventas de cargo*

y honores en el Antiguo Régimen, edited by Francisco Andújar Castillo and María del Mar Felices de la Fuente, 46–62. Madrid: Biblioteca Nueva, 2011.
Bethencourt, Francisco. *The Inquisition. A Global History, 1478–1834*. Cambridge: Cambridge University Press, 2009.
Bianchini, Janna. *Queen's Hand: Power and Authority in the Reign of Berenguela of Castile*. Philadelphia: University of Pennsylvania Press, 2012.
Black, John, Nigar Hashimzade, and Gareth Myles, eds. *A Dictionary of Economics*. 3rd ed. Oxford: Oxford University Press, 2009.
Bleiberg, Germán, ed. *Diccionario de Historia de España*. 2nd ed. Madrid: Revista de Occidente, 1969.
Bleichmar, Daniela. "Painting as Exploration: Visualizing Nature in Eighteenth-Century Colonial Science." In *Empires of Vision: A Reader*, edited by Martin Jay and Sumathi Ramaswamy, 64–90. Durham, NC: Duke University Press, 2014.
Blockmans, Wim. "Citizens and their Rulers." In *Empowering Interactions: Political Cultures and the Emergence of the State in Europe 1300–1900*, edited by Wim Blockmans, André Holenstein, and Jon Mathieu, 281–292. Farnham: Ashgate, 2009.
Blockmans, Wim, Jean-Philippe Genet, and Christoph Mühlberg. "Annexe 1: The Origin of the Modern State." In *L'état moderne: genèse. Bilans et perspective. Actes du colloque tenu au CNRS à Paris les 19–20 septembre 1989*, edited by Jean-Philiippe Genet, 285–303. Paris: Centre National de la Recherche Scientifique, 1990.
Bluteau, Rafael. *Vocabulario Portuguez e latino*, vol. 2. Coimbra: Collegio das Artes da Companhia de Jesu, 1712.
Böckenförde, Ernst-Wolfgang. *Geschichte der Rechts- und Staatsphilosophie. Antike und Mittelalter*. Tübingen: Mohr Siebeck, 2002.
Böttcher, Nikolaus. "Inquisición y limpieza de sangre en Nueva España." In *El peso de la sangre. Limpios, mestizos y nobles en el mundo hispánico*, edited by Nikolaus Böttcher, Bernd Hausberger, and Max S. Hering Torres, 187–217.
Böttcher, Nikolaus, Bernd Hausberger, and Max S. Hering Torres, eds. *El peso de la sangre. Limpios, mestizos y nobles en el mundo hispánico*. Mexico City: El Colegio de México, 2011.
Bonney, Richard. "France, 1494–1815." In *Rise of the Fiscal State in Europe, c. 1200–1815*, edited by Richard Bonney, 123–176. Oxford: Oxford University Press, 1999.
Bonney, Richard. "Early Modern Theories of State Finance." In *Economic Systems and State Finance*, edited by Richard Bonney, 163–231. Oxford: Clarendon Press, 1995.
Borah, Woodrow. *Justice by Insurance: The General Indian Court of Colonial Mexico and the Legal Aides of the Half-Real*. Berkeley: University of California Press, 1983.
Bordat, Josef. "Martín de Azpilcueta." In *Biographisch-Bibliographisches Kirchenlexikon*, edited by Traugott Bautz, vol. 30, 76–78. Nordhausen: Bautz, 2009.
Bourdieu, Pierre. "The Forms of Capital." In *Handbook of Theory and Research for the Sociology of Education*, edited by John G. Richardson, 241–58. New York: Greenwood, 1986.

Boyden, James M. *The Courtier and the King. Ruy Gómez de Silva, Philip II, and the Court of Spain*. Berkeley, Los Angeles: University of California Press, 1995.

Brading, David, *Miners and Merchants in Bourbon Mexico, 1763–1810*. Cambridge: Cambridge University Press, 1971.

Brading, David. "La monarquía católica." In *De los imperios a las naciones: Iberoamérica*, edited by Antonio Annino, Luis Castro Leiva, and François-Xavier Guerra, 15–46. Zaragoza: Ibercaja, Obra Cultural, 1994,

Brakensiek, Stefan. "Akzeptanzorientierte Herrschaft. Überlegungen zur politischen Kultur der Frühen Neuzeit." In *Die Frühe Neuzeit als Epoche*, edited by Helmut Neuhaus, 395–406. Munich: Oldenbourg, 2009.

Brakensiek, Stefan. "Ergebene Diener ihrer Herren? Herrschaftsvermittlung im alten Europa. Praktiken lokaler Justiz, Politik und Verwaltung im internationalen Vergleich." In *Ergebene Diener ihrer Herren? Herrschaftsvermittlung im alten Europa*, edited by Stefan Brakensiek and Heide Wunder, 1–22. Cologne: Böhlau, 2005.

Bravo Lira, Bernardino. *Derecho común y derecho propio en el Nuevo Mundo*. Santiago, Chile: Ed. Jurídica de Chile, 1989.

Bravo Lira, Bernardino. *El juez entre el derecho y la ley. Estado de derecho y derecho del Estado en el mundo hispánico, siglos xvi a xxi*. Santiago, Chile: Lexis Nexis, 2006.

Brendecke, Arndt. "Informing the Council. Central Institutions and Local Knowledge in the Spanish Empire." In *Empowering Interactions: Political Cultures and the Emergence of the State in Europe 1300–1900*, edited by Wim Blockmans, André Holenstein, and Jon Mathieu, 235–252. Farnham: Ashgate, 2009.

Brendecke, Arndt. *Imperio e información: funciones del saber en el dominio colonial español*. Frankfurt, Madrid: Vervuert / Iberoamericana, 2012.

Brundage, James Arthur. *The Medieval Origins of the Legal Profession: Canonists, Civilians, and Courts*. Chicago: University of Chicago Press, 2008.

Brunner, Otto, Werner Conze, and Reinhart Koselleck eds. *Geschichtliche Grundbegriffe. Historisches Lexikon zur politisch-sozialen Sprache in Deutschland*. Stuttgart: Klett-Cotta, 1978.

Burbank, Jane, and Frederick Cooper. *Empires in World History: Power and the Politics of Difference*. Princeton: Princeton University Press, 2010.

Burgos Lejonagoitia, Guillermo. *Gobernar las Indias: Venalidad y méritos en la provisión de cargos americanos, 1701–1746*. Almería: Universidad de Almería, 2014.

Burke, Peter. *What Is Cultural History*. Cambridge: Polity Press, 2008.

Burkholder, Mark. "An Empire beyond Compare." In *The Oxford History of Mexico*, edited by Michael C. Meyer and William H. Beezley, 115–149. Oxford: Oxford University Press, 2000.

Burkholder, Mark A. "Honest Judges Leave Destitute Heirs: The Price of Integrity in Eighteenth-Century Spain." In *Virtue, Corruption, and Self-Interest: Political Values in the Eighteenth Century*, edited by Richard K. Matthews, 247–269. Bethlehem, PA: Lehigh University Press, 1994.

Burkholder, Mark A. *Spaniards in the Colonial Empire: Creoles vs. Peninsulars?* Chichester, UK: Wiley-Blackwell, 2013.

Burkholder, Mark A., and Dewitt Samuel Chandler. *Biographical Dictionary of Audiencia Ministers in the Americas, 1687–1821.* Westport, CT: Greenwood Press, 1982.

Burkholder, Mark A., and D. S. Chandler. "Creole Appointments and the Sale of Audiencia Positions in the Spanish Empire under the Early Bourbons, 1701–1750." *Journal of Latin American Studies* 4, no. 2 (1972): 187–206.

Burkholder, Mark A., and D. S. Chandler. *From Impotence to Authority: The Spanish Crown and the American Audiencias, 1687–1808.* Columbia, MO: University of Missouri Press, 1977.

Burns, Kathryn. *Into the Archive: Writing and Power in Colonial Peru.* Durham, NC: Duke University Press, 2010.

Büschges, Christian. "Del criado al valido. El padronazgo de los virreyes de Nápoles y Nueva España (primera mitad del siglo XVII)." In *Las cortes virreinales de la Monarquía española: América e Italia. Actas del Coloquio Internacional, Sevilla, 1–4 Junio 2005*, edited by Francesca Cantú, 157–181. Rome: Viella, 2008.

Büschges, Christian, "Don Quijote in Amerika. Der iberoamerikanische Adel von der Eroberung bis zur Unabhängigkeit." In *Lateinamerika 1492–1850/70*, edited by Friedrich Edelmayer, Bernd Hausberger, and Barbara Potthast, 154–170. Vienna: ProMedia, 2005.

Cañeque, Alejandro. "Cultura vicerregia y estado colonial. Una aproximación crítica al estudio de la historia política de la Nueva España." *Historia Mexicana* 51, no. 1 (2001): 5–57.

Cañeque, Alejandro. *The King's Living Image: The Culture and Politics of Viceregal Power in Colonial Mexico.* New York: Routledge, 2004.

Cañizares-Esguerra, Jorge. *How to Write the History of the New World. Histories, Epistemologies, and Identities in the Eighteenth-Century Atlantic World.* Stanford, CA: Stanford University Press, 2001.

Cañizares-Esguerra, Jorge. *Puritan Conquistadors. Iberianizing the Atlantic, 1550–1700.* Stanford, CA: Stanford University Press, 2006.

Caño Ortigosa, José Luis. "La real hacienda en venta: los oficiales reales de Guanajuato (1665–1775)." In *La venta de cargos y el ejercicio del poder en indias*, edited by Julián Bautista Ruiz Rivera and Ángel Sanz Tapia, 139–156. León, Spain: Universidad de León, Secretariado de Publicaciones, 2007.

Cárceles de Gea, Beatriz. *Fraude y desobediencia fiscal en la Corona de Castilla en el siglo XVII (1621–1700).* Valladolid: Consejería de Educación y Cultura, 2000.

Cárdenas Gutiérrez, Salvador. "La lucha contra la corrupción en la Nueva España según la visión de los neoestoicos." *Historia Méxicana* 55, no. 3 (2006): 717–765.

Cardim, Pedro, Tamar Herzog, José Javier Ruis Ibáñez, and Gaetano Sabatini. Introduction to *Polycentric Monarchies: How did Early Modern Spain and Portugal Achieve and Maintain a Global Hegemony?*, edited by Pedro Cardim, Tamar Herzog, José Javier Ruis Ibáñez, and Gaetano Sabatin, 3–10. Brighton, UK: Sussex Academic Press, 2012.

Carmagnani, Marcello. "Una institución económica colonial: repartimiento de mercancías y libertad de comercio." *Historia Mexicana* 54, no. 1 (2004): 249–262.

Castejón, Philippe. "Colonia, entre appropriation et rejet: La naissance d'un concept (de la fin des années 1750 aux révolutions hispaniques)." *Mélanges de la Casa de Velázquez*. Nouvelle série, vol. 43, no. 1 (2013): 251–271.

Castellano, Juan Luis, and Jean-Pierre Dedieu, eds. *Réseaux, familles et pouvoirs dans le monde ibérique à la fin de l'Ancien Régime*. Paris: CNRS, D. L., 1998.

Castro, Concepción de. "Las secretarías de los consejos, las de estado y del despacho y sus oficiales durante la primera mitad del siglo xviii." *Hispania* 59, no. 201 (1999): 193–215.

Castro, Concepción de. *A la sombra de Felipe V. José de Grimaldo, ministro responsable (1703–1726)*. Madrid: Marcial Pons, Ediciones de Historia, 2004.

Castro Gutierrez, Felipe. "La fuerza de la ley y el asilo de la costumbre. Un proceso por fraudes y abusos en la real casa de Moneda de México." *Revista de Indias* 77, no. 271 (2017): 759–790. doi:10.3989/revindias.2017.022.

Castro Gutiérrez, Felipe. *Nueva ley y nuevo rey. Reformas borbónicas y rebelión popular en Nueva España*. Zamora: El Colegio de Michoacán; Mexico City: UNAM, 1996.

Castro Gutierrez, Felipe. "Del paternalismo autoritario al autoritarismo burocrático: Los éxitos y fracasos de José de Gálvez (1764–1767)." In *Mexico in the Age of Democratic Revolutions, 1750–1850*, edited by Jaime Rodríguez O., 21–33. Boulder, CO: Lynne Rienner Publications, 1994.

Castro Gutierrez, Felipe. "La visita del virrey conde de Galve a la Real Casa de Moneda de México, 1693." In *Comercio y minería en la historia de América Latina*, edited by José Alfredo Uribe Salas and Eduardo Flores Clair, 123–142. Mexico City: Universidad Michoacana de San Nicolás de Hidalgo, Instituto Nacional de Antropología e Historia, 2015.

Cavalcante de Oliveira Junior, Paulo. "Negócios de Trapaça: Caminhos y descaminhos na América portuguesa (1700–1750)." PhD diss., Universidade de São Paulo, 2002.

Chaturvedula, Nandini. "Entre particulares: venalidade na Índia portuguesa no século xvii." In *Cargos e ofícios nas monarquias ibéricas: provimento, controlo e venalidade (séculos xvii e xviii)*, edited by Roberta Stumpf and Nandini Chaturvedula, 267–278. Lisbon: CHAM, 2012.

Chuchiak, John, ed. *The Inquisition in New Spain, 1536–1820: A Documentary History*. Baltimore: The Johns Hopkins University Press, 2012.

Clavero Salvador, Bartolomé. *Antidora, antropología católica de la economía moderna*, Milano: Giuffrè Editore, 1991.

Clavero Salvador, Bartolomé. *Historia del derecho: derecho común*. Salamanca: Ediciones Universidad de Salamanca, 1994.

Coello de la Rosa, Alexandre, Claudia Contente, and Martín Rodrigo y Alharilla. "Introducció: Corrupció, cobdícia i bé públic al món hispànic (segles XVIII–XX)." *Illes i Imperis. Estudis d'història de les societats en el món colonial i postcolonial* 16 (2014): 7–12.

Comín Comín, Francisco, and Bartolomé Yun-Casalilla. "Spain: From Composite Monarchy to Nation-State, 1492–1914. An Exceptional State?" In *The Rise of Fiscal States: A Global History 1500–1914*, edited by Francisco Comín Comín, Bartolomé Yun-Casalilla, and Patrick K. O'Brien, 233–266. Cambridge: Cambridge University Press, 2012.

Contreras, Jaime. *Historia de la Inquisición Española (1478–1834). Herejías, delitos, y representación*. Madrid: Arco, 1997.
Connell, William F. *After Moctezuma: Indigenous Politics and Self-Government in Mexico City, 1524–1730*. University of Oklahoma Press, 2011.
Connell, William F. "Clients, Patrons, and Tribute: The Indigenous Aguilar Family in Mexico Tenochtitlan." In *Corruption in the Iberian Empires. Greed, Custom, and Colonial Networks*, edited by Christoph Rosenmüller, 63–85.
Condorelli, Orazio. "Diego de Covarrubias e i diritti degli Indiani." *Rivista Internazionale di Diritto Comune* 25 (2014): 207–267.
Cordero Fernández, Macarena. *Institucionalizar y desarraigar. Las visitas de idolatrías en la diócesis de Lima, siglo XVII*. Lima: Pontificia Universidad Católica del Perú, Instituto Riva-Agüero, 2016.
Costa, Luis Miguel. "Patronage and Bribery in Sixteenth-Century Peru: The Government of Viceroy Conde del Villar and the *Visita* of Licentiate Alonso Fernández de Bonilla." PhD diss., Florida International University, 2005.
Costa, Luis Miguel. "Prácticas corruptas o relaciones de patronazgo." In *'Dádivas, dones y dineros.' Aportes a una nueva historia de la corrupción en América Latina desde el imperio español hasta la modernidad*, edited by Christoph Rosenmüller and Stephan Ruderer, 27–60. Frankfurt, Madrid: Vervuert/Iberoamericana, 2016.
Cour, Anders La, and Holger Højlund. "Organizations, Institutions and Semantics: Systems Theory Meets Institutionalism." In *Luhmann Observed: Radical Theoretical Encounters*, edited by Anders La Cour and Andreas Philippopoulos-Mihalopoulos, 188–202. Basingstoke: Palgrave Macmillan, 2013.
Cruz Barney, Óscar. "Prólogo." In *Los abogados y la formación del Estado mexicano*, edited by Óscar Cruz Barney, Héctor Felipe Fix-Fierro, and Elisa Speckmann, xiii–xxvi. Mexico City: UNAM, Instituto de Investigaciones Jurídicas, 2013.
Cummins, Thomas B. F., and Emily A. Engel. "Introduction: Beyond the Normal; Collaborative Research and the Forensic Study of New World Manuscripts." In *Manuscript Cultures of Colonial Mexico and Peru*, edited by Thomas B. F. Cummins, Emily A. Engel, Barbara Anderson, and Juan M. Ossio A., 1–8. Los Angeles: Getty Publications, 2014.
Cutter, Charles R. "Community and the Law in Northern New Spain." *The Americas* 50, no. 4 (April 1994): 467–480.
Cutter, Charles. "The Legal System as a Touchstone of Identity in Colonial New Mexico." In *The Collective and the Public in Latin America: Cultural Identities and Political Order*, edited by Luis Roniger and Tamar Herzog, 57–70. Brighton, UK: Sussex Academic Press, 2000.
Dahlgren de Jordán, Barbro, ed. *Nocheztli, economía de una región. La grana cochinilla*. Mexico City: Porrúa, 1963.
Deans-Smith, Susan. *Bureaucrats, Planters, and Workers. The Making of the Tobacco Monopoly in Bourbon Mexico*. Austin: University of Texas Press, 1992.

Decock, Wim. *Theologians and Contract Law. The Moral Transformation of the Ius Commune (ca. 1500–1650)*. Leiden, Boston: Martinus Nijhoff Publishers, 2013.
Dedieu, Jean Pierre. "Acercarse a la venalidad." In *El poder del dinero. Ventas de cargos y honores en el Antiguo Régimen*, edited by Francisco Andújar Castillo and María del Mar Felices de la Fuente, 19–28. Madrid: Biblioteca Nueva, 2011.
Dedieu, Jean-Pierre. "La haute administration espagnole au XVIIIe siècle: Un projet." In *Les figures de l'administrateur: Institutions, réseaux, pouvoirs en Espagne, en France et au Portugal, 16e–19e siècle*, edited by Robert Descimon, Jean-Frédéric Schaub, and Bernard Vincent, 167–80.
Dedieu, Jean-Pierre. "Procesos y redes: La historia de las instituciones administrativas de la época moderna, hoy." In *La pluma, la mitra y la espada: Estudios de historia institucional en la edad moderna*, edited by Juan Luis Castellano, Jean-Pierre Dedieu, and María Victoria López-Cordón, 13–30. Madrid: Marcial Pons, 2000.
Deutsch, Andreas. "Beweis." In *Handwörterbuch zur deutschen Rechtsgeschichte (HRG)*, edited by Albrecht Cordes, Hans-Peter Haferkamp, Heiner Lück, Dieter Werkmüller, and Ruth Schmidt-Wiegand, 2nd ed., vol. 1, 559–566. Berlin: Erich Schmidt Verlag, 2008. www.hrgdigital.de/HRG.beweis.
Deutsch, Andreas. "Fälschungsdelikte." In *Handwörterbuch zur deutschen Rechtsgeschichte (HRG)*, edited by Albrecht Cordes, Hans-Peter Haferkamp, Heiner Lück, Dieter Werkmüller, and Ruth Schmidt-Wiegand. 2nd ed., vol. 1, 1489–1496. Berlin: Erich Schmidt Verlag, 2008. www.hrgdigital.de/HRG.faelschungsdelikte.
Dehouve, Danièle. "El crédito de repartimiento por los alcaldes mayores, entre la teoría y la práctica." In *El Crédito en Nueva España*, edited by María del Pilar Martínez López-Cano and Guillermina del Valle Pavón, 151–175. Mexico City: Instituto Mora, 1998.
Descimon, Robert. "La venalité des offices et la construction de l'État dans la France moderne: Des problèmes de la représentation symbolique aux problèmes du coût social du pouvoir." In *Les figures de l'administrateur: Institutions, réseaux, pouvoirs en Espagne, en France et au Portugal, 16e–19e siècle*, edited by Robert Descimon, Jean-Frédéric Schaub, and Bernard Vincent, 77–93.
Descimon, Robert, Jean-Frédéric Schaub, and Bernard Vincent, eds. *Les figures de l'administrateur: Institutions, réseaux, pouvoirs en Espagne, en France et au Portugal, 16e–19e siècle*. Paris: Editions de l'Ecole Hautes Études en Sciences Sociales, 1997
Deylen, Wiebke von. *Ländliches Wirtschaftsleben im spätkolonialen Mexiko. Eine mikrohistorische Studie in einem multiethnischem Distrikt: Cholula 1750–1810*. Hamburg: Hamburg University Press, 2003.
Dictionaire de la Academie Francaise. http://atilf.atilf.fr/dendien/scripts/tlfiv4/showps.exe?p=combi.htm;java=no.
Diego-Fernández Sotelo,Rafael, and María Pilar Gutiérrez Lorenzo. "Genealogía del proyecto borbónico. Reflexiones en torno al tema de las subdelegaciones." In *De reinos y subdelegaciones. Nuevos escenarios para un nuevo orden en la América borbónica*, edited by Rafael Diego-Fernández Sotelo, María

Pilar Gutiérrez Lorenzo, and Luis Alberto Arrioja Díaz Viruell, 17–48. Zamora: El Colegio de Michoacán, Universidad de Guadalajara, El Colegio Mexiquense, 2014.
Diego-Fernández Sotelo, Rafael. *El proyecto de José de Gálvez de 1774 en las ordenanzas de intendentes de Río de la Plata y Nueva España*. Zamora: El Colegio de Michoacán, 2016.
Domínguez, Ramón Joaquín. *Diccionario Nacional o Gran Diccionario Clásico de la Lengua Española (1846–47)*. 5th ed. Madrid, Paris: Establecimiento de Mellado, 1853.
Domínguez Ortiz, Antonio. "La venta de cargos y oficios públicos en Castilla y sus consecuencias Económicas y sociales." *Anuario de Historia Economica y Social* 3 (1975): 105–37.
Doyle, William. "Changing Notions of Public Corruption, c. 1770–c. 1850." In *Corrupt Histories*, edited by Emmanuel Kreike and William Chester Jordan, 83–95. Rochester: University of Rochester Press, 2004.
Doyle, William. *Venality: The Sale of Offices in Eighteenth–Century France*. Oxford: Clarendon Press, 1996.
Droste, Heiko. "Patronage in der Frühen Neuzeit: Institutionen und Kulturformen." *Zeitschrift für Historische Forschung* 30 (2003): 555–90.
Dubet, Anne. *La Hacienda real de la Nueva Planta (1713–1726), entre fraude y buen gobierno. El caso Verdes Montenegro*. Mexico City/ Madrid: Fondo de Cultura Económica, 2015.
Dubet, Anne. "La moralidad de los mentirosos: por un estudio comprensivo de la corrupción." In *Mérito, venalidad y corrupción*, edited by Francisco Andújar Castillo and Pilar Ponce-Leiva, 213–234.
Dülmen, Richard van. *Theater des Schreckens. Gerichtspraxis und Strafrituale in der frühen Neuzeit*. 6th ed. Munich: C. H. Beck, 2014.
Duve, Thomas. *Global Legal History: A Methodological Approach*. Max Planck Institute for European Legal History Research Paper Series no. 4. (2016). http://ssrn.com/abstract=2781104.
Duve, Thomas. *Sonderrecht in der Frühen Neuzeit. Studien zum ius singulare und den privilegia miserabilium personarum, senum und indorum in Alter und Neuer Welt*. Frankfurt: Vittorio Klostermann, 2008.
Duve, Thomas. "Von der Europäischen Rechtsgeschichte zu einer Rechtsgeschichte Europas in globalhistorischer Perspektive." *Rechtsgeschichte-Legal History* 20 (2012): 18–71. An amended version appeared as "Entanglements in Legal History: Concepts, Methods, Challenges." In *Entanglements in Legal History: Conceptual Approaches*, edited by Thomas Duve, 29–66. Frankfurt: Max Planck Institute for European Legal History, 2014.
Eagle, Marc. "Portraits of Bad Officials: Malfeasance in *Visita* Sentences from Seventeenth-Century Santo-Domingo." In *Corruption in the Iberian Empires. Greed, Custom, and Colonial Networks*, edited by Christoph Rosenmüller, 87–110.
Eagle, Marc. "Restoring Spanish Hispaniola, the First of the Indies: Local Advocacy and Transatlantic Arbitrismo in the Late Seventeenth Century." *Colonial Latin American Review* 23, no. 3 (2014): 384–412.

Ebert, Ina. "Fahrlässigkeit." In *Handwörterbuch zur deutschen Rechtsgeschichte (HRG)*, edited by Albrecht Cordes, Hans-Peter Haferkamp, Heiner Lück, Dieter Werkmüller, and Ruth Schmidt-Wiegand. 2nd ed., vol. 1, 1470–1474. Berlin: Erich Schmidt Verlag, 2008. www.hrgdigital.de/HRG.fahrlaessigkeit.

Eissa-Barroso, Francisco A. "De corregimiento a gobierno político-militar: el gobierno de Veracruz y la 'militarización' de cargos de gobierno en España e Indias durante los reinados de Felipe V." *Relaciones* 147 (2016): 13–49.

Eissa-Barroso, Francisco A. "La Nueva Granada en el sistema de Utrecht: Condiciones locales, contexto internacional, y reforma institucional." In *Resonancias Imperiales. América y el Tratado de Utrecht de 1713*, edited by Iván Escamilla, Matilde Souto, and Guadalupe Pinzón, 47–78.

Eissa-Barroso, Francisco A. "Of Experience, Zeal, and Selflessness: Military Officers as Viceroys in Early Eighteenth Century Spanish America." *The Americas* 68, no. 3 (2012): 317–345.

Eissa-Barroso, Francisco. "'Our Delivery Consists in Appointing Good Ministers': Corruption and the Dilemmas of Appointing Officials in Early Eighteenth-Century Spain." In *Corruption in the Iberian Empires. Greed, Custom, and Colonial Networks*, edited by Christoph Rosenmüller, 133–150.

Eissa-Barroso, Francisco A. "Politics, Political Culture, and Policy Making: The Reform of Viceregal Rule in the Spanish World under Philip V (1700–1746)." PhD diss., University of Warwick, 2010.

Eissa-Barroso, Francisco A. *The Spanish Monarchy and the Creation of the Viceroyalty of New Granada (1717–1739): The Politics of Early Bourbon Reform in Spain and Spanish America*. Leiden: Brill, 2016.

Elliot, John H. *The Count-Duke of Olivares. The Statesman in an Age of Decline*. New Haven and London: Yale University Press, 1986.

Elliott, John H. *Empires of the Atlantic World: Britain and Spain in America 1492–1830*. New Haven: Yale University Press, 2007.

Enciclopedia universal ilustrada europeo-americana. Vol. 61. Madrid: Espasa Calpe, 1991.

Engels, Jens Ivo. "Politische Korruption und Modernisierungsprozesse: Thesen zur Signifikanz der Korruptionskommunikation in der westlichen Moderne." In *Korruption: Historische Annäherungen an eine Grundfigur politischer Kommunikation*, edited by Niels Grüne and Simona Slanička, 35–54. Göttingen, Germany: Vanderhoek & Ruprecht. 2010.

Engels, Jens Ivo, Andreas Fährmeir, and Alexander Nützenadel, eds. "Einleitung." In *Geld–Geschenke–Politik. Korruption im neuzeitlichen Europa*. Historische Zeitschrift, Beihefte, NF., vol. 48, 1–15. Munich: Oldenbourg, 2009.

Escalona Lüttig, Huemac. "Rojo profundo: grana cochinilla y conflicto en la jurisdicción de Nexapa, Nueva España, siglo XVIII." PhD diss., Pablo de Olavide University, Seville, Spain, 2015.

Escamilla González, Francisco Iván. "Juan Manuel de Oliván Rebolledo (1676–1738): pensamiento y obra de un mercantilista novohispano." In *Historia del pensamiento económico: del mercantilismo al liberalismo*, edited by Pilar Martínez López-Cano and Leonor Ludlow, 109–130. Mexico City, UNAM, Instituto de Investigaciones Históricas, 2007.

Escamilla González, Francisco Iván. "La memoria de gobierno del virrey duque de Alburquerque, 1710." *Estudios de Historia Novohispana* 25 (2001): 157–78.
Escamilla González, Francisco Iván. "Nueva España ante la diplomacia de la era de Utrecht, 1716–1720: El caso de la guerra de la cuádruple alianza." In *Resonancias Imperiales. América y el Tratado de Utrecht de 1713*, edited by Iván Escamilla, Matilde Souto Mantecón, and Guadalupe Pinzón. 28–45.
Escamilla González, Francisco Iván, Matilde Souto Mantecón, and Guadalupe Pinzón Ríos. eds. *Resonancias Imperiales. América y el Tratado de Utrecht de 1713*. Mexico City: UNAM, Instituto de Investigaciones Históricas, Instituto de Investigaciones Dr. José María Luis Mora, 2016.
Escudero, José Antonio. "El gobierno central de las Indias: el consejo y las secretarías del despacho." In *El gobierno de un mundo. Virreinatos y audiencias en la América Hispánica*, edited by Feliciano Barrios, 95–118. Cuenca, Spain: Ediciones de la Universidad Castilla-La Mancha, Fundación Rafael del Pino, 2004.
Escudero, José Antonio. *Los orígenes del consejo de ministros en España*. Madrid: Editorial Complutense, 2001.
Farriss, Nancy M. *Maya Society under Colonial Rule. The Collective Enterprise of Survival*. Princeton: Princeton University Press, 1984.
Felices de la Fuente, María del Mar. *Condes, marqueses y duques. Biografías de nobles titulados durante el reinado de Felipe V*. Madrid: Doce Calles, Junta de Andalucía, 2013.
Felices de la Fuente, María del Mar. "Hacia la nobleza titulada: Los "méritos" para titular en el siglo XVII." In *Mérito, venalidad y corrupción*, edited by Francisco Andújar Castillo and Pilar Ponce-Leiva, 19–40.
Felices de la Fuente, María del Mar. *La nueva nobleza titulada de España y América en el siglo XVIII (1701–1746). Entre el mérito y la venalidad*. Almería: Universidad de Almería, 2012.
Feros, Antonio. *Kingship and Favoritism in the Spain of Philip III, 1598–1621*. Cambridge: Cambridge University Press, 2000.
Fernández, Roberto. *Carlos III*. Madrid: Arlanza, 2001.
Finnis, John. "Aquinas' Moral, Political, and Legal Philosophy." In *The Stanford Encyclopedia of Philosophy* (Fall 2011 Edition), edited by Edward N. Zalta. http://plato.stanford.edu/entries/aquinas-moral-political/.
Fischer, Karsten. "Korruption als Problem und Element politischer Ordnung." In *Geld–Geschenke–Politik: Korruption im neuzeitlichen Europa*, edited by Jens Ivo Engels, Andreas Fahrmeir, and Alexander Nützenadel, 49–65.
Foucault, Michel. *Discipline and Punish. The Birth of the Prison*. New York: Random House 1995.
Foucault, Michel. *The History of Sexuality: An Introduction*. Translated by Robert Hurley. New York: Vintage Books, 1978.
García García, Antonio. "Corrupción y venalidad en la magistratura mexicana durante el siglo XVIII." *Illes i Imperis. Estudis d'història de les societats en el món colonial i postcolonial* (Barcelona) 16 (2014): 13–38.
García García, Antonio. "La reforma de la plantilla de los tribunales americanos de 1701: El primer intento reformista del siglo XVIII." In *La venta de cargos y el*

ejercicio del poder en Indias, edited by Julián Ruiz Rivera and Ángel Sanz Tapia, 59–70. León, Spain: Universidad de León, Secretariado de Publicaciones, 2007.

García Cárcel, Ricard. *Felipe V y los españoles. Una visión periférica del problema de España*. Barcelona: Plaza & Janés, 2002.

García Cárcel, Ricard, and Rosa María Alabrús Iglesias. *España en 1700. Austrias o Borbones?* Madrid: Arlanza Ediciones, 2001.

Gardiner, John. "Defining Corruption." In *Political Corruption: Concepts and Contexts*, edited by Arnold J. Heidenheimer and Michael Johnston, 3rd ed., 25–40. New Brunswick, NJ: Transaction Publishers, 2002.

Garriga, Carlos. "Crimen corruptionis. Justicia y corrupción en la cultura del ius commune (Corona de Castilla, siglos XVI–XVII)." *Revista Complutense de Historia de América* 43 (2017): 21–48.

Garriga, Carlos. "Concepción y aparatos de la justicia: las Reales Audiencias de Indias." In *Convergencias y divergencias: México y Perú, siglos xvi–xix*, edited by Lilia Oliver. Mexico City: University of Guadalajara, El Colegio de Michoacán, 2006.

Garriga, Carlos. "Sobre el gobierno de la justicia en Indias (siglos xvi–xii)." *Revista de Historia del Derecho* 34 (2006): 67–160.

Gayol, Víctor. *Las reglas del juego*. Vol. 1 of *Laberintos de justicia: Procuradores, escribanos y oficiales de la Real Audiencia de México (1750–1812)*. Zamora: El Colegio de Michoacán, 2007.

Gayol, Víctor. *El juego de las reglas*. Vol. 2 of *Laberintos de justicia: Procuradores, escribanos y oficiales de la Real Audiencia de México (1750–1812)*. Zamora: El Colegio de Michoacán, 2007.

Gebhardt, Jürgen. "Ursprünge und Elemente des 'Korruptionsdiskurses' im westlichen Ordnungsdenken." In *Korruption und Governance aus interdisziplinärer Sicht: Ergebnisse eines Workshops des Zentralinstituts für Regionalforschung vom Mai 2001*, edited by Oskar Kurer, 15–38. Bad Windsheim: Degener, 2003.

Génaux, Maryvonne. "Corruption in English and French Fields of Vision." In *Political Corruption: Concepts and Contexts*, edited by Arnold J. Heidenheimer and Michael Johnston, 3rd ed. 107–21. New Brunswick, NJ: Transaction Publishers, 2002.

Génaux, Maryvonne. "Social Sciences and the Evolving Concept of Corruption." *Crime, Law & Social Change* 42, no. 1 (2004): 13–24.

Gerhard, Peter. *A Guide to the Historical Geography of New Spain*. Rev. ed. Norman: University of Oklahoma Press, 1993.

Gerhard, Peter. *México en 1742*. Mexico City: Porrúa, 1962.

Gil, Xavier. "Spain and Portugal." In *European Political Thought, 1450–1700: Religion, Law, and Philosophy*, edited by Howell A. Lloyd, Glenn Burgess, and Simon Hodson, 416–57. New Haven, CT: Yale University Press, 2007.

Granovetter, Mark S. "The Strength of Weak Ties." *American Journal of Sociology* 78, no. 6 (1973): 1360–1380.

Griffin, Miriam T. *Seneca on Society. A Guide to De Beneficiis*. Oxford: Oxford University Press, 2013.

Göhler, Gerhard, Ulrike Höppner, Sybille de la Rosa, and Stefan Skupien. "Steuerung jenseits von Hierarchie. Wie diskursive Praktiken, Argumente und

Symbole steuern können." *Politische Vierteljahresschrift* 51, no. 4 (2010): 691–720.
Gombrich, Ernst H. *The Uses of Images. Studies in the Social Function of Art and Visual Communication.* London: Phaidon Press, 1999.
Gómez, Inés. "Entre la corrupción y la venalidad: Don Pedro Valle de la Cerda y la visita al Consejo de Hacienda de 1643." In *Mérito, venalidad y corrupción*, edited by Francisco Andújar Castillo and Pilar Ponce-Leiva, 235–250.
Gómez García, Lidia. "La conformación de los ayuntamientos constitucionales en los pueblos indios de la jurisdicción de San Juan de los Llanos, Puebla, 1765–1824." In *Los actores locales de la nación en la América Latina: Análisis estratégicos*, edited by Evelyne Sanchez, 99–136.
Gómez Gómez, Amalia. *Las visitas de la Real Hacienda novohispana en el reinado de Felipe V (1710–1733)*. Seville: Escuela de Estudios Hispano-Americanos, 1979.
Gómez Urdáñez, José Luis. "Carvajal y Ensenada, un binomio político." In *Ministros de Fernando VI*, edited by José Luis Gómez Urdáñez and José Miguel Delgado Barrado, 65–92. Córdoba, Spain: Universidad de Córdoba, 2002.
Gómez Urdáñez, José Luis. *Fernando VI*. Madrid: Arlanza, 2001.
Gómez Urdáñez, José Luis. *El proyecto reformista de Ensenada*. Lleida: Milenio, 1996.
González Alonso, Benjamín. "Estudio preliminar." In *Política para corregidores y señores de vassallos, en tiempo de paz, y de guerra, y para juezes eclesiásticos y seglares [...]*, by Jerónimo Castillo de Bobadilla, edited by Sebastián Martín-Retortillo, 7–34. Madrid: Instituto de Estudios de Administración Local, 1978.
González Jiménez, Manuel, et al. *Instituciones y corrupción en la historia*. Valladolid: Universidad de Valladolid, 1998.
González González, Enrique, ed. *Proyecto de estatutos ordenados por el virrey Cerralvo (1626)*. Mexico City: UNAM, 1991.
González González, Enrique, and Víctor Gutiérrez Rodríguez. "Los catedráticos novohispanos y sus libros. Tres bibliotecas del siglo xvi." In *Dalla lectura all'e-learning*, edited by Andrea Romano. 83–103. Bologna: Clueb, 2015.
González Rodríguez, Jaime. "La condición del intelectual en México. Los juristas mexicanos en las audiencias de Nueva España entre 1600 y 1711." *Revista Complutense de Historia de América* 34 (2008): 157–182.
Goode, Catherine Tracy. "Merchant-Bureaucrats, Unwritten Contracts, and Fraud in the Manila Galleon Trade." In *Corruption in the Iberian Empires. Greed, Custom, and Colonial Networks*, edited by Christoph Rosenmüller, 171–197.
Graeff, Peter. "Prinzipal-Agent-Klient-Modelle als Zugangsmöglichkeit zur Korruptionsforschung. Eine integrative und interdisziplinäre Perspektive." In *Korruption: historische Annäherungen an eine Grundfigur politischer Kommunikation*, edited by Niels Grüne and Simona Slanička, 55–75. Göttingen: Vanderhoek, 2010.
Grafe, Regina. *Distant Tyranny: Markets, Power, and Backwardness in Spain, 1650–1800*. Princeton, NJ: Princeton University Press, 2012.

Grüne, Niels. "'Und sie wissen nicht, was es ist': Ansätze und Blickpunkte historischer Korruptionsforschung." In *Korruption: historische Annäherungen an eine Grundfigur politischer Kommunikation*, edited by Niels Grüne and Simona Slanička, 11–34. Göttingen: Vanderhoek, 2010.

Gruzinski, Serge. "The Walls of Images." In *Empires of Vision: A Reader*, edited by Martin Jay and Sumathi Ramaswamy, 47–63. Durham, NC: Duke University Press, 2014.

Guevara-Gil, Armando, and Frank Solomon. "A 'Personal Visit': Colonial Political Ritual and the Making of Indians in the Andes." *Colonial Latin American Review* 3, nos. 1–2 (1994): 3–36.

Guerra, François-Xavier. "De la política antigua a la política moderna. La revolución de la soberanía." In *Los espacios públicos en Iberoamérica. Ambigüedades y problemas. Siglos xviii–xix*, edited by François-Xavier Guerra, Annick Lempérière, et al. 109–139. Mexico City: Fondo de Cultura Económica, 1998.

Guerra, François-Xavier. *Modernidad e Independencias. Ensayos sobre las revoluciones hispánicas*. Mexico City: Fondo de Cultura Económica, Mapfre, 1992.

Guerra, François-Xavier. "Pour une nouvelle histoire politique: Acteurs sociaux et acteurs politiques." In *Structures et Cultures des Sociétés Ibéro-Américaines. Au-delà du Modèle-Économique: Coloque international en hommage au professeur Francois Chevalier, 29–30 avril 1988*. Maison des Pays Ibériques, Groupe Interdisciplinaire de Recherche et de Documentation sur l'Amérique Latine, 245–260. Paris: CNRS, 1990.

Gundermann, Iselin, ed. *Allgemeines Landrecht für die Preußischen Staaten 1794. Ausstellung des Geheimen Staatsarchivs Preußischer Kulturbesitz, 1994*. Mainz: Hase & Koehler, 1994.

Gutiérrez Rodríguez, Víctor. "El colegio novohispano de Santa María de Todos los Santos: alcances y límites de una institución colonial." *Estudios de historia social y económica de América* (Alcalá de Henares, Spain) 9 (1992): 23–35.

Guzmán Brito, Alejandro. "Prólogo." In *Derecho común y derecho propio en el Nuevo Mundo*, edited by Bernardino Bravo Lira, xi–xxxviii. Santiago, Chile: Ed. Jurídica de Chile, 1989.

Habermas, Jürgen. *The Structural Transformation of the Public Sphere: an Inquiry into a Category of Bourgeois Society*. Cambridge: Polity Press, 1996.

Härter, Karl. "Violent Crimes and Retaliation in the European Criminal Justice System between the Seventeenth and Nineteenth Century." *Max Planck Institute for European Legal History Research Paper Series* 1 (2013): 1–18. http://dx.doi.org/10.2139/ssrn.2218350.

Hamnett, Brian. "The Appropriation of Mexican Church Wealth by the Spanish Bourbon Government–The 'Consolidación de Vales Reales,' 1805–1809." *Journal of Latin American Studies* 1 (1969): 85–113.

Hamnett, Brian. *The Mexican Bureaucracy before the Bourbon Reforms, 1700–1770: A Study in the Limitations of Absolutism*. Glasgow: Institute of Latin American Studies, University of Glasgow, 1979.

Hamnett, Brian. "Neu-Spanien/Mexiko 1760–1821." In *Handbuch der Geschichte Lateinamerikas. Vol. 2. Lateinamerika von 1760 bis 1900*, edited

by Raymond Th. Buve and John R. Fisher, 142–189. Stuttgart: Klett-Cotta, 1992.
Hamnett, Brian. *Politics and Trade in Southern Mexico, 1750–1821*. Cambridge: Cambridge University Press, 1971.
Haring, C. H. *The Spanish Empire in America*. New York, Oxford University Press, 1947.
Hatton, Ragnhild Marie, Robert Oresko, G. C. Gibbs, and Hamish M. Scott. Introduction to *Royal and Republican Sovereignty in Early Modern Europe: Essays in Memory of Ragnhild Hatton*, edited by Ragnhild Marie Hatton, Robert Oresko, G. C. Gibbs, and Hamish M. Scott, 1–42. Cambridge: Cambridge University Press, 1997.
Hausberger, Bernd. "La conquista del empleo público en la Nueva España. El comerciante gaditano Tomás Ruiz de Apodaca y sus amigos, siglo xviii." *Historia Mexicana* 56, no. 3 (2007): 725–778.
Hausberger, Bernd. "Limpieza de sangre y construcción étnica de los vascos en el imperio español." In *El peso de la sangre. Limpios, mestizos y nobles en el mundo hispánico*, edited by Nikolaus Böttcher, Bernd Hausberger, and Max S. Hering Torres, 77–111.
Hausberger, Bernd, and Óscar Mazín. "Nueva España: Los años de autonomía." In *Nueva Historia general de México*, edited by Erik Velásquez García, Enrique Nalda, Pablo Escalante Gonzalbo, Bernardo García Martínez, Bernd Hausberger, Óscar Mazín Gómez, Dorothy Tanck de Estrada, et al. 263–307. Mexico City: El Colegio de México, 2010.
Heidenheimer, Arnold J., and Michael Johnston, eds. *Political Corruption: Concepts & Contexts*. New Brunswick, NJ: Transaction Publishers, 2002.
Hensel, Silke. "Symbolic Meaning of Electoral Processes in Mexico in the Early 19th Century." In *Constitutional Cultures. On the Concept and Representation of Constitutions in the Atlantic World*, edited by Silke Hensel, Ulrike Bock, Katrin Dircksen, and Hans-Ulrich Thamer, 375–402. Newcastle, UK: Cambridge Scholars Publishing, 2012.
Hering Torres, Max S. "Limpieza de sangre en España. Un modelo de interpretación." In *El peso de la sangre. Limpios, mestizos y nobles en el mundo hispánico*, edited by Nikolaus Böttcher, Bernd Hausberger, and Max S. Hering Torres, 29–62.
Hermann, Christian. "L'Arbitrisme: Un autre état pour un autre Espagne." In *Le premier âge de l'état en Espagne (1450–1700)*, edited by Christian Hermann, 239–256. Paris: Editions du Centre National de la Recherche Scientifique, 1989.
Hermann, Christian, and Jacques Marcadé. *Les royaumes ibériques au XVIIe siècle*. Paris: SEDES, 2000.
Herzog, Tamar. *Defining Nations. Immigrants and Citizens in Early Modern Spain and Spanish America*. New Haven: Yale University Press, 2003.
Herzog, Tamar. *Frontiers of Possession. Spain and Portugal in Europe and the Americas*. Cambridge, MA: Harvard, 2015.
Herzog, Tamar, "Ritos de control, prácticas de negociación: pesquisas, visitas y residencias y las relaciones entre Quito y Madrid (1650–1750)." In *Nuevas Aportaciones a la historia jurídica de Iberoamérica*, edited by

José Andrés-Gallego. Madrid: Fundación Histórica Tavera, Hernando de Larramendi/Mapfre, 2000. CD-ROM.

Herzog, Tamar. *Upholding Justice. Society, State, and the Penal System in Quito (1650–1750)*. Ann Arbor: University of Michigan Press, 2004.

Hespanha, António Manuel. *As vèsperas de Leviathan. Instituções e Poder Político. Portugal Sec. XVII.* Lisbon: Hespanha, 1986.

Hespanha, António Manuel. "Les autres raisons de la politique. L'économie de la grâce." In *Recherche sur l'histoire de l'État dans le monde ibérique (15e–20e siècle)*, edited by Jean-Frédéric Schaub, 67–86. Paris: Presses de l'École Normale Superieure, 1993. Spanish translation "La economía de la gracia." In *La Gracia del Derecho. Economía de la cultura en la edad moderna*. Madrid: Centro de Estudios Constitucionales, 1993.

Hespanha, António Manuel. "Paradigmes de légitimation, aires de gouvernement, traitement administratif et agents de l'administration." In *Les figures de l'administrateur. Institutions, réseaux, pouvoirs en Espagne, en France et au Portugal 16e–19e siècle*, edited by Robert Descimon, Jean-Frédéric Schaub, and Bernard Vincent, 19–28.

Hespanha, António Manuel. "Porque é que existe e em que é que consiste um direito colonial brasileiro." In *Brasil-Portugal: Sociedades, culturas e formas de governar no mundo português (séculos XVI–XVIII)*, edited by Eduardo França Paiva, 21–41. São Paulo: Annablume, 2006.

Hillebrand, Christian. *Die Real Audiencia in Mexiko*. Baden-Baden: Nomos, 2016.

Hintze, Otto. "Der Commissarius und seine Bedeutung in der allgemeinen Verwaltungsgeschichte." In *Staat und Verfassung. Gesammelte Abhandlungen zur allgemeinen Verfassungsgeschichte*, edited by Gerhard Oestreich, 242–274. Göttingen: Vandenhoek und Rupprecht, 1962.

Holenstein, André. "'Gute Policey' und lokale Gesellschaft. Erfahrung als Kategorie im Verwaltungshandeln des 18. Jahrhunderts." *Historische Zeitschrift*. New Series 31 (2001): 433–450.

Holenstein, André. "Introduction: Empowering Interactions: Looking at Statebuilding from Below." In *Empowering Interactions: Political Cultures and the Emergence of the State in Europe 1300–1900*, edited by Wim Blockmans, André Holenstein, and Jon Mathieu in collaboration with Daniel Schläppi, 1–31. Farnham, UK: Ashgate, 2009.

Holguín Callo, Oswaldo. *Poder, corrupción y tortura en el Perú de Felipe II. El Doctor Diego de Salinas (1558–1595)*. Lima: Fondo Editorial del Congreso del Perú, 2002.

Honores, Renzo. "El licenciado Polo Ondegardo y el debate sobre el Derecho Consuetudinario en los Andes del siglo XVI." Unpublished manuscript.

Huetz de Lemps, Xavier, *L'archipel des épices. La corruption de l'administration espagnole aux Philippines (fin xviiie–fin xixe siècle)*. Madrid: Casa de Velázquez, 2006.

"Imperator Caesar M. Aurelius Severus Alexander Augustus." In *Brill's Encyclopedia of the Ancient World*, edited by Hubert Cancik and Helmuth Schneider, vol. 13, 360–61. Leiden: Brill, 2008.

Irigoin, Alejandra, and Regina Grafe. "Bargaining for Absolutism: A Spanish Path to Nation-State and Empire Building." *HAHR* 88, no. 2 (2008): 173–209.
Iseli, Andrea. *Gute Policey. Öffentliche Ordnung in der Frühen Neuzeit*. Stuttgart: Ulmer, 2009.
Isenmann, Moritz. "Rector est Raptor. Korruption und ihre Bekämpfung in den italienischen Kommunen des späten Mittelalters." In *Nützliche Netzwerke und korrupte Seilschaften*, edited by Arne Karsten and Hillard von Thiessen, 208–230. Göttingen: Vandenhoeck & Rupprecht, 2006.
Israel, Jonathan I. *Radical Enlightenment: Philosophy and the Making of Modernity, 1650–1750*. Oxford: Oxford University Press, 2001.
Jansen, Dorothea. *Einführung in die Netzwerkanalyse. Grundlagen, Methoden, Forschungsbeispiele*. 2nd ed. Opladen: Leske + Budrich, 2003.
Jaumann, Herbert. *Handbuch Gelehrtenkultur der Frühen Neuzeit. Band 1: Bio-bibliographisches Repertorium*. Berlin, New York: Walter de Gruyter, 2004.
Jiménez Estrella, Antonio. "Servicio y mérito en el ejército de Felipe IV: la quiebra de la meritocracia en época de Olivares." In *Mérito, venalidad y corrupción*, edited by Francisco Andújar Castillo and Pilar Ponce-Leiva, 91–113.
Johnston, Michael. "The Search for Definitions: The Vitality of Politics and the Issue of Corruption." *International Social Science Journal* 48, no. 3 (1996): 149, 321–335.
Kagan, Richard L. *Lawsuits and Litigants in Castile, 1500–1700*. Chapel Hill: University of North Carolina Press, 1981.
Kamen, Henry. *Philip V of Spain: The King Who Reigned Twice*. New Haven, CT: Yale University Press, 2001.
Kamen, Henry. *Spain in the Later Seventeenth Century, 1665–1700*. London: Longman, 1980.
Kaufmann, Ekkehard. "Schuldstrafrecht." In *Handwörterbuch zur deutschen Rechtsgeschichte*, edited by Adalbert Erler, Ekkehard Kaufmann, and Ruth Schmidt-Wiegand, vol. 4, 1516–1517. Berlin: Erich Schmidt Verlag, 1990.
Kettering, Sharon. *Patrons, Brokers, and Clients in Seventeenth-Century France*. Oxford: Oxford University Press, 1986.
Klaveren, Jakob van, "Corruption as a Historical Phenomenon." In *Political Corruption. Concepts & Contexts*, edited by Arnold J. Heidenheimer and Michael Johnston, 83–94. New Brunswick: Transaction Publishers, 2002.
Klaveren, Jakob van. "Die historische Erscheinung der Korruption, in ihrem Zusammenhang mit der Staats-und Gesellschaftsstruktur betrachtet." *Vierteljahresschrift für Sozial-und Wirtschaftsgeschichte* 44, no. 4 (1957): 289–324.
Klaveren, Jakob van. "Die historische Erscheinung der Korruption. II. Die Korruption in den Kapitalgesellschaften, besonders in den Großen Handelskompanien, III. Die internationalen Aspekte der Korruption." *Vierteljahresschrift für Sozial- und Wirtschaftsgeschichte* 45, no. 4 (1958): 433–68, 469–504.
Klaveren, Jacob van. *Europäische Wirtschaftsgeschichte Spaniens im 16. und 17. Jahrhundert*. Stuttgart: Gustav Fischer, 1960.
Koch, Elisabeth. "Gerechter Preis." In *Handwörterbuch zur deutschen Rechtsgeschichte (HRG)*, edited by Albrecht Cordes, Hans-Peter Haferkamp, Heiner Lück, Dieter Werkmüller, and Ruth Schmidt-Wiegand. 2nd ed., vol. 2,

123–127. Berlin: Erich Schmidt Verlag, 2012. www.hrgdigital.de/HRG.gerechter_preis.

Koschaker, Paul. *Europa und das römische Recht*. Munich: C. H. Beck, 1966.

Koselleck, Reinhart. "Introduction and Prefaces to the Geschichtliche Grundbegriffe," trans. Michaela Richter. *Contributions to the History of Concepts* 6, no. 1 (2011): 8–22.

Koselleck, Reinhart. *Futures Past: On the Semantics of Historical Time*. Translated and with an introduction by Keith Tribe. New York City: Columbia University Press, 2004.

Koselleck, Reinhart. *The Practice of Conceptual History: Timing History, Spacing Concepts*. Stanford, CA: Stanford University Press, 2002.

Kuethe, Allan J, "Cardinal Alberoni and Reform in the American Empire." In *Early Bourbon Spanish America. Politics and Society in a Forgotten Era*, edited by Francisco A. Eissa-Barroso and Ainara Vázquez Varela, 23–39. Leiden: Brill, 2013.

Kuethe, Allan J. "Imperativos militares en la política comercial de Carlos III." In *Soldados del Rey. El ejército borbónico en América colonial en vísperas de la Independencia*, edited by Alan Kuethe and Juan Marchena, 149–161. Castelló de la Plana: Universitat Jaume Primer, 2005.

Kuethe, Allan J. "La política colonial de Felipe V y el proyecto de 1720." In *Orbis Incognitus: Avisos y legajos del Nuevo Mundo: Homenaje al Profesor Luis Navarro García*, vol. 1, edited by Fernando Navarro Antolín, 233–242. Huelva, Spain: Universidad de Huelva. 2007.

Kuethe, Allan J., and Kenneth J. Andrien. *The Spanish Atlantic World in the Eighteenth Century: War and the Bourbon Reforms, 1713–1796*. Cambridge: Cambridge University Press, 2014.

Kurer, Oskar. "Was ist Korruption? Der Stand der Diskussion um eine Definition von Korruption." In *Korruption und Governance aus interdisziplinärer Sicht*, edited by Oskar Kurer, 41–52. Neustadt: Degener, 2003.

Lane, Kris. "Corrupción y dominación colonial: el gran fraude a la Casa de la Moneda de Potosí en 1649." *Boletín del Instituto de Historia Argentina y Americana Dr. Emilio Ravignani* 43 (2015): 94–130.

Lane, Kris. "From Corrupt to Criminal: Reflections on the Great Potosí Mint Fraud of 1649." In *Corruption in the Iberian Empires. Greed, Custom, and Colonial Networks*, edited by Christoph Rosenmüller, 33–62.

Langer, Máximo. "The Long Shadow of the Adversarial and Inquisitorial Categories." In *The Oxford Handbook of Criminal Law*, edited by Markus D. Dubber and Tatjana Hörnle. Oxford: Oxford University Press, 2015. www.oxfordhandbooks.com/view/10.1093/oxfordhb/9780199673599.001.0001/oxfordhb-9780199673599-e-39.

Langue, Frédérique. "Los pardos venezolanos, ¿heterodoxos o defensores del orden social? Una revisión necesaria en el contexto de las conmemoraciones de la Independencia." In *Los actores locales de la nación en la América Latina: Análisis estratégicos*, edited by Evelyne Sanchez, 77–98.

Larkin, Brian. *The Very Nature of God. Baroque Catholicism and Religious Reform in Bourbon Mexico City*. Albuquerque, NM: University of New Mexico Press, 2010.

Bibliography

Lavrín, Asunción. "The Execution of the Law of the Consolidación in New Spain: Economic Aims and Results." *HAHR* 53, no. 1 (1973): 27–49.

Lepsius, Susanne. "Bartolus de Saxoferrato (1313/14–1357)." In *Handwörterbuch der deutschen Rechtsgeschichte (HRG)*, edited by Albrecht Cordes, Hans-Peter Haferkamp, Heiner Lück, Dieter Werkmüller, and Ruth Schmidt-Wiegand. 2nd ed., vol. 1, 450–453. Berlin: Erich Schmidt Verlag, 2008. www.hrgdigital.de/HRG.bartolus_de_saxoferrato_1313_14_1357.

Lepsius, Susanne. *Von Zweifeln zur Überzeugung. Der Zeugenbeweis im gelehrten Recht ausgehend von der Abhandlung des Bartolus von Sassoferrato.* Frankfurt: Klostermann, 2003.

Lempérière, Annick. *Entre Dieu et le roi, la république: México, XVIe–XIXe siècle.* Paris: Belles lettres, 2004.

Lentz, Mark. *Murder in Mérida, 1792. Violence, Factions, and the Law.* Albuquerque, NM: University of New Mexico Press, 2018.

León Sanz, Virginia. "La nobleza austracista. Entre Austrias y Borbones." In *Nobleza y Sociedad en la España Moderna II*, edited by María del Carmen Iglesias, 43–77. Madrid, Oviedo: Nobel, Fundación Banco Santander Central Hispano, 1997.

León Sanz, Virginia. "La llegada de los Borbones al trono." In *Historia de España: Siglo XVIII: La España de los Borbones*, edited by Ricardo García Cárcel, 41–111. Madrid: Cátedra, 2002.

Lindemann, Mary. "Dirty Politics or 'Harmonie'? Defining Corruption in Early Modern Amsterdam and Hamburg." *Journal of Social History* 45, no. 3 (2012): 582–604.

Lingelbach, Gerhard. "Arglist." In *Handwörterbuch der deutschen Rechtsgeschichte (HRG)*, edited by Albrecht Cordes, Hans-Peter Haferkamp, Heiner Lück, Dieter Werkmüller, and Ruth Schmidt-Wiegand. 2nd ed., vol. 1, 294–296. Berlin: Erich Schmidt Verlag, 2008. www.hrgdigital.de/id/arglist.html.

Lira, Andrés. "Dimension jurídica de la justicia. Pecadores y pecados en tres confesionarios de la Nueva España, 1545–1732." *Historia Mexicana* 55, no. 4 (2006): 1139–1179.

Llombard Rosa, Vicent. "El pensamiento económico de la Ilustración en España (1730–1812)." In *Economía y economistas españoles. Vol 3. La Ilustración*, edited by Enrique Fuentes Quintana. 7–89. Barcelona: Galaxia Gutenberg, 2000.

Llorente, Mercedes. "Mariana of Austria's Portraits as Ruler-Governor and *Curadora* by Juan Carreño de Miranda and Claudio Coello." In *Early Modern Habsburg Women: Transnational Contexts, Cultural Conflicts, Dynastic Continuities*, edited by Anne J. Cruz and Maria Galli Stampino, 197–222. Brookfield, VT: Ashgate, 2013.

Lockhart, James. *The Nahuas after the Conquest: A Social and Cultural History of the Indians of Central Mexico, Sixteenth through Eighteenth Centuries.* Stanford, CA: Stanford University Press, 1992.

Lohmann Villena, Guillermo. *Los ministros de la audiencia de Lima (1700–1821).* Sevilla: EEHA, 1974.

Lomnitz, Claudio, "Introducción." In *Vicios públicos, virtudes privadas: la corrupción en México*, edited by Claudio Lomnitz Adler. 11–30. Mexico City: CIESAS, 2000.

López i Camps, Joaquim E. "La embajada española del conde Ferdinand von Harrach y la formación del austracismo." In *Hispania-Austria III: Der Spanische Erbfolgekrieg: La Guerra de Sucesión española*, edited by Friedrich Edelmayer, Virginia León Sanz, and José Ignacio Ruiz Rodríguez, 11–26. Munich: Oldenbourg, 2008.

Loupès, Philippe, and Jean-Pierre Dedieu. "Pouvoir et vénalité des offices en Espagne: Corregidores et échevins, un groupe médian?" In *Les officiers "moyens" à l'époque moderne: France, Angleterre, Espagne*, edited by Michel Cassan, 153–180. Limoges, France: Presses Universitaires de Limoges. 1998.

Luhmann, Niklas. "Familiarity, Confidence, Trust: Problems and Alternatives." In *Trust: Making and Breaking Cooperative Relations*, edited by Diego Gambetta. Department of Sociology, University of Oxford, 2000. http://citeseerx.ist.psu.edu/viewdoc/download?doi=10.1.1.23.8075&rep=rep1&type=pdf.

Luhmann, Niklas. *Introduction to Systems Theory*. Edited by Dirk Baecker. Cambridge: Polity, 2013.

Luhmann, Niklas. *Legitimation durch Verfahren*. 6th ed. Frankfurt: Suhrkamp, 2001.

Luhmann, Niklas. "Operational Closure and Structural Coupling: The Differentiation of the Legal System." *Cardozo Law Review* 13, no. 5 (1992): 1419–1442.

Lynch, John. *The Hispanic World in Crisis and Change, 1598–1700*. Oxford: Blackwell, 1992.

Lynn, Kimberly. *Between Court and Confessional: The Politics of Spanish Inquisitors*. Cambridge: Cambridge University Press, 2013.

MacLachlan, Colin M. *Criminal Justice in Eighteenth Century Mexico: A Study of the Tribunal of the Acordada*. Berkeley and Los Angeles: University of California Press, 1974.

MacLachlan, Colin M. *Imperialism and the Origins of Mexican Culture*. Cambridge, MA: Harvard University Press, 2015.

MacLachlan, Colin M. *Spain's Empire in the New World: The Role of Ideas in Institutional and Social Change*. Berkeley: University of California Press, 1988.

Machuca, Laura. "El impacto del repartimiento de mercancías en la provincia de Tehuantepec durante el siglo xviii: los pueblos de la grana." In *Repartimiento forzoso de mercancías en México, Perú, y Filipinas*, edited by Margarita Menegus. 120–145. Mexico City: Instituto Mora, UNAM, 2000.

Machuca, Laura. "Los pueblos indios de Tehuantepec y el repartimiento de mercancías durante el siglo XVIII." MA Thesis, UNAM, 2000.

Magdaleno Redondo, Ricardo, ed. *Títulos de Indias. Catálogo XX del AGS*. Valladolid: Archivo General de Simancas, 1954.

Maravall, José Antonio. *Estado moderno y mentalidad social (siglos XV a XVII)*. 2 vols. Madrid: Ediciones de la Revista de Occidente, 1972.

Marichal, Carlos. *Bankruptcy of Empire: Mexican Silver and the Wars between Spain, Britain, and France, 1760–1810.* New York: Cambridge University Press, 2007.

Marichal, Carlos. "Rethinking Negotiation and Coercion in an Imperial State." *HAHR* 88, no. 2 (2008): 211–18.

Marichal, Carlos, and Matilde Souto Mantecón. "La nueva España y el financiamiento del imperio español en América: Los situados para el Caribe en el siglo XVIII." In *El secreto del imperio español: Los situados coloniales en el siglo XVIIII*, edited by Carlos Marichal and Johanna von Grafenstein, 61–93. Mexico City: El Colegio de México, Instituto Mora, 2012.

Martínez Shaw, Carlos, and Marina Alonso Mola. *Felipe V.* Madrid: Arlanza Ediciones, 2001.

Martins, José Antônio. "Os fundamentos da república e sua corrupçao nos *Discursos* de Maquiavel." PhD diss., Universidade de São Paulo, 2007.

Mathieu, Jon. "Statebuilding from Below – Towards a Balanced View." In *Empowering Interactions: Political Cultures and the Emergence of the State in Europe 1300–1900*, edited by Wim Blockmans, André Holenstein, and Jon Mathieu, 305–311. Farnham: Ashgate, 2009.

Mayagoitia, Alejandro. "Notas sobre las Reglas ciertas y precisamente necessarias para juezes y ministros [...] de Fray Jerónimo Moreno, O.P." *Anuario Mexicano de Historia del Derecho* 8 (1996): 309–336.

Mayagoitia, Alejandro, "Las últimas generaciones de abogados virreinales." In *Los abogados y la formación del Estado mexicano*, edited by Oscar Cruz Barney, Héctor Felipe Fix-Fierro, and Elisa Speckmann, 3–82. Mexico City: UNAM, Instituto de Investigaciones Históricas, Instituto de Investigaciones Jurídicas, Colegio de Abogados de México, 2013.

Mazín Gómez, Oscar. "Introducción." In *México en el mundo hispánico*, edited by Oscar Mazín Gómez, vol. 1, 15–18. Zamora: El Colegio de Michoacán, 2000.

Mazín Gómez, Oscar. "La nobleza ibérica y su impacto en la América española: tendencias historiográficas recientes." In *El peso de la sangre. Limpios, mestizos y nobles en el mundo hispánico*, edited by Nikolaus Böttcher, Bernd Hausberger, and Max S. Hering Torres, 63–76.

McFarlane, Anthony. "Hispanoamerika." In *Handbuch der Geschichte Lateinamerikas*, edited by Horst Pietschmann, vol. 1, 751–788. Stuttgart: Klett-Cotta, 1994.

McFarlane, Anthony. "Political Corruption and Reform in Bourbon Spanish America." In *Political Corruption in Europe and Latin America*, edited by Walter Little and Eduardo Posada Carbó, 41–63. London: Palgrave, Macmillan, 1996.

McKinley, Michelle A. *Fractional Freedoms. Slavery, Intimacy, and Legal Mobilization in Colonial Lima, 1600–1700.* Cambridge: Cambridge University Press, 2016.

Meccarelli, Massimo. "Dimensions of Justice and Ordering Factors in Criminal Law from the Middle Ages till Juridical Modernity." In *From the Judge's Arbitrium to the Legality Principle. Legislation as a Source of Law in Criminal Trials.* Comparative Studies in Continental and Anglo-American

Legal History, edited by Georges Martyn, Anthony Musson, and Heikki Pihlajamäki, vol. 31. 49–68. Berlin: Duncker & Humblot, 2013.

Meder, Stephan. *Rechtsgeschichte. Eine Einführung.* 5th amended ed. Cologne: Böhlau, 2014.

Menegus Bornemann, Margarita. "La economía indígena y su articulación al mercado en Nueva España. El repartimiento forzoso de mercancías." In *Repartimiento forzoso de mercancías en México, Perú, y Filipinas*, edited by Margarita Menegus. 9–64. Mexico City: Instituto Mora, UNAM, 2000.

Mirow, Matthew C. *Latin American Law: A History of Private Law and Institutions in Spanish America.* Austin: University of Texas Press, 2004.

Mitteis, Heinrich. *The State in the Middle Ages. A Comparative Constitutional History of Feudal Europe.* Amsterdam, Oxford: North Holland, 1975.

Moreno Cebrián, Alfredo. "Acumulación y blanqueo de capitales del Marqués de Castelfuerte (1723–1763)." In *El "Premio" de Ser Virrey. Los intereses públicos y privados del gobierno virreinal en el Perú de Felipe V*, edited by Alfredo Moreno Cebrián and Nuria Sala i Vila, 151–276. Madrid: CSIC, 2004.

Moreno Cebrián, Alfredo. "La confusión entre lo público y lo privado en el reinado de Felipe V." *Boletin de Historia y Antigüedades* 93, no. 835 (2006): 837–855.

Moreno Cebrián, Alfredo. *Corregidor de Indios y la economía peruana del siglo xviii (los repartos forzosos de mercancias).* Madrid: CSIC, 1977.

Moreno Cebrián, Alfredo. *El virreinato del marqués de Castelfuerte 1724–1736.* Madrid: Editorial Catriel, 2000.

Moreno Cebrián, Alfredo, and Núria Sala i Vila. *El "Premio" de Ser Virrey. Los intereses públicos y privados del gobierno virreinal en el Perú de Felipe V.* Madrid: CSIC, 2004.

Morris, Steven David, and Charles H. Blake, eds. *Corruption and Politics in Latin America: National and Regional Dynamics.* Boulder, CO: Lynne Rienner, 2010.

Möller, Horst. "Ämterkäuflichkeit in Brandenburg-Preußen im 17. und 18. Jahrhundert." In *Ämterkäuflichkeit: Aspekte sozialer Mobilität im europäischen Vergleich (17. und 18. Jahrhundert)*, edited by Klaus Malettke, 156–176. Berlin: Colloquium Verlag, 1980.

Mondragón Aguilera, Edgar Iván. "Atrapados por el procedimiento. Un proceso inquisitorial como espacio para el juego de estrategias." In *Los actores locales de la nación en la América Latina: Análisis estratégicos*, edited by Evelyne Sanchez. 41–76.

Moreno Gamboa, Olivia. "Historia de una librería novohispana del siglo xviii." MA Thesis, UNAM, 2006.

Moreno Gamboa, Olivia. "La imprenta y los autores novohispanos. La transformación de una cultura impresa colonial bajo el régimen borbónico (1701–1821)." PhD diss., UNAM, 2013.

Moreno Gamboa, Olivia, "Comercio y comerciantes de libros entre Cádiz y Veracruz en el tránsito hacia un nuevo orden (1702–1749)." In *Resonancias imperiales: América y la Paz de Utrecht de 1713*, edited by Iván Escamilla, Matilde Souto, and Guadalupe Pinzón, 275–308.

Mousnier, Roland. *The Organs of State and Society: The Institutions of France under the Absolute Monarchy, 1598–1789*, vol. 2. Translated by Arthur Goldhammer. Chicago: University of Chicago Press, 1984.
Mousnier, Roland. *La vénalité des offices sous Henri IV et Louis XIII*. 2nd ed. Paris: Presses Universitaires de France, 1971.
Moutin, Osvaldo Rodolfo. *Legislar en la América hispánica en la temprana edad moderna. Procesos y características de la producción de los Decretos del Tercer Concilio Provincial Mexicano (1585)*. Frankfurt: Max Planck Institute for European Legal History, 2016.
Moutoukias, Zacarias. "Negocios y redes sociales: modelo interpretativo a partir de un caso rioplatense (siglo XVIII)." *Caravelle* 67 (1997): 37–55.
Moutoukias, Zacarias. "Networks, Coalitions and Unstable Relationships: Buenos Aires on the Eve of Independence." In *The Collective and the Public in Latin America. Cultural Identities and Political Order*, edited by Tamar Herzog and Luis Roniger, 134–157. Brighton, UK: Sussex Academic Press, 2000.
Moutoukias, Zacarias. "Una forma de oposición: el contrabando." In *Metals and Monies in an Emerging Global Economy, An Expanding World. The European Impact on World History 1450–1800*, edited by Dennis O. Flynn and Arturo Giráldez, 19–54. Aldershot: Variorum, 1997.
Muldoon, James. "Extra ecclesiam non est imperium: The Canonists and the Legitimacy of Secular Power." *Studia Gratiana* 9 (1996): 553–580.
Muldoon, James. "Solórzano's De indiarum iure: Applying a Medieval Theory of World Order in the Seventeenth Century." *Journal of World History* 2, no. 1 (1991): 29–45.
Mumford, Jeremy Ravi. "Forgeries and Tambos: False Documents, Imagined Incas, and the Making of Andean Space." In *Corruption in the Iberian Empires. Greed, Custom, and Colonial Networks*, edited by Christoph Rosenmüller, 13–32.
Mumford, Jeremy Ravi. "Litigation as Ethnography in Sixteenth-Century Peru." *HAHR* 88, no. 1 (2008): 5–40.
Mumford, Jeremy Ravi. *Vertical Empire: The General Resettlement of Indians in the Colonial Andes*. Durham, NC: Duke University Press, 2012.
Münkler, Heribert. *Empires. The Logic of World Domination from Ancient Rome to the United States*. Translated by Patrick Camiller. Cambridge: Polity, 2007.
Nassehi, Armin. *Wie weiter mit Niklas Luhmann?* Hamburg: Hamburger Edition, 2008.
Nava Rodríguez, Teresa, and Gloria Franco Rubio. "Vénalité et futuras dans l'administration espagnole au XVIIIe siècle." In *Les figures de l'administrateur: Institutions, réseaux, pouvoirs en Espagne, en France et au Portugal, 16e–19e siècle*, edited by Robert Descimon, Jean-Frédéric Schaub, and Bernard Vincent, 95–108.
Navarro García, Luis. "Los Oficios vendibles en Nueva España durante la Guerra de Sucesión." *Anuario de Estudios Americanos* 32 (1975): 133–152.
Niermeyer, J. F., C. van de Kieft, and G. S. M. M. Lake-Schoonebeek. *Mediae Latinintatis Lexicon Minus*. Leiden: Brill, 1976.

Noejovich, Héctor Omar. "El consumo de azogue: ¿indicador de corrupción, del sistema colonial en el virreinato del Perú? (siglos xvi–xvii)." *Fronteras de la historia* 7 (2002): 77–98.

Ochoa Brun, Miguel Ángel. "Vida, obra y doctrina de Juan de Solórzano y Pereyra." In *Politica Indiana*, edited by Miguel Ángel Ochoa Brun, vol. 1, xiii–lxviii. Madrid: Atlas, 1972.

"Original Sin." In *The Oxford Dictionary of the Christian Church*, edited by F. L. Cross and E. A. Livingstone, rev. ed. Oxford: Oxford University Press, 2005, online ed. 2009. www.oxfordreference.com.

Otto, Jonathan. "Tiraquellus, Andreas (André Tiraqueau)." In *The Oxford International Encyclopedia of Legal History*, edited by Stanley N. Katz, Oxford: Oxford University Press. 2009, online ed. 2009. www.oxfordreference.com.

Owensby, Brian. *Empire of Law and Indian Justice in Colonial Mexico*. Stanford, CA: Stanford University Press, 2008.

Ouweneel, Arij. "El gobernador de Indios, el repartimiento de comercios y la caja de comunidad en los pueblos de Indios del México central (siglo xviii)." In *Repartimiento forzoso de mercancías en México, Perú, y Filipinas*, edited by Margarita Menegus, 65–97.

Ouweneel, Arij. *Shadows over Anáhuac. An Ecological Interpretation of Crisis and Development in Central Mexico, 1730–1880*. Albuquerque, NM: University of New Mexico Press, 1996.

Padgett, John F. and Christopher K. Ansell. "Robust Action and the Rise of the Medici." In *American Journal of Sociology* 98, no. 6 (1993): 1259–1319.

Pagden, Anthony. *Lords of All the World. Ideologies of Empire in Spain, Britain and France c. 1500–1800*. New Haven: Yale University Press, 1995.

Paquette, Gabriel B. *Enlightenment, Governance, and Reform in Spain and Its Empire, 1759–1808*. Houndmills, NY: Palgrave Macmillan, 2008.

"Para seguir con el debate en torno al colonialismo," *Nuevo Mundo Mundos Nuevos*, February 8, 2005. http://nuevomundo.revues.org/430.

Parry, J. H. *The Sale of Public Office in the Spanish Indies under the Habsburgs*. Berkeley, Los Angeles: University of California Press, 1953.

Pastor, Rodolfo. "El repartimiento de mercancías y los alcaldes mayores novohispanos. Un sistema de explotación, de sus orígenes a la crisis de 1810." In *El gobierno provincial en la Nueva España 1570–1787*, edited by Woodrow Borah. 2nd ed. 219–258. Mexico City: UNAM, 2002.

Phelan, John L. *The Kingdom of Quito in the Seventeenth Century: Bureaucratic Politics in the Spanish Empire*, Madison: University of Wisconsin Press, 1967.

Pearce, Adrian J. *The Origins of Bourbon Reform in Spanish South America, 1700–1763*. New York: Palgrave Macmillan, 2014.

Pearce, Adrian J. "Repercusiones comerciales del Tratado de Utrecht en Hispanoamérica." In *Resonancias imperiales: América y la Paz de Utrecht de 1713*, edited by Iván Escamilla, Matilde Souto, and Guadalupe Pinzón. 221–246.

Peck, Linda Levy. *Court, Patronage, and Corruption in Early Stuart England*. London: Routledge, 1993.

Pennington, Kenneth. "Bartolomé de las Casas." In *Great Christian Jurists in Spanish History*, edited by Rafael Domingo and Javier Martínez-Torrón, 98–115. Cambridge: Cambridge University Press, 2018.
Pennington, Kenneth. "Sovereignty and Rights in Medieval and Early Modern Jurisprudence: Law and Norms without a State." In *Roman Law as Formative of Modern Legal Systems: Studies in Honour of Wiesław Litewski*, edited by J. Sondel, J. Reszczyński, and P. Ściślicki, vol. 2, 25–36. Krakow: Jagiellonian University Press, 2003.
Peña Izquierdo, Antonio Ramón. *La casa de Palma: La familia Portocarrero en el gobierno de la Monarquía Hispánica (1665–1700)*. Córdoba, Spain: Universidad de Córdoba. 2004.
Peña Izquierdo, Antonio Ramón. "La crisis sucesoria de la monarquía española: El cardenal Portocarrero y el primer gobierno de Felipe V (1698–1705)." PhD diss., Universidad Autónoma de Barcelona. 2005.
Peralta Ruiz, Victor. *Patrones, clientes y amigos. El poder burocrático indiano en la España del siglo XVIII*. Madrid: Consejo Superior de Investigaciones Científicas, 2006.
Phipps, Elena. *Cochineal Red: The Art History of a Color*. New York: Metropolitan Museum of Art, 2010.
Pieper, Renate. *Die spanischen Kronfinanzen in der zweiten Hälfte des 18. Jahrhunderts (1753–1788). Ökonomische und soziale Auswirkungen*. Stuttgart: Franz Steiner 1988. Translated into Spanish as *La Real Hacienda bajo Fernando VI y Carlos III (1753–1788). Repercusiones económicas y sociales*. Madrid: Instituto de Estudios Fiscales. 1992.
Pieper, Renate, and Philipp Lesiak. "Redes mercantiles entre el Atlántico y el Mediterráneo en los inicios de la guerra de los treinta años." In *Redes sociales e instituciones comerciales en el imperio español, siglos xvii a xix*, edited by Antonio Ibarra and Guillermina del Valle Pavón, 19–39. Mexico City: UNAM, Instituto Mora, 2007.
Pietschmann, Horst. "Alcaldes Mayores, Corregidores und Subdelegados: Zum Problem der Distriktsbeamtenschaft im Vizekönigreich Neuspanien." *Jahrbuch für Geschichte von Staat, Wirtschaft und Gesellschaft Lateinamerikas* 9 (1972): 173–270.
Pietschmann, Horst. "Antecedentes políticos de México, 1808: Estado territorial, estado novohispano, crisis política y desorganización constitucional." In *México, 1808–1821. Las ideas y los hombres*, edited by Pilar Gonzalbo Aizpuru and Andrés Lira González, 23–70. México: Colegio de México, 2014.
Pietschmann, Horst. "El comercio de repartimientos de los alcaldes mayores y corregidores en la región de Puebla-Tlaxcala en el siglo XVIII." In *Estudios sobre política indigenista española en América, Simposio Hispanoamericano de Indigenismo Histórico. Terceras Jornadas Americanistas de la Universidad de Valladolid*, edited by Demetrio Ramos Pérez, vol. 3, 147–153. Valladolid: Universidad de Valladolid, 1977.
Pietschmann, Horst. "'Corrupción' en el virreinato novohispano: Un tercer intento de valoración." *E-Spania: Revue interdisciplinaire d'études*

hispaniques médiévales et modernes 16 (2013). http://e-spania.revues.org/22848.

Pietschmann, Horst, "Corrupción en las Indias Españolas: Revisión de un debate en la historiografía sobre Hispanoamérica colonial." *Memorias de la Academia Mexicana de la Historia* 40 (1997): 39–54.

Pietschmann, Horst. "Diego García Panés y Joaquín Antonio de Rivadeneira Barrientos, pasajeros en un mismo barco: Reflexiones en torno al México 'imperial' entre 1755 y 1808." In *Un hombre de libros: homenaje a Ernesto de la Torre Villar*, edited by Alicia Mayer and Amaya Garritz, 203–233. Mexico City: UNAM, 2012.

Pietschmann, Horst. "Justicia, discurso político y reformismo borbónico en la Nueva España del siglo xviii." In *Dinámicas del antiguo régimen y orden constitucional. Representación, justicia, y administración en Iberoamérica. Siglos xviii–xix*, edited by Marco Bellingeri, 17–54. Turin: Otto, 2000.

Pietschmann, Horst. *Die staatliche Organisation des kolonialen Iberoamerika*. Stuttgart: Klett-Cotta, 1980.

Pilo, Rafaella. *Juan Everardo Nithard y sus "causas no causas": Razones y pretextos para el fin de un valimiento*. Madrid: Silex, 2010.

Pinzón Ríos, Guadalupe. "El Tratado de Utrecht y sus repercusiones en los contactos marítimos entre Nueva España y Guatemala." In *Resonancias imperiales: América y la Paz de Utrecht de 1713*, edited by Iván Escamilla, Matilde Souto, and Guadalupe Pinzón. 275–308.

Pinzón Ríos, Guadalupe. "Un interinato contra las prácticas corruptas en Acapulco. El castellano Teodoro de Croix al arribo del galeón San Carlos de Borromeo (1766)." In *'Dádivas, dones y dineros.' Aportes a una nueva historia de la corrupción en América Latina desde el imperio español hasta la modernidad*, edited by Christoph Rosenmüller and Stephan Ruderer, 88–112.

Plescia, Joseph. "Judicial Accountability and Immunity in Roman Law." *American Journal of Legal History* 45, no. 1 (2001): 51–70.

Plumpe, Werner. "Korruption. Annäherung an ein historisches und gesellschaftliches Phänomen." In *Geld–Geschenke–Politik. Korruption im neuzeitlichen Europa*, edited by Jens Ivo Engels, Andreas Fahrmeir, and Alexander Nützenadel, 19–48.

Ponce-Leiva, Pilar. "Percepciones sobre la corrupción en la monarquía hispánica, siglos XVI y XVII." In *Mérito, venalidad y corrupción*, edited by Francisco Andújar Castillo and Pilar Ponce-Leiva, 193–211.

Ponce-Leiva, Pilar. "El valor de los méritos. Teoría y práctica política en la provisión de oficios (Quito, 1675–1700)." *Revista de Indias* 73, no. 258 (2013): 341–363.

Ponce-Leiva, Pilar, and Francisco Andújar Castillo. "Introducción." In *Mérito, venalidad y corrupción*. 7–17.

Ponce-Leiva, Pilar, and Francisco Andújar Castillo, eds. *Mérito, venalidad y corrupción en España y América*. Valencia: Albatros, 2016.

Poole, Stafford. *Pedro Moya de Contreras. Catholic Reform and Royal Power in New Spain, 1571–1591*. Berkeley: University of California Press, 1987.

Posthumus, Nicolaas Wilhelmus. *Nederlandsche Prijsgeschiedenis*, vol. 1. Leiden: Brill, 1943. In *Medieval and Early Modern Databank*. www2.scc.rutgers.edu/memdb/.
Prado, Fabricio. "Addicted to Smuggling: Contraband Trade in Eighteenth-Century Brazil and Rio de la Plata." In *Corruption in the Iberian Empires. Greed, Custom, and Colonial Networks*, edited by Christoph Rosenmüller, 197–214.
Premo, Bianca. "Custom Today: Temporality, Customary Law, and Indigenous Enlightenment." *HAHR* 94, no. 3 (2014): 355–80.
Prodi, Paolo. *Settimo non rubare. Furto e mercato nella storia dell'Occidente*. Bologna: Società editrice Il Mulino, 2009.
Puente Brunke, José de la. "Codicia y bien público: los ministros de la Audiencia en la Lima seiscentista." *Revista de Indias* 236, no. 66 (2006): 133–148.
Puente Luna, José Carlos de la, and Renzo Honores. "Guardianes de la real justicia: alcaldes de indios, costumbre y justicia local en Huarochirí colonial." *Histórica* (Lima) 40, no. 2 (2016): 11–47.
Puntoni, Pedro. "O governo-geral e o Estado do Brasil: poderes intermédios e administração (1549–1720)." In *O Brasil no império maritime português*, edited by Stuart Schwartz and Erik L. Myrup, 39–75. Bauru, Sao Paolo: EDUSC, 2009.
Quiroz, Alfonso W. *Corrupt Circles. A History of Unbound Graft in Peru*. Washington: Woodrow Wilson Center Press; Baltimore: The Johns Hopkins Press, 2008.
Ragon, Pierre. "Abusivo o corrupto? El conde de Baños, virrey de la Nueva España (1660–1664): De la voz pública al testimonio en derecho." In *Mérito, venalidad y corrupción*, edited by Francisco Andújar Castillo and Pilar Ponce-Leiva, 267–281.
Ramos, Frances. *Identity, Ritual, and Power in Colonial Puebla*. Tucson: University of Arizona Press, 2012.
Ramos, Frances. "Un puñal, un tóxico que quita la vida de toda una monarquía. Ceremonias públicas, sermones panegíricos, y el discurso antiinglés en la víspera de Utrecht." In *Resonancias imperiales: América y la Paz de Utrecht de 1713*, edited by Iván Escamilla, Matilde Souto, and Guadalupe Pinzón, 119–146.
Ramos, Frances. "Custom, Corruption, and Reform in Early Eighteenth-Century Mexico. Puebla's Merchant Priests versus the Reformist Bureaucrat." In *Corruption in the Iberian Empires. Greed, Custom, and Colonial Networks*, edited by Christoph Rosenmüller, 151–170.
Reinhard, Wolfgang. *Freunde und Kreaturen. "Verflechtung" als Konzept zur Erforschung historischer Führungsgruppen. Römische Oligarchie um 1600*. Munich: Ernst Vögel, 1979.
Reinhard, Wolfgang, *Geschichte der Staatsgewalt: Eine vergleichende Verfassungsgeschichte*, 3rd ed. Munich: C. H. Beck, 2003.
Reinhard, Wolfgang. "No Statebuilding from Below! A Critical Commentary." In *Empowering Interactions: Political Cultures and the Emergence of the State in Europe 1300–1900*, edited by Wim Blockmans, André Holenstein, and Jon Mathieu, 299–304. Farnham: Ashgate, 2009,

Reinhard, Wolfgang. "Resümee." In *Ämterkäuflichkeit: Aspekte sozialer Mobilität im europäischen Vergleich (17. und 18. Jahrhundert)*, edited by Klaus Malettke, 188. Berlin: Colloquium Verlag, 1980.

Reinhard, Wolfgang. "Staatsmacht als Kreditproblem: Zur Struktur und Funktion des frühneuzeitlichen Ämterhandels." In *Absolutismus*, edited by Ernst Hinrichs, 214–248. Frankfurt: Suhrkamp, 1986.

Reinhard, Wolfgang. Review of *Geld–Geschenke–Politik: Korruption im neuzeitlichen Europa*, edited by Engels, Fahrmeir, Nützenadel. *Historische Zeitschrift* 290, no. 1 (2010): 141–142.

Richter, Melvin. "A Note on the Text of Reinhart Koselleck: 'Offene Fragen an die Geschichtlichen Grundbegriffe.'" *Archiv für Begriffsgeschichte* 54 (2012): 249–266.

Riedel-Spangenberger, Ilona. "Nicolò de Tudeschi (1386–1445)." In *Biographisch-Bibliographisches Kirchenlexikon*, edited by Traugott Bautz, vol. 6, 696–701. Herzberg: Bautz, 1993.

Restall, Matthew. *The Maya World. Yucatec Culture and Society, 1550–1850*. Stanford, CA: Stanford University Press, 1997.

Ringrose, David R. *Spain, Europe, and the "Spanish Miracle," 1700–1900*. Cambridge: Cambridge University Press, 1996.

Riva Fernández, Amanda de la. *Guia de las actas del cabildo de la ciudad de México, 1731–1740*. Mexico City: UIA, DDF, 1988.

Robinson, O. F., T. D. Fergus, and W. M. Gordon. *European Legal History. Sources and Institutions*. Oxford: Oxford University Press, 2000.

Rodríguez O., Jaime. *"We Are Now the True Spaniards." Sovereignty, Revolution, Independence, and the Emergence of the Federal Republic of Mexico, 1808–1824*. Stanford, CA: Stanford University Press, 2012.

Rojas Aguirre, Luis Emilio. "Historia dogmática de la falsedad documental." *Revista de Derecho de la Pontificia Universidad Católica de Valparaíso* 39 (2012): 545–583.

Rojkind, Inés. "'El triunfo moral del pueblo.' Denuncias de corrupción y movilización política en Buenos Aires, a fines del siglo xix." In *'Dádivas, dones y dineros.' Aportes a una nueva historia de la corrupción en América Latina desde el imperio español hasta la modernidad*, edited by Christoph Rosenmüller and Stephan Ruderer, 169–188.

Rosenmüller, Christoph. "'Corrupted by Ambition:' Justice and Patronage in Imperial New Spain and Spain, 1650–1755." *HAHR* 96, no. 1 (2016): 1–37.

Rosenmüller, Christoph, ed. *Corruption in the Iberian Empires. Greed, Custom, and Colonial Networks*. Albuquerque, NM: University of New Mexico Press, 2017.

Rosenmüller, Christoph. "De lo innato a lo performativo: dos conceptos rivales de la corrupción, siglos xvii–xviii." In *'Dádivas, dones y dineros.' Aportes a una nueva historia de la corrupción en América Latina desde el imperio español hasta la modernidad*, edited by Christoph Rosenmüller and Stephan Ruderer, 61–86.

Rosenmüller, Christoph. "'El grave delito de … corrupcion.' La visita de la audiencia de México (1715–1727) y las repercusiones internas de Utrecht." In *Resonancias imperiales: América y la Paz de Utrecht de 1713*, edited by Iván Escamilla, Matilde Souto, and Guadalupe Pinzón, 79–118.

Rosenmüller, Christoph. "'The Indians... long for change:' The Secularization of Regular Parishes in New Spain, 1749–1755." In *Early Bourbon Spanish America. Politics and Society in a Forgotten Era*, edited by Francisco A. Eissa-Barroso and Ainara Vázquez Varela, 143–64. Leiden: Brill, 2013.

Rosenmüller, Christoph. "Mexico in Spain's Oceanic Empire, 1519–1821." In *Latin American History: Oxford Research Encyclopedias*, edited by William Beezley, 2016. http://latinamericanhistory.oxfordre.com/view/10.1093/acrefore/9780199366439.001.0001/acrefore-9780199366439-e-28.

Rosenmüller, Christoph. *Patrons, Partisans, and Palace Intrigues: The Court Society of Colonial Mexico, 1702–1710*. Latin American and Caribbean Series, no. 6. Calgary: Calgary University Press, 2008.

Rosenmüller, Christoph, and Stephan Ruderer, eds. *'Dádivas, dones y dineros.' Aportes a una nueva historia de la corrupción en América Latina desde el imperio español hasta la modernidad*. Frankfurt, Madrid: Vervuert/Iberoamericana, 2016.

Rubial García, Antonio. *Una monarquía criolla (La provincia agustina en el siglo XVII)*. Mexico City: Consejo Nacional para la Cultura y las Artes, 1990.

Rubio Mañé, José Ignacio. *Introducción al estudio de los virreyes de Nueva España, 1535–1746*. 2 vols. Mexico City: UNAM, 1959.

Ruderer, Stephan. "Corrupción y violencia. Una relación ambivalente en Argentina y Uruguay en el siglo xix." In *'Dádivas, dones y dineros.' Aportes a una nueva historia de la corrupción en América Latina desde el imperio español hasta la modernidad*, edited by Christoph Rosenmüller and Stephan Ruderer, 147–168.

Ruiz Rivera, Julián, and Ángel Sanz Tapia. "Presentación." In *La venta de cargos y el ejercicio del poder en Indias*, edited by Julián Ruiz Rivera and Ángel Sanz Tapia, 11–15. León, Spain: Universidad de León, Secretariado de Publicaciones. 2007.

Ruiz Torres, Pedro. *Reformismo e Ilustración. Historia de España*, vol. 5. Barcelona: Crítica, Marcial Pons, 2008.

Saguier, Eduardo. "La corrupción de la burocracia colonial borbónica y los orígenes del federalismo: El caso del Virreinato del Río de la Plata." *Jahrbuch für Geschichte Lateinamerikas* 29 (1992): 149–177.

Sala i Vila, Nuria. "Una corona bien vale un virreinato: El marqués de Castelldosrius, primer virrey borbónico del Perú (1707–1710)." In *El "Premio" de Ser Virrey. Los intereses públicos y privados del gobierno virreinal en el Perú de Felipe V*, edited by Alfredo Moreno Cebrián, and Nuria Sala i Vila, 17–150.

Sánchez Bella, Ismael. *Derecho Indiano: Estudios I. Las visitas generals en la América española (siglos XVI–XVII)*. Pamplona, Spain: Ediciones Universidad de Navarra, 1991.

Sanchez, Evelyne. "Introducción." In *Los actores locales de la nación en la América Latina: Análisis estratégicos*, edited by Evelyne Sánchez, 6–22. Puebla: Benemérita Universidad Autónoma de Puebla; Tlaxcala: El Colegio de Tlaxcala, 2011.

Sanchiz, Javier, "Lucas de Careaga, marqués de Santa Fe. La historia fugaz de un noble vasco en la Nueva España. Una biografía en construcción." In *Los vascos en las regiones de México. Siglos XVI–XX*, edited by Amaya Garritz. Vol. 3, 203–217. Mexico City: UNAM, Gobierno Vasco, 1997.

Sanchiz, Javier, and José I. Conde. *Títulos y dignidades nobiliarias en Nueva España*. In preparation.

Sanciñena Asurmendi, Teresa. *La audiencia en México en el reinado de Carlos III*. Mexico City: UNAM, Instituto de Investigaciones Históricas, 1999.

Sandoval, Irma Eréndira. ed. *Corrupción y Transparencia: Debatiendo las fronteras entre Estado, mercado y sociedad*. Mexico City: UNAM, 2009.

Sanz Ayán, Carmen. "Reformismo y Real Hacienda: Oropesa y Medinaceli." In *Nobleza y sociedad en la España moderna*, edited by Maria del Carmen Iglesias, 157–186. Madrid: Fundacion Cultural de la Nobleza Española, 1996.

Sanz Tapia, Ángel. "Aproximación al beneficio de cargos políticos americanos en la primera mitad del siglo XVIII." *Revista Complutense de Historia de América*, no. 24 (1998): 147–76.

Sanz Tapia, Ángel. *¿Corrupción o necesidad? La venta de cargos de gobierno americanos bajo Carlos II (1674–1700)*. Madrid: CSIC, 2009.

Sarabia Viejo, María Justina. *Don Luís de Velasco, virrey de Nueva España, 1550–1564*. Sevilla: CSIC, EEHA, 1978.

Scardaville, Michael C. "Justice by Paperwork: A Day in the Life of a Court Scribe in Bourbon Mexico City." *Journal of Social History* 36, no. 4 (2003): 979–1007.

Schaposchnik, Ana E. *The Lima Inquisition: The Plight of Crypto-Jews in Seventeenth-Century Peru* Madison: University of Wisconsin Press, 2015.

Schaub, Jean-Frédéric. "El pasado republicano del espacio público." In *Los espacios públicos en Iberoamérica: Ambigüedades y problemas, siglos XVIII–XIX*, edited by François-Xavier Guerra and Annick Lempérière, et al. 27–53.

Schlosser, Hans. *Neuere europäische Rechtsgeschichte. Privat- und Strafrecht vom Mittelalter bis zur Moderne*. 2nd ed. Munich: C. H. Beck, 2014.

Schmoeckel, Mathias. "Notorietät." In *Handwörterbuch der deutschen Rechtsgeschichte (HRG)*, edited by Albrecht Cordes, Hans-Peter Haferkamp, Heiner Lück, Dieter Werkmüller, and Ruth Schmidt-Wiegand. 2nd ed., vol. 3, 1985–1987. www.hrgdigital.de/HRG.notorietaet.

Schroeder, Susan. Introduction to *The Conquest All Over Again: Nahuas and Zapotecs Thinking, Writing, and Painting Spanish Colonialism*, edited by Susan Schroeder, 1–15. Brighton, UK: Sussex Academic Press, 2010.

Schroeder, Susan. "Chimalpahin Rewrites the Conquest. Yet Another Epic History?" In *The Conquest All Over Again*, edited by Susan Schroeder, 101–123.

Schwaller, John F. "*Alcalde* vs. Mayor: Translating the Colonial World." *The Americas* 69, no. 3 (2013): 391–400.

Schwartz, Stuart B. *Sovereignty and Society in Colonial Brazil. The High Court of Bahia and its Judges, 1609–1751*. Berkeley: University of California Press, 1973.

Scott, James C. *Comparative Political Corruption*. Englewood Cliffs, NJ: Prentice-Hall, 1972.

Sebastián, Javier Fernández, ed. *Diccionario político y social del mundo iberoamericano: Conceptos políticos fundamentales, 1770–1870, Iberconceptos 2*. Madrid: Universidad del País Vasco, 2014.
Skinner, Quentin. "On Intellectual History and the History of Books." *Contributions to the History of Concepts* 1, no. 1 (2005): 29–36.
Skinner, Quentin, and Javier Fernández Sebastián, "Intellectual History, Liberty and Republicanism: An Interview with Quentin Skinner." *Contributions to the History of Concepts* 3, no. 1 (2007): 103–123.
Socolow, Susan Migden. *The Women of Colonial Latin America*. 2nd ed. Cambridge: Cambridge University Press, 2015.
Souto, Matilde. "Tierra Adentro: los riesgos de permitir la internación de los flotistas gaditanos y los factores ingleses en Nueva España." In *Resonancias imperiales: América y la Paz de Utrecht de 1713*, edited by Iván Escamilla, Matilde Souto, and Guadalupe Pinzón, 247–274.
Speer, Heino. *Rechtshistorische Notizen und Texte*. http://drqerg.de/RHN/personen/.
Stagl, Jakob Fortunat. "Restitutio in integrum." In *Diccionario Histórico de Derecho Canónico en Hispanoamérica y Filipinas. Siglos XVI–XVIII*, edited by Thomas Duve, Osvaldo R. Moutin, and María del Pilar Mejía Quiroga. Frankfurt: Max Planck Institute of European Legal History, forthcoming.
Stein, Stanley J. "Bureaucracy and Business in the Spanish Empire, 1759–1804: Failure of a Bourbon Reform in Mexico and Peru." *HAHR* 61, no. 1 (1981): 2–28.
Stein, Stanley J., and Barbara H. Stein. *Apogee of Empire. Spain and New Spain in the Age of Charles III, 1759–1789*. Baltimore and London: The Johns Hopkins University Press, 2003.
Stein, Stanley J., and Barbara H. Stein. *Silver, Trade, and War. Spain and America in the Making of Early Modern Europe*. Baltimore, London: Johns Hopkins Press, 2000.
Stolleis, Michael. "Grundzüge der Beamtenethik (1550–1650)." In Michael Stolleis, *Ausgewählte Aufsätze und Beiträge*, edited by Stefan Ruppert and Miloš Vec, 41–72. Frankfurt: Vittorio Klostermann, 2011.
Stolleis, Michael. *Histoire du droit public en Allemagne. La théorie du droit public impérial et la science de la police 1600–1800*. Translated by Michel Senellart. Paris: Presse Universitaire de France, 1998.
Storrs, Christopher. *The Resilience of the Spanish Monarchy, 1665–1700*. Oxford: Oxford University Press, 2006.
Stumpf, Roberta. "Formas de venalidade de ofícios na monarquia portuguesa de século xviii." In *Cargos e ofícios nas monarquias ibéricas: Provimento, controlo e venalidade (séculos XVII–XVIII)*, edited by Roberta Stumpf and Nandini Chaturvedula, 279–298. Lisbon: Centro de História de Além-Mar, 2012.
Suter, Andreas. "Korruption oder Patronage? Außenbeziehungen zwischen Frankreich und der Alten Eidgenossenschaft als Beispiel (16. bis 18. Jahrhundert)." *Zeitschrift für Historische Forschung* 37, no. 2 (2010): 187–218.

Szászdi León-Borja, István. "Observaciones sobre la venta de los oficios en tiempos de Carlos I." In *La Venta de cargos y el ejercicio del poder en Indias*, edited by Julián Ruiz Rivera and Ángel Sanz Tapia, 19–32. León, Spain: Universidad de León, Secretariado de Publicaciones.

Tanck de Estrada, Dorothy, and Carlos Marichal. "¿Reino o colonia? Nueva España, 1750–1804." In *Nueva Historia General de México*, edited by Erik Velásquez García, et al. 307–353. Mexico City: El Colegio de México, 2010.

Tau Anzoátegui, Victor. *El Jurista en el Nuevo Mundo. Pensamiento. Doctrina. Mentalidad*. Frankfurt: Max Planck Institute for European Legal History, 2016.

Tau Anzoátegui, Víctor. "El poder de la costumbre. Estudios sobre el Derecho Consuetudinario en América hispana hasta la Emancipación." In *Nuevas aportaciones a la historia jurídica de Iberoamérica*, edited by José Andrés Gallego. Madrid: Fundación Histórica Tavera, Hernando de Larramendi / Mapfre, 2000. CD-ROM.

Tau Anzoátegui, Víctor. "Entre leyes, glosas y comentos. El episodio de la recopilación de Indias." In *Homenaje al Profesor Alfonso García-Gallo*, vol. 4, 267–283. Madrid: Editorial Complutense, 1996.

Taylor, William. *Drinking, Homicide, and Rebellion in Colonial Mexican Villages*. Stanford, CA: Stanford University Press, 1979.

TePaske, John J. "General Tendencies and Secular Trends in the Economies of Mexico and Peru, 1750–1810: The View from the *cajas* of Mexico and Lima." In *The Economies of Mexico and Peru During the Late Colonial Period 1760–1810*, edited by Nils Jacobsen and Hans-Jörg Puhle, 316–339. Berlin: Colloquium, 1986.

TePaske, John J., and Herbert S. Klein. *Ingresos y egresos de la Real Hacienda de Nueva España*. 2 vols. Mexico City: Instituto Nacional de Antropología e Historia, 1986–1988.

Thiessen, Hillard von. "Korruption und Normenkonkurrenz: Zur Funktion und Wirkung von Korruptionsvorwürfen gegen die Günstling-Minister Lerma und Buckingham in Spanien und England im frühen 17. Jahrhundert." In *Geld–Geschenke–Politik: Korruption im neuzeitlichen Europa*, edited by Jens Ivo Engels, Andreas Fahrmeir, and Alexander Nützenadel, 91–120.

Thompson, E. P. "The Moral Economy of the English Crowd in the Eighteenth Century." *Past and Present* 50 (1971): 76–136.

Thompson, I. A. A. "Absolutism, Legalism, and the Law in Castile, 1500–1700." In *Der Absolutismus–ein Mythos? Strukturwandel monarchischer Herrschaft in West-und Mitteleuropa (ca. 1550–1700)*, edited by Ronald G. Asch and Heinz Duchhardt, 185–227. Cologne: Böhlau, 1996.

Thompson, I. A. A. "*Do ut des*: La economía política del 'servicio' en la Castilla moderna." In *Servir al rey en la monarquía de los Austrias: Medios, fines y logros del servicio al soberano en los siglos XVI y XVII*, edited by Alicia Esteban Estríngana, 283–296. Madrid: Sílex, 2012.

Toribio Medina, José. *Historia de la Inquisición en México*. Mexico City: Ediciones Fuentes Cultural, 1905.

Torribio Medina, José. *La imprenta en México (1539–1821)*, vol. 4 (1718–1744). Mexico City: UNAM, 1989. Facsimile of the first edition, Santiago, Chile, 1911.

Torres Puga, Gabriel. "Fragmentos del proceso contra fray José de San Ignacio." Unpublished transcription of the inquisition trial record.

Torres Puga, Gabriel. *Opinión pública y censura en Nueva España. Indicios de un silencio imposible. 1767–1794*. Mexico City: El Colegio de México, 2010.

Torres Aguilar, Manuel. *Corruption in the Administration of Justice in Colonial Mexico. A Special Case*. Madrid: Dykinson, 2015.

Traslosheros Hernández, Jorge Eugenio. *La reforma de la iglesia del antiguo Michoacán. La gestión episcopal de fray Marcos Ramírez de Prado (1640–1666)*. Morelia: Universidad Michoacana de San Nicolás de Hidalgo, 1995.

Traslosheros Hernández, Jorge Eugenio, and Ana de Zaballa Beascoechea, eds. *Los indios ante los foros de justicia religiosa en la Hispanoamérica virreinal*. Mexico City: UNAM, 2010.

Tomás y Valiente, Francisco. *La venta de oficios en Indias (1492–1606)*. Madrid: Instituto de Estudios Administrativos, 1972.

Tomás y Valiente, Francisco. "Les ventes des offices publics en Castille aux XVIIe et XVIIIe siècles." In *Ämterkäuflichkeit: Aspekte sozialer Mobilität im europäischen Vergleich (17. und 18. Jahrhundert)*, edited by Klaus Malettke, 89–114. Berlin: Colloquium Verlag, 1980.

Tomás y Valiente, Francisco. *Los validos en la monarquía española del siglo XVII: Estudio institucional*. Madrid: Siglo Veintiuno, 1982.

Tutino, John. *Making a New World. Founding Capitalism in the Bajío and Spanish North America*. Durham, DC: Duke University Press, 2011.

Twinam, Ann. *Public Lives, Private Secrets: Gender, Honor, Sexuality and Illegitimacy in Colonial Spanish America*. Stanford, CA: Stanford University Press, 1999.

Twinam, Ann. *Purchasing Whiteness: Pardos, Mulattos, and the Quest for Social Mobility in the Spanish Indies*. Stanford, CA: Stanford University Press, 2015.

Uribe-Urán, Victor M. *Honorable Lives: Lawyers, Family, and Politics in Colombia, 1780–1850*. Pittsburgh: University of Pittsburgh Press, 2000.

Valle Menéndez, Antonio del. *Juan Francisco de Güemes y Horcasitas: Primer conde de Revillagigedo, Virrey de México: La historia de un soldado (1681–1766)*. Santander, Spain: Librería Estudio, 1998.

Vallejo, Jesús. "Acerca del fruto del árbol de los jueces. Escenarios de la justicia en la cultura del *ius commune*." In *La justicia en el derecho privado y en el derecho público. Series Anuario de la Facultad de Derecho de la Universidad Autónoma de Madrid 2*, edited by Liborio L. Hierro and Francisco J. Laporta, 19–46. Madrid: Universidad Autónoma de Madrid, 1998.

Vallejo, Jesús. "El cáliz de plata. Articulación de órdenes jurídicos en la jurisprudencia del ius commune." *Revista de Historia del Derecho* 38 (2009). www.scielo.org.ar/scielo.php?script=sci_arttext&pid=S1853-17842009000 200002&lng=es&nrm=iso.

Vallejo García-Hevia, José María. *Juicio a un conquistador. Pedro de Alvarado*. Madrid: Marcial Pons, 2008.

Van Young, Eric. *Hacienda and Market in Eighteenth-Century Mexico: The Rural Economy of the Guadalajara Region, 1675–1820.* 2nd ed. Lanham: Rowman & Littlefield Publishers, 2006.
Van Young, Eric. "The New Cultural History Comes to Old Mexico." *HAHR* 79, no. 2 (1999): 211–247.
Van Young, Eric. *The Other Rebellion: Popular Violence, Ideology, and the Mexican Struggle for Independence, 1810–1821.* Stanford, CA: Stanford University Press, 2001.
Veith, Werner. "Gerechtigkeit." In *Christliche Sozialethik. Ein Lehrbuch.* Vol. 1: *Grundlagen,* edited by Marianne Heimbach-Steins, 315–326. Regensburg: Pustet, 2004.
Villa-Flores, Javier. "Wandering Swindlers: Imposture, Style, and the Inquisition's Pedagogy of Fear in Colonial Mexico." *Colonial Latin American Review* 17 (2008): 251–272.
Villa-Flores, Javier. "Archivos y falsarios: producción y circulación de documentos apócrifos en el México borbónico." *Jahrbuch für Geschichte Lateinamerikas* 46, no. 1 (2009): 19–41.
Villella, Peter B. "Indian Lords, Hispanic Gentlemen: The Salazars of Colonial Tlaxcala." *The Americas* 69, no. 1 (2012): 1–36.
Voekel, Pamela. *Alone before God. The Religious Origins of Modernity in Mexico.* Durham, NC: Duke University Press, 2002.
Vorlander, Hans. "What is constitutional culture." In *Constitutional Cultures. On the Concept and Representation of Constitutions in the Atlantic World,* edited by Silke Hensel, Ulrike Bock, Katrin Dircksen, and Hans-Ulrich Thamer, 21–42. Newcastle, UK: Cambridge Scholars Publishing, 2012.
Walter, Uwe. "Patronale Wohltaten oder kriminelle Mobilisierung. Sanktion gegen unerlaubte Wahlwerbung im spätrepublikanischen Rom." In *Korruption. Historische Annäherungen an eine Grundfigur politischer Kommunikation,* edited by Niels Grüne and Simona Slanička, 145–166. Göttingen: Vanderhoek, 2010.
Waquet, Jean-Claude. *Corruption. Ethics and Power in Florence, 1600–1770.* Translated by Linda McCall. University Park: Pennsylvania State University Press, 1992. Originally published as *De la corruption: Morale et pouvoir à Florence aux xviie et xviiie siècles.* Paris: Librairie Arthème Fayard, 1984.
Waquet, Jean-Claude. "Some Considerations on Corruption, Politics and Society in Sixteenth and Seventeenth Century Italy." In *Political Corruption in Europe and Latin America,* edited by Walter Little and Eduardo Posada-Carbó, 21–40. London: Macmillan Press, 1996.
Wasserman, Stanley, and Katheryne Faust. *Social Network Analysis: Methods and Applications.* Cambridge, New York: Cambridge University Press, 1994.
Weber, Max. *Economy and Society. An Outline of Interpretive Sociology.* Edited by Günther Roth and Claus Wittich. Berkeley, Los Angeles: University of California Press, 1978. https://archive.org/stream/MaxWeberEconomyAndSociety#page/no.
Weimar, Peter "Bartolus of Saxoferrato." In *The Oxford International Encyclopedia of Legal History,* edited by Stanley N. Katz. Oxford: Oxford University Press, 2009. www.oxfordreference.com.

Westbrook, Raymond. "The origin of 'Laesio Enormis.'" *Revue internationale des droits de l'antiquité* 55 (2008): 39–52.
Whipple, Pablo. "Guerra a los abogados. La defensa libre y los debates sobre el monopolio de los abogados y la corrupción de la justicia peruana, 1841–1862." In *'Dádivas, dones y dineros.' Aportes a una nueva historia de la corrupción en América Latina desde el imperio español hasta la modernidad*, edited by Christoph Rosenmüller and Stephan Ruderer, 127–146.
Windler, Christian. "Bureaucracy and Patronage in Bourbon Spain," in *Observation and Communication: The Construction of Realities in the Hispanic World*, edited by Johannes-Michael Scholz, and Tamar Herzog, 299–320. Frankfurt: Vittorio Klostermann, 1997.
Wieacker, Franz. *A History of Private Law in Europe with Particular Reference to Germany*. Translated by Tony Weir. Oxford: Clarendon Press, 1995.
Yalí Román, Alberto. "Sobre alcaldías mayores y corregimientos en Indias: Un ensayo de interpretación." *Jahrbuch für Geschichte von Staat, Wirtschaft und Gesellschaft Lateinamerikas* 9 (1972): 1–39.
Yhmoff Cabrera, Jesús. *Catálogo de obras manuscritas en Latín de la Biblioteca Nacional de México*. Mexico City: UNAM, Instituto de Investigaciones Bibliográficas, 1975.
Yun Casalilla, Bartolomé, ed. *Las redes del imperio. Élites sociales en la articulación de la Monarquía Hispánica, 1492–1714*. Madrid: Marcial Pons; Seville: Universidad Pablo Olavide, 2009.
Yannakakis, Yanna. *The Art of Being In-Between: Native Intermediaries, Indian Identity, and Local Rule in Colonial Oaxaca*. Durham, NC: Duke University Press, 2008.
Yannakakis, Yanna, and Martina Schrader-Kniffki. "Between the 'Old Law' and the New: Christian Translation, Indian Jurisdiction, and Criminal Justice in Colonial Oaxaca." *HAHR* 96, no. 3 (2016): 517–548.
Zeitlin, Judith Francis. *Cultural Politics in Colonial Tehuantepec: Community and State among the Isthmus Zapotec, 1500–1750*. Stanford, CA: Stanford University Press, 2005.

Index

Acapulco, 147
Aguilera, Ana Ventura de, 175
Aguilera, Juan José, notary and interim fine collector, 211–213
Alberoni, Giulio, chief minister, 144, 145, 225, 228–229, 250, 252
Alburquerque, Duke of, viceroy, 225, 232
 and loss of patronage, 148–149
alcabala (sales tax), 120, 261
Alcalá de Henares, University of, 81, 130, 225, 276
alcalde (Native magistrate), 18, 33, 65, 96, 109
alcalde de crimen. *See* criminal judge
alcalde mayor, 33, 259–261
 as merchant, 93–122
 beneficio of, 123, 147
 viceregal patronage over, 147–149
alcalde ordinario, 33, 105, 135
altepetl (ethnic polity), 46
ambitus, 58
Amsterdam, 107, 109, 121
Anaya, José Antonio de, senior audiencia notary, 69–70, 200
Ángeles, Juana de los, 191
Antequera, 107, 113, 118, 119, 174, 184, *See* Oaxaca
 royal factory in, 116
Antunez Portugal, Domingo, jurist, 264
appeals, 246
appointments, royal sale of, 25, 54, 81, 259
 expansion of, 123–152

 of *alcaldes mayores*, 96–97
 of *audiencia* ministers, 238–243, 253
Aquinas, Thomas, 82, 127–129, 150, 264
Aragon, province or kingdom of, 47
Aramburu y Vilches, María Teresa de, 155, *See* Sánchez Morcillo, Pedro
Aranda, Teresa, 250, 252, *See* Suárez de Figueroa, Félix
arbitrio (judgment), 17, 29, 51, 62, 86, 91, 256
archbishop of Mexico, 230
Aristotle, 82
Armada, royal, 126, 228
Artiaga, Teresa de, 189
Atlacomulco, Santa María Nativitas, 32
Atlantic world, 21
attorneys
 absolved in *visita*, 201
 and custom, 27
 and negligence, 204
 and their sentences in Garzarón's *visita*, 213, 218
 college of, 23
 education of, 23
 in *plenaria*, 166
 negotiating bribes, 63
 representing Native community, 67
Austria, 21, 44, 227
Austria, Juan (José) de, 138–140, 142
Austria, Mariana of, 80, 102, 134–139, 259
Azpilcueta, Martín de, or Doctor Navarro, 56, 100, 126, 129–130, 265

334

Index

Bacon, Francis, 37
bankers, 81, 259
baratería, 2, 7, 60–61, 70, 91, 170, 204, 220, 256, 269
Barbero, María, 163
Bartolus de Sassoferrato, 16, 23, 78, 86, 88, 206
    Bartolists, his adherents, 15, 16
Baskes, Jeremy, 95
Basques, 35
Bavaria (Germany), 21
beneficio. *See* appointments, royal sale of
Berart y Gassol, Gabriel, jurist, 65, 220, 265
blacks, 19, 110, 153, 179
    as witnesses, 182
    charged illicit fees, 188, 201
Board of Trade, 228, 245
Bogotá (Colombia), 228
Bologna, Italy, 14
Borah, Woodrow, 197
Borromeo, Saint Charles de, 25
Bravo de Laguna, Juan, clergyman, 179–182
bribery, 55–70, 90, 160, 205, 241, 246, 261, 265, 267, 271, *See repentundarum*
Buenavista, Marquis of, 97
Burkholder, Mark A., 124, 152, 224

cabecera, 33, 96–97
Cádiz, 115, 229, 237, 245
    consulado of, 228
Cajetan, Thomas, theologian, 264
Calderón de la Barca, Miguel, civil judge, 229, 240, 253, 279
Campillo y Cosío, José, chief minister, 145
Cantabrana, Mariana de, 63
Cañeque, Alejandro, 268
Capuluapa, San Mateo de, 110
carcelaje, 188
Caribbean isles, 44
casa de contratación. *See* Board of Trade
Casafuerte, Marquis of, viceroy, 83, 85, 110, 144, 238, 245, 249, 252
Castillo de Bobadilla, Jerónimo, jurist, 15, 60, 61, 190, 205, 269
Catalonia, 47
Cerdán, Andrea, 178–182
Cervantes, Micaela de, 157, 258
Ceuta (North Africa), 226
Chandler, D. S., 124, 152, 224
Chapultepec Forest, 147

Charles II, king of Spain, 20, 39, 93, 130, 139, 143
Charles III, king of Spain, 84
Charles V (I), king of Spain and emperor, 58
China, 98, 104, 260
chino (Asian), 64, 171
Cholula, 118
Cicero, Marcus Tullius, Roman senator, 17, 55, 264
cochineal, 94, 101, 106–108, 112–115, 117, 118, 120, 121, 136, 147, 261
    and infestations, 119
    and Revillagigedo, 115
    price decline of, 106–109
    production of, 97
code
    French civil, 30
    new and systematic, 29–30, 51
    Prussian civil, 30
    Roman, 14
Coimbra, library of, 264
colegio mayor of All Saints, 234, 239
colegios mayores (study halls) in Spain, 81, 130, 225
    groups less tied to, 242
college of attorneys, 23
college of Christ, 147
Colombia, 228
common law. *See* law, common, of England
common madder, 107
concusión (violent extortion), 164, 269, 271, *See* extortion
confraternity, 45
Conquest of Mexico, 1, 44, 102
constable
    deputy jail, 217
    senior, Francisco de Fonseca Enríquez, 77, 186–188, 192–193, 248
consulado, 97, 228
    of Cádiz, 115
    of Guadalajara, 48
    of Mexico City, 97, 120, 245, 251
    of Seville, 228
    of Veracruz, 48
contract, 59
Corpus Christi, convent of, 251
Corpus Iuris Civilis. *See* law, Roman
Corral, Juan de Dios del, attorney, 218
corregidor (district judge), 15, 227
Cortes, parliament of estates, 39, 185

Cos y Cevallos, Juan Antonio de, *alcalde mayor*, 155–162
Council, 134, 262
   and patronage, 123, 126, 130
   of Castile, 58, 246, 249
   of Orders, 137
Council of the Indies, 3–4, 20, 139, 249
   and *ambitus repentundarum*, 58
   and college of attorneys, 24
   and conflict with Charles II, 39
   and customs, 28
   and its opposition to Garzarón's *visita*, 228, 245, 249–250
   and *parecer* of the prosecutor, 203
   and patronage, 135–139
   and *reales cédulas*, 34
   and *repartimiento*, 110
   and sentences, 70, 91, 164, 175, 183, 193, 195, 201, 203, 207, 209–211, 212
   and sentences for judges, 236, 237
   and sentences for officials, 237
   and sentences for *relatores* and attorneys, 213, 218
   and Valero as governor, 245
   assessing culpability, 221
council, municipal, 33, 45, 51, 72
   as jail, 217, 247
   of Tlaxcala, 171
court, royal, in Madrid, 43, 134, 135, 237, 243, 246, 249, 257, 263
court, viceregal, 106, 109, 197–201
Covarrubias, Diego, jurist, 21
coyote (person of mixed racial descent), 77
Coyotepec, 109
criminal judge, 28, 155–164, 178–183, 190–192, *See* Sánchez Morcillo, Pedro
Cruz, Andrés de la, alias the Eyebrow, 188
culpa (guilt), 204–206
   grave, 204
   gravísima, 205
   leve, 204
customs, 18–19, 33
   and judicial pluralism, 24–29, 215
   and notarial offices, 200
   and *repartimiento*, 112, 118
   and royal power, 39
   corrupting effects of, 31, 53, 65–67, 93
   in jail, 183
   Native, 18, 46
   of gifts, 62

Díaz de Bracamonte, Juan, civil judge, 62, 274
Digest, 14, 38
dolo (intent to do evil), 102, 205, 206, 220, 256
Domingo de Soto. *See* Soto, Domingo de, theologian
Dubet, Anne, 197

Ecatepec, Oaxaca, 108
elite
   American, 20
   and non-, 132
   and popular and middling groups, 267
   in provincial cities, 36
   novohispano, 51, 156
   traditional, 9, 54, 79–81, 90, 123, 143, 150, 259
   traditional, and Juan de Austria, 138
embezzlement, 85, 115, 268
Engels, Jens Ivo, 268
England, 44, 227
Enríquez de Ribera, Payo, fray, archbishop viceroy, 136, 147, 149
Ensenada, Marquis of la, chief minister, 83, 94, 95, 109, 114, 116, 121, 146, 148, 151, 261
evidence, standard of, 165–178
experts, legal, 11
extortion, 64, 164, 193, 196, 240, 241, 254, 255, 269, *See also concusión*

falsedad. *See* fraud
Farnese, Elizabeth, queen of Spain, 144, 222, 228, 229, 252
Farriss, Nancy, 48
Fernández de Otero, Antonio, jurist, 75, 78, 79
Fernández de Portocarrero, Luis Manuel, cardinal, 142, 143
Flores, Guillermo, 64
Florida, University of, 264
Foucault, Michel, 258
France, 21, 44, 56, 64, 85, 87, 104, 131, 206, 227, 231, 260, 263, 270
fraud, 78, 101, 161, 168, 194, 196, 197, 201, 202, 206–212, 220, 221, 235, 253, 256
fuero, 20

Galve, Count of, viceroy, 141
Gálvez, José de, *visitador*, 151, 241, 244, 244, 253, 260

García de Guesca, Diego, 155, 156, 157, 161
García de Guesca, José, *hacendado*, 155, 157, 159, 162, 164
García de Xismeros, Juan, notary and procurator, 162, 207, 209, 210, 213, 281
García García, Antonio, 54
Garriga, Carlos, 270
Garzarón, Francisco
  family and allies, 231–234
  final days, 251
  inquisitor of New Spain, 226–227
  methods of prosecution, 167–178
  origins, 225
  sentences of, 4, 90, 161, 196, 202–205, 235, 237
  staff, 173, 251
  visitador, appointment as, 227
Génaux, Marivonne, 270
Germany, 21, 30, 263
Gómez de Angulo, Felipe, vicar-general of Puebla, 162
González, Bernardo, 192
González, Juana Teresa, 32
Grégoire de Toulouse, Pierre, jurist, 264
Grimaldo, José de, chief minister, 144–145, 236
Guadalajara, 44
  archives of, 264
  audiencia of, 230
  cathedral chapter of, 251, 254
  treasury of, 87
Guatemala, 1, 107
  University of, 21
Guichicovi, San Juan Bautista, 104
Guzmán, Alonso de. *See* usher of the jail
gypsies. *See* Romany

Habsburg, House of. *See* Austria, Charles V, Charles II, Mariana of Austria, War of the Spanish Succession
sympathizers of, 224, 240
Havana, 237, 240
Hernández Bravo, Manuel, coachbuilder, 186
Hernández, Pedro, governor of Santa María Nativitas Atlacomulco, 32
Herzog, Tamar, 6, 37, 124
Hevia Bolaños, Juan de, 26, 264

Holy Roman empire. *See* Germany
Hospital of the Holy Trinity, 248
Huejotzingo, 118, 155, 157, 162, 164, 168, 194, 205, 258, 263
Huichapan, 215, 217
humanism, 17

Iberconceptos, 272
Inquisition, 226–227, 232, 251
Institutes, 14, 28
Italy, 14, 21, 228
ius commune, 15, 21–23, 82, 91, 255
Ixtepeji, Santa Catarina, 118

jail, 33, 111, 158, 162, 210, 211, 214, 217
  and Sánchez Morcillo, 247–249, 276
  in Puebla, 2
  in Tlaxcala, 156, 159, 170
  of the *audiencia*, 169, 171, 178–179, 181, 247
  practices, 183–193
Jalapa. *See* Xalapa
Jalapa root, 98
Jews, 19, 76, 160
Josefa Nicolasa. *See* Nieto, Juan Miguel
Juan Pascal, 156
Juan Salvador, 156
Juan, Jorge, naval officer, 83
Juana María, 32
judges, 31–34, 37, 73–76, 83, 86, 100, 102, 239–243
  acting as impartial public persons, 34
  unsuited, 75–81
juntas (committees), 42
jurists, 13, 15, 17
  and military officers, 85
  and *repartimiento*, 98
  and the systematic code, 29
  and torture, 185
  humanist, 16
  in Atlantic world, 21
  justifying verdicts, 196
justice
  administration of, 138, 141, 146
  and grace, 42
  and royal economic power, 42
  as bent by corruption, 53, 220, 255
  as defined by Thomas Aquinas, 127–128
  casuistic character of, 3, 255
  colonial system of, 154

justice (cont.)
  commutative, 127–128
  distributive, 62, 82, 85, 90, 91, 123, 128, 132–133, 137
  ordinary, 39
  restoration of, 51
  rigor of, 40, 41, 172
  six pillars of, 13–31
  social, 140
Justinian, emperor of Rome, 14
  legal collection of, 16, 18, 23, 50, 101

Kettering, Sharon, 268
Klaveren, Jacob van, 266
Koselleck, Reinhart, 271,

laesio enormis, 101, 102, 116, 118, 121
Lancina, Juan Alfonso de, xiii, 140
Larraga, Francisco, 264
law, 11–31
  canon, 15, 21, 58
  common, of England, 21, 165
  customary. *See* customs
  divine, 16
  humanist, 16–17
  natural, 11, 17–18, 51, 66, 215, 258
  Roman, 13–14, 16, 19, 21–23, 25–27, 30, 38, 50, 51, 58, 73, 75, 101
Law of Castile, 19, 25, 30, 57, 91, 183, 190, 194
Law of the Indies, 18–20, 25, 27, 51, 91
lawyers. *See* attorneys
Leyva, Marquis of, viceroy, 135
Lima, 26, 48, 77, 114
limpieza de sangre, 72
Linares, Duke of, viceroy, 69, 70, 93, 100, 121, 200, 229, 236
Louis I, king of Spain, 193, 243, 245–246, 249, 252
Louis XIV, king of France, 227
Luther, Martin, 217
Luz Alonso, María, 224

Macanaz, Melchor de, jurist, 30, 84
MacLachlan, Colin, 6, 268
Madre de Dios, Valentín de la, theologian, 204, 206
Madrid, 222, 225, 226, 227, 229, 231, 237, 245, 249, 250, 253, 254, 263, 264
Madrigal, Juan Esteban, slave, 4
Magdalena, 156

malversación. *See* embezzlement
Manila, 48, 64
  galleon, 155
María Josefa, 171
María Rosa, *india*, 32
María Teresa, *mulata*, 211
marrano, 76
Martín, Benito, 153
Martín, Juan, 111
Medellín, Count of, president of the Council of the Indies, 137–138
Medina del Castillo, Luis de, *alcalde mayor*, 104
Medina, Juana María de, inmate's wife, 188
Medinaceli, Duke of, 139–140
Meléndez, José, attorney, 131, 150
Mendo, Andrés, Jesuit, 41, 42, 133, 150
merchants, 153, 173, 226, 231, 244, 266
  and *repartimiento*, 94–100, 103, 107, 112–122
  as unsuited for judicial office, 78–79, 81, 90
  of Oaxaca, Puebla, and Mexico City, 98
merit, 71–74, 132–133
  and *beneficio*, 138
  and services, 141–142
  changing values of, 83–85
  lack of, 75–81
mestizo (person of mixed racial descent), 77
Metepec, 65, 67
Mexico, University of, 23, 243
Meztitlan, 25, 78, 90
Michoacan, 117, 135, 155, 239
Milpa Alta, 92
miserable person, 102–103, 175
monastery
  Dominican, imperial, in Mexico City, 198, 226, 227, 251
  Dominican, of Tehuantepec, 111
  of Saint Augustine, 4
Montezuma, María, 72
Montiel, Gregorio, 191–192
Moreno, Jerónimo, Dominican friar, 100–104, 121
Moreno, Juan Martín, jailer, 188, 189
Moscoso y Córdoba, Cristóbal de, councilor of Castile, 128, 129
Moya de Contreras, Pedro, *visitador* and archbishop, 243, 253
mulata/o, 2, 77, 163, 171, 181, 182, 192, 201, 211, 226, 231, 257, 262

mule drivers, 78
Murillo Velarde, Pedro, canonist, 100, 264

nation, Spanish, 228
Navarre, 225
negligence. See *culpa* (guilt)
Netherlands, The, 44
Neuburg, Mariana of, 141, 142
New Galicia, 44, 119, 243
New Granada, viceroyalty of, 48, 116, 245
New Spain
  and Atlantic trade, 47
  and *pueblos* and *alcaldes mayores*, 96
  and social bodies, 45
  aristocratic viceroys of, 128
  as core kingdom, 43–44
  expansion of administration, 87
  judges born in, 240
  military governors of, 146
Nexapa, 110, 135
Nieto, José Miguel, Native peon, 155, 156
noble, Native, 102, 109, 111, 113
  cacique (ethnic lord), 96, 111, 158, 170, 214
  nuns of the Corpus Christi convent, 251
  principal (lesser noble), 96, 109
North Africa, 226
notary *(escribano)*, 2, 4, 34, 37, 67–70, 73, 162–163, 165–166, 189–192
  notarial offices, 197–201
  of Garzarón, 173
Novels *(Corpus Iuris Civilis)*, 14

Oaxaca, 136, 147, 149, 263, See Antequera
  bishop of, 231, 249
  repartimiento in, 94–121
obedezco pero no cumplo (I obey but do not execute), 21
Olivares, Count-Duke of, chief minister, 262
onomasiology, 271
Oropesa, Count of, chief minister, 140–141, 142, 150
Otomí, 201, 214
Owensby, Brian, 197

Pablo Mateo, 156
Palafox, Juan de, bishop of Puebla and *visitador*, 135
Palanco, Francisco, bishop of Jaca, 82
Pamplona, 225
Panama, 47, 228

Patiño, José, chief minister, 145, 150, 250
Pátzcuaro, 239
Paz, Juan Raymundo de, official, 92
Peña, Juan Francisco de la, prosecutor, 174–175, 276
Pérez, Miguel, governor, 155, 162, 173, 221, 258
Peru, 47, 48, 89, 114, 119
  as core kingdom, 43
Philip IV, king of Spain, 138
Philip V, king of Spain, 131, 143–144, 151, 167, 222, 227, 243, 249, 252
Philippines, 44, 48
Pietschmann, Horst, 6
Pinto, Agustín Silvestre, *mulato* servant, 181–182, 194
Pividal, Ana, 230
plenaria, 166, 176
Poe, Edgar Allan, 165
Polybius, historian, 55, 71
Popocatepetl volcano, 106, 118
Portocarrero y Guzmán, Pedro, canon, 30, 71–72, 81, 129, 137, 264
Portugal, 235, 263
  king of, 42
prison. See jail
procurators *(procuradores)*, 7, 24, 26, 28, 65, 196
Prussia, 30
Puebla, 119, 162
  and *alcalde mayor*, 225, 232, 233
  and criminal prosecution, 153, 155, 156, 159, 164, 258, 263
  and José Joaquín Uribe, 233
  and military governor, 85
  and vicar-general, 162–163, 174
  and viceregal appointment of *alcalde mayor*, 147
pueblo (Native polity), 33, 46, 52, 96–97, 109
pulque, 65, 191
pulqueria (tavern), 230

Quadruple Alliance, 236
Querétaro, 215
Quevedo, Francisco de, poet, 14
Quiroz, Alfonso, 89
Quito, 2, 6, 37, 117, 124, 228

Ragon, Pierre, 268
Ramírez, Nicolasa, 63

Rastatt, treaty of. *See* Utrecht and Rastatt, treaties of
Reiffenstuel, Johann Georg, canonist, 21
relatores (salaried *audiencia* lawyers), 23, 213, 216, 244
repartimiento de mercancías, 92–122, 260
repentundarum, 58
restitutio in integrum, 103, 121, 260
Revillagigedo, Count of, viceroy, 126, 146–147, 151, 261, 263, 264
  and cochineal prices, 107
  and loss of patronage, 148–149
  and reform of *repartimiento*, 94, 114–117, 119–120, 121
  labeling financial officials as corrupt, 86
Ripperda, Baron of, chief minister, 249–250
Rivadeneyra, Tristán Manuel de, 230
robbery, 4, 170
Robledo, Pedro, notary, 60–61, 67–69, 210, 281
Roman law. *See* law, Roman
Romany (gypsies), 19
Rome, 270
Romero, María, 188

Saint Paul, 16, 75
Saint Paul, Augustinian church of, 217
Saint Peter, 16
Salamanca, University of, 81, 130, 225
Salazar, Juana de, 230
Salazar, Úrsula de, 167
San Antonio, Miguel de, theologian, 204–206, 264
San Cayetano, Juana de, jailed *mulata*, 171
Sánchez Morcillo, Pedro, criminal judge, 174, 194, 205, 221, 253, 276
  and *cacique* of Tlacotla, 171
  and his corruption trial, 153–164, 223, 237, 258, 263
  obtained prebendary, 250–251
Sandoval y Caballero, Micaela María de, 233, *See* Uribe, José Joaquín
Santa María, Francisco de, 163
Santander (Spain), 115
Santiago Tecali. *See* Tecali, Santiago (Puebla)
Santiago, knights of, military order, 72, 111
Sardinia, island of, 228, 229
Sassoferrato Bartolus de. *See* Bartolus de Sassoferrato
Saxony (Germany), 21

Schwartz, Stuart, 6, 267
Seijas y Lobera, Francisco de, 131
semasiology, 271
Seneca, Lucius Annaeus, Roman stoic, 74, 132, 150, 264
Severus Alexander, emperor of Rome, 25, 131, 144
Sevilla, Juan José, receptor, 179
Seville
  and Board of Trade, 245
  Archive of the Indies, 263
  consulado of, 228
  trade oligopoly, 47
Sicilia, José de, *mulato* shoemaker, 171
Sicily, island of, 228
Siena, Saint Bernard of, 269
Siete Partidas, 19, 25, 38, 66, 172, 183, 185, 194
Sigüenza, University of, 225
Sinaloa, 85
Skinner, Quentin, 272
social body, 45–47
  and porous identity of members, 45
Solís, Miguel, scribe, 69–70
Solórzano y Pereyra, Juan de, jurist, 19
  and distributive justice, 128
  and *restitutio in integrum*, 103
  and suitable *alcaldes mayores*, 74, 98
Soria, Jerónimo, civil judge, 174, 239–240
Soto, Domingo de, theologian, 73, 264
Sousa de Macedo, Antonio, jurist, 39
stoicism, 74, 132
Suárez de Figueroa, Félix, civil judge, 203, 245–247, 252, 275, *See* Aranda, Teresa
Suárez, Francisco, theologian, 39
sumaria, 165, 166, 167, 176, 179, 183

Tacuba, 131
Tantalus, 235
Tecali, Santiago (Puebla), 2
Tehuantepec
  and cochineal insects, 98
  and unpaid services, 110
  complaint against *alcalde mayor*, 104, 113
  discontent in 1715, 111
  Isthmus of, 109
  revolt of, 41, 105, 135
Tenochtitlan, *parcialidad* (neighborhood) of, 49
Teotitlan del Camino, 118
Tepeaca, 2

testimony, 180, 191
  discredited, 171
  Garzarón's assessment of, 202
  irregular evidence of three singular witnesses, 169–171, 258
  Native witnesses, 170
  regular evidence of two witnesses, 169, 171
Texas, 106
Texmelucan, San Martín, 156, 160
theft, 56, 220, 221
Tiraqueau, André (Andreas Tiraquellus), 17, 23
Tlacotla, 170
Tlalpujahua, 32
Tlaxcala, 34, 159, 162, 171, 263
Tochimilco, 105
Torres de Lima, Luis, political author, 74
torture, 65, 102, 153, 176, 185–186, 188, 243
  rack (*potro*), 185
Tula, 111
Turkish dye, 107

U.S.A., 263
Ulloa y Sevilla, Feliciano, notary of the provincial court, 211, 281
Ulloa, Antonio de, naval officer, 83
Uribe, José Joaquín, civil judge, 29, 198, 223, 232–234, 252, *See* Sandoval y Caballero, Micaela María de
usher
  of Puebla's vicar-general, 163
  of the *audiencia*, 18, 67, 200, 214
  of the jail, Alonso de Guzmán, 184, 188–189, 193
Utrecht and Rastatt, treaties of, 227

Valenzuela, Fernando, Queen Mariana's favorite, 135–139, 150
Valero, Marquis of, viceroy, 159, 279
  and dropsy, 238
  appointment of, 229
  as governor of the Council of the Indies, 245, 249
  opposed to Garzarón's *visita*, 177, 222, 234
  passing of, 251
  return to Spain, 237
Valladolid (Michoacan), 239

Valladolid, University of (Spain), 81, 130, 225
Van Young, Eric, 5
Veracruz, 115, 116, 173, 237, 247, 250
  and cochineal export prices, 106–109, 121
  and contraband trade, 231, 236
  and crime, 156
  and military governor, 85
  and Tlacotla, 170
  and *visitas*, 243
  consulado of, 48
Veytia Linage, Juan José, *alcalde mayor* of Puebla, 233, 274
Vienna (Austria), 21
Villa Alta
  and bribes for appointment as *alcalde mayor*, 136
  discontent in, 135, 143
  trade in, 113
visita. *See* Garzarón, Francisco
  historiography on, 223–225
  of Pedro Domingo Contreras, 251
  of Pedro Moya de Contreras, 243
  restoring Garzarón's *visita general*, 249
visitador
  as royal agent, 41–42
  prosecution methods of Francisco Garzarón, 167–178
visitador general (investigative judge). *See visitador*

War of the Spanish Succession, 143, 231

Xalapa, 102, 117
Ximénez, Bernabé, *cacique* of Tlacotla, 170
Xochimilco, 175, 211
Xuárez, Francisco, interpreter, 201, 214–215

Yannakakis, Yanna, 35
Yucatan, 48, 137, 138

Zacatecas, 87
zambalo (person of mixed racial descent), 77
Zapata y Sandoval, Juan, Augustinian, 133
Zapotecs, revolt of, 109
Zoquistlan, San Pablo (Puebla), 113

Other Books in the Series (continued from page ii)

99. *Black Saint of the Americas: The Life and Afterlife of Martín de Porres*, Celia Cussen
98. *The Economic History of Latin America since Independence, Third Edition*, Victor Bulmer-Thomas
97. *The British Textile Trade in South American in the Nineteenth Century*, Manuel Llorca-Jaña
96. *Warfare and Shamanism in Amazonia*, Carlos Fausto
95. *Rebellion on the Amazon: The Cabanagem, Race, and Popular Culture in the North of Brazil, 1798–1840*, Mark Harris
94. *A History of the Khipu*, Galen Brokaw
93. *Politics, Markets, and Mexico's "London Debt," 1823–1887*, Richard J. Salvucci
92. *The Political Economy of Argentina in the Twentieth Century*, Roberto Cortés Conde
91. *Bankruptcy of Empire: Mexican Silver and the Wars between Spain, Britain, and France, 1760–1810*, Carlos Marichal
90. *Shadows of Empire: The Indian Nobility of Cusco, 1750–1825*, David T. Garrett
89. *Chile: The Making of a Republic, 1830–1865: Politics and Ideas*, Simon Collier
88. *Deference and Defiance in Monterrey: Workers, Paternalism, and Revolution in Mexico, 1890–1950*, Michael Snodgrass
87. *Andrés Bello: Scholarship and Nation-Building in Nineteenth-Century Latin America*, Ivan Jaksic
86. *Between Revolution and the Ballot Box: The Origins of the Argentine Radical Party in the 1890s*, Paula Alonso
85. *Slavery and the Demographic and Economic History of Minas Gerais, Brazil, 1720–1888*, Laird W. Bergad
84. *The Independence of Spanish America*, Jaime E. Rodríguez
83. *The Rise of Capitalism on the Pampas: The Estancias of Buenos Aires, 1785–1870*, Samuel Amaral
82. *A History of Chile, 1808–2002, Second Edition*, Simon Collier and William F. Sater
81. *The Revolutionary Mission: American Enterprise in Latin America, 1900–1945*, Thomas F. O'Brien
80. *The Kingdom of Quito, 1690–1830: The State and Regional Development*, Kenneth J. Andrien
79. *The Cuban Slave Market, 1790–1880*, Laird W. Bergad, Fe Iglesias García, and María del Carmen Barcia
78. *Business Interest Groups in Nineteenth-Century Brazil*, Eugene Ridings
77. *The Economic History of Latin America since Independence, Second Edition*, Victor Bulmer-Thomas
76. *Power and Violence in the Colonial City: Oruro from the Mining Renaissance to the Rebellion of Tupac Amaru (1740–1782)*, Oscar Cornblit

75. *Colombia before Independence: Economy, Society, and Politics under Bourbon Rule*, Anthony McFarlane
74. *Politics and Urban Growth in Buenos Aires, 1910–1942*, Richard J. Walter
73. *The Central Republic in Mexico, 1835–1846, 'Hombres de Bien' in the Age of Santa Anna*, Michael P. Costeloe
72. *Negotiating Democracy: Politicians and Generals in Uruguay*, Charles Guy Gillespie
71. *Native Society and Disease in Colonial Ecuador*, Suzanne Austin Alchon
70. *The Politics of Memory: Native Historical Interpretation in the Colombian Andes*, Joanne Rappaport
69. *Power and the Ruling Classes in Northeast Brazil: Juazeiro and Petrolina in Transition*, Ronald H. Chilcote
68. *House and Street: The Domestic World of Servants and Masters in Nineteenth-Century Rio de Janeiro*, Sandra Lauderdale Graham
67. *The Demography of Inequality in Brazil*, Charles H. Wood and José Alberto Magno de Carvalho
66. *The Politics of Coalition Rule in Colombia*, Jonathan Hartlyn
65. *South America and the First World War: The Impact of the War on Brazil, Argentina, Peru and Chile*, Bill Albert
64. *Resistance and Integration: Peronism and the Argentine Working Class, 1946–1976*, Daniel James
63. *The Political Economy of Central America since 1920*, Victor Bulmer-Thomas
62. *A Tropical Belle Epoque: Elite Culture and Society in Turn-of-the-Century Rio de Janeiro*, Jeffrey D. Needell
61. *Ambivalent Conquests: Maya and Spaniard in Yucatan, 1517–1570, Second Edition*, Inga Clendinnen
60. *Latin America and the Comintern, 1919–1943*, Manuel Caballero
59. *Roots of Insurgency: Mexican Regions, 1750–1824*, Brian R. Hamnett
58. *The Agrarian Question and the Peasant Movement in Colombia: Struggles of the National Peasant Association, 1967–1981*, Leon Zamosc
57. *Catholic Colonialism: A Parish History of Guatemala, 1524–1821*, Adriaan C. van Oss
56. *Pre-Revolutionary Caracas: Politics, Economy, and Society 1777–1811*, P. Michael McKinley
55. *The Mexican Revolution, Volume 2: Counter-Revolution and Reconstruction*, Alan Knight
54. *The Mexican Revolution, Volume 1: Porfirians, Liberals, and Peasants*, Alan Knight
53. *The Province of Buenos Aires and Argentine Politics, 1912–1943*, Richard J. Walter
52. *Sugar Plantations in the Formation of Brazilian Society: Bahia, 1550–1835*, Stuart B. Schwartz
51. *Tobacco on the Periphery: A Case Study in Cuban Labour History, 1860–1958*, Jean Stubbs
50. *Housing, the State, and the Poor: Policy and Practice in Three Latin American Cities*, Alan Gilbert and Peter M. Ward

49. *Unions and Politics in Mexico: The Case of the Automobile Industry*, Ian Roxborough
48. *Miners, Peasants, and Entrepreneurs: Regional Development in the Central Highlands of Peru*, Norman Long and Bryan Roberts
47. *Capitalist Development and the Peasant Economy in Peru*, Adolfo Figueroa
46. *Early Latin America: A History of Colonial Spanish America and Brazil*, James Lockhart and Stuart B. Schwartz
45. *Brazil's State-Owned Enterprises: A Case Study of the State as Entrepreneur*, Thomas J. Trebat
44. *Law and Politics in Aztec Texcoco*, Jerome A. Offner
43. *Juan Vicente Gómez and the Oil Companies in Venezuela, 1908–1935*, B. S. McBeth
42. *Revolution from Without: Yucatán, Mexico, and the United States, 1880–1924*, Gilbert M. Joseph
41. *Demographic Collapse: Indian Peru, 1520–1620*, Noble David Cook
40. *Oil and Politics in Latin America: Nationalist Movements and State Companies*, George Philip
39. *The Struggle for Land: A Political Economy of the Pioneer Frontier in Brazil from 1930 to the Present Day*, J. Foweraker
38. *Caudillo and Peasant in the Mexican Revolution*, D. A. Brading, ed.
37. *Odious Commerce: Britain, Spain and the Abolition of the Cuban Slave Trade*, David Murray
36. *Coffee in Colombia, 1850–1970: An Economic, Social and Political History*, Marco Palacios
35. *A Socioeconomic History of Argentina, 1776–1860*, Jonathan C. Brown
34. *From Dessalines to Duvalier: Race, Colour and National Independence in Haiti*, David Nicholls
33. *Modernization in a Mexican Ejido: A Study in Economic Adaptation*, Billie R. DeWalt
32. *Haciendas and Ranchos in the Mexican Bajío, Léon, 1700–1860*, D. A. Brading
31. *Foreign Immigrants in Early Bourbon Mexico, 1700–1760*, Charles F. Nunn
30. *The Merchants of Buenos Aires, 1778–1810: Family and Commerce*, Susan Migden Socolow
29. *Drought and Irrigation in North-East Brazil*, Anthony L. Hall
28. *Coronelismo: The Municipality and Representative Government in Brazil*, Victor Nunes Leal
27. *A History of the Bolivian Labour Movement, 1848–1971*, Guillermo Lora
26. *Land and Labour in Latin America: Essays on the Development of Agrarian Capitalism in the Nineteenth and Twentieth Centuries*, Kenneth Duncan and Ian Rutledge, eds.
25. *Allende's Chile: The Political Economy of the Rise and Fall of the Unidad Popular*, Stefan de Vylder
24. *The Cristero Rebellion: The Mexican People between Church and State, 1926–1929*, Jean A. Meyer

23. *The African Experience in Spanish America, 1502 to the Present Day*, Leslie B. Rout, Jr.
22. *Letters and People of the Spanish Indies: Sixteenth Century*, James Lockhart and Enrique Otte, eds.
21. *Chilean Rural Society from the Spanish Conquest to 1930*, Arnold J. Bauer
20. *Studies in the Colonial History of Spanish America*, Mario Góngora
19. *Politics in Argentina, 1890–1930: The Rise and Fall of Radicalism*, David Rock
18. *Politics, Economics and Society in Argentina in the Revolutionary Period*, Tulio Halperín Donghi
17. *Marriage, Class and Colour in Nineteenth-Century Cuba: A Study of Racial Attitudes and Sexual Values in a Slave Society*, Verena Stolcke
16. *Conflicts and Conspiracies: Brazil and Portugal, 1750–1808*, Kenneth Maxwell
15. *Silver Mining and Society in Colonial Mexico: Zacatecas, 1546–1700*, P. J. Bakewell
14. *A Guide to the Historical Geography of New Spain*, Peter Gerhard
13. *Bolivia: Land, Location, and Politics since 1825*, J. Valerie Fifer, Malcolm Deas, Clifford Smith, and John Street
12. *Politics and Trade in Southern Mexico, 1750–1821*, Brian R. Hamnett
11. *Alienation of Church Wealth in Mexico: Social and Economic Aspects of the Liberal Revolution, 1856–1875*, Jan Bazant
10. *Miners and Merchants in Bourbon Mexico, 1763–1810*, D. A. Brading
9. *An Economic History of Colombia, 1845–1930*, by W. P. McGreevey
8. *Economic Development of Latin America: Historical Background and Contemporary Problems*, Celso Furtado and Suzette Macedo
7. *Regional Economic Development: The River Basin Approach in Mexico*, David Barkin and Timothy King
6. *The Abolition of the Brazilian Slave Trade: Britain, Brazil and the Slave Trade Question, 1807–1869*, Leslie Bethell
5. *Parties and Political Change in Bolivia, 1880–1952*, Herbert S. Klein
4. *Britain and the Onset of Modernization in Brazil, 1850–1914*, Richard Graham
3. *The Mexican Revolution, 1910–1914: The Diplomacy of Anglo-American Conflict*, P. A. R. Calvert
2. *Church Wealth in Mexico: A Study of the "Juzgado de Capellanias" in the Archbishopric of Mexico 1800–1856*, Michael P. Costeloe
1. *Ideas and Politics of Chilean Independence, 1808–1833*, Simon Collier

Printed in the United States
By Bookmasters